Lecture Notes of the Institute for Computer Sciences, Social Informatics and Telecommunications Engineering 211

More information about this series at http://www.springer.com/series/8197

Keping Long · Victor C. M. Leung
Haijun Zhang · Zhiyong Feng
Yonghui Li · Zhongshan Zhang (Eds.)

5G for Future Wireless Networks

First International Conference, 5GWN 2017
Beijing, China, April 21–23, 2017
Proceedings

 Springer

Editors
Keping Long
University of Science and Technology
Beijing
China

Victor C. M. Leung
The University of British Columbia
Vancouver, BC
Canada

Haijun Zhang
University of Science and Technology
Beijing
China

Zhiyong Feng
Beijing University of Posts
  and Telecommunications
Beijing
China

Yonghui Li
Centre of Excellence in Telecommunications
The University of Sydney
Maze Crescent
Australia

Zhongshan Zhang
University of Science and Technology
Beijing
China

ISSN 1867-8211   ISSN 1867-822X (electronic)
Lecture Notes of the Institute for Computer Sciences, Social Informatics
and Telecommunications Engineering
ISBN 978-3-319-72822-3   ISBN 978-3-319-72823-0 (eBook)
https://doi.org/10.1007/978-3-319-72823-0

Library of Congress Control Number: 2017962877

Printed on acid-free paper

This Springer imprint is published by Springer Nature
The registered company is Springer International Publishing AG
The registered company address is: Gewerbestrasse 11, 6330 Cham, Switzerland

Preface

The EAI International Conference on 5G for Future Wireless Networks (5GWN) is a comprehensive conference that focuses on 5G wireless networks. The main objective of 5GWN 2017, the first conference in the series, was to address and deliberate on the latest technical status and recent trends in the research and application of 5G technologies.

5GWN 2017 provided an opportunity for scientists, engineers, industrialists, scholars, and other professionals from all over the world to interact and exchange new ideas and research outcomes in related fields and to pursue possibilities for future collaboration. The conference is also aimed at gathering research contributions from the field of 5G wireless networks that address the major opportunities and challenges in applying 5G technologies to the understanding and designing of modern network systems, with an emphasis on both new analytical techniques and novel application scenarios.

The proceedings contain 64 papers that were selected from a total of 135 papers submitted to the conference. In the proceedings, readers can gather cutting-edge knowledge about the future 5G wireless networks. Each paper was presented, orally or as a poster, in the frame of the new analytical techniques and novel application scenarios, with topics on 5G networks including: non-orthogonal multiple access techniques; cognitive radio; channel modeling; D2D; performance analysis; cloud/CRAN-based 5G Networks; small cells; game theory; software-defined networks; heterogeneous networks; 5G ultra dense networks; self-organizing networks; network function virtualization; backhaul/fronthaul; resource allocation; big data; vehicular networks; massive MIMO; IoT; energy harvesting; radio resource management; caching; unlicensed spectrum (LTE-U); network slicing; full duplex techniques; and MmWave techniques.

We would like to express our grateful thanks to the conference program chairs and committee members, and all the reviewers for their great professionalism and efforts in reviewing the submitted papers. We also thank all the participants and sponsors for their valuable contributions to and support of 5GWN 2017.

14th December 2017

Keping Long
Victor C. M. Leung
Haijun Zhang
Zhiyong Feng
Yonghui Li
Zhongshan Zhang

Organization

Steering Committee

Steering Committee Chair

Imrich Chlamtac   CREATE-NET, Italy

Steering Committee

Victor C. M. Leung   The University of British Columbia, Canada
Haijun Zhang   The University of British Columbia, Canada

Organizing Committee

General Chairs

Keping Long   University of Science and Technology Beijing, China
Victor C. M. Leung   The University of British Columbia, Canada
Haijun Zhang   University of Science and Technology Beijing, China

Technical Program Committee Chairs

Zhiyong Feng   Beijing University of Posts and Telecommunications,
                               China
Yonghui Li   The University of Sydney, Australia
Zhongshan Zhang   University of Science and Technology Beijing, China

Symposium Chairs

PHY and Massive MIMO Symposium

Feifei Gao   Tsinghua University, China
Gang Wu   UESTC, China
Chengwen Xing   BIT, China
Kai Niu   BUPT, China

Wireless Access Technology and Heterogeneous Networks Symposium

Lingyang Song   Peking University, China
Tianyu Wang   University of California-Davis, USA
Chen Xu   North China Electric Power University, China

5G Networks Symposium

Xiang Cheng   Peking University, China
Chuan Huang   UESTC, China
Xiaotian Zhou   Shandong University, China

Communications Software, Services and SDN Symposium

Liang Zhou	Nanjing University of Posts and Telecommunications, China
Joel Rodrigues	University of Beira Interior, Portugal
Han Hu	Nanyang Technological University, Singapore

Future Trends and Emerging Technologies Symposium

Yongle Wu	Beijing University of Posts and Telecommunications, China
Shaoyong Zheng	Sun Yat-Sen University, China
Wenhua Chen	Tsinghua University, China

Workshops Chairs

Zhengguo Sheng	University of Sussex, UK
Lexi Xu	China Unicom, China

Publicity and Social Media Chair

Chunsheng Zhu	UBC, Canada

Sponsorship and Exhibits Chair

Renchao Xie	Beijing University of Posts and Telecommunications, China

Publications Chair

Chao Xu	Xidian University, China

Tutorials Chair

Chunxiao Jiang	Tsinghua University, China

Local Chairs

Yu Qiu	BUCT, China
Yanliang Chen	BUCT, China

Web Chair

Baobao Wang	BUCT, China

Conference Manager

Lenka Oravska	EAI - European Alliance for Innovation

Technical Program Committee

Alagan Anpalagan	Ryerson University, Canada
Mehdi Bennis	University of Oulu, Finland
Shengrong Bu	The University of Glasgow, UK
Wei Chen	Beijing Jiaotong University, China
Xianfu Chen	VTT Technical Research Centre of Finland, Finland
Zhiyong Chen	Shanghai Jiaotong University, China
Xiaoli Chu	University of Sheffield, UK
Lingjie Duan	Singapore University of Technology and Design
Lisheng Fan	Guangzhou University, China
Luoyi Fu	Shanghai Jiaotong University, China
Lin Gao	Chinese University of Hong Kong, SAR China
Fengkui Gong	Xidian University, China
Weisi Guo	University of Warwick, UK
Chunlong He	Shenzhen University, China
Mingyi Hong	Iowa State University, USA
Ekram Hossian	University of Manitoba, Canada
Wen Ji	Chinese Academy of Sciences, China
Chunxiao Jiang	Tsinghua University, China
Long Le	University of Quebec, Canada
Yuan Luo	Chinese University of Hong Kong, SAR China
Dusit Niyato	Nanyang Technological University, Singapore
Miao Pan	University of Houston, USA
Anibal Sanjab	Virignia Tech, USA
Omid Semiari	Virginia Tech, USA
Derrick Wing Kwan Ng	University of New South Wales, Australia
Wei Wang	University of Zhejiang, China
Yong Xiao	University of Houston, USA
Renchao Xie	Beijing University of Posts and Telecommunications, China
Chungang Yang	Xidian University, Xi'an, China
Guanding Yu	University of Zhejiang, China
Daqiang Zhang	Tongji University, China
Guopeng Zhang	China University of Mining and Technology, China
Tiankui Zhang	BUPT, China
Wensheng Zhang	Shandong University, China
Yan Zhang	Simula Research Laboratory, Norway
Yanru Zhang	University of Houston, USA

Contents

28 GHz MIMO Channel Characteristics Analysis for 5G Communication Systems

Suiyan Geng[1(✉)], Ningning Fan[1], Rui Zhang[2], and Xiongwen Zhao[1,2]

[1] North China Electric Power University, Beijing 102206, China
gsuiyan@ncepu.edu.cn
[2] National Key Laboratory of Electromagnetic Environment,
China Research Institute of Radiowave Propagation, Qingdao 266107, China

Abstract. In this paper, 28 GHz MIMO channel capacity and characteristics are analyzed, based on indoor propagation measurements carried out for both LOS and NLOS scenarios. Specifically, MIMO channel link budget, capacity, path loss, K-factor and delay spreads are studied based on experimental data. Results show that Gigabit capacity can be achieved in 28 GHz channel with MIMO (1 × 4) configuration in indoor corridor. RMS delay spread depends on both the size and scenario (LOS and NLOS) of environments. CDF of *K*-factor can be fitted with normal distribution in the LOS corridor. The provided parameters are useful for design of 5G wireless communication systems.

Keywords: Multiple-In Multiple-Out (MIMO) · Channel capacity
Link budget · Path loss · K-factor · Delay spread

1 Introduction

Gigabit millimeter wave indoor M2M (Machine-to-machine) communication technology is rising all over the world [1, 2]. At present, many countries and regions in the world have assigned 26 GHz to 38 GHz frequency band to the wireless broadband application in the local multipoint distribution system (Multipoint Distribution Systems Local, LMDS) [3, 4]. In particular, the FCC is proposing the use of spectrum at Ka-band (28 GHz and 39 GHz bands) for 5G mobile communications. At this frequency, the free space wavelength around 10 mm, enabling phased array antennas that can provide the bandwidth and be small enough to fit into mobile devices such as laptops, tablets and smartphones.

Multiple-in multiple-out (MIMO) technology has become one of the key technologies in the field of wireless communications. With the continuous development in recent years, MIMO technology will be more and more applied to a variety of wireless communication systems. In the wireless broadband access system, IEEE 802.16e, 802.11n and 802.20 which are being developed also adopt MIMO technology. MIMO technology can make full use of space resources and multiple antennas to improve the system capacity several times without increasing the spectrum resources or antenna transmit power.

The 28 GHz outdoor channel modeling has been studied in [5–7]. However, litter information on indoor channel characteristics in open literature. In this paper, the

© ICST Institute for Computer Sciences, Social Informatics and Telecommunications Engineering 2018
K. Long et al. (Eds.): 5GWN 2017, LNICST 211, pp. 1–7, 2018.
https://doi.org/10.1007/978-3-319-72823-0_1

28 GHz indoor MIMO channel capacity and characteristics are analyzed based on experimental measurements performed for both LOS and NLOS scenarios, for providing useful information on design of radio systems.

2 Measurement Environment and Campaigns

The 28 GHz indoor channel measurements were performed for both LOS and NLOS corridors in North China Electric power University (NCEPU). In the measurement, MIMO antennas were employed, i.e. antenna elements at transmitter (TX) and receiver (RX) are of 1 and 4 denoted as MIMO (1 × 4). In the measurements, the TX was fixed at certain position at the end of the corridor, and the RX was replaced with different positions along both LOS and NLOS routes. Figure 1 shows the measurement environment and scenarios. Specifically, 11 LOS positions (RX1 to RX11) and 3 NLOS positions (RX12 to RX14) were chosen, the LOS distance separations between TX and RX1 is 2.7 m, RX1 to RX10 is separated by 1.5 m and RX10 to RX11 is separated by 3 m. In NLOS case the TX and RX separations are of 3.4 m, 4.2 m and 5.5 m. The TX antenna was an omni-directional biconical horn (5 dBi gain), and the RX antenna was a 1 × 4 array, which was rotated in the azimuth plane from 0° to 360° (step length is 45°) at each measurement position. This means that 36 data was collected in each measurement position. The bandwidth (B) of system was chosen as 1 GHz in this measurement. Detailed information on measurement parameters and setup are summarized in Table 1.

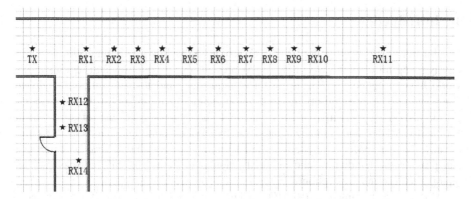

Fig. 1. 28 GHz channel measurements for both LOS (RX2-RX11) and NLOS (RX12-RX14) scenarios

Table 1. The 28 GHz channel measurement parameters

Measurement frequency	28 GHz
Frequency bandwidth	1 GHz
Code length	1024 ns
Delay resolution ratio	1 ns
TX power	18 dBm
TX antenna	Omni-directional biconical horn, 5 dBi gain
RX antenna	4 array antenna, 5 dBi gain
TX/RX antenna height	1.95/1.95 m

3   MIMO Channel Capacity Analysis

MIMO technology can make full use of space resources and use multiple antennas to improve the system capacity several times without increasing the spectrum resources or antenna transmit power. The application of MIMO technology makes the space become a kind of resource that can be used to improve performance and increase the coverage of wireless system.

3.1   MIMO Capacity

In MIMO, N_T and N_R are the number of TX and RX antennas, respectively. Assuming that all antenna signals are spatially uncorrelated, the maximum capacity in MIMO channel with given bandwidth B can be expressed as:

$$C_{MIMO} = B \log_2 \det \left(I + \frac{\rho}{N_T} HH^+ \right). \qquad (1)$$

where ρ denotes the average *SNR, I* is the identity matrix, and H is the normalized channel matrix, '+' denotes transpose conjugate.

For $B = 1$ GHz the CDF of MIMO channel capacity is shown in Fig. 2. It is seen that MIMO (4 × 4) capacity is about 2 times in MIMO (2 × 2) channel. MIMO (2 × 2) channel capacity is 1 about Gbps larger than in MIMO (1 × 4) channel at

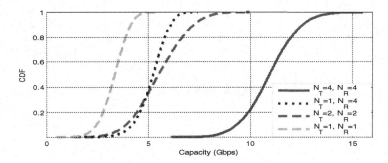

Fig. 2. CDF of MIMO channel capacity

$CDF = 0.8$. This is because in MIMO (2×2) the spatial multiplexing (number of parallel channels) makes information streams transmitted independently in channel.

3.2   MIMO Channel Link Budget Analysis

In wireless system, SNR is often determined from radio link budget as:

$$SNR = P_t + G_t + G_r - PL(d) - N_0 - IL. \tag{2}$$

where P_t is the transmitted power, G_t and G_r are the TX and RX antenna gains, PL is channel path loss, N_0 is the total noise power, IL denotes the total implementation loss at the TX and RX. Path loss (PL) can be modeled by mean path loss and fading margin σ [8]:

$$PL(d) = PL_0 + 10\,n\,\log(d/d_0) + \sigma \tag{3}$$

where PL_0 is the free space path loss at $d_0 = 1$ m, n is path loss exponent and σ is the standard deviation (STD) of fading margin in multipath channel.

Path loss model in the 28 GHz channel measurement is shown in Fig. 3. It is seen that PL exponent (n = 1.94) in LOS case is lower than free-space value of 2 due to the guided-wave effects in the corridor. The values of PL exponent n and shadowing STD σ are in consistent with the values reported in [1].

In order to estimate 28 GHz MIMO channel capacity, in Eq. (2), parameters $P_t = 18$ dBm, G_t and G_r are 5 dB which are chosen as the same values as measurement data. A total of 6 dB IL is estimated. The noise power is calculated as: $N_0 = 10\log 10(kTB) + NF$, where k is the Boltzmann's constant, $T = 290K$ (room temperature) and the noise figure NF is assumed to be 6 dB at receiver. Note that parameters of IL and NF are the same values as in [9] for a 60 GHz radio system. Figure 4 shows capacity vs. distance in the LOS corridor. It is seen that at the shortest TX-RX separation d = 2.7 m about 8 Gbps rate can be achieved in channel.

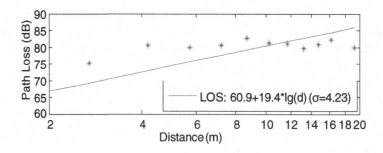

Fig. 3. Path loss model

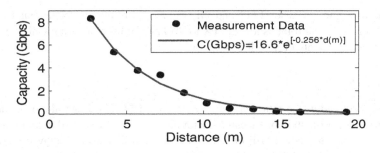

Fig. 4. Capacity vs. distance in the LOS corridor measurements

4 Channel Statistical Parameter Analysis

The statistical parameters and models of the channel are required to describe general channel properties which are useful for system design. Rms delay spread (DS) is very important and a common parameter for comparing different multipath channels in order to develop some general guidelines in system design. Rician K-factor is usually used to evaluate the performance of wireless systems.

4.1 Delay Spread

Rms delay spread is derived from the square root of the second central moment of a PDP. The formula for rms delay spread can be found in [8]. Figure 5(a) and (b) are the CDFs of RMS delay spreads in the LOS and NLOS corridor measurements, respectively. It is seen that the mean values of RMS delay spread in the LOS and NLOS corridor are of 26.4 ns and 27.6 ns, respectively. As the RMS delay spread depends on

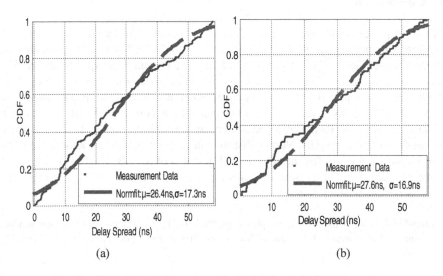

Fig. 5. CDF of RMS delay spread in (a) LOS and (b) NLOS corridors

both the size and scenario (LOS and NLOS) of environments. Note that the LOS corridor measurement route is longer (TX to RX11 is 19 m) comparing with the NLOS corridor measurements (TX to RX14 is 5 m).

4.2   K-factor

K-factor is defined as the ratio between the powers of LOS path and the other random multipaths. The estimation of Ricean K-factor has been widely studied in literature. The moment estimation method [10] of K-factor is used in this work. Figure 6 shows the CDF of K-factor in the LOS corridor measurements. It is seen that normal distribution can fit well with the measurement data. The mean value of K-factor is of 5.5 dB (with STD of 7.1 dB) in the LOS corridor measurements.

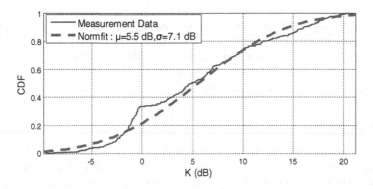

Fig. 6. CDF of K-factor in the LOS corridor measurements

5   Conclusion

This paper presented an investigation of channel characteristics based on experimental measurements performed at 28 GHz for both LOS and NLOS scenarios. Specifically, MIMO channel link budget, capacity, path loss, K-factor and delay spreads are studied based on experimental data. Results show that Gigabit capacity can be achieved in 28 GHz channel with MIMO (1 × 4) configuration in indoor environment. The mean values of RMS delay spread in the LOS and NLOS corridors are of 26.4 ns and 27.6 ns, respectively. RMS delay spread depends on both the size and scenario (LOS and NLOS) of environments. Normal distribution can fit well with K-factor in the LOS corridor measurements. The mean value of K-factor is of 5.5 dB (with STD of 7.1 dB) in the environment. The presented results are useful for design of 28 GHz high rate wireless communication systems.

Acknowledgments. This work is supported by National Key Laboratory of Electromagnetic Environment, China Research Institute of Radiowave Propagation under grant No. JW2016-014.

References

1. Rappaport, T.S., MacCartney, G., et al.: Wideband millimeter-wave propagation measurements and channel models for future wireless communication system design. IEEE Trans. Commun. **63**(9), 3029–3056 (2015)
2. Hu, Y., Ji, B.F., Huang, Y.M., et al.: Energy-efficient resource allocation algorithm for massive MIMO OFDMA downlink system. J. Commun. **36**(7), 40–47 (2015). (in Chinese)
3. Hur, S., Cho, Y.J., Lee, J., et al.: Synchronous channel sounder using horn antenna and indoor measurements on 28 GHz. In: IEEE International Black Sea Conference on Communications and Networking, pp. 83–87 (2014)
4. Gu, Z.Q., Zhang, Z.P.: Nonlinear robust precoding for coordinated multipoint transmission. J. Commun. **36**(10), 140–148 (2015). (in Chinese)
5. Psychoudakis, D., Zhou, H., Biglarbegian, B., et al.: Mobile station radio frequency unit for 5G communications at 28 GHz. In: 2016 IEEE MTT-S International Microwave Symposium (IMS), San Francisco, CA, pp. 1–3 (2016)
6. Kim, M., Liang, J., Lee, J., et al.: Directional multipath propagation characteristics based on 28 GHz outdoor channel measurements. In: 10th European Conference on Antennas and Propagation (EuCAP), Davos, pp. 1–5 (2016)
7. Wang, G., Liu, Y., Qi, X.: Study on the propagation characteristics of 28 GHz radio wave in outdoor microcellular. In: 2015 Asia-Pacific Microwave Conference (APMC), Nanjing, pp. 1–3 (2015)
8. Geng, S., Vainikainen, P.: Experimental investigation of the properties of multiband UWB propagation channels. In: IEEE International Symposium on Personal, Indoor and Mobile Radio Communications (PIMRC 2007), Greek, 3–7 September 2007
9. Yong, S.K., Chong, C.C.: An overview of multigigabit wireless through millimeter wave technology: potentials and technical challenges. EURASIP J. Wirel. Commun. Netw. **1**, 1–10 (2007)
10. Greenstein, L.J., Michelson, D.G., Erceg, V.: Moment-method estimation of the Ricean K-factor. IEEE Commun. Lett. **3**(6), 175–176 (1999)

A Caching Strategy Based on User Interest in Content-Centric Network

Yuehua Huo[1], Yanyu Sun[2], Yu Zhang[3], Donglin Cui[2],
Weiqiang Fan[2], and Yinlong Liu[3($\boxtimes$)]

[1] Center of Modern Education Technology,
China University of Mining and Technology, Beijing 100083, China
[2] School of Mechatronics and Information Engineering,
China University of Mining and Technology, Beijing 100083, China
[3] Institute of Information Engineering, Chinese Academy of Sciences,
Beijing 100093, China
huoyh@cumtb.edu.cn

Abstract. In Content-Centric Networking, content caching is a critical issue. At present, most researches on content network caching mainly focus on network resource utilization, while user interest is neglected. In this paper, we propose a caching strategy based on user interest in the Content-Centric Networking. Firstly, it divides the users into several interest groups. Then get the appropriate caching probability for each node by using grey relational analysis method. Simulation results show that the caching strategy proposed in this paper can achieve higher cache hit ratio and less average hop count than Leave copy everywhere (LCE) and ProbCache.

Keywords: Content-Centric Networking · Caching strategy · User interest
Grey relational analysis

1 Introduction

Content-Centric Networking (CCN) is an innovative network model, and it can achieve the content dissemination effectively. Reference [1] pointed out that CCN content retrieval depends on content rather than IP address. In the research field of CCN, network caching is a very important issue. In [2], the author proposes a strategy for allocating more cache space to important nodes. This strategy needs to measure the importance of each node in the network. Caching metrics such as content popularity, different application classes, and content type were considered in [3, 4]. Reference [3] explored that caching only most popular contents could reduce content copies and cache load at each node. Content types can be used to decide which content files will be cached first [4].

Leave copy everywhere (LCE) and ProbCache are two simple and common strategies. LCE strategy means all nodes along he delivery path cache contents. Reference [5] presented a ProbCache strategy that designed a caching probability with a function of the remained cache capability and the hop reduction from the router to the

© ICST Institute for Computer Sciences, Social Informatics and Telecommunications Engineering 2018
K. Long et al. (Eds.): 5GWN 2017, LNICST 211, pp. 8–18, 2018.
https://doi.org/10.1007/978-3-319-72823-0_2

content store. The above two strategies mainly considered single layer caching metrics. It is not efficient and cannot improve cache performance very well.

5G (5th-generation) is the fifth generation of mobile communication technology short [6], the existing wireless access technology (including 2G, 3G, 4G and WiFi) technology evolution, 5G system development will be for the 2020 mobile communications needs, Including key technologies such as architecture, wireless networking, wireless transmission, new antenna and radio frequency, and new spectrum development and utilization. In this paper, we design a caching strategy based on user interests (CSUI) in CCN. This strategy is implemented by dividing the interest groups and computing the probability of each node in the return path using the grey relational analysis method. Simulation results show that the strategy improves the cache hit ratio and reduces the average number of hops.

2 Related Works

2.1 Introduction of CCN

The traditional IP network has a long exploratory stage. At the beginning, it was designed for less users, easy application, small flow rate and other characteristics. In this way, it establish a simple and clear network architecture. It is very suitable for the requirement of using Internet at that time. However, with the rapid growth in network size and offered application type, the simple and clear network architecture has become more and more complicated. Figure 1 shows the difference between the traditional IP network and Content-Centric Networking.

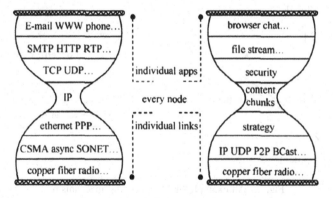

Fig. 1. The difference between the traditional IP network and Content-Centric Networking

From the Fig. 1, we can see the CCN replaced the original IP layer with content identify layer. The middle of the CCN network architecture becomes a simple structure again. Therefore, this new network architecture works more efficiently than the current complicated network architecture.

The mechanism of CCN is on the base of content which is named [7]. CCN takes full advantage of the network equipment's characteristics of big capacity memory and low storage cost. Applying the caching mechanism appropriately can further promote the network performance. Comparing with traditional IP network, in which requirements can be satisfied by the producer, requirements in CCN can also be responded by the intermediate nodes as long as this intermediate node has cached the required content before [8].

If this intermediate node does not have cached this content, it will forward the interest packet to neighbor nodes. This process will continue until the content is satisfied by the provider or the hit node. Then, the hit node or the provider will respond with a data packet [9]. When the data packet is transmitted along the reverse path, the intermediate node which is on the reverse path can cache the content into its content store.

When the content store becomes full, it will adopt the replacement policy in order to make a decision on removing one content from the store for the new content.

From Fig. 2, we can see when a user R1 requests a content, it first sends the interest packet to node P1. However, P1 does not have this requested content. So, P1 forwards the interest packet hop by hop until it finds the node P which can satisfy the requested content. Then P sends data packet along the reverse path and nodes which are on the reverse path cache the requested content in their content stores. Next time, when user R2 requests the same content, the node P1 can satisfy the request. Therefore, P1 responds the request and send the content back to R2.

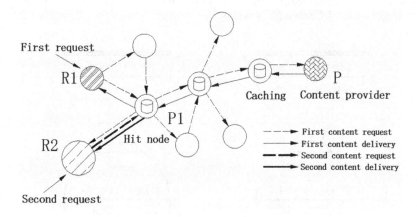

Fig. 2. An example of CCN caching mechanism

2.2 Grey Relational Analysis

The grey relational analysis method is used to compute the two parameters of each node's cache probability: the betweenness B [10, 11] and the cache replacement rate R. In the topology, betweenness is a useful way to judge the importance of nodes in the network. The higher the betweenness is, the more important the node is. The betweenness of user u_j is shown as:

$$B(u_j) = \sum_{s \neq u \neq t \in U} \frac{N_{s,t}(u_j)}{N_{s,t}} \tag{1}$$

Where $N_{s,t}$ is the number of the shortest paths from node s to node t. $N_{s,t}(u_j)$ represents the number of the shortest paths from node s to node t through node u_j.

The caching replacement rate $R(u_j)$ is denoted as:

$$R(u_j) = \frac{\sum_{i=1}^{M} S_j(c_i)}{C(u_j)} \tag{2}$$

Where $C(u_j)$ is the cache size of u_j and $S_j(c_i)$ represents the total number of replaced content for T_1 seconds in the content store of u_j.

Along the delivery path, interest packet is transmitted. During the transmission, interest packet records two caching parameters vectors of each node in the path. We define two parameters vector as a binary group, which is represented as $(B(u_j), R(u_j))^T$. The providers or the hit nodes receive the interest packet and extract the set of the binary groups regarding as comparative sequences. Based on Grey Relational Analysis, the providers or the hit nodes compute the caching probability and response a data packet with computed caching probability. The data packet is forwarded along the reverse path [12].

3 Caching Strategy Based on User Interests (CSUI)

3.1 Resource Matrix Construction Based on Dichotomy Network

A system that has a large number of individuals and interpersonal interactions can be abstracted as a complex network. According to the quantity of node types in the network, the complex network can be classified as single peak network, bipartite network and other forms. Bipartite network has been a research focus.

Bipartite network is made up of two types of nodes and links between two types of nodes. There is no link between the same types of node [13].

Different users may have the same interest, the same user may have multiple interests, so the users and the interests generate relations. The existence of interests depends on the users, because there is no users to have interests, interests do not exist. The interaction between users and interests can be considered a resource allocation process. We think nodes in the same group have similar resource vectors. Therefore, dividing groups toward nodes can be transformed into clustering row vectors of the resource distribution matrix.

Users-interests presents a characteristic of bipartite [14]. We assume the top nodes in bipartite network as users and bottom nodes as interests (see Fig. 3). The initial distribution of resources on the top nodes are x, y and z (see Fig. 3).

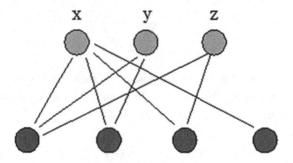

Fig. 3. The initial distribution of resources

All the nodes' resource in the network can be expressed as three-dimensional vectors:

$$
\begin{pmatrix} x_1 \\ x_2 \\ x_3 \\ y_1 \\ y_2 \\ y_3 \\ y_4 \end{pmatrix} = \begin{pmatrix} 7/12 & 5/12 & 5/12 \\ 5/24 & 5/12 & 1/6 \\ 5/24 & 1/6 & 5/12 \\ 1/4 & 1/2 & 1/2 \\ 1/4 & 1/2 & 0 \\ 1/4 & 0 & 1/2 \\ 1/4 & 0 & 0 \end{pmatrix} \begin{pmatrix} x \\ y \\ z \end{pmatrix}
\tag{3}
$$

Where x_1, x_2, x_3 represents the resource of the top nodes, y_1, y_2, y_3, y_4 represents the resource of bottom nodes. The matrix that on the right side of the equation is resource distribution matrix.

3.2   Divide Users into Interest Group

Divide users into interest group by K-means clustering and F-statistics [15], select K objects as initial cluster center. Then by using the method of iteration, we can divide objects into different groups. Our purpose is to make objects that in the same group have a big similarity and objects that in the different group have a small similarity.

Assume the resource distribution matrix is $U = (u_1, u_2, \ldots, u_{m+n})^T$, $u_j = (x_{j1}, x_{j2}, \ldots, x_{jm})$ (the number of users is m; the number of interests is n). K is the group number. n_i is the number of nodes in ith group. These nodes are: u_1^i, u_2^i to $u_{n_i}^i$. $u^i = (x_1^i, x_2^i, \ldots, x_m^i)$ is the ith group's cluster center.

$$
x_k^i = \frac{1}{n_i} \sum_{j=1}^{n_i} x_{jk}
\tag{4}
$$

The definition of F-statistics is

$$F = \frac{\sum_{i=1}^{K} \frac{n_i \|u^i - u\|^2}{K-1}}{\sum_{i=1}^{K} \sum_{j=1}^{n_i} \frac{n_i \|u_j^i - u^i\|^2}{n-K}} \tag{5}$$

The longer the distance between external groups, the shorter the distance in internal groups, the bigger value of the F-statistics. Therefore, when the value of F-statistics reaches its maximum, the effect of dividing groups is the best.

3.3   Calculate the Caching Probability Based on Grey Relational Analysis

When a user requests content c_i, the interest packet adds the binary group information of the requester

$$X_j = (B(u_j), R(u_j))^T \tag{6}$$

The node receives interest packet from the previous neighbor node, if the content store has not the requested content, interest packet is added into binary group information of the node, then it is forwarded to the next hop along the path. If the content store has the requested content [16], they extract the binary groups of the interest packet as the comparative sequences.

The distance from requester to the providers or hit nodes is n hops. The information matrix A′ is denoted as:

$$A' = \left(X_1', X_2', \ldots, X_n' \right)$$
$$= \begin{pmatrix} x_1'(1) & x_2'(1) & \ldots & x_n'(1) \\ x_1'(2) & x_2'(2) & \ldots & x_n'(2) \end{pmatrix} \tag{7}$$

Since each attribute has different ranges, we need to normalize attributes before we calculate the grey grade. The $x_i(k)$ is normalized as:

$$x_i(k) = \frac{x_i'(k) - \min_{1 \leq i \leq n} \{x_i'(k)\}}{\max_{1 \leq i \leq n} \{x_i'(k)\} - \min_{1 \leq i \leq n} \{x_i'(k)\}} \tag{8}$$

$$x_i(k) = \frac{\max_{1 \leq i \leq n} \{x_i'(k)\} - x_i'(k)}{\max_{1 \leq i \leq n} \{x_i'(k)\} - \min_{1 \leq i \leq n} \{x_i'(k)\}} \tag{9}$$

Where k = 1, 2. Pay attention to (8) is used for the-larger-the-better attributes while (9) is used for the-smaller-the-better attributes. Based on this, we can get

$$A = (X_1, X_2, \ldots, X_n)$$
$$= \begin{pmatrix} x_1(1) & x_2(1) & \ldots & x_n(1) \\ x_1(2) & x_2(2) & \ldots & x_n(2) \end{pmatrix} \tag{10}$$

Define reference sequence

$$X_0 = (x_0(1), x_0(2), \ldots, x_0(m))^T = (1, 1, \ldots 1)^T \tag{11}$$

Calculate grey relational coefficient

$$\rho(x_0(j), x_i(j)) = \frac{\Delta_{\min} + \tau \Delta_{\max}}{|x_0(j) - x_i(j) + \mu \Delta_{\max}|} \tag{12}$$

$$\Delta_{\min} = \min_{1 \le i \le n, 1 \le j \le m} |x_0(j) - x_i(j)| \tag{13}$$

$$\Delta_{\max} = \max_{1 \le i \le n, 1 \le j \le m} |x_0(j) - x_i(j)| \tag{14}$$

Where u is distinguishing coefficient, and $\tau \in [0, 1]$. The larger grey relation coefficient is, the closer $x_i(j)$ is to $x_0(j)$.

The grey relation grade p_i can be calculated as

$$p_i = \sum_{j=1}^{m} a_j \rho(x_0(j), x_i(j)) \tag{15}$$

Where $\sum_{j=1}^{m} a_j = 1$ and a_j represents the weight of j_{th} attribute.

Providers or hit nodes send data packet that the requester is requiring. Data packet carries above calculated grey relation grades along the reverse path [17]. Intermediate node receives data packet and caches content with the corresponding caching probability, which is equal to the node grey relational grade.

4   Simulation Analysis

4.1   Simulation Environment

We use the software ndnSIM [18] to simulate the GRA-based caching strategy. It is a chunk-level simulator developed in the NS-3 framework.

The network topology is a 7 * 7 grid network.

We evaluate our caching strategy by comparing two common caching strategies.

(1) LCE, all nodes along the delivery path cache the content.
(2) ProbCache, by which nodes along the delivery path cache the content with the fixed probability 0.5.

In the evaluation, we consider the independent variable as cache size which is the cache capacity in terms of content units. The cache size ranges from 50 to 200.

4.2   Evaluation Metrics

Caching hit ratio is defined as:

$$\beta = \frac{S}{R} \tag{16}$$

Where S denotes the numbers of requests satisfied by caching node, and R represents the total number of requests in the network.

Caching hit ratio gain β_{gain}

$$\beta_{gain} = \frac{\beta - \beta_{LCE}}{\beta_{LCE}} \tag{17}$$

Where β is the hit ratio of caching strategy, and β_{LCE} is the hit ratio of LCE.

Average hops

Average hops indicates the delay for user to fetch the content and it is a good way to estimate the access delay to the content. The same as the β_{gain}, hop reduction ratio η is represented as:

$$\eta = \frac{H - h}{H} \tag{18}$$

Where H is the average hops from user to the content provider or hid nodes in the LCE strategy, h is the average hops from the user to content provider or hit nodes for CSUI and ProbCache.

4.3   Simulation Diagram

In order to better verify the performance of CSUI strategy, the following experiment was done to draw the relationship between the cache hits and the average hops corresponding to different cache sizes.

From Fig. 4, we can see that the cache hit ratio of all compared caching strategies increases as the cache size increases. When the cache size become larger, the better diversity of cached contents will satisfy more requests. We can calculate that our CSUI strategy can achieve about 13%–27% cache hit ratio gain compared with LCE and ProbCache as the cache size changes.

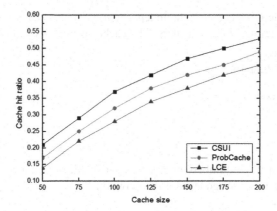

Fig. 4. Caching hit ratio with different cache sizes

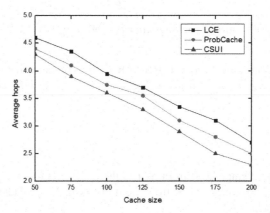

Fig. 5. Average hops with different cache sizes

Figure 5 illustrate the average hops and hop reduction ratio for each strategy with different cache sizes respectively. When the cache size is 50, the average hops reduction is little, about 4%. However, when the cache size is 200, hop reduction can reach 11%.

Therefore, it is obvious that our strategy CSUI performs better than LCE and ProbCache.

5   Conclusion

In this paper, we design a caching strategy that considers the interest of CCN users. On the basis of dichotomous network, we divide the users into appropriate interest groups, and then use the grey correlation analysis method to calculate the cache probabilities of each node in each interest group. This is a CCN caching strategy that takes into account user interest. Simulation results show that compared with LCE and ProbCache caching strategies, the strategy of this paper (CSUI) achieves higher cache hit ratio and fewer average hops.

References

1. Naboulsi, D., Fiore, M., Ribot, S., Stanica, R.: Large-scale mobile traffic analysis: a survey. IEEE Commun. Surv. Tutor. **18**(1), 124–161 (2015). IEEE Communications Society Press
2. Wu, Y., Zhang, P.: Study on bipartite networks. Complex Syst. Complex. Sci. **7**, 1–12 (2010)
3. Bernardini, T., Festor, O.: MPC: popularity-based caching strategy for content centric networks. In: 2013 IEEE International Conference on Communications, Budapest, pp. 3619–3623. IEEE Press (2013)
4. Diallo, M., Fdida, S., Sourlas, V., Flegkas, P., Tassiulas, L.: Leveraging caching for internet-scale content-based publish/subscribe networks. In: 2011 IEEE International Conference on Communications, Japan, pp. 1–10. IEEE Press (2011)
5. Xu, Y., Li, Y., Lin, T., Ci, S.: A novel cache size optimization scheme based on manifold learning in content centric networking. J. Netw. Comput. Appl. **37**, 273–281 (2014)
6. Zhang, H., Dong, Y., Cheng, J., Hossain, M.J., Leung, V.C.M.: Fronthauling for 5G LTE-U ultra dense cloud small cell networks. IEEE Wirel. Commun. **23**, 48–53 (2016)
7. Cheng, Y., Afanasyev, A., Wang, L., Zhang, B., Zhang, L.: Adaptive forwarding in named data networking. ACM SIGCOMM Comput. Commun. Rev. **42**, 62–67 (2012)
8. Chai, W.K., He, D., Psaras, I., Pavlou, G.: Cache "Less for More" in information-centric networks (extended version). Comput. Commun. **36**, 758–770 (2013)
9. Chai, W.K., He, D., Psaras, I., Pavlou, G.: Cache "Less for More" in information-centric networks. In: Bestak, R., Kencl, L., Li, L.E., Widmer, J., Yin, H. (eds.) NETWORKING 2012. LNCS, vol. 7289, pp. 27–40. Springer, Heidelberg (2012). https://doi.org/10.1007/978-3-642-30045-5_3
10. Xu, L., Luan, Y., Cheng, X., Cao, X., Chao, K., Gao, J., Wang, S.: WCDMA data based LTE site selection scheme in LTE deployment. In: International Conference on Signal and Information Processing, Networking and Computers, Beijing, pp. 249–260. CRC Press (2015)
11. Ahlgren, B., Dannewitz, C., Imbrenda, C.: A survey of information centric networking. IEEE Commun. Mag. **50**, 26–36 (2012)
12. Jacobson, V., Smetters, D.K., Thornton, J., Plass, M., Briggs, N., Braynard, R.: Networking named content. In: 2009 ACM Conference on Emerging Networking Experiments and Technologies, Rome, pp. 1–12. ACM Press (2009)
13. Jacobson, V., Smetters, D., Thornton, J., Plass, M., Briggs, N., Braynard, R.: Networking named content. Commun. ACM **55**, 117–124 (2012)
14. Carofiglio, G., Gallo, M., Muscariello, L.: Modeling data transfer in content-centric networking. In: Proceedings of the 23rd International Teletraffic Congress, San Francisco, pp. 111–118. IEEE Computer Society (2011)
15. Katsaros, K., Xylomenos, G., Polyzos, G.C.: Multi cache: an overlay architecture for information-centric networking. Comput. Netw. **55**, 936–947 (2011)
16. Rossi, D., Rossini, G.: Caching performance of content centric networks under multi-path routing (and more). Technical report, Telecom Paris Tech (2011)

17. Zhang, L., Estrin, D., Burke, J., Jacobson, V.: Named data networking (NDN) project. Transp. Res. Rec. J. Transp. Res. Board **1892**, 227–234 (2012)
18. Xu, L., Chen, Y., Kok, K.C., John, S., Laurie, C.: Self-organising cluster-based cooperative load balancing in OFDMA cellular networks. Wiley Wirel. Commun. Mob. Comput. **15**, 1171–1187 (2015)

Node Localization Based on Multiple Radio Transmission Power Levels for Wireless Sensor Networks

Yikang Xing[1,2], Wei Huangfu[1,2(✉)], Xiaoming Dai[1,2],
and Xiaoyan Hu[3]

[1] University of Science and Technology Beijing, Beijing, China
huangfuwei@ustb.edu.cn
[2] Beijing Engineering and Technology Research Center for Convergence
Networks and Ubiquitous Services, Beijing, China
[3] China Mobile Group Design Institute Co., Ltd., Beijing, China

Abstract. The range-free node localization techniques are attractive in wireless sensor networks. However, only based on the connectivity information, the range-free schemes are usually not accurate. The transmission radio power of the sensor nodes is often adjustable and multiple levels of the transmission power correspond to multiple levels of the communication radius. Thus an improved range-free node localization algorithm inspired by multiscale virtual forces is proposed, which adopts multiscale connectivity information. The simulation results showed that the proposed approach performs well in various scenario and the localization accuracy is improved.

Keywords: Node localization · Range-free · Wireless sensor networks
Virtual force field · Multiscale virtual forces

1 Introduction

The Internet of Things (IOT) in 5G wireless networks is predicted to connect billions of smart devices over the next decades [1]. Wireless Sensor Networks (WSN) [2–4] are fundamental in the IOT. The position information of sensor nodes is widely used in many areas such as routing, surveillance and monitoring. A large number of localization algorithms have been proposed.

The node localization can be obtained with the Global Positioning System (GPS). However, it requires that all the devices are equipped with GPS modules and thus it is considered to be a costly solution in terms of money and power consumption. Also, the node position can be calculated with the help of anchor nodes. These techniques are usually economical [5] and can be classified into two categories: range-based techniques and range-free ones.

The range-based techniques usually need to measure distance with additional devices. The range-based techniques perform well with accurate distance measurements. On the contrary, the range-free algorithms only depend on the connectivity information among sensor nodes, which have some advantages such as low energy

© ICST Institute for Computer Sciences, Social Informatics and Telecommunications Engineering 2018
K. Long et al. (Eds.): 5GWN 2017, LNICST 211, pp. 19–27, 2018.
https://doi.org/10.1007/978-3-319-72823-0_3

consumption, low cost, low noise sensitivity and high-efficiency. Many improved range-free algorithms have been proposed, and there is still a great room for improvement in localization accuracy of such range-free algorithms [6].

Note that the Radio Frequency (RF) chips which are equipped in the sensor nodes can broadcast packets with different radio power levels, and different power levels have different communication ranges. This feature may help the range-free localization schemes to obtain high localization accuracy. In this paper, an improved range-free node localization algorithm inspired by Multiscale Virtual Forces (MVF) based on multiple transmission power levels is proposed.

The organization of the paper is as follows. In Sect. 2, we review the related to range-free algorithms. In Sect. 3, we present the system model and the details of MVF algorithm. In Sect. 4, we present simulation results in various situations. Section 5 concludes this paper.

2   Related Work

Nodes localization problems have been studied for many years. A number of techniques are proposed.

Distance Vector-Hop (DV-Hop) [7] is a kind of typical range-free localization algorithm. The location process is divided into the three phase. In the first phase, nodes obtain the smallest hop-count from anchor nodes using typical distance vector exchange protocols. In the second phase, the distance matrix between nodes and anchor nodes is estimated. In the third phase, the nodes calculate their own position using the maximum likelihood estimation method [8]. Multidimensional Scaling (MDS-MAP) [9, 10] is another kind of typical localization algorithm for both range-free and range-based circumstances. It uses the distance matrix or hop matrix to solve the eigenvectors related to the top two maximum eigenvalues to construct a two-dimensional relative map. Although many improved algorithms have been proposed, the range-free techniques also suffer from the low localization accuracy and the high computational complexity.

The Virtual Forces algorithm (VF) [11] aims to get effective deployment which can provide good coverage and connectivity. Each sensor node behaves as a source of virtual force. If two sensor nodes are placed close enough, i.e. the distance between two nodes is shorter than the threshold, there will exist a virtual repulsive force. On the contrary, if a pair of nodes is too far apart from each other, there will be a virtual attractive force.

The VF algorithm combines the ideas of potential field and disk packing. The idea of VF algorithm can also be used in node localization [12]. If we consider the connectivity between any pair of nodes in the wireless sensor network as a constraint condition and construct virtual force model according to these conditions. We can use these virtual forces to push the unknown nodes to where they should be. The VF algorithm uses the neighbor lists of sensor nodes to estimate the absolute location with the help of anchor nodes. This algorithm belongs to Heuristic-based location estimation techniques. The VF algorithm can usually obtain high localization accuracy than other range-free algorithms.

3 Node Localization Algorithm with Multiscale Virtual Forces

We propose a novel algorithm named Multiscale Virtual Forces (MVF). This new algorithm extends the advantages of range-free localization algorithm: low energy consumption, low cost and low noise sensitivity. Compare with the traditional VF algorithm, the new algorithm uses multiple groups of neighbor information of each sensor node. Each sensor node broadcasts packets with multiple transmission power, each different transmission power level leads to different information. Thus it help obtain higher accuracy than the traditional virtual force algorithm.

In this section, we will propose a node localization algorithm inspired by the multiscale virtual forces corresponding to multi-level transmission power in wireless sensor networks. The underlying assumptions and the localization algorithm are described as follows.

3.1 Assumptions

We have the following assumptions:

- Each sensor node has its unique ID (identification) and can set its RF chip to various radio power levels.
- Each sensor node is fixed during the positioning process.
- For any pair of sensor nodes there exists at least one routing path, i.e. all sensor nodes are connected.
- There are a certain number of anchor nodes, which have the GPS modules. It means these anchor nodes can obtain the location information.

3.2 System Model

All the N sensor nodes including anchor nodes are $s_1, s_2, \cdots, s_N$ deployed in the sensing field. The coordination of node $s_i (1 \leq i \leq N)$ is (x_i, y_i). We also let $\vec{s}_i$ denote the vector (x_i, y_i). Each sensor node has K transmission power levels: $P_1, P_2, \cdots, P_K (P_1 < P_2 < \cdots < P_K)$, which corresponds to a series of communication radius: $r_1, r_2, \cdots, r_K (r_1 < r_2 < \cdots < r_K)$ (Fig. 1).

For any pair of sensor node (s_i, s_j), we define neighbor index $n_1(i,j)$, $n_2(i,j), \cdots, n_K(i,j)$ as

$$
\begin{aligned}
n_1(i,j) &= \begin{cases} 1, & d_{ij} \leq r_1 \\ 0, & d_{ij} \geq r_1 \end{cases} \\
n_2(i,j) &= \begin{cases} 1, & d_{ij} \leq r_2 \\ 0, & d_{ij} \geq r_2 \end{cases} \\
&\vdots \\
n_K(i,j) &= \begin{cases} 1, & d_{ij} \leq r_K \\ 0, & d_{ij} \geq r_K \end{cases},
\end{aligned}
\tag{1}
$$

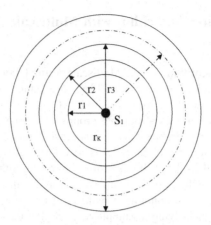

Fig. 1. Multiscale communication radius

where d_{ij} is the Euclidean distance between s_i and s_j.

$$d_{ij} = \sqrt{(x_i - x_j)^2 + (y_i - y_j)^2} \tag{2}$$

Every sensor node has an initial position. We assume that the initial position of unknown node s_i is $\vec{\hat{s}}_i = (\hat{x}_i, \hat{y}_i)$, where $\hat{x}_i$ and $\hat{y}_i$ generated randomly. For each anchor nodes s_i, the initial position $(\hat{x}_i, \hat{y}_i)$ is its actual position (x_i, y_i).

We define multiscale virtual force $f_1(i,j), f_2(i,j), \cdots, f_K(i,j)$ as

$$
\begin{aligned}
\vec{f_1}(i,j) &= \begin{cases} \lambda(\vec{\hat{s}}_i - \vec{\hat{s}}_j), & \hat{d}_{ij} > r_1 \text{ and } n_1(i,j) = 1 \\ -\lambda(\vec{\hat{s}}_i - \vec{\hat{s}}_j), & \hat{d}_{ij} < r_1 \text{ and } n_1(i,j) = 0 \\ 0, & else \end{cases} \\[2mm]
\vec{f_2}(i,j) &= \begin{cases} \lambda(\vec{\hat{s}}_i - \vec{\hat{s}}_j), & \hat{d}_{ij} > r_2 \text{ and } n_2(i,j) = 1 \\ -\lambda(\vec{\hat{s}}_i - \vec{\hat{s}}_j), & \hat{d}_{ij} < r_2 \text{ and } n_2(i,j) = 0 \\ 0, & else \end{cases} \\[2mm]
&\qquad\qquad\qquad \vdots \\[2mm]
\vec{f_k}(i,j) &= \begin{cases} \lambda(\vec{\hat{s}}_i - \vec{\hat{s}}_j), & \hat{d}_{ij} > r_k \text{ and } n_k(i,j) = 1 \\ -\lambda(\vec{\hat{s}}_i - \vec{\hat{s}}_j), & \hat{d}_{ij} < r_k \text{ and } n_k(i,j) = 0 \\ 0, & else \end{cases}
\end{aligned}
\tag{3}
$$

$$\hat{d}_{ij} = \sqrt{(\hat{x}_i - \hat{x}_j)^2 + (\hat{y}_i - \hat{y}_j)^2}, \tag{4}$$

where $\hat{d}_{ij}$ is the Euclidean distance between estimated nodes location $\vec{\hat{s}}_i$ and $\vec{\hat{s}}_j$; λ is a positive parameter called the learning rate; $\lambda(\vec{\hat{s}}_i - \vec{\hat{s}}_j)$ represents the attractive force between two nodes, and $-\lambda(\vec{s}_i - \vec{s}_j)$ represents the repulsive force.

We define the net force on a node s_i is the vector sum of all the above the forces:

$$F_i = \sum_{L=1}^{K} \sum_{j=1, i \neq j}^{N} \vec{f}_L(i,j) \tag{5}$$

3.3 Operation of the Localization Algorithm

The detailed steps of the MVF algorithm are as follows:

Step 1. All the sensor nodes broadcast packets with transmission power: $P_1, P_2, \cdots, P_K$. The data packets include ID of the source node, the information of

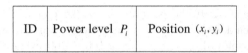

ID	Power level P_i	Position (x_i, y_i)

Fig. 2. The packet structure

transmission power level and the current position of the sensor node (Fig. 2).

Step 2. If node s_i can receive the packets broadcasted with power P_K from s_j, we can know that $d_{ij} \leq r_k$. Node receives all the packets and organizes the information

Table 1. The information of packets that the sensor node receives and organizes

j	1	2	...	N
$n_1(i,j)$	1	1	...	0
$n_2(i,j)$	1	1	...	0
...	...	...	...	...
$n_K(i,j)$	0	1	...	0

into Table 1 where i and j are ID of the destination node and source node:

Step 3. Each sensor node sends the table to the center node.

Step 4. The center node collects all the table of sensor nodes. Then the location data is calculated with the following algorithm.

We assume that the initial position of each unknown node is $\vec{s}_i^{(0)} = (\hat{x}_i^{(0)}, \hat{y}_i^{(0)})$, $1 \leq i \leq N$. Then we can use (3) (4) to calculate $f_1^{(0)}(i,j), f_2^{(0)}(i,j), \cdots, f_K^{(0)}(i,j)$ and use (5) to calculate the net force $F_i^{(0)}$. New estimated by locations $(\hat{x}_i^{(1)}, \hat{y}_i^{(1)})$ are calculated.

$$(\hat{x}_i^{(1)}, \hat{y}_i^{(1)}) = \vec{\hat{s}}_i^{(1)} = \vec{\hat{s}}_i^{(0)} + \alpha F_i^{(0)} \tag{6}$$

Here the symbol α is a coefficient to indicates the virtual inertia of the nodes.

Step 5. We use the new locations to repeat Step. 4 for the next movement. After the number of iteration reaches M (the max number of iterations), the algorithm stops. We denote the final results as

$$\vec{\hat{s}}_i = \vec{\hat{s}}_i^{(M)} = (\hat{x}_i^{(M)}, \hat{y}_i^{(M)}), 1 \leq i \leq N \tag{7}$$

Step 6. The center node sends the final positions to all sensor nodes.

4 Performance Evaluation

In order to assess and verify the performance of the proposed algorithm, multiple simulations have been done using python, numpy and matplotlib. All the sensor nodes in the network are deployed randomly in area 100×100 (where the distance unit is arbitrary) and the number of sensor nodes is N. We compare the MVF algorithm and other similar algorithm, including the basic DV-Hop algorithm, MDS-MAP algorithm and the VF algorithm. In all of the experiments, the metric used to evaluate the localization methods is the Mean Localization Error (MLE).

$$MLE = \frac{1}{N} \sum_{i,j=1}^{N} \sqrt{(x_i - \hat{x}_i)^2 + (y_i - \hat{y}_i)^2}, \tag{8}$$

where $(\hat{x}_i, \hat{y}_i)$ are the coordinates of the estimated location of s_i and (x_i, y_i) are the coordinates of the actual location of node s_i.

We denote VF(r) as the node localization algorithm with Single Virtual Force, MDS-MAP(r) as the algorithm with MDS-MAP, DV-Hop(r) as the node localization algorithm with DV-Hop, where r represents the communication radius corresponding to the power. We denote MVF $(r_1, r_2, \cdots, r_K)$ as the node localization algorithm with Multiscale Virtual Forces, $r_1, r_2, \cdots, r_K$ represent the multiscale communication radius sequence.

Figure 3 shows the iteration times of two localization algorithm with VF and MVF. The number of sensor nodes is 100 and the density of anchor nodes is 15%. The communication radius of MVF algorithm is set to 10, 15, 20. In order to compare VF and MVF algorithm, the communication radius of VF algorithm is set to 10, 15, 20 respectively. We find that when the iteration count of VF and MVF algorithms increase, the localization errors of the algorithm decreases. When the iteration count reach about 100, the localization errors of both VF and MVF algorithms tend to be

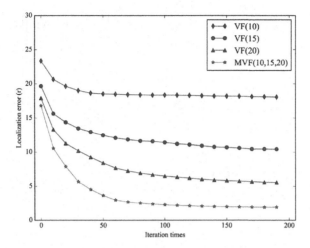

Fig. 3. Localization performance comparison at different iteration times

steady. The localization errors of MVF algorithms are lower than all the VF algorithms obviously.

Figure 4 shows the localization errors of MVF algorithm is lower than other algorithm if the ratio of the anchor nodes is big enough. Note that the MVF algorithm uses the multiple communication ranges. The wide communication range is for coarse-grained positioning and the narrow communication range is for fine-grained

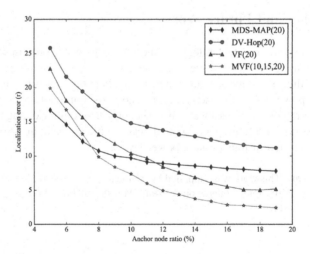

Fig. 4. Localization performance comparison at different ratio of anchor node

positioning. Thus the connectivity information for different communication range improves the performance of the MVF algorithm.

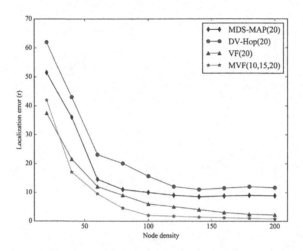

Fig. 5. Localization performance comparison at different node density

Figure 5 shows the localization error at different node density. The iteration count is 100 and the ratio of anchor nodes is 15%. We find that with the increasing of the node density, the localization errors of these algorithm decreases. When the node density is greater than 100, the localization errors of these algorithms tend to be steady. The localization error of MVF algorithm is lower than other algorithms if the node density is reasonable high.

5   Conclusion and Future Work

Positioning is an important technology for the IOT. This paper proposes an improved node localization algorithm in wireless sensor networks. It does not require additional hardware and thus suits for a wide range of application scenarios. It depends on multiple radio power levels to reach high-precision positioning. The results show that our algorithm can obtain higher localization accuracy than other existing algorithms in the dense networks. Our future work will address the fundamental questions of how to choose the best group of transmission power levels.

Acknowledgement. This work was supported by National Natural Science Foundation of China (No. 61370191) and the Joint Foundation of MoE (Ministry of Education) and China Mobile Group (No. MCM20160103).

References

1. Condoluci, M., Araniti, G., Mahmoodi, T., Dohler, M.: Enabling the IoT machine age with 5G: machine-type multicast services for innovative real-time applications. IEEE Access **4**, 5555–5569 (2016)

2. Akyildiz, I.F., Su, W., Sankarasubramaniam, Y., Cayirci, E.: A survey on sensor networks. IEEE Commun. Mag. **40**(8), 102–114 (2002)
3. Hutchison, D.: Self-Organization in Sensor and Actor Networks. Wiley, Hoboken (2007)
4. Zhang, Z., Long, K., Wang, J., Dressler, F.: On swarm intelligence inspired self-organized networking: its bionic mechanisms, designing principles and optimization approaches. IEEE Commun. Surv. Tutor. **16**(1), 513–537 (2014). First Quarter
5. Kuriakose, J., Amruth, V., Nandhini, N.S.: A survey on localization of wireless sensor nodes. In: 2014 International Conference on Information Communication and Embedded Systems (ICICES), Chennai, pp. 1–6 (2014)
6. Zanaj, E., Elbasani, E., Alinci, M., Kotobelli, E., Zanaj, B.: Application of the localization algorithms in WSN. In: 2014 49th International Universities on Power Engineering Conference (UPEC), Cluj-Napoca, pp. 1–5 (2014)
7. Niculescu, D., Nath, B.: DV based positioning in ad hoc networks. J. Telecommun. Syst. **22**, 267–270 (2003)
8. Liu, Y., Zhang, Y.: A better range-free localization algorithm in wireless sensor networks. In: 2016 International Symposium on Computer, Consumer and Control (IS3C), Xi'an, pp. 132–135 (2016)
9. Shang, Y., Ruml, W., Zhang, Y., Fromherz, M.P.J.: Localization from mere connectivity. In: Proceedings of the 4th ACM International Symposium on Mobile Ad Hoc Networking and Computing (2003)
10. Shang, Y., Rumi, W., Zhang, Y., Fromherz, M.: Localization from connectivity in sensor networks. IEEE Trans. Parallel Distrib. Syst. **15**(11), 961–974 (2004)
11. Zou, Y., Chakrabarty, K.: Sensor deployment and target localization based on virtual forces. In: Twenty-Second Annual Joint Conference of the IEEE Computer and Communications, INFOCOM 2003, vol. 2, pp. 1293–1303. IEEE Societies, San Francisco, CA (2003)
12. Awad, F.H.: Wireless location estimation using virtual forces. In: 2015 IEEE International Conference on Computer and Information Technology; Ubiquitous Computing and Communications; Dependable, Autonomic and Secure Computing; Pervasive Intelligence and Computing (CIT/IUCC/DASC/PICOM), Liverpool, pp. 1481–148 (2015)
13. Assaf, A.E., Zaidi, S., Affes, S., Kandil, N.: Low-cost localization for multihop heterogeneous wireless sensor networks. IEEE Trans. Wirel. Commun. **15**(1), 472–484 (2016)
14. Han, G., Jiang, J., Zhang, C., Duong, T.Q., Guizani, M., Karagiannidis, G.K.: A survey on mobile anchor node assisted localization in wireless sensor networks. IEEE Commun. Surv. Tutor. **18**(3), 2220–2243 (2016). Third Quarter
15. Zaidi, S., El Assaf, A., Affes, S., Kandil, N.: Accurate range-free localization in multi-hop wireless sensor networks. IEEE Trans. Commun. **64**(9), 3886–3900 (2016)
16. Jayasumana, A.P., Paffenroth, R., Ramasamy, S.: Topology maps and distance-free localization from partial virtual coordinates for IoT networks. In: 2016 IEEE International Conference on Communications (ICC), Kuala Lumpur, pp. 1–6 (2016)
17. Chen, Y.S., Deng, D.J., Teng, C.C.: Range-based localization algorithm for next generation wireless networks using radical centers. IEEE Access **4**, 2139–2153 (2016)

End-to-End Transmission Performance Optimization Based Routing Selection Algorithm for Software Defined Networking

Guixiang Jiang[✉], Rong Chai, and Haipeng Li

Key Lab of Mobile Communication Technology,
Chongqing University of Posts and Telecommunications, Chongqing, China
825882445@qq.com, chairong@cqupt.edu.cn, lihaipeng814@qq.com

Abstract. Software-defined networking (SDN) is a new networking paradigm enabling innovation through decoupling control plane from data plane and providing programmability for network application development. Specific research focus has been placed to achieve route optimal selection in SDN scenario. In this paper, we study the problem of route selection for a user flow in a SDN scenario consisting of a number of switches and propose an end-to-end transmission performance optimization based routing selection algorithm. We jointly consider the characteristics of user flow and service capability of the network, and formulate the arrival curve of user flow and the service curve of switches by applying Network Calculus theory. The transmission performance of user flow, defined as effective bandwidth is evaluated and the route offering the maximum effective bandwidth is selected as the optimal route. Numerical results demonstrate the effectiveness of the proposed algorithm.

Keywords: SDN · Routing algorithm · Network calculus
Effective bandwidth

1 Introduction

The rapid growth of data services with different quality of service (QoS) requirements poses challenges to network architecture and management mechanisms. Traditional Internet technologies can hardly meet the increasing service requirements due to tightly coupled control and date plane, inflexible network architecture and complicated network and service management mechanisms. To tackle these challenges, software-defined networking (SDN) technology has been proposed [1].

As an emerging network technology, SDN is one of the most promising approaches to dynamically programming networks and managing user services via building customized solutions which are manageable, dynamic, cost-effective and adaptable. In SDN, controllers in control plane are responsible for controlling and managing data forwarding devices such as switches in a centralized

© ICST Institute for Computer Sciences, Social Informatics and Telecommunications Engineering 2018
K. Long et al. (Eds.): 5GWN 2017, LNICST 211, pp. 28–37, 2018.
https://doi.org/10.1007/978-3-319-72823-0_4

manner, thus achieving the separation between data forwarding plane and the control plane. This new network technology permits separating network control functions, e.g., routing from switches so that routing algorithms can be designed in controllers [2,3].

In recent years, the problem of routing algorithm design for SDN has been stressed and several routing algorithms have been proposed. Some references consider applying network function virtualization (NFV) technology to achieve performance enhancement of routing algorithms in SDN. In [4], the authors present a QoS-aware virtualization-enabled routing framework to fulfill the QoS requirement of multiple clients in a SDN. To isolate and prioritize tenants from different clients, a network virtualization algorithm is designed to create a subnet for each tenant, and then a QoS-aware routing algorithm is proposed to maximize the minimum residue bandwidth of links. The authors in [5] present an approach for building multicast mechanisms over SDN. By applying NFV technology, transcoding functions are embedded into some of the servers, switches or routers. A multicast routing algorithm is then proposed to ensure each multicast flow traverses through the nodes embedded NFV technology before reaching the destination, while the total routing cost is minimized at the same time.

User QoS requirements and network characteristics are jointly considered in routing algorithm for SDN. In [6], the authors propose a probabilistic QoS routing mechanism for SDN which jointly considers link probability and bandwidth availability of the network. By applying Bayes theorem and Bayesian network model, link probability is determined based on which the path consisting of the links of the highest probabilities is selected under that satisfies the bandwidth constraint. The authors in [7] stress resource requirements of flows in the core network. Defining resource requirements including transmission bandwidth and flow tables as resource preference, the authors quantize the resource preference of different network flows based on analytic hierarchy process (AHP) method and propose a resource preference aware routing algorithm which matches each flow to the path with the largest preference degree.

In [8], the authors consider transmitting a set of unicast sessions in SDN with each session having a QoS requirement on transmission throughput. Assuming each session is associated with a collection of packet forwarding rules, the authors propose a rule multiplexing scheme, in which the same set of rules is deployed on the common nodes of multiple paths. Based on the multiplexing scheme, a route selection and rule placement strategy is proposed with the objective of minimizing rule space occupation of all the sessions.

In previous works, the transmission characteristics such as network bandwidth and throughput are taken into account in designing optimal routing strategy, however, the end-to-end transmission performance fails to be stressed, which may result in undesired transmission performance. In this paper, we study the problem of routing algorithm design for one user flow in SDN. Particularly, we consider service preference on high data rate and propose an end-to-end transmission performance optimization based routing algorithm. To quantitatively analyze the end-to-end transmission performance of user flow, we apply Network

Calculus theory, which enables the joint consideration of the service arrival characteristics of the user flow and the serving ability of the intermediate switches, thus achieving comprehensive evaluation of the transmission performance of user flow.

The rest of this paper is organized as follows. Section 2 describes the system model considered in this paper. Section 3 discusses the optimal route selection algorithm. In Sect. 4, we examine the end-to-end transmission performance of user flow. Simulation results are presented in Sect. 5. Finally, Sect. 6 concludes the paper.

2   System Model

In this paper, we consider a SDN model as shown in Fig. 1. The system consists of one SDN controller and a number of switches. We assume that a user flow needs to be transmitted from a source switch (SS) to a destination switch (DS). In the case that no direct transmission link between SS and DS exists, route selection strategy should be designed for the user flow.

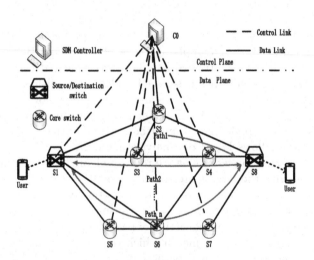

Fig. 1. System model

We assume in the SDN scenario considered, there exists M_0 switches in addition to SS and DS. For convenience, we denote Φ as the set containing all the switches. To characterize the connection status between switches, we introduce binary connection identifiers. Let $\delta_{i,j}$ denote the connection identifier between switch i and switch j, i.e., $\delta_{i,j} = 1$ if switch i is an adjacent node of switch j, thus there exists an available link between switch i and switch j; otherwise, $\delta_{i,j} = 0$, $i \in \Phi$, $j \in \Phi, i \neq j$. In this paper, we assume that the network topology is given, hence, $\delta_{i,j}$ are known constants.

3   Optimal Route Selection Algorithm Description

In this paper, we assume that the user flow has a minimum data rate requirement, to reduce the computation complexity of route selection, we first propose a candidate route selection scheme based on user rate requirement and network characteristics, and then an optimal route selection is proposed to select the optimal route among all the candidate routes.

3.1   Candidate Route Selection Scheme

Given a SDN scenario, we first search for all the possible routes connecting SS and DS. We assume that the number of possible routes connecting SS and DS is M, and denote the mth route as L_m. For convenience, we denote the switches along L_m as $S_{m,0}$, $S_{m,1}$, $\cdots$, S_{m,N_m}, where N_m denotes the link number of L_m. We can obtain that L_m is an available route connecting SS and DS provided that $S_{m,0}$ and S_{m,N_m} are respectively SS and DS and the following condition meets. For simplicity, we assume that the jth switch of L_m is labeled as the m_jth switch of the network, $1 \leq j \leq N_m$, we can achieve that the m_{j-1}th switch and the m_jth switch should be adjacent nodes of the network, i.e.,

$$\delta_{m_{j-1}, m_j} = 1. \tag{1}$$

Denote the data rate of L_m as R_m, $1 \leq m \leq M$, we define R_m^0 as the minimum data rate of all the links of L_m, i.e.,

$$R_m^0 = \min\{R_{m,j}^0\}, \ 1 \leq j \leq N_m \tag{2}$$

where $R_{m,j}^0$ denotes the data rate of the jth link of L_m. In this paper, we assume that the link capacity is large enough, thus the data rate of one link is determined by the port rate of the two switches being connected by the link. We denote the import and outport rate of $S_{m,j}$ as $R_{m,j}^{in}$ and $R_{m,j}^{out}$, respectively, $0 \leq j \leq N_m$. The data rate of the jth link of L_m can be defined as the smaller one of the outport rate of $S_{m,j-1}$ and the import rate of $S_{m,j}$, $1 \leq j \leq N_m$, which can be expressed as:

$$R_{m,j}^0 = \min\{R_{m,j-1}^{out}, R_{m,j}^{in}\}, \ 1 \leq j \leq N_m \tag{3}$$

Assuming user flow has a minimum data rate requirement, denoted by R^{min}, only the routes meeting this constraint can be selected as the transmission route. Denoting Ψ as the set of the candidate routes, we obtain:

$$\Psi = \{L_m | R_m^0 \geq R^{min}, \ 1 \leq m \leq M\}. \tag{4}$$

3.2   Optimal Route Selection Strategy

To obtain the optimal route, we examine the transmission performance of all the candidate routes, and select the one offering the best performance. In particular, we focus on the end-to-end transmission performance and evaluate the throughput of the candidate routes by jointly considering the characteristics of user flow and the service capability of the switches. Denote T_m, $1 \leq m \leq M$, as the throughput of the mth route, we obtain the optimal route, denoted by L_{m^*} as:

$$L_{m^*} = \mathrm{argmax}\ \{T_m\}. \tag{5}$$

The detail evaluation of T_m will be discussed in the following section.

4   End-to-End Transmission Performance Evaluation

In this section, the transmission performance of the candidate routes between SS and DS is evaluated based on Network Calculus theory [9], which is an efficient tool to analyze flow control problems in networks mainly from a lower bound (i.e., worst case) perspective. The essential idea of network calculus is to transform complex non-linear network systems into analytically tractable linear systems by using alternate algebras, i.e., the min-plus algebra and max-plus algebra.

4.1   Brief Introduction of Network Calculus Theory

In this subsection, some concepts defined in the theory of network calculus will be introduced briefly.

Definition 1: Min-plus Convolution. Let f and g be two functions or sequences of time, the min-plus convolution of f and g is defined as follows:

$$(f \otimes g)(t) = \begin{cases} \inf_{0 \leq s \leq t} \{f(t-s) + g(s)\}, & t > 0 \\ 0, & t < 0. \end{cases} \tag{6}$$

Definition 2: Arrival Curve. Given a wide-sense increasing function $\alpha(t)$ defined for $t \geq 0$, a flow $F(t)$ is constrained by $\alpha(t)$ if for all $s \leq t$, following inequality holds:

$$F(t) - F(s) \leq \alpha(t-s), \tag{7}$$

we say that $\alpha(t)$ is the arrival curve of $F(t)$.

Definition 3: Service Curve. Consider a system S and a flow with the input and output functions respectively being $F(t)$ and $O(t)$ passing through S, we say that S offers a service curve $\beta(t)$ to the flow if and only if $\beta(t)$ meets following conditions:

$$\beta(0) = 0, \tag{8}$$

$$O(t) \geq (F \otimes \beta)(t). \tag{9}$$

Definition 4: Effective Bandwidth. Consider a flow with arrival curve $\alpha(t)$ passing through a system S, for a given delay $L = \theta + \frac{s_b}{r}$, where θ and s_b denote respectively the service delay and the burst tolerance of S, and r denotes the service rate of S, we define the effective bandwidth of the flow, denoted by $e_L(\alpha)$, as the required throughput at t to serve the flow in a work conserving manner, i.e.:

$$e_L(\alpha) = \sup_{s \geq 0}\{\frac{\alpha(s)}{s + L}\}. \tag{10}$$

From the definition of effective bandwidth, it can be seen that effective bandwidth represents the maximum transmitted data packets for a given time interval, thus is equivalent to transmission throughput, which can be applied to characterize the end-to-end transmission performance of the mth candidate route, i.e., T_m in (5), when the flow with arrival function being $\alpha(t)$ passes through a system with the service curve being $\beta(t)$. In the following subsections, we will examine the transmission performance of candidate routes based on Network Calculus theory. The arrival curve of user flow and the service curve of switches are formulated, then the effective bandwidth of each route is evaluated.

4.2   Modeling Arrival Curve of User Flow

In this paper, referring to [10], we characterize the arrival curve of user flow as traffic-specification (T-SPEC) model [11]. We define the set of T-SPEC parameters $(r^{(m)}, s^{(m)}, r^{(s)}, s^{(b)})$, where $r^{(m)}$ and $s^{(m)}$ represent the maximum arrival rate and the maximum packet size, respectively, $r^{(s)}$ and $s^{(b)}$ represent the sustainable arrival rate and the burst tolerance, respectively, the arrival curve of the user flow can be modeled as:

$$\alpha(t) = \min\{r^{(m)}t + s^{(m)}, r^{(s)}t + s^{(b)}\}. \tag{11}$$

4.3   Modeling Service Curve of Switches

In this paper, we assume that the switches are latency-rate (LR) system, of which the service curve can be characterized by the service rate and the transmission latency. For the jth switch of L_m, the service curve can be modeled as:

$$\beta_{m,j}(t) = R_{m,j}(t - \theta_{m,j})^+ \tag{12}$$

where $R_{m,j}$ and $\theta_{m,j}$ are respectively the service rate and the latency of the jth switch of L_m, $(x)^+ = \max\{x, 0\}$. According to Network Calculus theory, the joint service curve of L_m can be expressed as:

$$\beta_m(t) = \beta_{m,1}(t) \otimes \beta_{m,2}(t) \cdots \otimes \beta_{m,N_m}(t) = R_m(t - \theta_m)^+ \tag{13}$$

where $R_m = \min\{R_{m,1}, R_{m,2}, \cdots, R_{m,N_m}\}$, $\theta_m = \sum_{j=1}^{N_m} \theta_{m,j}$.

4.4   Effective Bandwidth of the Candidate Routes

Substituting $\alpha(t)$ obtained in (11) into (10), and calculating L based on $\beta_m(t)$ obtained in (13), after some simple mathematical manipulations, we can obtain the effective bandwidth when the user flow transmitting through L_m, i.e.,

$$T_m = \max \left\{ r^{(s)}, \frac{s^{(m)}}{\theta_m}, \frac{(s^{(m)} + r^{(m)}\Gamma_m)}{\Gamma_m + \theta_m} \right\} \tag{14}$$

where $\Gamma_m = (s^{(b)} - s^{(m)})/(r^{(m)} - r^{(s)})$.

5   Performance Evaluation

In this section, we examine the performance of the proposed routing selection algorithm via simulation. We consider a SDN scenario with the size being 100×100 consisting of a SS, a DS and multiple intermediate switches. We assume that all the switches are randomly located in a area. In the simulation, the numbers of intermediate switches are chosen from 6 to 12, the parameters of the arrival curve of the user flow and those of switches are randomly chosen within certain range, as shown in Table 1. For a randomly generated position distribution of switches and the characteristics of arrival curve and service curve, the proposed routing selection algorithm as well as the one proposed in [6] are conducted. The simulation results are averaged over 1000 independent adaptation processes where each adaptation process involves different positions of switches and various characteristics of arrival curve and service curve.

Table 1. Simulation parameters

Parameter name	Value
Peak rate (r^m) (Mbps)	1.5–10
Maximum packet size (s^m) (Kbit)	1–400
Average rate (r^s) (Mbps)	0.7–3.5
Burst tolerance (s^b) (Kbit)	38–140
Equivalent service rate ($R_{m,j}$) (Mbps)	10–100
Equivalent latency ($\theta_{m,j}$) (ms)	10–60
The service rate of switches (Mbps)	10–80
The simulation iteration	1000

The simulation results are averaged over 1000 independent adaptation processes where each adaptation process involves different positions of switches. The detailed parameters used in the simulation are shown in Table 1. Fig. 2 shows the effective bandwidth versus the number of switches. It can be seen from the figure that the effective bandwidth increases with the increase of the number of

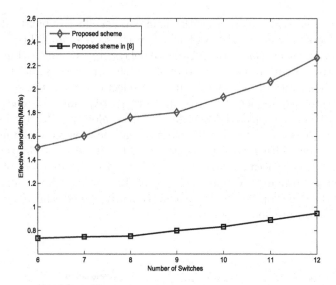

Fig. 2. Effective bandwidth versus the number of the switches

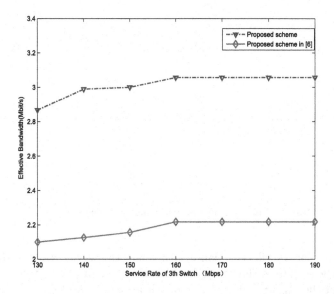

Fig. 3. Effective bandwidth versus service rate

switches, this is because for a large number of switches may offer more options in route selection compared to small number of switches, resulting in better transmission performance in turn. Comparing the results obtained from our proposed scheme and the one proposed in [6], we can see our proposed scheme offers better effective bandwidth than previous scheme. The reason is that our proposed scheme aims of selecting the route with the maximum effective bandwidth, which jointly considers the characteristics of user flow and service capability of switches, including both transmission rate and service delay, while the algorithm proposed in [6] only stresses the transmission rate of switches. In Figs. 3 and 4, we examine the characteristics of one switch on route selection, for instance, we change the service rate and service delay of the third switch, and examine the effective bandwidth of the selected route. In Fig. 3, we plot the effective bandwidth versus the service rate of the third switch. It can be seen from the figure that the effective bandwidth increases slightly with the increase of the service rate of the switch, this is because higher service rate of the switch will offer better transmission performance. Comparing the results obtained from our proposed scheme and the one proposed in [6], we can see our proposed scheme offers better performance than previous scheme.

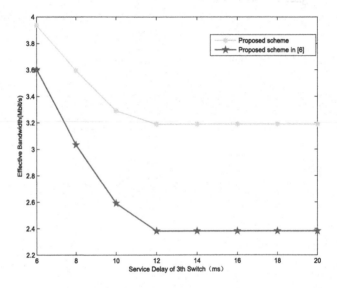

Fig. 4. Effective bandwidth versus service delay

In Fig. 4, we plot the effective bandwidth versus the service delay of the third switch. It can be seen from the figure that the effective bandwidth decreases with the increase of the service delay of the switch for small service delay, then the effective bandwidth will not change clearly with the increase of the service delay. This is because higher service delay of the switch will result in small effective bandwidth. However, as the service delay is relatively high, the optimal route obtained based on the proposed route selection algorithm may not involve the third switch due to its deteriorated performance, thus the achieved effective bandwidth will not change. Comparing the results obtained from our proposed scheme and the one proposed in [6], we can see our proposed scheme offers better performance.

6   Conclusion

In this paper, we propose an optimal route selection algorithm for SDN which aims of achieving end-to-end performance optimization of user flow. Through applying Network Calculus theory, we jointly take into account the characteristics of arrival curve and switches of the network, formulate the transmission performance of user flow as effective bandwidth, and then the route offering the maximum effective bandwidth is selected as the optimal route. The numerical results demonstrate that compared to previous algorithm, our proposed algorithm achieves much better performance in terms of effective bandwidth.

Acknowledgement. This work is supported by the National Science and Technology Specific Project of China (2016ZX03001010-004) and the 863 project (2014AA01A701), the special fund of Chongqing key laboratory (CSTC) and the project of Chongqing Municipal Education Commission (Kjzh11206).

References

1. Matias, J., Garay, J., Toledo, N., et al.: Toward an SDN-enabled NFV architecture. IEEE Commun. Mag. **53**(4), 187–193 (2015)
2. Gantz, J., Reinsel, D.: Extracting value from chaos, Idcemc2 Report, pp. 1–12. Framingham, MA, USA, White Paper, June 2011
3. Adami, D., Antichi, G., Garroppo, R.G., et al.: Towards an SDN network control application for differentiated traffic routing. In: IEEE International Conference on Communications (ICC) (2015)
4. Porxas, A.X., Lin S.C., Luo, M.: QoS-aware virtualization-enabled routing in software-defined networks. In: IEEE International Conference on Communications (ICC), pp. 5771–5776, June 2015
5. Zhang, S.Q., Zhang, Q., Bannazadeh, H., et al.: Routing algorithms for network function virtualization enabled multicast topology on SDN. IEEE Trans. Netw. Serv. Manag. **12**(4), 580–594 (2015)
6. Al-Jawad, A., Trestian, R., Shah, P., et al.: BaProbSDN: A probabilistic-based QoS routing mechanism for software defined networks. In: IEEE Network Softwarization (NetSoft), London, pp. 1–5, June 2015
7. Lee, D., Hong, P., Li, J.: RPA-RA: a resource preference aware routing algorithm in software defined network. In: IEEE Global Communications Conference (GLOBE-COM), San Diego, pp. 1–6 (2015)
8. Huang, H., Guo, S., Li, P., et al.: Joint optimization of rule placement and traffic engineering for QoS provisioning in software defined network. IEEE Trans. Comput. **64**(12), 3488–3499 (2015)
9. Le Boudec, J.-Y., Thiran, P. (eds.): Network Calculus: A Theory of Deterministic Queuing Systems for the Internet. LNCS, vol. 2050. Springer, Heidelberg (2001). https://doi.org/10.1007/3-540-45318-0
10. Shenker, C.P.S., Guerin, R.: Specification of guaranteed quality of service, RFC2212 (1997)
11. Liu, Y., Jiang, Y.: Stochastic Network Calculus. Springer, London (2008). https://doi.org/10.1007/978-1-84800-127-5

Research on Video Services with QoE Perception Over Future Wireless Networks

Qinghua Zhu[1]([✉]), Jinglu Zhang[1], Gongsheng Zhu[1],
and Xiaokui Chen[2]

[1] School of Telecommunication Engineering,
Beijing Polytechnic, Beijing 100176, China
3170312109@QQ.com
[2] Beijing University of Posts and Telecommunications, Beijing 100876, China

Abstract. Research on video services with QoE (quality of experience) perception, through the analysis of the characteristics of the video service as well as its service quality influence and combined with the practical application of the scene, this paper presents a QoE perception model based on the characteristics of video frame. Based on MPEG compression coding and the independence between the video frames are proposed by this paper, and discussed the frame structure and the effect of FLR for QoE of video services. Simulation results show that QoE perception model proposed can effectively evaluate the influence of FLR of QoE of video services, and has very strong practicability of this scene in the real-time video transmission. The results show that in order to ensure the QoE, the packet loss of video frames must control in the process of transfer.

Keywords: Wireless video services · QoE perception
Future wireless network

1 Introduction

With the rapid development and wide application of in 5G wireless network, video streaming has taken up most of today's network traffic, and the digital video services have brought new challenges to the future wireless network [1, 2], which mainly reflect in: the evaluation on service quality is experiencing the transformation from QoS to QoE [3]. In the conventional mobile communication system, the band width, time delay, jitter, packet loss rate and other QoS parameters are typically considered as the indicator of measuring service quality. For the mobile Internet business especially the video services, the corresponding evaluation of the service quality is not only related to the transmission parameters of the wireless network physical layer, but also related to service characteristics and users' experience environment, and therefore QoE is generally used for evaluating the user quality. QoE is an application and service-level protection mechanism. The service quality evaluated from the perspective of users is not only based on the relevant QoS parameters, but also combined with the service characteristics, which can be better able to reflect the users' subjective feelings. QoS/QoE requirements are varied for different types of services [4–7]. For example, the files downloading, web pages browsing and other data services do not have the

© ICST Institute for Computer Sciences, Social Informatics and Telecommunications Engineering 2018
K. Long et al. (Eds.): 5GWN 2017, LNICST 211, pp. 38–51, 2018.
https://doi.org/10.1007/978-3-319-72823-0_5

real-time requirements, but they have the clear requirements for the accuracy of the transmission data; for example, the real-time video services are more sensitive to time delay, so it's essential to make sure that data can be transmitted timely.

The video service QoE perception algorithm plays a significant role in video call, video conferencing, video surveillance, and video on demand and other fields, which is the feedback measurement of users towards the video service quality, but even an important tool to guarantee video quality [8, 9].

The video quality is originally reflected through people's subjective visual feeling towards the video, but because people's subjective evaluation will require a lot of time and efforts, and the differences between individuals have a larger impact on the evaluation results, people are in an urgent demand for some objective, quantitative mathematical model to express their subjective feeling towards the wireless video. This requires to starting from the basic characteristics of the video services of the wireless network to build an video QoE perception system that can penetrate into the wireless network and meet different demands, so as to improve the accuracy of video quality assessment and increase the utilization of wireless network resources as much as possible, safeguarding the service quality of future wireless network.

Currently, the QoE subjective and QoE objective evaluation methods are mainly used as the video service QoE assessment method. Among them, the subjective QoE perception method is to let the subjects to continuously watch the test sequence in a controlled environment, which will be lasted for about 10–30 min, and then is to conduct the subjective ratings for the watched video sequences, thus to finally calculate MOS (Mean Opinion Score). Wherein the controlled environment includes: The selection of the test environment, the viewing distance, the test material (video sequences), and the intervals of time display of the test sequence, etc. For subjective quality assessment method, currently the widely used method is mainly from ITU organization, including DSCQS (Double Stimulus Continuous Quality Scale), SSCQE (Single Stimulus Continuous Quality Scale), DSIS (Double stimulus Impairment Scale), ACR (Absolute Category Rating) and PC (Pair Comparison), etc.

The objective QoE perception method of video quality is to use a mathematical model to analyze the test sequence, thus to finally obtain the perception results of the video quality. The objective perception method can be divided into the following three types according to whether there's the original video for reference: FR (Full-Reference), RR (Reduce-Reference) and NR (No-Reference). The corresponding full reference evaluation method requires a full video reference to compare its quality with the distorted test sequence, thereby getting the score. Reduced reference evaluation method is mainly to discover the distortion through comparison of the extracted reduced reference, so these reference characteristics should be able to better reflect the distortion of coding and channel transmission. The vast majority of the algorithm is to extract the characteristic of space-time domain, as well as to extract the video image edges, but there's also the algorithm of extracting the values calculated based on the pixel values, such as the mean, standard deviation, etc., in addition, there's also the algorithm of extracting video spatial or temporal activity [10] (video activity describes the strong extent of the visual perception motion of video sequences to users [11]). Saviotti proposed evaluation method based on digital watermark, adding watermark in a video image to predict the video distortion at the receiving end through measurement of the watermark image distortion [12]. No-reference evaluation method does not require any reference information, and it derives the video distortion directly through the evaluation of the distortion video. The method has a very great significance for future wireless video services, and it can reduce the transmission content compared with the two evaluation methods of full reference and reduced reference, thereby reducing the band width. However, since no-reference algorithm is too complicated, there's limited research results currently.

The subjective evaluation method is not widely used due to its low real-time, cost of manpower and resources, while the objective method is to use the mathematical models, there's no need to consume too much manpower. In the objective evaluation method, the results of full reference are closer to the results of human eye perception; and the results of the reduced reference are worse than the results of the full reference and it requires the additional band width to transmit the reference signal, therefore, it has little research significance; no-reference method is with higher practical value, because it can use the video features captured currently within a short time to directly obtain the video QoE indicators, which is with the characteristics of simple calculation and high real-time, and therefore it is also the research focus.

Through the study of QoE perception method based on pixel-domain and QoE method based on frame characteristics, this thesis uses mutual independence between MPEG-based coding-decoding characteristics and video frames to propose the transmission strategy with a combination of modulation and coding strategy, video packet re-transmission, and service quality, and also the study of the impact of frame structure and frame loss rate on QoE, and builds the objective evaluation model of the video service transmission.

2 Service Quality Evaluation Method Based on Video Frame Characteristics

The wireless video quality is closely related to its consistency of time domain, this feature determines the real-time of video services, and even does not allow the video to have any Caton phenomenon. In addition, the video quality is also greatly related to the audio corresponding to videos, and therefore it needs the received video and audio information to be strictly synchronous, there's even more strict requirement for the synchronization between voice and image of the video on demand, video conferencing, if the voice is not exactly match with the image, it will seriously affect the viewing effects of the audience. Since the real-time video feature, the corresponding evaluation also needs to have real-time feature. Thus, although the full-reference video quality evaluation method have better performance, it can't meet the requirements, therefore, this thesis adopts the no-reference video quality evaluation method considering the frame loss rate based on video frame characteristics.

In MPEG coding and decoding, the image group includes three categories of frame, namely I-frame, B-frame and P-frame, the loss of different categories of frame will have different impacts on decoding quality of the receiving end [13]. The method proposed in this thesis is to use the independence between MPEG-based coding-decoding characteristics and video frames to study the impact of the frame structure and frame loss rate on QoE.

2.1 MPEG Image Group

The MPEG (Moving Pictures Experts Group) is a video compression coding standard, which mainly uses inter-frame compression coding technology with motion compensation to reduce the temporal redundancy; using DCT (Discrete Cosine Transform) technology to reduce the spatial redundancy of the image, the use of the entropy coding is to reduce the statistical redundancy in terms of information expression. In order to save network band width, video data will be transmitted after being encoded. There are three types of frames in MPEG standard video coding sequence: I-frame (Intra-coded Picture), P-frame (Predictive-coded Picture), B-frame (Bidirectional Predicted Picture). Wherein I-frame is to code by using its own information without any reference to other frames; P-frame refers to the preceding I-frame or P-frame, and it is to code based on the motion differences; B-frame is to make the bidirectional coding by using P-frame before and after it, so it is with the higher compression ratio. When decoding, if B-frame loss will not cause too much impact, P-frame loss will not affect the I-frame, but it will affect P-frame and B- frame associated with it, I-frame loss will make P-frame and B-frame associated with it can't be decoded, so the loss of different frames will have varied impacts on QoE [14].

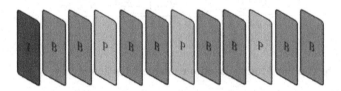

Fig. 1. Open GOP structure diagram

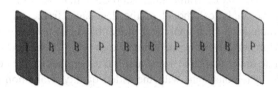

Fig. 2. Closed GOP structure diagram

According to the distance between I-frames in a video sequence, all of the frames are divided into GOP (Group of Picture), so there's only one I-frame in each GOP. A common GOP structure is generally described by using (N, M), wherein N is the distance between one I-frame and the next I-frame, M is the distance between

I-frame and the next P-frame. For example, one GOP may be such a composition: IBBPBBPBBPBB, which is referred to as (12, 3), where 12 represent the length of GOP, 3 is the distance between I-frame and P-frame. For such a frame, the last B-frame is coded with reference to I-frame of the next GOP, and such GOP is called as the open GOP, as shown in Fig. 1. The other is such as GOP of (10, 3): IBBPBBPBBP, the last B-frame is with the reference to P-frame in GOP, so such GOP is called as the closed GOP as shown in Fig. 2. Suppose N represents the total number of I-frame, P-frame and B-frame in one GOP, and N_I, N_P and N_B respectively represents the number of I-frame, P-frame and B-frame, thus it may be inferred that for an open GOP, the number of P-frame is $N/M - 1$, and for a closed GOP, the number of P-frame is $(N - 1)/M$, the number of B-frame is $N - N_P - 1$. Therefore, regarding to any kind of GOP, there will be the following formula:

$$N_I = 1$$
$$N_P = [(N - 1)/M]$$
$$N_B = N - [(N - 1)/M] - 1. \tag{1}$$

In the formula (1), $[a]$ represents the rounding of a. In an open GOP, $N_B = (N_P + 1) \times (M - 1)$, and in a closed GOP, $N_B = N_P \times (M - 1)$, this thesis uses a variable φ to represents the type of GOP, when $\varphi = 1$, GOP is an open GOP, when $\varphi = 0$, indicating that GOP is a closed GOP. Therefore, φ value can be calculated directly from GOP result, as shown in formula (2):

$$\varphi = \frac{N_B}{M - 1} - N_P = \frac{N - 1 - \frac{N-1}{M}}{M - 1} - \frac{N - 1}{M}. \tag{2}$$

2.2   QoE Perception Model Based on Frame Characteristics

Decodable frame rate refers to the part of the video frames that can be completely and correctly seen by users after they are decoded by the Player, so it is directly related to the user perception and only related to the video signal received by users. The literature [15] introduces the decodable frame rate, supposing that the loss of each frame is independent, and the analytical model of the decodable frame rate depends on the probability of a frame loss, such analytical model has been used in some research on wireless transmission network. In some other studies [16, 17], they compare PSNR and decodable frame rate under the same scene and frame parameters, the conclusion is that decodable frame rate is consistent with the video quality evaluation result based on PSNR, both can reflect the visual effect quality shown by the video to users, so MOS video quality can be estimated by decodable frame rate at the reasonable estimation accuracy.

Decodable frame rate can evaluate the video quality by spending less time on the receiving end to assess the video quality. Decodable frame rate is also known as Q, in this thesis Q will be used as the assessment measurement of video services in the wireless network.

Prior to the video transmission, the first is to divide each frame of the images of video data into certain number of data packets for transmission, real-time transmission of video services is conducted according to the corresponding needs, since there's large amount of data and demanding real-time, UDP connection is generally adopted for transmission of video data in order to avoid the network collapse. However, the characteristics of best efforts of UDP show that the non-reliability of UDP is bound to make the packet loss become a problem must be considered, the missing of a packet in one frame will make the whole video impossible to be decoded, and this will certainly affect the video QoE, and it is also a major factor affecting QoE in wireless network video services.

Different types of frame loss will make the number of decodable frame loss to be varied, herein the decodable frame rate is defined as Q to represent the quality of the video sequence, and Q represents the ratio of the number of decodable frame and the total number of received frame. Supposing, and respectively represents the loss probability of I-frame, P-frame and B-frame, and there's the mutual independence between frames, then for an open GOP structure that can be expressed as (N, M), the decodable frame rate Q of its video sequence can be derived as follows:

(1) The mathematical expectation for calculating the number of decodable I-frame is N_{DI}. In a GOP, I-frame is to code by using its own information without any reference to other frames, therefore $N_{DI} = (1 - FLR_I)$;

(2) The mathematical expectation for calculating the number of decodable P-frame is N_{DP}. In a GOP, only when the preceding I-frame and P-frame can be decoded, can P-frame be decoded accordingly. $S(P_n)$ represents probability for n^{th} P-frame to be decoded:

$$S(P_1) = (1 - FLR_I) * (1 - FLR_P)$$
$$S(P_2) = (1 - FLR_I) * (1 - FLR_P)^2$$
$$\ldots$$
$$S(P_{N_P}) = (1 - FLR_I) * (1 - FLR_P)^{N_P}$$

Thus, there's:

$$N_{DP} = \sum_{i=1}^{N_P} S(P_i) = (1 - FLR_I) \sum_{i=1}^{N_P} (1 - FLR_P)^{N_P}. \tag{3}$$

(3) The mathematical expectation for calculating the number of decodable P-frame is N_{DB}. In a GOP, only when the preceding or the following I-frame and P-frame can be decoded, can P-frame be decoded accordingly. Especially the last B-frame is based on the preceding P-frame coding and following I-frame coding, thus the last B-frame is affected by two I-frames. $S(B_n)$ represents the probability for n^{th} B-frame can be decoded:

$$S(B_1) = (1 - FLR_I) * (1 - FLR_P) * (1 - FLR_B)$$
$$S(B_2) = (1 - FLR_I) * (1 - FLR_P)^2 * (1 - FLR_B)$$
$$\cdots$$

$$S(B_{\frac{N}{M}-1}) = (1 - FLR_I) * (1 - FLR_P)^{\frac{N}{M}-1} * (1 - FLR_B)$$

$$S(B_{\frac{N}{M}}) = (1 - FLR_I)^2 * (1 - FLR_P)^{\frac{N}{M}-1} * (1 - FLR_B)$$

Therefore, the formula (4) is concluded:

$$N_{DB} = (M - 1) \sum_{i=1}^{\frac{N}{M}} S(B_i) = (M - 1)(1 - FLR_I)(1 - FLR_B)$$
$$\left[\sum_{j=1}^{\frac{N}{M}-1} (1 - FLR_P)^j (1 - FLR_B) + (1 - FLR_I)(1 - FLR_P)^{\frac{N}{M}-1} \right]. \quad (4)$$

(4) Calculate the ratio of decodable frame Q, as shown in formula (5).

$$Q = \frac{N_{DI} + N_{DP} + N_{DB}}{N}. \quad (5)$$

Formula (5) can be further expressed as:

$$Q = \frac{(1 - FLR_I) + (1 - FLR_I) \sum_{i=1}^{N_P} (1 - FLR_P)^i}{N}$$
$$+ \frac{(M - 1)(1 - FLR_I)(1 - FLR_B) \left[\sum_{i=1}^{N_P} (1 - FLR_P)^i + (1 - FLR_I)(1 - FLR_P)^{N_P} \right]}{N}.$$

$$(6)$$

The last part $(1 - FLR_I)(1 - FLR_P)^{N_P}$ of formula (6) is only related to the last B-frame that needs to take a reference of the decoding I-frame in the following GOP, so decodable frame rate Q of the video sequence for any GOP structure can be expressed as:

$$Q = \frac{(1 - FLR_I) + (1 - FLR_I) \sum_{i=1}^{N_P} (1 - FLR_P)^i}{N}$$
$$+ \frac{(M - 1)(1 - FLR_I)(1 - FLR_B) \left[\sum_{i=1}^{N_P} (1 - FLR_P)^i + \varphi(1 - FLR_I)(1 - FLR_P)^{N_P} \right]}{N}.$$

$$(7)$$

Q is a measurement of the video quality of the receiving end, and we have finally established the method for video QoE assessment based on frame loss rate.

Formula (7) can be further simplified, it is considered that there's little change of the frame loss rate of a video sequence, therefore, it is assumed that each type of frames has the same frame loss rate, if the frame loss rate of I-frame, P-frame and B-frame is the same when there's the transmission of the video services, namely, $FLR = FLR_I = FLR_P = FLR_B$, then

$$Q = \frac{(1 - FLR) + (1 - FLR) \sum_{i=1}^{N_P} (1 - FLR)^i}{N}$$
$$+ \frac{(M - 1)(1 - FLR)^2 \left[\sum_{i=1}^{N_P} (1 - FLR)^i + \varphi(1 - FLR)^{N_P + 1} \right]}{N}. \tag{8}$$

3 Simulation Results and Performance Analysis

3.1 Experimental Network and Its Encoding Parameter Setting

Figure 3 is the architecture of the experimental network, the entire network environment is built based on NS2 [18] environment. Network has two emission sources, one is to generate the background stream of CBR (Constants Bit Rate), which is to transmit the CBR data packet at a rate of 1 Mbps; and the other is to generate MPEG4 video stream, which is to transmit the data packet at a rate of 10 Mbps. The router is to connect the wireless network at a rate of 10 Mbps, the connection frequency is 1 ms. The wireless network is to transmit the data to the mobile endpoint via WLAN at a rate of 11 Mbps.

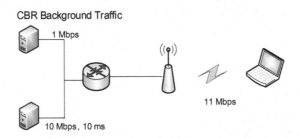

Fig. 3. Experimental network architecture

In the simulation, this thesis assumes that: (1) when connected to the network, there is no loss of the video packet; (2) the loss of a video packet will make it impossible to decode the entire video frame.

In this thesis, the video can be divided into three types according to the time characteristics and space characteristics: SM (Slight Movement), GW (Gentle Walking) and RM (Rapid Movement). Parameter settings based on application layer and the transport layer are as shown in Table 1.

Table 1. Parameter values of application layer and the transport layer:

Video sequences	Frame rate (fbps)	Transmission rate (kb/s)	Link rate (kb/s)	FLR
SM	10, 15, 30	18	32, 64, 128	0.01, 0.05, 0.1, 0.15, 0.2
		44		
		80		
GW	10, 15, 30	18	128, 256, 384	0.01, 0.05, 0.1, 0.15, 0.2
		44		
		80		
RM	10, 15, 30	80	384, 512, 768	0.01, 0.05, 0.1, 0.15, 0.2
		104		
		512		

3.2   Comparative Analysis of Q and PSNR

The experiment of this thesis is to use PSNR and Q indicators in Evalvid [19] to study the effectiveness of video service quality evaluation. Three different types of videos are used respectively in the simulation, namely, foreman, highway and coastguard. Figure 4 is the Q and PSNR comparative figure of different types of videos.

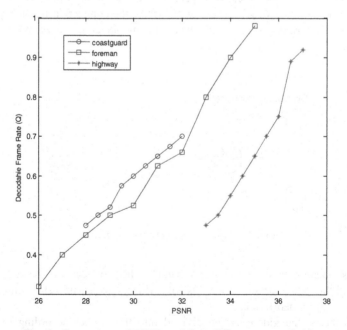

Fig. 4. Comparison of PSNR and Q in different types of video

It can be known from the simulation results that when Q is increased, PSNR is also increased accordingly. Based on the relationship between Q and PSNR, it can be considered that Q indicator is the same to PSNR to reflect the service quality of the video.

3.3   Analysis of Factors Affecting Q

Figure 5 compares the effect of changes in B-frame on video quality. Figures 6 and 7 respectively compares the impact of the total length of the video frame on video quality under the condition of open and closed GOP. Figure 8 compares the impact of frame on video quality whether GOP is open.

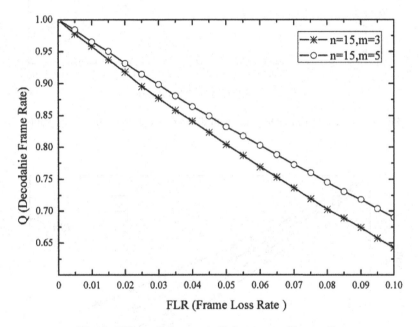

Fig. 5. Effects of changes in B frames on video quality

Through the analysis, it can be found that: (1) With the increase of video frame loss rate, the video quality at the receiving end shows the decreasing trend, and therefore in the wireless video transmission, it's essential to minimize the frame loss rate as much as possible in order to improve the quality of the service experience; (2) when the frame loss rate is smaller, the more B-frames in a sequence, the higher the video quality; (3) when the frame loss rate is smaller, the longer a GOP sequence, its video quality will be lower; (4) when the frame loss rate is smaller, there's little impact on the corresponding service quality whether a video frame is open.

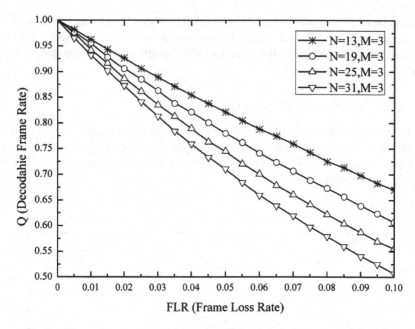

Fig. 6. Effects of open GOP video with different length frame on video quality

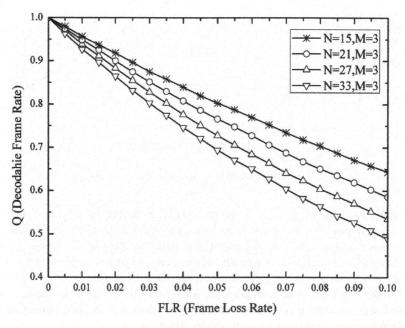

Fig. 7. Effects of closed GOP video with different length frame on video quality

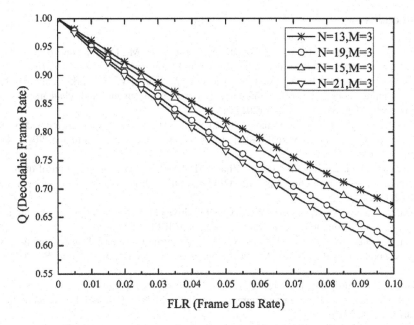

Fig. 8. The effect of video quality in open or closed GOP

4 Conclusion

The wireless network services are with the interaction, real-time, integration and other characteristics, thus the evaluation model is required to be a non-parameter evaluation model with good real-time. The impact of wireless network on the video is mainly for the packet loss resulting in frame loss, so this thesis is committed to finding a frame-level evaluation model. The perception method based on the pixel domain is simple and intuitive, and easy to calculate, but it only considers the energy of the signal, overlooking the impact of video content on the perception quality, which sometimes makes the results to be inconsistent with human eye perception, especially for the same original signal, two distortion signals with the same PSNR are not necessarily the same. In addition, PSNR needs to take a longer time to compare the corresponding frames of the original video and distortion video to obtain the evaluation parameters, and therefore it does not meet the requirements. This thesis presents a transmission strategy with a combination of modulation and coding strategy, video packet retransmission and service quality can meet the needs of future wireless network for the video services.

References

1. Zhang, H., Dong, Y., Cheng, J., Hossain, M., Leung, V.C.M.: Fronthauling for 5G LTE-U ultra dense cloud small cell networks. IEEE Wirel. Commun. **23**(6), 48–53 (2016)
2. Zhang, H., Liu, N., Chu, X., Long, K., Aghvami, A., Leung, V.: Network slicing based 5G and future mobile networks: mobility, resource management, and challenges. IEEE Commun. Mag. **55**(8), 138–145 (2017)
3. Shao, H., Lu, L., Wen, X., Zhang, H., Chen, Y., Hong, Y.: Content-aware video QoE coverage analysis in heterogeneous wireless networks. Wirel. Pers. Commun. **90**(2), 487–502 (2016)
4. Shao, H., Wen, X., Jing, W., Lu, Z., Zhang, H., Chen, Y.: Joint optimization of quality of experience and power consumption in OFDMA multi-cell networks. IEEE Commun. Lett. **20**(2), 380–383 (2016)
5. Ma, W., Zheng, W., Zhang, H., Wen, X.: MOS-driven energy efficient power allocation for wireless video communications. In: Proceedings of IEEE Globecom (2012)
6. Ma, W., Zheng, W., Zhang, H., Wen, X., Lu, Z.: Distortion-guaranteed energy saving power allocation for downlink OFDMA multiuser video transmission. J. Inf. Comput. Sci. **9**, 3011–3019 (2012)
7. Gómez, G., Hortigüela, L., Pérez, Q., Lorca, J., García, R., Aguayo-Torres, M.C.: YouTube QoE evaluation tool for android wireless terminals. EURASIP J. Wirel. Commun. Netw. **2014**, 1–14 (2014)
8. He, S., Tang, A., Zhang, H.: High-performance implementation of OFDM-MIMO base-band in wireless video system. Inf. Technol. J. **13**, 1678–1685 (2014)
9. Shen, Y., Jiang, C., Quek, T., Zhang, H., Ren, Y.: Device-to-device cluster assisted downlink video sharing - a base station energy saving approach. In: Proceedings of IEEE GlobalSIP, Atlanta, Georgia, USA (2014)
10. Yang, C., Ro, C.W.: Resource utilization and QoS analysis for differentiated services in wireless cellular networks. In: 2012 8th International Conference on IEEE Computing and Networking Technology (ICCNT), pp. 264–267 (2012)
11. Huo, Y., Jing, T., Zhang, D., Feng, Y.: Error distribution feedback quantization scheme based on HVS. In: Signal Processing, vol. 25, no. 4, pp. 537–542 (2009)
12. Bucciol, P., et al.: Cross. In: Global Telecommunications Conference, GLOBECOM 2004, vol. 5, pp. 3027–3031. IEEE (2004)
13. Khan, A., Sun, L., Ifeachor, E.: Impact of video content on video quality for video over wireless networks. In: Fifth International Conference on Autonomic and Autonomous Systems, ICAS 2009, pp. 277–282. IEEE (2009)
14. Ma, X., Liu, J., Jiang, H.: Energy-efficient mobile data uploading from high-speed trains. Mob. Netw. Appl. **17**(1), 143–151 (2012)
15. Cheng, R.S., et al.: Improving performance of MPEG-based stream by SCTP multi-streaming mechanism. In: 2010 5th International ICST Conference on Communications and Networking in China (CHINACOM), pp. 1–6 (2010)
16. Ke, C.H., et al.: An evaluation framework for more realistic simulations of MPEG video transmission. J. Inf. Sci. Eng. **24**(2), 425–440 (2008)
17. Singh, K.D., Rubino, G.: Quality of experience estimation using frame loss pattern and video encoding characteristics in DVB-H networks. In: Packet Video Workshop International 2011, pp. 150–157 (2011)

18. NS2. http://www.isi.edu/nsnam/ns/
19. Klaue, J., Rathke, B., Wolisz, A.: EvalVid – a framework for video transmission and quality evaluation. In: Kemper, P., Sanders, William H. (eds.) TOOLS 2003. LNCS, vol. 2794, pp. 255–272. Springer, Heidelberg (2003). https://doi.org/10.1007/978-3-540-45232-4_16

Tree-LSTM Guided Attention Pooling
of DCNN for Semantic Sentence Modeling

Liu Chen[1,3(✉)], Guangping Zeng[1,3], Qingchuan Zhang[2,3],
and Xingyu Chen[1,3]

[1] School of Computer and Communication Engineering,
University of Science and Technology Beijing, Beijing, China
chenliueve@163.com, zgp@ustb.edu.cn, cscserer@sina.com
[2] School of Computer and Information Engineering,
Beijing Technology and Business University, Beijing, China
zqcl982@126.com
[3] Beijing Key Laboratory of Knowledge Engineering for Materials Science,
Beijing, China

Abstract. The ability to explicitly represent sentences is central to natural
language processing. Convolutional neural network (CNN), recurrent neural
network and recursive neural networks are mainstream architectures. We introduce a novel structure to combine the strength of them for semantic modelling of
sentences. Sentence representations are generated by Dynamic CNN (DCNN, a
variant of CNN). At pooling stage, attention pooling is adopted to capture most
significant information with the guide of Tree-LSTM (a variant of Recurrent NN)
sentence representations. Comprehensive information is extracted by the pooling
scheme and the combination of the convolutional layer and the tree long-short
term memory. We evaluate the model on sentiment classification task. Experiment results show that utilization of the given structures and combination of
Tree-LSTM and DCNN outperforms both Tree-LSTM and DCNN and achieves
outstanding performance.

Keywords: Dynamic Convolutional Neural Network (CNN)
Tree-Structured Long-Short Term Memory (Tree-LSTM)
Attention Pooling · Semantic Sentence Modeling

1 Introduction

The sentence modelling problem is an essential component of natural language processing (NLP) and has drawn mass attention recently. The objective of sentence
modelling is to analyze and represent the semantic content of a sentence for purposes of
sentiment analysis, document summarization, machine translation, discourse analysis,
etc. [1]. Sentence features, the key of sentence modeling, are usually extracted from
features of word representations.

With advances in word vector representation [2, 3], word vectors become a common practice of word representation for classification. Vector representations of words
can even preserve the semantic relationship [4]. In the vector space, words with similar
semantics lie close in Euclidean or cosine distance.

© ICST Institute for Computer Sciences, Social Informatics and Telecommunications Engineering 2018
K. Long et al. (Eds.): 5GWN 2017, LNICST 211, pp. 52–59, 2018.
https://doi.org/10.1007/978-3-319-72823-0_6

Recently, neural network methods have achieved outstanding performance namely recursive neural networks (Recursive NN) [5], recurrent neural networks (Recurrent NN) [6] and convolutional neural networks (CNN) [7].

The recursive neural networks of [5, 8, 9] rely on syntactic parse trees and recursively compose sentence representation from child nodes in the parse tree. The learning performance of recursive neural networks depends much on the construction of the textual tree which can be quite time-consuming.

The recurrent neural networks of [10, 11] compose word vectors from one end to the other stores the information of all previous contexts in a fixed-sized hidden layer. RNNs with Long Short-Term Memory (LSTM) units [12] have re-emerged as a popular architecture due to their representational power and effectiveness at dealing with vanishing gradient problem and capturing long-term dependencies. Studies of [12, 13] proposed an improved variant of Recurrent NN which integrate Recursive NNs by feeding syntactic parse tree into LSTM.

CNN was originally proposed in computer vision [14], and recently it becomes popular in NLP tasks. Different from Recursive and Recurrent NNs, CNN encodes word vectors by convolution operation and generates a fixed-sized high-level representation by pooling. [7] proposed a Dynamic Convolutional Neural Network (DCNN) with multiple layers of convolutional and dynamic pooling operations which handles input sentences of varying length and forms feature maps which is capable of explicitly capturing syntactic or semantic relations between nonconsecutive parts within the input sentence.

In this paper, we introduce an attention pooling dynamic CNN architecture (abbreviated to AP-DCNN) to combine the benefits of CNN, Recursive and Recurrent NNs with attention pooling schema. The AP-DCNN can be considered a variant of APCNN in [15] where the attention pooling scheme is proposed. The Tree-LSTM model [16] is employed to enhance the information extraction capability of the pooling layer. The Tree-LSTM model is also concatenated with the convolutional structure to extract comprehensive information, namely historical, future and local context information, of any position in a sequence at the testing phase.

We conduct experiments on sentiment analysis task of Stanford Treebank Datasets and results show that utilization of the given structures and combination of Tree-LSTM and DCNN leads to better performance.

2   The Proposed AP-DCNN Model

The architecture of the AP-DCNN model is shown in Fig. 1. The following subsections describe the proposed model in detail.

2.1   Word Embedding

The input of the model is N sentences with variable lengths. Each sentence S is constituted by words which are represented by vectors. Recent researches have demonstrated that continuous word representation is a popular and powerful method for sentence classification tasks. A word vector can be formed as follows:

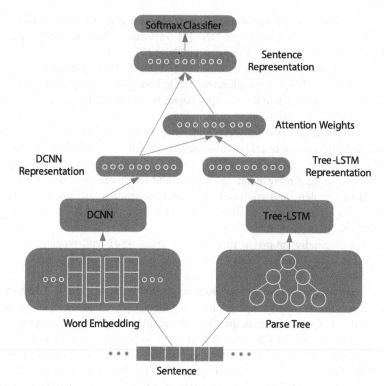

Fig. 1. Architecture of AP-DCNN. Convolution filters perform convolutions on the input sentence matrix to generate local Sentence representations. An attention pooling scheme is used to integrate local representations into the final sentence representation with attention weights. These weights are composed by comparing local representations with Tree-LSTM based sentence representation by position and optimized during the training phase.

$$x = Wp, \tag{1}$$

where $p \in \mathbb{R}^V$ is a one-hot vector where the position the word appears is 1 while the others are 0, $W \in \mathbb{R}^{d \times V}$ is a word-representation matrix, in which the i th column is the vector representation of the i th word in the vocabulary, and V denotes the vocabulary size.

We adopt the publicly available word2vec vectors as initial word embedding matrices to make adequately use of semantic and grammatical associations of words. The vectors, with dimension of 300, are trained on 100 billion words from the Google News by using the continuous bag-of-words method [3] and maximizing the average log probability of all the words [17]. Words not present in the set of pre-trained words are initialized randomly.

2.2   DCNN Based Sentence Representation

Convolutional layers play significant roles in the success of the CNN because they can encode significant information contained in input data with significantly fewer parameters than other deep learning architectures. We adopt the Dynamic Convolutional Neural Network (DCNN) for the semantic modelling of sentences. The network uses Dynamic k-Max Pooling [7], a global pooling operation over linear sequences. The network handles input sentences of varying length and induces a feature graph over the sentence which is capable of explicitly capturing short and long-range relations.

The convolution operation at layer l is conducted between k_l filters $W_l^T \in \mathbb{R}^{md \times k_l}$ and a concatenation vector $c_{l-1_{i:i+m-1}}$ which represents a window of m features starting from the ith feature in the feature maps conducted in the last layer while $l = 1$ represents the word embedding in the origin sentence.

The term d is the dimension of word embedding. Multiple filters with differently initialized weights are used to improve the model's learning capability.

The number of filters k_{top} is determined using cross-validation and the convolution operation is governed by:

$$c_{l_i} = g\left(W_l^T c_{l-1_{i:i+m-1}} + b_l\right) \in \mathbb{R}^{k_i}, \tag{2}$$

where k_l denotes the number of filters in the current convolutional layer l, using:

$$k_l = \max\left(k_{top}, \left\lceil \frac{L-l}{L} T \right\rceil\right), \tag{3}$$

where L is the total number of convolutional layers in the network.

Following the approach in [4, 18], we also use filters with varying convolution window sizes to form parallel DCNNs so that they can learn multiple types of embedding of local regions so as to complement each other to improve model accuracy. Sentence representations produced by all the distinct DCNNs are concatenated to form the final feature vector as an input to the top SoftMax classifier.

2.3   Tree-LSTM Based Sentence Representation

Tree-LSTM is a variant of LSTM. A Tree-LSTM unit (indexed by j) contains input and output gates i_j and o_j, a memory cell c_j and hidden state h_j as a standard LSTM do, while contains one forget gate f_{jk} for each child k, which is the difference. This allows the Tree-LSTM unit to selectively incorporate information from each child. A Tree-LSTM unit at each node takes an input word vector x_j which depends on the tree structure used for the network. Given a tree, let $C(j)^K$ denote the set of K children of node j. The transition proceeds as follows:

$$i_j = \sigma\left(W^{(i)}x_j + \sum_{k\in C(j)^K} U_k^{(i)}h_{jk} + b^{(i)}\right), \tag{4}$$

$$f_{jk} = \sigma\left(W^{(f)}x_j + \sum_{l\in C(j)^K} U_{kl}^{(i)}h_{jl} + b^{(f)}\right), \tag{5}$$

$$o_j = \sigma\left(W^{(o)}x_j + \sum_{k\in C(j)^K} U_k^{(o)}h_{jk} + b^{(o)}\right), \tag{6}$$

$$u_j = tanh\left(W^{(u)}x_j + \sum_{k\in C(j)^K} U_k^{(u)}h_{jk} + b^{(u)}\right), \tag{7}$$

$$c_j = i_j \odot u_j + \sum_{k\in C(j)^K} f_{jk} \odot c_k, \tag{8}$$

$$h_j = o_j \odot tanh(c_j), \tag{9}$$

where in Eq. (5), $k \in C(j)^K$.

We use binary tree LSTM ($K = 2$) because it suits more to constituency trees we use. When the forgetting node has only one child, the model can be considered as the standard LSTM. We denote the sentence representation as $\tilde{s}$.

2.4 Attention Pooling

In the attention pooling stage, we compare DCNN-based sentence representation and Tree-LSTM based sentence representation to calculate the attention weights. By controlling the output dimension of the Tree-LSTM same as the number of convolutional filters k_{top}, we are able to map the both representations into the space of the same dimension. The higher the similarity between the DCNN sentence representation and Tree-LSTM representation, the bigger attention weight is assigned to DCNN representation. The attention weights is given by:

$$\alpha_i = \frac{exp(sim(c_i, \tilde{s}))}{\sum_{i=1}^{T} exp(sim(c_i, \tilde{s}))}. \tag{10}$$

The function sim denotes a method to measure similarity between inputs where cosine similarity is adopted. The final sentence representation guided by the attention weights is calculated by:

$$s = \alpha \odot c \in \mathbb{R}^T. \tag{11}$$

The final sentence representation forms the input of the top classifier.

2.5 Softmax Classifier

The sentence representation s is naturally regarded as an input to the top classifier during the training phase while $[s, \tilde{s}]$ is used at the testing phase. A linear transformation layer and a softmax layer are added at the top of the model to produce conditional probabilities over the class space. To avoid overfitting, dropout with a masking probability p is applied to the penultimate layer. The key idea of dropout is to randomly drop units (along with their connections) from the neural network during the training phase [19]. This output layer is calculated as follows:

$$z = \begin{cases} W_s(s \odot q) + b_s & \text{training phase} \\ W_s([s, \tilde{s}]) + b_s & \text{testing phase} \end{cases}, \tag{12}$$

$$y_c = \frac{exp(z_c)}{\sum_{c' \in C} exp(z'_c)}, \tag{13}$$

where q is the masking vector with dropout rate p which is the probability of dropping a unit during training, and C is the class number. In addition, a $l - 2$ norm constraint of the output weights W s is imposed during training as well.

Let $\tilde{y}_c$ denotes the label of a sentence. Cross entropy loss function is given by:

$$\mathbb{L} = -\sum_{i \in N} \sum_{c \in C} \tilde{y}_c(S_i) log(y_c(S_i)), \tag{14}$$

where $\tilde{y}_c$ codes in 1-of-K schema whose dimension corresponding to the true class is 1 while all others being 0. The parameters to be determined by the model include all the weights and bias terms in the convolutional filters, the Tree-LSTM and the softmax classifier. The attention weights will be updated during the training phase. Word embeddings are fine tuned as well. Optimization is performed using the Adadelta update rule of [20], which has been shown as an effective and efficient back-propagation algorithm.

3   Experiments and Results

3.1   Classification

In this section, we evaluate the performance of the proposed model on the Stanford Sentiment Treebank [21] benchmark dataset and compare it with several state-of-the-art approaches.

The Stanford Sentiment Treebank contains about 11,800 sentences from the movie reviews. The sentences were parsed with the Stanford parser [22]. There are two subtasks: binary classification of sentences excluding neutral reviews with class distribution of 4955/4663., and fine-grained classification over five classes: very positive, positive, neutral, negative, very negative, with class distribution of 1837/3118/2237/3147/1516. Standard binarized constituency parse trees are provided for each sentence in the dataset, and each node in these trees is annotated with a sentiment label.

[23] provide a guide regarding CNN architecture and hyperparameters for practitioners who deploy CNNs for sentence classification tasks. We initialized our word representations using publicly available 300-dimensional word2vec vectors. Word representations were updated during training with a learning rate of 0.1. The DCNN has two wide convolution layers with filters whose width is 7 and 5 respectively [7] and

100 feature maps. The networks use the *tanh* non-linear function. DCNN models were trained using Adadelta with a learning rate of 0.05 and a minibatch size of 50.

The output dimension of the Tree-LSTM is set the same as the number of feature maps in order to compare Tree-LSTM representations with DCNN representations. The training batch size is set as 100.

All parameters were regularized with a per-minibatch L2 regularization strength of 10–4. The sentiment classifier was additionally regularized using dropout with a dropout rate of 0.5.

3.2 Result

Table 1. Accuracy (%) of our model and other methods from literature. The presented results are the test set accuracy of the run with the highest accuracy on the validation set.

Method	Fine-grained	Binary
CNN-non-static	48.0	87.2
CNN-multichannel	47.4	88.1
DCNN	48.5	86.8
LSTM	46.4	84.9
Bidirectional LSTM	49.1	87.5
Tree-LSTM	51.0	88.0
APCNN	50.1	89.9
This work	50.6	88.7

Experiment results against other methods are listed in Table 1. The performance of AP-DCNN outperforms the state-of-the-art models like BLSTM and APCNN on the fine-grained classification subtask and achieves accuracy comparable to APCNN and Tree LSTM on the binary classification subtask.

4   Conclusion

In the present work, a new neural semantic sentence model termed Attention Pooling DCNN has been successfully developed. We introduce Tree-LSTM to attention mechanism to model sentence. Our model is able to capture long term and syntactic information. We evaluated the learned semantic sentence representations on sentiment classification task with very satisfactory results and good performance.

Acknowledgements. This research was supported by National High-tech R&D Program (863 Program No 2015AA015403) and National Natural Science Foundation of China (No 61370131).

References

1. LeCun, Y., Bengio, Y., Hinton, G.: Deep learning. Nature **521**(7553), 436–444 (2015)
2. Bengio, Y., Ducharme, R., Vincent, P., Jauvin, C.: A neural probabilistic language model. J. Mach. Learn. Res. **3**(Feb), 1137–1155 (2003)
3. Mikolov, T., Sutskever, I., Chen, K., Corrado, G.S., Dean, J.: Distributed representations of words and phrases and their compositionality, pp. 3111–3119 (2013)
4. Kim, Y.: Convolutional neural networks for sentence classification. arXiv preprint arXiv: 1408.5882 (2014)
5. Socher, R., Pennington, J., Huang, E.H., Ng, A.Y., Manning, C.D.: Semi-supervised recursive autoencoders for predicting sentiment distributions. In: Association for Computational Linguistics, pp. 151–161 (2011)
6. Lawrence, S., Giles, C.L., Fong, S.: Natural language grammatical inference with recurrent neural networks. IEEE Trans. Knowl. Data Eng. **12**(1), 126–140 (2000)
7. Kalchbrenner, N., Grefenstette, E., Blunsom, P.: A convolutional neural network for modelling sentences. arXiv preprint arXiv:1404.2188 (2014)
8. Socher, R., Lin, C.C., Manning, C., Ng, A.Y.: Parsing natural scenes and natural language with recursive neural networks, pp. 129–136 (2011)
9. Socher, R., Manning, C.D., Ng, A.Y.: Learning continuous phrase representations and syntactic parsing with recursive neural networks, pp. 1–9 (2010)
10. Funahashi, K., Nakamura, Y.: Approximation of dynamical systems by continuous time recurrent neural networks. Neural Netw. **6**(6), 801–806 (1993)
11. Schuster, M., Paliwal, K.K.: Bidirectional recurrent neural networks. IEEE Trans. Sig. Process. **45**(11), 2673–2681 (1997)
12. Hochreiter, S., Schmidhuber, J.: Long short-term memory. Neural Comput. **9**(8), 1735–1780 (1997)
13. Graves, A., Schmidhuber, J.: Framewise phoneme classification with bidirectional LSTM and other neural network architectures. Neural Netw. **18**(5), 602–610 (2005)
14. LeCun, Y., Bottou, L., Bengio, Y., Haffner, P.: Gradient-based learning applied to document recognition. P IEEE **86**(11), 2278–2324 (1998)
15. Er, M.J., Zhang, Y., Wang, N., Pratama, M.: Attention pooling-based convolutional neural network for sentence modelling. Inf. Sci. **373**, 388–403 (2016)
16. Tai, K.S., Socher, R., Manning, C.D.: Improved semantic representations from tree-structured long short-term memory networks. arXiv preprint arXiv:1503.00075 (2015)
17. Mikolov, T., Chen, K., Corrado, G., Dean, J.: Efficient estimation of word representations in vector space. arXiv preprint arXiv:1301.3781 (2013)
18. Johnson, R., Zhang, T.: Effective use of word order for text categorization with convolutional neural networks. arXiv preprint arXiv:1412.1058 (2014)
19. Srivastava, N., Hinton, G.E., Krizhevsky, A., Sutskever, I., Salakhutdinov, R.: Dropout: a simple way to prevent neural networks from overfitting. J. Mach. Learn. Res. **15**(1), 1929–1958 (2014)
20. Zeiler, M.D.: ADADELTA: an adaptive learning rate method. arXiv preprint arXiv:1212. 5701 (2012)
21. Socher, R., Perelygin, A., Wu, J.Y., Chuang, J., Manning, C.D., Ng, A.Y., Potts, C.: Recursive deep models for semantic compositionality over a sentiment treebank, p. 1642. Citeseer (2013)
22. Klein, D., Manning, C.D.: Accurate unlexicalized parsing. In: Association for Computational Linguistics, pp. 423–430 (2003)
23. Zhang, Y., Wallace, B.: A Sensitivity Analysis of (and Practitioners' Guide to) Convolutional Neural Networks for Sentence Classification. arXiv preprint arXiv:1510.03820 (2015)

Multi-base Station Energy Cooperation Based on Nash Q-Learning Algorithm

Yabo Lv, Baogang Li, Wei Zhao$^{(\boxtimes)}$, Dandan Guo, and Yuanbin Yao

Department of Electronics and Communication Engineering,
North China Electric Power University, Baoding 071000, Hebei, China
yabolv@163.com, baogangli@ncepu.edu.cn,
andyzhaoster@163.com, guodanstyle@163.com,
hdyaoyuanbin@outlook.com

Abstract. In view of the current energy problems of communication base station, a multi-base station energy cooperation strategy is proposed to reduce the energy consumption of power grid, which is introducing renewable energy and energy cooperation between the base station based on the Nash-Q learning algorithm. We analyze the packet rate and throughput of the system under the proposed approach. The simulation results show that the proposed algorithm can enhances the adaptability to the changing environment, effectively improve the system capacity.

Keywords: Multi-agent reinforcement learning · Nash equilibrium
Q-learning · Energy harvesting

1 Introduction

Recently, with the arrival of the fifth generation (5G) and the rapid development of the cellular network [1, 2], the number of users and the corresponding traffic have greatly increased. Therefore, the energy consumption in cellular networks has also increased significantly. According to the statistics, the cellular network consumes more than 0.5% of the global energy supply [3], the figure will increase as users' demand grows. In some mountainous areas, grasslands and other special areas, communication base stations are not usually directly connected to the grid, so it is necessary to introduce the wind power, solar power or other renewable energy in the base station. Because of the instability and uneven distribution of renewable energy, it is difficult for a single base station to achieve the optimal utilization of energy, and energy cooperation between the base stations can solve the above problems.

The optimal energy allocation based on the off-line algorithm, assuming the non-causal information of the energy and data are known ahead at the transmitter [4]. The other is the study based on the online algorithm, assuming that the transmitter can not know the statistical information ahead [5]. In [6], a distributed reinforcement learning algorithm is proposed to solve the problem of energy cooperation between multi-base stations. In [7], based on a complete model, which is unrealistic, it is difficult or even impossible to obtain such a priori knowledge in reality. [8] studies the single-step TD algorithm only modifies the estimate of the neighbor state, leading to

© ICST Institute for Computer Sciences, Social Informatics and Telecommunications Engineering 2018
K. Long et al. (Eds.): 5GWN 2017, LNICST 211, pp. 60–68, 2018.
https://doi.org/10.1007/978-3-319-72823-0_7

algorithm convergence is too slow. Maximize energy efficiency under power constraints in each sub-channel is considered [9–12].

In this paper, we consider a wireless communication system equipped with an energy harvesting device and a limited-capacity rechargeable battery,the base station can maintain system operation by harvesting renewable energy. Because of the uneven distribution of energy, a single base station can not meet the requirements, to solve this problem, we start with general-sum stochastic games, combining with reinforcement learning, propose an on-line algorithm. and apply proposed algorithm to energy coordination in wireless communication systems. The simulation results show the superiority of the proposed algorithm. We compare the data rate under the presence of energy cooperation, and obtain the desired experimental results.

The remainder of the paper is organized as follows. Section 2 describes the system model, while Sect. 3 presents the optimization algorithm, and Sect. 3 also details how the problem is solved using proposed algorithm. Simulation results are presented in Sect. 4. Finally, the conclusion is given in Sect. 5.

2 System Model

We consider a wireless communication system equipped with an energy harvesting device and a rechargeable battery with limited storage capacity, assuming energy and data packets arrive at each time slot (TS), the channel conditions being constant during each TS, and changes from one TS to the next TS. We believe that the packet transmission has a strict transmission delay constraints, that is, the data packets must be sent or be dropped before the next TS arrivals, and the arrival of data and energy in each TS follows a first-order discrete-time Markov model. System model is shown in Fig. 1. There are energy and data package arriving at the transmitter i at TS t, the energy which in battery can cooperate with other base station (BS) through power line or radio frequency, user 1 and user 2 connect BS1 and BS2 respectively.

Where $D_i(t)$ is the data packet arriving at the BS i in the TS t, wherein the data packet satisfies $D_i(t) \in D = \{d_1, d_2 \ldots d_N\}$, N is the number of elements in D, and d_i represents the type of the packet; $p_d(d_j, d_k)$ is the probability that the packet changes from state d_j to d_k. $\varepsilon_i(t)$ is the energy harvested by the BS i in TS t, denoted as $\varepsilon_i(t) \in E^H = \{e_1, e_2 \ldots e_N\}$, and N represents the number of elements in E^H, e is the energy harvested in each TS, $p_e(e_j, e_k)$ is the probability that the harvested energy from e_j to e_k in the next TS. $H_i(t)$ is the channel state of the BS i in TS t, denoted by $H_i(t) \in H = \{h_1, h_2 \ldots h_N\}$, and $p_h(h_j, h_k)$ is the probability that the next slot channel state is converted from h_j to h_k. $f_1(t)$ is the energy that BS1 transmits to BS2 in TS t, $f_2(t)$ is the energy transmitted by BS2 to BS1 in slot t, K indicates energy transfer efficiency, with $0 < K < 1$, The battery capacity is $B_{\max}$, At any time, the battery power to meet the $0 \leq B_i(t) \leq B_{\max}$, when the battery is full, the harvested energy is no longer stored in the battery.

At the beginning of the TS t, the transmitter can obtain the channel state $H_i(t)$ and packet $D_i(t)$. According to the Shannon formula, the energy needed to send the packet $E_i^T(t)$ can be calculated, and the packet can be successfully transmitted by the energy

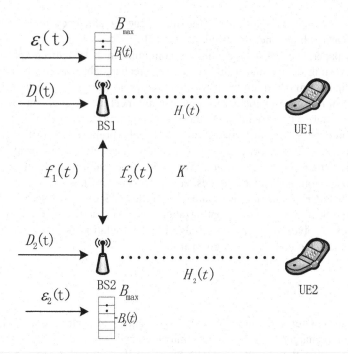

Fig. 1. System model

consumption. According to the causality of energy harvesting, It can be seen that the energy harvested in TS t can only be used in its subsequent time slot, then the next slot battery energy meets:

$$B_1(t+1) = \min\{B_1(t) + \varepsilon_1(t) - f_1(t) + kf_2(t) - a_1(t)E_1^T(t), B_{\max}\} \tag{1}$$

$$a_1(t)E_1^T(t) \le B_1(t) \tag{2}$$

$$B_2(t+1) = \min\{B_2(t) + \varepsilon_2(t) - f_2(t) + kf_1(t) - a_2(t)E_2^T(t), B_{\max}\} \tag{3}$$

$$a_2(t)E_2^T(t) \le B_2(t) \tag{4}$$

The objective of this paper is to maximize the average transmission data rate of the system, which is given by:

$$\bar{r}(t) = \max \lim_{T \to \infty} \frac{1}{T} \sum_{i=1}^{N} \sum_{t=0}^{T} a_i D_i \tag{5}$$

S.t. (1) (2) (3) and (4).

3 Optimization Algorithm Analysis

3.1 Basic Q-Learning Algorithm

The Q-learning algorithm was first proposed by C. Watkins in his PhD thesis. The algorithm can only be assumed to be a Markov decision process model based on the underlying system. The system does not need to know other priori information, and the algorithm can converge to the optimal strategy by learning to enhance the discount return value. The iterative calculation formula is

$$Q(s_t, a_t) = Q(s_t, a_t) + l(r(s_t, a_t) + \gamma \, maxQ(s_{t+1}, a_{t+1}) - Q(s_t, a_t)) \qquad (6)$$

Where (s_t, a_t) is the state-action pair of MDP at time t, s_{t+1} is the state at time $t + 1$, $r(s_t, a_t)$ is the return at time t, and $l > 0$ is the learning factor. When certain conditions are satisfied, the algorithm converges to the optimal solution [13].

From Eq. (6), it can be seen that the update of Q-learning-valued function is carried out in an iterative way. The value function is the expectation of the reward discount after the action a_t selected according to a certain policy under the state s_t. There are two ways to achieve Q learning: One method is to use lookup table, the other is the use of neural network. This paper uses lookup table method. In the initialization phase, all states and actions are initialized to discrete quantities, and the value functions are learned according to algorithmic flow and constraints.

3.2 Nash Q Learning Algorithm

Hu and others in 1998 proposed the Nash-Q algorithm, which extends the multi-agent learning to complete information non-cooperative general and stochastic game with incompletely antagonistic interests [14].

First, we give the definition of Nash equilibrium: Nash equilibrium is a joint strategy, in this state, each participant's strategy for other participants are excellent. In a random game process, Nash equilibrium is a n-tuple stratergy $(\pi_*^1, \cdots, \pi_*^n)$, such that for all $s \in S, i = 1, \cdots, n$, there are:

$$v^i(s, \pi_*^1, \cdots, \pi_*^n) \geq v^i(s, \pi_*^1, \cdots, \pi_*^{i-1}, \pi_*^i, \pi_*^{i+1}, \cdots, \pi_*^n) \qquad (7)$$

There $\pi_i \in \Pi_i$, Π_i for the agent i available strategies.

In the Nash Q-learning algorithm, the Nash equilibria are used to define the value functions. In this case, the agents can observe each other to obtain information such as the action taken and the reward they get, etc., and to update their own valued functions. The value function of other agents is modeled. In a game with n players, the Q value of all agents in the same state forms a countermeasure form, $Q_t^1(s), \ldots, Q_t^n(s)$, and the value function update formula of Nash Q-learning algorithm is:

$$Q_{t+1}^i(s_t^i, a_t^1 \ldots a_t^n) = (1 - \alpha_t)Q_t^i(s_t^i, a_t^1 \ldots a_t^n) + \alpha_t\left[r_t^i + \beta NashQ_t^i(s')\right] \tag{8}$$

S.t. $NashQ_t^i(s') = \pi^1(s') \ldots \pi^n(s') \cdot Q_t^i(s')$

$\pi^1(s') \ldots \pi^n(s')$ is the Nash equilibrium solution of Q value in the state s'. Indicates that the participant i selects the winning function of the Nash equilibrium solution under state s'.

At the same time, the agent needs to update the value function of other agents by the following equation:

$$Q_{t+1}^j(s_t^j, a_t^1 \ldots a_t^n) = (1 - \alpha_t)Q_t^j(s_t^j, a_t^1 \ldots a_t^n) + \alpha_t\left[r_t^j + \beta NashQ_t^j(s')\right] \tag{9}$$

S.t. $NashQ_t^j(s') = \pi^1(s') \ldots \pi^n(s') \cdot Q_t^j(s'), \quad i \neq j$

Given the Nash Q-learning algorithm steps, the learning process of the agent i can be described as follows:

Initialization:

Set initial time index $t \leftarrow 0$, initial state $s_t^i = s_0^i$.

For all $s_t^i \in S$, $a_t^i \in A$, $i = 1, 2, \cdots, n$, $t = 0, 1, \cdots$, the initialized value functions $Q_t^i(s_t^i, a_t^1 \ldots a_t^n) = 0$, $Q_t^j(s_t^j, a_t^1 \ldots a_t^n) = 0$, $j = 1, 2 \cdots n$, and $j \neq i$.

Repeat the following steps until the condition is met:

(a) observe the current state s_t^i, according to the rules and learning process to get $Q_t^i(s_t^i, a_t^1 \ldots a_t^n)$ and $Q_t^j(s_t^j, a_t^1 \ldots a_t^n)$, according to the greedy strategy to select action a_t^i;

(b) Observe the joint reward $r_t^1 \ldots r_t^n$ and joint action $a_t^1 \ldots a_t^n$ in the current state and update the value functions of themselves and other agents according to (8) and (9).

(c) Let $t = t + 1$, observe the next state s'.

In this section, we consider two base stations, and each base station can be regarded as an agent with learning ability. Agent i calculates $\pi^1(s')\pi^2(s')$ for the stage game $(Q_t^1(s')Q_t^2(s'))$, and update the Q-value according to (8) and (9). the state set consists of four parts: the harvested energy, arrival data, channel state, and battery capacity. At TS t, the state is represented by $S_t = <\varepsilon(t), D(t), H(t), B(t) >$, according to the following simulation parameters set, the system is divided into 48 discrete state. And the action set is represented by $A_t = <a(t), f(t) >$, where $a(t) = <0, 1 >$ is whether to send data packets, $f(t) = <0, 2 >$ Which indicates the energy of cooperation between the two BS, whether the action can be performed is governed by Eqs. (2) and (4).

4   Simulation Results Analysis

In this paper, simulation parameters similar to the paper [5] are used. Assuming the length of each TS is $\Delta_{TS} = 10\,\text{ms}$, the time that the transmitter transmits data is $\Delta_{Tx} = 5\,\text{ms}$, the available bandwidth is $W = 2\,\text{MHz}$, the noise power spectral density of Gaussian channel is $N_0 = 10^{-20.4}\,\text{W/Hz}$, The basic energy unit is $2.5\,\mu\text{j}$, assuming that the transmitter in time slot t, the available energy unit is $\varepsilon_i(t) = \{0, 5\}\mu j$, the packet size is $D_i(t) = \{300, 600\}$ bit/s, the channel state is $H_i(t) = \{1.655 \times 10^{-13}, 3.311 \times 10^{-13}\}$; set to harvested energy in each TS, the arrival of the packet, the channel state are random.

In order to ensure the reliable transmission of data, it is necessary to calculate the energy required to transmit data in each state. From the channel capacity formula (Shannon formula) under the Gaussian channel, can be described as

$$D_i(t) = W\Delta_{Tx} \log_2(1 + \frac{H_i(t)P}{WN_0}) \tag{10}$$

The channel capacity may be approximately equal to

$$D_n \approx \frac{\Delta_{Tx}H_nP}{\log(2)N_0} \tag{11}$$

Where is the energy required to transmit the data in the TS, so we get the energy required to reliably send a packet is:

$$E_i^T = f_e(D_i(t), H_i(t)) = \frac{D_i(t)\log(2)N_0}{H_i(t)} \tag{12}$$

In the simulation, taking into account the causal nature of energy harvesting, the renewable energy harvested by the base station is used in the following TS, the system depends on the current battery remaining capacity to determine whether to send data packets and co-energy, the data package will be sent successfully if the energy in battery is enough in current TS, otherwise the package will be dropped.

Figure 2 Shows the relationship between the number of learning iterations and the transmission data rate. It can be seen that the system throughput increases with the number of learning times. When the number of iterative times reaches 600, the data rate reaches 77 kb/s, and the learning data rate is no longer significantly improved and stable. The learning process has been gradually completed. The blue curve is the data rate under the greedy strategy. If the greedy strategy is adopted, only the local optimal solution is adopted. The throughput of the system is 52 kb/s, its throughput is much lower than the Nash Q learning algorithm. It can be seen that the Nash Q learning algorithm can effectively improve the data rate of the system.

The impact of battery capacity on the system throughout shown in Fig. 3. With the battery capacity increases, the system throughout gradually increased, because the energy harvesting probability is a fixed value, in a continuous period of time, the system will harvest more renewable energy, increased battery capacity can store more available electrical energy, which can send more data during no energy harvesting time, so an appropriate increase in battery capacity will help improve the system throughout. From the curve, we can see that as the battery capacity increases, the data rate increases slowly, the growth rate decreased significantly when the rate increase to 80 kb/s, because the system throughout is not only determined by the battery capacity, but also by the packet size, capture Energy probability, channel state and other factors.

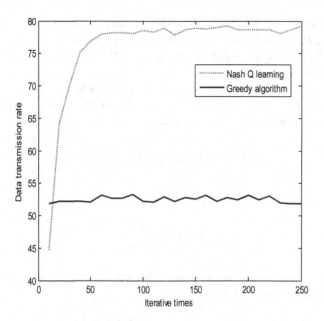

Fig. 2. Influence of iteration times on rate

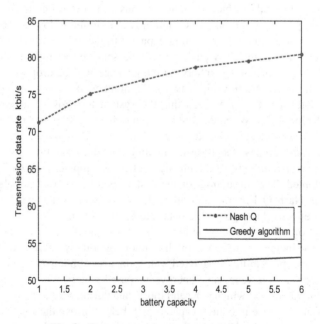

Fig. 3. Battery capacity on the rate of impact

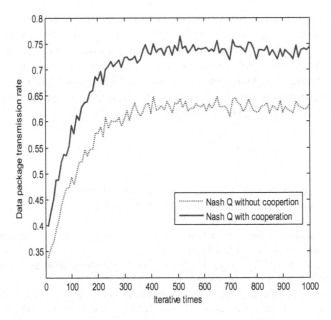

Fig. 4. Effect of energy cooperation on transmit rate under Q-Learning

Figure 4 shows the impact of energy cooperation on the successful transmission of data packets to the base station. From the simulation results, we can see that when the energy cooperation is not carried out between the base stations, the data packets transmission rate of the system is as high as 60%. When the energy cooperation is carried out, The two base stations can share the excess energy, the current state of excess energy sharing to another energy-poor base stations, the data packet rate can be up to 73%. From the comparison we can conclusion that the cooperation energy have a significance on improving the data transmission rate.

5 Conclusion

In order to reduce the energy consumed by the communication base station and increase the flexibility of the deployment of the base station, more and more researchers consider the use of renewable energy to the base station power supply. This paper have studied the energy allocation and the energy cooperation between off-grid base stations. Based on the knowledge of game theory, we have proposed an online energy management method. The simulation results of Nash Q learning algorithm have shown that the information rate of the system can be improved effectively with the agent learning process. It has been shown that, multi-base station energy cooperation method is superior to single base station communication system. For the off-grid connected base station rechargeable battery capacity, we can conclusion that the appropriate increase in battery capacity can increase the system speed.

The following research will be carried out from the following three aspects: The reinforcement learning algorithm is applied to solve the energy optimization problem in the coexistence scenario of grid and renewable energy. Improvement of reinforcement learning algorithm, the emphasis is on improving the robustness and convergence speed of the algorithm, reducing the complexity of multi-agent learning and exploring the method of solving the dimension problem. Consider the co-optimization of energy efficiency and spectral efficiency.

References

1. Zhang, H., Dong, Y., Cheng, J., Hossain, M.J., Leung, V.C.M.: Fronthauling for 5G LTE-U ultra dense cloud small cell networks. IEEE Wirel. Commun. **23**(6), 48–53 (2016)
2. Zhang, H., Liu, N., Chu, X., Long, K., Aghvami, A., Leung, V.: Network slicing based 5G and future mobile networks: mobility, resource management, and challenges. IEEE Commun. Mag. **55**(8), 138–145 (2017)
3. Tombaz, S., Vastberg, A., Zander, J.: Energy-and cost-efficient ultrahigh-capacity wireless accross. IEEE Wirel. Commun. **18**(5), 18–24 (2011)
4. Gong, J., Zhou, S., Niu, Z.: Optimal power allocation for energy harvesting and power grid coexisting wireless communication systems. IEEE Trans. Commun. **61**(7), 3040–3049 (2013)
5. Pol Blasco, D., Dohler, M.: A learning theoretic approach to energy harvesting communication system optimization. IEEE Trans. Wirel. Commun. **12**(4), 1872–1882 (2013)
6. Lin, W.T., Lai, I.W., Lee, C.H.: Distributed energy cooperation for energy harvesting nodes using reinforcement learning. In: 2015 IEEE 26th Annual International Symposium on Personal, Indoor, and Mobile Radio Communications (PIMRC), Hong Kong, pp. 1584–1588 (2015)
7. Udenze, A., McDonald-Msier, K.: Discrete time markov based optimisation for dynamic control of transmitter power in wireless sensor networks. In: IET Proceedings of the 3rd UK Embedded Forum, Newcastle, UK, 2–3 April (2007)
8. Alhajry, M., Alvi, F., Ahmed, M.: TD(λ) and q-learning based ludo players. In: IEEE Conference on Computation Intelligence and Games (CIG), pp. 83–90 (2012)
9. Li, W., Zhang, H., Zheng, W., Su, T., Wen, X.: Energy-efficient power allocation with dual-utility in two-tier OFDMA femtocell. In: Proceedings of IEEE Globecom (2012)
10. Liu, H., Zheng, W., Zhang, H., Zhang, Z., Wen, X.: An iterative two-step algorithm for energy efficient resource allocation in multi-Cell OFDMA networks. In: Proceedings of IEEE WCNC (2013)
11. Ma, W., Zheng, W., Zhang, H., Wen, X.: MOS-driven energy efficient power allocation for wireless video communications. In: Proceedings of IEEE Globecom (2012)
12. Zhang, Z., Zhang, H., Lu, Z., Zhao, Z., Wen, X.: Energy-efficient resource optimization in OFDMA-based dense femtocell networks. In: Proceedings of IEEE ICT (2013)
13. Dayan, W.P.: Q-Learning. Mach. Learn. **38**(2), 362–399 (2002)
14. Hu, J.L., Wellmam, M.P.: Multiagent reinforcement learning: theoretical framework and an algorithm. In: 15th International Conference on Machine Learning, Washington, pp. 242–249 (1999)

Crowdfunding Assisted Cellular System Analysis and Application

Mingqiang Yuan, Xinzhou Cheng, Tao Zhang$^{(\boxtimes)}$, Yongfeng Wang,
Lexi Xu, Chen Cheng, Haina Ye, and Weiwei Chen

Network Technology Research Institute, China United Network Technology
Corporation, Beijing, People's Republic of China
zhangtl76@chinaunicom.cn

Abstract. In this paper, a novel crowdfunding assisted cellular system analytical (CCSA) scheme is designed. Its basic idea is that mobile terminals collect cellular system related data from different telecom operators continuously, including signal strength, signal quality, data rate, delay etc. Mobile terminals automatically report the collected data to the analytical system periodically. Then, the analytical system analyses the performance and competitiveness level among telecom operators, as well as seeking the problem area for each telecom operator. Compared to driving test (DT) and call quality test (CQT), the CCSA scheme can save the capital expenditure (CAPEX) and effectively analyse the user experience in the cellular system.

Keywords: Cellular system · Mobile terminal · Crowdfunding · APP

1 Introduction

In the past decade, mobile internet experiences fast developments and popularization [1, 2]. The mobile internet reshapes the traditional inter-personal communication and effectively promotes the resources integration in the society [3, 4]. In the mobile internet era, a series of techniques (e.g., big data, data mining, deep learning etc.) become the driving force of enterprise transformation [5, 6]. These techniques are also key to industry upgrading in many traditional industries.

For telecom operators, the big data analysis is vital for mobile cellular system operation and optimization [7, 8]. Employing big data analysis, telecom operators can be aware of user preference, service feature, system performance, terminal characteristics [9, 10]. In this way, telecom operators can grasp the service/operation problems and system development trends [11, 12]. Then, telecom operators can put forward the solution to these service/operation problems, thus continuously improving the Quality of Service (QoS) and providing relevant measures for the cellular system operation [13, 14]. In the traditional cellular system performance analysis, acquiring other telecom operator's data is difficult with high cost, as well as deviation from the user's real perception [15, 16]. This paper tries to address above mentioned problems and designs a novel crowdfunding assisted cellular system analytical (CCSA) scheme. Initially, application (APP) equipped in mobile terminals collect cellular system related data from different telecom operators continuously. Then, mobile terminals automatically

K. Long et al. (Eds.): 5GWN 2017, LNICST 211, pp. 69–78, 2018.
https://doi.org/10.1007/978-3-319-72823-0_8

report these collected data to analytical system periodically. Finally, the analytical system analyses the performance and competitiveness level among telecom operators, as well as seeking the problem area for each telecom operator.

2 Crowdfunding Assisted Cellular System Analytical Scheme

2.1 System Architecture

The basic structure of the proposed crowdfunding assisted cellular system analytical scheme is shown in Fig. 1. The CCSA scheme has two characteristics. The first characteristic is the active data acquisition. For a specific geographic area, mobile terminals and APP periodically collect both the system related data and the service related information. Then mobile terminals and APP report these data to the background server for storage. These collected/stored data can be used in the optimization supporting system and planning & supporting platform etc. The second characteristic is to seek the cellular system problem interactively. The CCSA scheme employs user's data to assess the cellular system and find the problem.

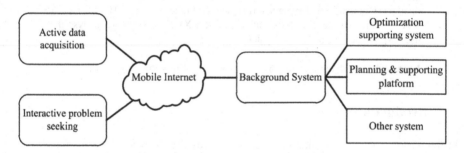

Fig. 1. Basic structure of the CCSA scheme

2.2 Key Indicator

The mobile terminal, especially the smart phone, can be regarded as an integrated sensor system, as well as a comprehensive information processing system. From the perspective of information collection, a smart phone can be regarded as an integrated sensor system. In addition to detection of the wireless environment information, the smart phone also integrates Global Positioning System (GPS), gyroscopes, light sensors, distance sensors, gravity sensors, magnetic sensors, acceleration sensors etc. [9]. Based on these sensors, the smart phone can perceive and record a large amount of information. Based on the Application Programming Interface (API) of mobile terminal operation system, developers can access to the public resources of the mobile terminal, as well as access to the user's information. A series of information can be collected via the API, such as phone number, signal strength, network condition, time information, camera condition, accelerometer information, location information etc. Hence, API also brings the opportunity of comprehensive analysis. From the perspective of cellular system analysis, we mainly collect the following data:

(1) 2G, 3G, 4G mobile system basic information: Cell identification (CI), location area code (LAC), IP address, network identification etc. [17].

(2) User location information: Longitude, latitude, altitude etc.

(3) Wireless environment information: Received signal level (RxLev) in 2G, received signal code power (RSCP) in 3G, reference signal received power (RSRP), signal to interference plus noise ratio in 4G [2, 4].

(4) User perception information: Uplink data rate, downlink data rate, delay etc.

(5) Terminal related information: International mobile subscriber identification number (IMSI), international mobile equipment identity (IMEI), terminal brand etc.

2.3 Key Technology

Data collection is the first step of the CCSA scheme, as shown in Fig. 2. Some service related characters can only be collected when the user undergoes services. In order to drop the worthless raw data, the data pre-process is implemented.

Fig. 2. Data collection and pre-process procedure

2.3.1 Device Collection

Device collection gets data from the operating system APIs. Appropriate APIs are chosen and packaged to Software Development Kit (SDK). And then certain logical operation is implemented to get the final results. This can be applied to Android operation system [18].

2.3.2 Service Collection

Some data are collected when users undergo the service, such as user data volume, service speed, time delay. Actually, most of the perceptive indexes are collected in this stage. Downlink speed and uplink speed are calculated as (1) and (2), respectively. In addition, the APIs involved are listed in Table 1 [18].

$$Speed_{downlink} = \frac{dataVolume_{downlink}}{\Delta time} \tag{1}$$

$$Speed_{uplink} = \frac{dataVolume_{uplink}}{\Delta time} \tag{2}$$

Table 1. APIs for speed calculation

Description	Method name	Purpose
Get current timestamp	System. currentTimeMillis()	To calculate time
Received bytes	getTotalRxBytes()	To calculate downlink speed
Sent bytes	getTotalTxBytes()	To calculate uplink speed
Received byte in mobile network	getMobileRxBytes()	To calculate downlink speed in cellular network
Sent byte in mobile network	getMobileTxBytes()	To calculate uplink speed in cellular network

2.3.3 Property Association

For further analysis, we associate the data with social properties, such as geographic information [19, 20]. Based on GPS information, the geographic association is utilized to classify points to certain areas, including the linear scene and the polygonal scene. As shown in Fig. 3, the beam method is applied to decide whether a point is in a certain polygon. The main idea is that: if the point is in the polygon, there are odd crossover point between the beam of point and the polygon; otherwise, there are even crossover points.

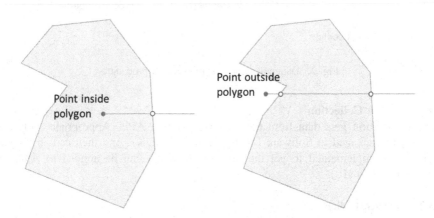

Fig. 3. Beam method to judge whether a point is in a polygon

Besides, the CCSA scheme needs commercial channels to popularize the SDK, in order to release the SDK to more phones. Ordinarily, there are several ways to popularize the SDK. To develop and operate an application is a direct way, however, the cost is high. Another way is to develop an application service platform, where statistic analysis for application operation is supplied for free. When the SDK from our service platform is bundled in any APP, the app plays a role as a data collector, continuously supplying user data. At the same time, the SDK obtains huge number of data in mobile terminals.

3   CCSA Scheme Application

3.1   Main Application Aspects

The crowdfunding data can be applied in the following four aspects:

(1) Network Analysis: The crowdfunding data contains the information of operators' network parameters and network signal. We can get the network overall performance from different dimensions and be aware of the gap with competitors, so that we can provide data support for network construction and optimization [21, 22].
(2) User Analysis: The crowdfunding data also includes the user information, such as the user phone number, IMSI etc. [19]. Based on different user groups' service perception, we can focus on customer care and support for the VIP subscribers.
(3) Terminal Analysis: The crowdfunding data also contains the terminal information. Therefore, we can analyze the terminal performance in the network, thus to provide support for terminal marking [5].
(4) Other Analysis: In addition to the analysis of the cellular system, the crowdfunding data analysis can also be used in WIFI network evaluation.

3.2   Network Competitiveness Analysis

It is beneficial to carry out cellular system competiveness analysis based on the crowdfunding data, leading to a wider coverage, a lower cost of data acquisition and a more accurate user perception. Compared with traditional DT/CQT methods, the CCSA scheme has obvious advantages to provide effective supports for network development and construction.

3.2.1   Network Competitiveness Analysis Process
The overall process for dealing with the smart phone APP data is shown as Fig. 4.

Fig. 4. Overall process for dealing with the smart phone APP data

The first and second step are data cleaning and data warehousing, respectively. The data that is out of reasonable range or incomplete ones should be cleaned [23]. Besides, each sample point should contain the required fields for analysis. After data cleaning, the structured data are saved in a database for subsequent statistical analysis.

The third step is data preprocessing. The main work of data preprocessing is to decide each sample data point's features, e.g., the terminal brand model belonging, the operator belonging, the network type belonging and the geographic area belong.

The fourth and fifth step are algorithm formulating and data analysis, respectively. Network competitiveness analysis can be carried out in two dimensions. The first dimension is from different aspects (such as the network coverage, delay, service speed rate) to set up a single parameter evaluation algorithm to reveal single network parameter competitiveness among telecom operators. The second dimension is to set up an operator network competitiveness comprehensive evaluation system, the overall comprehensive score of network competitiveness for each operator can be obtained.

In the last result demonstration step, the result of the single parameter and comprehensive network competitiveness can be demonstrated in various forms such as diagrams, maps and so on.

3.2.2   Single Parameter Network Competitiveness Analysis

The single parameter network competitiveness analysis can be divided into five aspects: the network scale competitiveness analysis, the network coverage competitiveness analysis, the network quality competitiveness analysis, the network speed rate competitiveness analysis and the network service time delay competitiveness analysis. Each can be processed from different time granularity (month/quarter/year) and geographical granularity (provinces/cities/scene/grid).

(1) Network Scale Competitiveness Analysis
   Operator network scale competitiveness analysis consists of three aspects: the number of users, sampling points and cells. These aspects can reflect the operators' user market share distribution and network size, as exemplified in Fig. 5.

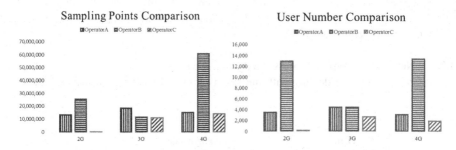

Fig. 5. Exemplified results of network scale competitiveness

(2) Network Coverage Competitiveness Analysis
   Coverage competitiveness analysis can be evaluated via good coverage sample point ratio and 4G network sample point ratio. Percentage of good coverage sample point can be used as indicators for evaluation of 2G (RSSI), 3G (RSCP) and 4G (RSRP) coverage performance, which is defined as: the number of sample point that its signal strength is greater than a certain threshold accounted for the proportion of all sampling points, as shown in Fig. 6. While the 4G network sample point ratio is used to evaluate operators' 4G signal coverage competitiveness, which can be defined as: the sample points generated by 4G users in the

4G network users in the 4G network accounted for the proportion of total sampling points of these users in 2/3/4G.

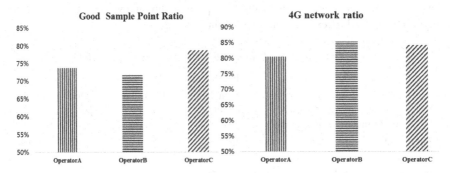

Fig. 6. Exemplified results of network coverage competitiveness

(3) Network Quality Competitiveness Analysis

Operator network quality competitive analysis can be evaluated via good signal quality sampling point ratio. 4G good signal quality sampling point ratio is defined as the number of sample point that its signal quality SINR is greater than a certain threshold accounted for the proportion of all sampling points.

(4) Network Speed

Download (downlink) speed and upload (uplink) speed are applied to evaluate the operator competitiveness of speed, as exemplified in Fig. 7. The download speed and upload speed are affected by the behavior of users.

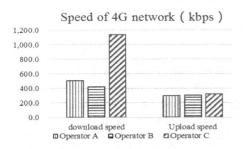

Fig. 7. Results of speed in 4G

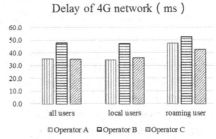

Fig. 8. Results of delay in 4G

(5) Network Delay

Network delay is defined as the delay of ping to some typical website, such as SINA, TAOBAO, YOUKU, IQIYI and etc., which is designed according to specific requirements. Network delay includes the delay of each website and the average delay of all websites, which measures the level of user perception immediately, as exemplified in Fig. 8.

3.2.3   Global Competitiveness Analysis of Network

In the above subsection, we evaluate the competitiveness of each operator by its coverage, interference and perception respectively. However, to evaluate the competitiveness of each operator synthetically, we propose an analysis system based on Analytic Hierarchy Process, which is shown in Table 2.

Table 2. Operator network competitiveness evaluation system (4G)

	Cover			Interference	Perception		
Index	Good sample point ratio	Proportion of 4G users in 4G network		Signal quality	Download speed	Upload speed	Delay
Weight	30%	10%		10%	20%	10%	20%

The score of each index is computed as (3).

$$Score = \frac{x_i}{max(\mathbf{x})}(i = 1, 2, 3) \tag{3}$$

Where x_i is the value of each index and $\mathbf{x}$ is a one-dimensional set composited by three operators. Specially, the score of delay is as (4). A higher score reflects a less delay.

$$Score_{timedelay} = \frac{min(\mathbf{x})}{x_i}(i = 1, 2, 3) \tag{4}$$

The competence of each operator is computed as (5).

$$Competence_{LTE} = Score_{coverage} \times k_{coverage} + Score_{4Gratio} \times k_{4Gratio}$$
$$+ Score_{upspeed} \times k_{upspeed} + Score_{downspeed} \times k_{downspeed} + Score_{timedelay} \times k_{timedelay} \tag{5}$$

where *Score* is the level of each index and k is the weight of each index.

Based on practical data and requirements, we present an example result in Table 3. The result of operator competitiveness evaluation via the CCSA scheme shows that Operator B (0.93) > Operator C (0.82) > Operator A (0.81). This means the network of Operator B is the best while the Operator C and the Operator A have similar competition level.

Table 3. 4G network of operator competitiveness evaluation (Example)

Index	Good sample point ratio	Proportion of 4G users in 4G network	Download speed	Upload speed	Delay	Competence
Weight	30%	20%	20%	10%	20%	
Operator A	0.88	0.82	0.80	0.58	0.82	0.81
Operator B	1.00	0.98	1.00	1.00	0.67	0.93
Operator C	0.90	1.00	0.58	0.35	1.00	0.82

4   Conclusion

In this paper, we design a crowdfunding assisted cellular system analytical (CCSA) scheme, including its framework, mainly-used indicators, key technologies as well as channel expansions. In terms of application, we introduce the content, application of direction, flow and case of this system. As a novel method, the CCSA scheme changes the traditional mode of network analysis, expands the category of network analysis, benefits the network quality of network and expands the range of users. In the future, the contents of the analysis would be further enriched, and the collection of data would be more normalized and persistent. In addition, the combination of data from the OSS and the BSS domain will be enhanced and the CCSA scheme will be constructed to realize normalizing analysis and application.

References

1. Cao, Y., Sun, Z., Wang, N., Riaz, M., Cruickshank, H., Liu, X.: Geographic-based spray-and-relay (GSaR): an efficient routing scheme for DTNs. IEEE Trans. Veh. Technol. **64**(4), 1548–1564 (2015)
2. Xu, L., Cheng, X., Liu, Y., Chen, W., Luan, Y., Chao, K., Yuan, M., Xu, B.: Mobility load balancing aware radio resource allocation scheme for LTE-advanced cellular networks. In: IEEE International Conference on Communication Technology, pp. 806–812. IEEE Press, Hangzhou (2015)
3. Cheng, C., Cheng, X., Yuan, M., Xu, L., Zhou, S., Guan J., Zhang, T.: Spectrum allocation based on data mining in heterogeneous cognitive wireless networks. In: International Conference on Signal and Information Processing, Networking and Computers, pp. 315–324. CRC Press Taylor & Francis Group, Beijing (2015)
4. Xu, L., Luan, Y., Cheng, X., Cao, X., Chao, K., Gao, J., Jia, Y., Wang, S.: WCDMA data based LTE site selection scheme in LTE deployment. In: International Conference on Signal and Information Processing, Networking and Computers, pp. 249–260. CRC Press Taylor & Francis Group, Beijing (2015)
5. Cheng, X., Xu, L., Zhang, T., Jia, Y., Yuan, M., Chao, K.: A novel big data based telecom operation architecture. In: International Conference on Signal and Information Processing, Networking and Computers, pp. 385–396. CRC Press Taylor & Francis Group, Beijing (2015)
6. Zhang, H., Dong, Y., Cheng, J., Hossain, M.J., Leung, V.C.M.: Cooperative interference mitigation and handover management for heterogeneous cloud small cell networks. IEEE Wirel. Commun. **22**(3), 92–99 (2015)
7. Xu, L., Chen, Y., Chai, K.K., Schormans, J., Cuthbert, L.: Self-organising cluster-based cooperative load balancing in OFDMA cellular networks. Wiley Wirel. Commun. Mob. Comput. **15**(7), 1171–1187 (2015)
8. Wang, W., Xu, L., Zhang, Y., Zhong, J.: A novel cell-level resource allocation scheme for OFDMA system. In: International Conference on Communications and Mobile Computing, pp. 287–292. IET Press, Kunming (2009)
9. Cao, Y., Wang, N., Kamel, G., Kim, Y.J.: An electric vehicle charging management scheme based on publish/subscribe communication framework. IEEE Syst. J., 1–14 (2015). https://doi.org/10.1109/JSYST.2015.2449893

10. Liu, Y., Xu, L., Chen, Y., Fan, Y., Xu, B., Nie, J.: A novel power control mechanism based on interference estimation in LTE cellular networks. In: IEEE International Symposium on Communications and Information Technologies, pp. 397–401. IEEE Press, Qingdao (2016)

11. Xu, L., Chen, Y., Gao, Y., Cuthbert, L.: A self-optimizing load balancing scheme for fixed relay cellular networks. In: IET International Conference on Communication Technology and Application, pp. 306–311. IET Press, Beijing (2011)

12. Cui, G., Lu S., Wang, W., Wang, C., Zhang, Y.: Decentralized antenna selection with no CSI sharing for multi-cell MU-MIMO systems. In: IEEE International Symposium on Personal and Indoor, Mobile Radio Communications, pp. 2319–2323. IEEE Press, Sydney (2012)

13. Zhang, T., Cheng, X., Yuan, M., Xu, L., Cheng, C., Chao, K.: Mining target users for mobile advertising based on telecom big data. In: IEEE International Symposium on Communications and Information Technologies, pp. 296–301. IEEE Press, Qingdao (2016)

14. Cui, G., Lu, S., Wang, W., Zhang, Y., Wang, C., Li, X.: Uplink coordinated scheduling based on resource sorting. In: IEEE Vehicular Technology Conference, pp. 1–5. IEEE Press, Quebec (2012)

15. Xu, L., Luan, Y., Cheng, X., Xing, H., Liu, Y., Jiang, X., Chen, W., Chao, K.: Self-optimised joint traffic offloading in heterogeneous cellular networks. In: IEEE International Symposium on Communications and Information Technologies, pp. 263–267. IEEE Press, Qingdao (2016)

16. Cao, Y., Wang, N., Sun, Z., Cruickshank, H.: A reliable and efficient encounter-based routing framework for delay/disruption tolerant networks. IEEE Sens. J. **15**(7), 4004–4018 (2015)

17. Xu, L., Chen, Y., Chai, K.K., Luan, Y., Liu, D.: Cooperative mobility load balancing in relay cellular networks. In: IEEE International Conference on Communication in China, pp. 141–146. IEEE Press, Xi'an (2013)

18. Android. Introduction to Android (2016). http://wear.techbrood.com/guide/index.html

19. Cheng, X., Yuan, M., Xu, L., Zhang, T., Jia, Y., Cheng, C., Chen, W.: Big data assisted customer analysis and advertising architecture for real estate. In: IEEE International Symposium on Communications and Information Technologies, pp. 312–317. IEEE Press, Qingdao (2016)

20. Xu, L., Chen, Y., Chai, K.K., Zhang, T., Schormans, J., Cuthbert, L.: Cooperative load balancing for OFDMA cellular networks. In: European Wireless, pp. 1–7. VDE Verlag GMBH, Poznan (2012)

21. Zhao, L., Al-Dubai, A.Y., Li, X., Chen, G.: A new efficient cross-layer relay node selection model for wireless community mesh networks. Comput. Electr. Eng. (2017). https://doi.org/10.1016/j.compeleceng.2016.12.031

22. Xu, L., Luan, Y., Cheng, X., Fan, Y., Zhang, H., Wang, W., He, A.: Telecom big data based user offloading self-optimisation in heterogeneous relay cellular systems. Int. J. Distrib. Syst. Technol **8**(2), 27–46 (2017)

23. Ye, H., Cheng, X., Yuan, M., Xu, L., Gao, J., Cheng, C.: A survey of security and privacy in big data. In: IEEE International Symposium on Communications and Information Technologies, pp. 268–272. IEEE Press, Qingdao (2016)

SWAT Hydrological Model and Big Data Techniques

Xi Guo$^{(\boxtimes)}$, Biao Wang, Wei Xiong, and Shisheng Jin

GuiZhou Provincial Meteorological Administration Information Center,
GuiYang, GuiZhou, China
guoxiguoxi1989@163.com

Abstract. Meteorological and hydrological data includes a wide range
of items with complex format and large scale. In the era of big
data, it brings great opportunities and challenges to meteorology and
hydrology services. Because isolated information resources and industry data barriers bring incomplete data parameters, which makes the
hydrological model simulate inaccurately. This paper mainly discusses
the application of big data technology in Hydro-Meteorological industry. Firstly, it introduces the background and principal of hydrological SWAT model. Secondly, this paper proceeds the SWAT simulation
and estimates runoff prediction of WangMo river in GuiZhou province,
and analyzes simulation results. Finally, it proposes a big data platform architecture design combines with SWAT hydrological model as
future research direction. Big data platform will provide libraries of
integrated model, method, component, knowledge database for Hydro-
Meteorological resources management. It also offers decision-making for
flood control, water shortage, water pollution incidents.

Keywords: Hydro-meteorological model · Big data · SWAT model
Forecasting model

1   Introduction

Hydrological model is one of the hot spots and important branches in research
of hydrology. It is an important tool of studying the hydrology natural law and
solving relative practical problems. At present, a new generation of distributed
hydrological model has greatly broaden simulation fields, which changes water
yield vary simulation in single way to water ecological diversified situation. The
rapid development technologies of computer, remote sensing, and geographic
information system has greatly promoted hydrological model. However, the distributed hydrological model is not mature enough. It often performs problems
in following aspects: parameter estimation and model checking of hydrological

This project has been funded with support by 2017 Youth Technology Foundation
of GuiZhou Provincial Meteorological Administration.

© ICST Institute for Computer Sciences, Social Informatics and Telecommunications Engineering 2018
K. Long et al. (Eds.): 5GWN 2017, LNICST 211, pp. 79–88, 2018.
https://doi.org/10.1007/978-3-319-72823-0_9

system complexity, different space-time scales of hydrological and spatial parameters variability, different time scales of water cycling dynamic mechanism, and the limitations of data, etc.

At present, facing water issues in the rapid development of society, distributed hydrological model is an effective tool to explore complex hydrological process mechanism for water problems. It becomes an indispensable means for hydrological cycle research, and this will become opportunities and challenges for vast number of Hydro-Meteorological scientists.

2   Hydrological Model SWAT with Big Data Techniques

2.1   Background of SWAT Model

SWAT is a watershed scale model developed by the US Department of Agricultural Research Center USDA-ARS. The purpose of the model is to predict the impact of long-term land management influences on water, sediment and agricultural pollutants in complex watersheds with diversity of soil, land use and management conditions [1]. This section introduces the basic structure of SWAT model, hydrological cycle of land stage, and analyzes the characteristics of model. Finally, in Sect. 3, we simulated WangMo river of climate change on hydrological cycle influenced by SWAT model and put forward the prospects of hydrological model future work in big data field.

2.2   Hydrological Cycle of Land Stage

Water balance is a very important process in SWAT basin simulation. The hydrological simulation of basin can be divided into two main parts: the first part is about land stage hydrological cycle, water quantity control, sediment and nutrients, pesticides; the second part is river hydrological cycle calculation stage, which can be defined as the movement of water and sediment until the export process [2]. Hydrological cycle of SWAT model is mainly composed of following components: climate, hydrology, sediment, crop growth, soil temperature, nutrients, pesticides and agricultural management. The hydrological cycle water balance equation is as follow:

$$SW_t = SW_0 + \sum_{i=1}^{t}(R_{day} - Q_{surf} - E_a - W_{seep} - Q_{gw}) \tag{1}$$

SW_t is final moisture content of soil (mm), SW_0 is soil moisture content at earlier stage (mm), t is step (day), R_{day} is rainfall for the i day (mm), Q_{surf} is surface runoff for the i day (mm), E_a is the evaporation for the i day, W_{seep} is infiltrating and side-flow for the i day of soil bottom section (mm), Q_{gw} is water flow for the i day (mm) [3].

1. Weather and Climate: Watershed climate provides moisture and energy inputs, which controls the water balance. The climatic variables required by SWAT are daily precipitation, maximum/minimum temperature, solar radiation, wind speed and relative humidity. The model reads measured data, and generate climate automatically by weather generator.

2. Hydrological Process: During the precipitation process, it may be intercepted in vegetation canopy or directly drop to soil surface. Soil surface moisture will infiltrate into the soil or generate profile runoff, which moves relatively fast and causes short-term river response when it runs into river. Infiltration of water can be retained in soil, and then be evaporated, or move slowly to surface water system. The physical processes involved include: canopy storage, infiltration, redistribution, evapotranspiration, side runoff, surface runoff, and return flow.

3. Erosion: Calculate the erosion of each HRU and sediment by soil loss equation (MUSLE). MUSLE uses runoff to simulate erosion and sediment yield, which can improve the prediction accuracy of model, and estimate the single storm sediment yield. The hydrological model supports net runoff and peak flow rate, which can be used to calculate runoff erosivity combined with subbasin. Erosion produced by rainfall runoff is calculated by Modified Universal Soil Loss Equation (MUSLE), and the formula is below:

$$Y = 11.8(Q \times pr)^{0.56} K_{USLE} \times C_{USLE} \times P_{USLE} \times LS_{USLE} \qquad (2)$$

Y is quantity of soil erosion (t), Q is surface runoff (mm), pr is peak runoff (m^3/s), K_{USLE} is soil erosion, C_{USLE} is vegetation cover and crop management factor, P_{USLE} is conservation measure factor, LS_{USLE} is terrain factor.

4. Nutrients and Pesticides: SWAT model can track the migration and transformation of nitrogen and phosphorus in several forms. Nutrients run into the river by surface runoff and interflow, and be transported to river downstream. SWAT model simulates the surface runoff carrying pesticides into river, through the leakage into the soil profile and aquifer.

5. Agriculture Management: SWAT model can define in each HRU about the start date of growing season, the time and amount of fertilization, the use of pesticides and irrigation of farming schedule according to the management measures. Beyond these basic management measures, model includes grazing, automatic fertilization and irrigation, as well as every possible water management options. The latest improvement in land management is the integration of sediment and nutrient loads from urban runoff [4].

2.3 Model Structure

Once the SWAT model determines the main river water, sediment, nutrients and pesticides load, river network load is calculated by HYMO command structure. In order to track the material flow in the river, SWAT model simulates the chemical conversion of the river, and computation involves: surface runoff, soil water, groundwater, river, and the confluence of the water storage. The model structure diagram is in Fig. 1. SWAT model has various parameters, mainly include: DEM, spatial distribution of hydro-meteorological station data, soil type and land use, series of evaporation and river data, etc. The list of input parameters could be referred in Table 1.

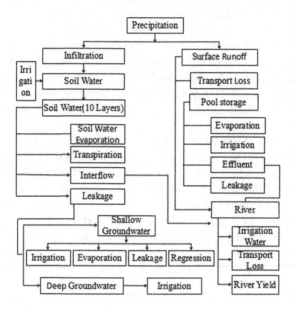

Fig. 1. SWAT model structure

3   WangMo River Simulation on SWAT Model

WangMo river is located in the middle of WangMo county, GuiZhou province, which is slope zone transition of Yunnan-Guizhou plateau to Guangxi hilly, and basin is consisted of karst and normal landform. Annual rainfall is 1249.3 mm, flood season happens concentratively between April and October, and rainy season accounted for 83.14% of the whole year. This river is one of the main branches of BeiPan river, and rises in DaYi village of WangMo county north, run into BeiPan river in WangMo county boundary. The study area is the main stream of river basin, the coordinate is 106°2′–106°12′E, 25°9′–25°23′N. WangMo river is 74 km long, drop height 1050 m, basin area 554 km². Main tributaries includes: NaBa river, NaGuo river, NaChao river, SongLin river. River basin belongs to the seasonal mountain river, and flood varies along with the rainfall. Since year of 70s, there has been occurred dozens of severe floods, collapse, landslide, debris flow and other geological disasters. At present, there are few research about WangMo river basin runoff. In this section, we use SWAT model to study various factors on the WangMo basin runoff, which can be based on the analysis of climate change, land use, and land cover.

Table 1. SWAT model input datasets

Type	Shape	Parameter	Source
Digital elevation data	Raster	Elevation, Slope length, River slope direction	STRM3 arc-seconds
Land use data	GRID	Leaf area index, Vegetation root depth, Runoff curve number, Pipe layer height, Manning coefficient	GLC2000 Lucc 1 km
Soil type	GRID	Density, Saturated water conductivity, Water retention rate, Particle content, Root depth	HWSD
Meteorological data	DBF table	Max–Min temperature, Daily precipitation, Relative humidity, Solar radiation and Wind speed	Meteorological CMADS
Hydrological data	DBF table	Daily flow, Monthly flow, etc.	Hydrological site data
Land management info.	x	Farming methods, Vegetation type, Irrigation methods, Fertilization time and quantity	Investigation of statistics

SWAT is a data driven model and it requires several types of data, which are listed in Table 1. Digital Elevation Data (DEM) were obtained from Shuttle Radar Topography Mission (STRM3), NASA and NIMA, U.S. Land cover datasets were adopted from GLC2000 LUCC 1 km CHINA, and China area datasets is cut from the global data [5]. Soil datasets were from Harmonized World Soil Database (HWSD). Weather datasets were collected from China Meteorological Assimilation Driving Datasets for SWAT model (CMADS) [5]. Different processes have been carried out when databases were established. Considering hydrological behavior of the basin with losing productive soil and water as runoff problems, the study took with SWAT2012 integrated with Arc GIS10.3.1 to evaluate the surface runoff watershed of WangMo river [6]. SWAT model is physically based and computationally efficient, uses readily available inputs and enables users to study long-term impacts. To use the model estimates WangMo river basin runoff, firstly, we need to setup a new SWAT project and load the existed WangMo river DEM from disk and define the river network. Figure 2 shows the processes of running SWAT model. The key procedures of modeling is as follow:

- Load or select the SWAT extension checking the relative box in the BASINS Extension Manager (Models category). Add three types of nodes: the rivers export, entry and source point. Generally speaking, one natural basin only has one export.
- Delineate the watershed and define the Hydrological Response Units (HRU). We obtained watershed map when calculated the sub-basin and activated reservoir button.

- Edit SWAT databases and make database index (data including: soil, slope, land use, weather, etc.). Model analyzes land use, soil coverage and HRU and make them overlay together. This is the most complex step, because when establish database, you need calculate lots of parameters by equations.
- Define the weather data with weather generator (data including: relative humidity, solar radiation, and wind speed).
- Set up and run SWAT simulation, after then, apply the default input files writer.
- Analyze, plot and graph SWAT output (SWATOutput.mdb) with Origin.

Fig. 2. SWAT model simulation of WangMo river

3.1 Results and Discussion

From the simulation of SWAT model, we obtain relationship between precipitation and runoff in the watershed of WangMo river, which could be referred to Fig. 3, and the simulation period is the average of each month from year 2008 to 2016. Firstly, it reflects the effect of rainfall intensity. When a rainstorm occurs in the watershed, it generates large runoff, which makes the runoff appear large jump in result graph. However, in the period of drought, due to the lack of rainfall, runoff decreases [7,8]. In the case of heavy rainstorm, soil water conservation is difficult to play an effective role. At present, due to human activities, it causes serious damage to the environment, which also makes the relationship between runoff and rainfall become complicated [9]. While upstream desertification phenomenon occurs, it makes groundwater become lower, and reduces runoff storage. The soil moisture content of various effects will make the runoff results different.

When analyzing the relation between precipitation and runoff by SWAT model, we supposed that temperature T is a constant, and then change the value of precipitation. We found that there was a positive correlation between precipitation and runoff and the result is shown in Fig. 4. When precipitation P1 increased by 40%, the runoff increased 115.43 mm, and increased by 71.2% on

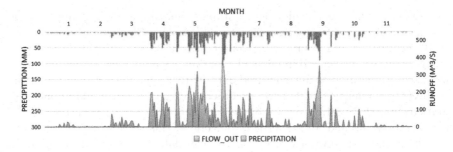

Fig. 3. SWAT model results

the basis of the original runoff; When P2 increased by 20%, the runoff increased 61.42 mm, and increased by 35.23% on the basis of the original runoff; When the P3 was reduced by 15%, the runoff was reduced 41.55 mm, which was reduced by 25.24% on the basis of the original runoff; When the P4 was reduced by 30%, the runoff was reduced 79.48 mm, which was reduced by 54.87% on the basis of the original runoff.

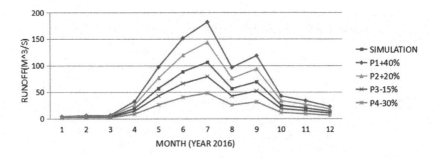

Fig. 4. Runoff variation with precipitation

3.2 Big Data with Hydrological Models

The arrival of big data era has brought hydro-meteorological information opportunities and challenges. This section introduces how to enhance the theoretical basis of hydrological model with big data support, broaden model's applicability, and propose a framework of intelligent real-time hydrological model of big data driven; discuss on the aspects that we can spare effort to study hydrological model forecasting precision of big data techniques. More and more people understand and pay close attention to hydro-meteorological model with big data, which will be widely used in society [10,11]. Big data needs new processing mode to have a strong decision-making capability, process optimization of massive, high growth rate and diversification of datasets. In other words, if we take big data as an industry, the key of achieving profitability such industry is to improve the data processing capacity by making value-added data [12,13].

At present, water resource data center mainly uses relational database to manage structured data and implement geographic spatial data extending; organizing semi-structured or unstructured data by relational database and file storage directory management. For water conservancy data storage and application requirements, the existing data storage structure has a bottleneck on aspects of data processing and analyzing [14]. Therefore, this section puts forward an idea about the structure of hydrological model data center based on big data platform, including data collection, data storage, data processing and analysis, and data application of four layers, which can be referred in Fig. 5.

Hydrological forecasting plays a very important role in flood control and disaster reduction. Due to the climate change and human activities, the basic law of hydrology has changed a lot, and those past hydrological models can not meet the needs of sustainable development of social economy. The hydrological runoff monitoring, rainfall, DEM and soil vegetation, remote sensing images bring increasing rich elements of big data. Research of new hydrology forecast technology driven by big data has become an inevitable way to solve above problems.

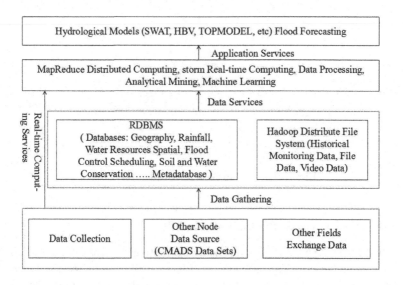

Fig. 5. SWAT model on big data platform

In the background of big data, we can conduct the thorough research from the following several aspects about hydrological law in big data mining, runoff theory method, and the cloud stage of real-time efficient forecasting technology.

- Research on flood characteristic pattern and parameter geography big data mining method. This could study from the characteristics of storm flood and construct a typical watershed model library.
- Research on precise hydrological model and big data driven intelligent real-time forecast model, flood forecast integration and real-time correction method, which is based on water storage capacity curve and terrain index of semi distributed dynamic combination in order to improve the prediction accuracy of semi-humid and semi-arid.
- Study on redistribution of flow along the side and water unit exchange between grid adaptive distributed simulation technology and precise prediction of watershed, which could achieve arbitrary grid unit flow and water level, improve the accuracy of real-time flood forecasting in complex basin.
- Research of water conservancy satellite remote sensing monitoring system and hydrological forecasting cloud platform, in order to achieve an integrate multi system running environment. Multi particle splitting, loose coupling and service collaboration technology could achieve hydro-meteorological flood forecast transferring, which can improve the efficiency, expand forecast period, and improve the accuracy of hydrological forecasting.

Flood forecasting plays a very important role in flood control and disaster reduction. Due to climate change, human activities, social economy development, flood forecasting encounters new problems and challenges. Study on the development of runoff theory, and create model of complex river basin and high accuracy flood forecasting, which has become the key technical points of national flood control. In the future, we can carry out the research and application of flood forecasting methods base on the data mining and big data techniques according to researches aspects above.

4   Conclusion

To develop a suitable model for the hydrological process for a river basin is the most important aspect for water resource management. SWAT hydrological model is applied to WangMo, GuiZhou watershed in order to assess the relationship between runoff and precipitation. Input datasets DEM, STRM3, HWSD, GLC2000, CMADS are quite applicable to run the SWAT model for the basin. The performance and applicability of SWAT model was successfully evaluated through model calibration. Average annual prediction of stream flow is 95.54 mm. As this model has a broaden functions, the model can be utilized not only as a potential tool for water resource management, but also help assess different land management and evaluate the effect of climate change on soil erosion.

Big data technology promotes water conservancy data acquisition, management and application of the rapid development. This paper also proposes a big data technology data center architecture of hydrological model, and to demonstrate how it can improve the management. And MapReduce series big data technology break through traditional data analysis perspective in a completely different way, in order to build the flood forecasting model in a more accurate way.

References

1. Ning, J., Liu, G., Liu, Q., Xie, C.: The hydrologic response unit (HRU) on SWAT model. Adv. Water Sci. **23**(1) (2012)
2. Sun, R., Zhang, X.: The Basin runoff study based on SWAT model. Geogr. Sci. Dev. **30**(3), 28–32 (2010)
3. Gassman, P.W., Reyes, M.R., Green, C.H., Arnold, J.G.: The Soil and Water Assessment Tool Historical Development. Applications and Future Research Directions. Center for Agricultural and Rural Development Lowa State University, Working Paper 07–WP 443
4. Jayakrishnan, R., Srinivasan, R., Santhi, C., Arnold, J.G.: Advances in the application of the SWAT model for water resources management. Hydrol. Process. **19**, 749–762 (2005)
5. This data set is provided by Cold and Arid Regions Science Data Center at Lanzhou. http://westdc.westgis.ac.cn
6. Source for this dataset was Global Land Cover 2000 database. European Commission, Joint Research Centre (2003). http://www-gem.jrc.it/glc2000/
7. Xu, L., Luan, Y., Cheng, X., Cao, X., Chao, K., Gao, J., Jia, Y., Wang, S.: WCDMA data based LTE site selection scheme in LTE deployment. In: International Conference on Signal and Information Processing, Networking and Computers (ICSINC), Beijing, China, pp. 249–260. CRC Press, Taylor and Francis Group (2015)
8. Xu, L., Chen, Y., Chai, K. K., Luan, Y., Liu, D.: Cooperative mobility load balancing in relay cellular networks. In: IEEE International Conference on Communication in China (ICCC), Xi'an, China, pp. 141–146. IEEE Press (2013)
9. Xu, L., Cheng, X., Liu, Y., Chen, W., Luan, Y., Chao, K., Yuan, M., Xu, B.: Mobility load balancing aware radio resource allocation scheme for LTE-advanced cellular networks. In: IEEE International Conference on Communication Technology (ICCT), Hangzhou, China, pp. 806–812. IEEE Press (2015)
10. Cao, Y., Wang, N., Sun, Z., Cruickshank, H.: A reliable and efficient encounter-based routing framework for delay/disruption tolerant networks. IEEE Sens. J. **15**(7), 4004–4018 (2015)
11. Cao, Y., Sun, Z., Wang, N., Riaz, M., Cruickshank, H., Liu, X.: Geographic-based spray-and-relay (GSaR): an efficient routing scheme for DTNs. IEEE Trans. Veh. Technol. **64**(4), 1548–1564 (2015)
12. Rui, X.: Hydrology and big data. In: Advances in Science and Technology of Water Resources, vol. 36. College of Hydrology and Water Resources, Hohai University (2016)
13. Xu, L., Chen, Y., Gao, Y., Cuthbert, L.: A self-optimizing load balancing scheme for fixed relay cellular networks. In: IET International Conference on Communication Technology and Application (ICCTA), Beijing, China, pp. 306–311. IET Press (2011)
14. Xu, L., Luan, Y., Cheng, X., Xing, H., Liu, Y., Jiang, X., Chen, W., Chao, K.: Self-optimised joint traffic offloading in heterogeneous cellular networks. In: IEEE International Symposium on Communications and Information Technologies (ISCIT), Qingdao, China, pp. 263–267. IEEE Press (2016)

A Survey on Security Issues in Big Data of Ubiquitous Network

Yuehua Huo[1], Yanyu Sun[2], Weiqiang Fan[2], Xinzhou Cheng[3], Dong Li[1], and Yinlong Liu[4(✉)]

[1] Center of Modern Education Technology,
China University of Mining and Technology, Beijing 100083, China
[2] School of Mechatronics and Information Engineering,
China University of Mining and Technology, Beijing 100083, China
[3] China Unicom Network Technology Research Institute, Beijing 100048, China
[4] Institute of Information Engineering, Chinese Academy of Sciences,
Beijing 100093, China
huoyh@cumtb.edu.cn, chinahuo007@163.com

Abstract. In the ubiquitous network, these many devices generate a huge amount of data. The sharp increase of the diverse devices has led to the various heterogeneous data types and the booming growth of the data, that is, the ubiquitous network will bring big data. Due to the heterogeneity and ubiquitous nature of ubiquitous networks, the big data of ubiquitous network faces a broad and growing range of security threats and challenges. Based on the basic knowledge of the big data of ubiquitous network, this paper analyzes the security threats in the process of data collection, storage, processing and application. System elaborated the big data of ubiquitous network encryption and integrity protection, access control, privacy protection, attack detection, security technology research status. The research direction and future development direction are also discussed in this paper.

Keywords: Ubiquitous network · Big data · Information security · Intelligent

1 Introduction

With the rapid development of network technology, both at home and abroad pay more and more attention to the study of ubiquitous network, increasing investment, making the network is widely used in social and economic sustainable development and national development strategy, extensive penetration as part of the network in all walks of life, become strategy core of each country. A large number of sensor networks, RFID [1] and other widely used, so that everything can be data, people realize that the nature of the world is the data, and the data will gradually completely change the future of the world.

Nowadays, the ubiquitous network plays a central role in the national strategic development, triggered unprecedented national investment and the further research of many scholars, and aiming at security problems exist in the process of its development, put forward the solution. The United States proposed broadband urban planning [2],

© ICST Institute for Computer Sciences, Social Informatics and Telecommunications Engineering 2018
K. Long et al. (Eds.): 5GWN 2017, LNICST 211, pp. 89–98, 2018.
https://doi.org/10.1007/978-3-319-72823-0_10

the plan for the arrival of the network to pave the way at the same time, will be in the United States to set up a wide range of urban broadband network. The South Korean government also proposed the "U-Korea" strategic plan [3], ubiquitous sensor network, broadband network integration and IPv6 core network is included in the investment plan of infrastructure construction, the construction of a part of achievements in the promotion, in city management, medical treatment, military has been widely used. In China, some research on the ubiquitous network is gradually carried out, such as "perception of China", "U-Beijing" and "U-Qingdao" [4] is one of the typical representative.

With the extensive application of 4G network, 5G [5, 6] as a new wireless access technology is gradually into people's lives, it has more powerful features, will be a true sense of the integration of the network [5, 7]. In this paper, according to the characteristics of ubiquitous network data, generally reveal: safety issues faced in the ubiquitous network of different network structure and big data in different data processing stages, and the corresponding solutions and technology.

2   Big Data of Ubiquitous Network

2.1   The Concept and Characteristics of Big Data of Ubiquitous Network

Ubiquitous network is wider than the web of things, more extensive content. It is generally believed that the sensor network, the sensor node is composed of a large number of networking, personal and social network etc., which refers to at any time (Anytime) of any location (Anywhere) of any person (Anyone) and (Anything) any communication [8].

Big data [9], also known as mass data, refers to the size of the data involved to a huge scale cannot be artificial or computer, within a reasonable time to achieve interception, management, processing, and sorting into human interpretations of the form of information. Ubiquitous network is the root of big data, has a close connection, the network application can promote the research of big data. Big data is the resources and wealth, big data analysis makes the decision more scientific, more intelligent terminals, will promote the ubiquitous network more intelligent and more widely used to promote its further rapid development. Big data generated by the ubiquitous network, due to the large amount of data and fast generation and often change characteristics [10], if the encryption and decryption technology and traditional hash algorithm [11] to achieve the integrity of the identification and authentication of data, the efficiency is low and it is hard to meet the real-time, consistency and synchronization so on. The ubiquitous network is still in the stage of the Internet of things, big data mining, analysis and processing methods are not mature, at the same time, we must face many security problems of big data, in the ubiquitous network, and more complex than ever. Therefore, it is necessary for the ubiquitous network security key problems on the big data of research, for the application of ubiquitous network and big data cleared.

2.2 Security Challenges for Big Data of Ubiquitous Networks

The doubling of the amount of data challenges the ability to store data; the traditional database lacks strong scalability and better system availability, and cannot effectively store unstructured and semi-structured data such as video and audio. Cloud storage in the application of big data to bring development opportunities at the same time, also brought a huge security risk. First of all, the user data storage and security entirely by the cloud computing provider is responsible for the data is transparent to the provider. Second, in the cloud storage, the user's data is stored in the Internet server, an increase of unauthorized access to security issues.

With the increasing scale of data, the time of analysis and processing is correspondingly longer and longer, and the time requirement of information processing is getting higher and higher under big data condition. The processing of big data requires more simple and effective artificial intelligence algorithm and new problem solving method. Discover new methods, predict predictability of threats, and detect and judge unknown threats. The Prism Plan is a case of a large data technology for security analysis. The basic principle is to discover potentially dangerous situations by collecting various types of data from various countries, using safety-related data and threatening security analysis. Identify the threat before it occurs.

3 Security Problems in Big Data of Ubiquitous Network

3.1 Security Threats in the Acquisition Process

Most of the current privacy protection using location, identifier, anonymous connection and other methods. But in practice, in addition to face the threat of personal privacy, people through the vast amounts of data, analysis of people's living state and behavior, prediction, through anonymous protection in today's era of big data is not fully achieve the purpose of privacy protection. On the one hand, due to the current lack of user data collection, storage, management and use of norms, lack of supervision and effective management, mainly rely on self-discipline, cannot guarantee the user privacy information purposes; On the other hand, the data traceability and intelligent analysis technology in the big data age can analyze the sensitive information such as data sources and obtain the privacy data [12].

3.2 Security Threats to Stored Procedures

The arrival of cloud storage, big data applications with more development opportunities, but also with a huge security risk. Firstly, cloud computing providers are fully responsible for the storage and security of user data, the data provider is transparent. Secondly, in the cloud storage, the user's data is stored in the Internet server, an increase of unauthorized access to security issues. As shown in Fig. 1, it analyzed cloud storage ubiquitous network data security; research on big data security of ubiquitous network based on cloud storage includes data integrity protection and access control.

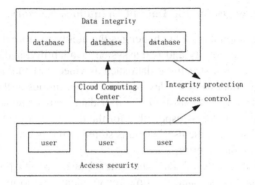

Fig. 1. Big data security analysis of cloud storage

3.3 Process Security Threats

In terms of pattern matching algorithms. In English character environment, classic DFSA application efficiency is very high, if utilized directly match characters, the construction of a Chinese character storage expansion problems when a Hash table. To this end, Shen Zhou [13], Wong [14], Gao Peng [15], respectively, put forward different algorithms. In text content analysis, the text content analysis in cloud content monitoring, the depth of the user identification of suspicious information, but also can find the current flow of hot information.

3.4 Application Process Security Threats

In the ubiquitous network environment, the content of the network is richer, and the flooding of reactionary, pornographic, violent and other undesirable contents has become a problem to be solved urgently [16]. How to ensure the legitimacy and health of data content has become a big data analysis And big data security research areas of hot issues, and cause more and more attention.

4 Security Technology in Big Data of Ubiquitous Network

4.1 Data Encryption

Research on Cloud Storage Key Management and Auditing Proxy Mechanism, Cloud Storage Service (Cloud Storage Service). In addition to the general personal data storage, but also to allow enterprises or data owners (Data Owner, DO) to facilitate the sharing of data services. But when DO wants to share specific data, especially secret information to a specific group or individual, the data access control and key management information security issues need to be considered. Zhao [17] proposed a classification proxy re-encryption technique, which enables data distributors to implement fine-grained categorization control of ciphertext delegation. Wu [18] gives a proxy-re-encryption algorithm with no certificate and an identity-based key escrow protocol. Liang [19] studied the identity-based revocable proxy re-encryption mechanism. Fang [20] proposed an anonymous conditional proxy re-encryption scheme and a fuzzy condition proxy re-encryption scheme [21] to improve the performance of the algorithm.

4.2 Integrity Protection

Integrity protection consists mainly of two components, POR and PDP. Literature [22] builds a hierarchical architecture that provides high availability and integrity protection for data by combining two-dimensional RS coding with a challenge-response mechanism. Literature [23] gives a method to determine the integrity of the data. That is, the authentication element is generated from each file data block, in the challenge of the challenge - response mechanism, adopt the method of pseudo random, draw a small amount of data blocks, judgment data integrity can be achieved through authentication of authentication element. Literature [24] proposed method based on the pattern of challenge - response "Data type to hold Proof" (Proof of Data Possession, PDP), namely in outsourcing Data, detect is greater than a certain percentage of Data corruption. Literature [25] to solve files in multiple servers distributed storage situation, proposed the CPDP (Cooperative Provable Data Possession). The proposed scheme utilizes a homomorphic authentication response to combine responses from different cloud servers into a single response message. Currently, the big data integrity of the cloud to verify mainly rely on a third party to complete. According to whether to allow the restoration of the original data, the current data integrity verification protocol can be divided into two categories: only to verify data integrity of the PDP protocol and allow recovery of data POR protocol. Data integrity verification of the general process shown in Fig. 2.

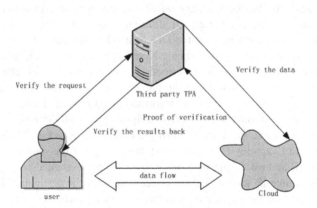

Fig. 2. Data integrity verification of the general process

4.3 Access Control

In the aspect of access control, the decryption rules are embedded in the encryption algorithm through the algorithms of KP-ABE and CP-ABE [26] (ABE), which can avoid the frequent occurrence of ciphertext access control Key distribution cost.

However, when the control strategy changes dynamically, the data owner (the Data Owner) is required to re-encrypt the data. In literature [27], Cloud service providers (cloud service provider, CSP) agent in order to reach the goal of user revocation, the cipher text from an encrypted access structure to another encrypted access structure. Undo unit has a certain limitation of the scheme, a single user cannot complete the revocation, only is a set of properties. Literature [28] cipher text access control scheme is put forward, to support fine-grained access control strategy, but when undo attribute and user privileges, DO the calculation of the price has a linear relation with the data file size. In summary, for the purpose of profit-making CSP, cannot effectively guarantee security.

4.4 Privacy Protection

Ubiquitous network game model of big data privacy protection required game basic research. Based on the previous research, we have fully understood the privacy requirements and the basic technical means at all levels. It is proposed that participants, strategy (attack and defense strategy, behavior rule set), information collection (common knowledge) Action and action sequences, utility (payment) functions and other basic elements of the game to abstract and extract. Based on the ubiquitous network heterogeneity, diversity of unstructured characteristics of big data, both offensive and defensive behavior, the environment, the diversity of information, the incomplete information dynamic game, combined with Bayesian equilibrium subgame perfect Nash equilibrium, and the Bayesian inference method, the optimal privacy policy.

4.5 Attack Detection

DDoS attack detection has been a very important research topic in network intrusion detection. In recent years, a variety of different types of detection platforms and algorithms have been proposed to solve DDoS attacks, and many technical problems have been solved and many achievements have been made. Among them, the information entropy power system is described as random degree of effective index, gradually become the research focus in the network anomaly traffic analysis and detection. We based on the theory of information entropy and chaos phase space reconstruction theory, through the in-depth study of typical DDoS attack scenario, put forward the following two methods for intrusion detection: Detection Method Based on Tsalli Entropy and Lyapunov Exponent. First, the entropy of the source IP address and the destination IP address in the network traffic packet is counted to reflect the randomness of the source IP address and the concentration of the destination IP address in the response attack. On the basis, the Lyapunov exponent in chaos theory is introduced to calculate the degree of separation between the source IP address entropy and the destination IP address entropy, and the attack traffic is distinguished from the normal traffic. Detection Method Based on Markov Chain and Kolmogorov Entropy. By analyzing the degree of protocol dependency of various network packets in attack traffic, the Markov chain model is established, and the complex Markov chain model is simplified by entropy rate sequence, and the chaotic phase space reconstruction is introduced. The data is reconstructed by using the geometric invariant feature

Kolmogorov entropy of the phase space to reflect the inherent chaos of the network traffic model to achieve the purpose of detecting the attack. The above research has basically reflected the advantages of information entropy theory in the analysis of network anomalies and network intrusion, so the above research provides a theoretical basis for big data analysis.

5 Prospect of Security Technology in Big Data of Ubiquitous Network

5.1 Technical Level

On the technical level, the subsystems are independent and closely integrated with each other. Each part belongs to an indivisible whole, it will be the perfect fusion of the subsystems together. In general can be divided into the ubiquitous network, the security of data architecture and technical analysis, related research in information industry and the practical application of hercynian information industry, and a few kinds big data pretreatment method in between data key security study four blocks of the model.

By analyzing the security requirements at different levels of the ubiquitous network and different stages of big data, the preprocessing technology of big data in the ubiquitous network, the application technology in the information industry and the specific key security models are studied. In turn, these three aspects of research are the key to promoting the development and application of large-scale data security technologies.

The big data preprocessing technology is the foundation of the research on the concrete data security model of the big data network. It can also be used in the actual information industry to solve the difficult problems in the application of the information industry and promote its further healthy development.

As shown in Fig. 3, the big data processing from front to back into data collection, data transmission, data analysis, data analysis at different stages. Then the security problems faced by different stages are analyzed. The security techniques and methods that may be adopted in each stage are determined. For example, the integrity of the big data transmission stage can be verified by digital watermarking technique.

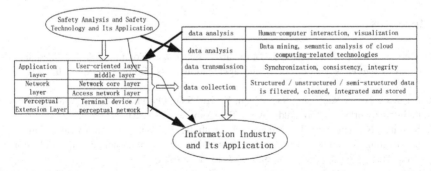

Fig. 3. Ubiquitous network and big data architecture, security requirements and technical analysis and application

5.2 Management Level

In the case of big data, a large number of users need to implement the rights management, and the user specific authority requirements unknown. In the face of unknown large amounts of data and users, it is very difficult to set the role in advance. Construction of important sensitive equipment and carrier management and monitoring system architecture and standards, and based on RFID and other Internet of things technology, from the production to the retirement of the whole life cycle management and control system to complete the relevant standards development, system development work.

First of all, the establishment of content monitoring knowledge model; then, based on "people, behavior, content," the sensitive data-aware platform, the generalized network of information data sets for preliminary screening, reduce the amount of redundant information; Finally, the establishment of dynamic awareness of the network, the suspicious, potential portals, forums and users real-time tracking analysis, so that quickly found, in time to stop. The practical application of big data in the information industry can lead to further improvement of big data analysis methods and help to improve the management level. The security model can be applied directly to the real information industry.

6 Conclusion

According to the characteristics of big data, we fully analyze the security problems and research status, and on this basis, we look at the research direction at the technical and management level. Therefore, the research on the big data and security in the network has far-reaching theoretical significance and practical application value. The research on it is not only necessary in the construction of the theoretical system, the key technology and the improvement of the security problems, Mode, laws and regulations and other aspects of exploration, but also need to carry out theoretical validation and demonstration of its application, it is better for the community to provide services. Analysis and utilization of big data in the ubiquitous network can make the future more common in the network will be more intelligent.

References

1. Van den Elzen, S.V., Wijk, J.J.: Multivariate network exploration and presentation: from detail to overview via selections and aggregations. Vis. Comput. Graph. **20**, 2310–2319 (2014)
2. Xu, X.Q., He, G.N., Zhang, S.Q., Chen, Y., Xu, S.G.: On functionality separation for green mobile networks: concept study over LTE. Commun. Mag. **51**, 82–90 (2013)
3. Kushiro, N., Higuma, T., Nakata, M., Kubota, H., Sato, K.: Practical solution for constructing ubiquitous network in building and home control system consumer electronics. IEEE Trans. Consum. Electron. **53**, 1387–1392 (2007)
4. Saito, H., Kagami, O., Umehira, M., Kado, Y.: Wide area ubiquitous network: the network operator's view of a sensor network. Commun. Mag. **46**, 112–120 (2008)

5. Zhang, H., Dong, Y., Cheng, J., Hossain, M., Leung, V.C.M.: Fronthauling for 5G LTE-U ultra dense cloud small cell networks. IEEE Wirel. Commun. **23**, 48–53 (2016)

6. Xu, L., Chen, Y., Chai, K.K.: Cooperative mobility load balancing in relay cellular networks. In: 2013 IEEE/CIC International Conference on Communications in China, Xi'an, pp. 141–146. IEEE Press (2013)

7. Xu, L., Cheng, X., Liu, Y.: Mobility load balancing aware radio resource allocation scheme for LTE-advanced cellular networks. In: IEEE International Conference on Communication Technology, Hangzhou, pp. 806–812. IEEE Press (2015)

8. Chung, Y.F., Tsai, M.Y., Wu, E.P., Chiang, D.L., Lee, C.C., Hsiao, T.C., Chen, T.S.: Bed site health care video-phone system. Appl. Mech. Mater. **284–287**, 1636–1641 (2013)

9. Hashem, I.A.T., Yaqoob, I., Anuar, N.B.: The rise of "big data" on cloud computing: review and open research issues. Inf. Syst. **47**, 98–115 (2015)

10. Guo, F., Wang, J.M., Li, D.Y.: Finger printing relational databases. In: ACM Symposium on Applied Computing, Dijon, pp. 487–492. ACM Press (2006)

11. Jiang, C.X., Sun, X.M., Yi, Y.Q., Yang, H.F.: Research on database public watermarking algorithm based on JADE algorithm. J. Syst. Simul. **18**, 1781–1785 (2006)

12. Zhang, H., Xing, H., Cheng, J., Nallanathan, A., Leung, V.: Secure resource allocation for OFDMA two-way relay wireless sensor networks without and with cooperative jamming. IEEE Trans. Ind. Inf. **12**, 1714–1725 (2016)

13. Shen, C., Wang, Y.C., Liu, G.S.: Improved algorithm of multi-pattern matching for Chinese string. Acta Agron. Sin. **21**, 27–32 (2002)

14. Zhao, J., Zheng, W., Wen, X., Zhang, H., Lu, Z., Jing, W.: Research on the resource allocation of OFDMA relay network based on secrecy ratio. J. Electron. Inf. Technol. **36**, 2816–2821 (2014)

15. Zhao, J., Lu, Z., Wen, X., Zhang, H., He, S., Jing, W.: Resource management based on security satisfaction ratio with fairness-aware in two-way relay networks. Int. J. Distrib. Sens. Netw. **2015**, 11 (2015)

16. Wang, T., An, B.Y., Peng, Z., Zhang, G.L., Zhong, B.N.: Blue card-green communications for exchanging information of mobile users. J. Comput. Inf. Syst. **10**, 8153–8160 (2014)

17. Schell, R.: Security — a big question for big data. In: 2013 IEEE International Conference on Big Data, Santa Clara, p. 5. IEEE Press (2013)

18. Bowers, K.D., Luels, A., Oprea, A.: Hail: a high-availability and integrity layer for cloud storage. In: 16th ACM Conference on Computer and Communications Security, Chicago, pp. 187–198. ACM Press (2009)

19. Zhao, J., Feng, D.G., Yang, L.: CCA-secure type-based proxyre-encryption without pairings. Acta Electron. Sin. **39**, 2513–2519 (2011)

20. Wu, X.X., Li, X.U., Zhang, X.W.: A certificateless proxyre-encryption scheme for cloud-based data sharing. In: 18th ACM Conference on Computer and Communications Security, Chicago, pp. 869–871. ACM Press (2011)

21. Liang, K., Liu, J.K., Wong, D.S., Susilo, W.: An efficient cloud-based revocable identity-based proxy re-encryption scheme for public clouds data sharing. In: Kutyłowski, M., Vaidya, J. (eds.) ESORICS 2014, Part I. LNCS, vol. 8712, pp. 257–272. Springer, Cham (2014). https://doi.org/10.1007/978-3-319-11203-9_15

22. Weng, J., Deng, R.H., Ding, X.H.: Conditional proxyre-encryption secure against chosen-ciphertext attack. In: ACM ASIACCS 2009, pp. 322–332 (2009)

23. Fang, L.M., Wang, J.D., Ge, C.P.: Fuzzy conditional proxyre-encryption. Sci. China Inf. Sci. **56**, 1–13 (2015)

24. Han, H., Wen, Y.G., Chua, T.S., Li, X.L.: Toward scalable systems for big data analytics: a technology tutorial. IEEE Access **2**, 652–687 (2014)

25. Yang, C., Liu, C., Nepal, S., Chen, J.: A time efficient approach for detecting errors in big sensor data on cloud. IEEE Trans. Parallel Distrib. Syst. **26**, 329–339 (2015)
26. Zhang, G.L., Wang, Z.N., Du, J.X., Wang, T., Jiang, Z.N.: A generalized visual aid system for teleoperation applied to satellite servicing. Int. J. Adv. Robot. Syst. **11**, 1–7 (2014)
27. Yi, X.M., Liu, F.M., Liu, J.C., Hai, J.: Building a network highway for big data: architecture and challenges. IEEE Netw. **28**, 5–13 (2014)
28. Liang, X., Cao, Z., Lin, H.: Attribute based proxy re-encryption with delegating capabilities. In: 4th International Symposium on Information, Computer and Communications Security, pp. 276–286. ACM Press, New York (2009)

Telecom Big Data Based User Analysis and Application in Telecom Industry

Guanglu Shao, Weiwei Chen, Xinzhou Cheng, Lexi Xu[✉],
Tao Zhang, and Chen Cheng

China United Network Technology Corporation,
Beijing, People's Republic of China
xulx29@chinaunicom.cn

Abstract. Due to the fast progress of mobile internet and smart phone, telecom operators store massive telecom big data. In this paper, we utilize telecom big data for the user analysis and application. Initially, this paper studies the content of telecom big data. Then, 360-degree user portrait is drawn via three types of factors, including user's information, user's consumption behavior and service behavior. Based on the user portrait, this paper seeks 4G potential users via data mining technique, which includes the business understanding, data preparation, model building, model training, model evaluation and model deployment steps. Based on the 4G potential users, the marketing department can accelerate the transferring process from 2G/3G users to 4G users.

Keywords: Telecom big data · 4G · Telecom operator · Data mining
User portrait

1 Introduction

The telecom industry experiences fast progress in the past decade [1, 2]. The dramatically increased network capacity and transmission rate allow a large number of users to get access to networks [3, 4]. The telecom industries generate abundant information, which is called telecom big data [5]. It's generally known that telecom big data brings great opportunity for telecom operators [6, 7].

Recently, telecom operators utilize telecom big data to generate value and bring profits, the value chain of telecom big data includes four stages, as shown in Fig. 1.

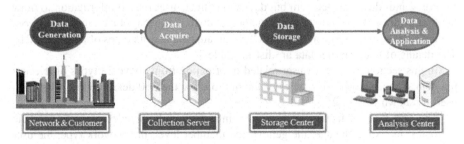

Fig. 1. Value chain of telecom big data

© ICST Institute for Computer Sciences, Social Informatics and Telecommunications Engineering 2018
K. Long et al. (Eds.): 5GWN 2017, LNICST 211, pp. 99–109, 2018.
https://doi.org/10.1007/978-3-319-72823-0_11

The first stage is the data generation stage since customers generate abundant data during the telecom services [8]. As the channel to bear these services, networks also generate massive signaling data and service data [9, 10]. According to the data source, telecom big data includes BSS data and OSS data. BSS data includes customer personal information, voice billing details, data billing details, monthly billing etc. OSS data includes measurement report (MR), counter, performance indicator, call detailed record (CDR), engineering parameters etc. [11, 12].

The second stage is the data collection stage. The widely used method is telecom operators set acquisition equipment in the network interface, thus collecting the data stream, which pass the network interface. Typical network interfaces include A and Abis interface in the switching network, Gb and Gn interface in GPRS, lu-PS and lu-CS interface in 3G, S1 and X2 interface in LTE [13, 14].

After collecting the data stream, in the third data storage stage, telecom operators can resolve data stream and form new-structure data, which suit for storage. Then, telecom operators store these data. Since telecom big data has the characteristics of large volume, effective storage is vital and cloud mechanism is a promising technique to store telecom big data in the future [15].

The key of big data era is to seek the data value in the data analysis and application stage [16, 17]. On one hand, telecom big data can be utilized in the telecom industry, for example, telecom big data based network planning and optimisation, telecom big data assisted market strategy, value-added service, telecom big data analysis of network quality and performance [18, 19]. On the other hand, telecom big data can be also utilized for the relevant industries, for example, advertisement, smart finance, transport, epidemic control, human flow control, public sentiment monitoring etc. [20].

In order to study the telecom big data application in the telecom industry, this paper analyses the content of telecom big data and then draw the 360-degree user portrait, including the characteristics, the resident area, the mainstream services and other preferences of users. According to the user information and behavior, this paper uses data mining technique to seek 4G potential users for telecom operators.

This paper is organised as follows: Sect. 2 describes the user portrait. Section 3 introduces the data mining process and presents 4G potential users analysis in details. Conclusions are given in Sect. 4.

2   360 Degree User Portrait Analysis

Section 2 introduces the telecom big data and extracts user related information to draw the user portrait. According to the data source, there are twenty-three types of telecom big data, including seventeen types of OSS domain data and six types of BSS data [21]. The details of telecom big data are list in Table 1.

In this section, we extract user related information from above 23 types of telecom big data. Then, we get three types of factors to draw the 360-degree portrait for each user, as shown in Fig. 2.

The first type of factors is the user's information. It includes a series of static attributes, including the age, the gender, the member level, the network type, the user state etc. [15, 22].

Table 1. Telecom big data source

Index	Category	Data source
1	OSS domain	Engineering parameters
2		DT/CQT data
3		IU-PS/Gn/S1 interface data
4		CDR (call detailed record) data
5		MR (measurement report) data
6		Wireless traffic statistical data
7		Wireless parameters
8		Core network data
9		Alarm data
10		Wireless call trace data
11		Equipment version and patch
12		Equipment load data
13		Wireless counter data
14		Core network counter data
15		Complaint data
16		Voice detail data
17		Resource configuration data
18	BSS domain	User detailed information
19		Monthly bill data
20		Voice service detail data
21		Data service detail data
22		Product information
23		Terminal information

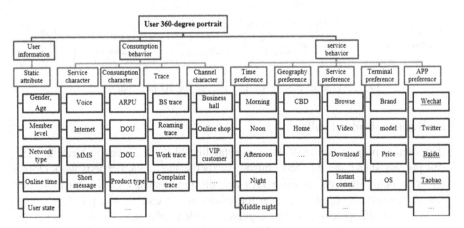

Fig. 2. 360-degree portrait for each user

The second type of factors is the user's consumption behavior. It includes four types of sub-factors, including the service character, the consumption character, the trace, and the channel character [17, 23].

The third type of factors is the service behavior. It includes five types of sub-factors, including the time preference, the geography preference, the service preference, the terminal preference, and the Application (APP) preference [23].

After drawing the 360-degree portrait of each user, we further analyze the user-group. This user-group analysis aims at studying the corresponding group of user (e.g., potential value user-group, Iphone terminal user-group, 4G migrated user-group, youth user-group etc.), according to a specific service requirement or a specific character [19, 24]. Typical user-group/clustering analysis algorithms include K-Means algorithm, Clarans algorithm, Focused-Clarans algorithm, K-Medoids algorithm etc. [25, 26].

On the basis of the 360-degree portrait and the user-group clustering analysis, we can jointly analyse the user information, the consumption behavior, the service behavior, as well as the network performance [27, 28]. In all, the 360-degree portrait and the user-group analysis help telecom operators identify serving users and be aware of the user-group precisely.

3 Data Mining Process for 4G Potential Users

3.1 Overall Process of 4G Data Mining

This section discusses the process of data mining for the 4G potential users targeting. The data mining process for working a machine learning (ML) problem is illustrated in Fig. 3. The whole process consists of six phases. This process provides a good coverage of the steps needed, starting with business understanding, data preparation, model building, model training, model evaluation, model deployment.

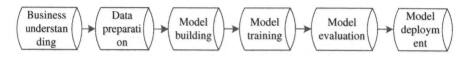

Fig. 3. Overall process of data mining for 4G potential users

3.2 Business Understanding

A data mining project starts with the understanding of the business problem [26, 29]. In this process, data mining experts, business experts, and domain experts work closely together to define the project objectives and the requirements from a business perspective. The project objective is then formulated into a data mining problem.

As for the 4G potential users targeting problem, the purpose is to target the potential users from existing 2G or 3G users. It is because the potential 4G users will contribute a lot to the growth of the services traffic in the near future. In addition, LTE network deployment is undergoing rapidly in China, telecom operators are trying to persuade 2G or 3G users to camp on LTE network to provide more efficient data services and better user experience, as well as the guaranteed quality of service (QoS) [2, 21].

3.3 Data Preparation

It is generally known that machine learning algorithms learn from data. The quality of the training data is vital factor that impacts the model performance. Therefore, it is critical that ML algorithm has the appropriate data for the problem formulation.

For the data preparation, the first step is collecting the data related with the problem. And then we try to be aware of the details of the data. The next step is to identify data quality problems such as data missing problem, data transformation etc. With regarding the problem in this paper, the user basic information, user consumption information, user service behavior information are needed.

3.4 Model Building

Model building actually is defining the abstract problem in a mathematical way that can be understood by machine. For a certain problem, you can select and apply various mining functions because you can use different mining functions for the same type of data mining problem. For example, Logistic Regression, Decision Tree, Support Vector Machine can all be used to deal with the classification problem [23]. However, different kinds of algorithm has its own applicable scenario and require specific data types.

For this paper, apparently this is a problem of classification, which aims to distinguish the potential 4G users from all the telecom subscribers. The two different groups can be expressed in Eq. (1):

$$4G\_potential\_user\_(Q_i) = \begin{cases} 1, & Q_i \text{ is } 4G\_potential\_user \\ 0, & Q_i \text{ is not } 4G\_potential\_user \end{cases} \tag{1}$$

Then the problem of this paper can be showed in the following linear mathematical model:

$$y = \theta^T z = \theta_0 + \theta_1 z_1 + \theta_2 z_2 +, \ldots, + \theta_n z_n \tag{2}$$

where θ is the weighting value, z is the feature vector.

3.5 Model Training

The process of model training is to train the model built in previous part by using training data. After the training process, we can get a ML model that attempts to predict whether a new user will be a potential 4G user or not.

During the model training process, another import issue can determine the corresponding features. This process is called the feature engineering, which aims to transform original data into features that make ML algorithm work precisely.

The feature engineering can be divided into several parts. Firstly, select the relevant variables to the target based on the understanding of the data, as for the topic in this paper, the user smartphone network type, the user traffic consumption etc. will have great influence to the 4G user prediction. Secondly, feature construction and feature selection. Sometimes, the feature can be obtained directly from the raw data, and for other times, we have to do some transformation to generate some more powerful features. Then we can evaluate each feature's contribution to the accuracy of the model, the unimportant features will be eliminated. Thirdly, we will check weather this set of features will work with the model precisely. We will choose the set of features generated the better prediction result. Lastly, if the prediction result is not ideal, then go back to the beginning part to create more features until the model result is well. From the above steps, we can see that the process of feature engineering is an iterative process.

For model training part in this paper, because this is a classification problem, we will choose the classic LR algorithm [15] to predict the 4G potential users. LR algorithm is a binary classification problems predict a binary outcome (one of two possible classes). LR generates the coefficients of a formula to predict a logit transformation of the probability of presence of the target of interest.

$$logit(p) = \beta_0 + \beta_1 z_1 + \ldots + \beta_k z_k \tag{3}$$

where p is the probability of presence of the target of interest and total k independent features $z = (z_1, z_2, \ldots, z_k)$.

The logit transformation is defined as the logged odds:

$$odds = \frac{p}{1-p} \tag{4}$$

where p can be denoted in the Eq. (5):

$$P(Y = 1 \mid z) = \frac{1}{1 + e^{-g(z)}} \tag{5}$$

where $g(z) = \beta_0 + \beta_1 z_1 + \ldots + \beta_k z_k$, β is the regression coefficient [26]. Similarity, we can define the probability of absence of the characteristic of interest:

$$P(Y = 0 \mid z) = 1 - P(Y = 1 \mid z) = 1 - \frac{e^{g(z)}}{1 + e^{g(z)}} = \frac{1}{1 + e^{g(z)}} \tag{6}$$

Based on Eqs. (5) and (6), the Eq. (4) can be expressed as:

$$\log(\frac{p}{1-p}) = \log(e^{g(z)}) = g(z) = \beta_0 + \beta_1 z_1 + \ldots + \beta_k z_k \tag{7}$$

In Eq. (7), the coefficient β is what we want to learn from the training data. The cost function can be denoted as:

$$L(\beta) = \prod P(y_i = 1 \mid z_i)^{y_i} (1 - P(y_i = 1 \mid z_i))^{1-y_i} \tag{8}$$

We can get the value of each β coefficient via GD (Gradient Descent) algorithm.

3.6 Model Evaluation

Model evaluation metrics are used to assess goodness of fit between model and data, to compare different models, and to reveal the accuracy of the model predictions. Actually, there are many ways to do the model evaluation, such as the Confidence Interval, Confusion Matrix, Gain and Lift Chart and ROC curve etc. In terms of the classification problem in this paper, we introduce Confusion Matrix method to measure the model's performance.

A confusion matrix is a $N \times N$ matrices. N is the number of classifications. A 2×2 *confusion matrix* for two classes (Positive and Negative) is presented in Table 2.

Table 2. Parameters in confusion matrix

		Target	
		Positive	Negative
Model	Positive	T_{11}	T_{12}
	Negative	T_{21}	T_{22}

From Table 2, we can see that the performance of the classification models can be evaluated using the data in the matrix. T_{11} is called correct positive prediction, these are cases in which we predicted yes (they are the potential 4G users), and they are actually potential 4G users. Similarly, T_{12} is called incorrect positive prediction, T_{21} is called correct negative prediction, T_{22} is called incorrect negative prediction.

Various measures can be derived from a confusion matrix [26]. The first metric is $M_{Accuracy}$, calculated by Eq. (9). $M_{Accuracy}$ reflects the proportion of the total number of predictions that were correct.

$$M_{Accuracy} = \frac{T_{11} + T_{22}}{T_{11} + T_{21} + T_{12} + T_{22}} \tag{9}$$

The second metric is $M_{Precision}$, calculated by Eq. (10). $M_{Precision}$ reflects the proportion of actual positive cases which are correctly identified.

$$M_{Precision} = \frac{T_{11}}{T_{11} + T_{12}} \tag{10}$$

The third metric is M_{Recall}, calculated by Eq. (11). M_{Recall} reflects the proportion of positive cases that were correctly identified.

$$M_{Recall} = \frac{T_{11}}{T_{11} + T_{21}} \tag{11}$$

Finally, we can get the ideal data model for the targeting for 4G potential users.

3.7 Model Deployment

After the model is validated, telecom operator can apply this model to 4G potential user classification. For each existing 2G or 3G user, this model will present the classification results. A data mining process continues after a solution is deployed. Data mining is an iterative process, since both the data and services are changing during the process.

3.8 Application Deployment and Results Analysis

This paper applies the proposed data mining algorithm based 4G potential users prediction in the city central area of China (named as A-city). Table 3 and Fig. 4 show the mining results. There are 1807674 2G mobile users in A-city. Employing our proposed data mining algorithm, 108000 of 2G users are predicted as 4G potential users. Then, market department of the telecom operator utilises this potential users list to take relevant marketing measures/methods to persuade these users transferring from 2G to 4G. Finally, 58423 2G users transfer to 4G successfully. Therefore, the *4G user conversion rate* reaches 54.10% (namely, 58423/108000) under 2G scenario.

Similarly, from Table 3 and Fig. 4, there are 1063955 3G users in A-city. The proposed data mining algorithm predicts that 335000 3G users are 4G potential users. After employing marketing measures/methods by the market department of the telecom operator, 216581 3G users transfer to 4G successfully. Hence, the *4G user conversion rate* reaches 64.65% (namely, 216581/335000) under 3G scenario.

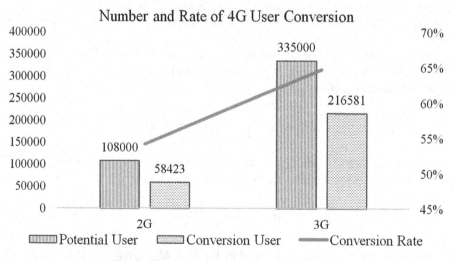

Fig. 4. Number and rate of 4G user conversion

Table 3. Application scenario and results

Network type	4G User conversion rate			
	Total user	4G Potential user prediction	4G Conversion user	Conversion rate
2G	1807674	108000	58423	54.10%
3G	1063955	335000	216581	64.65%

Figure 5 shows the 4G potential users distribution in the downtown of A-city. Red area reflects that this area has a large number of 4G potential users. From Fig. 5(a), most of 2G–to–4G potential users are gathered in the very city center. Since many 3G users surf on the mobile internet, these users are easily upgrade to 4G users. Compared to 2G–to–4G potential users, 3G–to–4G potential users have larger distribution, as shown in Fig. 5(b).

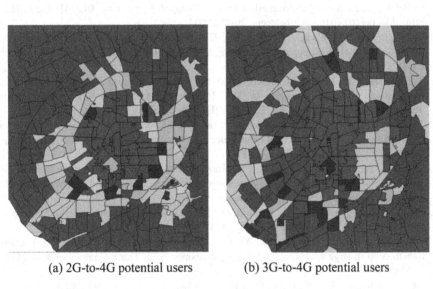

(a) 2G-to-4G potential users   (b) 3G-to-4G potential users

Fig. 5. Distribution of 4G potential users

4   Conclusion

This paper investigates on telecom big data based user analysis and application for telecom operators. Initially, this paper studies the content of telecom big data. Then, 360-degree user portrait is drawn via three types of factors, including user's information, user's consumption behavior and service behavior. Based on the user portrait, this paper employs data mining to seek 4G potential users. The data mining process includes the business understand, data preparation, model building, model train, model evaluation and model deployment steps. Overall, effectively targeting 4G potential users can benefit telecom operators.

References

1. Cao, Y., Wang, N., Sun, Z., Cruickshank, H.: A reliable and efficient encounter-based routing framework for delay/disruption tolerant networks. IEEE Sens. J. **15**(7), 4004–4018 (2015)
2. Xu, L., Luan, Y., Cheng, X., Cao, X., Chao, K., Gao, J., Jia, Y., Wang, S.: WCDMA Data based LTE Site Selection Scheme in LTE Deployment. In: International Conference on Signal and Information Processing, Networking and Computers, pp. 249–260. CRC Press, Taylor & Francis Group, Beijing (2015)
3. Zhang, H., Dong, Y., Cheng, J., Hossain, M.J., Leung, V.C.M.: Cooperative interference mitigation and handover management for heterogeneous cloud small cell networks. IEEE Wirel. Commun. **22**(3), 92–99 (2015)
4. Xu, L., Chen, Y., Chai, K.K., Schormans, J., Cuthbert, L.: Self-organising cluster-based cooperative load balancing in OFDMA cellular networks. Wiley Wireless Commun. Mob. Comput. **15**(7), 1171–1187 (2015)
5. Zhao, L., Al-Dubai, A.Y., Li, X., Chen, G.: A new efficient cross-layer relay node selection model for wireless community mesh networks. Comput. Electr. Eng. **61**, 361–372 (2017). https://doi.org/10.1016/j.compeleceng.2016.12.031
6. Cao, Y., Sun, Z., Wang, N., Riaz, M., Cruickshank, H., Liu, X.: Geographic-based Spray-and-Relay (GSaR): an efficient routing scheme for DTNs. IEEE Trans. Veh. Technol. **64**(4), 1548–1564 (2015)
7. Xu, L., Chen, Y., Gao, Y., Cuthbert, L.: A Self-Optimizing Load Balancing Scheme for Fixed Relay Cellular Networks. In: IET International Conference on Communication Technology and Application, pp. 306–311. IET Press, Beijing (2011)
8. Wang, W., Xu, L., Zhang, Y., Zhong, J.: A novel cell-level resource allocation scheme for OFDMA system. In: International Conference on Communications and Mobile Computing, pp. 287–292. IET Press, Kunming (2009)
9. Zhao, L., Li, Y., Meng, C., Gong, C., Tang, X.: A SVM based routing scheme in VANETs. In: IEEE International Symposium on Communications and Information Technologies, pp. 380–383. IEEE Press, Qingdao (2016)
10. Zhang, H., Dong, Y., Cheng, J., Hossain, M.J., Leung, V.C.M.: Fronthauling for 5G LTE-U ultra dense cloud small cell networks. IEEE Wirel. Commun. **23**(6), 48–53 (2016)
11. Deng, Y., Wang, L., Zaidi, S.A.R., Yuan, J., Elkashlan, M.: Artificial-noise aided secure transmission in large scale spectrum sharing networks. IEEE Trans. Commun. **64**(5), 2116–2129 (2016)
12. Xu, L., Cheng, X., Liu, Y., Chen, W., Luan, Y., Chao, K., Yuan, M., Xu, B.: Mobility load balancing aware radio resource allocation scheme for LTE-Advanced cellular networks. In: IEEE International Conference on Communication Technology, pp. 806–812, IEEE Press, Hangzhou (2015)
13. Xu, L., Chen, Y., Chai, K. K., Luan, Y., Liu, D.: Cooperative mobility load balancing in relay cellular networks. In: IEEE International Conference on Communication in China, pp. 141–146. IEEE Press, Xi'An (2013)
14. 3GPP TR 36.814: Further Advancements for E-UTRA Physical Layer Aspects (2010)
15. Zhang, T., Cheng, X., Yuan, M., Xu, L., Cheng, C., Chao, K.: Mining target users for mobile advertising based on telecom big data. In: IEEE International Symposium on Communications and Information Technologies, pp. 296–301. IEEE Press, Qingdao (2016)
16. Landset, S., Khoshgoftaar, T.M., Richter, A.N., Hasanin, T.: A survey of open source tools for machine learning with big data in the Hadoop Ecosystem. J. Big Data **2**(1), 24 (2015)

17. Cheng, C., Cheng, X., Yuan, M., Song, C., Xu, L., Ye, H., Zhang, T.: A novel cluster algorithm for telecom customer segmentation. In: IEEE International Symposium on Communications and Information Technologies, pp. 324–329. IEEE Press, Qingdao (2016)
18. Liu, Y., Xu, L., Chen, Y., Fan, Y., Xu, B., Nie, J.: A novel power control mechanism based on interference estimation in LTE cellular networks. In: IEEE International Symposium on Communications and Information Technologies, pp. 397–401. IEEE Press, Qingdao (2016)
19. Xing, H., Xu, L., Qu, R., Qu, Z.: A quantum inspired evolutionary algorithm for dynamic multicast routing with network coding. In: IEEE International Symposium on Communications and Information Technologies, pp. 186–190. IEEE Press, Qingdao (2016)
20. Cao, Y., Wang, N., Kamel, G., Kim, Y.J.: An electric vehicle charging management scheme based on publish/subscribe communication framework. IEEE Syst. J. **11**(3), 1822–1835 (2015). https://doi.org/10.1109/JSYST.2015.2449893
21. Xu, L., Luan, Y., Cheng, X., Fan, Y., Zhang, H., Wang, W., He, A.: Telecom big data based user offloading self-optimisation in heterogeneous relay cellular systems. Int. J. Distrib. Syst. Technol. **8**(2), 27–46 (2017)
22. Xu, L., Chen, Y., Chai, K.K., Liu, D., Yang, S., Schormans, J.: User relay assisted traffic shifting in LTE-Advanced systems. In: IEEE Vehicular Technology Conference, pp. 1–7. IEEE Press, Dresden (2013)
23. Cheng, X., Xu, L., Zhang, T., Jia, Y., Yuan, M., Chao, K.: A novel big data based telecom operation architecture. In: International Conference on Signal and Information Processing, Networking and Computers, pp. 385–396. CRC Press Taylor & Francis Group, Beijing (2015)
24. Xu, L., Luan, Y., Cheng, X., Xing, H., Liu, Y., Jiang, X., Chen, W., Chao, K.: Self-optimised joint traffic offloading in heterogeneous cellular networks. In: IEEE International Symposium on Communications and Information Technologies, pp. 263–267. IEEE Press, Qingdao (2016)
25. Cao, Y., Wang, N., Kamel, G.: A publish/subscribe communication framework for managing electric vehicle charging. In: IEEE International Conference on Connected Vehicles and Expo, pp. 318–324. IEEE Press, Vienna (2014)
26. Cheng, X., Yuan, M., Xu, L., Zhang, T., Jia, Y., Cheng, C., Chen, W.: Big data assisted customer analysis and advertising architecture for real estate. In: IEEE International Symposium on Communications and Information Technologies, pp. 312–317. IEEE Press, Qingdao (2016)
27. Cui, G., Lu, S., Wang, W., Zhang, Y., Wang, C., Li, X.: Uplink coordinated scheduling based on resource sorting. In: IEEE Vehicular Technology Conference, pp. 1–5. IEEE Press, Quebec (2012)
28. Cui, G., Lu S., Wang, W., Wang, C., Zhang, Y.: Decentralized antenna selection with no CSI sharing for multi-cell MU-MIMO systems. In: IEEE International Symposium on Personal and Indoor, Mobile Radio Communications, pp. 2319–2323. IEEE Press, Sydney (2012)
29. Xie, L., Pan, D.: On customer segmentation and retention of telecom broadband in Pearl River Delta. Chinese Control Conference, pp. 5564–5568 (2010)

Coverage Optimization in Self-organizing Small Cells

Yu Chen[1($\boxtimes$)], Wei Li[2], Xiuqing Yang[1], Yi Hu[1], and Qinghua Zhu[1]

[1] School of Telecommunication Engineering,
Beijing Polytechnic, Beijing 100176, China
buptchen@163.com
[2] The State Radio Monitoring Center, Beijing 100037, China

Abstract. Heterogeneous two-tier network with hybrid deployed small cells and macrocells is a promising solution for fifth generation (5G) wireless networks. However, with the higher and higher spectrum band used in 5G, the coverage and capacity of indoor environment is not good enough for the users' increasing demand. In this paper, we proposed a self-organizing capacity and coverage optimization scheme using power adaptation to enhance the capacity and improve the coverage. Simulation results show that the proposed self-organizing scheme can effectively improve the capacity and coverage.

Keywords: Small cells · Coverage optimization
Capacity optimization · Self-organizing network

1 Introduction

In recent years, the mobile data usage has grown by 70–200% per annum. More worryingly, the bursty nature of wireless data traffic makes traditional network planning for capacity obsolete. Currently, heterogeneous small cell network with overlay femtocells and macrocell is a most promising solution for the wireless cellular communications of the future [1]. The use of femtocell, which is considered a promising technique, can provide an effective solution to tackle the challenges in this respect [2,3]. In heterogeneous small cell network, low power small cells (such as picocell, relay and femtocell) together with macrocells, can improve the coverage and capacity of cell-edge users and hotspot by exploiting the spatial reuse of spectrum [2]. Small cells can also offload the explosive growth of wireless data traffic from macrocells [3–5]. For example, in an indoor environment WiFi and femtocells can offload most of the data traffic from macrocells [5–7]. For mobile operators, small cells such as femtocells can reduce the capital expenditure (CAPEX) and operating expenditure (OPEX) because of the self-installing and self-operating features of femto basestations [7,8]. The femtocell combined with cognitive radio can further improve the system performance [9,10]. Resource allocation of small cells was studied in [9,10]. The authors addressed many critical issues on femtocells, such as interference mitigation, spectrum access, resource allocation, and quality-of-service (QoS) provisioning [11–13].

© ICST Institute for Computer Sciences, Social Informatics and Telecommunications Engineering 2018
K. Long et al. (Eds.): 5GWN 2017, LNICST 211, pp. 110–119, 2018.
https://doi.org/10.1007/978-3-319-72823-0_12

In the Long Term Evolution (LTE) system, with the demand of home eNB (HeNB) deployment within the residual area, the interference between macro eNB and HeNB becomes major obstacle for operators to deploy HeNB. Figure 1 illustrates a result we simulate the coverage of Macro and home eNB with unsuitable transmit power [7]. In this figure, the red zone is covered by Macro eNB and the green zone is covered by HeNB. We can see there are three apartments which are supposed to be covered by Macro eNB covered by a neighbor HeNB in zone 1. As a result, the UE is in the three apartments can't work normally because they aren't the members of the closed subscriber group (CSG) HeNB and can't connect to Macro eNB neither. On the other hand, in zone 2 we can see that HeNB can't cover the whole apartment and that means the end-user who buys HeNB can't get the advantage from HeNB. From the above description, we can summary the main issues of HeNB from the coverage aspect as following:

- If transmit power of HeNB is large, non-CSG UEs which is supposed to connect to MeNB will be affected.
- If transmit power of HeNB is small, some place can't be covered by HeNB and CSG UEs will be affected.

The number of HeNB involved in a wide-scale deployment will be orders of magnitude more than the numbers commonly associated with cells used in macro eNB deployments. With such large numbers, the conventional manual approach to cell-planning and deployment of base stations would not be feasible due to the resulting prohibitively high costs. HeNBs therefore have to be deployed by the end-users themselves, and the HeNB must be able to auto-configure all the required parameters and self-optimize them during operation with minimal human intervention. In this paper, a detail coverage and capacity optimization (CNC) solution will be proposed which includes the self configuration and the self optimization. Both of two parts will adjust the transmit power to optimize the coverage of HeNB in the different stage of HeNB running.

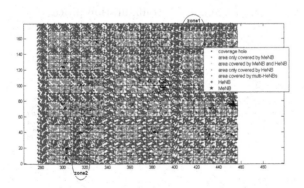

Fig. 1. Coverage overview in dense-urban scenario.

2   Detailed Algorithm

2.1   Self Configuration

After power on, HeNB can detect the wireless environment with a downlink receiver. HeNB can get the RSRP of Macro eNB and its neighbor HeNBs from this detection. Self configuration process will use the detection result to configure a suitable transmit power for the HeNB.

- HeNB has a small coverage area and the boundary is defined as the place that is x2 dB away from HeNB.
- A close-by MUE or HUE has similar RSRP as the detection of HeNB.
- The SINR of a HUE received from the HeNB is more than x3 dB means HUE is covered by a HeNB.
- The SINR of a MUE received from the Macro eNB is more than x1 dB means MUE is covered by a Macro eNB.

With the above assumption, the basic concept of algorithm in self configuration process can be described as following:

- Maintain an SINR is less than x3 dB for a HUE located more than X2 dB away from HeNB
- Maintain an SINR is more than x1 dB for a MUE located more than x2 dB away from HeNB

Figure 2 illustrates how to determine the transmit power of a HeNB [7]. The left figure shows the suitable transmit power of HeNB is supposed to guarantee the HUE is on the boundary has a SINR that is less than x3 dB, thus the HeNB can't affect the MUE. The right figure shows the suitable transmit power of HeNB is supposed to guarantee the MUE which is on the boundary has a SINR that is more than x1 dB.

Here is the detail algorithm.

Figure 3 is the flowchart about self configuration process.

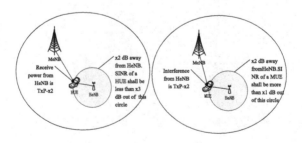

Fig. 2. How to determine the transmit power of a HeNB.

Algorithm 1. Accumulated-Payoff Based Snowdrift Game

1: **Input** The RSRP of Macro eNB and the neighbor HeNB detected by the considered HeNB Process:

2: **Calculate** the RSRP of a HUE which is on the boundary from HeNB: $TxP_{HeNB}1 - x2$

3: **Calculate** the interference of the HUE from the Macro eNB and the neighbor HeNB $\sum\limits_{i=1}^{N_2} 10^{RxP_i/10}$

   Where: N_2 is the number of the Macro eNB and the all neighbor HeNB RxP_i is the RSRP of the i-th Macro eNB or HeNB. The unit is dBm

4: **Calculate** the SINR of the HUE $(TxP_{HeNB}1 - x2) - 10*\log_{10}(\sum\limits_{i=1}^{N_2} 10^{RxP_i/10} + noise)$

   Where: is the basic noise and its unit is mW.

5: **Guarantee** this SINR is less than x3 dB

$$(TxP_{HeNB}1 - x2) - 10*\log_{10}(\sum_{i=1}^{N_2} 10^{RxP_i/10} + noise) < x3 \qquad (1)$$

6: **Calculate** the RSRP of a MUE which is on the boundary from Macro eNB: RxP_{MeNB}

   Where: the unit of RxP_{MeNB} is dBm.

7: **Calculate** the interference of the MUE from the HeNB $10^{(TxP_{HeNB}2 - x2)/10}$

   Where: the unit of $TxP_{HeNB}2$ is dBm

8: **Calculate** the interference of the MUE from the Macro eNB and the neighbor HeNB $\sum\limits_{i=1}^{N_1} 10^{RxP_i/10}$

   Where: N_1 is the number of the Macro eNB and the all HeNB except the considered HeNB RxP_i is the RSRP of the i-th Macro eNB or HeNB. The unit is dBm

9: **Calculate** the SINR of the MUE $RxPMeNB - 10*\log 10(10^{(TxP_{HeNB}2 - x2)/10} + \sum\limits_{i=1}^{N_1} 10^{RxP_i/10} + noise)$

10: **Guarantee** this SINR is more than x1 dB $RxPMeNB - 10*\log 10(10^{(TxP_{HeNB}2 - x2)/10} + \sum\limits_{i=1}^{N_1} 10^{RxP_i/10} + noise) > x1$

11: **Get** the minimum of these two TxP $Txp_{HeNB} = \min(Txp_{HeNB}1, Txp_{HeNB}2)$

12: **Output:** Txp_{HeNB}

2.2   Self Optimization

Boundary Algorithm. In the self configuration process, the boundary is fixed, actually in real environment, the size of an apartment or a house is various, we are supposed to get the real boundary of every HeNB coverage area. In the self configuration process, SON system can't get any information but the RSRP of Macro eNB and neighbor HeNBs. According to the detection we can't determine the exactly boundary. In the self optimization process, there are HUEs work in the coverage area of HeNB, we can use the measurement of HUE to determine the boundary. Since when HUE enter an apartment, its RSRP from HeNB will have a big change because of the penetration loss of wall, we can use the path-loss form HeNB as the radius of the HeNB coverage. Although according to the position of a HeNB, this kind of radius isn't an concise value, i.e. when HeNB is near to the window (left in Fig. 4), or in the corner (right in Fig. 4). But when the HeNB is in the central of apartment (in Fig. 5), the boundary is suitable. And we know that this kind of boundary depends on the real size of apartment or house, it's better than a fixed boundary, also, we can optimize the transmit power in next optimization process.

About this adaptive boundary, there is another thing to be considered. The measurement report will be sent to eNB only when A3 event occur. However, when UE enter or go out the door, A3 event doesn't occur always. So, we need a new trigger for it. Here we define a threshold $Thres_{boundary}$, and a event B_T that the change of RSRP from HeNB between successive two measurements is more than $Thres_{boundary}$. Once B_T occurs, the measurement the bigger RSRP is in will be sent to HeNB. For boundary determination, a measurement period T is needed, boundary is supposed to be determined in two successive T. once occurs, HeNB will determine the boundary with the RSRP reported by UE from the this event B_T. The fixed boundary will be the initial value of the boundary. If SON server gets a boundary from HeNB, use it in the self optimization process, if not, use the initial value, namely, the fixed boundary. Figure 6 is the relationship between boundary process and the self optimization process. Before t_0, there is no boundary is calculated, self optimization process will use the fixed boundary; when B_T occurs at time 3T, SON server will calculate a boundary

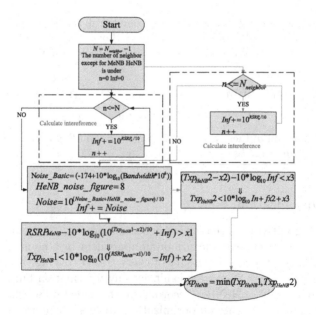

Fig. 3. Self configuration flowchart.

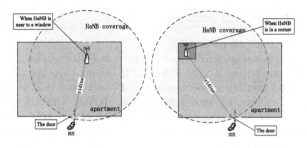

Fig. 4. Unsuitable position of HeNB.

with two successive measured RSRP, hence when t_0 comes, the boundary has been calculated, self optimization can use the new boundary.

Here is the algorithm.

Simulation Plan

- Run simulation in every position in Fig. 5.
- Run simulation with same penetration loss of outdoor wall and separating wall, the penetration loss can be 10 and 20 dB.
- Compare the performance of our CNC solution and other similar CNC solution.

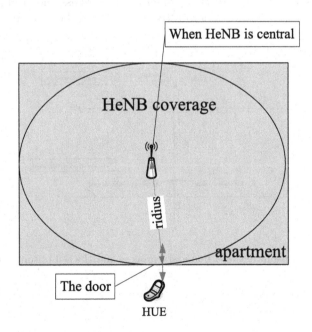

Fig. 5. Suitable position of HeNB.

Algorithm 2. Boundary Algorithm

1: **Input** The RSRP measured by HUE.

2: In T time, get the average RSRP, and regard it as RSRPi, in next T time, get the average RSRP, and regard it as RSRPi+1. If the change between this measurement RSRPi+1and the previous measurement RSRPi isn't more than the $Thres_{boundary}$, do nothing; if crosses it, record the bigger RSRP. $|RSRP_i - RSRP_{i+1}| > Thres_{boundary}$ $RSRP_{boundary} = \max(RSRP_i, RSRP_{i+1})$ Where: $RSRP_i$ is the averaged RSRP of HUE in ith T time period $RSRP_{boundary}$ is the RSRP used to calculate house boundary

3: **Get** the $RSRP_{boundary}$ and report the $RSRP_{boundary}$ to HeNB. If there is no $RSRP_{boundary}$ can be got, doesn't report anything to HeNB.

4: When HeNB get the report from HUE, it will calculate the boundary with its transmit power and sends the path-loss to SON server. HeNB will save the boundary for further self optimization. If SON server doesn't receive any boundary, use the fixed boundary and enter the next T time to get a suitable boundary. $boundary = TxP_{HeNB} - RSRP_{average}$ If don't get a boundary: $boundary = boundary_{fixed}$ Where: the unit of $boundary$ is dB

5: **Output:** Output: $boundary$

2.3   Shadowing Fading Model

Log-normal shadowing will be applied in our simulation. The standard deviation for HeNB is assumed to be 10 dB, for Macro eNB, it is assumed to be 8 dB. The auto-correlation distance for Macro eNB is assumed to be 50 m and for HeNB, it is 3 m.

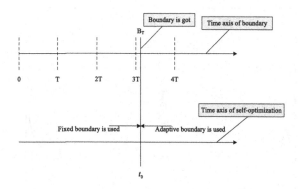

Fig. 6. The relationship between boundary process and the self optimization process.

3   Simulation Result

3.1   Coverage and Capacity

In this simulation, the blocks will be put into Position 1, Position 2 and Position 3 and get the coverage ratios of Macro eNB and HeNB. When simulator running, the penetration loss of wall will be set to 10 dB or 20 dB. But in each simulation, the penetration loss is a fixed value.

Simulation Results in Position 1. The optimized coverage ratio value of macro eNB and HeNB and comparisons with coverage ratio value of macro eNB and HeNB with fixed power of HeNB when penetration loss = 10 dB is shown in the following table and figure (Table 1).

The distribution of optimized transmitted power of HeNB is shown in the following figure where Y axis is the number of HeNB with the same optimized transmitted power and the X axis is the transmitted power of each HeNB. The average transmit power is -16.66 dBm.

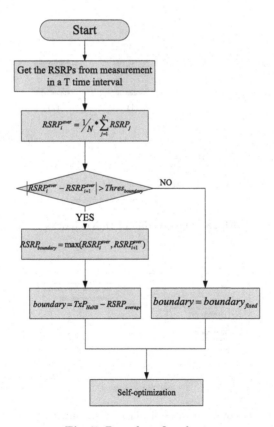

Fig. 7. Boundary flowchart.

Table 1. Parameters assumption.

			Optimized	20 dBm	0 dBm	−10 dBm	−20 dBm
Position1	10 dB	MeNB coverage ratio	90.99%	20.17%	59.72%	83.66%	96.34%
		HeNB coverage ratio	75.63%	95.76%	94.90%	90.18%	74.06%
	20 dB	MeNB coverage ratio	90.05%	35.23%	72.12%	84.23%	92.59%
		HeNB coverage ratio	91.88%	96.44%	96.17%	95.17%	91.52%
Position2	10 dB	MeNB coverage ratio	89.70%	15.47%	48.95%	74.46%	91.50%
		HeNB coverage ratio	82.27%	95.86%	95.69%	92.92%	81.69%
	20 dB	MeNB coverage ratio	87.33%	28.09%	65.88%	80.59%	89.46%
		HeNB coverage ratio	93.37%	95.96%	95.97%	95.52%	92.81%
Position3	10 dB	MeNB coverage ratio	90.22%	16.97%	53.80%	78.10%	93.36%
		HeNB coverage ratio	91.56%	96.20%	95.73%	93.04%	82.77%
	20 dB	MeNB coverage ratio	89.94%	31.85%	67.86%	81.56%	91.78%
		HeNB coverage ratio	93.22%	96.32%	96.26%	95.66%	93.09%

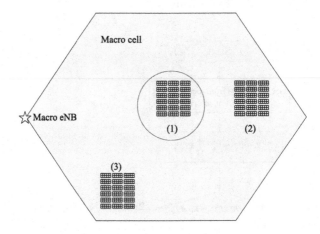

Fig. 8. The position of HeNB blocks

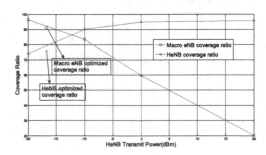

Fig. 9. Comparisons of coverage ratio of macro eNB and HeNB with optimized and fixed power of HeNB.

4 Conclusion

Our optimized target is that, first, the coverage ratio of macro eNB is more than required coverage ratio, then, maximize the coverage ratio of HeNB. The following table gives the summary results for CNC. From the table list above, We can see that the optimized coverage ratio of macro eNB is very near the required coverage ratio of macro eNB 90%. The optimized coverage ratio of HeNB is very big than that of the most fixed transmitted power when macro eNB meets coverage target. From the above results, we can see that the optimized coverage ratio is similar to that of −20 dBM, this is because the HeNB in our simulation conditions is still densely deployed, so the inter-interference among HeNB is high, as a result, the transmitted power of HeNB after optimization shall not be high, if the HeNB is sparse deployed, the optimized power of HeNB shall be higher than −20 dBM.

References

1. Zhang, H., Chu, X., Wen, X.: 4G Femtocells: Resource Allocation and Interference Management. Springer, New York (2013). https://doi.org/10.1007/978-1-4614-9080-7
2. Claussen, H., Ho, L.T.W., Samuel, L.G.: Self-optimization of coverage for femtocell deployments. In: Wireless Telecommunications Symposium, 2008, WTS 2008, pp. 278–285. IEEE (2008)
3. Zhang, H., Jiang, C., Cheng, J., Leung, V.C.M.: Cooperative interference mitigation and handover management for heterogeneous cloud small cell networks. IEEE Wirel. Commun. **22**(3), 92–99 (2015)
4. Peng, M., Liang, D., Wei, Y., et al.: Self-configuration and self-optimization in LTE-advanced heterogeneous networks. IEEE Commun. Mag. **51**(5), 36–45 (2013)
5. Zhang, H., Chu, X., Guo, W., Wang, S.: Coexistence of wi-fi and heterogeneous small cell networks sharing unlicensed spectrum. IEEE Commun. Mag. **53**(3), 158–164 (2015)
6. Bennis, M., Perlaza, S.M., Blasco, P., et al.: Self-organization in small cell networks: a reinforcement learning approach. IEEE Trans. Wirel. Commun. **12**(7), 3202–3212 (2013)
7. Zhang, H., Jiang, C., Hu, Q., Qian, Y.: Self-organization in disaster resilient heterogeneous small cell networks. IEEE Netw. **30**(2), 116–121 (2015)
8. Fehske, A.J., Viering, I., Voigt, J., et al.: Small-cell self-organizing wireless networks. Proc. IEEE **102**(3), 334–350 (2014)
9. Zhang, H., Jiang, C., Beaulieu, N., Chu, X., Wen, X., Tao, M.: Resource allocation in spectrum-sharing OFDMA femtocells with heterogeneous services. IEEE Trans. Commun. **62**(7), 2366–2377 (2014)
10. Bennis, M., Simsek, M., Czylwik, A., et al.: When cellular meets WiFi in wireless small cell networks. IEEE Commun. Mag. **51**(6), 44–50 (2013)
11. Zhang, H., Jiang, C., Mao, X., Chen, H.: Interference-limited resource optimization in cognitive femtocells with fairness and imperfect spectrum sensing. IEEE Trans. Veh. Technol. **65**(3), 1761–1771 (2015)
12. Mhiri, F., Sethom, K., Bouallegue, R.: A survey on interference management techniques in femtocell self-organizing networks. J. Netw. Comput. Appl. **36**(1), 58–65 (2013)
13. Chen, C.S., Baccelli, F., Roullet, L.: Joint optimization of radio resources in small and macro cell networks. In: IEEE 73rd Vehicular Technology Conference, VTC Spring, 2011, pp. 1–5. IEEE (2011)

Expectation Maximization for Multipath Detection in Wideband Signals

Salem Salem[1] and Mohamed El-Tarhuni[2($\boxtimes$)]

[1] Phoenicia University, Beirut, Lebanon
[2] American University of Sharjah, Sharjah, UAE
mtarhuni@aus.edu

Abstract. In this paper, a new technique for delay estimation of multipath components in wideband communication systems is proposed. The proposed scheme uses the Expectation Maximization algorithm at the output of an energy detector in order to separate the multipath components from the noise components. The proposed scheme provides comparable performance to the conventional scheme based on maximum energy detector in terms of detection probability. However, it has two major advantages over the conventional scheme that make it more attractive in practical applications. Firstly, the proposed scheme does not require prior knowledge of the number of multipath components; and, secondly, it does not need to use a threshold to decide on the presence or absence of multipath components.

Keywords: Expectation Maximization · Delay estimation · Wideband signals

1 Introduction

Wideband digital communication over wireless channels has been a very important topic over the past several years. This continues to motivate the development of mobile radio systems that could support high rate applications with tens of Mbps speed through wideband transmission. Furthermore, ultra wideband (UWB) systems are of great interest for achieving even higher data rates and accurate localization applications [1]. However, as a consequence of using wideband signals, multipath propagation is the main characteristic of the wireless channel. The deployed systems need to not only mitigate the interference caused by multipath but also to exploit the diversity available in the multiple received copies of the transmitted signal. Hence, for such communication systems to operate properly, it is very crucial to device effective schemes for detecting multipath components. Another reason to detect multipath components is to improve the performance of location finding systems such as the Global Positioning Systems (GPS) and Global Navigation Satellite Systems (GNSS) [2–4].

There have been many techniques for delay estimation based on correlation and matched filtering for wideband systems using spread spectrum transmission [5–7]. All these schemes utilize the pseudo random (PN) code used in generating the spread spectrum signal to search for the multipath delays over a search window of a range of possible delays. The search window is typically searched at a discrete step that is a fraction of the PN code chip duration to produce a set of correlation results. These results

© ICST Institute for Computer Sciences, Social Informatics and Telecommunications Engineering 2018
K. Long et al. (Eds.): 5GWN 2017, LNICST 211, pp. 120–131, 2018.
https://doi.org/10.1007/978-3-319-72823-0_13

are typically compared to a preset threshold to decide on how many multipath components are present and what their delays are.

In [8], multipath detection was done for a receiver with soft handover conditions with either full scanning or sequential scanning of all available multipath components is performed. The proposed scheme used the combined signal-to-noise ratio (SNR) to decide on the selection of the multipath components. Multipath detection based on per path signal-to-noise and interference was introduced in [9]. The authors extended their work to a system with space-time spreading in [10] and interference cancellation. In [11], selection of multipath components for a generalized rake (G-Rake) received based on a maximal weight criterion to maximize the signal energy and minimize interference was presented.

As indicated earlier, one of the most important reasons for multipath detection is to improve the accuracy of positioning systems. Multipath results in ranging errors that could lead to significant error in estimating the location. Most of the techniques presented in the literature were devised to mitigate the impact of multipath by compensating for the presence of multipath or eliminating the multipath after been detected [12–14]. Other techniques were recently introduced to mitigate multipath delays that are closely spaced to within a fraction of a chip [15, 16].

One of the difficult tasks in implementing an effective multipath detection scheme is the selection of the threshold to decide if a multipath component exists at a particular delay or not. The threshold is usually set to maximize the probability of correctly detecting the presence of the multipath component (detection probability) while minimizing or fixing the probability of deciding that a multipath component exists at a particular delay while no signal was present (called false alarm probability). The challenge comes from the fact that the threshold needs to be continuously optimized to maintain the desired performance due to the variation in the wireless channel. Furthermore, a major drawback of most existing multipath detection schemes is that they assume the number of multipath components in the received signal is known to the receiver apriori and they just need to estimate the delays for these components. This assumption is not realistic since the number of multipath components is actually a random value that depends on the physical objects surrounding the transmitter and receiver and how the transmitted wave is affected by these objects. This is further complicated because, in a mobile radio system, the physical objects vary as the transmitter, receiver, or both move during the data transmission leading to variation in the number of multipath components and their delays. These variations are especially significant for fast moving terminals.

In this paper, we develop a multipath detection scheme that overcomes both of the above issues. Namely, the proposed scheme does not use a threshold at all so there is no issue with setting the threshold value and optimizing it over time. Furthermore, the proposed scheme detects all multipath components without assuming prior knowledge of how many paths exist in the received signal. The proposed scheme works by modeling the multipath detection problem as a mixture model generated from two independent and unknown distributions; one for the noise and one for the signal. Then, each correlation result obtained from a conventional search algorithm is classified to belong to either the noise or signal distribution using the Expectation Maximization (EM) algorithm.

2 System Model

Let us consider a wideband signal generated using a PN code of length N and transmitted over a frequency-selective Rayleigh fading channel with L paths each with delay $\tau_l \in \{0, 1, 2, \ldots, N-1\}$. We assume L to be a random integer value to be estimated by the receiver as well as to estimate the delays corresponding to these paths. The equivalent baseband transmitted signal from the mth user can be written as

$$s_m(t) = \sqrt{P_m} \sum_i d_i^{(m)} \sum_{k=0}^{N-1} c_m[k] p(t - iT_b - kT_c), \tag{1}$$

where P_m is the transmitted power, $\left\{ d_i^{(m)} \in \pm 1 \right\}$ is the ith information bit, $\{ c_m[k] \in \pm 1 \}$ is the PN code of the desired user, N is the PN code length which is the same as the number of chips pet bit, i.e. $N = T_b/T_c$, T_b is the bit duration, T_c is the chip duration, and $p(t)$ is the chip pulse shape.

The signal goes through a mobile radio channel and the received signal in presence of multiuser interference is written as

$$r(t) = \sum_{m=1}^{M} \sum_{l=1}^{L} \alpha_l^{(m)}(t) s_m(t - \tau_{ml}) + w(t), \tag{2}$$

where $\alpha_l^{(m)}(t)$ and τ_{ml} are the channel gain and path delay for the lth path of the mth user, respectively, M is the number of users, and $w(t)$ is an additive Gaussian noise (AWGN) with zero mean and two-sided power spectral density $N_0/2$. The received base-band signal is sampled at a multiple of the chip rate such that there are N_s samples per chip.

To find the delays of these multipath components, the received signal is correlated with different versions of the PN code each shifted with a specific delay offset within a search window of N_D offsets. The smallest shift between the different PN codes is called the step size, Δ, which is typically equal to 1-chip period or 1/2-chip. The correlation is done over a long period of time to ensure that enough signal energy is collected before making a decision. This period is typically the same as the PN code duration for short codes or could be a fraction of the PN code duration for long codes. Without loss of generality, we assume that the first user is the desired user and a step size of 1-chip is used, the correlation for every possible offset within the search window is calculated as:

$$h_n(v) = \frac{1}{N} \sum_{k=n}^{n+N} r[k] c_1[k+v] = f_{1n}(v) + f_{In}(v) + f_{wn}(v), \tag{3}$$

where $n = 0, 1, 2, \ldots$, and $v = 0, 1, 2, \ldots, N_D - 1$. The term $f_{1n}(v)$ depends on the autocorrelation function of the desired user, while $f_{In}(v)$ depends on the cross-correlation function between the desired user and the other users. Finally, $f_{wn}(v)$ represents the AWGN contribution. The first term in (3) can be represented as:

$$f_{1n}(v) = \begin{cases} \sqrt{E_b} \alpha_l^{(1)}(n) & v = \tau_{1l} \\ 0 & otherwise \end{cases}, \tag{4}$$

where $E_b = T_b P_1$ is the energy per bit for the first user and $\alpha_l^{(1)}(n)$ is the channel coefficient for the first user during the nth bit duration. When a large number of users exist in the system, the second term in (3) can be represented by a Gaussian process with zero-mean and variance σ_I^2.

The receiver non-coherently combines the correlation results for the same offset over multiple bits to obtain the energy estimates at every offset as

$$x(v) = \frac{1}{N_a} \sum_{i=1}^{N_a} |h_i(v)|^2. \tag{5}$$

In a conventional multipath detection algorithm, the set of energy estimates $\{x(v)\}$ is compared to a preset threshold and the values that exceed this threshold indicate a presence of a multipath component at that delay offset. Optimization of this threshold is considered as a difficult task for the conventional algorithm. Another option is to choose the offsets with L largest energy values as the multipath components. This assumes that the detector knows in advance that there are L paths in the received signal. Such assumption is not realistic since the number of paths depends on the channel conditions and varies in a non-deterministic way with time.

Our proposed scheme for multipath detection is presented in the next section to overcome both restrictions of the conventional scheme. The proposed scheme uses the energy estimates in (5) to find the maximum likelihood estimates of the delay offsets based on an iterative Expectation Maximization (EM) algorithm.

3 Expectation Maximization

Suppose a mixture model is composed from K independent, unknown probability distributions. Let $\mathbf{P} = \{p_k | k = 1...K\}$ be a set of prior probabilities of each kth distribution, where

$$\sum_{k=1}^{K} p_k = 1, \tag{6}$$

Let $\phi = \{\phi_k | k = 1...K\}$ be a set of parameters that define the K distributions, where each kth distribution is defined by its parameters ϕ_k. Given a set of N_D observed data points $\mathbf{X} = \{x_v | v = 1...N_D\}$ drawn from this mixture model, what are the parameters ϕ and prior probabilities $\mathbf{P}$ that most likely generated $\mathbf{X}$?

The probability of a data point x_v is

$$p(x_v|\boldsymbol{\phi}) = \sum_{k=1}^{K} p(x_v|\phi_k)p_k, \tag{7}$$

therefore the log-likelihood of the mixture model is

$$\ell(\boldsymbol{\phi}) = \sum_{v=0}^{N_D-1} \log\left(\sum_{k=1}^{K} p(x_v|\phi_k)p_k\right). \tag{8}$$

The parameters $\boldsymbol{\phi}$ and prior probabilities $\mathbf{P}$ can be estimated by maximizing (8). This is achieved by taking the derivative of (8) with respect to $\boldsymbol{\phi}$ and $\mathbf{P}$ then setting it to zero. For simple models, a solution could be achieved as an explicit function of $\mathbf{X}$. However, for models that are more complex a numerical solution is achieved through optimization methods, such as the Expectation Maximization algorithm [17]. The EM algorithm is a numerical method for maximizing (8) by iteratively estimating the mixture model parameters and the prior probabilities. The EM algorithm starts with an initial set of mixture model parameters $\boldsymbol{\phi}$. After that, it iterates between the two following steps:

1. **Expectation step:** Maximize (8) with respect to prior probabilities $\mathbf{P}$, subject to constraints in (6). For this one may use Lagrange multipliers [18]

$$\mathcal{L}(\boldsymbol{\phi}) = \sum_{v=0}^{N_D-1} \log\left(\sum_{k=1}^{K} p(x_v|\phi_k)p_k\right) - \lambda\left(\sum_{k=1}^{K} p_k - 1\right). \tag{9}$$

Taking the derivative of (9) with respect to $p(k)$ and equating to zero we get

$$\Delta_{p(k)}\mathcal{L}(\boldsymbol{\phi}) = \sum_{v=0}^{N_D-1} \frac{p(x_v|\phi_k)}{\sum_{k=1}^{K} p(x_v|\phi_k)p_k} - \lambda = 0. \tag{10}$$

After some manipulation, we get

$$p_k^{(new)} = \frac{N_K}{N_D}, \tag{11}$$

where

$$N_k = \sum_{v=0}^{N_D-1} \frac{p_k p(x_v|\phi_k)}{\sum_{k=1}^{K} p_k p(x_v|\phi_k)} = \sum_{v=0}^{N_D-1} w_{vk}, \tag{12}$$

where we define w_{vk} as

$$w_{vk} = \frac{p_k p(x_v|\phi_k)}{\sum_{k=1}^{K} p_k p(x_v|\phi_k)}. \tag{13}$$

2. **Maximization step:** Maximize (8) with respect to mixture model parameters ϕ by taking the derivative with respect to all model parameters, equating to zero, and finding a solution set.

$$\Delta_\phi \ell(\phi) = \sum_{v=0}^{N_D-1} \frac{p_k \Delta_\phi p(x_v|\phi_k)}{\sum_{k=1}^{K} p_k p(x_v|\phi_k)} = 0, \tag{14}$$

where the outcome of (14) is dependent on the probability distribution assumption.

The above two steps are repeated until the value of the log-likelihood function (8) ceases to change. In the next section we discuss the problem of multipath detection from the maximum likelihood approach.

4   Problem Formulation

Let $\mathbf{X} = \{x_v|v = 0, 1, 2, \ldots N_D - 1\}$ be a set of N_D possible delays, where each value x_v is calculated as in (5). The set $\mathbf{X}$ contains an unknown number of signal delays, denoted N_1, and the remainder are noise delays, denoted by N_2, where

$$N_1 + N_2 = N_D. \tag{15}$$

Our goal is to correctly classify each delay x_v as a signal or noise delay. This problem can be viewed as a classic mixture model problem: Given a set of observed points $\mathbf{X}$ generated from two independent and unknown distributions $\mathcal{Q}_1$ and $\mathcal{Q}_2$, where $\mathcal{Q}_1$ stands for a noise distribution and $\mathcal{Q}_2$ stands for a signal distribution, what are the parameters and prior probabilities of these two distributions that most likely generated $\mathbf{X}$? Once we estimate the distribution parameters, we can classify a delay x_v to correspond to a signal complement if $p(x_v|\mathcal{Q}_2) > p(x_v|\mathcal{Q}_1)$ else it is classified as a noise component. Using the Central Limit Theorem, we may assume that $\mathcal{Q}_1$ and $\mathcal{Q}_2$ follow a Gaussian distribution, if enough bits are used to generate $\mathbf{X}$ in (5). The mixture model likelihood function in (8) becomes

$$\ell(\phi) = \sum_{v=0}^{N_D-1} \log \left(\sum_{k=1}^{K} \frac{1}{\sqrt{2\pi}\sigma_k} e^{-\frac{(x_v-\mu_k)^2}{2\sigma_k^2}} p_k \right). \tag{16}$$

Our goal is to find the prior probabilities p_k as well the distribution parameters μ_k and σ_k that most likely generated $\mathbf{X}$. Using the EM algorithm outlined previously, we start with an initial set of model parameters ϕ and prior probabilities p_k and we iterate between calculating the prior probabilities and model parameters:

1. Expectation step:

$$p_k^{(new)} = \frac{1}{N_D} \sum_{v=0}^{N_D-1} w_{vk},$$ (17)

where

$$w_{vk} = \frac{\frac{p_k}{\sqrt{2\pi}\sigma_k} e^{-\frac{(x_v - \mu_k)^2}{2\sigma_k^2}}}{\sum_{k=1}^{K} \frac{p_k}{\sqrt{2\pi}\sigma_k} e^{-\frac{(x_v - \mu_k)^2}{2\sigma_k^2}}}.$$ (18)

2. Maximization step:

$$\Delta_{\mu_k}\ell(\phi) = \sum_{v=0}^{N_D-1} \frac{p_k \Delta_{\mu_k} p(x_v|\phi_k)}{\sum_{k=1}^{K} p_k \Delta_{\mu_k} p(x_v|\phi_k)} = 0,$$

$$\Rightarrow \sum_{v=0}^{N_D-1} \frac{p_k p(x_v|\phi_k)}{\sum_{k=1}^{K} p_k p(x_v|\phi_k)} \times \left(-\frac{(x_v - \mu_k)}{\sigma_k^2}\right) = 0,$$

$$\Rightarrow \sum_{v=0}^{N_D-1} w_{vk} \times \left(-\frac{(x_v - \mu_k)}{\sigma_k^2}\right) = 0.$$

After some manipulation, we get

$$\mu_k = \frac{\sum_{v=0}^{N_D-1} w_{vk} x_v}{\sum_{v=0}^{N_D-1} w_{vk}}.$$ (19)

Now taking the derivative with respect to σ_k we get

$$\Delta_{\sigma_k}\ell(\phi) = \sum_{v=0}^{N_D-1} \frac{p_k \Delta_{\sigma_k} p(x_v|\phi_k)}{\sum_{k=1}^{K} p_k p(x_v|\phi_k)} = 0,$$

$$\Rightarrow \sum_{v=0}^{N_D-1} w_{vk} \left[-\frac{1}{\sigma_k} + \frac{2(x_v - \mu_k)^2}{2\sigma_k^3}\right] = 0,$$

$$\Rightarrow \sum_{v=0}^{N_D-1} w_{vk} \left[-\sigma_k^2 + (x_v - \mu_k)^2\right] = 0.$$

After some manipulation, we get

$$\sigma_k^2 = \frac{\sum_{v=0}^{N_D-1} w_{vk}(x_v - \mu_k)^2}{\sum_{v=0}^{N_D-1} w_{vk}}. \tag{20}$$

We stop the EM iterations when the log likelihood in (16) stops changing after each iteration. The delays are then classified based on their posterior probability: A delay x_v is classified as a signal delay if $p(x_v|\mathcal{Q}_2) > p(x_v|\mathcal{Q}_1)$, else it is classified as a noise delay.

We initialize the model parameters and prior probabilities as follows:

1. Assume signal and noise classes $\mathcal{Q}_1$ and $\mathcal{Q}_2$ are equally probable, with $p_1 = p_2 = 0.5$

2. Initialize class means as: $\mu_k = \min(\mathbf{X}) + k\left(\frac{\max(\mathbf{X})-\min(\mathbf{X})}{3}\right)$

   where min and max are the minimum and maximum values of $\mathbf{X}$, respectively. The 3 in the denominator places μ_1 at a third of the range of $\mathbf{X}$ and μ_2 at two-thirds of the range. It ensures the means are well spaced out and symmetric within $\mathbf{X}$.

3. Initialize class standard deviations as $\sigma_k = \frac{\sigma_{\mathbf{X}}}{2}$, where $\sigma_{\mathbf{X}}$ is the standard deviation of the entire data set $\mathbf{X}$. Any other initialization of the standard deviations is possible, so long as the initializations are not extremely unequal, which might cause one class to dominate erroneously.

5   Simulation Results

In this section, we compare simulation results from our EM-based algorithm to the conventional algorithm of picking the N_D delays with the highest power. For our EM-based algorithm, the number of multipath delays is not known apriori, whereas for the conventional algorithm the number of delays N_D is assumed known.

Our simulation is based on the case where the paths are widely spaced apart (multiples of chips apart). In general, performance is affected by three factors: number of delay paths (N_D), number of non-coherent accumulations (N_a), and the signal-to-noise ratio (SNR). For each variation of the factors we run the simulation 500 times. We consider a trial successful if the algorithm correctly finds at least half the multipath delays without adding a noise delay, else if is considered a failure. The probability P_D is the percentage of the 500 trials that were successful.

Figure 1 shows the probability of multipath detection when the number of non-coherent accumulations and the SNR are fixed, and only the number of delay paths is varied. Two simulations are shown, the first where $SNR = -15\,\text{dB}$ (per chip), and $N_a = 200$, and the second where $SNR = -20\,\text{dB}$ and $N_a = 50$. The results show that the performance of our EM-based algorithm improves as the number of signal delays increases. This is expected with any statistical based approach: as more data is available for a model, the model estimate improves.

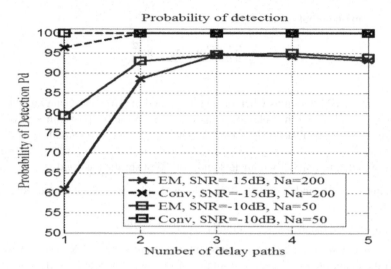

Fig. 1. Detection probability for different number of delay paths.

The results of varying the number of non-coherent accumulations N_a while fixing the SNR and number of delay paths is shown in Fig. 2. Two simulations are shown, the first where $SNR = -15$ dB and the number of delay paths is $N_D = 3$ and the second is where $SNR = -20$ dB and the number of delay paths is $N_D = 4$. The figure shows that P_D improves as N_a increases for both the conventional algorithm and our EM based algorithm. The performance of our EM-based algorithm is comparable to the conventional methods, but trails in the required number of non-coherent accumulations for proper performance. At lower number of non-coherent accumulations, the delays are

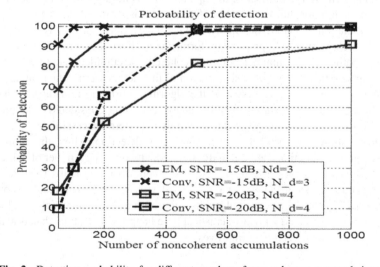

Fig. 2. Detection probability for different number of non-coherent accumulations.

sometimes too close to each other to be properly separated by the EM algorithm, and hence the lower performance at lower N_a. As the number of accumulations increases, the classes are more distinct, and performance of the EM algorithm increases to become comparable to the conventional algorithm.

Figure 3 shows the effect of SNR on performance, while keeping the number of delay paths to 5. The figure shows two simulations, one for $N_a = 100$ and one for $N_a = 200$. As expected, as SNR decreases performance decreases. This effect is compounded if the number of non-coherent accumulations is also decreased. Note that our EM-based algorithm outperforms the conventional algorithm at lower number of accumulations N_a. This is due to the fact that the conventional algorithm has to pick N_D delays, and noise delays can be dominant at low SNR and low N_a, whereas our EM-based algorithm does not make any assumptions about the number of delays.

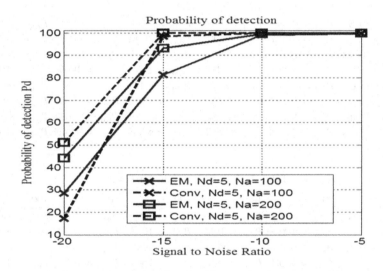

Fig. 3. Detection probability for different Signal to Noise Ratios

Tables 1, 2 and 3 show detailed comparison results of our EM-based algorithm to the conventional algorithm, where a simulation is considered a success if at least 50% of the signal delays are detected without adding a noise delay. Each experiment is repeated 500 times.

The data shows that our scheme performs comparably to the conventional one, without prior knowledge of the number of signal delays or a preset threshold. It generally requires more accumulations N_a for the same performance, and the performance increases as the number of delays N_D increases. This is typical of any statistical algorithm where performance increases when more data is available for parameter estimation.

Table 1. Simulation results for $L = 1$.

N_a	50	100	200	500	1000
SNR = −5 dB	P_{EM} = 98.4% P_{conv} = 100%	P_{EM} = 100% P_{conv} = 100%	P_{EM} = 100% P_{conv} = 100%	P_{EM} = 100% P_{conv} = 100%	P_{EM} = 100% P_{conv} = 100%
SNR = −10 dB	P_{EM} = 79.4% P_{conv} = 100%	P_{EM} = 92.2% P_{conv} = 100%	P_{EM} = 98.4% P_{conv} = 100%	P_{EM} = 99.8% P_{conv} = 100%	P_{EM} = 99.8% P_{conv} = 100%
SNR = −15 dB	P_{EM} = 19% P_{conv} = 62%	P_{EM} = 33.2% P_{conv} = 82.7%	P_{EM} = 61% P_{conv} = 96.4%	P_{EM} = 88.2% P_{conv} = 100%	P_{EM} = 96.6% P_{conv} = 100%
SNR = −20 dB	P_{EM} = 1.8% P_{conv} = 22.8%	P_{EM} = 2.6% P_{conv} = 28.2%	P_{EM} = 8.6% P_{conv} = 39.4%	P_{EM} = 16% P_{conv} = 66%	P_{EM} = 37% P_{conv} = 90.8%

Table 2. Simulation results for $L = 3$.

N_a	50	100	200	500	1000
SNR = −5 dB	P_{EM} = 100% P_{conv} = 100%	P_{EM} = 100% P_{conv} = 100%	P_{EM} = 100% P_{conv} = 100%	P_{EM} = 100% P_{conv} = 100%	P_{EM} = 100% P_{conv} = 100%
SNR = −10 dB	P_{EM} = 94.6% P_{conv} = 100%	P_{EM} = 99% P_{conv} = 100%	P_{EM} = 99.8% P_{conv} = 100%	P_{EM} = 100% P_{conv} = 100%	P_{EM} = 100% P_{conv} = 100%
SNR = −15 dB	P_{EM} = 68.8% P_{conv} = 91.4%	P_{EM} = 82.8% P_{conv} = 99.6%	P_{EM} = 94.6% P_{conv} = 100%	P_{EM} = 97.6% P_{conv} = 100%	P_{EM} = 99.6% P_{conv} = 100%
SNR = −20 dB	P_{EM} = 21.8% P_{conv} = 12.8%	P_{EM} = 26.8% P_{conv} = 29.2%	P_{EM} = 45.2% P_{conv} = 63.8%	P_{EM} = 73.6% P_{conv} = 98.4%	P_{EM} = 87.4% P_{conv} = 100%

Table 3. Simulation results for $L = 5$.

N_a	50	100	200	500	1000
SNR = −5 dB	P_{EM} = 99.8% P_{conv} = 100%	P_{EM} = 99.8% P_{conv} = 100%	P_{EM} = 100% P_{conv} = 100%	P_{EM} = 100% P_{conv} = 100%	P_{EM} = 100% P_{conv} = 100%
SNR = −10 dB	P_{EM} = 93.8% P_{conv} = 100%	P_{EM} = 99.2% P_{conv} = 100%	P_{EM} = 99.6% P_{conv} = 100%	P_{EM} = 100% P_{conv} = 100%	P_{EM} = 100% P_{conv} = 100%
SNR = −15 dB	P_{EM} = 61% P_{conv} = 75.8%	P_{EM} = 81.4% P_{conv} = 98.6%	P_{EM} = 93.2% P_{conv} = 100%	P_{EM} = 98.4% P_{conv} = 100%	P_{EM} = 99.8% P_{conv} = 100%
SNR = −20 dB	P_{EM} = 18.2% P_{conv} = 3.4%	P_{EM} = 28.4% P_{conv} = 17.2%	P_{EM} = 44.2% P_{conv} = 51.2%	P_{EM} = 77% P_{conv} = 96%	P_{EM} = 91.4% P_{conv} = 100%

6   Conclusion

We proposed an algorithm for multipath estimation in wideband communication systems. The proposed scheme is based on classifying an energy detector search results into either a signal component of a noise component using the Expectation Maximization algorithm. Simulation results have shown that the performance of our EM-based algorithm is comparable to the conventional energy detector scheme but without the need for prior knowledge of the number of multipath components and without the need to use a preset threshold for detecting the multipath components.

References

1. Meissner, P., Leitinger, E., Witrisal, K.: UWB for robust indoor tracking: weighting of multipath components for efficient estimation. IEEE Wireless Commun. Lett. **3**(5), 501–504 (2014)
2. Chen, X., Dovis, F., Peng, S., Morton, Y.: Comprehensive studies of GPA multipath mitigation methods performance. IEEE Trans. Aerosp. Electron. Syst. **49**(3), 1555–1568 (2013)
3. Qu, B., Wei, J., Tang, Z., Yan, T., Zhou, Z.H.: Analysis of combined effects of multipath and CW interference on coherent delay lock loop. Wireless Pers. Commun. **77**(3), 2213–2233 (2014)
4. Wildemeersch, M., Slump, C., Rabbachin, A.: Acquisition of GNSS signals in urban interference environment. IEEE Trans. Aerosp. Electron. Syst. **50**(2), 1078–1091 (2014)
5. Holmes, J.: Coherent Spread Spectrum systems. R.E. Krieger Pub. Co., Malabar (1990)
6. Simon, M., Omura, J., Scholtz, R., Levitt, B.: Spread Spectrum Communications Handbook. McGraw-Hill Telecom Engineering, Electronic edn. McGraw-Hill Education, New York (2001)
7. Braun, W.R.: PN acquisition and tracking performance in DS/CDMA systems with symbol-length spreading sequences. IEEE Trans. Commun. **45**(12), 1595–1601 (1997)
8. Choi, S., Alouini, M.S., Qaraqe, K.A., Yang, H.C.: Finger assignment schemes for rake receivers with multiple-way soft handover. IEEE Trans. Wireless Commun. **7**(2), 495–499 (2008)
9. Abou-Khousa, M., Ghrayeb, A., El-Tarhuni, M.: An efficient multipath detection scheme for CDMA systems. IEEE Trans. Wireless Commun. **6**(8), 2776–2781 (2007)
10. Abou-Khousa, M., Ghrayeb, A., El-Tarhuni, M.: A multipath detection scheme for CDMA systems with space-time spreading. IEEE Trans. Veh. Technol. **57**(1), 146–156 (2008)
11. Fulghum, T., Cairns, D.A., Cozzo, C., Wang, Y.P.E., Bottomley, G.E.: Adaptive generalized rake reception in DS-CDMA systems. IEEE Trans. Wireless Commun. **8**(7), 3464–3474 (2009)
12. Van Nee, R.D.J.: The multipath estimating delay lock loop. In: ISSTA 1992, pp. 39–42, August 1992
13. Wilde, A.: The generalized delay-locked loop. Wireless Pers. Commun. **8**(2), 113–130 (1998)
14. Sheen, W.H., Tai, C.H.: A noncoherent tracking loop with diversity and multipath interference cancellation for direct-sequence spread-spectrum systems. IEEE Trans. Commun. **46**(11), 1516–1524 (1998)
15. Brenneman, M., Morton, Y., Zhou, Q.: GPS multipath detection with ANOVA for adaptive arrays. IEEE Trans. Aerosp. Electron. Syst. **46**(3), 1171–1184 (2010)
16. Closas, P., Fernandez-Prades, C.: A statistical multipath detector for antenna array based GNSS receivers. IEEE Trans. Wireless Commun. **10**(3), 916–929 (2011)
17. Dempster, P., Laird, N.M., Rubin, D.B.: Maximum likelihood from incomplete data via the EM algorithm. J. Roy. Stat. Soc. B **39**(1), 1–38 (1977)
18. Arfken, G., Weber, H.: Mathematical Methods for Physicists. Elsevier, Amsterdam (2005)

Dynamic Resource Orchestration of Service Function Chaining in Network Function Virtualizations

Bangchao Yu[1,2,3(✉)], Wei Zheng[1,2,3], Xiangming Wen[1,2,3], Zhaoming Lu[1,2,3], Luhan Wang[1,2,3], and Lu Ma[1,2,3]

[1] Beijing Laboratory of Advanced Information Networks, Beijing, China
yubc0321@gmail.com, zhengweius@163.com,
lzy_0372@163.com, wluhan@bupt.edu.cn
[2] Beijing Advanced Innovation Center for Future Internet Technology,
Beijing, China
[3] Beijing Key Laboratory of Network System Architecture and Convergence,
Beijing University of Posts and Telecommunications, Beijing, China

Abstract. Network Functions Virtualization is a new network architecture framework and is revolutionizing the way networking service that how to design and deploy. NFV promotes virtualizing network functions and improves the flexibility to resource orchestration for request service function chains. However, how to find the most suitable resource in NFV-based network resource is a challenge. This paper presents a comprehensive state of the NFV resource orchestration by introducing a dynamic resource orchestration architecture that can configure dynamic resources. With consideration of load balance, energy cost and resource consumption, the resource orchestration is formulated as a multi-objective optimal problem. Finally, a multi-objective simulated annealing algorithm is used to obtain the optimal resource strategy to deploy network functions. Simulation results show that the solution for dynamic resource orchestration can achieve approximate optimal solution in acceptable time and reduce 8% energy consumption with a 0.89 Jain's fairness index.

Keywords: NFV · Service function chains · Performance optimization
Resource orchestration

1 Introduction

Network Function Virtualization (NFV) is revolutionizing the way networking service are designed and deployed, and is a promising technique to meet the requirements of explosive data traffic in fifth generation (5G) mobile communications [1]. Compared to traditional network where dedicated hardware is required for each function (manually installed into the network), the NFV virtualizes the network functions (NFs) (e.g., local cache, firewalls, load balancers, databases), which can be hosted on commodity hardware (i.e., industry standard servers, storage and switches). NFV transforms the way that how network operators architect their infrastructure by leveraging the full-blown virtualization technology to separate software instance from hardware

© ICST Institute for Computer Sciences, Social Informatics and Telecommunications Engineering 2018
K. Long et al. (Eds.): 5GWN 2017, LNICST 211, pp. 132–145, 2018.
https://doi.org/10.1007/978-3-319-72823-0_14

platform and by decoupling functionally from location for faster networking service [2]. These functions decoupled from the underlying hardware are knows as Virtualized Network Functions (VNFs).

Under the paradigm of NFV, the networks provide considerably more flexibility, leads to efficient and scalable resource usage and reduce costs. Despite the emergence of NFV, deploying and orchestrating VNFs still requires more research and development. To facilitate the service management in NFV environments, service function chaining technique is proposed. A SFC is describes the various NFs and how they interact to provide a complete network service [3]. In order to offer various service, the operator needs to configure the networking infrastructure to direct the right traffic through the right service chain. Since the deployment and management of NFs providing the services usually require a significant capital investment, the operators are seeking ways to optimize the resource utilization of theses NFs. The key to exploiting the potential of the NFV based networks is the issue of resource orchestration in SFC.

Resource Orchestration (RO) is the set of operations that cloud providers and application owners undertake for selecting, deploying, monitoring, and dynamically controlling the configuration of hardware and software resources as a system of quality of service-assured components that can be seamlessly delivered to end users [4]. Orchestration can significantly reduce the cost and the time required for provisioning new services with respect to today's standards by allowing the joint allocation of different types of physical or virtual resource.

However, there are still many issues that need to be tackled in the resource orchestration of SFC. In [5], the authors study the network slicing based on 5G and future mobile network. One is to achieve dynamic variation of service resource requirements arise from a number of factors, including resource capacity demand, failures, end-user access patterns, and variations in resource prices. The other is configuring dynamic resources. The impetus behind NFV environment if the ever-increasing demand to manage growth and increase computing flexibility by dynamic scaling up or down resources based on demand [2]. Moreover, dynamic configuration of resources is a complex issue because of lack of visibility and control across heterogeneous services at different layers.

Recently, there have been many efforts on how to configure dynamic resources from both academia and industry. In [6], the authors study the problem of dynamic and programing resource orchestration in Mobile Cloud Computing (MCC) environment, and propose a multi-objective particle swarm optimization algorithm by considering resource choice for complicated service where multiple tasks are composed together. Another work in [7] studies NFV resource allocation problem, and proposed a coordinated approach Jointly Optimize the Resource Allocation in NFV (JoraNFV) to jointly optimization three phases in NFV resource allocation. While initial research results are promising, more than that, in many case designing effective dynamic resource orchestration techniques that cope with large-scale NFV environment remains a deeply challenging problem.

In this paper, we focus on the configuring dynamic resources orchestration in NFV environment. More specifically, we search for the optimal resource strategies and dynamically configure resource to meet requirements and constraints. To solve this problem, we propose a dynamic resource orchestration framework that contains a software defined architecture along with the multi-objectives optimization algorithm aiming to obtain the optimal resource configurations.

The rest of this paper is organized as follows: Some related works are presented in Sect. 2. After that, we present the dynamic resource orchestration architecture in Sect. 3. The algorithm to solve configuring dynamic resource problem is introduced in Sect. 4. Section 5, we report performance evaluation results. Section 6 concludes this paper.

2   Related Works

Over the last few years, some works have already been done to study resource orchestration in NFV environment.

Recent studies show that, in an enterprise network, the number of middle-boxes is comparable with the number of routers and switches needed to maintain the operation of the network [8]. Sherry et al. [9] presents a comprehensive state of the art of NFV-RA by introducing a novel classification of the main approaches that pose solutions to solve the resource allocation of demanded network services in NFV-based network infrastructure. He proposed three different stages of NFV-RA. In addition, NFV facilitates installation and deployment of VNFs on general purpose server [10, 11], thus allowing dynamic migration of VNFs form one server to another, that is, to any place of the network [12].

In [13], a two-layer home-to-home cloud framework which allows intra-home resources to be shared among consumer electronic devices and inter-home resources to be shared among neighboring houses is proposed to find the most suitable resources in the home cloud. But the optimal orchestration strategy in [13] fails to scale or down resources based on demand dynamically.

VNFs can be deployed and reassigned to share different physical and virtual resource of the infrastructure, so as to guarantee scalability and performance requirements. Tao et al. [14] work on the resource service composition in industry grid system, and exploit the standard particle swarm algorithm to find the solution. In [15], the authors propose two heuristic algorithms to optimize middle-box placement problem. One is greedy algorithm, and the other is simulated annealing algorithm. Their simulation results show that the Simulated Annealing algorithm outperforms the Greedy algorithm. However, the resource orchestration techniques mentioned above don't effectively support dynamic resource configuration. For example, service or dataflow can't be dynamically and automatically partitioned or migrated arbitrarily from one cloud service to another if demand cycles increase.

Therefore, the dynamic resource orchestration in the NFV environment should take the CPUs and energy consumption into consideration. In this work, a dynamic NFV-based resource orchestration architecture and a multi-object simulated annealing is proposed to find the appropriate solution for service to meet requirement and constraints.

3   System Architecture

3.1   NFV-Based Resource Orchestration Architecture

In this section we present the proposed integrated NFV Resource Orchestration and Management Architecture in order to deploy Virtual Network Functions (VNFs) on top of an integrated cloud and network platform (i.e., NFV infrastructure (NFVI)). The NFVI is composed of heterogeneous multi-domain and multi-layer transport networks with heterogeneous transport and control technologies interconnecting distributed Databases Centers, providing computing, storage, and network resources. Today, cloud computing systems follow a service-driven, layered software architecture model, with Software as a service, Platform as a service, Infrastructure as a service. On top of this physical infrastructure, we deploy an NFVI virtualization layer responsible for virtualizing the computing, storage, and network resources of the NFVI by means of a virtualized infrastructure manager.

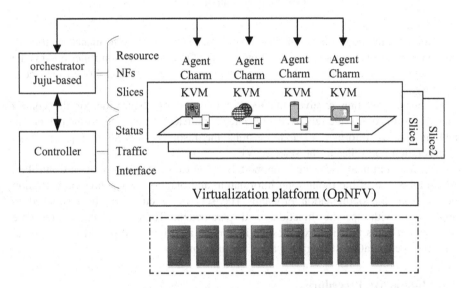

Fig. 1. NFV-based Resource Orchestration System

As shown in Fig. 1, the NFV based Resource Orchestration System is composed of Resource and Management Controller, VNFs (for example, database appliance, load balancer, auto scaling, virtualized HSS, virtualized MME, virtualized S-PGW) and the physical infrastructure. The Resource and Management Controller as well as Orchestration Controller is a centered controller for resource orchestration by interacting with distributed flexible Agents. The communication and monitoring functions for the resources are encapsulated in the Agents.

3.2   Resource Orchestration Controller

The Resource Management and Orchestration Controller is composed of three functional modules: monitor function, decision function and execution function, as show in Fig. 2(a). They are responsible for the set of operations that cloud providers and application owners undertake for selecting, deploying, monitoring, and dynamically controlling the configuration of hardware and software. The abstract resource and management orchestration operations in the lifecycle of an application or service are resource selection, deployment, monitoring and control, as shown in Fig. 2(b).

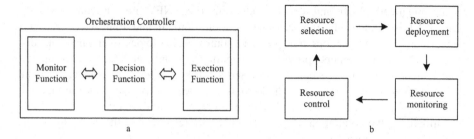

Fig. 2. Orchestration controller and operations

Monitor Function collects and aggregates the status and performance metrics of consumer electronic devices. By this function, the Orchestration Controller obtains the resource parameters such as CPU, storage and communication capability, or the Cache memory.

Decision Function receives the register message of connection, or the control message from Agent, and records the resource parameters. It also gathers the perceiving and monitoring information, and transmits the resource orchestration policy from orchestration controller to the selected VFs.

Execution Function is calculation module in the Resource Orchestration Controller, which takes use of the monitoring information and obtains the resource orchestration policy from the optimization problem. The service function can be abstracted to application with specific functions and parameters. Then according to resource requirements, this function executes the intelligent algorithm and provides the optimal resource orchestration strategy for a virtual function.

3.3   Interactive Procedure

The could computing resources may not stick to only one service or platform, so taking advantage of virtualization resource has become a key issue. Based on this, our goal is to achieve the automatic management of Virtual functions (VFs) and service orchestration, meeting the quality of service (QoS)-assured components that can be seamlessly delivered to end users. In Fig. 3, for collecting the resource status, Orchestration Controller subscribes the information for each Agent. When the user's behavior or the timer is triggered, Agent sends the information to the monitor function box in Orchestration Controller. When a service's request arrives at the Orchestration Controller, it finishes the virtualization resource orchestration (in the Decision Function box) and transmits the strategies to the Execution Function box.

When Agent receives the strategy, it performs the service management or deployment and executes the service. After that, it collects the result of its previous services, updates the results, deletes the records of itself and transmits the results to the

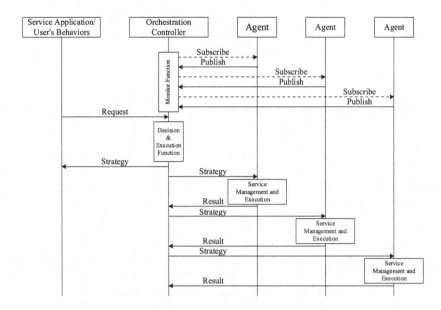

Fig. 3. Interactive procedure for resource orchestration

Orchestration Controller. The interaction message of Agents and Orchestration Controller are implemented by using Representational State Transfer (REST) Application Programming Interfaces (APIs) that is easy for extending.

4 Resource Orchestration Algorithm

4.1 Problem Definition

Figure 4 depicts the basic resource orchestration in NFV resource management. The left part is the service chaining which consist of function units (VFs) hosted on NFV nodes. By isolation, multiple VFs can run on the same physical could server, e.g. three units on Infrastructure-based resource area A and four units on Infrastructure-based resource area B. It should be noted than the CPU, storage, and network resources in A and B is different. On the right part of Fig. 4, there is mapping part from physical resources to virtual resources. The NFV resource are abstracted to services with specific functions and parameters. The VFs in a complicated service chaining is modeled as dataflow graph and denoted by Directed Acyclic Graph, depicted in Fig. 3. Due to the difference existing in the hardware resources, the appropriate resource is chosen for VFs according to the global optimization goal during user's behaviors. As the metrics such as resource cost, resource availability and CPU load average are not relevant or not following the same trend or even conflicting with each other, improving one metric may result in the deterioration of another one.

The multi-objective resource orchestration is to find a solution set Resource Orchestration Path (ROP_{SET}) in which each solution ROP_d has extreme optional value of aggregated metric, i.e.

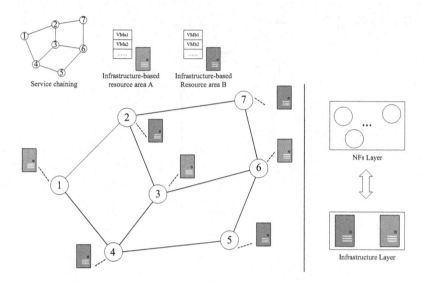

Fig. 4. Example of resource orchestration in NFV

$$\min F(ROP_d) = \alpha \cdot \min E(ROP_d) + \beta \cdot \min C(ROP_d) + \gamma \cdot \min L(ROP_d) \quad (1)$$

where $d = 1, \ldots, n$; $ROP_d \in ROP_{set}$, $\alpha + \beta + \gamma = 1$, $E(ROP_d)$, $C(ROP_d)$ and $L(ROP_d)$ are the energy consumption, resource charges and CPU load average of ROP_d respectively. F is the target vector function.

Energy consumption ($E_S^{r,i}$) means the total energy consumption of service i when VFs node is hosted on the resource r. It is determined by the amount of transmitted data. e_{trans}^r is the energy consumption of transmitting per unit (bit) data to resource r. V_{load}^i is the data volume of service i deploy to the NFV resource and $V_{interact}^i$ is interaction data volume between NFV resource and resource orchestration controller during the service i execution. e_{comput} is the energy consumption of computing per unit (bit) data and V_{comput}^i is the local data volume of the service i.

$$E_S^{r,i} = e_{trans}^r \cdot (V_{load}^i + V_{interact}^i) + e_{comput} \cdot V_{comput}^i \quad (2)$$

Resource charges ($C_S^{r,i}$) refers to the price pay for the specific NFV resource r where service i will be offload to. Let $c_{storage}^r$ be the storage charge of selected resource r, c_{comput}^r be the computing charge of selected resource r, and $c_{commun}^{r,c}$ be the communication cost from resource r to resource orchestrator controller when service i will be offloaded to. $V_{commun}^{r,c}$ is the data volume transmitted from resource r to resource orchestrator controller.

$$C_S^{r,i} = c_{storage}^r + c_{comput}^r + c_{commun}^{r,c} \cdot V_{commun}^{r,c} \quad (3)$$

CPU load average ($L_s^{r,i}$) represents the average system load over a period of time. An idle computer has a number of 0. Each process using or waiting for CPU increments the load number. For single-CPU systems that are CPU bound, one can think of load average as a percentage of system utilization during the respective time period. For system with multiple CPUs, one must divide the number by the number of processors in order to get a comparable percentage. l_A^i is the CPU load average of infrastructure-based resource area A when service i is hosted and n_A is the total number of service hosted on A.

$$L_S^{r,i} = \min\left[\sum_{i=0}^{n_A} l_A^i, \sum_{i=0}^{n_B} l_B^i, \cdots\right] \tag{4}$$

4.2 Resource Orchestration Algorithm

The resource orchestration is to select the optimal from all possible candidates considering multiple objectives (e.g. energy consumption, resource cost, resource availability), which is known as multi-objective optimization problem. We take use of the Multi-Objective Simulated Annealing (MOSA) algorithm to solve this problem, for it is a general random search framework that can get near-optimal solutions of combinational optimization problems. Besides, the advantage of MOSA is it can keep improving the solution effectively if time allows.

Algorithm: MOSA for the dynamic resource orchestration

Inputs: temperature T; parameter λ; probability set p
Output: resource orchestration strategy ROP_d
// Initialization
$T(t) = \lambda T$, $t = t_0$, $p(\Delta F) = e^{-\Delta F/t}$, $IteNum = L \cdot |ROP_{set}|$, $i = 0$
while $i < IteNum$ **do**

    $ROP_e \leftarrow$ generate neighbor of ROP_d

    calculate $\Delta F = F(ROP_e) - F(ROP_d)$, $p(\Delta F)$

    if $\Delta F < 0$ **then**

        $ROP_d \leftarrow ROP_e$

      if $rand(0,1) < p(\Delta F)$ **then**

        $ROP_d \leftarrow ROP_e$ with probability p

    end

  end

  $i = i + 1$

  if $mod(i, L) == 0$ **then**

    $t \leftarrow$ update temperature t

  end

Return ROP_d

The MOSA algorithm for resource orchestration is stepped as follows:

5 Performance Evaluation

5.1 Simulation Scenarios

The implementation set-up consists of a test bed with seven VMs of desktop PCs performing as the NFV clouding computing resource. The VFs are all configured with 1 GB memory, CPU 3.2 GHz, gigabit Ethernet network interfaces, and Linux operating system, and are deployed with the Resource Controller for orchestration resources.

In the simulation scenarios, we generate specific service function chain that include different types services which hosted on NFV based resources. For each component service, the V_{load}^i, $V_{interact}^i$, V_{comput}^i and $V_{commun}^{r,c}$ are generated according to a uniform distribution. We generated serval resource providers to represent different NFV based resources with e_{trans}^r, e_{comput}, $c_{storage}^r$, c_{comput}^r and $c_{commun}^{r,c}$ follow a uniform distribution. The detailed setting is shown in Table 1. The resource parameters of service functions are generated while the service function is getting started. The available time T_{start} and T_{end} are set to 0 and 5 min, respectively. And we take an example of a service function chain that contains NFs and dataflow depicted in Fig. 5.

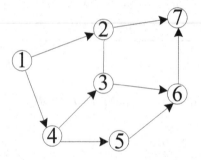

Fig. 5. Service dataflow in simulation scenarios

Table 1. Simulation parameters

NFV resource		Service		MOSA	
Parameters	Values	Parameters	Values	Parameters	Values
e_{trans}^r	[1, 5]	V_{load}^i	[10,80]	α	0.3
e_{comput}	3	$V_{interact}^i$	[10,50]	β	0.4
$c_{storage}^r$	[1, 10]	V_{comput}^i	[20,100]	λ	0.3
c_{comput}^r	[20,50]	$V_{commun}^{r,c}$	[5,30]	l_A^i	[0.1,0.7]
$c_{commun}^{r,c}$	[0,1]				

5.2 Simulation Results

In order to evaluate the performance of the proposed Resource Orchestration Architecture and the MOSA algorithm, we carried out the evaluation through a combination of testbed based experiments and numerical simulations. We use the testbed to evaluate the real service functions in small scale network with different physical infrastructures. In our evaluation, we compare the proposed algorithms against a baseline algorithm (Greedy Algorithm) and a basic resource orchestration (without any algorithm).

(1) *Energy evaluation*

To evaluate the performance of MOSA algorithm, we generate seven NFs that contains multiple instances hosted on different hardware resources in total. The physical hardware is different in computing resource, storage resources, etc. We started the resource orchestration with MOSA algorithm at 40 min when the virtual machine was deployed, for the installation and configuration of service functions.

As shown in the Fig. 6, we can observe that MOSA-based approach slightly outperforms GA-based, and both MOSA and GA-based approach outperform basic RO without any algorithm in the runtime of orchestration operations. There are mainly due to two reasons. Firstly, both MOSA and GA-based approach are taking the energy consumption into consideration before configuring resources. Second reason is the CPU load average of hardware or software resource are also considered in MOSA approach, which is related to the energy consumption. On average, the MOSA-based approach will reduce 8% energy consumption than basic RO and reduce 3% than GA-based algorithm.

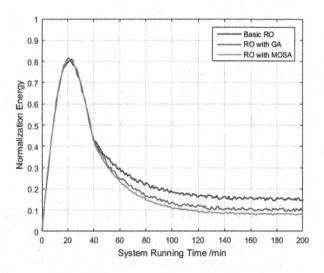

Fig. 6. Energy consumption of infrastructure

(2) *Load evaluation*

In the MOSA algorithm, we considered the CPU load average of the physical infrastructure or service functions. The Jain's Fairness Index indicates the fairness of different algorithm for resource invocation [16]. It is defined as follows:

$$f(x_1, x_2, x_3, \ldots, x_n) = \frac{\left(\sum_{i=1}^{n} x_i\right)^2}{n \sum_{i=1}^{n} x_i^2} \tag{5}$$

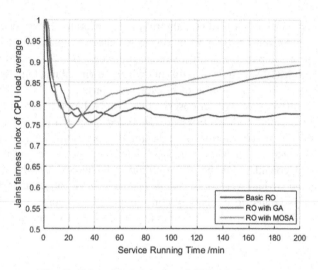

Fig. 7. Jain's fairness index of CPU load average

The Jain's Fairness Index was calculated for each of SFs and is shown in Fig. 7. It can be observed that the fairness is improved with the MOSA-based or GA-based approach compared to basic RO. The Jain's index can achieve about 0.89 with MOSA and 0.87 with GA, which is higher than basic RO with about 0.77. It shows that, considering CPU load average and configuring dynamic resources, MOSA approach perform consistently on different resources. The Jain's index of MOSA becomes better when the network scale becomes larger and larger, and more instances are deployed, which also make resources more fair.

(3) *Execution Time*

To evaluate the execution time, we use MOSA and GA-based approach to deploy service functions chain on different physical infrastructure. The request service chain contains 7 VNFs and the number of virtual nodes in network is set from 10 to 100 with an interval of 10. The simulation result is shown in Fig. 8. With the increase of the number of nodes, the execution time are increasing, but the MOSA and GA-based approach take less time than basic resource orchestration without any algorithm. The MOSA-based approach can hit optimal solutions of configure dynamic resource in acceptable time.

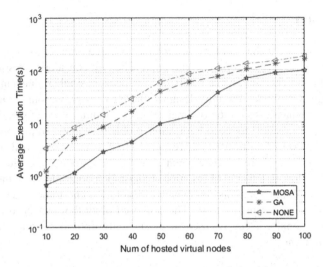

Fig. 8. Execution time performance of algorithms

(4) *Multi-object evaluation*

To facilitate understanding results, we use the three-dimensional figures to show the optimal solutions in resource orchestration. The result is shown in Fig. 9. It contains 30 instances of service functions for each algorithm. Pentagram represent the value of MOSA algorithm in the objective space. We can find that the MOSA can obtain more optimal results than GA algorithm and basic resource orchestration.

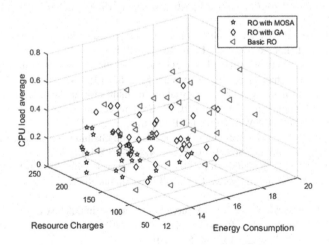

Fig. 9. Comparisons of resource orchestration results

6   Conclusion

In this paper, we target the problem of dynamic resource orchestration in NFV environment. Our work goes beyond existing approaches by considering resource choice for service function chaining, while others mainly focus on single influencing factors or static deployment problem. We thus designed the NFV-based Resource Orchestration Architecture to dynamic select the optimal resource candidates for VNFs. We defined the resource orchestration as an optimization problem with the multi-objective, i.e. energy consumption of infrastructure, resource charges and CPU load average. To obtain the optimal results for resource orchestration, we introduce the Multi-Objective Simulated Annealing in the core of resource orchestration controller. Simulation results show that the multiple solutions for dynamic resource orchestration can archive the optimal solutions in acceptable time. The proposed algorithm can be used in many scenarios, for example, it can be used to dynamically optimize service functions in NFV-based environment.

Acknowledgment. This work is supported by a grant from the National High Technology Research and Development Program of China (863 Program), No. 2014AA01A701, and Beijing Municipal Science and technology Commission research fund project No. Z161110005000000.

References

1. Zhang, H., et al.: Fronthauling for 5G LTE-U ultra dense cloud small cell networks. IEEE Wireless Commun. **23**(6), 48–53 (2016)
2. Chiosi, M., et al.: Network functions virtualisation: an introduction, benefits, enablers, challenges and call for action. In: SDN and OpenFlow World Congress (2012)
3. Halpern, J., Pignataro, C.: Service Function Chaining (SFC) Architecture. No. RFC 7665 (2015)
4. Ranjan, R., et al.: Cloud resource orchestration programming: overview, issues, and directions. IEEE Internet Comput. **19**(5), 46–56 (2015)
5. Zhang, H., et al.: Network slicing based 5G and future mobile networks: mobility, resource management, and challenges. IEEE Commun. Mag. **55**, 138–145 (2017)
6. Qi, Q., et al.: Dynamic resource orchestration for multi-task application in heterogeneous mobile cloud computing. In: 2016 IEEE Conference on Computer Communications Workshops (INFOCOM WKSHPS). IEEE (2016)
7. Wang, L., et al.: Joint optimization of service function chaining and resource allocation in network function virtualization. IEEE Access **4**, 8084–8094 (2016)
8. Fiorani, M., et al.: Challenges for 5G transport networks. In: 2014 IEEE International Conference on Advanced Networks and Telecommunications Systems (ANTS). IEEE (2014)
9. Sherry, J., Ratnasamy, S., At, J.S.: A survey of enterprise middlebox deployments (2012)
10. Herrera, J.G., Botero, J.-F.: Resource allocation in NFV: a comprehensive survey. IEEE Trans. Netw. Serv. Manage. **13**, 518–532 (2016)
11. Hirschman, B., et al.: High-performance evolved packet core signaling and bearer processing on general-purpose processors. IEEE Network **29**(3), 6–14 (2015)
12. Bronstein, Z., et al.: Uniform handling and abstraction of NFV hardware accelerators. IEEE Network **29**(3), 22–29 (2015)

13. Qi, Q., et al.: Resource orchestration for multi-task application in home-to-home cloud. IEEE Trans. Consum. Electron. **62**(2), 191–199 (2016)
14. Tao, F., et al.: Resource service composition and its optimal-selection based on particle swarm optimization in manufacturing grid system. IEEE Trans. Industr. Inf. **4**(4), 315–327 (2008)
15. Liu, J., et al.: Improve service chaining performance with optimized middlebox placement. IEEE Trans. Serv. Comput. **10**(4), 560–573 (2017)
16. Ma, W.-M., et al.: Utility-based fairness power control scheme in OFDMA femtocell networks. Dianzi Yu Xinxi Xuebao(J. Electron. Inf. Technol.) **34**(10), 2287–2292 (2012)

Support Recovery for Multiband Spectrum Sensing Based on Modulated Wideband Converter with SwSOMP Algorithm

Zhuhua Hu[1,2], Yong Bai[1,2(✉)], Yaochi Zhao[2], and Yiran Zhang[2]

[1] State Key Laboratory of Marine Resource Utilization in South China Sea,
Hainan University, No. 58, Renmin Avenue, Haikou 570228, Hainan Province,
People's Republic of China
{eagler_hu,bai}@hainu.edu.cn
[2] College of Information Science and Technology, Hainan University, No. 58,
Renmin Avenue, Haikou 570228, Hainan Province, People's Republic of China

Abstract. The Modulated Wideband Converter (MWC) can provide a sub-Nyquist sampling approach to sense sparse multiband analog signals and reconstruct the frequency support set. However, the existing SOMP reconstruction algorithms need a priori information of signal sparsity. This paper applies the SwOMP algorithm to the CTF (Continuous-To-Finite) block of MWC. The SwSOMP algorithm uses stage-wise weak selection in SOMP, and it can reduce computational cost and solve large scale problems. It does not need prior information of signal sparsity, and the frequency support can be reconstructed blindly. The simulation results demonstrate that, MWC system with SwSOMP algorithm, compared with the SOMP algorithm, can use less number of channels, achieve higher percentage of correct support recovery blindly, and reduce the sampling rate of the system.

Keywords: Spectrum sensing · MWC · sub-Nyquist sampling
Compressed sensing · Stage-wise weak Simultaneous OMP(SwSOMP)

1 Introduction

Spectrum sensing is often necessary in communication applications, such as Cognitive Radio (CR) [1]. Its aim is to solve the spectrum crowdedness. CR should be able to reliably monitor the spectrum and detect the primary users (PUs) activity. Then, secondary users (SUs) would opportunistically access frequency bands left vacant by PUs. Therefore, support recovery of signals is pivotal to exploit the vacant bands in wideband spectrum. Generally, the sparse multi-band analog signal is transmitted in CR network. Multiband RF signals occupy a fairly wideband range, while the frequency band of each RF signal is narrow and distributed within the given bandwidth without intersecting.

At the receiver, if the Nyquist sampling theorem is used to reconstruct the high frequency multiband analog signal, it brings the sampling system a burden of ultra-high sampling rate and massive sampling data [2]. Therefore, in order to achieve sub-Nyquist sampling rate, the compressed sensing theory [3] must be extended to the

© ICST Institute for Computer Sciences, Social Informatics and Telecommunications Engineering 2018
K. Long et al. (Eds.): 5GWN 2017, LNICST 211, pp. 146–159, 2018.
https://doi.org/10.1007/978-3-319-72823-0_15

analog domain. First came the method based on AIC (Analog-to-Information Conversion) [4, 5]; However, the application scenarios of AIC is limited, and sampling efficiency for the multiband signal is low. For this reason, a variety of novel sub-Nyquist sampling structures have emerged such as CRD (Constrained Random Demodulation) [6], random equivalent sampling [7] and MWC (Modulated Wideband Converter) [8]. The sub-Nyquist sampling method of MWC is proposed by Yonina Eldar and can be applied in the field of radar [9], broadband communication [10] and cognitive radio spectrum sensing [11, 12].

The accurate reconstruction of the signal support set is the core problem of MWC system. At present, MWC mainly uses CTF (Continuous-To-Finite) reconstruction block [13]. SOMP (Simultaneous Orthogonal Matching Pursuit) algorithm [14] can be used commonly as the reconstruction algorithm in CTF block. SOMP is simple and easy to realize, but its probability of correct reconstruction is not high enough [15]. Under the case of no noise, the required number of channels for accurate reconstruction is much higher than the theoretical lower bound. In practical applications, the channels must be implemented by the hardware, which will greatly increase the development cost of the system. In addition, the sparsity of signal has to be used as a priori information for the reconstruction. However, it is difficult to obtain in the CR environment. Therefore, it is important to investigate better reconstruction algorithms which do not depend on the signal sparsity, and can significantly improve the percentage of the support recovery and can reduce the number of required sampling channels.

To address the existing problems, this paper applies the SwSOMP (Stage-wise weak Simultaneous OMP) algorithm based on SwOMP [16] to the support recovery of MWC. The SwSOMP algorithm uses stagewise weak selection in SOMP, it further improves StOMP (Stage-wise OMP) [17] and optimizes the threshold settings for the selection of atoms, which can reduce the dependency for the observation matrix. It can reduce computational cost and solve large scale problems. It does not need prior information of signal sparsity, and the frequency support can be reconstructed blindly. This paper applies the SwSOMP algorithm to the CTF (Continuous-To-Finite) block of MWC. The simulation results demonstrate that, MWC system with SwSOMP algorithm can use less number of channels, achieve higher percentage of correct support recovery blindly, and further reduce the sampling rate of the system.

The remainder of this paper is organized as follows. In Sect. 2 we introduce the signal model and principles of MWC system. Section 3 describes the method of support recovery of MWC with SwSOMP algorithm. Section 4 gives the simulation results and discussion. Section 5 concludes this paper.

2 Signal Model and Principles of MWC System

2.1 Sparse Multiband Signal Model

Sparse multiband signal is often found in the CR environment [18]. Suppose that the received signal $x(t)$ is a sparse bandpass analog signal. Its spectrum is distributed in the frequency range $[-f_{nyq}/2, f_{nyq}/2]$, and f_{nyq} is the Nyquist sampling rate of the signal. Assume that the spectrum of $x(t)$ only contains N sub-bands whose bandwidth are

$B_i \le B$ $(N \ge i > 0)$ (without considering the symmetric band), and the sub-bands do not overlap. B is the maximum bandwidth of the sub-bands. The center carrier frequency of each sub-band is unknown. All unions of sub-bands and the maximum bandwidth B can be expressed as:

$$P_{2N} = \bigcup_{1}^{N} \{(a_i, b_i) \cup (-b_i, -a_i)\} \quad B = \max_i (b_i - a_i) \tag{1}$$

The minimum needed sampling rate of the multi-band signal, the Landau rate [19], is defined as:

$$M(P_{2N}) = 2 \sum_{i=1}^{N} (b_i - a_i) \tag{2}$$

As is shown in Fig. 1, the entire frequency band is divided into L continuous narrow bands, and each band's bandwidth is not larger than B. Adding the symmetric parts, the spectrum of $x(t)$ in the entire frequency band has at most $2N$ parts with signal energy. The bands are designated as $[1, \ldots, L]$, then the set of the indices of sub-band $X_i(f)$ is called the support set of signal $x(t)$ which is defined as $\Lambda = \operatorname{supp}(X(f))$. The frequency bands corresponding to the indices are called the support bands. Since $2N \ll L$, $x(t)$ can be viewed as a sparse multiband signal.

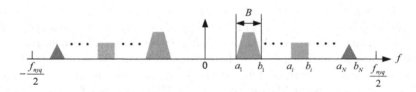

Fig. 1. Spectrum structure of sparse multiband signal

In summary, the support bands of $x(t)$ must meet the following two conditions: (1) it has to be distributed in a very wide frequency range; (2) the signals only exist in a few discrete frequency bands.

2.2 Sampling Scheme for MWC System

MWC contains a number of sampling channels, and each channel structure is the same, which is composed of the mixer, low-pass filter and ADC. The structure of the system is shown in Fig. 6(a). The received signal $x(t)$ is input into m parallel channels at the same time, each of which multiplies different patterns of periodic mixing signal $p_i(t)$ to realize the shifting from the frequency spectrum of $x(t)$ signal to baseband. The $p_i(t)$ of each channel is uncorrelated, and the cycle of $p_i(t)$ is $T_p = 1/f_p$. M is used to show the number of random alternating times of ± 1 in a cycle. Mf_p is defined as the alternating frequency of the mixing signal. The waveform of $p_i(t)$ is shown in Fig. 2. After mixing, the signal passes through lowpass filter whose cut-off frequency is $1/2T_s$, as is shown in Fig. 3. It finally passes through ADC at sampling rate is $f_s = 1/T_s$ and acquires M groups of low-speed digital sampling sequence $y_i[n]$.

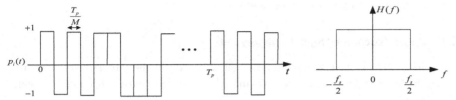

Fig. 2. Periodic mixing signal of the ith channel   **Fig. 3.** Ideal low-pass filter.

On the analysis of the ith channel, the Fourier series expansion of the random mixing function $p_i(t)$ is:

$$p_i(t) = \sum_{l=-\infty}^{\infty} c_{il} e^{j2\pi f_p lt} \tag{3}$$

The coefficient $c_{il} = d_l \sum_{k=0}^{L-1} \alpha_{ik} e^{-j\frac{2\pi}{L}lk}$, $\alpha_{ik} \in \{-1, +1\}$. When $l = 0$, $d_0 = 1/L$, and when $l \neq 0$, $d_l = (1 - e^{-j\frac{2\pi l}{L}})/j2\pi l$.

Then, after passing through the lowpass filter with frequency characteristic $H(f) = \begin{cases} 1 & |f| \leq f_s/2 \\ 0 & |f| > f_s/2 \end{cases}$, the relationship between the DTFT (Discrete Time Fourier Transform) of $y_i[n]$ and $x(t)$'s Fourier transform $X(f)$ is obtained by sampling is as follows:

$$Y_i(e^{j2\pi fT_s}) = \sum_{l=-L_0}^{L_0} c_{il} X(f - lf_p) \tag{4}$$

In (4), $f \in [-f_s/2, f_s/2]$, and L_0 is the smallest integer that makes $L = 2L_0 + 1 \geq F = f_{nyq}/f$. The Eq. (4) shows that the spectrum of the output sequence $Y_i[n]$ is changed to the weighted sum of original signal spectrum $X(f)$ with a f_p step shifts, and the spectral segment with a width of f_s is intercepted by a low-pass filter. If taking $Y_i(e^{j2\pi fT_s})$ as the ith component of m dimensional column vectors, $X(f - lf_p)$ as the lth components of the $2l_0 + 1$ dimensional column vectors $z(f)$, (4) can be expressed as:

$$y(f) = \Phi z(f), \quad f \in [-f_s/2, f_s/2] \tag{5}$$

In (5), Φ is a $m \times L$ matrix. $\Phi_{il} = c_{i,-l} = c_{il}*, 1 \leq i \leq m$, and $m < L$. Applying IDTFT (Inverse Discrete Time Fourier Transform) transform on (5), we can get the corresponding relationship between the sequence $Z[n] = [z_1[n], z_2[n], \ldots, z_L[n]]^T$ and the sampling data $Y[n] = [y_1[n], y_2[n], \ldots, y_m[n]]^T$.

$$Y[n] = \Phi Z[n] \tag{6}$$

For any frequency $f \in [-f_s/2, f_s/2]$, (6) can be viewed as a typical compressed sensing problem, where an observed vector Y is known to recover an unknown sparse vector Z. Therefore, it is viable to recover the support bands of the signal by using the reconstruction algorithms of compressed sensing.

2.3 Reconstruction of Signal Support Set

Since $m < L$, (5) is an underdetermined equation. To get the unique solution to the equation, the sampling parameters of the MWC system must meet the following conditions [8]:

(1) $f_s \geq f_p \geq B, \frac{f_s}{f_p} < \frac{M_{\min}+1}{2}$;

(2) $m \geq 2K = 4N$, K is the sparsity of the sparse vector $z(f)$. N is the number of signal bands without considering the symmetric bands;

(3) The number of ± 1 symbols in a periodic sequence $p_i(t)$ must satisfy $M \geq M_{\min} = \left\lceil \frac{f_{nyq}}{f_p} \right\rceil$. If $f_s = f_p$, then $M_{\min} = L$;

(4) Any $4N$ column of the matrix Φ is linearly independent.

It has been pointed out in [3] that the sparse solution for (5) is a NP-hard problem. Nonetheless, such a problem can be transformed into a minimization of the l_1 norm problem provided that the number of sampling channels $m \geq cK \log(L/K)$. c is a constant, and K is the sparsity (i.e. the number of signal bands). It can be known that the value of m is much greater than $2K$.

The crucial problem of reconstruction is to reconstruct the sparse $Z[n]$ from the sampling sequences $Y[n]$. Since the signal frequency is continuous in $[-f_s/2, f_s/2]$, (5) is infinite dimensional, i.e., contains infinite number of SMV (Single Measurement Vector) problem. A CTF block is proposed for reconstruction in [13], as shown in the Fig. 4. It was proposed as a transformation framework from infinite dimension to finite dimension (Multiple Measurement Vectors, MMV) [15]. Support bands Λ of the signal can be estimated by CTF, through which the signal $x(t)$ can be further recovered. SOMP algorithm can be used to the reconstruction in MWC, which achieves reconstruction in [8]. The experimental results show that algorithm can achieve high percentage of correct reconstruction when $m \geq 2K \log(L/K)$, but there is still a large gap compared with the theoretical lower bound.

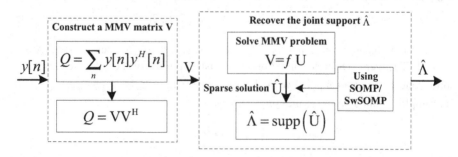

Fig. 4. Schematic diagram of the CTF block.

3 Support Recovery of MWC with SwSOMP Algorithm

As mentioned in the introduction, the SOMP reconstruction algorithm has many shortcomings. As a result, in terms of the success rate of recovery, the needed minimum number of channels, the reconstruction under low SNR and the maximum number of bands that can be reconstructed, the reconstruction algorithm of MWC still has a large space for improvement.

SwSOMP adopts the idea of stage-wise. First, atoms are selected according to the principles of correlation, using threshold to select atoms matched with residual. The difference with SOMP algorithm is that it does not always choose the most relevant matching atom in each iteration, but finds a number of atoms in each iteration according to atomic selection criteria. Then support set and support matrix are updated, least square method is used to obtain an approximate solution, and the residual is updated finally. At last, the support Λ is obtained after the end of the iterations. The procedure of SwSOMP algorithm is shown in the Fig. 5.

The threshold of the atomic selection of the algorithm is defined as:

$$th = \alpha \ \max_i |g_i| \tag{7}$$

where g represents the correlation matrix obtained after inner product operation with observation matrix Φ and the residual. (7) finds out the largest correlated data in the matrix and uses its index in the matrix to find the corresponding atom in the column of Φ. The chosen atom is most relevant with the residual. α is known as weakness parameter and $\alpha \in (0, 1]$. The reason of such a threshold selection is that the obtained largest value of the inner product operation sometimes may not be the most relevant one. According to (7), the updated expression of the corresponding support set in SwSOMP is:

$$\Lambda_k = \Lambda_{k-1} \cup \{i : |g_i| \geq th\} \tag{8}$$

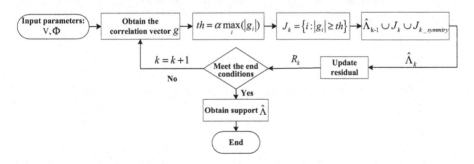

Fig. 5. Procedure of SwSOMP algorithm.

Although the StOMP algorithm does not rely on the signal sparsity, but there is a close relationship between the settings of selection threshold and observation matrix. Threshold obtained in [17] is only for random Gaussian matrix, thus limits the application of StOMP. On the other hand, the SwOMP algorithm has no strict requirement for the observation matrix, and does not need to know the signal sparsity, thus reduces the matching times, and improves the efficiency of the reconstruction. In the corresponding MMV problem of MWC, compared to the SMV problem handled in SwOMP, the one-dimensional sampling vector becomes two-dimensional sampling matrix Y. The MWC reconstruction process with SwSOMP algorithm is shown in Fig. 6.

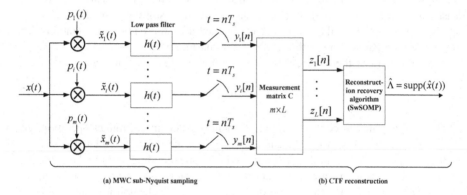

Fig. 6. MWC reconstruction process with SwSOMP.

The SwSOMP algorithm is a greedier approach for finding sparse solutions of underdetermined system. It selects several new elements in each iteration. The algorithm is described as Table 1. In Table 1, e_j is the unit column vector of the jth element that equals 1. The function of *diag* is to take the diagonal elements of the matrix. $\Lambda_{symmetry}$ is the symmetric support bands. $\Phi_{\hat{\Lambda}_k}$ is the sub-matrix of observation matrix, and $\Phi_{m \times L}$ corresponds to the support band $\hat{\Lambda}_k$.

Table 1. The reconstruction algorithm of support with SwSOMP

Input:	observation matrix $\Phi_{m \times L}$;
	mesurements $V_{m \times d}$;
	iterations *Iters*;
	the threshold of the residual ε_1;
	the threshold of the ratio of residual to estimated solution ε_2.

Initialization: the initial support of the signal band $\hat{\Lambda}_0 = \varnothing$, initial residual $R_0 = V$.

For $k = 1$ to *Iters*

Identification: $g = \left\| \sum_{j=1}^{d} \left| \Phi^H (R_{k-1} e_j) \right| \right\|_2 ./ \sqrt{diag(\Phi^H \Phi)}$.

$$J_k = \left\{ i : g_i \geq \alpha \max_i (g_i) \right\}.$$

$$\Lambda_{symmetry} = L + 1 - J_k.$$

Augmentation: $\hat{\Lambda}_k = \hat{\Lambda}_{k-1} \bigcup J_k \bigcup \Lambda_{symmetry}$, then obtain $\Phi_{\hat{\Lambda}_k}$.

Estimation: $\hat{\Theta}_k = \Phi_{\hat{\Lambda}_k}^{+} V$, and $\Phi_{\hat{\Lambda}_k}^{+} = (\Phi_{\hat{\Lambda}_k}^{H} \Phi_{\hat{\Lambda}_k})^{-1} \Phi_{\hat{\Lambda}_k}^{H}$.

Update the residual: $R_k = V - \Phi_{\hat{\Lambda}_k} \hat{\Theta}_k$.

if $\|R_k\|_2 \leq \varepsilon_1 \| \left(\|R_k\|_2 / \left\| \Phi_{\hat{\Lambda}_k} \hat{\Theta}_k \right\|_2 \leq \varepsilon_2 \right)$

      break;

   end

   $k = k + 1$;

End

Output: joint support set of the signal $\hat{\Lambda}_K$.

4   Simulation Results and Discussion

In our simulation, the correct support recovery of MWC refers to the criteria of the successful recovery in [8, 13], i.e., when the estimated support set $\hat{\Lambda}$ and real support set Λ meets the condition $\hat{\Lambda} \supseteq \Lambda$ and $\Phi_{\downarrow \hat{\Lambda}}$ is a full-rank matrix with columns. In order to validate the effectiveness of the proposed algorithm, signals with Sinc waveforms are used to carry out simulations, and we compare the performances of SOMP and SwSOMP algorithms on the support recovery under different number of bands, sampling channel numbers, and SNRs.

The sparse wideband analog signal with noise is generated by

$$x(t) = \sum_{i=1}^{N/2} \sqrt{E_i B_i} \mathrm{sinc}(B_i(t - \tau_i)) \cos(2\pi f_i(t - \tau_i)) + n(t) \qquad (9)$$

In (9), E_i, B_i, f_i and τ_i represent energy factor, bandwidth, carrier frequency and time offset of the produced ith signal, respectively. N represents the number of the symmetric bands. $n(t)$ is Gaussian white noise. The following procedure is repeated 500 times to calculate the percentage of correct support recovery.

(1) Generate the mixing signal $p_i(t)$ randomly;
(2) Generate the carrier frequency f_i in the interval $[-f_{nyq}/2, f_{nyq}/2]$ randomly;
(3) Generate new Sinc signal according to f_i;
(4) Using SOMP and SwSOMP respectively to estimate the support set and determine whether it is correctly recovered.

4.1 Impact of the Weakness Parameters on the Support Recovery

In the simulations, the parameters of the signal are $N = 6$ (3 pairs of symmetry), $E_i \in \{1, 2, 3\}$, $B_i \in \{50, 50, 50\}$ MHz, $\tau_i \in \{0.4, 0.7, 0.2\}$ µs, and carrier frequency f_i is randomly distributed in $[-f_{nyq}/2, f_{nyq}/2]$, and $f_{nyq} = 10$ GHz. The MWC sampling parameters are $L_0 = 97$, $L = 2L_0 + 1 = 195$, $f_s = f_p = f_{nyq}/L = 51.28$ MHz, and $m = \{15, 20, 25, 30, 35\}$. The reconstruction parameter is $\alpha \in (0, 1]$, and its initial value is 0.1 with 0.1 as the increasing interval, and here *Iters* = 10 because the iteration times of SWOMP has nothing to do with the signal sparsity. The $SNR = \{10, 20, 30\}$ dB. N is the band number of the signal, and m is the number of the MWC channels.

When α varies from 0.1 to 1, the percentage of correct support recovery is shown in Fig. 7 under the different number of channels m and different SNR. It can be seen from Fig. 7, SwSOMP algorithm performs best for the support recovery when $\alpha = 0.9$ for the effective channel number. Therefore, α is set to 0.9 in the following experiments.

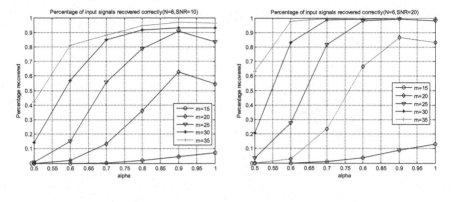

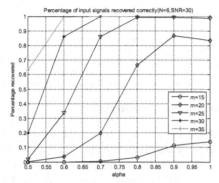

Fig. 7. Impact of α on the support recovery.

4.2 Impact of the Number of Sampling Channels on Support Recovery

The impact of the number of channels on the support recovery are investigated by using SOMP and SwSOMP algorithm. Figure 8 shows the percentages of correct recovery with SwSOMP and SOMP algorithms when the number of channels m is increased in the interval $[15, 40]$, and other parameters are the same as in Sect. 4.1. It can be seen from Fig. 8 that the performance of the recovery is improved by 12.4% when $m = 22$ with SwSOMP algorithm compared to that with SOMP algorithm. When $m = 25$, the percentage of correct recovery reaches 90% using SwSOMP algorithm, while the percentage of correct recovery can reach 90% when $m = 30$ using SOMP algorithm. Therefore, the SwSOMP algorithm can achieve higher reconstruction rate with less number of channels, which can save the hardware cost. Since the number of channels is directly related with the total sampling rate f_Σ ($f_\Sigma = mf_s$), SwSOMP algorithm can also reduce the system sampling rate by using less number of channels.

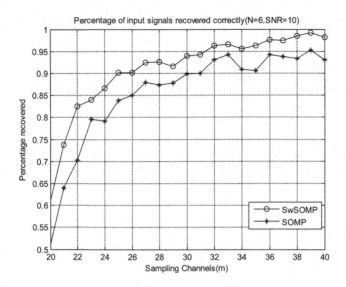

Fig. 8. Impact of the number of sampling channels on support recovery.

4.3 Impact of SNR on the Support Recovery

Now we consider about the impact of SNR on the support recovery by using two algorithms. The values of SNR are taken from the interval $[6, 20]$, $m = \{20, 25\}$, other parameters are the same as in Sect. 4.1. It can be seen from Fig. 9, when the number of channels is 25, SwSOMP algorithm achieves better recovery than SOMP algorithm in low SNR. When SNR = 6 dB and $m = 25$, the correct reconstruction with SwSOMP algorithm is improved 15% compared to that with SOMP algorithm. It can be seen that the correct reconstruction rate with SwSOMP algorithms is better than SOMP algorithm when the number of the channels is 20 and 25.

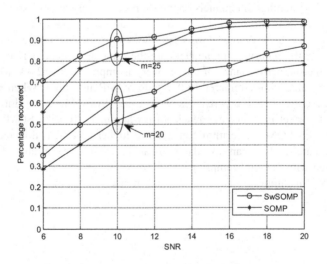

Fig. 9. Impact of SNR on the support recovery.

4.4   The Relationship Between the Number of Bands and the Support Recovery

The effects of number of frequency bands (i.e. signal sparsity) on the support recovery are investigated by using the two algorithms. The number of symmetric bands are taken from the interval $[2, 16]$. The relevant parameters setting are as follows, $SNR = 15$, $m = \{20, 25\}$, $E_i \in \{1, 2, 3, 4, 5, 6, 7, 8\}$, $\tau_i \in \{0.4, 0.7, 0.2, 0.9, 1.2, 1.5, 1.8, 2.1\}$ μs, and settings of other parameters are the same as in Sect. 4.1. It can be seen from the Fig. 10, when $N < 8$, the SwSOMP algorithm has a better performance. However, when $N = 8$, the performance has a sharp decline. It almost loses the ability of recovery when $N \geq 10$. It is mainly due to the fact that the signal can no longer be viewed as sparse signal under such circumstances. As a whole, SwSOMP algorithm performs better than SOMP algorithm under the cases of different number of bands.

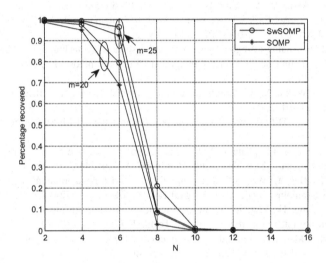

Fig. 10. The effects of number of signal bands on the support recovery.

5   Conclusion

Aiming to improve the performance of sensing multiband sparse signal in practice, this paper applies the SwSOMP algorithm to the CTF reconstruction block of MWC. The SwSOMP algorithm first obtains the largest matched inner-product value with the residual, which multiplies with the weakness parameter, and then obtains the atomic selection threshold. One or more atoms may be selected in each iteration, as a result of which the accuracy of matching the most relevant atoms is improved. Furthermore, the algorithm can reconstruct the support set of the signal blindly without knowing the signal sparsity in advance. By simulation experiments, we investigated the performance of SwSOMP algorithm in MWC and the impacting parameters. Compared with SOMP algorithm, SwSOMP algorithm has shown its advantages to be used in MWC for spectrum sensing on improving the percentage of correct recovery, reducing the number of required sampling channels, and decreasing the total sampling rate of the system.

Acknowledgments. This paper was supported by the National Natural Science Foundation of China (Grant No. 61561017), Open Sub-project of State Key Laboratory of Marine Resource Utilization in South China Sea (Grant No. 2016013B), Hainan Province Natural Science Foundation of China (Grant No. 617033), Doctoral Candidate Excellent Dissertation Cultivating Project of Hainan University, and Postgraduate Practice and Innovation Project of Hainan University. Oriented Project of State Key Laboratory of Marine Resource Utilization in South China Sea (Grant No. DX2017012).

References

1. Cohen, D., Akiva, A., Avraham, B., et al.: Centralized cooperative spectrum sensing from sub-nyquist samples for cognitive radios. In: IEEE International Conference on Communications (ICC), pp. 8–12. IEEE Press, London (2015)
2. Walden, R.H.: Analog-to-digital converters and associated IC technologies. In: Proceedings of IEEE Compound Semiconductor Integrated Circuits Symposium, pp. 1–2. IEEE Press, Monterey (2008)
3. Candes, E.J., Wakin, M.B.: An introduction to compressive sampling. IEEE Signal Process. Mag. **25**(2), 21–30 (2008)
4. Healy, D., Brady, D.J.: Compression at the physical interface. IEEE Signal Process. Mag. **25** (2), 67–71 (2008)
5. Tropp, J.A., Laska, J.N., Duarte, M.F., et al.: Beyond Nyquist: efficient sampling of sparse band-limited signals. IEEE Trans. Inf. Theory **56**(1), 520–544 (2010)
6. Harms, A., Bajwa, W.U., Calderbank, R.: A constrained random demodulator for sub-Nyquist sampling. IEEE Trans. Signal Process. **61**(3), 707–723 (2013)
7. Zhao, Y., Wang, H., Zhuang, X., et al.: Frequency domain sensing system using random modulation pre-integrator. IET Sci. Meas. Technol. **7**(3), 166–170 (2013)
8. Mishali, M., Eldar, Y.C.: From theory to practice: sub-Nyquist sampling of sparse wideband analog signals. IEEE J. Sel. Top. Sign. Process. **4**(2), 375–391 (2010)
9. Eldar, Y.C., Levi, R., Cohen, A.: Clutter removal in Sub-Nyquist radar. IEEE Signal Process. Lett. **22**(2), 177–181 (2015)
10. Lexa, M.A., Davies, M.E., Thompson, J.S.: Reconciling compressive sampling systems for spectrally sparse continuous-time signals. IEEE Trans. Signal Process. **60**(1), 155–171 (2012)
11. Shilian, Z., Xiaoniu, Y.: Wideband spectrum sensing in modulated wideband converter based cognitive radio system. In: 11th International Symposium on Communications and Information Technologies, pp. 114–119. IEEE Press, Hangzhou (2011)
12. Cohen, D., Akiva, A., Avraham, B., et al.: Distributed cooperative spectrum sensing from Sub-Nyquist samples for cognitive radios. In: 16th International Workshop on Signal Processing Advances in Wireless Communications (SPAWC), pp. 336–340. IEEE Press, Stockholm (2015)
13. Mishali, M., Eldar, Y.C.: Blind multiband signal reconstruction: compressed sensing for analog signals. IEEE Trans. Signal Process. **57**(3), 993–1009 (2009)
14. Tropp, J.A., Gilbert, A.C., Strauss, M.J.: Algorithms for simultaneous sparse approximation. Part I: greedy pursuit. Signal Process. **86**(3), 572–588 (2006)

15. Chen, J., Huo, X.: Theoretical results on sparse representations of multiple-measurement vectors. IEEE Trans. Signal Process. **54**(12), 4634–4643 (2006)
16. Blumensath, T., Davies, M.E.: Stagewise weak gradient pursuits. IEEE Trans. Signal Process. **57**(11), 4333–4346 (2009)
17. Donoho, D.L., Tsaig, Y., Drori, I., et al.: Sparse solution of underdetermined systems of linear equations by stagewise orthogonal matching pursuit. IEEE Trans. Inf. Theory **58**(2), 1094–1121 (2012)
18. Yang, P., Fan, Y., Huang, Z.T., et al.: Single channel spectrum sensing technique based on sub-Nyquist sampling. J. Natl. Univ. Defense Technol. **35**(4), 121–127 (2013)
19. Landau, H.J.: Necessary density conditions for sampling and interpolation of certain entire functions. Acta Math. **117**, 37–52 (1967)

Traffic Scheduling Algorithms for OFDM Based Radio Systems

Liang Li[1(✉)], Yirong Wang[2], Hao Zhang[3], Zhaoyan Qu[1],
Siyuan Zhang[1], Yu Zhang[1], and Xiongwen Zhao[1]

[1] North China Electric Power University, Beijing 102206, China
liliang2587@163.com, faszh@yeah.net
[2] Guodiantong Corporation, State Grid Information
and Telecommunications Group, Beijing 100070, China
wangyirong@sgitg.sgcc.com.cn
[3] State Grid Shandong Electric Power Corporation,
Economic and Technical Research Institute, Jinan 257000, Shandong, China

Abstract. In this paper, traffic scheduler for OFDM based radio system is studied in detail according to the traffic classes and Round-Robin (RR) series algorithms. The quantum, quanta and weights for the weighted deficit RR (WDRR) in downlink, and the basic quantity, quantity, weights for the weighted RR (WRR) in uplink are derived, respectively. The comprehensive traffic scheduler and algorithms are offered for the OFDM based radio systems.

Keywords: Traffic scheduling · OFDM · RR · DRR · WRR · WDRR

1 Introduction

Traffic scheduling algorithms for OFDM based radio systems, such as WLAN, LTE and WiMAX etc. is of importance in mobile wireless communication systems, and scheduling is also important in 5G networks [1, 2]. In the MAC layer, a very important issue is how to schedule the MAC protocol data units (MPDUs), and then complete to fill the created downlink (DL) and uplink (UL) frames. A large number of traffic scheduling algorithms for wireline networks have been proposed in the literature [3]. However, these algorithms cannot be directly applied to wireless networks because of fundamental differences between these two types of networks. For OFDM based scheduling algorithms, e.g. Round-Robin (RR), WRR (Weighted RR), DRR (Deficit RR), DWRR (Deficit-Weighted RR), and proportional fair (PF) etc. are introduced [3–9], the proportional fair scheduler is of interest in LTE and WiMAX. However, the main drawbacks of the scheduler are that the algorithms assume there are infinite packets to be transmitted at time zero and no packet arrivals, which is not a real-time scheduler. Moreover, the proportional fair scheduling algorithms are complicated to be implemented in practical applications. The criteria for selecting scheduling algorithms for OFDM based radio systems are: QoS requirement and simple to be implemented. Round-Robin scheduler can be unfair if different flows have different packet sizes. The DWRR and WRR are the improved Round-Robin family schedulers which can meet both of the criteria mentioned above. In this paper, the

© ICST Institute for Computer Sciences, Social Informatics and Telecommunications Engineering 2018
K. Long et al. (Eds.): 5GWN 2017, LNICST 211, pp. 160–169, 2018.
https://doi.org/10.1007/978-3-319-72823-0_16

explicit values of the weights for the DWRR and WRR are derived for the DL and UL. The basic quantum and quanta for the traffic in the DL, the basic quantity, the quantities of scheduled traffic for the UL are studied and offered. The priority scheduler, the DWRR and WRR scheduling algorithms, and the parameters introduced for using the algorithms have clear physical meanings and also easy to be implemented.

2 Traffic Scheduler for OFDM Based Radio Systems

The scheduler for OFDM based radio systems consists of five classes of traffic in common, namely, UGS (unsolicited grant), ertPS (extended real-time polling), rtPS (real-time polling), nrtPS (non-real-time polling), and BE (best effort) services. UGS can be a CBR (Constant Bit Rate) application, e.g. VoIP (Voice over IP) or video conference. ertPS/rtPS/nrtPS/BE can be, e.g. VoIP (Voice over IP) with VAD (Voice Activity Detection)/video and audio streaming (VAS)/FTP (File Transfer Protocol)/ web browsing http applications. The aforementioned traffic classes are for mobile WiMAX, but they can be also applied to WLAN and LTE and other OFDM based radio systems.

The diagram of the scheduler is shown in Fig. 1. We use the priority scheduler for the prioritized traffic. The priority orders of the traffic classes are: (i) MAC management & control messages, (H)ARQ [(hybrid) Automatic Repeat-reQuest)], (N)ACKs [(Non) Acknowledgements] and re-transmission, (ii) UGS, (iii) ertPS, (iv) rtPS, (v) nrtPS, and (vi) BE. We schedule (i) (ii) (iii) traffic when they are available, then the traffic in items (iv)–(vi) classes are scheduled by using DWRR (Deficit Weighted Round-Robin) and WRR (Weighted Round-Robin) algorithms for the DL and UL, respectively. In this paper, we take the joint traffic applications of the rtPS and nrtPS and give the weights and the scheduled traffic. The key reason is that both rtPS and nrtPS traffic have the

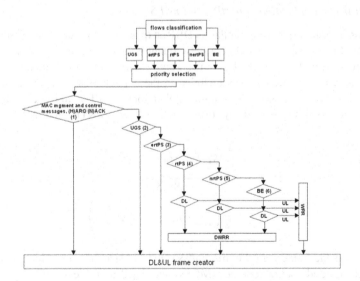

Fig. 1. Traffic scheduler for OFDM based radio systems.

bandwidth requirement. After scheduling items (i)–(iii) traffic, if not enough bandwidth as required in the rtPS and nrtPS traffic, then both should share the available bandwidth. Therefore, when implementing the DWRR and WRR, their weights and the quantity of scheduled traffic are independent. After this step, the rtPS traffic is scheduled first due to its sensitive to delay. The weights for the DWRR and WRR for the DL and UL, the basic quantum, quanta for the DL traffic, and the basic quantity, quantities of scheduled traffic for the UL will be studied in detail in Sects. 3 and 4.

3 The Basic Quantum, Quanta and Weights for the DL Traffic Applications

Assume that the rtPS, nrtPS, and BE traffic classes can have different applications, e.g. rtPS class can have video conference, streaming video, streaming audio, and broad-casting etc. These applications can have different minimum reserved traffic rates $\{MRTR_i\}_{rtPS}$, and maximum sustained traffic rates $\{MSTR_i\}_{rtPS}$, where i means a specific application for rtPS class, and {} means the assemble of applications. Same as in nrtPS traffic class, the applications (e.g. FTP, web browsing, P2P, large media downloads etc.) can have $\{MRTR_i\}_{nrtPS}$ and $\{MSTR_i\}_{nrtPS}$ as well. For the applications (e.g. small scale data transfer, web browsing etc.) in BE class, they're with $\{MSTR_i\}$ but without $\{MRTR_i\}$. In the following discussions, we merge the applications of the rtPS and nrtPS classes and denote their MRTR and MSTR assembles as $\{MRTR_i\}$ and $\{MSTR_i\}$ by removing the traffic classes in the subscripts. Within an application, all the flows (or users) have the same MSTR and MRTR, and the MSTR of an application is greater than its MRTR. The MSTR and MRTR can be the operation and management (O&M) parameters and will be decided by network operators or the agreed parameters between operators and the users.

(a) *Joint traffic applications for rtPS and nrtPS*

DWRR in principle is very similar as DRR, a quantum is needed first to schedule a traffic flow. In this paper, we define a basic quantum and weights for the applications when implementing the DWRR. Using the weights and defined basic quantum, we can get the quanta for the traffic flows included in the applications, and further to implement the DWRR algorithms. For joint applications of rtPS and nrtPS, the basic quantum (in slots) is defined by using both of the MRTR and MSTR of the applications.

$$Q_B = \frac{\sum_i (MSTR_i + MRTR_i)/2 * T_{frame}}{8 * S}$$
$$= \frac{1}{2}\left(\sum_i Q_{i,min} + \sum_i Q_{i,max}\right) \tag{1}$$

where T_{frame} is the frame period in ms, and S is the slot size in bytes, which depends on the modulation and coding schemes (MCSs) and listed in Table 1.

Table 1. Slot sizes for different MCSs in WiMAX

Modulation	QPSK	QPSK	16QAM	16QAM	64QAM	64QAM	64QAM
Coding rate	1/2	3/4	1/2	3/4	1/2	2/3	3/4
Slot size/Bytes	6	9	12	18	18	24	27

In (1), MSTR is in Kbps. The basic quantum is defined for a frame, and the traffic is scheduled frame by frame. $Q_{i,\min}$ and $Q_{i,\max}$ are the minimum and maximum quanta for application i and can be calculated as follows

$$Q_{i,\min} = \frac{MRTR_i * T_{\text{frame}}}{8 * S} \tag{2}$$

$$Q_{i,\max} = \frac{MSTR_i * T_{\text{frame}}}{8 * S} \tag{3}$$

The weights of DWRR can be defined and calculated as

$$W_i = \frac{MSTR_i}{\sum\limits_i MSTR_i} \tag{4}$$

In (4), the weights have been normalized. The larger the MSTR, the larger the weight for an application. The weight defined in (4) is fair regarding of each application. We define the quantum for application i as

$$Q_i = Q_B \cdot W_i \tag{5}$$

From (1), it's seen that if the application types and the corresponding MSTRs and MRTRs are pre-decided, the basic quantum Q_B is fixed. The quantum for a specific application i is defined and calculated as a product of the basic quantum and its weight, which means that when an application with a larger weight, then it can have larger quantum. Q_i shown in (5) generally is larger than $Q_{i,\min}$, but less than $Q_{i,\max}$, namely $Q_{i,\min} \le Q_i \le Q_{i,\max}$. Let's start prove this inequality. From (1), when using $Q_{i,\max}$ instead of $Q_{i,\min}$

$$\begin{aligned} Q_B &= \frac{1}{2}\left(\sum_i Q_{i,\min} + \sum_i Q_{i,\max}\right) \\ &\le \frac{1}{2}\left(\sum_i Q_{i,\max} + \sum_i Q_{i,\max}\right) = \sum_i Q_{i,\max} \end{aligned} \tag{6}$$

From (4), (5) and (6), we can get

$$
\begin{aligned}
Q_i = Q_B \cdot W_i &\leq \sum_i Q_{i,\max} \cdot \frac{MSTR_i}{\sum_i MSTR_i} \\
&= \frac{\sum_i MSTR_i \cdot T_{\text{frame}}}{8 * S} \cdot \frac{MSTR_i}{\sum_i MSTR_i} \\
&= \frac{MSTR_i \cdot T_{\text{frame}}}{8 * S} \\
&= Q_{i,\max}
\end{aligned}
\tag{7}
$$

which means that $Q_i \leq Q_{i,\max}$. In (1), when using $Q_{i,\min}$ instead of $Q_{i,\max}$, we can get

$$
\begin{aligned}
Q_B &= \frac{1}{2}\left(\sum_i Q_{i,\min} + \sum_i Q_{i,\max}\right) \\
&\geq \frac{1}{2}\left(\sum_i Q_{i,\min} + \sum_i Q_{i,\max}\right) = \sum_i Q_{i,\min}
\end{aligned}
\tag{8}
$$

From (4), (5) and (8), we can have

$$
\begin{aligned}
Q_i = Q_B \cdot W_i &\geq \sum_i Q_{i,\min} \cdot \frac{MSTR_i}{\sum_i MSTR_i} \\
&= \frac{\sum_i MRTR_i \cdot T_{\text{frame}}}{8 * S} \cdot \frac{MSTR_i}{\sum_i MSTR_i} = C
\end{aligned}
\tag{9}
$$

Because of $MRTR_i \leq MSTR_i$, and $\dfrac{\sum_i MRTR_i}{\sum_i MSTR_i} \leq 1$, from (9), we can get

$$
\begin{aligned}
C &\leq \frac{\sum_i MRTR_i}{\sum_i MSTR_i} \frac{MRTR_i \cdot T_{\text{frame}}}{8 * S} \\
&\leq \frac{MRTR_i \cdot T_{\text{frame}}}{8 * S} = Q_{i,\min}
\end{aligned}
\tag{10}
$$

From (9) and (10), $Q_i \geq C$ and $Q_{i,\min} \geq C$, which means that Q_i can be either larger or smaller than $Q_{i,\min}$. However, if the weight in (4) can also be defined by the MRTR (We expected that this can be happen due to when an application with larger MSTR, then it's with larger MRTR as well, so the weights can be kept as constant), then

$$W_i = \frac{MRTR_i}{\sum\limits_i MRTR_i} = \frac{MSTR_i}{\sum\limits_i MSTR_i} \tag{11}$$

In such a case, from (5), (8), and (11)

$$Q_i = Q_B \cdot W_i \geq \sum_i Q_{i,\min} \cdot \frac{MRTR_i}{\sum\limits_i MRTR_i} \tag{12}$$

$$= \frac{\sum\limits_i MRTR_i \cdot T_{\text{frame}}}{8 * S} \cdot \frac{MRTR_i}{\sum\limits_i MRTR_i}$$

$$= \frac{MRTR_i \cdot T_{\text{frame}}}{8 * S} = Q_{i,\min}$$

It means that $Q_i \geq Q_{i,\min}$, then the inequality of $Q_{i,\min} \leq Q_i \leq Q_{i,\max}$ keeps. The equal sign can be taken when $Q_{i,\min} = Q_{i,\max}$ by assuming that the MRTR is equal to the MSTR. From the results of the above discussions, we can get the following conclusions:

① The inequality $Q_{i,\min} \leq Q_i \leq Q_{i,\max}$ is true when the weight can be defined and calculated by Eq. (11).
② In this paper, we define the weight by Eq. (4), then the quantum Q_i can be either larger or smaller than $Q_{i,\min}$.

In conclusion ②, when $Q_i \leq Q_{i,\min}$, we should assign the quantum Q_i as $Q_{i,\min}$ so that it can guarantee the requirement of the minimum reserved traffic rate of the application. The general quantum can be expressed as follows when taking into consideration of (5)

$$Q_i = \begin{cases} Q_B \cdot W_i, & Q_{i\min} < Q_B \cdot W_i \\ Q_{i\min}, & \text{otherwise} \end{cases} \tag{13}$$

(b) *Demonstration examples*

For joint applications of the rtPS and nrtPS traffic classes, assume the {MSTR} are within 10 Kbps–2 Mbps, and we have six applications with {MSTR} = {10 100 300 600 1000 2000} in Kbps. The frame period is 5 ms, and the QPSK(1/2) MCS is applied with slot size of 6 bytes.

Example 1: Let MRTR = {5 50 150 300 500 1000}. For each application, the MRTR is taken as the half of its MSTR. The purpose is that the same weights can be remained by using either the MSTRs or the MRTRs defined in (11). The results are shown in Fig. 2(a) which shows that $Q_{i,\min} < Q_i < Q_{i,\max}$. The basic quantum Q_B in this case is about 313 slots (1878 bytes).

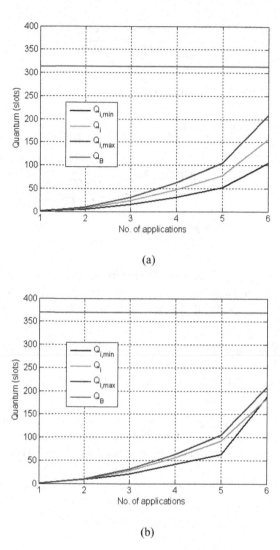

(a)

(b)

Fig. 2. Quanta relationships among $Q_{i,\min}$, Q_i and $Q_{i,\max}$. (a) The same weights can be defined by either the MSTRs or the MRTRs as in (11). (b) The weights are defined only by the MSTRs as in (4).

Example 2:   Let MRTR = {5 80 200 400 600 1800}. For every application, the MRTR is taken randomly a smaller value than the corresponding MSTR. The results are shown in Fig. 2(b). It shows that Q_i is less than $Q_{i,\max}$. However, it cannot always keep that $Q_{i,\min}$ is less than Q_i. The basic quantum Q_B is about 370 slots (2220 bytes).

(c) *Traffic applications for BE class*

For BE applications, there are no $\{MRTR_i\}$ QoS parameters, the basic quantum can be calculated by the $\{MSTR_i\}$. The basic quantum in (1) now is changed as

$$Q_B = \frac{\sum_i MSTR_i * T_{\text{frame}}}{8 * S} \tag{14}$$

Using (14) and the weights defined in (4). Then the quantum for application i is

$$Q_i = Q_B \cdot W_i = \frac{\sum_i MSTR_i * T_{\text{frame}}}{8 * S} * \frac{MSTR_i}{\sum_i MSTR_i}$$

$$= \frac{MSTR_i * T_{\text{frame}}}{8 * S} = Q_{i,\text{max}} \tag{15}$$

which means that the flows (or users) within an application, e.g. web browsing, will contend the available bandwidth. Once the contention is successful, then the traffic can be scheduled based on its MSTR. BE traffic has no QoS requirement and the MSTR is the only parameter available for scheduling the traffic. Figure 3 shows the flowchart of how the quanta and weights are defined and calculated in Sect. 3 as a summary.

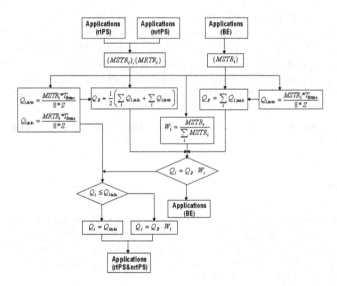

Fig. 3. The quanta and weights for the DL traffic applications using DWRR

4 Basic Quantity, Quantity of Scheduled Traffic and Weights for the UL Traffic

For the UL scheduling, the priority orders of the traffic classes are the same as in the DL. The difference is that in the UL we use WRR to schedule rtPS, nrtPS and BR traffic. For a specific application in the DL, the quantum Q_i and weight W_i are needed when implementing DWRR. While implementing the WRR algorithms in the UL, we need to know the weight and also the scheduled quantity of traffic for an application in a frame. For the WRR scheduling algorithm, it has no quantum concept, however we can use the scheduled quantity of traffic X instead of quantum Q in Sect. 3, then all the equations for the DL scheduling can be applied to the UL case. The specific replacements are as follows: we use the basic scheduled traffic X_B to replace of the basic quantum Q_B, use scheduled traffic X_i to replace the quantum Q_i, use the minimum and maximum scheduled traffic $X_{i,\min}$ and $X_{i,\max}$ for application i to replace the minimum and maximum quanta $Q_{i,\min}$ and $Q_{i,\max}$, respectively. Then we can get the corresponding formulas for scheduling the UL traffic as well for WRR.

5 Conclusion

The priority scheduler in this paper clearly shows that what kind of traffic class should be scheduled first for OFDM based radio systems. It can meet the QoS requirements both in throughput and delay. The DWRR and WRR algorithms are used further to schedule the rtPS, nrtPS and BE traffic in the DL and UL, respectively. DWRR and WRR have very clear physical meanings, they are straight forward algorithms to be implemented and are also very efficient scheduling algorithms. Moreover, we developed the basic quantum, quanta and weights for the applications in the DL by using WDRR as well as the basic quantity, the quantity of scheduled traffic, and the weights for the UL by using WRR for OFDM based system, such as mobile WiMAX.

Acknowledgement. This work is supported by the Department of Science and Technology, State Grid, China.

References

1. Zhang, H., Dong, Y., Cheng, J., Hossain, M., Leung, V.C.M.: Fronthauling for 5G LTE-U ultra dense cloud small cell networks. IEEE Wirel. Commun. **23**(6), 48–53 (2016)
2. Zhang, H., Liu, N., Chu, X., Long, K., Aghvami, A., Leung, V.: Network slicing based 5G and future mobile networks: mobility, resource management, and challenges. IEEE Commun. Mag. **55**(8), 138–145 (2017)
3. Zhang, H.: Service disciplines for guaranteed performance service in packet-switching networks. Proc. IEEE **83**, 1374–1396 (1995)
4. Fattah, H., Leung, C.: An overview of scheduling algorithms in Wireless Multimedia Networks. IEEE Wirel. Commun. **9**(5), 76–83 (2002)

5. Chaskar, H.M., Malhow, U.: Fair scheduling with tunable latency: a Round-Robin approach. IEEE/ACM Trans. Netw. **11**(4), 592–601 (2003)
6. Shreedhar, M., Varghese, G.: Efficient fair queuing using deficit Round-Robin. IEEE/ACM Trans. Netw. **4**(3), 375–385 (1996)
7. Cicconeti, C., et al.: Quality of service support in IEEE 802.16 networks. IEEE Netw. **20**(2), 50–55 (2006)
8. Sayenko, A., et al.: Ensuring the QoS requirements in 802.16 scheduling. In: Proceedings of the ACM/IEEE International Symposium on Modeling, Analysis and Simulation of Wireless and Mobile Systems (2006)
9. Veselinovic, N., Zhao, X., Casey, T., Nurmi, J.: Quality of experience in IEEE 802.16e. In: Proceedings of the 11th International Symposium on Wireless Personal Multimedia Communications (2008)
10. So-In, C., Jain, R., Tamimi, A.-K.: Scheduling in IEEE 802.16e mobile WiMAX networks: key issues and a survey. IEEE J. Sel. Areas Commun. **27**(2), 156–171 (2009)
11. Huang, C.-Y., Juan, H.-H., Lin, M.-S., Chang, C.-J.: Radio resource management of heterogeneous services in mobile WiMAX systems. IEEE Wirel. Commun. **14**(1), 20–26 (2007)
12. Esmailpour, A., Nasser, N.: Dynamic QoS-based bandwidth allocation framework for broadband wireless networks. IEEE Trans. Veh. Technol. **60**(6), 2690–2700 (2011)
13. Kang, X., Wang, W., Jaramillo, J.-J., Ying, L.: On the performance of largest-deficit-first for scheduling real-time traffic in wireless networks. IEEE/ACM Trans. Netw. **24**(1), 72–84 (2016)
14. Mehrjoo, M., Awad, M.K., Dianati, M., Shen, X.: Design of fair weights for heterogeneous traffic scheduling in multichannel wireless networks. IEEE Trans. Commun. **58**(10), 2892–2902 (2010)
15. Zheng, Q., Zheng, K., Zhang, H., Leung, V.C.M.: Delay-optimal virtualized radio resource scheduling in software-defined vehicular networks via stochastic learning. IEEE Trans. Veh. Technol. **65**(10), 7857–7867 (2016)
16. Ma, W., Zhang, H., Zheng, W., Wen, X., Lu, Z.: A novel QoS guaranteed cross-layer scheduling scheme for downlink multiuser OFDM systems. In: Proceedings of IEEE ICOEIS (2012)
17. Ma, W., Zhang, H., Wen, X., Zheng, W., Lu, Z.: Utility-based cross-layer multiple traffic scheduling for MU-OFDMA. Adv. Inf. Sci. Serv. Sci. **3**(8), 122–131 (2011)
18. Han, B., Zhao, S., Yang, B., Zhang, H., Chen, P., Yang, F.: Historical PMI based multi-user scheduling for FDD massive MIMO systems. In: Proceedings of the IEEE Vehicular Technology Conference (VTC), Nanjing, 15–18 May 2016
19. Zhang, H., Jiang, C., Beaulieu, N.C., Chu, X., Wen, X., Tao, M.: Resource allocation in spectrum-sharing OFDMA Femtocells with heterogeneous services. IEEE Trans. Commun. **62**(7), 2366–2377 (2014)
20. Zhang, H., Jiang, C., Mao, X., Chen, H.-H.: Interference-limit resource optimization in cognitive Femtocells with fairness and imperfect spectrum sensing. IEEE Trans. Veh. Technol. **65**(3), 1761–1771 (2016)

Coverage Performance in Cognitive Radio Networks with Self-sustained Secondary Transmitters

Xiaoshi Song$^{(\boxtimes)}$, Xiangbo Meng, Yuting Geng, Ning Ye, and Jun Liu

Northeastern University, Shenyang 110819, China
`songxiaoshi@cse.neu.edu.cn`

Abstract. In this paper, we investigate the opportunistic spectrum access (OSA) of self-sustained secondary transmitters (STs) in cognitive radio (CR) network to improve both the spectral efficiency and energy efficiency. Particularly, by utilizing energy harvesting, the STs are assumed to be able to collect and store ambient powers for data transmission. An energy harvesting based OSA protocol, namely the EH-PRA protocol, is considered, under which a ST is eventually allowed to launch the transmission only if its battery level is larger than the transmit power and the estimated interference perceived at the active primary receivers (PRs) is lower than a threshold N_{ra}. Given that the battery capacity of STs is infinite, we derive the transmission probability of STs. We then characterize the coverage performance of the CR network. Finally, simulation results are provided for the validation of our analysis.

Keywords: Cognitive radio network · Energy harvesting
Opportunistic spectrum access · Stochastic geometry
Transmission probabilty · Coverage probability · Spatial throughput

1 Introduction

Energy harvesting [1–5], widely believed as a promising solution of power generation for next generation wireless networks, has attracted tremendous interests over recent years. By utilizing energy harvesting as energy sources for wireless networks, the corresponding energy costs as well as the adverse effects to the environment can be significantly reduced. Further, the wireless networks powered by energy harvesting can be flexibly deployed without the need of power grid [6].

In addition to energy efficiency, spectral efficiency is another important issue in mobile networking. Particularly, how to effectively exploiting the underutilized spectrum resources in mobile networks is consider to be the key challenges for the enhancement of spectral efficiency [7,8]. To address this issue, technologies of CR [9,10] based OSA [11–13] are proposed such that the under-utilized spectrum of the primary network can be effectively reused by the secondary network.

© ICST Institute for Computer Sciences, Social Informatics and Telecommunications Engineering 2018
K. Long et al. (Eds.): 5GWN 2017, LNICST 211, pp. 170–181, 2018.
https://doi.org/10.1007/978-3-319-72823-0_17

In this paper, to simultaneously improve the energy efficiency and spectral efficiency of the mobile networks [15–17], the energy harvesting based OSA is investigated under the CR paradigm. Particularly, with energy harvesting, the STs become self-sustained. The energy efficiency of the CR network is thereby significantly improved. On the other hand, thanks to the OSA of STs, the spectral efficiency of the CR network can also be improved.

Energy harvesting powered CR networks has been widely studied over recent years [18–24]. In [18], assuming perfect spectrum sensing, the myopic spectrum access policy was studied to maximize the throughput of self-sustained STs powered by energy harvesting. Further, in [19,20], Park et $al.$ evaluated the effect of sensing error and temporal correlation of the primary traffic on the throughput of CR network. In [21], Pappas et $al.$ investigated the maximum stable throughput region for CR networks with self-sustained primary transmitters (PTs). In [22], Yin et $al.$ optimized the cooperation strategy of self-sustained STs to maximize the achievable throughput of the CR network. Further, in [23], with STs powered by energy harvesting, Yin et $al.$ proposed a generalized multi-slot spectrum sensing strategy which jointly optimized the save-ratio, sensing duration, sensing threshold as well as fusion rule to protect the primary transmissions. In [24], Chung et $al.$ maximized the average throughput of the energy harvesting powered CR network by optimizing the sensing duration and energy detectors sensing threshold of STs. It is worth noting that [18–24] do not consider the impact of the locations of PTs and STs on the performance of the CR network.

In this paper, different from [18–24], we consider the CR networks powered by energy harvesting with Poisson distributed PTs and STs. By applying energy harvesting, the STs are assumed to be able to collect and store ambient powers for data transmissions. Given sufficient energy stored in the batteries, the corresponding STs (denoted by eligible STs) are then allowed to launch the transmissions only if its estimated inference perceived at the active PRs is lower than a predefined threshold N_{ra}. We call this kind of OSA protocol as the energy harvesting based PRA protocol. Given that the battery capacity of STs is infinite, we derive the transmission probability for secondary network. We then characterize the coverage probability of the primary and secondary networks. Finally, simulation results are provided for the validation of our analysis.

2   System Model

We studied a CR network on $\mathbb{R}^2$. The PTs have higher priority for utilizing the spectrum, while the STs can only opportunistically access the spectrum by exploiting the spatial holes of the primary network. The PTs and STs are modeled by two independent HPPPs with intensities given by μ_0 and λ_0, respectively. For each PT, its associated PR is at a distance of d_p away in a random direction. Similarly, for each ST, its associated SR is at a distance of d_s away in a random direction. As such, the PRs and SRs also follow two independent HPPPs with their respective intensities given by μ_0 and λ_0.

With energy harvesting, the STs are assumed to be able to collect and store ambient powers for data transmissions. Particularly, the energy harvested by the

ST located at position $\mathbf{y} \in \mathbb{R}^2$ in the t-th time slot is modeled by a nonnegative random variable $Z_t^s(\mathbf{y})$ as

$$\mathbf{E}\big[Z_t^s(\mathbf{y})\big] = \nu_e^s, \tag{1}$$

$$\mathbf{Var}\big[Z_t^s(\mathbf{x})\big] = \delta_e^s. \tag{2}$$

Further, it is assumed that the PTs, PRs and SRs are powered by reliable energy sources.

For the primary network, the PTs independently access the spectrum with probability ρ_p [27]. For the secondary network, the EH-PRA protocol is applied, under which a ST is allowed to transmit only if the battery level is larger than the transmit power P_s and the spatial spectrum hole of the primary network is detected.

Let $\mathbf{B}_s$ denote the battery capacities for STs. Further, let P_p and P_s be the transmit powers of PTs and STs. Then, given $S_t^s(\mathbf{y})$ as the battery level of ST located at positions $\mathbf{y} \in \mathbb{R}^2$ in the t-th slot, it can be obtained that

$$S_t^s(\mathbf{y}) = \min\left(S_{t-1}^s(\mathbf{y}) + Z_t^s(\mathbf{y}) - P_s \cdot \mathcal{G}_t^s, \mathbf{B}_s\right), \tag{3}$$

where

$$\mathcal{G}_t^s = \mathbf{1}_{S_{t-1}^s(\mathbf{y}) \geq P_s} \cdot \mathbf{1}_{M_t^{ra}(\mathbf{y}) \leq N_{ra}}, \tag{4}$$

$\mathbf{1}_{\mathcal{A}}$ denotes the indicator function with respect to event $\mathcal{A}$.

For the primary network, the locations of active PTs/PRs follow a HPPP with density $\mu_p = \mu_0 p_p$. For the secondary network, under the energy harvesting based PRA protocol, the density of the point process formed by the active STs in the t-th time slot is given by $\mu_t^s = \eta_t^s \lambda_0$, where

$$\eta_t^s = \mathbb{E}\left[\mathbf{1}_{S_{t-1}^s(\mathbf{y}) \geq P_s} \cdot \mathbf{1}_{M_t^{ra}(\mathbf{y}) \leq N_{ra}}\right]. \tag{5}$$

The propagation channel is modeled by

$$l(r) = h \cdot r^{-\alpha}, \tag{6}$$

where h denotes the exponentially distributed small-scale Rayleigh fading with unit mean, r denotes the transmission distance, and α denotes the path-loss exponent [30]. The SIR targets for primary and secondary networks are denoted by θ_p and θ_s, respectively.

3   Transmission Probability with Infinite Battery Capacity

In this section, assuming infinite battery capacity for STs, we derive the corresponding transmission probabilities η^s. Particularly, based on (3), by letting $\mathbf{B} \to \infty$, it can be easily obtained that

$$S_t^s(\mathbf{y}) = S_{t-1}^s(\mathbf{y}) + Z_t^s(\mathbf{y}) - P_s \cdot \mathcal{G}_t^s. \tag{7}$$

where $\mathcal{G}_t^s$ are defined in (4), respectively. Then, based on (5), we characterize the transmission probability η^s of STs in the following theorems.

Theorem 1. *For CR network with self-sustained STs, assuming infinite battery capacity and under the EH-PRA protocol, η^s is given by*

$$\eta^s = \min\left(Q_{ra}, \frac{\nu_e^s}{P_s}\right). \tag{8}$$

where

$$Q_{ra} = \exp\left\{-2\pi\mu_p \frac{\Gamma(\frac{2}{\alpha})(\frac{P_p}{N_{ra}})^{\frac{2}{\alpha}}}{\alpha}\right\}. \tag{9}$$

Proof. The proof is omitted due to space limitation.

Remark 3.1. Based on Theorem 1, the intensity of the point process formed by active STs can be immediately obtained as

$$\lambda_s = \min\left(\lambda_0 Q_{ra}, \lambda_0 \frac{\nu_e^s}{P_s}\right). \tag{10}$$

4   Coverage Probability in Primary Network with Infinity Battery Capacity

4.1   Conditional Distribution of Active STs

To derive the coverage probability of primary transmission, we focus on a typical PR $\mathbf{R}_p$ at the origin with its associated PT $\mathbf{T}_p$ at a distance of d_p away in random direction. Then, by Slivnyak's theorem [35], it can be easily verified that the rest of the active PRs/PTs follow a HPPP with intensity μ_p. For the secondary network, we denote $\Phi_{ra}^{\mathbf{R}_p}(u)$ as the point process formed by the active STs on a circle of radius u centered at $\mathbf{R}_p$. Then, we derive the conditional distribution of the active STs in the following lemma.

Lemma 1. *For CR network with self-sustained STs, assuming infinite battery capacity and under the EH-PRA protocol, $\Phi_{ra}^{\mathbf{R}_p}(u)$ is isotropic with respect to $\mathbf{R}_p$ and its intensity $\lambda_{ra}^{\mathbf{R}_p}(u)$ is given by*

$$\lambda_{ra}^{\mathbf{R}_p}(u) = \min\left(\lambda_0 Q_{ra}\mathcal{P}(u), \lambda_0 \frac{\nu_e^s}{P_s}\right), \tag{11}$$

where

$$\mathcal{P}(u) = \left(1 - e^{-\frac{N_{ra}u^\alpha}{P_p}}\right). \tag{12}$$

Proof. The proof is omitted due to space limitation.

It is worth noting that under the EH-PRA protocol, $\Phi_{ra}^{\mathbf{R}_p}(u)$ does not follow a HPPP. Then, due to the fact that the higher order statistics of $\Phi_{ra}^{\mathbf{R}_p}(u)$ are intractable, the coverage performance of the primary network is difficult to be completely characterized. To address this issue, similar to [13, 36–39], we make the following approximation on $\Phi_{ra}^{\mathbf{R}_p}(u)$.

Assumption 1. $\Phi_{ra}^{\mathbf{R}_p}(u)$ *follows a HPPP with intensity given by* $\lambda_{ra}^{\mathbf{R}_p}(u)$.

Under Assumption 1, we then characterize the coverage performance of the primary network in the following subsection.

4.2   Coverage Probability with Energy Harvesting Based PRA Protocol

Theorem 2. *For CR network with self-sustained STs, under Assumption 1, the coverage probability of the primary network is given by*

$$\tau_p^{ra} = \exp\left\{ -\frac{2\pi^2}{\alpha \sin\left(\frac{2\pi}{\alpha}\right)} \theta_p^{\frac{2}{\alpha}} d_p^2 \mu_p \right\}$$

$$\times \exp\left\{ -2\pi\lambda_0 Q_{ra} \int_0^\zeta (1 - \varrho(u))\,\mathcal{P}(u)u\,du \right\} \tag{13}$$

$$\times \exp\left\{ -2\pi\lambda_0 \frac{\nu_e^s}{P_s} \int_\zeta^\infty (1 - \varrho(u))\,u\,du \right\}.$$

where

$$\zeta = \left(-\frac{P_p}{N_{ra}} \ln\left(1 - \frac{\eta^s}{Q_{ra}} \right) \right)^{\frac{1}{\alpha}},$$

and

$$\varrho(u) = \int_0^{\frac{N_{ra}u^\alpha}{P_p}} e^{-\frac{\theta_p P_s g u^{-\alpha}}{P_p d_p^{-\alpha}}} \times \frac{e^{-g}}{1 - e^{-\frac{N_{ra}u^\alpha}{P_p}}} dg.$$

Proof. See Appendix A.

5   Coverage Probability in Secondary Network with Infinity Battery Capacity

5.1   Conditional Distributions of Active PTs and STs

To derive the coverage probability of the secondary network, we focus on a typical SR $\mathbf{R}_s$ at the origin with its associated ST $\mathbf{T}_s$ at a distance of d_s away in random direction. Let $\Psi_{ra}^{\mathbf{T}_s}(r)$ be the point process formed by the active PRs on a circle of radius r centered at $\mathbf{T}_s$ under the ER-PRA protocol. Then, $\Psi_{ra}^{\mathbf{T}_s}(r)$ is characterized as follows.

Lemma 2. *For CR network with self-sustained STs, under the ER-PRA protocol,* $\Psi_{ra}^{\mathbf{T}_s}(r)$ *follows a HPPP with intensity* $\psi_{ra}^{\mathbf{T}_s}(r)$ *given by*

$$\psi_{ra}^{\mathbf{T}_s}(r) = \mu_0 \rho_p \mathcal{P}(r), \tag{14}$$

where

$$\mathcal{P}(r) = \left(1 - e^{-\frac{N_{ra}r^\alpha}{P_p}} \right). \tag{15}$$

Proof. Based on Lemma 5.1 in [13], it can be easily verified that $\Psi_{ra}^{\mathbf{T}_s}(r)$ follows a HPPP with density $\psi_{ra}^{\mathbf{T}_s}(r)$ as given by (14).

Let $\Upsilon_{ra}^{\mathbf{T}_s}(r)$ be the point process formed by the active PTs on a circle of radius r centered at $\mathbf{T}_s$ under the ER-PRA protocol. Then, with Lemma 2, $\Upsilon_{ra}^{\mathbf{T}_s}(r)$ is derived in the following lemma.

Lemma 3. *For CR network with self-sustained STs, under the ER-PRA protocol, $\Upsilon_{ra}^{\mathbf{T}_s}(r)$ follows a HPPP with intensity $\mu_{ra}^{\mathbf{T}_s}(r)$, which is upper-bounded by*

$$\mu_{ra}^{\mathbf{T}_s}(r) \leq \mu_0 \rho_p \mathcal{P}(r + d_p). \tag{16}$$

Proof. Based on Lemma 2, it can be easily verified that $\Upsilon_{ra}^{\mathbf{T}_s}(r)$ follows a HPPP and the upper bound on $\mu_{ra}^{\mathbf{T}_s}(r)$ is given by $\psi_{ra}^{\mathbf{T}_s}(r + d_p)$.

For the secondary network, we denote $\Phi_{ra}^{\mathbf{T}_s}(r)$ as the point process formed by the active STs on a circle of radius r centered at $\mathbf{T}_s$ under the energy harvesting based PRA protocol. Then, with Lemma 2, the conditional distribution of $\Phi_{ra}^{\mathbf{T}_s}(r)$ under the energy harvesting based PRA protocol is characterized as follows.

Lemma 4. *For an overlay CR network with self-sustained STs, under the energy harvesting based PRA protocol, conditioned on a typical SR at the origin, $\Phi_{ra}^{\mathbf{T}_s}(r)$ is isotropic around $\mathbf{T}_s$, and the corresponding density, denoted by $\lambda_{ra}^{\mathbf{T}_s}(r)$, is bounded by*

$$\mathcal{K} \leq \lambda_{ra}^{\mathbf{T}_s}(r) \leq \mathcal{D}, \tag{17}$$

where

$$\mathcal{D} = \min\left(\lambda_0 \beta_{ra},\ \lambda_0 \frac{\nu_e^s}{P_s}\right),$$

$$\mathcal{K} = \min\left(\lambda_0 Q_{ra},\ \lambda_0 \frac{\nu_e^s}{P_s}\right),$$

and

$$\beta_{ra} = \exp\left\{-2\pi \int_0^\infty e^{-\frac{N_{ra} r^\alpha}{P_p}} \mu_{ra}^{\mathbf{T}_s}(r) r\, dr\right\}. \tag{18}$$

Proof. Based on Lemma 5.3 in [13], (17) is immediately obtained. This thus completes the proof of Lemma 4.

It is worth noting that under the ER-PRA protocol, similar to the primary network case, $\Phi_{ra}^{\mathbf{T}_s}(r)$ or does not follow a HPPP. As such, the coverage probability of the secondary network under the energy harvesting based PRA protocol is difficult to be derived. To tackle this difficulty, we make the following approximation on $\Phi_{ra}^{\mathbf{T}_s}(r)$.

Assumption 2. *Under the ER-PRA protocol, $\Phi_{ra}^{\mathbf{T}_s}(r)$ follows a HPPP with intensity $\lambda_{ra}^{\mathbf{T}_s}(r)$.*

With Assumption 2, we then derive the coverage probability of the secondary network under the ER-PRA protocol in the following subsection.

5.2   Coverage Probability with PRA Protocol

Under the energy harvesting based PRA protocol, we denote $\Upsilon_{ra}^{\mathbf{R}_s}(u)$ as the point process formed by the active PTs on a circle of radius u centered at $\mathbf{R}_s$. Then, based on Lemma 3, it can be easily verified that $\Upsilon_{ra}^{\mathbf{R}_s}(u)$ does not follow a HPPP. Let $\mu_{ra}^{\mathbf{R}_s}(u)$ be the average density of $\Upsilon_{ra}^{\mathbf{R}_s}(u)$. Then, we characterize $\mu_{ra}^{\mathbf{R}_s}(u)$ in the following lemma.

Lemma 5. *Under the ER-PRA protocol, $\mu_{ra}^{\mathbf{R}_s}(u)$ is upper bounded by*

$$\mu_{ra}^{\mathbf{R}_s}(u) \leq \mu_0 \rho_p \mathcal{P}(u + d_p + d_s). \tag{19}$$

Proof. Based on Lemma 3, it can be easily verified that the highest density of $\mu_{ra}^{\mathbf{R}_s}(u)$ is $\mu_{ra}^{\mathbf{T}_s}(u + d_s)$.

Based on Lemma 5, we then derive the coverage probability of the secondary network under the ER-PRA protocol in the following theorem.

Theorem 3. *For CR network with self-sustained STs, under the ER-PRA protocol, based on Assumption 2, the coverage probability of the secondary network is lower-bounded by*

$$\tau_s^{ra} \geq \exp\left\{-\frac{2\pi^2}{\alpha \sin\left(\frac{2\pi}{\alpha}\right)}\theta_s^{\frac{2}{\alpha}}d_s^2 \mathcal{D}\right\}$$

$$\times \exp\left\{-2\pi\mu_0\rho_p \int_0^\infty \left(\frac{1 - e^{-\frac{N_{ra}(u+d_p+d_s)^\alpha}{P_p}}}{1 + \frac{P_s u^\alpha}{\theta_s P_p d_s^\alpha}}\right) u\, du\right\}, \tag{20}$$

Proof. By applying Lemmas 4 and 5, (20) is readily obtained.

6   Numerical Results

In this section, simulation results are provided to validate our analytical results. Throughout this section, unless specified otherwise, we set $\mu_p = 0.1$, $\lambda_0 = 0.1$, $P_p = 5$, $P_s = 2$, $d_p = d_s = 1$, $\theta_p = \theta_s = 3$, and $\alpha = 4$.

Figure 1 plots the analytical and simulation results on the transmission probability of the STs versus μ_p under the EH-PRA protocol. It is observed that the transmission probability of STs under the EH-PRA protocol are piecewise functions with μ_p, which are intuitively expected from Theorem 1. It is also observed that the simulation results are in accordance with our analytical results.

Figure 2 shows the coverage probability of primary network under the EH-PRA protocol. It is observed that the simulated values fit closely to our analytical values, which thereby shows that Assumption 1 is valid.

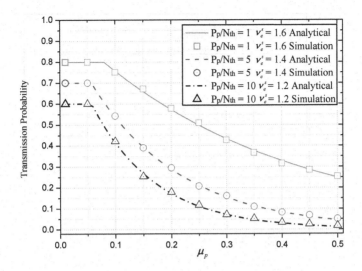

Fig. 1. Transmission probability of STs.

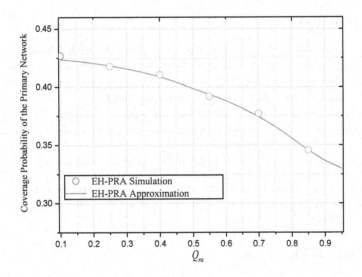

Fig. 2. Coverage probability of primary network.

Figure 3 plots the analytical and simulation results on the coverage probability of the secondary network under the EH-PRA protocol. As observed from Fig. 3, the lower bound on the coverage probability of the secondary network derived in Theorem 3 under Assumption 2 is effective.

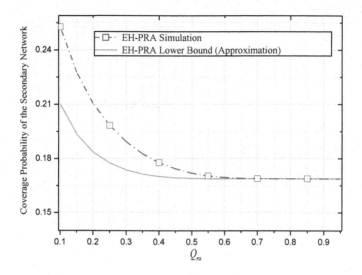

Fig. 3. Coverage probability of secondary network.

7   Conclusions

This paper has studied the performance of CR networks with self-sustained STs. Upon harvesting sufficient energy, the STs opportunistically access the spectrum if the estimated interference at the active PRs is lower than a predefined threshold N_{ra}. Assuming infinite battery capacity, we derived the transmission probability of STs. We then characterized the coverage probabilities of the primary and secondary networks. Simulation results are provided to validate our analysis.

Acknowledgements. This work is supported in part by Fundamental Research Funds for the Central Universities under Grant No. N150403001, the National Natural Science Foundation of China under Grant 61671141, U14331156, 1151002, 61401079, 61501038, and the Major Research Plan of the National Natural Science Foundation of China under Grant 91438117, 91538202.

A   Proof of Theorem 2

Proof. With the energy harvesting based PRA protocol, given a typical PR located at the origin, the received SIR is given by

$$\text{SIR}_p = \frac{P_p h_0 d_p^{-\alpha}}{\sum\limits_{i \in \Pi_p^t} P_p h_i |\mathbf{X}_i|^{-\alpha} + \sum\limits_{j \in \Pi_s^{ra}} P_s g_j |\mathbf{Y}_j|^{-\alpha}}. \tag{21}$$

It is worth noting that under the EH-PRA protocol, at the typical PR, the received interference from the j-th active ST is constrained as $P_s g_j |\mathbf{Y}_j|^{-\alpha} \leq \frac{P_s N_{ra}}{P_p}$. Therefore, under Assumption 1, the coverage probability of the primary network with the EH-PRA protocol is given by

$$\tau_p^{ra} = \Pr\left\{ \mathrm{SIR}_p \geq \theta_p \middle| g_j |\mathbf{Y}_j|^{-\alpha} \leq \frac{N_{ra}}{P_p} \right\}$$

$$= \Pr\left\{ \frac{P_p h_0 d_p^{-\alpha}}{\sum\limits_{i \in \Pi_p^t} P_p h_i |\mathbf{X}_i|^{-\alpha} + \sum\limits_{j \in \Pi_s^{ra}} P_s g_j |\mathbf{Y}_j|^{-\alpha}} \geq \theta_p \middle| g_j |\mathbf{Y}_j|^{-\alpha} \leq \frac{N_{ra}}{P_p} \right\}$$

$$= \mathbb{E}_{\mathbf{X}}\left[\prod_{i \in \Pi_p^t} \mathbb{E}_h\left[e^{-\frac{\theta_p h_i |\mathbf{X}_i|^{-\alpha}}{d_p^{-\alpha}}} \right] \right]$$

$$\times \mathbb{E}_{\mathbf{Y}}\left[\prod_{j \in \Pi_s^{ra}} \mathbb{E}_g\left[e^{-\frac{\theta_p P_s g_j |\mathbf{Y}_j|^{-\alpha}}{P_p d_p^{-\alpha}}} \middle| g_j \leq \frac{N_{ra} |\mathbf{Y}_j|^{\alpha}}{P_p} \right] \right] \tag{22}$$

$$\overset{(a)}{=} \exp\left\{ -\frac{2\pi^2}{\alpha \sin\left(\frac{2\pi}{\alpha}\right)} \mu_p \theta_p^{\frac{2}{\alpha}} d_p^2 \right\} \times \exp\left\{ -2\pi \int_0^\infty \mathcal{G} \cdot \lambda_{ra}^{\mathbf{R}}(u) u\, du \right\}$$

$$\overset{(b)}{=} \exp\left\{ -\frac{2\pi^2}{\alpha \sin\left(\frac{2\pi}{\alpha}\right)} \theta_p^{\frac{2}{\alpha}} d_p^2 \mu_p \right\} \times \exp\left\{ -2\pi \lambda_0 \frac{\nu_e^s}{P} \int_\zeta^\infty (1 - \varrho(u))\, u\, du \right\}$$

$$\times \exp\left\{ -2\pi \lambda_0 Q_{ra} \int_0^\zeta (1 - \varrho(u))\, \mathcal{P}(u) u\, du \right\}.$$

where (a) follows from the fact that the probability density function of g conditioned on $g \leq t$ is given by

$$f(g|g \leq t) = \frac{e^{-g}}{1 - e^{-t}},$$

$$\mathcal{G} = 1 - \int_0^{\frac{N_{ra} u^\alpha}{P_p}} e^{-\frac{\theta_p P_s g u^{-\alpha}}{P_p d_p^{-\alpha}}} \times \frac{e^{-g}}{1 - e^{-\frac{N_{ra} u^\alpha}{P_p}}} dg,$$

and (b) follows from (8). This thus completes the proof of Theorem 2.

References

1. Ellabban, O., Abu-Rub, H., Blaabjerg, F.: Renewable energy resources: current status, future prospects and their enabling technology. Renew. Sustain. Energy Rev. **39**, 748–764 (2014)
2. Hasan, Z., Boostanimehr, H., Bhargava, V.K.: Green cellular networks: a survey, some research issues and challenges. IEEE Commun. Surv. Tutor. **13**(4), 524–540 (2011)
3. Kwasinski, A., Kwasinski, A.: Increasing sustainability and resiliency of cellular network infrastructure by harvesting renewable energy. IEEE Commun. Mag. **53**(4), 110–116 (2015)
4. Gunduz, D., Stamatiou, K., Michelusi, N., Zorzi, M.: Designing intelligent energy harvesting communication systems. IEEE Commun. Mag. **52**(1), 210–216 (2014)

5. Han, T., Ansari, N.: Powering mobile networks with green energy. IEEE Wirel. Commun. **21**(1), 90–96 (2014)

6. Zhao, N., Yu, F.R., Leung, V.C.M.: Wireless energy harvesting in interference alignment networks. IEEE Commun. Mag. **53**(6), 72–78 (2015)

7. Zhang, H., Jiang, C., Beaulieu, N.C., Chu, X., Wen, X., Tao, M.: Resource allocation in spectrum-sharing OFDMA femtocells with heterogeneous services. IEEE Trans. Commun. **62**(7), 2366–2377 (2014)

8. Zhang, H., Chu, X., Guo, W., Wang, S.: Coexistence of Wi-Fi and heterogeneous small cell networks sharing unlicensed spectrum. IEEE Commun. Mag. **53**(3), 158–164 (2015)

9. Wang, B., Liu, K.J.R.: Advances in cognitive radio networks: a survey. IEEE J. Sel. Top. Sig. Process. **5**(1), 5–23 (2011)

10. Zeng, Y.H., Liang, Y.-C., Hoang, A.T., Zhang, R.: A review on spectrum sensing for cognitive radio: challenges and solutions. EURASIP J. Adv. Sig. Process. (2010). Article ID 381465

11. Zhao, Q., Sadler, B.: A survey of dynamic spectrum access. IEEE Sig. Process. Mag. **24**(3), 79–89 (2007)

12. Zhang, R., Liang, Y.C., Cui, S.: Dynamic resource allocation in cognitive radio networks. IEEE Sig. Process. Mag. **27**(3), 102–114 (2010)

13. Song, X., Yin, C., Liu, D., Zhang, R.: Spatial throughput characterization in cognitive radio networks with threshold-based opportunistic spectrum access. IEEE J. Sel. Areas Commun. **32**(11), 2190–2204 (2014)

14. Tandra, R., Mishra, S., Sahai, A.: What is a spectrum hole and what does it take to recognize one. Proc. IEEE **97**(5), 824–848 (2009)

15. Zhang, H., Jiang, C., Beaulieu, N., Chu, X., Wang, X., Quek, T.: Resource allocation for cognitive small cell networks: a cooperative bargaining game theoretic approach. IEEE Trans. Wirel. Wirel. Commun. **14**(6), 3481–3493 (2015)

16. Zhao, X., Yang, C., Yao, Y., Chen, Z., Xia, B.: Cognitive and cache-enabled D2D communications in cellular networks, November 2015. http://arxiv.org/abs/1509.04747

17. Wang, X., Chen, M., Taleb, T., Ksentini, A., Leung, V.C.M.: Cache in the air: exploiting content caching and delivery techniques for 5G systems. IEEE Commun. Mag. **52**(2), 131–39 (2014)

18. Park, S., Lee, S., Kim, B., Hong, D., Lee, J.: Energy-efficient opportunistic spectrum access in cognitive radio networks with energy harvesting. In: Proceedings of ACM International Conference on Cognitive Radio and Advanced Spectrum Management, Barcelona, Spain (2011)

19. Park, S., Kim, H., Hong, D.: Cognitive radio networks with energy harvesting. IEEE Trans. Wirel. Commun. **12**(3), 1386–1397 (2013)

20. Park, S., Hong, D.: Achievable throughput of energy harvesting cognitive radio networks. IEEE Trans. Wirel. Commun. **13**(2), 1010–1022 (2014)

21. Pappas, N., Jeon, J., Ephremides, A., Traganitis, A.: Optimal utilization of a cognitive shared channel with a rechargeable primary source node. In: Proceedings of IEEE Information Theory Workshop, Paraty, Brazil (2011)

22. Yin, S., Zhang, E., Qu, Z., Yin, L., Li, S.: Optimal cooperation strategy in cognitive radio systems with energy harvesting. IEEE Trans. Wirel. Commun. **13**(9), 4693–4707 (2014)

23. Yin, S., Qu, Z., Li, S.: Achievable throughput optimization in energy harvesting cognitive radio systems. IEEE J. Sel. Areas Commun. **33**(3), 407–422 (2015)

24. Chung, W., Park, S., Lim, S., Hong, D.: Spectrum sensing optimization for energy-harvesting cognitive radio systems. IEEE Trans. Wirel. Commun. **13**(5), 2601–2613 (2014)
25. Gallager, R.G.: Stochastic Processes Theory for Applications. Cambridge University Press, Cambridge (2013)
26. Baccelli, F., Błaszczyszyn, B.: Stochastic geometry and wireless networks. NOW Found. Trends Netw. (2010)
27. Baccelli, F., Błaszczyszyn, B., Mühlethaler, P.: Stochastic analysis of spatial and opportunistic aloha. IEEE J. Sel. Areas Commun. **27**(7), 1029–1046 (2009)
28. Kingman, J.F.C.: Poisson Processes. Oxford University Press, Oxford (1993)
29. Stoyan, D., Kendall, W., Mecke, J.: Stochastic Geometry and Its Applications, 2nd edn. Wiley, Chichester (1996)
30. Weber, S., Andrews, J., Jindal, N.: The effect of fading, channel inversion, and threshold scheduling on ad hoc networks. IEEE Trans. Inf. Theor. **53**(11), 4127–4149 (2007)
31. Vaze, R.: Transmission capacity of spectrum sharing ad hoc networks with multiple antennas. IEEE Trans. Wirel. Commun. **10**(7), 2334–2340 (2011)
32. Huang, K., Lau, V.K.N., Chen, Y.: Spectrum sharing between cellular and mobile ad hoc networks: transmission-capacity trade-off. IEEE J. Sel. Areas Commun. **27**(7), 1029–1046 (2009)
33. Lee, J., Andrews, J.G., Hong, D.: Spectrum-sharing transmission capacity. IEEE Trans. Wirel. Commun. **10**(9), 3053–3063 (2011)
34. Lee, J., Andrews, J.G., Hong, D.: The effect of interference cancellation on spectrum-sharing transmission capacity. In: Proceedings of IEEE Conference on Communications, Kyoto, Japan (2011)
35. Haenggi, M., Andrews, J., Baccelli, F., Dousse, O., Franceschetti, M.: Stochastic geometry and random graphs for the analysis and design of wireless networks. IEEE J. Sel. Areas Commun. **27**(7), 1029–1046 (2009)
36. Lee, C., Haenggi, M.: Interference and outage in Poisson cognitive networks. IEEE Trans. Wireless Commun. **11**(4), 1392–1401 (2012)
37. Nguyen, T., Baccelli, F.: A probabilistic model of carrier sensing based cognitive radio. In: Proceedings of IEEE Symposium on New Frontiers in Dynamic Spectrum Access Networks, Singapore, April 2010
38. Hasan, A., Andrews, J.: The guard zone in wireless ad hoc networks. IEEE Trans. Wirel. Commun. **6**(3), 897–906 (2007)
39. Lee, S.H., Huang, K.B., Zhang, R.: Opportunistic wireless energy harvesting in cognitive radio networks. IEEE Trans. Wirel. Commun. **12**(9), 4788–4799 (2013)
40. Huang, K.: Spatial throughput of mobile ad hoc networks with energy harvesting. IEEE Trans. Inf. Theor. **59**(11), 7597–7612 (2013)

A Novel Algorithm of UAV-Mounted Base Station Placement and Frequency Allocation

Xu Shen$^{(\boxtimes)}$, Zhiqing Wei, and Zhiyong Feng

Beijing University of Posts and Telecommunications, Beijing, China
xushen@bupt.edu.cn

Abstract. UAV equipped with base stations have recently gained significant development in cases of the terrestrial base station may not satisfy the communication command. Due to the agility and flexibility of UAV, it is used widely in disaster resilience, scenarios of unexpected and temporary events. Although UAV-mounted base station provides a fast coverage for the terrestrial users, the placement of UAVs is a problem to solve, especially the area to be covered is large which need multi-UAVs to cooperate to provide coverage. The difference of terrestrial and air-to-ground channel makes it a new coverage problem. Besides, the interference from UAVs requires a technique to manage the spectrum. In this paper, we formulate the placement of UAV as a 3-D problem, and then proposed a soft frequency reuse scheme to dynamically manage frequency resource. Simulations results show the algorithm is feasible to operate on resource-limited UAV platforms.

Keywords: Unmanned Aerial Vehicles
Mobile base station placement · User coverage · Soft Frequency Reuse
Spectrum allocation

1 Introduction

With the development of wireless communication, next generation wireless networks are in increasing demand of high reliability and availability. This adoption is motivated by the situations which are unexpected or temporary. Be in a disaster, the fixed infrastructure could be damaged by floods, earthquake or tsunamis, the wireless networks is destroyed, and could hinder the rescue works. Or in battlefields or rural area, it is impossible to invest an infrastructure. In these cases, utilizing unmanned aerial vehicles (UAVs) is a feasible solution for realizing wireless networks. However, how to place a UAV-mounted base station to benefit and assist the network on the ground at most is one of the biggest challenges.

Although there have been amounts of works on UAV-aided networks, the placement of UAV-mounted base station is still at its infancy. The authors in [1] uses p UAVs to serve terrestrial users, which the capacity of the each UAV is constrained. They use K-means to partition the terrestrial users to be served by

© ICST Institute for Computer Sciences, Social Informatics and Telecommunications Engineering 2018
K. Long et al. (Eds.): 5GWN 2017, LNICST 211, pp. 182–193, 2018.
https://doi.org/10.1007/978-3-319-72823-0_18

the UAVs, the other unsupported users are served by fixed base stations. In [2], an algorithm of offload as many users as possible from the station on the ground is proposed, the authors study the placement of a single UAV-mounted base station. An algorithm with successive placement along a spiral path towards the center is presented [3]. In [4,5], the positioning of UAVs as relays is discussed, but the placement of UAV is on a line which is not in accordance with practical coverage. The Interference of UAV-mounted base station with underlaid D2D network is further investigated in [6]. However, some of the works don't cover all the users to be served on the ground, some of the work consists of only one UAV-mounted base station, there are not multi-UAVs to cooperate to cover the users. Besides, the works doesn't determine the height of UAV-mounted base station. Since the character of the air-to-ground channel is different from the terrestrial channel, solve the problem of placement of UAV must take the height parameter into consideration.

After the placement of UAV-mounted base stations is determined, we should consider the spectrum allocation of UAV-mounted base stations. The frequency resource is limited, in order to satisfy data rate demand, it should adopt frequency reuse scheme in each cell. This will cause inter-cell interference of the UAV cells. Especially the UAV is deployed according to the nodes on the ground, if the distribution of the nodes is inhomogenous, the coverage of adjacent UAV-mounted base station may overlap, it makes the interference more severe. Soft frequency reuse (SFR) is a widely used scheme to deal with inter-cell interference in conventional terrestrial cells. In this paper, we design a similar scheme to allocate the frequency resource.

SFR is a spectrum reuse method which is used for improving spectrum efficiency and reduce interference in LTE networks in [7]. The frequency is divided into groups for center region and edge region. Meanwhile, power control is used with SFR. The authors in [8] divide the bandwidth into two segments, allocating them to center region and edge region respectively with different power level. In [9], a multi-level SFR is proposed, the spectrum is divided into three segment and the adjacent cells rotate the use of these segment to reduce interference.

To the best of our knowledge, the works presented have not considered UAV cells frequency reuse. In this paper, we first place the UAV-mounted base stations according to the distribution of nodes on ground to cover all nodes. Then we choose an optimal height of each UAV-mounted base station due to the implicit relation of coverage radius and height which can be seen from the air-to-ground channel. Sine the 3-D placement of UAV is solved, we determine the spectrum allocation and power control of UAV stations with interference limitation among neighboring cells. Diverging from with resource scheduling beforehand, the algorithm we proposed is dynamically allocating spectrum and adjust according to network traffic distribution.

The rest of the paper is organized as follows. In Sect. 2, we describe the system model and discuss the air-to-ground channel in detail. Then we present the two main problems, the placement of UAV-mounted base station and the frequency reuse pattern. Next, in Sect. 3, the algorithm of the solution to the problem mentioned above is proposed. In Sect. 4, numerical simulations to validate our algorithms is presented. Finally, Sect. 5 concludes this paper.

2   System Model

UAV-mounted mobile base station is used to provide coverage for users in terrestrial network without fixed infrastructure, achieve the connectivity of the network in disasters and relay for the nodes in remote area. UAV-mounted base station differs from other base stations. In contrary of the macro cell base stations that used in cellular networks, the base stations on UAV platform can adjust its position according to the distribution of users on the horizontal plane. Besides, UAV platform differs from other High Altitude Platforms reaching the upper layers of the stratosphere, UAV platforms are more easily to employ.

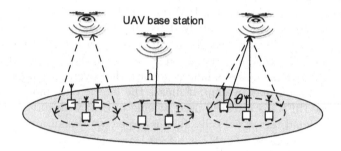

Fig. 1. A wireless network with UAV-mounted base stations

2.1   Channel Model

We consider a wireless network with K users on the ground, denoted by $\mathcal{K} = \{1, 2, \cdots K\}$. Assuming that the location information of these nodes is known by UAV-mounted base stations. Each of the known locations is given by two-dimensional coordinates (x_i, y_i). The characteristic of UAV-mounted base station is utilizing air-to-ground link. Air-to-ground channel distinguishes from the terrestrial channel such as Rayleigh channel or Rice channel. Although different literature use these channels to study air-to-ground channel widely, it is not in accordance with practical propagation. This is due to the high probability of Line-of-Sight (LoS) propagation in the air-to-ground channel. Some works on characterizing the air-to-ground channel are available. One of the most complete models is derived in [10] with the help of the channel proposed by ITU [11], which is based on classifying the signal arriving at the receivers into two propagation groups statistically. We adopt this channel in this paper.

The occurrence of two dominant propagation groups LoS group and NLoS group correspond to the LoS condition. The probability of having LoS users depend on the elevation angle θ, as Fig. 1 shows. For the ith user on the ground located at (x_i, y_i), the horizontal distance r_i between a UAV at (x_U, y_U) is $\sqrt{(x_i - x_U)^2 + (y_i - y_U)^2}$. For a UAV at the altitude h, the angle between user i with it is calculated as $\theta = \arctan(h/r_i)$. According to [10], the LoS probability is given by

$$P_{LoS} = \frac{1}{1 + a \exp(-b[\theta - a])}, \tag{1}$$

where a and b are constant parameters depends on the environment such as suburban, urban, etc. the probability of NLoS is $P_{NLoS} = 1 - P_{LoS}$.

Assuming the transmitter and receiver antennas is isotropic, the expectation of path loss between a UAV-mounted base station and a terrestrial user is denoted as PL, $PL = P_{LoS} \times \mathrm{PL}_{LoS} + P_{NLoS} \times \mathrm{PL}_{NLoS}$, where PL_{LoS} and PL_{NLoS} representing the path loss of different signal groups in air-to-ground link. According to [10], PL measured in db is

$$PL = \frac{A}{1 + a \exp(-b[\theta - a])} + 10 \log(h^2 + r^2) + B, \tag{2}$$

where $A = \eta_{LoS} - \eta_{NLoS}$, η_{LoS} and η_{NLoS} are the losses corresponding to the LoS and NLoS groups in db, $B = 20 \log f + 20 \log(4\pi/c) + \eta_{NLoS}$, f is the carrier frequency.

2.2   UAV-Mounted Base Station Placement

We aim to deploy UAV-mounted base stations so that a terrestrial user is covered by at least one UAV station. Denote the set of UAV-mounted base stations by $\mathcal{M} = \{1, 2, \cdots M\}$. The placement of UAV-mounted base stations is a comprehensive problem which is different from the cell base station on the ground. This is because that determine the location of the UAV-mounted base station is actually choosing the projection coordinates on the horizontal plane (x_j, y_j), $j \in \mathcal{M}$, and altitude of UAV h_j in addition.

The position information of users to be served by a UAV-mounted base station is known, so the area to be covered is determined. However, the coverage area of a UAV is unknown in advance, this is because that UAV-mounted base station coverage radius depends on the height of a UAV, which is to be determined. Due to the characteristic of air-to-ground, the coverage radius of a UAV-mounted base station is not a monotonic function of its height, which can be seen from the path loss expression (2).

Unlike terrestrial cells such as macro or micro cells which are fixed, UAV-mounted base station adjusts the position to serve users on the ground in accordance with the distribution of users changing. So the position of UAV-mounted base station that can bring the network maximum coverage is to be found to accommodate the mobility of user on the ground.

Besides, the bandwidth of a UAV is limited, which means the data rate of a UAV is limited. A UAV-mounted base station can only serve some users on the ground with limited resources. We assume that the total available bandwidth of a

UAV is divided into L different links, which means it can serve L terrestrial users at the same time. In order to cover all the users on the ground, it needs multi-UAVs to cooperate to provide coverage for the area. So the amount of UAV-mounted base stations and the placement of the UAVs need to be determined jointly.

2.3 Frequency Reuse Pattern Allocation

We consider downlink transmission in UAV aided networks since downlink traffic load is larger than uplink. We assume UAV-mounted base station adopts Frequency Division Duplexing (FDD), and the total bandwidth is divided into four segments (i.e., F_1, F_2, F_3, F_4) which are to be assigned to different part of the area as Fig. 2 shows. The distribution of nodes in horizontal plane is not homogenous, some areas where users have heavy traffic to transmit forming hot-spot areas. UAV-mounted base stations to serve users on the ground are more dense in these areas intuitively and vice versa. Due to the mobility of UAV-mounted base station, the UAV-mounted base stations are distributed in accordance with the distribution of traffic on the ground, the UAVs are evenly distributed, so sometimes the UAV cells overlap in edge. In order to decrease interference of adjacent UAV cells, we adopt SFR scheme to allocate different spectrum in cell edges. According to the four-color problem of graph theory, in order to allocate different spectrum in different UAV cells, we need four frequency segments. We propose a novel soft frequency reuse scheme to allocate the spectrum, which means distributing the spectrum according to 4-color frequency reuse pattern. First, a frequency segment is assigned to the edge of the area covered by a UAV-mounted base station, then we use a SINR-based criterion to allocate the other three segments, more details of the algorithm can be found in Sect. 3.

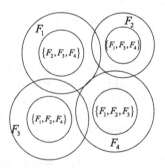

Fig. 2. Frequency reuse examples for 4-color frequency reuse pattern

3   UAV Placement and Resource Allocation Algorithm

In this section, we propose an efficient algorithm to solve UAV-mounted base stations placement problem to provide coverage for all users on the ground in the condition that the users a UAV-mounted base station can serve are limited. Then we propose a practical SFR scheme, to allocate frequency resources for planning UAV cells purpose.

3.1   UAV-Mounted Base Station Placement

The main idea of the UAV-mounted base station placement algorithm is to use divide-and-conquer which is a recursive technique. Due to the resources a UAV-mounted base station has are limited, including spectrum, the storage capacity and the battery, a UAV-mounted base station can only serve a certain number of users on the ground. As noted earlier in this paper, we assume that the spectrum a station holds is divided into L sub-carrier, namely, a UAV-mounted base station can serve at most L users at the same time. The coverage problem is formulated to use M UAV base stations to provide coverage for all the ground users cooperatively.

Since the locations of users on the ground are known to UAV-mounted base stations, first, we place a UAV-mounted base station in the middle of the area to be covered. The UAV-mounted base station detects the amount of the users, if the number of users is larger than L, then we add the number of UAV-mounted base stations to provide service for the target area. We divide the target area into four equal parts. This is because that a square is more accordant with the coverage circle a UAV-mounted base station projection on the ground. A square area is isotropic in four directions and can jointly cover a destination area seamlessly and reduce the occurrence of outlier users to be served.

Then place UAV-mounted base stations in the center of every newly divided square region, UAV-mounted base stations detect whether the nodes in the square area it guarantee to cover is provided coverage. If the amount of the terrestrial users is still larger than a UAV-mounted base station can serve at the same time, L, then repeat the steps above until the number of nodes a UAV serve is small or equal to L. After a UAV-mounted base station is placed, namely a sub-square area is covered by a station, the adjacent UAVs repeat this algorithm to place the next UAV-mounted base station until all users are covered. As a result, the process of determining the placement of UAV-mounted base station uses the recursive technique, which divides the area continuously. We therefore name our proposed algorithm as the divide-and-conquer algorithm, which is summarized in Algorithm 1.

Then the radius of each UAV-mounted base station cell can be calculated. It equals the distance between the projection point of the UAV and the node which is farthest to it. This base station placement method is simple and easy to operate on the UAV platform and saves computational resources for UAV which only has small storage to compute. For our divide-and-conquer algorithm, the complexity is relatively low, reducing energy consumption benefits for UAV platform of limited battery. Besides, this algorithm considers the inhomogenous distribution of the traffic on the ground, it places UAV-mounted base stations according to the distributions of the terrestrial under their conditions where the number of users a UAV-mounted base station can serve is limited. In hot spots,

---

Algorithm 1. Divide-and-Conquer Placement Algorithm

Input: terrestrial users location information, (x_i, y_i), $i \in \mathcal{K}$
Output: UAV-mounted base stations set $\mathcal{M}$, with locations (x_j, y_j), $i \in \mathcal{M}$
    Initialization: uncovered terrestrial users location; $\mathcal{M} = \emptyset$, $m = 1$.
1: **while** the number of users served by a UAV-mounted base station $> L$ **do**
2:    Place a UAV-mounted base station in the center of the area to be covered, and detect the amount of users on the ground.
3:    If the amount of users to be served is larger than L, divide the area into four equals part, repeat step 2.
4:    Else $\mathcal{M} \leftarrow \mathcal{M} \cup \{m\}$, $m \leftarrow m + 1$.
5: **end while**

---

the UAV-mounted base stations are more than in the area a relatively small number of users locate in.

3.2 Frequency Reuse Pattern Allocation

In this section, we address the issue of spectrum allocation and power control of UAV-mounted base stations. In order to solve these problems, we fist should determine the height of each UAV-mounted base station. This is because that the coverage radius of a UAV-mounted base station does not only depend on the transmitting power but also the height of a UAV. In the case that coverage radius of a UAV cell is determined, the height has an influence on the transmitting power and the interference of each other.

As described above, the air-to-ground link is different to the terrestrial channel. The power of signal is not a monotone decreasing function of distance but depends on elevation angle θ. To illustrate this, we plot the radius-altitude curve according to expression (2). We assume a path loss threshold, when path loss exceeds this threshold, the user is out of coverage of the UAV-mounted base station. As plots in Fig. 3, as to the same path loss, the UAV-mounted base station at different height corresponds to different coverage radius. An inflection point can be seen on each curve, which means for a given path loss, there is an optimum height can provide a maximum coverage. The optimum height means an optimum elevation angle θ. However, the path loss equation is implicit, there is not an explicit function of the coverage radius R with elevation θ. We find this optimum point by setting the derivative of the radius R with respect to elevation angle θ equals to zero, which yields as follows:

$$\frac{20}{\ln(10)} \tan(\theta_{OPT}) + \frac{abA \exp(-b[\theta_{OPT} - a])}{[aexp(-b[\theta_{OPT} - a]) + 1]^2} = 0. \tag{3}$$

From Eq. (3), we can know that the optimum elevation angle θ only depends on parameters a, b, and A conditioning on environments (i.e. urban, suburban). This also explains the straight line in Fig. 3, in the same environment the optimum θ is at the same value. We use the optimum θ to determine the height of the UAV.

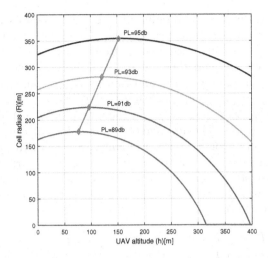

Fig. 3. Cell radius vs. UAV-mounted base station altitude for different pathloss in an urban environment

Since the radius and height of a UAV-mounted base station are determined, the issue of spectrum allocation and power control is to be solved. Here we adopt a soft frequency reuse scheme to allocate spectrum. The coverage area of a UAV-mounted base station is divided into cell edge and cell centers as depicts in Fig. 4 We set a guard band at the cell edge of each UAV. In order to make any two adjacent cells have different spectrum at the edge, the frequency is divided into four segments according to the four-color problem of graph theory. Four spectrum F_1, F_2, F_3, F_4 are available for a UAV-mounted base station.

First, a UAV-mounted base station can sense the guard frequency band which the UAV-mounted base station adjacent to it use. According to the graph coloring problem, the UAV-mounted base station selects a segment different from the segment adjacent cells use, then allocate to its edge region. The other segment is allocated to its center region. We propose an algorithm to design the transmitting power and radius of different frequency segment according to the power of signal and interference.

The useful signal a terrestrial user receives should be larger than a threshold that the signal can be accepted correctly, this yields follows:

$$10\log(P_1) - PL \geq 10log(P_{RXth}),\qquad(4)$$

where P_{TX} and P_{RXth} are transmitting power of a UAV-mounted base station and the receiving signal power of a user on the ground. The formulation is evaluated in db. The signal received at the user in edge region is the smallest due to its largest path loss, in order to satisfy the condition in inequation (4), the power of guard segment should be larger than or equal to the P_{TX} derived when using the path loss of the very point at the edge of the UAV-mounted base station coverage area.

For determining the power and radius of other segments, we take two adjacent UAV cells as an example. As shown in Fig. 4, point p_1 and point p_2 are the projection point of UAV-mounted base stations, their coordinates are (x_1, y_1) and (x_2, y_2) respectively, and their guard segment is F_1 and F_2. We assume a point p_3 on the line between p_1 and point p_2, the coordinate of which is $(x_1 + t(x_2 - x_1), y_1 + t(y_2 - y_1))$, where $t \in (0, 1)$.

In cell 1, segment F_1 is used in edge region, and in cell 2, the same segment is used in center region. The interference caused by adjacent cell should be restricted to guarantee communication quality, we set a SIR threshold of the same spectrum segment. We assume point p_3 is the very furthest node to the UAV-mounted base station in cell 2 using segment F_1, so the distance between p_3 and p_2 is the coverage radius of segment F_1 in cell 2. In order to satisfy the condition above, we have

$$10 \log(P_2) - PL_{23} \geq 10 log(P_{RXth}),$$
$$10 \log(P_2) - PL_{23} - (10 \log(P_1) - PL_{13}) \geq 10 \log(SIR_{th}), \tag{5}$$

where PL_{ij} representing the path loss between node i, j, and P_i denoting the transmitting power of node i. Substituting the path loss equation, the coordinates of every point, the power and radius of different spectrum segment can be derived.

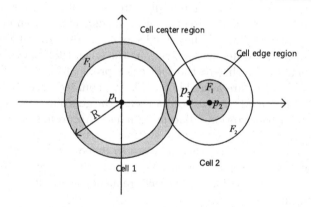

Fig. 4. Single adjacent interfering cell model

4   Numerical Results

Figure 5 illustrates a result of our algorithm in a snapshot, we apply our divide-and-conquer placement algorithm to cover 200 users on the ground. The users are randomly and independently distribute in a square area of $2.6 \, \text{km}^2$. The simulation parameter of the air-to-ground channels presented in Table 1 are derived from [2,10]. It is assumed that a UAV-mounted base station can serve at most 40 users at the same time. After dividing the area into small squares, the position

Table 1. Simulation parameters

Description	Parameter	Value
System frequency	f_c	2.5 GHz
Difference of path loss between two propagation groups	A	-20
Parameter for dense urban environment	a	4.88
Parameter for dense urban environment	b	0.43

of a UAV-mounted base station is determined, the radius is then calculated and the optimum height of UAVs is derived by solving the 3-D placement problem using the algorithm proposed above. Note that the UAV cells size is not equivalent, this is due to the distribution of nodes on the ground. Each terrestrial user is supplied coverage by a UAV-mounted base station. Some nodes are on the edge of the UAV cell, and some area isn't covered by a UAV-mounted base station, this means that the transmitting power of UAV is not wasted, and the algorithm is efficient.

Figure 6 shows the frequency allocation using the algorithm we propose. We choose a snapshot of the wireless networks. In this figure, frequency segments are noted next to the edge of circles with different radius, which means within the coverage circle, this segment is available. The coverage radius of different frequency segments are unequal, it depends on the interference of the same segment used in UAV cells surrounding it. We can further see that edge region of the UAV cells is separated by guard segment which decreases the interference from adjacent cells. The other frequency segment is allocated in the center area of the UAV cell to reuse to elevate spectrum efficiency. This algorithm is flexible and simple to operate on UAV platform which is power and capacity constrained.

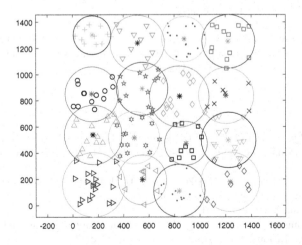

Fig. 5. Placement of UAV-mounted base stations to cover all users on the ground

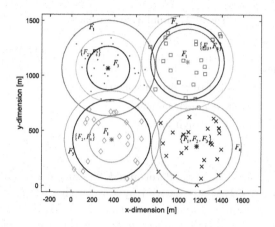

Fig. 6. Frequency allocation scheme in each UAV cells

5   Conclusion

In this paper, we have proposed a novel UAV-mounted base station placement solution for coverage problem, termed as divide-and-conquer algorithm. The proposed algorithm is low-complexity and occupies small storage, it is suitable to operate on UAV which is battery and storage constrained platform. Using this algorithm the UAV-mounted base stations which can serve a fixed number of users at the same time can cooperate to cover all terrestrial users. In addition, we have presented a soft frequency reuse scheme, the allocations of transmit power and spectrum segment are not fixed prior, it is dynamically deployed according to the position and interference of adjacent UAV cells. The algorithm achieves a good performance. We believe that these algorithms can provide guidelines for UAV-mounted base station design.

Acknowledgment. This work was supported by the National Natural Science Foundation of China (No. 61601055, No. 61631003), and the National Science Fund for Distinguished Young Scholars (No. 61525101).

References

1. Boris, G., Jacek, K., Luiz, A.D.: Deployment of UAV-mounted access points according to spatial user locations in two-tier cellular networks. In: 2016 Wireless Days, pp. 1–5 (2016)
2. Yaliniz, R.I.B., Elkeyi, A., Yanikomeroglu, H.: Efficient 3-D placement of an aerial base station in next generation cellular networks. In: IEEE International Conference on Communications (2016)
3. Lyu, J., Yong, Z., Rui, Z., Teng, J.L.: Placement optimization of UAV-mounted mobile base stations. http://arxiv.org/abs/1612.01047
4. Rohde, S., Putzke, M., Wietfeld, C.: Ad hoc self-healing of OFDMA networks using UAV-based relays. Ad Hoc Netw. **11**(7), 1893–1906 (2013)

5. Li, X., Guo, D., Yin, H., Wei, G.: Drone-assisted public safety wireless broadband network. In: Wireless Communications and Networking Conference Workshops, pp. 323–328. IEEE (2015)
6. Mozaffari, M., Saad, W., Bennis, M., Debbah, M.: Unmanned aerial vehicle with underlaid device-to-device communications: performance and tradeoffs. IEEE Trans. Wirel. Commun. **15**(6), 3949–3963 (2016)
7. Soft Frequency Reuse Scheme for UTRAN LTE, 3rd Generation Partnership Project. http://www.3gpp.org
8. Lopez-Perez, D., Chu, X., Vasilakos, A.V., Claussen, H.: Power minimization based resource allocation for interference mitigation in OFDMA Femtocell networks. IEEE J. Sel. Areas Commun. **32**(2), 333–344 (2014)
9. Giambene, G., Le, V.A., Bourgeau, T., Chaouchi, H.: Soft frequency reuse schemes for heterogeneous LTE systems. In: IEEE International Conference on Communications, pp. 3161–3166 (2015)
10. Al-Hourani, A., Kandeepan, S., Lardner, S.: Optimal lap altitude for maximum coverage. IEEE Wirel. Commun. Lett. **3**(6), 569–572 (2014)
11. Propagation data and prediction methods required for the design of terrestrial broadband radio access systems operating in a frequency range from 3 to 60 GHz. In: International Telecommunication Union Radiocommunication Sector (ITU-R), Recommendation ITU-R P.1410-5 (2012)

Throughput Analysis for Full-Duplex Based Device-to-Device Communications

Yajun Shang[1], Xuehan Meng[1], Xiaomeng Chai[1], Tong Liu[2], and Zhongshan Zhang[1(✉)]

[1] Technology Research Center for Convergence Networks and Ubiquitous Services, University of Science and Technology Beijing (USTB), Beijing 100083, China
zhangzs@ustb.edu.cn
[2] Department of Information and Communication Engineering, Harbin Engineering University, 145 Nantong Street, Harbin, China
liutong@hrbeu.edu.cn

Abstract. The throughput of Device-to-device (D2D) enabled underlaying cellular networks is analyzed, with either full duplex (FD) or conventional half duplex (HD) transmission mode considered in D2D links. Despite of the severe interference imposed on the cellular users (CUs) by the FD based D2D (FD-D2D) links, the FD-D2D mode always exhibits its superiority in terms of the network throughput due to its reduced large-scale fading as well as low transmit-power essences. Numerical results show that the proposed FD-D2D mechanism is capable of substantially improving the network throughput.

Keywords: Device-to-device · Full duplex · Throughput · Interference

1 Introduction

With the rapid development of wireless communication techniques, the existed cellular networks become more and more insufficient for supporting the customers' exponentially growing data traffic demands [1,2]. In order to successfully relieve the heavy burden of base stations (BSs), Device-to-Device (D2D) communication technique allowing proximity users to communicate directly with each other without relying on the intervention of BS has exhibited several promising advantages in terms of cell throughput [3], spectral efficiency [4], users' end-to-end latency [5], radio coverage [6], power consumption [7] and traffic offloading capabilities [8], etc. Unlike the traditional BS-centric communications, D2D mode possess the characteristics of shorter radio-propagation distance and lower transmit power, thus leading to a higher signal-to-interference-plus-noise ratio (SINR) at the receiver. Up to now, D2D technique has attracted a wide attention in both academia and industry [9,10].

Unlike the conventional half duplex (HD) mode, which has been widely adopted in the existed D2D studies [8,11], the full duplex (FD) mode is capable of supporting concurrent transmission and reception in a single time/frequency

© ICST Institute for Computer Sciences, Social Informatics and Telecommunications Engineering 2018
K. Long et al. (Eds.): 5GWN 2017, LNICST 211, pp. 194–205, 2018.
https://doi.org/10.1007/978-3-319-72823-0_19

channel so as to (in theory) improving the attainable spectral efficiency by a factor of two [12–15]. However, FD mode suffers from a performance degradation due to the impact of self-interference (SI) [16], which can be substantially reduced by employing the state-of-the-art SI cancellation techniques [13].

All the above-mentioned issues have motivated us to investigate the combination of D2D communications and FD techniques [11]. However, there still exist several challenges to address in D2D systems. For example, interference management constitutes a major concern of D2D-enabled cellular networks. To implement the practical D2D-based systems, the D2D links can either be allocated a dedicated resource (i.e. be orthogonal to the cellular bandwidth) [17] or be allowed to reuse the cellular's resources [18]. Relative to the former, the same spectrum is shared between the cellular and the D2D systems in the latter scenario, leading to a more efficient resource utilization but also a much more severe interference problem (e.g. cellular-to-D2D interference, D2D-to-D2D interference, etc.). As compared with the HD mode, the FD based D2D (FD-D2D) mode will lead to more serious interference problem. Specifically, the D2D-induced interference may even deteriorate the throughput of the geographically closed D2D pairs.

In light of the fact that the D2D mode is essentially service-oriented and a D2D link is created when and only when a service demand emerges between a pair of D2D-enabled users, the mute duration of the D2D links can still be regarded as the interference-free period of the conventional cellular users (CUs). In this case, it would be critical to complete a given D2D service as quick as possible in order to minimize the impact of D2D-imposed interference. Therefore, an efficient and straightforward way to improve the throughput of CUs might resort to the capability of suppressing the duration of D2D-induced interference. As compared to the HD mode, FD mode is (in theory) capable of doubling the data transmission rate of a given D2D link, corresponding to cut the D2D-imposed interference period by half. For a given block of data to be shared between D2D pairs, FD-D2D is found to be helpful to substantially expedite the completion of D2D services. Although the average interference strength imposed on the CUs by FD-D2D users becomes higher than that induced by the transmissions of HD-mode D2D pairs, the accumulated performance losses observed in the CUs due to the FD-D2D induced interference are still lower than that induced by the latter, because the average transmission time of a given data needed in the latter is almost two times of that of the former. From this point of view, it would be beneficial to improving the throughput of the D2D-aided cellular networks by adopting FD mode rather than HD mode.

In this paper, we investigate the technique of FD-D2D under the scenario of spatially distributed multiple cells by analyzing the network throughput. The main contributions of this paper are reflected as follows. Based on the theory of stochastic geometry, a theoretical framework is established for modelling and analyzing either the cellular/D2D links' data rate and the throughput of the whole network by considering both the FD and HD modes. We analyze the throughput gain brought about by enabling FD-D2D in cellular networks.

Despite of a higher interference than the HD mode may be imposed by employing FD-D2D, the latter still exhibits its superiority in terms of the network throughput due to its short-distance-communication essence and lower power consumption, provided that the SI power can be suppressed to a low enough level[1].

The remainder of this paper is organized as follows. In Sect. 2, the system mode for D2D-aided underlaying cellular networks is described. The theoretical analysis for the transmission rates in both the FD and the HD modes will be presented in Sect. 3, followed by numerical results given by Sect. 4. Finally, Sect. 5 concludes this paper.

Notation: $\mathcal{STP}_{\{\bullet\}}$ denotes the successful transmission probability of a link, $\mathcal{L}\{\bullet\}$ denotes the Laplace transforms of a random variable, $\mathbb{P}\{\bullet\}$ represents the probability of a event, $\mathbb{E}\{\bullet\}$ denotes the expectation, and $R_{\{\bullet\}}$ denotes the throughput of a link.

2 Uplink System Model for FD-D2D Based Underlaying Cellular Networks

In this paper, we consider a cellular system comprising multiple BSs and mobile user equipments (UEs). Without loss of generality, we assume that the BSs are spatially distributed inside a given geographical area according to a homogeneous Poisson point process (PPP) Φ_b of intensity λ_b. Furthermore, both the conventional CUs and the DUs can be served by the system, in which the CUs and DUs are also assumed to be geographically scattered according to independent homogeneous PPPs Φ_c and Φ_d, with intensities of λ_c and λ_d, respectively. We assume that each DU has an opportunity to find a matched DU close to it to constitute a D2D pair, in which the average length of the established D2D links is represented by D_d. In addition, a constant transmit power is assumed in each user, with P_c and P_d denoting the transmit power of CUs and DUs, respectively.

We consider an FD-D2D based underlaid HD cellular network, in which the conventional cellular links are assumed to be operated in HD mode, whereas the D2D links are operated at the FD mode. Furthermore, the uplink recourses are employed for facilitating the D2D communications. Without loss of generality, the general (large-scale) power law propagation model and the (small-scale) Rayleigh fading channels are adopted in both the cellular/D2D links and the interference links. In addition, we assume that all the above-mentioned links in our model are independent and identically distributed (i.i.d.) random variables with $h_{ij} \sim \exp(1), i, j \in \{\Phi_b, \Phi_c, \Phi_d\}$.

In the following, we assume that an orthogonal resource can be assigned to each CU for effectively mitigating the intra-cell interference. The receive SINR of both the conventional cellular links and the D2D links can be expressed as

---

[1] According to [13], SI-cancellation capability of up to 110 dB can be attained by employing proper spatial suppression, analog- and digital-domain cancellations.

$$\text{SINR}_c = \frac{P_c h_{cb} d_{cb}^{-\alpha}}{I_{dc} + I_{cc} + \sigma^2}, \tag{1}$$

$$\text{SINR}_d = \frac{P_d h_d D_d^{-\alpha}}{I_{cd} + I_{dd} + I_{SI} + \sigma^2}, \tag{2}$$

respectively, where $I_{dc} = 2 \sum_{\Phi_d} P_d h_{d_i b} r_{d_i b}^{-\alpha}$ denotes the interference power imposed

on CUs by FD-DUs, $I_{cc} = \sum_{\Phi_c / c_0} P_c h_{c_i b} r_{c_i b}^{-\alpha}$ represents the interference among

CUs, $I_{cd} = \sum_{\Phi_c} P_c h_{c_i d} r_{c_i d}^{-\alpha}$ stands for the interference power imposed on DUs by

CUs, $I_{dd} = 2 \sum_{\Phi_d} P_d h_{d_i d} r_{d_i d}^{-\alpha}$, represents the interference among FD-DUs, $I_{SI} = P_d c_{si}$ denotes the residual SI observed in the FD devices after performing SI cancellation, and c_{si} denotes the SI cancellation coefficient (a larger coefficient corresponds to a higher SI cancellation capability). Furthermore, σ^2 denotes the Additive-White Gaussian Noise (AWGN) covariance.

Note that the average length of D2D links (corresponding to the transmitter-receiver distance) is shorter than that of the cellular and/or interference links. Furthermore, the average interference strength imposed on BSs by the active FD-mode DUs is much higher than that imposed by the HD-mode DUs. It would thus be reasonable to assume that the former is two times of the latter. In other words, the interference induced by an FD-D2D pair comes from both the transmitter and the receiver, resulting in a two-fold interference strength compared to that induced by the HD-mode D2D pair, in which case only one out of the D2D peers is allowed to transmit in each time.

We further define the successful transmission probability (STP) as *the probability that the quality of a randomly chosen link successfully reaches its predetermined target SINR threshold* ε. The STP of a typical cellular or D2D link can thus be define as

$$STP_c = \Pr\left(\frac{P_c h_{cb} d_{cb}^{-\alpha}}{I_{dc} + I_{cc} + \sigma^2} > \varepsilon\right) \tag{3}$$

and

$$STP_d = \Pr\left(\frac{P_d h_d D_d^{-\alpha}}{I_{cd} + I_{dd} + I_{SI} + \sigma^2} > \varepsilon\right), \tag{4}$$

respectively.

3 Throughput for FD-D2D Based Underlaying Cellular Networks

In this section, the throughput for D2D based underlaying cellular networks will be analyzed. The SI cancellation is assumed to be already performed (but the residual SI power is always non-zero). The theory of stochastic geometry can be employed for modelling and analyzing the throughput of the proposed system by considering both the FD and HD modes.

According to the tractable analysis of PPP in [19], each CU will always preferentially communicate with the BS having the highest RSS (i.e. the geographically closest BS), leading to the probability density function (PDF) of the random CU-BS distances r as

$$f_r(r) = e^{-\pi\lambda_b r^2} 2\pi\lambda_b r. \tag{5}$$

3.1   STP of a Typical Cellular Links

From the Slivnyaks theorem [20], the statistical property of a typical node located at a specific position holds true for any generic node located at any generic location. Without loss of generality, we assume that the CU of interest is located at the origin of the plane and receives signals from the closest BS. The STP of a typical cellular link in a general FD-D2D underlaying cellular network can be derived as

$$STP_c^f = \int_0^\infty \mathcal{L}_{I_{cc}}\left(\frac{\varepsilon r^\alpha}{P_c}\right) \mathcal{L}_{I_{dc}}\left(\frac{\varepsilon r^\alpha}{P_c}\right)$$
$$\times e^{-\frac{\varepsilon r^\alpha \sigma^2}{P_c}} e^{-\lambda_b \pi r^2} 2\pi\lambda_b r \mathrm{d}r, \tag{6}$$

where $\mathcal{L}_{I_{cc}}(s)$ and $\mathcal{L}_{I_{dc}}(s)$ denote the Laplace transforms (evaluated at s) of random variables I_{cc} and I_{dc}, respectively, as defined by

$$\mathcal{L}_{I_{cc}}\left(\frac{\varepsilon r^\alpha}{P_c}\right) = \exp\left[\frac{-2\pi\lambda_b r^2 \varepsilon}{\alpha - 2} {}_2F_1\left(1, \frac{\alpha - 2}{\alpha}; 2 - \frac{2}{\alpha}; -\varepsilon\right)\right] \tag{7}$$

and

$$\mathcal{L}_{I_{dc}}\left(\frac{\varepsilon r^\alpha}{P_c}\right) = \exp\left[-2^{\frac{2}{\alpha}}\left(\frac{P_d}{P_c}\right)^{\frac{2}{\alpha}} \pi r^2 \lambda_d \varepsilon^{\frac{2}{\alpha}} \frac{1}{\mathrm{sinc}(\frac{2}{\alpha})}\right], \tag{8}$$

respectively, the function ${}_2F_1(a, b; c; z)$ denotes the hypergeometric function, and $\mathrm{sinc}(x) = \dfrac{\sin(\pi x)}{\pi x}$.

3.2   STP of a Typical FD-D2D Links

In the proposed FD-D2D based underlaying cellular networks, a given FD-D2D link also suffers from interference induced by various sources, including the conventional CUs, the neighboring FD-D2D pairs and the residual SI at the FD devices, etc. The STP of a typical FD-D2D link in a general FD-D2D underlaying cellular network is given by

$$STP_d^f = \mathcal{L}_{I_{cd}}\left(\frac{\varepsilon D_d^\alpha}{P_d}\right) \mathcal{L}_{I_{dd}}\left(\frac{\varepsilon D_d^\alpha}{P_d}\right) e^{-\varepsilon c_{si} D_d^\alpha} e^{-\frac{\varepsilon D_d^\alpha \sigma^2}{P_d}}, \tag{9}$$

where $\mathcal{L}_{I_{cd}}(s)$ and $\mathcal{L}_{I_{dd}}(s)$ denote the Laplace transforms (evaluated at s) of random variables I_{cd} and I_{dd}, respectively, as defined by

$$\mathcal{L}_{I_{cd}}\left(\frac{\varepsilon D_d^\alpha}{P_d}\right) = \exp\left[-\pi\lambda_b D_d^2\left(\frac{P_c}{P_d}\right)^{\frac{2}{\alpha}}\varepsilon^{\frac{2}{\alpha}}\frac{1}{\text{sinc}(\frac{2}{\alpha})}\right] \qquad (10)$$

and

$$\mathcal{L}_{I_{dd}}\left(\frac{\varepsilon D_d^\alpha}{P_d}\right) = \exp\left[-2^{\frac{2}{\alpha}}\pi\lambda_d D_d^2\varepsilon^{\frac{2}{\alpha}}\frac{1}{\text{sinc}(\frac{2}{\alpha})}\right], \qquad (11)$$

respectively.

3.3   Throughput Analysis for the FD-D2D Based Underlaying Cellular Networks

From information theory [21], the average throughput of a typical CU/DU can be defined as

$$R = \mathbb{E}[\log(1 + \text{SINR})] = \int_{\varepsilon>0}\frac{\mathbb{P}(\text{SINR} > \varepsilon)}{\varepsilon + 1}d\varepsilon. \qquad (12)$$

The throughput of a typical cellular link and FD-D2D link can thus be derived as

$$\begin{aligned} R_c^f &= \int_{\varepsilon>0}\frac{STP_c^f}{\varepsilon+1}d\varepsilon \\ &= \int_0^\infty\int_0^\infty\exp\left\{-\pi r^2\left[\frac{2\lambda_b\varepsilon}{\alpha-2}M + \left(2\frac{P_d}{P_c}\right)^{\frac{2}{\alpha}}\varepsilon^{\frac{2}{\alpha}}N\right]\right\} \\ &\quad\times\exp\left(-\frac{\varepsilon r^\alpha\sigma^2}{P_c} - \lambda_b\pi r^2\right)2\pi\lambda_b rdr\frac{1}{\varepsilon+1}d\varepsilon \end{aligned} \qquad (13)$$

and

$$\begin{aligned} R_d^f &= \int_{\varepsilon>0}\frac{STP_d^f}{\varepsilon+1}d\varepsilon \\ &= \int_0^\infty\exp\left\{-\frac{\pi D_d^2\varepsilon^{\frac{2}{\alpha}}}{\text{sinc}(\frac{2}{\alpha})}\left[\lambda_b\left(\frac{P_c}{P_d}\right)^{\frac{2}{\alpha}} + 2^{\frac{2}{\alpha}}\lambda_d\right]\right\} \\ &\quad\times\exp\left(-\varepsilon c_{si}D_d^\alpha - \frac{\varepsilon D_d^\alpha\sigma^2}{P_d}\right)\frac{1}{\varepsilon+1}d\varepsilon, \end{aligned} \qquad (14)$$

respectively.

Note that the impact of thermal noise will no longer dominate the performance degradation of the D2D-aided networks, which should be interference limited. In this case, it would be reasonable to assume that $\sigma^2 \to 0$, thus enabling the throughput of the FD-D2D underlaying cellular networks to be simplified as

$$R^f = \lambda_b R_c^f + 2\lambda_d R_d^f, \qquad (15)$$

where

$$R_c^f = \int_0^\infty \frac{1}{\varepsilon + 1} \times \frac{1}{\frac{2\varepsilon}{\alpha - 2} M + \left(2\frac{P_d}{P_c}\right)^{\frac{2}{\alpha}} \varepsilon^{\frac{2}{\alpha}} \frac{N}{\lambda_b} + 1} d\varepsilon \qquad (16)$$

and

$$R_d^f = \int_0^\infty \frac{1}{\varepsilon + 1} \exp\left\{ -\frac{\pi D_d^2 \varepsilon^{\frac{2}{\alpha}}}{\mathrm{sinc}(\frac{2}{\alpha})} F - \varepsilon c_{si} D_d^\alpha \right\} d\varepsilon, \qquad (17)$$

respectively, where $F = \left[\lambda_b \left(\frac{P_c}{P_d} \right)^{\frac{2}{\alpha}} + 2^{\frac{2}{\alpha}} \lambda_d \right]$.

For purposes of performance comparison, we also derive the throughput under HD mode, as given by

$$R^h = \lambda_b R_c^h + \lambda_d R_d^h, \qquad (18)$$

where

$$R_c^h = \int_0^\infty \frac{1}{\varepsilon + 1} \times \frac{1}{\frac{2\varepsilon}{\alpha - 2} M + \left(\frac{P_d}{P_c}\right)^{\frac{2}{\alpha}} \varepsilon^{\frac{2}{\alpha}} \frac{N}{\lambda_b} + 1} d\varepsilon \qquad (19)$$

and

$$R_d^h = \int_0^\infty \frac{1}{\varepsilon + 1} \times \exp\left\{ -\frac{\pi D_d^2 \varepsilon^{\frac{2}{\alpha}}}{\mathrm{sinc}(\frac{2}{\alpha})} \left[\lambda_b \left(\frac{P_c}{P_d} \right)^{\frac{2}{\alpha}} + \lambda_d \right] \right\} d\varepsilon, \qquad (20)$$

respectively. Evidently, the superiority of FD-mode over HD-mode is mainly reflected in the potential factor-2 throughput gain. However, this gain is not attainable in practical designs mainly due to the impact of residual SI as well as the other non-linear distortions [13]. Since the HD mode may occasionally outperform the FD mode in terms of attainable throughput if the residual SI power in the FD devices is high, the latter maintains its advantages only if the SI power can be sufficiently suppressed.

4   Numerical Results

In this section, we evaluate the spectral efficiency gain offered by underlaying cellular networks, which combines the benefits of both the FD mode and D2D communications. The uplink band is shared between the conventional CUs and the D2D links, with i.i.d. Rayleigh fading considered. Furthermore, the path-loss exponent is set to $\alpha = 4$ (i.e. corresponding to the typical urban environment).

In the following simulations, an area of $4000 \times 4000\,\mathrm{m}^2$ square serving 5 BSs and 30 D2D links (deployed according to independent PPP) is considered. Furthermore, an orthogonal resource allocation among CUs is assumed. In addition, the average length of D2D links is assumed to be 50 m, with the transmit powers of CUs and DUs assumed to be 30 dBm and 20 dBm, respectively. Finally, the noise power spectrum density is assumed to be −174 dBm/Hz. The detailed parameter settings are shown in Table 1.

As shown in Fig. 1, the numerical results can well validate the theoretical analysis. In the presence of low SI-cancellation capability (i.e. a relatively higher power of residual SI is imposed on the FD devices), the HD mode based D2D outperforms the FD-D2D mode in terms of the spectral efficiency. However, the FD-D2D mode exhibits its superiority over its FD counterpart if the SI-cancellation capability becomes higher than 85 dB.

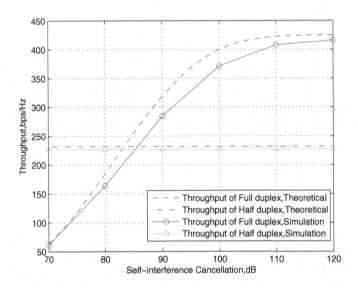

Fig. 1. Performance comparison of HD-D2D and FD-D2D in terms of throughput by considering variant SI cancelation.

Figure 2 illustrates the performance comparison between HD-D2D and FD-D2D modes in terms of spectral efficiency under various number of D2D links. Evidently, the spectral efficiency can be improved as the number of D2D link increases. However, the approach of improving the spectral efficiency by infinitely increasing the number of D2D links is shown to be un-sustainable. As illustrated in Fig. 3, when we shrink the simulation area from $4000 \times 4000\,m^2$ to $1000 \times 1000\,m^2$ (i.e. corresponding to magnifying the density of DUs), the spectral efficiency may be eroded by further increasing the D2D numbers once it approaches a critical threshold. We may explain it as follows: In scenarios with sparse D2D distributions, activating more D2D pairs implies contributing more throughput via D2D links. In scenarios with dense D2D distributions, on the other hand, the whole system becomes interference-overloaded, in which case the performance improvement brought about by increasing D2D pairs cannot

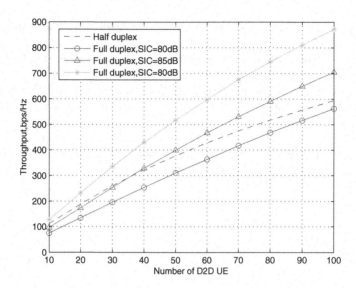

Fig. 2. Performance comparison of HD-D2D and FD-D2D in terms of throughput under different D2D-density settings (sparse scenario is considered).

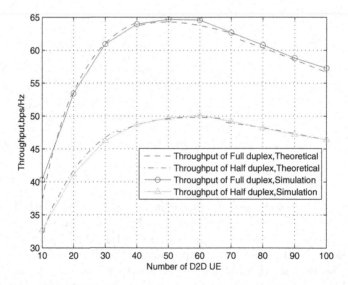

Fig. 3. Performance comparison of HD-D2D and FD-D2D in terms of throughput under different D2D-density settings (dense scenario is considered).

counter-balance the throughput losses induced by the severe interference imposed by D2D links. Furthermore, a further observation in Fig. 2 indicates that the performance gap between the FD-D2D and the HD-D2D modes becomes larger as the number of D2D pairs increases (i.e. the superiority of the FD-D2D mode is enhanced). Anyway, as long as the DU density is below the tolerable threshold, increasing the number of D2D pairs (i.e. corresponding to decreasing the distance between peer DUs) will always enables a better FD mode communication.

Table 1. Default key parameters in the simulation

Parameter	Physical Mean	Value
P_c	Power of CU	30 dBm
P_d	Power of DUs	20 dBm
α	Path loss coefficient	4
D_d	The average distance between a pair of D2D peers	50 m
σ^2	Power level of thermal noise	-174 dBm/Hz
	Simulation area	4000 m × 4000 m
N_b	Number of BS	5
N_d	Number of D2D link	30
k	Cellular Link Protecting Radius Coefficient	0.5–0.7
c_{si}	SI cancellation coefficient	100 dB

5   Conclusions

In this paper, benefits brought about by implementing FD-D2D aided cellular networks in terms of spectral efficiency was analyzed, showing that the FD-D2D communication is capable of improving the sum-rate of the network due to its speciality of short link distance and lower transmit power, despite of a much more severe interference than the HD-D2D mode imposed on it. Furthermore, it was shown that the attainable performance gain in terms of throughput cannot be infinitely increased by simply increasing the number of D2D links, because the CUs may become interference overloaded, in which case the performance gain brought by increasing the number of D2D links cannot counter-balance the throughput loss induced by the severe interference.

Acknowledgement. This work was supported by the key project of the National Natural Science Foundation of China (No. 61431001), the open research fund of National Mobile Communications Research Laboratory, Southeast University (No. 2017D02), Key Laboratory of Cognitive Radio and Information Processing, Ministry of Education (Guilin University of Electronic Technology), and the Foundation of Beijing Engineering and Technology Center for Convergence Networks and Ubiquitous Services. The corresponding author is Dr. Zhongshan Zhang.

References

1. Zhang, Z., Long, K., Wang, J.: Self-organization paradigms and optimization approaches for cognitive radio technologies: a survey. IEEE Wirel. Commun. Mag. **20**(2), 36–42 (2013)
2. Zhang, Z., Long, K., Wang, J., Dressler, F.: On swarm intelligence inspired self-organized networking: its bionic mechanisms, designing principles and optimization approaches. IEEE Commun. Surv. Tuts. **16**(1), 513–537 (2014). First Quarter
3. Liu, Z., Peng, T., Peng, B., Wang, W.: Sum-capacity of d2d and cellular hybrid networks over cooperation and non-cooperation. In: 2012 7th International ICST Conference on Communications and Networking in China (CHINACOM), pp. 707–711. IEEE (2012)
4. Abu Al Haija, A., Vu, M.: Spectral efficiency and outage performance for hybrid d2d-infrastructure uplink cooperation. IEEE Trans. Wirel. Commun. **14**(3), 1183–1198 (2015)
5. Lianghai, J., Klein, A., Kuruvatti, N., Schotten, H.D.: System capacity optimization algorithm for d2d underlay operation. In: 2014 IEEE International Conference on Communications Workshops (ICC), pp. 85–90. IEEE (2014)
6. Liu, J., Zhang, S., Nishiyama, H., Kato, N., Guo, J.: A stochastic geometry analysis of d2d overlaying multi-channel downlink cellular networks. In: INFOCOM (2015)
7. Fodor, G., Dahlman, E., Mildh, G., Parkvall, S., Reider, N., Miklos, G., Turanyi, Z.: Design aspects of network assisted device-to-device communications. IEEE Commun. Mag. **50**(3), 170–177 (2012)
8. Lei, L., Kuang, Y., Shen, X., Lin, C., Zhong, Z.: Resource control in network assisted device-to-device communications: solutions and challenges. IEEE Commun. Mag. **52**(6), 108–117 (2014)
9. Asadi, A., Wang, Q., Mancuso, V.: A survey on device-to-device communication in cellular networks. IEEE Commun. Surv. Tuts. **16**(4), 1801–1819 (2014). Fourth quarter
10. ElSawy, H., Hossain, E., Alouini, M.-S.: Analytical modeling of mode selection and power control for underlay d2d communication in cellular networks. IEEE Trans. Comm. **62**(11), 4147–4161 (2014)
11. Feng, D., Lu, L., Yuan-Wu, Y., Li, G., Li, S., Feng, G.: Deviceto-device communications in cellular networks. IEEE Commun. Mag. **52**(4), 49–55 (2014)
12. Zhang, Z., Chai, X., Long, K., Vasilakos, A.V., Hanzo, L.: Full duplex techniques for 5G networks: self-interference cancellation, protocol design, and relay selection. IEEE Commun. Mag. **53**(5), 128–137 (2015)
13. Zhang, Z., Long, K., Vasilakos, A.V., Hanzo, L.: Full-duplex wireless communications: challenges, solutions and future research directions. Proc. IEEE **104**(7), 1369–1409 (2016)
14. Goyal, S., Liu, P., Panwar, S.S., Difazio, R., Yang, R., Bala, E., et al.: Full duplex cellular systems: will doubling interference prevent doubling capacity? IEEE Commun. Mag. **53**(5), 121–127 (2015)
15. Zhang, H., Tabassum, H., Hossain, E., Kim, D.I.: Medium access control design for full duplex wireless systems: challenges and approaches. IEEE Commun. Mag. **53**(5), 112–120 (2015)
16. Wang, L., Tian, F., Svensson, T., Feng, D., Song, M., Li, S.: Exploiting full duplex for device-to-device communications in heterogeneous networks. IEEE Commun. Mag. **53**(5), 146–152 (2015)

17. Zhou, B., Hu, H., Huang, S.-Q., Chen, H.-H.: Intracluster device-to-device relay algorithm with optimal resource utilization. IEEE Trans. Veh. Technol. **62**(5), 2315–2326 (2013)
18. Feng, D., Lu, L., Yuan-Wu, Y., Li, G.Y., Feng, G., Li, S.: Device-to-device communications underlaying cellular networks. IEEE Trans. Comm. **61**(8), 3541–3551 (2013)
19. Andrews, J.G., Baccelli, F., Ganti, R.K.: A tractable approach to coverage and rate in cellular networks. IEEE Trans. Commun. **59**(11), 3122–3134 (2011, 2016)
20. Chiu, S.N., Stoyan, D., Kendall, W.S., Mecke, J.: Stochastic Geometry and Its Applications. Wiley, New York (2013)
21. Cover, T.M., Thomas, J.A.: Elements of Information Theory. Wiley, New York (1991, 2016)

Joint Mode Selection and Resource Allocation in Underlaying D2D Communication

Wei Zhang, Wanbing He, Dan Wu[✉], and Yueming Cai

Institute of Communications Engineering, PLA UST, Nanjing 210007, Jiangsu,
People's Republic of China
greenery_jul@sina.com, hewanbing0502@icloud.com,
wujing1958725@126.com, caiym@vip.sina.com

Abstract. Device-to-device (D2D) communication as an underlay to cellular networks is a promising technology to improve network capacity and user experience. However, it depends on elegant resource management between cellular users and D2D pairs. In this work, we study the problem of D2D communication underlaying cellular networks sharing uplink resources, which focuses on maximizing the sum rate of D2D pairs while guaranteeing the quality of existing cellular users. A three-step scheme is proposed. We first conduct mode selection to decide whether a D2D pair can share links with a cellular user. And then, we match a cellular user with each D2D pair based on the principle of fairness and try to maximize the sum rate of D2D pairs. Finally, a joint power control strategy is developed and a closed-form of solution is provided. The superiority of the proposed scheme is demonstrated in the numerical results.

Keywords: D2D communication · Mode selection · Resource allocation
Non-convexity · Joint optimization

1 Introduction

With the explosive growth of information and the increasing demand of user experience, device-to-device (D2D) technique, as an effective method to relieve the traffic load of cellular networks and improve local service flexibility, has attracted much attention in recent years [1]. By enabling two users in proximity to communicate directly without being relayed by a base station (BS), D2D communication can bring four types of benefits, that is, proximity gain, reuse gain, hop gain and paring gain, which may achieve higher rate, lower power consumption and more efficient resource utilization [2]. Thus, introducing D2D communications into cellular networks is worth consideration.

However, enabling D2D communication in a cellular network poses some inevitable challenges [3, 4]. It will generate interference between D2D pairs and cellular users due to the sharing of links and furthermore it may decrease the QoS (Quality of Service) of

This work is supported by the National Natural Science Foundation of China (No. 61671474, No. 61371122).

both users. As such, an elegant resource management to coordinate with the interference is in urgent demand [5, 6]. Resource management includes mode selection and resource allocation, which refers to the allocation of link and power. D2D communication underlaying cellular networks can either exploit cellular mode, in which the communication will be relayed by the BS, or communicate directly sharing links with primary cellular users, referred to as reuse mode, which can further improve the spectral efficiency [7]. Link allocation should be jointly considered with mode selection, that is, a D2D pair with reuse mode chooses which cellular user to share its link. Power control includes power allocation among D2D pairs, as well as cellular users, which will ultimately achieve optimal network performance with limited power resource.

There are some existing works that study resource management for D2D communication underlaying cellular networks. In particular, an interference limited area (ILA) is suggested in [8], where a D2D pair cannot be admitted to reuse the links of cellular users to decrease their quality of communication. To further mitigate the interference from D2D transmission to cellular communication, a distance-based resource allocation scheme is developed in [9], based on the outrage probability analysis while restricting the maximum transmit power of D2D pairs. [10] provides an optimal resource sharing strategy based on convex optimization, to maximize the rate of one D2D pair which can share the link resources of all the cellular users in the cell. However, there is only one D2D pair considered. In [11], a heuristic algorithm is proposed to match D2D pairs and cellular users, which chooses the cellular users with higher channel gain to share with D2D pairs with lower interference gain, while in that case, coordination between both of the users is not considered. [12] jointly considers three respects of resource management, which exploits maximum weight bipartite matching based scheme to choose cellular partners for D2D pairs to maximize the network throughput.

Motivated by the above literature, we investigate D2D communication underlaying a multi-user cellular network sharing uplink resources. We aim to design a resource management scheme which jointly considers mode selection, link allocation and power control to maximize the sum rate of D2D pairs, and meanwhile, to guarantee the QoS of both cellular users and D2D pairs. The contributions are summarized as follows:

(i) We consider multiple D2D pairs and multiple cellular users in a cell, rather than only one D2D pair. And we model a joint mode selection and resource allocation optimization problem, where the QoS requirements of both cellular users and D2D pairs are simultaneously considered. Moreover, we constrain the total power budget of D2D pairs.

(ii) We formulate the uplink resource sharing problem into a non-convex optimization problem, and then, we divide it into three serial subproblems and obtain the closed-form of the solution. Firstly, we decide an interference limited area (ILA) for each potential D2D pair and then conduct mode selection based on a minimum distance metric. Then, we allocate the links of cellular users based on a principle of fairness to maximize the sum rate of D2D pairs, which will achieve the tradeoff between the efficiency and the fairness of the network [13]. Moreover, we use Lagrangian Algorithm to simultaneously allocate the power for both cellular users and D2D pairs.

The remainder of the paper is organized as follows. In Sect. 2, we describe the network model and formulate the optimization problem. The joint mode selection and resource allocation algorithm is illustrated in Sect. 3. Section 4 presents the numerical results to demonstrate the performance of the proposed scheme. Finally, Sect. 5 concludes the paper.

2 Problem Formulation

We consider a single cell, where there exist one BS, L cellular users and M D2D pairs, and the later compose the sets $\mathcal{C} = \{1, \ldots, L\}$ and $\mathcal{D} = \{1, \ldots, M\}$, respectively, as shown in Fig. 1. We assume that each cellular user occupies a frequency band normalized to be one, and then, the transmission links are orthogonal. In order to improve spectrum efficiency, we exploit the underlaying D2D communication sharing uplink resources with reuse mode. As such, the mutual interference among D2D pairs and cellular users may become more serious. To facilitate manipulation, we assume that the link of each cellular user is reused by at most one D2D pair. However, for those lacking in a proper cellular partner, the D2D pairs conduct cellular mode to communicate through the BS.

Considering the resource sharing between cellular users and D2D pairs, the SINR of cellular user i and D2D pair j sharing the link of user i are given respectively by

$$\xi_i^c = \frac{p_i h_i^c}{\sigma_N^2 + q_j g_{j,i}^d} \tag{1}$$

$$\xi_j^d = \frac{q_j h_j^d}{\sigma_N^2 + p_i g_{i,j}^c} \tag{2}$$

where σ_N^2 represents Gaussian noise variance on each channel of cellular user i and D2D pair j. h_i^c is denoted as the channel gain from cellular user i to the BS. Similarly, denote $g_{i,j}^c$, h_j^d, and $g_{j,i}^d$ as the channel gain between cellular user i and the receiver of D2D pair j, between the transmitter to the receiver of D2D pair j and between the transmitter of D2D pair j to the BS on frequency i, respectively. Let p_i and q_j represent the transmit power of cellular user i and D2D pair j, respectively.

Thus, their rate can be expressed as

$$R_i^c(p_i, q_j) = log_2(1 + \xi_i^c) \tag{3}$$

$$R_j^d(p_i, q_j) = log_2(1 + \xi_j^d) \tag{4}$$

Our goal is to maximize the total rate of D2D pairs, and also satisfy the requirements of cellular users and D2D pairs, in terms of their individual rate and power limit, and the total power budget for all D2D pairs sharing the links. The joint mode selection and resource allocation optimization problem in D2D communication underlaying cellular system is formulated as

$$\text{maximize} \quad \sum_{j=1}^{N} R_j^d(p_i, q_j) \tag{5}$$

$$\text{subject to} \quad R_i^c(p_i, q_j) \geq \rho_i, \forall i \in \mathcal{C} \tag{5a}$$

$$R_j^d(p_i, q_j) \geq \gamma_j, \forall j \in \mathcal{S} \tag{5b}$$

$$0 \leq p_i \leq P_i, \forall i \in \mathcal{C} \tag{5c}$$

$$0 \leq q_j \leq Q_j, \forall j \in \mathcal{S} \tag{5d}$$

$$\sum_{j=1}^{N} q_j \leq Q \tag{5e}$$

where $\mathcal{S}(\mathcal{S} \subseteq \mathcal{D}, \mathcal{S}\{1, \ldots, N\})$ denotes the set of D2D pairs. ρ_i and γ_j represent the rate threshold of cellular user i and potential D2D pair j, respectively, and hence, (5a) and (5b) ensure that both cellular users and potential D2D pairs reach their minimum QoS requirements in terms of rate. (5c) and (5d) guarantee that the transmit power of cellular users and potential D2D pairs are within the maximize limit P_i and Q_j, respectively. (5e) represents Q is the total power budget of the D2D pairs on all links.

Since it is a nonconvex problem, it is difficult to find the solution of (5). To facilitate manipulation, we will transform it into a convex one and provide a fully analytical characterization of the optimized solution to (5). We divide the optimization problem into three subproblems since the matching process of D2D pairs and cellular users belongs to the problem based on discrete space, while the power allocation problem belongs to continuous space.

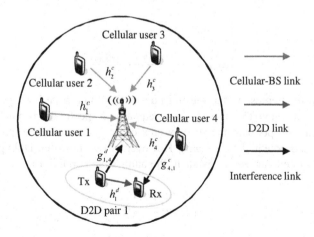

Fig. 1. System model of D2D communication underlaying cellular networks.

3 Joint Mode Selection and Resource Allocation Algorithm

In this section, to solve the joint mode selection and resource allocation optimization problem in underlaying D2D communication, we divide the joint optimization problem into three subproblems, referred as mode selection, link allocation and power control. Then, we propose an optimization algorithm and analyze the properties of the scheme.

3.1 Distance-Oriented Admission Control of D2D Pairs

Before introducing D2D pairs into the cellular network, we first consider which mode to choose for them. That is, we need to determine whether a potential D2D pair can reuse the links of existing cellular users. If a potential D2D pair is admitted, it selects reuse mode, and furthermore, we need to decide a reuse cellular partner for it. If not, its communication will be relayed by the BS with cellular mode.

For each potential D2D pair, if it is admitted to reuse a cellular user's link, the constraints in (5a), (5b), (5c), (5d) must be primarily satisfied. As such, we obtain a set of reuse candidates for potential D2D pair j and denote them as $\mathcal{R}_j$ and then potential D2D pair j is admitted if $\mathcal{R}_j = \emptyset$. Since the channel condition and the mutual interference mainly depend on distance, we will divide an ILA for each potential D2D pair based on the distance between two kinds of users, outside of where the cellular candidates in $\mathcal{R}_j$ are distributed.

It can be verified that it is a linear programming problem, and hence, there will be a feasible area for potential D2D pair j, as the shadow part shown in Fig. 2. The line l_c and l_d represent constraints (5a) and (5b) with equality, respectively. Let $p_{i,\min}$ and $q_{j,\min}$ denote the minimum power of cellular user i and D2D pair j, respectively, which indicate there is no link sharing and no interference between them.

To guarantee that there will be a feasible root of the linear programming problem, point T, $(p_{i,T}, q_{j,T})$, as shown in Fig. 2, must be within the square area, that is, they satisfy constraints (5c) and (5d). And then, there may be feasible power for both cellular user i and potential D2D pair j in the shadow area. Computing the intersection of l_c and l_d in the first place, and point T, $(p_{i,T}, q_{j,T})$ can be expressed as

$$
\begin{cases}
p_{i,T} = \dfrac{(2^{\rho_i}-1)\sigma_N^2 [h_j^d + (2^{\gamma_j}-1)g_{j,i}^d]}{h_i^c h_j^d - (2^{\rho_i}-1)(2^{\gamma_j}-1)g_{i,j}^c g_{j,i}^d} \\[4mm]
q_{i,T} = \dfrac{(2^{\gamma_j}-1)\sigma_N^2 [h_i^c + (2^{\rho_i}-1)g_{i,j}^c]}{h_i^c h_j^d - (2^{\rho_i}-1)(2^{\gamma_j}-1)g_{i,j}^c g_{j,i}^d}
\end{cases}
\tag{6}
$$

where $p_{i,T}$ and $q_{i,T}$ represent the transmit power of cellular user i and potential D2D pair j to meet constraints (5a) and (5b) with equality, respectively. If point T is within the square area, any point in the shadow area can manage a feasible power pair for cellular user i and potential D2D pair j. However, if not, potential D2D pair j cannot reuse the link of cellular user i. As such, the admissible condition is,

$$
\begin{cases}
0 < p_{i,T} \le P_i \\
0 < q_{j,T} \le Q_j
\end{cases}
\tag{7}
$$

Accordingly, combining with the distance based path loss model, $h_{i,j} = K d_{i,j}^{-\alpha}$, we can impose a distance control between cellular users and potential D2D pairs to decide $\mathcal{R}_j$. Denote $L_{i,j}$ as the distance between cellular user i and the receiver of potential D2D pair j. We have the following proposition that characterizes the admission control of a potential D2D pair.

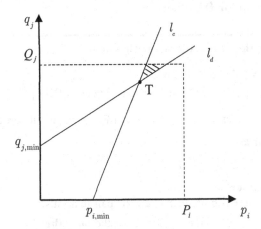

Fig. 2. Admission control of D2D pair j.

Proposition 1. *Potential D2D pair j can be admitted to reuse the link of cellular user i, if and only if $L_{i,j} \geq L_{i,j}^{\min}$, where $L_{i,j}^{\min}$ is the minimum distance limit between cellular user i and the receiver of potential D2D pair j, and it is given by, (i)*
$$\left\{ \frac{K P_i (2^{\rho_i}-1)(2^{\gamma_j}-1) g_{j,i}^d}{P_i h_i^c h_j^d - (2^{\rho_i}-1)\sigma_N^2 [h_j^d + (2^{\gamma_j}-1) g_{j,i}^d]} \right\}^{\frac{1}{\alpha}}, \text{ if } \log_2(1 + \frac{P_i h_i^c}{Q_i g_{j,i}^d + \sigma_N^2}) \leq \rho_i. \text{ (ii) } [\frac{K(2^{\rho_i}-1)(2^{\gamma_j}-1)(Q_j g_{j,i}^d + \sigma_N^2)}{Q_j h_i^c h_j^d - (2^{\gamma_j}-1)\sigma_N^2 h_i^c}]^{\frac{1}{\alpha}},$$
if $\log_2(1 + \frac{P_i h_i^c}{Q_i g_{j,i}^d + \sigma_N^2}) \leq \rho_i$.

Proof. According to constraint (7), we can simplify it into the following

$$g_{i,j}^c \leq \begin{cases} \frac{P_i h_i^c h_j^d - (2^{\rho_i}-1)\sigma_N^2 [h_j^d + (2^{\gamma_j}-1) g_{j,i}^d]}{P_i (2^{\rho_i}-1)(2^{\gamma_j}-1) g_{j,i}^d} = g_c \\[2ex] \frac{Q_j h_i^c h_j^d - (2^{\gamma_j}-1)\sigma_N^2 h_i^c}{(2^{\rho_i}-1)(2^{\gamma_j}-1)(Q_j g_{j,i}^d + \sigma_N^2)} = g_d \end{cases} \tag{8}$$

To move a step forward, it can be transformed into

$$g_{i,j}^c \leq \begin{cases} g_c, & \log_2(1 + \frac{P_i h_i^c}{Q_i g_{j,i}^d + \sigma_N^2}) \leq \rho_i \\[2ex] g_d, & \log_2(1 + \frac{P_i h_i^c}{Q_i g_{j,i}^d + \sigma_N^2}) > \rho_i \end{cases} \tag{9}$$

Finally, we can get the distance limit $L_{i,j}^{\min}$ according to path loss model.

Thus, we set an ILA for each potential D2D pair, and a potential D2D pair can only match with the cellular users outside of its ILA, since the mutual interference between them cannot be too serious to decrease their QoS, or the D2D pair must be far enough from the potential cellular partner. If there is no cellular user outside of a potential D2D pair's ILA, it can only select cellular mode, instead.

3.2   Link Allocation for D2D Pairs

Algorithm: Link Allocation Algorithm

1:    $\mathcal{S}$: List of D2D pairs

2:    $\mathcal{R}_j$: List of reuse cellular candidates of D2D pair j

3:    $\mathcal{M}$: List of D2D pairs with $|\mathcal{R}_j|$ in increasing order

4: **for all** $j \in \mathcal{S}$ **do**

5:        find $|\mathcal{R}_j| = 1$

6: **end for**

7: **if** there is more than one D2D pair that satisfies

8:    $|\mathcal{R}_j| = 1$ and the $i \in \mathcal{R}_j$ is the same **then**

9:    find $j^* = \arg\ \max_{i \in \mathcal{R}_{j^*}} R_j^d(p_i, q_{j^*})$ and D2D pair

10:    j^* reuse the link of cellular user i

11:    delete i from other D2D pairs' $\mathcal{R}_j$ and upgrade

12:    $|\mathcal{R}_j|$ and $\mathcal{M}$

13: **end if**

14: **for all** $j \in \mathcal{S} \setminus \{j^*\}$

15:        choose cellular users in $\mathcal{R}_j$ for D2D pair j in

16:        the order of $\mathcal{M}$

17: **end for**

18: find $\max \sum_{j \in \mathcal{S}} R_i^d(p_i, q_j)$

Here, we investigate how to choose a cellular user in $\mathcal{R}_j$ for D2D pairs with reuse mode to maximize the rate of all these D2D pairs while guaranteeing that each of them can access a cellular candidate to share its link.

Without loss of generality, we assume that each cellular user and D2D pair has the same transmit power respectively, which ensures that every D2D pair has the same chance to reuse links and the same chance for cellular users to be reused. According to the previous subsection, we have determined $\mathcal{R}_j$ for each D2D pair and $\mathcal{S}$ by finding D2D pair j when it satisfies $\mathcal{R}_j = \emptyset$.

There are three steps in the link allocation algorithm. We firstly calculate $|\mathcal{R}_j|$, which denotes the number of $\mathcal{R}_j$, and obtain $\mathcal{M}$, which contains the D2D pairs with $|\mathcal{R}_j|$ in increasing order. According to this, we can try to allocate cellular users with priority to those with less candidates and ensure each D2D pair will find a partner. Then, considering that different D2D pairs may have only one cellular candidate, if there is more than one D2D pair that can only share the link of cellular user i, we allocate link i to D2D pair j^* which can achieve the maximum rate, as shown in line 4 to 13. Finally, we match the remaining D2D pairs with cellular candidates in the order of $\mathcal{M}$, as line 14 to 17 indicate. And we will find a union of D2D-cellular pairs which can maximiz $\sum_{j \in \mathcal{S}} R_i^d(p_i, q_i)$. Therefore, we can guarantee a kind of fairness for D2D pairs, and also achieve the maximum benefit in that case.

3.3   Optimal Power Control for Cellular Users and D2D Pairs

In previous subsections, we have matched D2D pair with appropriate cellular users. Hence, we denote the cellular user and its link which is reused by D2D pair j as index j as well. We rewrite problem (5) as,

$$\text{maximize} \quad \sum_{j=1}^{N} R_j^d(p_j, q_j) \tag{10}$$

$$\text{subject to} \quad R_j^c(p_j, q_j) \geq \rho_j, \forall j \in \mathcal{C} \tag{10a}$$

$$R_j^d(p_j, q_j) \geq \gamma_j, \forall j \in \mathcal{S} \tag{10b}$$

$$0 \leq p_j \leq P_j, \forall j \in \mathcal{C} \tag{10c}$$

$$0 \leq q_j \leq Q_j, \forall j \in \mathcal{S} \tag{10d}$$

$$\sum_{j=1}^{N} q_j \leq Q \tag{10e}$$

Then, we denote $\alpha_j = h_j^c/\sigma_N^2$, $\beta_j = h_j^d/\sigma_N^2$, $\gamma_j = g_j^d/\sigma_N^2$, and $\theta_j = g_j^c/\sigma_N^2$ as the normalized channel gains. And the rate of D2D-cellular pair j is expressed as,

$$R_j^c(p_j, q_j) = log_2(1 + \frac{p_j \alpha_j}{1 + q_j \gamma_j}) \tag{11}$$

$$R_j^d(p_j, q_j) = log_2(1 + \frac{q_j \beta_j}{1 + p_j \theta_j}) \tag{12}$$

Now, we will propose an optimal power control strategy for all these paired users to solve the problem in (10).

Proposition 2. *Denote* (p_j^*, q_j^*) *as the optimal power allocation for problem (10), and* $k_j = 2^{P_j} - 1$. *Then, for all* $j = 1, \ldots, N$, *we define* $A_j = k_j \gamma_j \theta_j (\alpha_j \beta_j + k_j \gamma_j \theta_j)$, $B_j = (\alpha_j + k_j \theta_j)(2k_j \gamma_j \theta_j + \alpha_j \beta_j)$, $C_j = (\alpha_j + k_j \theta_j)(\frac{\alpha_j + k_j \theta_j - \alpha_j \beta_j}{\lambda})$ *and renew* $Q_j = $ $\min\left\{Q_j, \frac{\alpha_j P_j - k_j}{k_j \gamma_j}\right\}$. *We can get the optimal solution as, (i) if* $\sum_{j=1}^{N} Q_j \leq Q$, *then,* $q_j^* = Q_j$,

$p_j^* = \frac{k_j(1 + \gamma_j Q_j)}{\alpha_j}$. *(ii) if* $\sum_{j=1}^{N} Q_j > Q$, *then,* $q_j^* = \left[\frac{\sqrt{B_j^2 - 4A_j C_j(\lambda)} - B_j}{2A_j}\right]_0^{Q_j}$, $p_j^* = \frac{k_j(1 + \gamma_j q_j^*)}{\alpha_j}$, *where*

$[\cdot]_0^{Q_j}$ *indicates the projection onto the interval* $[0, Q_j]$.

Proof. The rate of D2D pair j defined in (12) is monotonically decreasing by increasing p_j, when q_j is fixed. Moreover, to satisfy the constraint in (10a), we can get $p_j \geq \frac{k_j(1 + \gamma_j q_j)}{\alpha_j}$, and hence, the optimal p_j^* is obtained when $p_j^* = p_{j,min} = \frac{k_j(1 + \gamma_j q_j)}{\alpha_j}$. Then, we substitute it into (12) and it can be further expressed as

$$R_j^d(p_j^*, q_j) = \log_2\left(1 + \frac{\alpha_j \beta_j q_j}{\alpha_j + k_j \theta_j + k_j \gamma_j \theta_j q_j}\right) \tag{13}$$

Now, we investigate how to decide q_j in (13) to maximize the sum rate of D2D pairs.

Denote $h(q_j) = \frac{\alpha_j \beta_j q_j}{\alpha_j + k_j \theta_j + k_j \gamma_j \theta_j q_j}$, we can easily confirm that

$$h'(q_j) = \frac{\alpha_j \beta_j (\alpha_j + k_j \theta_j)}{(\alpha_j + k_j \theta_j + k_j \gamma_j \theta_j q_j)^2} \geq 0 \tag{14}$$

$$h''(q_j) = -\frac{2k_j \alpha_j \beta_j \gamma_j \theta_j (\alpha_j + k_j \theta_j)}{(\alpha_j + k_j \theta_j + k_j \gamma_j \theta_j q_j)^3} \leq 0 \tag{15}$$

It is obviously that $h(q_j)$ is a concave function and increases by increasing q_j, which contributes to that $R_j^d(p_j^*, q_j)$ is also a concave function and increases with the increasing of q_j. Now, we have transformed the problem in (5) which is nonconvex into a convex one indicated in (10).

In order to maximize $R_j^d(p_j^*, q_j)$ in (13), it is essential to determine the feasible region of q_j. The power constraint in (10c) is equal to $q_j \leq \frac{\alpha_j P_j - k_j}{k_j \gamma_j}$, therefore, we renew the power limit as $Q_j = \min\left\{Q_j, \frac{\alpha_j P_j - k_j}{k_j \gamma_j}\right\}$. To solve the problem in (10), we consider two different situations, (i) if $\sum_{j=1}^{N} Q_j \leq Q$, we can take $q_j^* = Q_j$ to maximize $R_j^d(p_j^*, q_j^*)$.

And accordingly, $p_j^* = \frac{k_j(1 + \gamma_j Q_j^*)}{\alpha_j}$. (ii) if $\sum_{j=1}^{N} Q_j > Q$ we use Lagrangian Algorithm to solve the problem: $l(q,\lambda) = \ln 2 \sum_{j=1}^{N} \log_2(1 + \frac{\alpha_j \beta_j q_j}{\alpha_j + k_j \theta_j + k_j \gamma_j \theta_j q_j}) + \lambda(Q - \sum_{j=1}^{N} q_j)$ with $\lambda \geq 0$.

Then, we will illustrate how to find the optimal solution with the constraint $\sum_{j=1}^{N} q_j^* = Q$.

The first partial derivative of $l(q,\lambda)$ with respect to λ is given as,

$$\frac{\partial l(q,\lambda)}{\partial q_j} = \frac{\alpha_j \beta_j (\alpha_j + k_j \theta_j)}{(\alpha_j + k_j \theta_j + k_j \gamma_j \theta_j q_j)^2 + \alpha_j \beta_j q_j (\alpha_j + k_j \theta_j + k_j \gamma_j \theta_j q_j)} - \lambda \qquad (16)$$

The solution of problem (10) is equal to that $\frac{\partial l(q,\lambda)}{\partial q_j} = 0$ and it is obvious that there will be a feasible solution only when λ is positive. Therefore, we can get a quadratic equation expressed as $A_j q_j^{*2} + B_j q_j^* + C_j(\lambda) = 0$, with $A_j, B_j, C_j(\lambda)$ defined in proposition 2, and the projection of the positive solution for the equation is onto $[0, Q_j]$.

By now, we are able to investigate how to get a proper λ to determine q_j^*, which is difficult with direct computing. We can primarily confirm an interval $[0, \lambda_{max}]$, where $\lambda_{max} = \max_{j \in S} \left\{ \frac{\alpha_j \beta_j}{\alpha_j + k_j \theta_j} \right\}$, according to $C_j(\lambda) \leq 0$, which ensures $B_j^2 - 4A_j C_j(\lambda)$ in proposition 2 positive. Moreover, given the condition that q_j^* is monotonically decreasing as λ increases, and that we can absolutely find a positive root in the feasible region, bisection method is exploited to obtain the optimal λ^*. Thus, we can finally determine an optimal λ^* to get the power allocation strategy as (p_j^*, q_j^*).

4 Numerical Results

The simulation setup is as follows: Consider a hexagonal cell with a radius of 250 m, where the BS is centered, and some cellular users and potential D2D pairs are randomly where the BS is centered, and some cellular users and potential D2D pairs are randomly distributed. Each potential D2D transmitter is 50 m away from its receiver. The power spectral density of additive white Gaussian noise is 10^{-8} W/Hz, and the QoS threshold of cellular users is $\rho_i = \gamma_j = 1$ bit/s. It is verified in [10] that the maximum SNR of cellular user i is $\alpha_i P_i$, and without loss of generality, we set P_i for each cellular user so that they can reach the same maximum SNR.

Figure 3 shows the sum rate of D2D pairs at different total D2D SNR, which is denoted by Q/σ_N^2 [10], comparing the performance with different amount of cellular users. As the number of cellular users increases, the rate of D2D pairs derived by our proposed scheme also increases, however, the speed of the increasing is slower gradually. When there are only 8 or 16 cellular users for the 4 D2D pairs we set in the cell, the sum rate of the D2D pairs increases obviously. However, when the amount of cellular users is up to 32 and above, the performance tends to approach. Note that, for a fixed amount of D2D pairs, if there exists only a small number of cellular candidates, there is a larger space for them to improve the performance, and their rate will increase dramatically with the increasing of cellular users. While if they have well enough cellular candidates to choose, they can achieve a fairly high rate as a whole and the effect of increasing cellular users is less obvious.

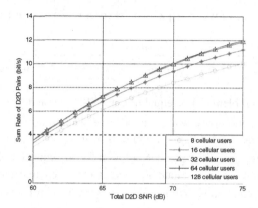

Fig. 3. The sum rate of D2D pairs versus total D2D SNR with different amount of cellular users.

As Fig. 4 indicates, the sum rate of D2D pairs is almost linearly increased by increasing the power limit of each D2D pair. And at a fixed power limit, the D2D pairs with more cellular users to reuse perform better. Actually, with D2D power limit increasing, D2D pairs will choose different cellular users to reuse and they are more likely to obtain higher rate.

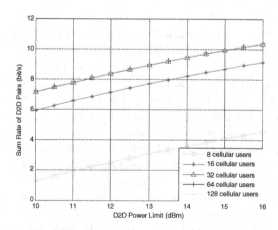

Fig. 4. The sum rate of D2D pairs versus D2D power limit with different amount of cellular users.

To comparison, we compare the proposed scheme to two other algorithms,

(i) Global search: it doesn't divide an ILA for D2D pairs or consider fairness when D2D pairs choose cellular candidates to share. Since the global search only deals with link allocation, we incorporate the proposed power control strategy into it.
(ii) Suboptimal power control [10]: it is based on waterfilling algorithm, in which the cellular users simply use their maximum power.

We consider a cell with 16 cellular users and 4 potential D2D pairs. Figure 5 indicates that the proposed scheme can obtain higher D2D rate than suboptimal power control strategy, while lower than global search. After ILA division in the first step, our proposed scheme performs better than global search in pairing, in terms of computational complexity. And the suboptimal power control only optimizes the power of D2D pairs with a fixed cellular users' power. As shown in Fig. 6, with the increasing of total D2D SNR, the average energy efficiency of cellular users is monotonically decreasing. Since D2D pairs use a higher power and then cause more severe interference to their shared cellular users, cellular users have to increase their transmit power to reach the rate threshold. The proposed scheme can perform better than two other algorithms with regard to energy efficiency of cellular users. As the simulation result indicates, D2D pairs tend to choose cellular users which are far away from them and the BS which cause less interference in global search, and in that case, cellular users will use a higher transmit power. Moreover, in the suboptimal power control scheme, cellular users simply use their fixed maximum power. Then, by jointly optimizing the power of D2D-cellular pair while satisfying the total SNR constraint, our scheme achieves better performance.

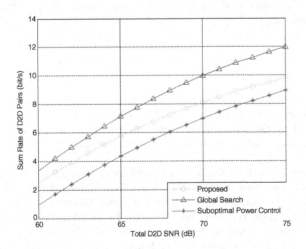

Fig. 5. The sum rate of D2D pairs versus total D2D SNR.

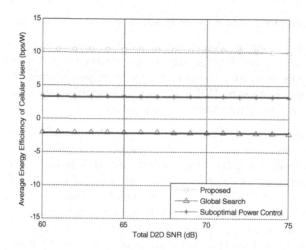

Fig. 6. Average energy efficiency of cellular users versus total D2D SNR.

5 Conclusion

In this paper, we investigated D2D communication as an underlay sharing uplink resources in cellular networks and proposed a joint mode selection and resource allocation scheme which jointly considers mode selection, link allocation and power control. In particular, we maximized the sum rate of D2D pairs with guaranteed QoS requirements of existing cellular users, as well as D2D pairs. Moreover, we set a fairness principle to ensure that each D2D pair shares links with a cellular user. Simulation results demonstrated that the proposed scheme brings substantial performance improvements.

References

1. Feng, D., Lu, L., Wu, Y.Y., Li, G.Y., Li, S., Feng, G.: Device-to-device communications in cellular networks. IEEE Commun. Mag. **52**(4), 49–55 (2014)
2. Wei, L., Hu, R.Q., Qian, Y., Wu, G.: Enable device-to-device communications underlaying cellular networks: challenges and research aspects. IEEE Commun. Mag. **52**(6), 90–96 (2014)
3. Wu, D., Wang, J., Hu, R.Q., Cai, Y.: Energy-efficient resource sharing for mobile device-to-device multimedia communications. IEEE Trans. Veh. Technol. **63**(5), 2093–2103 (2014)
4. Wu, D., Cai, Y., Hu, R.Q., Qian, Y.: Dynamic distributed resource sharing for mobile D2D communications. IEEE Trans. Wireless Commun. **14**(10), 5417–5429 (2015)
5. Zhang, H., Jiang, C., Beaulieu, N.C., Chu, X., Wen, X., Tao, M.: Resource allocation in spectrum-sharing OFDMA femtocells with heterogeneous services. IEEE Trans. Commun. **62**(7), 2366–2377 (2014)
6. Zhang, H., Jiang, C., Beaulieu, N.C., Chu, X., Wang, X., Quek, T.: Resource allocation for cognitive small cell networks: a cooperative bargaining game theoretic approach. IEEE Trans. Wireless Commun. **14**(6), 3481–3493 (2015)

7. Asadi, A., Wang, Q., Mancuso, V.: A survey on device-to-device communication in cellular networks. IEEE Commun. Surv. Tuts. **16**(4), 1801–1818 (2014). Fourth quarter
8. Min, H., Lee, J., Park, S., Hong, D.: Capacity enhancement using an interference limited area for device-to-device uplink underlaying cellular networks. IEEE Trans. Wireless Commun. **10**(12), 3995–4000 (2011)
9. Duong, Q., Shin, O.: Distance-based interference coordination for device-to-device communications in cellular networks. In: Proceedings of Ubiquitous and Future Networks (ICUFN), pp. 776–779, Da Nang, July 2013
10. Wang, J., Zhu, D., Zhao, C., Li, G.Y., Lei, M.: Resource sharing of underlaying device to device and uplink cellular communications. IEEE Commun. Lett. **17**(6), 1148–1151 (2013)
11. Meshgi, H., Zhao, D., Zheng, R.: Joint channel and power allocation in underlay multicast device-to-device communications. In: Proceedings of the IEEE International Conference on Communications (ICC), pp. 2937–2942, London, June 2015
12. Feng, D., Lu, L., Wu, Y.Y., Li, G.Y., Feng, G., Li, S.: Device-to-device communications underlaying cellular networks. IEEE Trans. Commun. **61**(8), 3541–3551 (2013)
13. Zhang, H., Jiang, C., Mao, X., Chen, H.H.: Interference-limit resource optimization in cognitive femtocells with fairness and imperfect spectrum sensing. IEEE Trans. Veh. Technol. **65**(3), 1761–1771 (2016)

PAPR Reduction with Amplitude Clipping and Subband Filter in Filtered-OFDM System

Changsen Nie and Yong Bai[(✉)]

State Key Lab of Marine Resource Utilization in South China Sea,
College of Information Science and Technology, Hainan University,
58 Renmin Ave., Haikou 570228, Hainan, China
bai@hainu.edu.cn

Abstract. To reduce the PAPR (Peak-to-Average Power Ratio) in the Filtered-OFDM (F-OFDM) system, we propose an amplitude clipping method working together with the subband filter in the F-OFDM system. Firstly, a power level is preset to clip the real and imaginary parts of F-OFDM signals for reducing the peak energy of transmitted signals. Then the spectrum leakage and distortion caused by amplitude clipping are mitigated by the designed subband filter of F-OFDM system. The simulation results demonstrate that such a combined method can suppress PAPR effectively and maintains good BER (Bit Error Rate) performance compared with the traditional OFDM system.

Keywords: F-OFDM · PAPR · Subband filter · Amplitude clipping

1 Introduction

OFDM (Orthogonal Frequency Division Multiplexing) [1, 2] is the main multi-carrier modulation technology that is widely used in 4G system. OFDM offers a considerable high spectral efficiency, power efficiency, and immunity to the frequency selective fading channels. There are more challenges for 5G mobile communication technologies to support stricter transmitting requirements. F-OFDM (Filtered-OFDM) [3–5], OFDM with subband filter, is proposed by Huawei as an approach to reduce high frequency spectrum leakage and large out-of-band interference for 5G system [6–8].

One challenging issue in OFDM system is high Peak-to-Average Power Ratio (PAPR) of transmitted signals. F-OFDM signals also consist of many independent and orthogonal sub-carriers, and have the problem of high PAPR [9–11]. Meanwhile, the subband filter in the F-OFDM system can also increase the PAPR. Hence, efficient PAPR reduction is needed for F-OFDM system. The PAPR reduction schemes can mainly be categorized into signal scrambling techniques (e.g., block codes and PTS) and signal distortion techniques such as amplitude clipping. Amplitude clipping [12, 13] is the simplest technique for PAPR reduction. It is a predistortion technology that basically clips the parts of the signals when they are above a preset clipping level. However, clipping method introduces both in-band distortion and out-of-band radiation into OFDM signals, which degrades the system performance such as BER and spectral efficiency. To counter the drawbacks of amplitude clipping, one filter can be added after clipping to reduce the in-band distortion and out-of-band radiation.

© ICST Institute for Computer Sciences, Social Informatics and Telecommunications Engineering 2018
K. Long et al. (Eds.): 5GWN 2017, LNICST 211, pp. 220–227, 2018.
https://doi.org/10.1007/978-3-319-72823-0_21

This paper proposes to reduce PAPR of F-OFDM system [14, 15] by amplitude clipping and subband filtering. With our proposed method, the PAPR of the F-OFDM system can be reduced, and the out-of-band radiation caused by amplitude clipping can be reduced by the inherent subband filter in F-OFDM system. Hence, it is not necessary to design a special filter after clipping in our approach. The simulation results demonstrated that our proposed method can suppress PAPR effectively and still maintains a good BER performance in F-OFDM system.

This paper is organized as follows. In Sect. 2, we describe the PAPR reduction method for F-OFDM system by using amplitude clipping and subband filter. Section 3 presents and discusses the simulation results of our proposed method. Section 4 concludes this paper.

2 F-OFDM with Amplitude Clipping and Subband Filter

F-OFDM is an improvement on the basis of OFDM. F-OFDM has lower out-of-band leakage by dividing the whole band into multiple subbands and add subband filter in the sender and receiver of OFDM system. This helps F-OFDM system to have higher spectral efficiency compared with OFDM. Moreover, F-OFDM system enables flexible waveforms in the 5G networks. Each subband of F-OFDM system can be processed independently by configuring different parameters, such as sub-carrier spacing, IFFT points and CP (Cyclic Prefix) length, to make the waveform meet the requirements for different 5G scenarios. The system model of F-OFDM system is shown in Fig. 1. Compared with traditional OFDM system, the F-OFDM system adds two new modules, subcarrier mapping and subband filter.

To reduce the high PAPR in F-OFDM system, our proposal utilizes amplitude clipping technology and the subband filter in F-OFDM system. The added clipping module (in red color) is shown in Fig. 1. The power level is preset to control the peak values of F-OFDM signals, and the spectrum leakage can be suppressed by the designed subband filter.

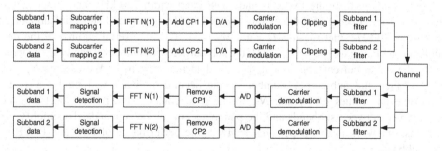

Fig. 1. F-OFDM system model with PAPR reduction (Color figure online)

2.1   Subcarrier Mapping

The F-OFDM algorithm need to give index numbers of all subcarriers and map different subband data to different sub-carriers separated in frequency domain. The sub-carrier mapping function ensures that different subbands are configured with different parameters for simultaneous transmission and the signals can be decoupled in the receiver.

Figure 2 shows an example by taking two subbands. It is assumed that the number of subcarriers of the first subband is M_1, the number of subcarriers of the second subband is M_2, and the size of IFFT points is 2048. The serial number of 2048 subcarriers is $[K_{min}\ K_{max}]$. K_{min} and K_{max} is the integers within the scope of $[-1023, 1024]$. We suppose the number of subcarriers of guard band for the first subband is N_1, and the number of subcarriers of guard band for the second subband is N_2.

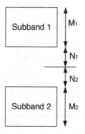

Fig. 2. Subcarrier mapping between subbands

The serial number of the sub-carriers of the second subband can be calculated by

$$[\frac{K_{max}+N_1}{2}+N_2+1, \frac{K_{max}+N_1}{2}+N_2+M_2] \tag{1}$$

There $K_{max}+N_1$ must be an even number.

For example, there are two subbands with band width 720 kHz, and suppose that the sub-carrier spacing of the first subband is 15 kHz, the second subband sub-carrier spacing is 30 kHz, that means $M_1 = 48$, $M_2 = 24$. Then the serial number of the first subband can be set as $[-24,-1]$ $[1,24]$, the sub-carrier with number 0 can be considered to be the direct current component without data mapping in it. We assume $N_1 = 0$, $N_2 = 1$, then the sub-carrier number of the second subband will be $[14,37]$. To determine the values of N_1 and N_2, we need to consider the power spectrum, the interference between subbands and the parameters of all the subbands. To simplify the analysis, our work in this paper only analyzes the performance of PSD and PAPR in one subband.

2.2   The PAPR Reduction with Amplitude Clipping

PAPR is defined as the ratio of maximum peak power and mean power, which is represented as

$$PAPR_{dB} = 10 \lg \left\{ \frac{\max\limits_{0 \leq n < N} (|x_n|^2)}{\frac{1}{N} \sum_{n=0}^{N-1} |x_n|^2} \right\} \tag{2}$$

Complementary cumulative distribution function (CCDF) can be used to evaluate the performance of PAPR. CCDF shows the possibility of PAPR that exceeds a given threshold. Amplitude clipping technology reduces the peak energy of signal by setting a power level. However, traditional amplitude clipping method can lead to signal distortion and out-of-band leakage after clipping process, and it needs to add a filter to mitigate this issue. Our proposal combines the subband filter in F-OFDM system and amplitude clipping technology. Thus, the subband filter plays another role in our approach to mitigate the drawbacks of amplitude clipping. The subband filter in F-OFDM system can reduce frequency spectrum leakage and out-of-band interference effectively. Hence, it is not necessary to design a special filter after clipping in our proposed approach. Meanwhile, F-OFDM system divides the whole band into multiple subbands, and we can perform clipping and filtering in each subband.

Denote the send signals as x_n, the clipping process on the real part and imaginary part of the transmitted signals can be represented as

$$\text{Re}(X_n) = \begin{cases} \text{Re}(x_n) & |x_n| \leq A \\ p \times \text{Re}(x_n) & |x_n| > A \end{cases} \tag{3}$$

$$\text{Im}(X_n) = \begin{cases} \text{Im}(x_n) & |x_n| \leq A \\ p \times \text{Im}(x_n) & |x_n| > A \end{cases} \tag{4}$$

where X_n is the F-OFDM signal after clipping, A is the given power threshold, p is the limiting factor with scope of $[0,1]$. The peak energy of F-OFDM signal can be suppressed directly by clipping process. Then X_n will be filtered by the subband filter, which can reduce the out-of-band leakage effectively and improve the performance of transmitted signals. In Sect. 3, the simulation results will demonstrate that our proposed method can suppress PAPR effectively and still maintains good BER performance in F-OFDM system.

2.3   Design of Subband Filter

It can be noted in the F-OFDM system block diagram that the F-OFDM signal is transformed to the time domain after IFFT before the subband filter. It is discrete time domain signal on each sub-carrier. We need to design D/A transfer filter $g(t)$ to transfer the discrete signal to continuous wave signal (e.g., rectangular wave, square-root raised cosine wave). To reduce high PAPR of the signal, the signal is clipped after carrier modulation by setting a power level to reduce peak energy and the clipped signal is further filtered by the subband filter. The subband filter can reduce the out-of-band leakage and the signal distortion caused by clipping process. The design of subband filter uses the traditional window function method, that is to add different window functions to the Sinc function in time domain. It can be expressed by

$$W_{\sin c} \times W_{win} = W_{filter} \tag{5}$$

The design of subband filter in this paper is based on Hanning window which is known as cosine square or ascending cosine window. The time domain form of Hanning window can be expressed as

$$W(n) = \frac{1}{2}\left[1 - \cos\left(\frac{2\pi n}{N-1}\right)\right]R_N(n) \tag{6}$$

The spectral function of Hanning window can be represented as

$$W(e^{j\omega}) = \left\{0.5W_R(\omega) + 0.25\left[W_R\left(\omega - \frac{2\pi}{N-1}\right) + W_R\left(\omega + \frac{2\pi}{N-1}\right)\right]\right\}e^{-j\left(\frac{N-1}{2}\right)\omega} \tag{7}$$

$$= W(\omega)e^{-j\left(\frac{N-1}{2}\right)\omega} \tag{8}$$

where $W_R(e^{j\omega}) = W_R(\omega)e^{-j\left(\frac{N-1}{2}\right)\omega}$.

When N is very greater than 1, it can be approximated as

$$W(\omega) \approx 0.5W_R(\omega) + 0.25\left[W_R\left(\omega - \frac{2\pi}{N}\right)\right] + W_R\left(\omega + \frac{2\pi}{N}\right) \tag{9}$$

The sum of the three parts makes the sidelobe largely canceled out, and energy is more concentrated in the main lobe.

When designing the subband filter, the filter length N need to be chosen to be an appropriate value because larger N helps to reduce the spectrum leakage but may lead to larger PAPR and degrade the BER performance.

3 Simulation and Discussion

3.1 Simulation Parameters of F-OFDM System

In the simulated F-OFDM system, the size of IFFT is 2048, the number of effective sub-carriers is 336, and the other sub-carriers are set to zero. The sub-carrier spacing is set to 15 kHz according to 3GPP standard, then the subband band width is 5.04 MHz. In addition, the CP length is 128. Table 1 shows the parameters of F-OFDM system for simulation. We choose 4QAM as the modulation method on the subcarriers. The sending signal before the subband filter is rectangular wave signal. The order of the subband filter $(N - 1)$ is chosen to be 128 to balance the tradeoff between the spectrum leakage reduction and the BER performance.

Table 1. Parameters of simulation

Parameter	Sub-band
Modulation system	4QAM
Sub-carrier spacing	15 kHz
FFT points	2048
Used sub-carriers	336
CP length	128
Bandwidth	5.04 MHz
Symbol period	1/15 K = 66.67us
Carrier frequency	76.8 MHz

3.2 Simulation Results and Discussion

Figure 3 shows the respective PSD (Power Spectrum Density) of clipping OFDM signal and clipping F-OFDM signal. We can see that the subband filter results in smaller out-of-band leakage in the clipping F-OFDM signal than that in the clipping OFDM signal, and the clipping F-OFDM signal has better PSD performance compares with clipping OFDM signal. Note that

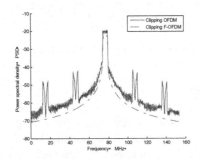

Fig. 3. PSD of clipping OFDM signal and clipping F-OFDM signal

Figure 4 shows the CCDF of OFDM signal, F-OFDM signal, clipping OFDM signal and clipping F-OFDM signal. The simulation results show that the subband filter deteriorates the PAPR performance such that the PAPR of F-OFDM signal is higher than that of OFDM signal. We can see clearly that the PAPR of clipping F-OFDM signal is much lower than that of the F-OFDM signal, which means our proposed method can reduce PAPR effectively.

Figure 5 shows the BER performance of OFDM and F-OFDM system. It can be seen that clipping F-OFDM system has a better BER performance than the clipping OFDM system. The BER of clipping F-OFDM system is a little bit higher than that of F-OFDM due to the fact that the clipping process causes out-of-band interference. Then we can know that our proposed method not only has good PAPR performance but also maintains good BER performance.

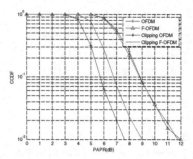

Fig. 4. PAPR of OFDM and F-OFDM

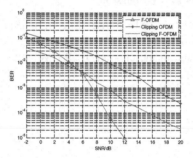

Fig. 5. BERs of OFDM and F-OFDM

4 Conclusion

Filter-OFDM signals for 5G wireless system also have the problem of high PAPR like OFDM system. This paper proposes to reduce the PAPR of F-OFDM system by amplitude clipping and subband filtering. Our proposed approach can suppress the PAPR of the F-OFDM system and reduce the in-band distortion and out-of-band radiation by the inherent subband filter in F-OFDM system. Thus, the subband filter plays another role in our approach to mitigate the drawbacks of amplitude clipping. Hence, it is not necessary to design a special filter after clipping as is required when using amplitude clipping in the traditional OFDM system. We investigated our proposal by simulation according to the 3GPP transmission parameters and we demonstrated that our proposed method can suppress PAPR effectively and maintains a good BER performance in F-OFDM system.

Acknowledgments. This paper was supported by the National Natural Science Foundation of China (Grant No. 61561017), National Science & Technology Pillar Program (Grant No. 2014BAD10B04), Hainan Province Major Science & Technology Project (Grant No. ZDKJ2016015), Open Sub-project of State Key Laboratory of Marine Resource Utilization in South China Sea (Grant No. 2016013B), and Hainan Province Natural Science Foundation of China (Grant No. 617033).

References

1. Hmood, J.K., Noordin, K.A.: Mitigation of phase noise in all-optical OFDM systems based on minimizing interaction time between subcarriers. J. Opt. Commun. **355**, 313–320 (2015)
2. Berbra, K., Barkat, M.: A fast spectrum sensing for CP-OFDM cognitive radio based on adaptive thresholding. J. Sig. Process. **128**, 252–261 (2016)
3. Zhang, X., Jia, M., Chen, L., Ma, J.: Filtered-OFDM - enabler for flexible waveform in the 5th generation cellular networks. In: 2015 IEEE Global Communications Conference (GLOBECOM), pp. 1–6. IEEE Press, New York (2015)
4. Abdoli, J., Jia, M., Ma, J.: Filtered OFDM: a new waveform for future wireless systems. In: 2015 IEEE 16th International Workshop on Signal Processing Advances in Wireless Communications (SPAWC), pp. 66–70. IEEE Press, New York (2015)
5. Huawei, HiSilicon: R1-164033, f-OFDM scheme and filter design. Nanjing, China (2016)
6. GokulRaj, N., Umapathy, K.: 5G wireless mesh network 802.11 s load balancing architecture for 802.11 Bgn radio-PCI interface. J. Procedia Comput. Sci. **87**, 252–257 (2016)
7. Panwar, N., Sharma, S., Singh, A.K.: A survey on 5G: the next generation of mobile communication. Phys. Commun. J. **18**, 64–84 (2016)
8. Tong, W., Ma, J., Huawei, P.Z.: Enabling technologies for 5G air-interface with emphasis on spectral efficiency in the presence of very large number of links. In: 2015 21st Asia-Pacific Conference on Communications, Kyoto, Japan, pp. 184–187 (2016)
9. Singh, S., Kumar, A.: Performance analysis of adaptive clipping technique for reduction of PAPR in alamouti coded MIMO-OFDM systems. J. Procedia Comput. Sci. **93**, 609–616 (2016)
10. Zhou, J., Zhang, Z., Zhang, T.: A combined PAPR-reduction technique for asymmetrically clipped optical OFDM system. J. Opt. Commun. **366**, 451–456 (2016)
11. Naeiny, M.F., Marvasti, F.: Iterative clipping recovery in spatially multiplexed OFDM systems. J. Sci. Iran. **19**, 739–744 (2012)
12. Wang, Y.C., Luo, Z.Q.: Optimized iterative clipping and filtering for PAPR reduction of OFDM signals. In: IEEE Transactions on Communications, pp. 33–37. IEEE Press, New York (2011)
13. AliHemmati, R., Azmi, P.: Clipping distortion mitigation in OFDM systems over fading channels by using DFT-based method. J. Comput. Electr. Eng. **31**, 431–443 (2005)
14. Petra, W., Jamal, B., Katsutoshi, K.: Adaptive filtered OFDM with regular resource grid. In: 2016 IEEE International Conference on Communications Workshops, pp. 462–467. IEEE Press, New York (2016)
15. Cheng, X., He, Y., Ge, B.: A filtered OFDM using FIR filter based on window function method. In: IEEE Vehicular Technology Conference. IEEE Press, New York (2016)

Throughput Maximization for Two-Hop Decode-and-Forward Relay Channels with Non-ideal Circuit Power

Hengjing Liang[1,2]([✉]), Xiaojie Wen[2], Chuan Huang[1,2], Zhi Chen[1,2], and Shaoqian Li[1,2]

[1] National Key Laboratory of Science and Technology on Communications,
University of Electronic Science and Technology of China,
Chengdu, People's Republic of China
lianghj@hotmail.com, {huangch,chenzhi,lsq}@uestc.edu.cn
[2] Beijing Institute of Satelite Information Engineering,
Beijing, People's Republic of China
ziwen7189@aliyun.com

Abstract. This paper studies the throughput maximization problem for a two-hop relay channel considering non-ideal circuit power. In particular, the relay operates in a half-duplex manner, and the decode-and-forward (DF) relaying scheme is adopted. Considering the extra power consumption by the circuits, the optimal power allocation to maximize the throughput of the considered system over the infinite time horizon is investigated. By transforming the non-convex problem into the quasiconcave one, the closed-form solution shows that the source and the relay transmit with certain probability, which is determined by the average power budget, circuit power consumption, and channel gains. Numerical results show that the optimal power allocation scheme outperforms other conventional schemes.

Keywords: Green communication · Relay channel
Throughput maximization · Optimal power allocation
Decode-and-forward (Df)

1 Introduction

Green communication has drawn great attention during the past years. The energy consumed by communication networks constitute a large portion of total energy consumption, and will still go up in the future [1]. The growing cost of fossil fuel energy calls for both environmental and economical demands and motivations for the design of green communications.

Circuit energy consumption amounts for a significant part of the total energy consumption [2]. In order to save energy, green communication associated with

This work was supported by the National Natural Science Foundation of China under Grand No. 61401030.

non-ideal circuit power needs to be designed both energy and spectrum efficiently. In [3], a link adaptation scheme that balances circuit power consumption and transmission power was proposed in frequency-selective channels. Energy efficiency (EE) maximization problems with circuit energy consumption was also considered in orthogonal frequency division multiple access in [4]. A throughput optimal policy considering circuit power was proposed for point-to-point channels with energy harvesting transmitter [5].

Relaying has been considered as a promising technique to mitigate fading and extend coverage in wireless networks [6]. The capacity of a classical three-node relay channel, consisting of a source, a destination, and a single half-duplex DF relay, was investigated in [7]. Green communication problems in relay networks were discussed in [8–10]. In [8,9], energy minimization problems considering channel state information acquiring energy and signaling overhead were investigated in single relay selection schemes, respectively. In [10], non-zero circuit power consumption was considered for a total energy minimization problem in multihop relay channels. Most of the existing problems associated with the non-ideal circuit power consumptions focused on the total energy consumption minimization, whereas the throughput maximization problems were rarely investigated.

In this paper, throughput maximization for a two-hop half-duplex Gaussian relay channels considering non-ideal circuit power is studied over the infinite time horizon. The transceiver circuitry consumes a constant amount of power in the active mode and negligible power in the sleep mode. Under this setup, the optimal power allocations for the throughput maximization of the two-hop relay channel is investigated. By solving a max-min problem, the optimal power allocation shows that the source and the relay transmit either at a certain portion of time slots or constantly according to different average power budgets, circuit power consumptions, and channel power gains. Then, the average throughput and asymptotic analysis of the relay channel is studied. Finally, simulation results show that the optimal power allocation scheme outperforms other conventional schemes.

The rest of this paper is organized as follows. Section 2 introduces the signal model of this paper. Section 3 introduces the power consumption model. Section 4 studies the optimal power allocation and the throughput performances in low SNR and high SNR regimes. Section 5 evaluates the throughput performances by simulations and finally Sect. 6 concludes the paper.

2   Signal Model

This paper considers a two-hop relay channel as shown in Fig. 1, which consists of a source, a destination, and a half-duplex relay. The source sends information to the destination via the relay, and the direct link is unavailable. Slotted transmission scheme is adopted, and each time slot is with duration T.

Then, channel input and output relationship of the considered relay channel is introduced. Denote the channel coefficients of the source-relay and the relay-destination links as g_{SR} and g_{RD}, respectively, and then the channel power gains of the two links are given by

$$h_{SR} = |g_{SR}|^2, \quad h_{RD} = |g_{RD}|^2, \tag{1}$$

which are all constants across the time slots.

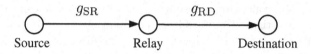

Fig. 1. A two-hop relay channel.

When the DF relaying scheme is adopted, it operates in a half-duplex manner (one time slot is then divided into two phases), and the information encoding and decoding processes are described as follows:

1. In the first phase of time slot i, the source transmits $x(i)$ to the relay with power $P_S(i)$;
2. Then, the received signal at the relay during the first phase of time slot i is given as

$$y_R(i) = g_{SR}x(i) + n_R(i), \tag{2}$$

where $n_R(i)$ is the independent and identically distributed (i.i.d.) circularly symmetric complex Gaussian (CSCG) noise with zero mean and unit variance. Next, the relay decodes the source message, re-encodes it into a new signal $\tilde{x}(i)$, and forwards $\tilde{x}(i)$ to the destination with power $P_R(i)$.

3. Finally, the destination receives the signals over the second phase of time slot i, and the received signal $y_D(i)$ at the destination is given as

$$y_D(i) = g_{RD}\tilde{x}(i) + n_D(i), \tag{3}$$

where $n_D(i)$ is the i.i.d. CSCG noise with zero mean and unit variance.

For the purpose of exposition, consider the case that the two phases in one time slot are with equal length. Thus, the transmission rate for the DF relaying scheme at time slot i is given as [7]

$$R(i) = \frac{1}{2} \min \{ \mathcal{C}(P_S(i) h_{SR}), \mathcal{C}(P_R(i) h_{RD}) \}, \tag{4}$$

where $\mathcal{C}(x) = \log_2(1+x)$ denotes the capacity of the additive white Gaussian noise channel, where x is the signal-to-noise ratio (SNR) of the channel.

3   Power Consumption Model

In this subsection, power consumption model considering the non-ideal circuit power is discussed. The transceiver circuitry works in two modes: when a signal is transmitting, all circuits work in the *active mode*; and when there is no signal to transmit, they work in the *sleep mode*.

Active mode: The consumed power is mainly comprised of the transmission power and the circuit power. The transmission power is determined by the power allocation $P_S(i)$ and $P_R(i)$. The circuit power consists of the following two parts: the transmitting circuit power P_{ct} comes from the power consumed by the mixer, frequency synthesizer, active filter, and digital-to-analog converter [2]; and the receiving circuit power P_{cr} is composed of the power consumption of the mixer, frequency synthesizer, low noise amplifier, intermediate frequency amplifier, active filter, and analog-to-digital converter [2]. Constant circuit power model is considered in this paper, i.e., P_{ct} and P_{cr} are constants [2]. In the sequel, superscripts "S", "R", and "D" are added to P_{ct} and P_{cr} to distinguish the power consumed at the source, relay, and destination, respectively.

Sleep mode: It has been shown that the power consumption P_{sp} in the sleep mode is dominated by the leaking current of the switching transistors and is usually much smaller than that in the active mode [2]. Therefore, the power consumption in the sleep mode is set as $P_{sp} = 0$. It is worth pointing out that the results of this paper can be readily extended to the case of $P_{sp} \neq 0$ by deducting P_{sp} from the average power budget and the power consumption in the active mode.

In general, the circuit power consumed in the active mode is larger than that in the sleep mode, i.e.,

$$P_{cr} > P_{ct} > P_{sp}. \tag{5}$$

Thus, smartly operating between the two modes can potentially save a significant amount of energy.

Based on the power model discussed above, the power consumptions for the considered DF relaying is computed as: Denote α as the total circuit power consumption in the active mode, and it is the sum of the transmitting circuit power at the source and the relay, the receiving circuit power at the relay and the destination, i.e.,

$$\alpha = \frac{1}{2}\left(P_{ct}^S + P_{cr}^R\right) + \frac{1}{2}\left(P_{ct}^R + P_{cr}^D\right), \tag{6}$$

where the $\frac{1}{2}$ penalty is due to the half-duplex constraint for the considered relaying scheme. With the defined α and $P_{sp} = 0$, the total power consumption at time slot i is given as

$$P_{total}(i) = \begin{cases} 0 & P_S(i) = 0, P_R(i) = 0 \\ \frac{1}{2}\left(P_S(i) + P_R(i)\right) + \alpha & P_S(i) > 0, P_R(i) > 0, \end{cases} \tag{7}$$

where the $\frac{1}{2}$ penalty is also due to the half-duplex constraint for the considered relaying scheme. Then, the average power constraint is defined over N time slots, as N goes to infinity, i.e.,

$$\lim_{N \to \infty} \frac{1}{N} \sum_{i=1}^{N} P_{\text{total}}(i) \leq P_0, \tag{8}$$

where $P_0 \geq 0$ is the power budget.

4   Optimal Power Allocation

In this section, the optimal power allocation and throughput performance of the considered relaying scheme is studied.

4.1   Problem Formulation

The goal is to determine $\{P_S(i)\}$ and $\{P_R(i)\}$ such that the long term average throughput subject to the average power constraint defined in (8) is maximized over N time slots as $N \to \infty$, i.e., solve the following optimization problem

$$\mathcal{C}_{\text{DF}}(P_0) = \max_{\{P_S(i)\},\{P_R(i)\}} \lim_{N \to \infty} \frac{1}{N} \sum_{i=1}^{N} R(i) \tag{9}$$

$$\text{s.t.} \quad (8), \ P_S(i) \geq 0, \ P_R(i) \geq 0, \tag{10}$$

where $R(i)$ is given in (4).

It can be checked that the objective function (9) is nonnegative and concave [11]. Thus, it is easy to check [5] that the optimal power allocation of problem (9)–(10) is given as: Transmit with power $P_S(i) = P_S > 0$ and $P_R(i) = P_R > 0$ over p portion of time slots and keep silent for the rest of the slots, where P_S and P_R are constants. As a result, problem (9)–(10) can be reformulated as

$$\mathcal{C}_{\text{DF}}(P_0) = \max_{\{P_S, P_R, p\}} \frac{p}{2} \min \{\mathcal{C}(P_S h_{\text{SR}}), \mathcal{C}(P_R h_{\text{RD}})\} \tag{11}$$

$$\text{s.t.} \quad \left(\frac{1}{2}P_S + \frac{1}{2}P_R + \alpha\right) \cdot p \leq P_0, \tag{12}$$

$$0 \leq p \leq 1, \ P_S \geq 0, \ P_R \geq 0, \tag{13}$$

where (12) is obtained from (8).

It is easy to check that to achieve the optimal value of problem (11)–(13), constraint (12) must be satisfied with equality; otherwise, increasing the transmission power or transmission probability could still boost the average throughput. Thus it follows that the optimal transmission probability $p^* = \frac{2P_0}{P_S + P_R + 2\alpha}$. Hence, problem (11)–(13) can be further simplified as

$$\mathcal{C}_{\text{DF}}(P_0) = \max_{\{P_S, P_R\}} \frac{\min \{\mathcal{C}(P_S h_{\text{SR}}), \mathcal{C}(P_R h_{\text{RD}})\}}{P_S + P_R + 2\alpha} \cdot P_0 \tag{14}$$

$$\text{s.t.} \quad P_S + P_R \geq 2P_0 - 2\alpha, \tag{15}$$

$$P_S \geq 0, \ P_R \geq 0, \tag{16}$$

where (15) is obtained by substituting p^* into the constraint $0 \leq p \leq 1$.

4.2   Optimal Power Allocation

In this subsection, the optimal power allocation for problem (14)–(16) is investigated.

For objective function (14), the maximum value is achieved when $\mathcal{C}(P_S h_{SR}) = \mathcal{C}(P_R h_{RD})$; otherwise, decrease the source or relay power could still achieve the same average throughput. Thus, it can be obtained from $\mathcal{C}(P_S h_{SR}) = \mathcal{C}(P_R h_{RD})$ that $P_R = \frac{P_S h_{SR}}{h_{RD}}$. Substituting $P_R = \frac{P_S h_{SR}}{h_{RD}}$ into (14) and (15), problem (14)–(16) can be rewritten as

$$\mathcal{C}_{DF}(P_0) = \max_{P_S \geq 0} \frac{h_{RD}\mathcal{C}(P_S h_{SR})}{(h_{SR} + h_{RD})P_S + 2h_{RD}\alpha} \cdot P_0 \tag{17}$$

$$\text{s.t.} \quad (h_{SR} + h_{RD})P_S \geq 2h_{RD}(P_0 - \alpha). \tag{18}$$

Since objective function (17) is a concave function divided by a linear function, it is quasiconcave over $P_S > 0$ [11]. Define

$$P_{ee} \triangleq \arg\max_{P_S \geq 0} \frac{P_C h_{RD}\mathcal{C}(P_S h_{SR})}{(h_{SR} + h_{RD})P_S + 2h_{RD}\alpha}, \tag{19}$$

which achieves the maximum value of (17) without considering constraint (18). Then, the optimal power allocation of problem (9)–(10) and the average throughput for the considered relaying scheme are given in the following proposition.

Proposition 1. *The optimal power allocation for problem (9)–(10) is given as: Transmit with power value (P_S^*, P_R^*) over p^* portion of time slots and keep silent for the rest of slots, where*

$$P_S^* = \max\left(P_{ee}, \frac{2h_{RD}}{h_{SR} + h_{RD}}(P_0 - \alpha)\right), \tag{20}$$

$$P_R^* = \frac{h_{SR}}{h_{RD}}P_S^*, \tag{21}$$

and $p^* = \frac{2P_0}{P_S^* + P_R^* + 2\alpha}$. With the optimal power allocation, the average throughput $\mathcal{C}_{DF}(P_0)$ defined in (9) is given as

$$\mathcal{C}_{DF}(P_0) = \begin{cases} \frac{h_{RD}\mathcal{C}(P_{ee}h_{SR})}{(h_{SR}+h_{RD})P_{ee}+2h_{RD}\alpha} \cdot P_0 & 0 \leq P_0 \leq \frac{h_{SR}+h_{RD}}{2h_{RD}}P_S + \alpha \\ \frac{1}{2}\mathcal{C}\left(\frac{2h_{SR}h_{RD}}{h_{SR}+h_{RD}}(P_0 - \alpha)\right) & P_0 > \frac{h_{SR}+h_{RD}}{2h_{RD}}P_S + \alpha. \end{cases} \tag{22}$$

Proof. Since objective function (17) is quasiconcave over $P_S > 0$, it is increasing if $0 \leq P_0 \leq \frac{h_{SR}+h_{RD}}{2h_{RD}}P_S + \alpha$ and decreasing if $P_0 > \frac{h_{SR}+h_{RD}}{2h_{RD}}P_S + \alpha$. Thus, with the constraint (18), $P_S^* = \max\left(P_{ee}, \frac{2h_{RD}}{h_{SR}+h_{RD}}(P_0 - \alpha)\right)$ achieves the maximum value of problem (17)–(18).

Then, $P_R^* = \frac{h_{SR}}{h_{RD}}P_S^*$ is obtained from $P_S h_{SR} = P_R h_{RD}$. Substituting P_S^* and P_R^* into objective function (17), the average throughput $\mathcal{C}_{DF}(P_0)$ is obtained as (22).

Thus, Proposition 1 is proved.   □

Remark 1. Based on Proposition 1, it is worth noting that the transmission scheme given in Proposition 1 is to transmit with an on-off structure when the average power budget P_0 is small to maximize the EE of the considered relay channel, and transmit constantly when the average power budget P_0 is large to maximize the spectral efficiency. It is also worth noticing that P_{ee} can be efficiently obtained by a simple bisection search.

4.3 Asymptotic Analysis

In this subsection, the asymptotic performance for the considered relaying scheme is analyzed.

Low SNR Regime: As $P_0 \to 0$, the average throughput for the considered relaying scheme at the low SNR regime is given in (22):

$$C_{DF}(P_0) = \frac{\mathcal{C}(P_{ee}h_{SR})h_{RD}}{(h_{SR} + h_{RD})P_{ee} + 2h_{RD}\alpha} \cdot P_0. \tag{23}$$

It is interesting to note that $C_{DF}(P_0)$ is a linear function of the average power budget P_0 at the low SNR regime. The scaling factors $\frac{\mathcal{C}(P_{ee}h_{SR})h_{RD}}{(h_{SR}+h_{RD})P_{ee}+2h_{RD}\alpha}$ is the maximum EE of the considered relaying scheme.

High SNR Regime: Based on the results in (22), as $P_0 \to \infty$, the average throughput of the considered relaying scheme at the high SNR regime is asymptotically given as

$$C_{DF}(P_0) \approx \frac{1}{2}\log_2\left(\frac{2h_{SR}h_{RD}}{h_{SR} + h_{RD}}(P_0 - \alpha)\right). \tag{24}$$

It is obvious that the multiplexing gain of the considered relaying scheme is $\frac{1}{2}$, which is due to the half duplex constraint.

5 Numerical Results

In this section, simulations are performed to compare the performances of the proposed optimal power allocation for the two-hop relay transmission (THRT) and various suboptimal schemes.

- DLT: denotes direct link transmission, whose power allocation is to transmit with power value $P_S^* = \max(P_{ee1}, P_0 - \alpha_A)$ over p^* portion of time slots and keep silent for the rest of the slots, where $P_{ee1} \triangleq \arg\max\limits_{P_S>0} \frac{\mathcal{C}(P_S h_{SD})}{P_S+\alpha_A}$ and $p^* = \frac{P_A}{P_S^*+\alpha_A}$, α_A is the total power consumption for DLT, and h_{SD} is the channel gain of the source-destination link.
- CDLT: denotes constant direct link transmission, which transmits only with the direct link every time slot. The power allocation for CDLT is given as

$$P_S^* = \begin{cases} P_0 - \alpha_A & P_0 > \alpha_A \\ 0 & \text{otherwise.} \end{cases} \tag{25}$$

– CTHRT: denotes constant two-hop relay transmission, where the source transmits to the destination via the relay every time slot. The power allocation for CTHRT is given as

$$(P_S^*, P_R^*) = \begin{cases} \left(P_S^*, \frac{h_{SR}}{h_{RD}} P_S^*\right) & P_0 > \alpha \\ (0,0) & \text{otherwise}, \end{cases} \tag{26}$$

where $P_S^* = \max\left(P_{ee}, \frac{2h_{RD}}{h_{SR}+h_{RD}}(P_0 - \alpha)\right)$.

5.1   Average Power Budgets vs. Throughput

Figure 2 compares the performances of several transmission schemes at both low and high SNR regimes. The circuit power consumptions are set as $\alpha = 0.18$ W and $\alpha_A = 0.2$ W. The channel gains are set as $h_{SD} = 1$, $h_{SR} = 10$, $h_{RD} = 3$. It is easy to see that in the low SNR regime, the throughput curve of THRT outperforms other throughput curves, which suggests that THRT is more energy efficient than other transmission schemes. As P_0 increases, the curves of THRT and CTHRT coincide, and the curves of DLT and CDLT coincide. when $P_0 = 0.8$ W, throughput performance of THRT/CTHRT is about 0.3 b/s/Hz larger than that of DLT/CDLT.

In high SNR regime, the curves of THRT and CTHRT coincide, and the curves of DLT and CDLT coincide. The curves of DLT and CDLT outperforms the curves of THRT and CTHRT, which is due to the $\frac{1}{2}$ multiplexing gain of THRT and CTHRT. As P_0 increases, the throughput gap between the curves of

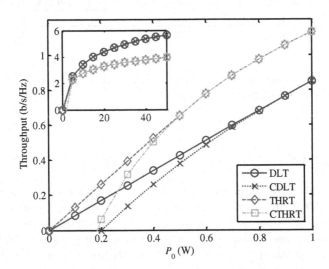

Fig. 2. The relationship between the power budget and the average throughput in low SNR and high SNR regimes.

DLT/CDLT and THRT/CTHRT enlarges, and the throughput performance of DLT/CDLT approaches twice as much as that of THRT/CTHRT.

5.2   Channel Gain h_{SR} vs. Throughput

In this subsection, the average throughput of THRT is compared with different channel gain h_{SR} and circuit power consumption α. The channel gain is set as $h_{RD} = 2$. The average power budget is set as $P_0 = 1$ W. The circuit power consumptions are set as $\alpha = 0.12$, 0.16, 0.2, 0.24, 0.28 W, respectively.

Figure 3 shows that the increase in h_{SR} leads to the increase in the average throughput. Besides, it can be concluded from the figure that as α increases, more power is consumed on the circuits, which leads to the decrease in the average throughput.

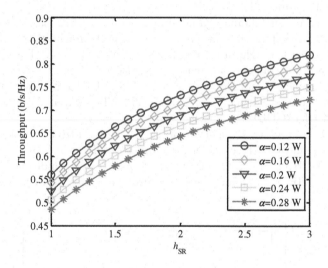

Fig. 3. The relationship between the channel gain h_{SR} and the average throughput with different circuit power consumption α.

6   Conclusion

In this paper, the throughput optimal power allocation for a two-hop relay channel with non-ideal circuit power was studied. By discovering the structure of the optimal power allocation, the non-convex problem was transformed into a quasi-concave problem. The closed-form solution showed that the source and the relay transmit with certain probability, which is determined by the average power budget, circuit power consumption, and channel gains. Then, asymptotic analysis was given, and finally, numerical results showed that the proposed optimal power allocation outperforms other suboptimal schemes.

References

1. Li, G.Y., Xu, Z., Xiong, C., Yang, C., Zhang, S., Chen, Y., Xu, S.: Energy-efficient wireless communications: tutorial, survey, and open issues. IEEE Wirel. Commun. Mag. **18**(6), 28–35 (2011)
2. Cui, S., Goldsmith, A.J., Bahai, A.: Energy-constrained modulation optimization. IEEE Trans. Wirel. Commun. **4**(5), 2349–2360 (2005)
3. Miao, G., Himayat, N., Li, G.Y.: Energy-efficient link adaptation in frequency-selective channels. IEEE Trans. Commun. **58**(2), 545–554 (2010)
4. Xiong, C., Li, G.Y., Zhang, S., Chen, Y., Xu, S.: Energy- and spectral-efficiency tradeoff in downlink OFDMA networks. IEEE Trans. Wirel. Commun. **10**(11), 3874–3886 (2011)
5. Xu, J., Zhang, R.: Throughput optimal policies for energy harvesting wireless transmitters with non-ideal circuit power. IEEE J. Sel. Areas Commun. **32**(2), 322–332 (2014)
6. Laneman, J.N., Tse, D.N.C., Wornell, G.W.: Cooperative diversity in wireless networks: efficient protocols and outage behavior. IEEE Trans. Inf. Theory **50**(12), 3062–3080 (2004)
7. Høst-Madsen, A., Zhang, J.: Capacity bounds and power allocation for wireless relay channels. IEEE Trans. Inf. Theory **51**(6), 2020–2040 (2005)
8. Madan, R., Mehta, N.B., Molisch, A.F., Zhang, J.: Energy-efficient cooperative relaying over fading channels with simple relay selection. IEEE Trans. Wirel. Commun. **7**(8), 3013–3025 (2008)
9. Zhou, Z., Zhou, S., Cui, J., Cui, S.: Energy-efficient cooperative communication based on power control and selective single-relay in wireless sensor networks. IEEE Trans. Wirel. Commun. **7**(8), 3066–3078 (2008)
10. Brante, G., Kakitani, M.T., Souza, R.D.: Energy efficiency analysis of some cooperative and non-cooperative transmission schemes in wireless sensor networks. IEEE Trans. Commun. **59**(10), 2671–2677 (2011)
11. Boyd, S., Vandenberghe, L.: Convex Optimization. Cambridge University Press, Cambridge (2004)

Big Data-Driven Vehicle Mobility Analysis and Design for 5G

Ruoxi Sun[(✉)], Kai Zhang, and Yong Ren

Department of Electronic Engineering, Tsinghua University, Beijing 100084, China
xysrx@163.com, zhang-k16@mails.tsinghua.edu.cn, reny@tsinghua.edu.cn

Abstract. Each generation of communication technology has a subversion, 5G will have a greater bandwidth, high carrier frequency, extreme base station and device densities, especially in vehicular network. Mobility models play a pivotal role in vehicular network, especially for routing policy evaluation. Relying on big data technology, the big data aided vehicle mobility analysis and design gets a lot of attentions. In this paper, we commerce with introducing the data set, i.e., a big GPS data set in Beijing. Then, a novel vehicle and location collaborative mobility scheme is proposed relying the GPS data set. We evaluate its performance based on degree distribution, duration distribution and interval time distribution. Our works may help the mobility design in vehicular networks.

Keywords: Big data · Vehicle mobility · 5G

1 Introduction

Each generation of communication technology has a subversion, 5G will have a greater bandwidth, high carrier frequency and extreme base station and device densities, especially in vehicular network [4,6]. The growing number of vehicles and the peoples in city, resulting in traffic congestion and automobile exhaust, which greatly reduces people's life travel experience. To address these issue, many schemes have been proposed, and intelligent transportation system (ITS) is one of them. Thanks to the accumulation of vehicle data and the maturer big data technology, such as parallel computing, machine learning and deep learning, the vehicular network analysis and design based on big data has got more and more attention.

As we all known, vehicular network is a dynamic network [1,5,8]. Therefore, the mobility models are of great importance for evaluating the performance of upper-layer protocol, and incorrect mobility model even lead to wrong conclusions. In present stage, GPS data for the analysis of the mobility model has got widespread concern. For vehicular network, mobility models can be roughly divided into four categories [1]: synthetic models, survey-based models, traffic simulator-based models and the trace-based models. Synthetic models, which is based on mathematical models, is capable of reflecting a realistic physical

© ICST Institute for Computer Sciences, Social Informatics and Telecommunications Engineering 2018
K. Long et al. (Eds.): 5GWN 2017, LNICST 211, pp. 238–245, 2018.
https://doi.org/10.1007/978-3-319-72823-0_23

effect, such as random way point [7] and weighted waypoint model [9]. Survey based Models get the models property by surveys, and the agenda-based mobility model [11] is a typical example. And the traffic simulator-based models is obviously, which are generated form traffic simulator, such as SUMO [13], VISSIM [14] and TraNS [15]. And the big data contributes to the trace-based models [16].

In fact, the big data for mobility model analysis is not limited in the race-based models. Specifically, the model based on social network belong to the first category [1–3,10,12,18]. Gonzalez et al. [17] analyzed the data collected tracing mobile phone users, and found that most people traveled around their familiar place. Song et al. [18] analyzed the distribution of time interval, i.e., how much time a user stayed at a location, and found the a truncated power law distribution. Based on real trajectory data, Musolesi et al. [19] modeled social relationships by interaction matrix, and the value of matrix elements represented the relationship between the two users.

Relying on the vehicle GPS data, we conduct the relevant research and our original contributions are as follows:

- Mobility model design: Inspired form the recommended system, we proposed three novel vehicular mobility models, which approximates real data and is easy to interpret.
- Real-world dataset evaluation: Relying on the vehicle GPS data in Beijing, we evaluate our scheme.

The remainders of this article are outlined as follows. In Sect. 2, we introduce the mobility models and relevant indicators. Section 3 establishes the performance comparison in degree distribution, duration distribution and interval time distribution, followed by the conclusion in Sect. 4.

2   System Model

In this section, we commerce with introducing the mobility model designed in Sect. 2.1. Then, in Sect. 2.2, we specify the evaluating indicator, which is utilized for mobility scheme comparison in this paper.

2.1   Mobility Model

We first need to explain the reasons for introducing social attributes. For a specific vehicle, we plot all positions in the given time zone. The corresponding results are presented in the Fig. 1.

As can be seen from the diagram, the driver has a preference for position. And this property is a traditional random walk mobility model can not be reflected.

Typical social features based mobility model need a interaction matrix, i.e., R, to reflect the relationship between two vehicles or a vehicle to a location. In this paper, we also consider the distance martrix, i.e., D. And the relationship

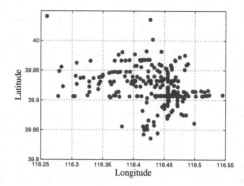

Fig. 1. Moving track of a vehicle.

and the distance of i and j is represented by R_{ij} and D_{ij}. The movement of vehicle could be modeled by the Markov process, which can be defined as:

$$Q_{ij} = \frac{R_{ij}D_{ij}}{\sum_{j=1}^{m} R_{ij}D_{ij}} \qquad (1)$$

Based on the different definitions of social properties in R, the related solutions include the random initialization scheme (RIS), the global critical location assessment scheme (GCLAS) and the personalized important location assessment scheme (PCLAS).

Specifically, if the values in R are random given, then the random initialization scheme are achieved. In the random initialization scheme (RIS), the R_{ij} is given by:

$$R_{ij} = rand(1), \qquad (2)$$

where $rand(1)$ means a random number between 0 and 1.

Based on the global critical location assessment, i.e., the probability of each site being accessed is proportional to its frequency, we get the global critical location assessment scheme. In global critical location assessment scheme (GCLAS), the R_{ij} is given by:

$$R_{ij} = \frac{\sum_v \sum_t transit_{i \to j}}{\sum_v \sum_t \sum_k transit_{i \to k}}, \qquad (3)$$

where v reflects a vehicle, t means a specific time and k denotes any position that connects with position i.

Considering the individual characteristics of the vehicle, we evaluate the importance of the location based on the specific vehicle history data, which lead to the personalized important location assessment scheme. In the personalized important location assessment scheme (PCLAS), the R_{ij} is given by:

$$R_{ij}^k = \frac{\sum_t transit_{i \to j}^k}{\sum_t \sum_k transit_{i \to j}^k}. \qquad (4)$$

And the Q_{ij} should be modified as follows:

$$Q_{ij}^k = \frac{R_{ij}^k D_{ij}}{\sum_{j=1}^m R_{ij}^k D_{ij}} \tag{5}$$

Besides, we adopt the real track data, simplified trajectory data and random walk as a comprising. Specifically, we map the real track data (RTD) into a 25*25 grid network, then we get the simplified trajectory data (STD). The mobility in random walk scheme (RWS) assumes all the vehicles' movements are random.

2.2 Evaluating Indicator

Specifically, VANETs can be viewed as a time variant graph $\mathcal{G} = (No, E, \mathcal{T}, \rho)$. Vehicles compose the entity in No set and the relationship between them is the E set. In this paper, the relationship represents a communication link. In dynamic network, this relationship may chance over time, so T represents the survival time and T represents the time domain, which satisfy $T \subseteq \mathcal{T}$. $\rho : E \times \mathcal{T} \to \{0, 1\}$ indicates survival function, which reflects whether a given edge exists at a given time slot. For time vary graph, there are two important parameters, the duration of the connection and the length of time interval. In other words

- the duration of the connection: starting from the entity i and entity j connection, to the first break time point, $\rho_{ij}(T) = 1$ was established in this time range;
- the length of time interval: starting from the entity i and entity j break, to the first connection time point, $\rho_{ij}(T) = 0$ was established in this time range.

And these two parameters will be utilized later to evaluate our mobility model.

3 Scheme Comparison

In this section, we conduct some simulation analysis on mobility models on the vehicular networks relying on the dataset introduced in Subsect. 3.1. We consider three typical indicators, i.e., degree distribution, duration distribution and interval time distribution, in mobility model assessment. And the relevant results and analysis are presented in Sects. 3.2, 3.3 and 3.4, respectively.

3.1 Dataset Analysis

This dataset records around ten thousand vehicles' GPS data in Beijing. For each vehicle, the travel track of the vehicle is recorded for several days.

And the Fig. 2 depicts the whole vehicle distribution in a specific time. This figure is not only a good reflection of the spatial distribution of vehicles, while reflecting the characteristics of Beijing's road network structure, i.e., the grid network topology.

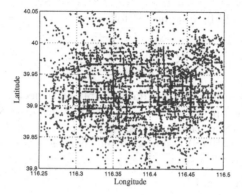

Fig. 2. System model.

3.2 Degree Distribution Comparison

In this subsection, we evaluate the mobility models based on degree distribution. Actually, the degree distribution is a very vital indicator in complex network, especially in distinguishing network types.

Based on the above five mobility schemes specified in Sect. 3.2 and the real data, we plot their degree distribution in Fig. 3. From the results, we can easily find that the real data network shows the characteristics of scale-free. However, both the simplified trajectory data and other four mobility schemes are more like a Gaussian distribution network.

3.3 Duration Comparison

In network communication field, we may pay more attention to the latter two indicators. So in this section, we explore their performance in duration distribution.

The Fig. 4 represents their comparison in duration distribution. In addition to the simplified trajectory data being closer to the real data, the other four schemes converge. As can be seen from the local magnification in Fig. 4, although the latter four programs close to each other, GCLAS and PCLAS is closer to the real data.

3.4 Interval Time Comparison

Similarly, in this section we explore their performance in interval time distribution.

The results are revealed in Fig. 5. We can see that the GCLAS and PCLAS scheme is closer to the simplified trajectory data, which can verify its superiority.

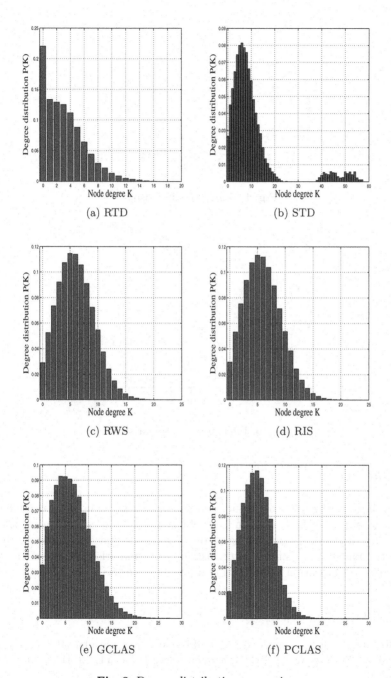

(a) RTD

(b) STD

(c) RWS

(d) RIS

(e) GCLAS

(f) PCLAS

Fig. 3. Degree distribution comparison

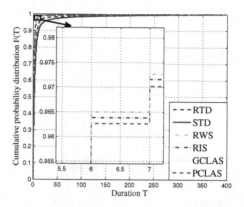

Fig. 4. Duration comparison

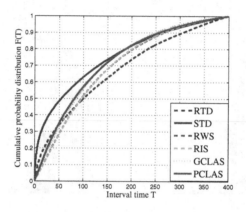

Fig. 5. Interval time comparison

4   Conclusion

To sum, inspired by user to product collaboration scheme in the recommended system, we propose the corresponding vehicle to location collaboration scheme in vehicular network. Based on degree distribution comparison, duration distribution comparison and interval time distribution comparison, the performances of the vehicle to location collaboration scheme are verified.

References

1. Harri, J., Filali, F., Bonnet, C.: Mobility models for vehicular ad hoc networks: a survey and taxonomy. IEEE Commun. Surv. Tutor. **11**, 19–41 (2009). Fourth Quarter
2. Jiang, C., Chen, Y., Liu, K.J.R.: Graphical evolutionary game for information diffusion over social networks. IEEE J. Sel. Top. Sig. Process **8**(4), 524–536 (2014)

3. Jiang, C., Chen, Y., Liu, K.J.R.: Evolutionary dynamics of information diffusion over social networks. IEEE Trans. Sig. Process **62**(17), 4573–4586 (2014)
4. Andrews, J.G., Buzzi, S., Choi, W., Hanly, S.V., Lozano, A., Soong, A.C., Zhang, J.C.: What will 5G be? IEEE J. Sel. Areas Commun. **32**(6), 1065–1082 (2014)
5. Jiang, C., Zhang, H., Ren, Y., Chen, H.: Energy-efficient non-cooperative cognitive radio networks: micro, meso and macro views. IEEE Commun. Mag. **52**(7), 14–20 (2014)
6. Wang, J., Jiang, C., Han, Z., Ren, Y., Hanzo, L.: Network association strategies for an energy harvesting aided super-wifi network relying on measured solar activity. IEEE J. Sel. Areas Commun. **34**(12), 3785–3797 (2016)
7. Bettstetter, C., Resta, G., Santi, P.: The node distribution of the random waypoint mobility model for wireless ad hoc networks. IEEE Trans. Mob. Comput. **2**(3), 257–269 (2003)
8. Wang, J., Jiang, C., Zhi, B., Quek, T.Q.S., Ren, Y.: Mobile data transactions in device-to-device communication networks: pricing and auction. IEEE Wirel. Commun. Lett. **5**(3), 300–303 (2016)
9. Hsu, W., Merchant, K., Shu, H., Hsu, C., Helmy, A.: Weighted waypoint mobility model and its impact on ad hoc networks. ACM SIGMOBILE Mob. Comput. Commun. Rev. **9**(1), 59–63 (2005)
10. Wang, J., Jiang, C., Quek, T.Q.S., Wang, X., Ren, Y.: The value strength aided information diffusion in socially-aware mobile networks. IEEE Access **4**, 3907–3919 (2016)
11. Zheng, Q., Hong, X., Liu, J.: An agenda based mobility model21. In: Proceedings of the 39th Annual Symposium on Simulation, pp. 188–195. IEEE Computer Society, April 2006
12. Wang, J., Jiang, C., Quek, T.Q.S., Ren, Y.: The value strength aided information diffusion in online social networks. In: IEEE Global Conference on Signal and Information Processing (GlobalSIP), pp. 1–6, December 2016
13. Sommer, C., German, R., Dressler, F.: Bidirectionally coupled network and road traffic simulation for improved ivc analysis. IEEE Trans. Mob. Comput. **10**(1), 3–15 (2011)
14. Fellendorf, M., Vortisch, P.: Microscopic traffic flow simulator vissim. In: Barceló, J. (ed.) Fundamentals of Traffic Simulation. ISOR, vol. 145, pp. 63–93. Springer, New York (2010). https://doi.org/10.1007/978-1-4419-6142-6_2
15. Piorkowski, M., Raya, M., Lugo, A.L., Papadimitratos, P., Grossglauser, M., Hubaux, J.-P.: Trans: realistic joint traffic and network simulator for vanets. ACM SIGMOBILE Mob. Comput. Commun. Rev. **12**(1), 31–33 (2008)
16. Kim, M., Kotz, D., Kim, S.: Extracting a mobility model from real user traces. In: INFOCOM, vol. 6, pp. 1–13 (2006)
17. Gonzalez, M.C., Hidalgo, C.A., Barabasi, A.-L.: Understanding individual human mobility patterns. Nature **453**(7196), 779–782 (2008)
18. Song, C., Koren, T., Wang, P., Barabasi, A.-L.: Modelling the scaling properties of human mobility. Nat. Phys. **6**(10), 818–823 (2010)
19. Musolesi, M., Mascolo, C.: Designing mobility models based on social network theory. ACM SIGMOBILE Mob. Comput. Commun. Rev. **11**(3), 59–70 (2007)

Complexity Analysis of Massive MIMO Signal Detection Algorithms Based on Factor Graph

Zhichao Yao[✉], Chao Dong, Kai Niu, and Zhiqiang He

Key Lab of Universal Wireless Communications,
Beijing University of Posts and Telecommunications, Beijing, China
{mr_cuber,dongchao,niukai,hezq}@bupt.edu.cn

Abstract. Massive MIMO technology is one of the most promising concepts in 5G wireless system. In the uplink of a massive MIMO system, complexity and performance of signal detection are two key issues been concerned simultaneously. Many message passing algorithms based on factor graph have claimed to achieve nearly optimal performance at low complexity. A unified factor graph model is introduced to describe two typical message passing algorithm,approximate message passing (AMP) and message passing detection (MPD). By analyzing different message calculation methods in the two algorithms, their computational complexity and performance are given in detail. Simulation results have shown that MPD exceeds AMP in both complexity and performance.

Keywords: Massive MIMO · Signal detection · Factor graph
Message passing · Channel hardening · Computation complexity

1 Introduction

Massive MIMO with tens of hundreds of antennas at the BS can significantly improve the system capacity and spectrum efficiency, which is considered as a candidate technology for 5G standards [1]. However, as the number of antennas grows, the computational complexity of detectors has become the bottleneck of its hardware implementation. Some detectors that work well in traditional MIMO fail in massive MIMO. For example, the complexity of optimal maximum likelihood (ML) detector scales exponentially in the number of transmit antennas, and conventional linear detectors like zero-forcing (ZF) and minimum-mean-square-error (MMSE) involve complicated matrix inversion, are difficult to simultaneously satisfy high-performance and low-complexity requirement of massive MIMO. Thus, finding a low-complexity detection algorithm on the uplink in massive MIMO, while maintaining good performance, is necessary.

Researches have shown that iterative detection algorithms based on factor graph can achieve performance that close to ML, meanwhile the computation complexity scales linearly, rather than exponentially in the number of transmit antennas [2–4]. There are two main directions to solve this problem. One is message passing algorithm working in complex-value domain [2,3]. The other

© ICST Institute for Computer Sciences, Social Informatics and Telecommunications Engineering 2018
K. Long et al. (Eds.): 5GWN 2017, LNICST 211, pp. 246–256, 2018.
https://doi.org/10.1007/978-3-319-72823-0_24

is message passing exploiting channel-hardening working in real-value domain [4]. These algorithms all claim that nearly ML performance has been achieved, but computation complexity comparison between these algorithms has not been done so far.

Therefore, in this paper, we select two typical algorithms, approximate message passing (AMP) and message passing detection (MPD) representing those two directions previously mentioned. First we described these two algorithms by using unified system model and message passing graphical model, then compared their computation complexity and performance in detail.

The rest of the paper is organized as follows. We first introduce the system model in Sect. 2. Two message passing detection algorithms based on factor graph are described in Sect. 3. Complexity analysis and simulation results are presented in Sects. 4 and 5, respectively. Section 6 concludes this paper.

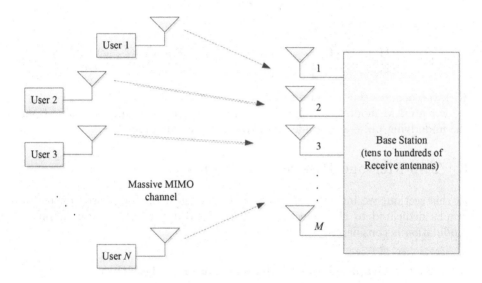

Fig. 1. Multi-user massive MIMO system on the uplink

2   System Model

Consider a multi-user massive MIMO system with N independent users, where each user is equipped with one transmit antenna, and the receiver is equipped with an array of M antennas, M is in the range of tens to hundreds [5]. System load factor φ is defined as N/M. The system model is illustrated in Fig. 1. For each user, every Q information bits are mapped to one modulation symbol. Let $\mathbf{x}_c = [x_1^c, x_2^c, ...x_N^c]^T$ be the transmitted vector from all the users, where $x_n^c \in \mathbb{B}$ is the symbol transmitted from the nth user and $\mathbb{B}$ is the modulation alphabet. Let $\mathbf{H}_c \in \mathbb{C}^{M \times N}$ denote the channel gain matrix and h_{ij}^c denote the complex channel gain from the jth user to the ith BS antenna. The elements of $\mathbf{H}_c$, which follow $\mathbb{CN}(0,1)$, are assumed to be independent identically distributed (i.i.d.). It is assumed that the N transmitters and the receiver are perfect synchronized and all channel gains are known at the receiver. Then the received vector can be presented as

$$\mathbf{y}_c = \mathbf{H}_c \mathbf{x}_c + \mathbf{n}_c, \tag{1}$$

where $\mathbf{n}_c$ is the additive white Gaussian noise (AWGN) vector whose entries follow $\mathbb{CN}(0,\sigma_n^2)$. The average received SNR per receive antenna is given by $\gamma = NE_s/\sigma_n^2$, where E_s is the average per transmitted symbol.

The MPD algorithm to be introduced works in real-value domain, so (1) can be written as

$$\mathbf{y} = \mathbf{H}\mathbf{x} + \mathbf{n}, \tag{2}$$

where

$$\mathbf{H} \triangleq \begin{bmatrix} \Re(\mathbf{H}_c) & -\Im(\mathbf{H}_c) \\ \Im(\mathbf{H}_c) & \Re(\mathbf{H}_c) \end{bmatrix}, \mathbf{y} \triangleq \begin{bmatrix} \Re(\mathbf{y}_c) \\ \Im(\mathbf{y}_c) \end{bmatrix}, \mathbf{x} \triangleq \begin{bmatrix} \Re(\mathbf{x}_c) \\ \Im(\mathbf{x}_c) \end{bmatrix}, \mathbf{n} \triangleq \begin{bmatrix} \Re(\mathbf{n}_c) \\ \Im(\mathbf{n}_c) \end{bmatrix},$$

$\Re(\cdot),\Im(\cdot)$ denotes the real and imaginary part, respectively.

For a QAM modulation alphabet $\mathbb{B}$, the elements of $\mathbf{x}$ will take value from the underlying pulse-amplitude modulation (PAM) alphabet $\mathbb{A}$.

3   Two Message Passing Algorithms

In this section, we introduce two message passing algorithms based on factor graphs dedicated to the detection of massive MIMO. 16-QAM gray-mapping modulation is considered.

3.1   Factor Graph Model of Message Passing Algorithm

Detection algorithms based on FG (Factor Graph) is briefly introduced in this section [2]. Consider the MIMO system model in (1) or (2), each entry of the received vector (or observation vector) is seen as a function node $f_j, j = 1, 2, n\_f$(number of function nodes) in a factor graph, and each transmitted symbol as a variable node $x_i, i = 1, 2, n\_x$(number of variable nodes). Figure 2 illustrates this graph model. The job of MIMO detection is using the knowledge of received vector and channel matrix to obtain an estimate of transmitted vector. Message passing algorithms are carried out on the factor graph by passing messages between the variable and function nodes.

3.2   MPD Algorithm

As proposed in [4], the MPD algorithm exploits channel hardening that occurs in massive MIMO channel.

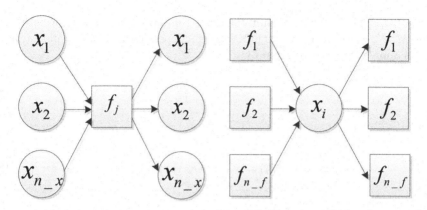

Fig. 2. Message passing between function and variable nodes on FG

Channel Hardening. As the dimension of the channel gain matrix $\mathbf{H}$ increases, the off-diagonal terms of the $\mathbf{H}^T\mathbf{H}$ matrix become increasingly weaker compared to the diagonal terms. This phenomenon is called channel hardening in [6].

In Sect. 3.2, we will work with approximations to the off-diagonal terms of the $\mathbf{H}^T\mathbf{H}$ matrix, which achieves very good performance in large dimensions at low-complexity.

MPD Algorithm. By performing matched filter operation on (2), we have

$$\mathbf{H}^T\mathbf{y} = \mathbf{H}^T\mathbf{H}\mathbf{x} + \mathbf{H}^T\mathbf{n}. \tag{3}$$

From (3), we write the following:

$$\mathbf{z} = \mathbf{G}\mathbf{x} + \mathbf{v}, \tag{4}$$

where

$$\mathbf{z} \triangleq \frac{\mathbf{H}^T\mathbf{y}}{M}, \mathbf{y} \triangleq \frac{\mathbf{H}^T\mathbf{H}}{M}, \mathbf{x} \triangleq \frac{\mathbf{H}^T\mathbf{n}}{M}.$$

The ith element of $\mathbf{z}$ can be written as

$$z_i = G_{ii}x_i + \underbrace{\sum_{j=1,j\neq i}^{2N} G_{ij}x_j + v_i}_{\triangleq k_i} \tag{5}$$

where G_{ij} is the (i,j)th of $\mathbf{G}$, x_i is the ith element of x, and

$$v_i = \sum_{j=1}^{2N} \frac{H_{ji}n_j}{M} \tag{6}$$

is the ith element of v, where H_{ji} is the (j,i)th element of H. The variable k_i defined in (5) denotes the interference-plus-noise term, which involves the off-diagonal elements of $\mathbf{G}$(i.e., H_{ji}, $i \neq j$). The distribution of k_i is approximated as $\mathbb{CN}(\mu_i, \sigma_i^2)$. By central limit theorem, this approximation is accurate for large M, N. Since the elements in $\mathbf{x}$, $\mathbf{v}$ are independent, the mean and variance in this approximation are given by

$$\mu_i = \mathbb{E}(k_i) = \sum_{j=1, j \neq i}^{2N} G_{ij} \mathbb{E}(x_j) \tag{7}$$

$$\sigma_i^2 = \operatorname{Var}(k_i) = \sum_{j=1, j \neq i}^{2N} G_{ij}^2 \operatorname{Var}(x_j) + \sigma_v^2. \tag{8}$$

Denoting the probability of the symbol x_j as $p_j(s)$,we have

$$\mathbb{E}(x_j) = \sum_{\forall s in \mathbb{A}} s p_j(s), \operatorname{Var}(x_j) = \sum_{\forall s in \mathbb{A}} s^2 p_j(s) - \mathbb{E}(x_j)^2$$

where $\sigma_v^2 = \sigma_n^2/2M$. Due to the above Gaussian approximation, the *a posteriori* probability (APP) of x_i being $s \in \mathbb{A}$ is computed as

$$p_i(s) \propto \exp\left(\frac{-1}{2\sigma_i^2}(z_i - G_{ii}s - \mu_i)^2\right). \tag{9}$$

Message Passing. First of all, because of the above matched filter operation, observation vector became a $2N \times 1$ vector, which means that the number of function and variable nodes is $2N$. As shown in Fig. 3, the messages passed from variable node x_j to any function node are $\mathbb{E}(x_j)$ and $\operatorname{Var}(x_j)$, the computation of which needs $p_i(s)$. Then, we use the knowledge of $\mathbf{G}$, i.e. channel matrix and the message passed to function node f_j to compute the mean μ_i and variance σ_i^2 of interference-plus-noise term k_j. Moreover, $p_i(s)$ is computed using μ_i, σ_i^2 and jth elements in observation vector. As we can see, the major difference in Fig. 3 comparing to Fig. 2 is that computation of messages coming from x_j only needs the messages from function node f_j, rather than all $2N$ function nodes. Therefore, computation complexity of MPD is significantly reduced.

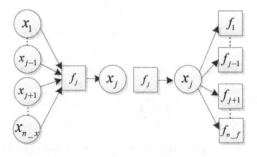

Fig. 3. Message passing between function and variable nodes for MPD

Damping Message. In the above graphical model, the message passing algorithm may fail to converge, and even if it does converge, the estimated probabilities may be far from exact. In [7], a damping method intended to improve the rate of convergence is proposed. The damped message to be passed in iteration t is computed as a weighted average of the message in iteration $t-1$ and the message computed at the tth iteration with a damping factor $\Delta \in [0,1)$. In [3], it is shown that $\Delta = 0.33$ is optimal, Thus, let $\tilde{p}_i^t$ be the computed probability at the tth iteration, the message at the end of tth iteration is

$$p_i^t = (1 - \Delta)\,\tilde{p}_i^t + \Delta p_i^{t-1}. \tag{10}$$

The algorithm is initialized with $p_i(s) = 0.25, \forall s \in \mathbb{A}$ and terminates after a fixed number of iterations. Finally, the bit as

$$\Pr(b_i^p = 1) = \sum_{\forall s \in \mathbb{A}: p\text{th bit in } s \text{ is } 1} p_i(s), \tag{11}$$

where b_i^p is the pth bit in the ith user's symbol. A hard estimate of bit b_i^p can be obtained as

$$b_i^p = \begin{cases} 1 \; if \; \Pr(b_i^p = 1) > 0.5 \\ 0 \; otherwise. \end{cases}$$

3.3 AMP Algorithm

Message passing algorithms referred as AMP (Approximate Message Passing) based on factor graph and its variants are proposed in [2]. In typical AMP algorithm, the message is modeled as Gaussian random variable. In addition, the messages of all the edges shown in Fig. 2 should be calculated. The focus of AMP is mainly on the mean and variance updating in message passing. In the following, $\mathcal{N}_{\mathbb{C}}(x; a, b) = (\pi b)^{-1}\exp(-|x - a|^2/b)$ denotes complex Gaussian function, where x, a, b denotes the random variable, the mean, the variance, respectively. The conditional probability $p(\mathbf{y}_c|\mathbf{x}_c)$ can be factorized into:

$$p(\mathbf{y}_c|\mathbf{x}_c) = \prod_j p_j(y_j^c|\mathbf{x}_c), \tag{12}$$

where

$$p_j(y_j^c|\mathbf{x}_c) = \frac{1}{\pi \sigma_n^2} \exp\left(-\frac{|y_j^c - \sum_i h_{ji}^c x_i^c|^2}{\sigma_n^2}\right). \tag{13}$$

This factorization is represented by the factor graph in Fig. 2. Let $\mu_{x_i \to f_j}^t(x_i^c)$ denotes the message sent from the variable node x_i to the function node f_j in the tth iteration, and let $\mu_{f_j \to x_i}^t(x_i^c)$ denotes the opposite message. The message-update rules are given by

$$\mu_{x_i \to f_j}^t(x_i^c) = \prod_{j' \neq j} \mu_{f_{j'} \to x_i}^{t-1}(x_i^c), \tag{14}$$

$$\mu_{f_j \to x_i}^t (x_i^c) = \sum_{\mathbf{x} \backslash x_i} p_j(y_j^c | \mathbf{x}_c) \prod_{i' \neq i} \mu_{x_{i'} \to f_j}^t (x_{i'}^c). \tag{15}$$

As the symbols take on values in the discrete set $\mathbb{B}$, the computation of $\mu_{f_j \to x_i}^t (x_i^c)$ in (15) requires exponential time to marginalize out the random vector $\mathbf{x} \backslash x_i$. To reduce complexity, x_i^c is considered as a continuous random variable and the message $\mu_{x_i \to f_j}^t (x_i^c)$ is approximated into a complex Gaussian function $\hat{\mu}_{x_i \to f_j}^t (x_i^c) = \mathcal{N}_{\mathbb{C}}(x_i^c; \bar{x}_{x_i \to f_j}^t, \bar{w}_{x_i \to f_j}^t)$, where the parameters $\bar{x}_{x_i \to f_j}^t$ and $\bar{w}_{x_i \to f_j}^t$ are transmitted symbols' mean and variance, $\mu_{f_j \to x_i}^t (x_i^c)$ can be calculated by integration:

$$\begin{aligned} \mu_{f_j \to x_i}^t (x_i^c) &= \int_{\mathbf{x} \backslash x_i} p_j(y_j^c | \mathbf{x}_c) \prod_{i' \neq i} \mathcal{N}_{\mathbb{C}}(x_i^c; \bar{x}_{x_i \to f_j}^{t-1}, \bar{w}_{x_i \to f_j}^{t-1}) \\ &= \mathcal{N}_{\mathbb{C}}(h_{ji}^c x_i^c; \theta_{f_j \to x_i}^t, \gamma_{f_j \to x_i}^t) \end{aligned} \tag{16}$$

where the parameters $\theta_{f_j \to x_i}^t$ and $\gamma_{f_j \to x_i}^t$ are given by

$$\theta_{f_j \to x_i}^t = y_j - \sum_{i' \neq i} h_{ji} \bar{x}_{x_i \to f_j}^t = \underbrace{y_j - \sum_i h_{ji} \bar{x}_{x_i \to f_j}^t}_{\theta_{f_j}^t} + h_{ji} \bar{x}_{x_i \to f_j}^t, \tag{17}$$

and

$$\gamma_{f_j \to x_i}^t = \sigma_n^2 + \sum_{i' \neq i} |h_{ji'}|^2 \bar{w}_{x_{i'} \to f_j}^t = \underbrace{\sigma_n^2 + \sum_i |h_{ji}|^2 \bar{w}_{x_i \to f_j}^t}_{\gamma_{f_j}^t} - |h_{ji}|^2 \bar{w}_{x_i \to f_j}^t. \tag{18}$$

Then, by substituting $\mu_{f_j \to x_i}^{t-1} (x_i^c) = \mathcal{N}_{\mathbb{C}}(h_{ji}^c x_i^c; \theta_{f_j \to x_i}^{t-1}, \gamma_{f_j \to x_i}^{t-1})$ into (14), $\mu_{x_i \to f_j}^t (x_i^c)$ can be normalized as

$$\mu_{x_i \to f_j}^t (x_i^c) = \frac{\mathcal{N}_{\mathbb{C}}(x_i^c; \alpha_{x_i \to f_j}^{t-1}, \beta_{x_i \to f_j}^{t-1})}{\sum_{x_i^c \in \mathbb{B}} \mathcal{N}_{\mathbb{C}}(x_i^c; \alpha_{x_i \to f_j}^{t-1}, \beta_{x_i \to f_j}^{t-1})} \tag{19}$$

where $\alpha_{x_i \to f_j}^{t-1}$ and $\beta_{x_i \to f_j}^{t-1}$ are given by

$$\alpha_{x_i \to f_j}^{t-1} = \left(\sum_{j' \neq j} \frac{|h_{j'i}|^2}{\gamma_{f_{j'} \to x_i}^{t-1}} \right)^{-1} = \left(\underbrace{\sum_j \frac{|h_{ji}|^2}{\gamma_{f_j \to x_i}^{t-1}}}_{(\alpha_{x_i}^{t-1})^{-1}} - \frac{|h_{ji}|^2}{\gamma_{f_j \to x_i}^{t-1}} \right)^{-1} \tag{20}$$

$$\beta_{x_i \to f_j}^{t-1} = \alpha_{x_i \to f_j}^{t-1} \sum_{j' \neq j} \frac{h_{j'i}^* \theta_{f_{j'} \to x_i}^{t-1}}{\gamma_{f_{j'} \to x_i}^{t-1}} = \alpha_{x_i \to f_j}^{t-1} \left(\underbrace{\sum_j \frac{h_{ji}^* \theta_{f_j \to x_i}^{t-1}}{\gamma_{f_j \to x_i}^{t-1}}}_{\tau_{x_i}^{t-1}} - h_{ji}^* \theta_{f_j \to x_i}^{t-1} \right).$$

$$(21)$$

In (17–21), $\theta_{f_j}^t$, $\gamma_{f_j}^t$, $\alpha_{x_i}^t$, $\tau_{x_i}^t$ are used to reduce complexity. After Tth iterations, the probability of transmitted symbol from ith user been $x_i^c \in \mathbb{B}$ is

$$p(x_i^c) = \mathcal{N}_{\mathbb{C}}(x_i^c; \xi_{x_i}^T, \alpha_{x_i}^T), \tag{22}$$

where $\xi_{x_i}^T = \tau_{x_i}^T \alpha_{x_i}^T$. A hard estimate of symbol x_i^c can be obtained as

$$x_i^c = \arg \max p(x_i^c). \tag{23}$$

4   Complexity Analysis

The complexity is evaluated in terms of floating-point operations(FLOPs) as in [2]. A FLOP is assumed to be either a real multiplication or a real summation here. Transposition, Hermitian transposition, conjugate, and real/imaginary operator require no FLOP. It is also assumed that the operation of exponent can be implemented by a look-up table. Note that the multiplication of two complex numbers needs six FLOPs.

4.1   Complexity of MPD

In the preprocessing stage, the MPD algorithm requires $8MN$, $16MN^2$, $4N^2$ FLOPs for the calculation of $\mathbf{z}$, $\mathbf{G}$, $|\mathbf{G}|^2$ respectively. For computing the messages at nodes in each iteration, $\mathbb{E}(x_j)$ needs $14N$ FLOPs, $\mathrm{Var}(x_j)$ needs $18N$ FLOPs, $\{\mu_i, i \in \{1, 2, ...2N\}\}$ need $2N(4N-3)$ FLOPs, $\{\sigma_i^2, i \in \{1, 2, ...2N\}\}$ need $2N(4N-2)$ FLOPs, $\{\tilde{p}_i^t(s), i \in \{1, 2, ...2N\}, s \in \mathbb{A}\}$ need $2N \times 4 \times 6$ FLOPs, the normalization of $\tilde{\mathbf{p}}$ needs $2N \times 7$ FLOPs. Finally, at the end of each iteration, damping of messages need $2N \times 4 \times 3$ FLOPs.

4.2   Complexity of AMP

In the preprocessing stage, the AMP algorithm requires $3MN$ FLOPs to compute $|\mathbf{H_c}|^2$. For computing the downward messages at the variable nodes, $\{\mu_{x_i \to f_j}^t(x_i^c), \forall i, \forall j\}$ and $\{\bar{x}_{x_i \to f_j}^t, \bar{w}_{x_i \to f_j}^t, \forall i, \forall j\}$ need $(11|\mathbb{B}| - 1)MN$ FLOPs and $(6|\mathbb{B}| + 1)MN$ FLOPs, respectively. For computing the upward messages at the function nodes, $\{\gamma_{f_j \to x_i}^t, \gamma_{f_j}^t, \theta_{f_j \to x_i}^t, \theta_{f_j}^t, \forall i, \forall j\}$ need $13MN$ FLOPs. For computing the messages at the variable nodes, $\{\alpha_{x_i \to f_j}^t, \alpha_{x_i}^t, \beta_{x_i \to f_j}^t, \tau_{x_i}^t, \forall i, \forall j\}$ need $16MN-3N$ FLOPs.

4.3   Complexity Comparison

Total complexity per iteration for MPD, AMP is listed in Table 1.

Table 1. Complexity Comparison of MPD and AMP

Algorithm	Preprocessing	Per iteration
MPD	$16MN^2+8MN+4N^2$	$16N^2+108N$
AMP	$3MN$	$(17|\mathbb{B}| + 29)MN\text{-}3N$

5   Simulation Results

Simulation results all base on the same assumption. System model (1) or (2) is used for simulation. For each simulated point, a minimum of 100 bit errors were counted.

First, a massive MIMO system with $N = 16$ users and $M = 128$ receiving antennas is considered. Figure 4 presents the BER performance of MPD and AMP with the number of iterations. It can be seen that 8 iterations are enough for both MPD and AMP to converge at SNR $= 6$ dB and SNR $= 8$ dB.

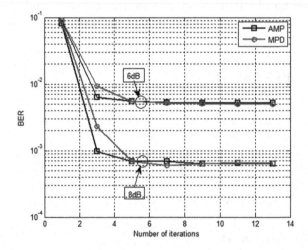

Fig. 4. BER performance versus number of iterations for MPD and AMP in a 16×128 system

Furthermore, Fig. 5 presented complexity versus number of users with fixed receiving antenna number, M $= 128$. The number of iterations is set to be 8. It is shown in Fig. 5 that AMP needs more than ten times FLOPs than MPD at lightly loaded system (let's say, $\varphi < 0.1$). However, as the load factor grows, the complexity of MPD increase faster than AMP. In [3], several variants of AMP that can significantly reduce complexity are proposed.

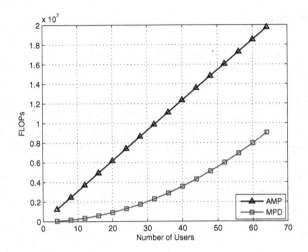

Fig. 5. Complexity versus number of users with $M = 128$

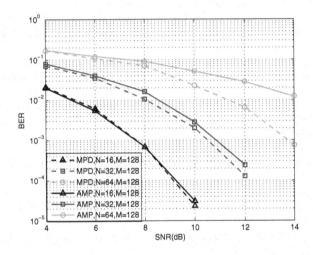

Fig. 6. BER performance of MPD and AMP for different values of $N(=16, 32, 64)$ and fixed $M = 128$

Figure 6 presents the BER performance of MPD and AMP for a fixed number of receiver antennas at the BS ($M = 128$) and varying number of users ($N = 16$, 32, 64). The number of iterations is big enough to converge. It can be observed that when $N = 16$, MPD performs as well as AMP, when $N = 32$, MPD outperforms AMP by about 0.2 dB to achieve BER of 10^{-3}, when $N = 64$, MPD performs much better than AMP.

6   Conclusions

In this paper, we introduced a unified message passing graphical model based on factor graph to describe two detection algorithms dedicated to massive MIMO. Then detailed computation complexity is analyzed in detail in the terms of FLOP. Simulation results had shown that thanks to channel hardening phenomenon, the computation complexity of MPD is far less than AMP. In addition, as the load factor grows, MPD outperformed AMP. Therefore, MPD is a promising signal detection algorithm for massive MIMO.

Acknowledgement. This paper is supported by the National Natural Science Foundation of China (No. 61171099 & No. 61671080).

References

1. Larsson, E., Edfors, O., Tufvesson, F.: Massive MIMO for next generation wireless systems. IEEE Commun. Mag. **52**(2), 186–195 (2013)
2. Som, P., Datta, T., Srinidhi, N., Chockalingam, A.: Low-complexity detection in large-dimension MIMO-ISI channels using graphical models. IEEE J. Sel. Top. Sig. Process. **5**(8), 1497–1511 (2011)
3. Wu, S., Kuang, L., Ni, Z., Lu, J., Huang, D., Guo, Q.: Low-complexity iterative detection for large-scale multiuser MIMO-OFDM systems using approximate message passing. IEEE J. Sel. Top. Sig. Process. **8**(5), 902–915 (2014)
4. Narasimhan, T.L., Chockalingam, A.: Channel hardening-exploiting message passing (CHEMP) receiver in large-scale MIMO systems. IEEE J. Sel. Top. Sig. Process **8**(5), 847–860 (2013)
5. Guo, R., Li, X., Fu, W., Hei, Y.: Low-complexity signal detection based on relaxation iteration method in massive MIMO systems. Commun. China **12**(Supplement), 1–8 (2015)
6. Hochwald, B.M., Marzetta, T.L., Tarokh, V.: Multiple-antenna channel hardening and its implications for rate feedback and scheduling. IEEE Trans. Inf. Theory **50**(9), 1893–1909 (1909)
7. Pretti, M.: A message-passing algorithm with damping. J. Stat. Mech. Theory Exp. **2005**(11), 283–292 (2005)

Per-Antenna Maximum Likelihood Detector for Massive MIMO

Senjie Zhang$^{(\boxtimes)}$, Zhiqiang He, and Baoyu Tian

Key Laboratory of Universal Wireless Communications, Ministry of Education,
Beijing University of Posts and Telecommunications, Beijing 100876, China
{senjie.zhang,hezq,tianbaoyu}@bupt.edu.cn

Abstract. Massive multiple-input multiple-output (MIMO) systems
have attracted extensive attention recently due to their potentials to provide high system capacity. The uplink receiver of massive MIMO is with
very high complexity due to the large number of antennas at base station,
while the processing time budget reduces in order of magnitude due to
the low latency requirement in next generation wireless systems like 5G.
In this paper, a per-antenna maximum likelihood (PAML) detector is
proposed to address this issue. The proposed PAML detector separates
and distributes ML detection to a group of observation nodes (VNs).
Each VN associates with a receiving antenna and extracts a fraction
of soft information using ML detection. The soft information from all
VNs is accumulated before being delivered to channel decoder. Thus the
degree of parallelism scales up with antenna number. Furthermore, VN
of PAML detector works independently each other. High localization
benefits parallel processing a lot. Simulation results show that PAML
detector approaches ML detector and outperforms MMSE detector.

Keywords: Massive MIMO · Maximum likelihood detection · MLD
Belief propagation · BP · Parallel processing · 5G

1 Introduction

Massive multiple-input multiple-output (MIMO) systems, also called as large-
scale antenna systems, attracted extensive attention in the past few years as a
promising key technology for next generation wireless systems like 5G [1].

In massive MIMO, dozens of or even hundreds of antennas are employed at
base station (BS) [2,3]. The number of receiving antennas is much higher than
the number of concurrent uplink user equipment (UE). Large antenna array provides high degrees of freedom and increase the system capacity significantly [4–6].
Although asymptotical analysis based on random matrix theory demonstrates
that massive MIMO systems can achieve the capacity gain with simple signal
processing methods, traditional MIMO detectors are still favorite for robust to
different channel models. Due to the large number of antennas, traditional MIMO
detectors become very complicated.

© ICST Institute for Computer Sciences, Social Informatics and Telecommunications Engineering 2018
K. Long et al. (Eds.): 5GWN 2017, LNICST 211, pp. 257–264, 2018.
https://doi.org/10.1007/978-3-319-72823-0_25

Another important point is the low latency requirements for next generation wireless systems like 5G [7]. A widely accepted end-to-end latency value is 1us. The time budget for signal processing may reduce to be lower than 500 ns. It makes the design of massive MIMO detector further challenging. Various algorithms were proposed to reduce complexity of massive MIMO detector, e.g. Neumann series expansion [5] and Gauss-Seidel method [8]. However these algorithms does not exploit the parallelism among receiving antennas so they are not efficient for low latency processing.

Belief propagation (BP) detector serves as an alternative solution to this problem [9–11]. In BP detector, the MIMO channel at a given subcarrier is represented by a factor graph where each receiving antenna is referred as an observation node (VN) and each UEs transmitted constellation symbol as a symbol node (SN). VN and SN is equivalent to variable node and check node in LDPC. Thus BP algorithm can be applied for detection in similar manner as its application in LDPC decoders. BP detector requires exchanging belief information between observation nodes and symbol nodes iteratively. The amount of information exchanged is very high. And iterative processing is less attractive for low latency processing, although BP detector is with high degree of parallelism.

Based on BP detector, in this paper we proposed the per-antenna maximum likelihood (PAML) detector for massive MIMO. PAML detector has similar framework with BP detector, while it replaces BP detectors SN with code block node (CN), i.e. PAML detector treats each UEs code block (cross multiple subcarriers) as the check node in LDPC.

In PAML detector, a group of VNs are employed. Each VN associates with a receiving antenna. From its associated antenna, VN extracts the log-likelihood ratio (LLR) for multiple UEs code blocks using maximum likelihood detection (MLD) described in [12]. The CN of PAML detector accumulates the LLR from different VNs and deliver the combined LLR to channel decoders. The enhanced LLR of each UE, extracted by channel decoder, can be used for a priori information to VNs. By utilizing the diversity provided by channel coding, this improvement reduces iteration number. At typical massive MIMO scenario, where the number of receiving antennas is much higher than the number of concurrent uplink UEs, PAML detector with two iterations outperforms MMSE detector and approaches traditional ML detector. Compared with MMSE and traditional ML detector, PAML detector is more suitable for low latency parallel processing.

The rest of the paper is organized as follows. Section 2 describes the system model. Section 3 presents details of PAML detector. Numerical simulation results are given in Sect. 4. Section 5 concludes the entire paper.

Notation: In this paper, lower-case and upper-case boldface letters are used to denote vectors and matrices, respectively. The operations $(\cdot)^H$ and $E\{\cdot\}$ stand for conjugate transpose and expectation, respectively. The entry in the i-th row and j-th column of $\boldsymbol{A}$ is a_{ij}; the k-th entry of $\boldsymbol{a}$ is a_k.

2   System Model

Consider a MIMO-OFDM system with M uplink UEs, each with a single antenna, and one BS having a large number of receiving antennas. Let N denote the number of BS antennas; N is in the range of tens to hundreds. In massive MIMO, $M \ll N$.

Given that the system has Q subcarriers, and the number of bits carried per constellation symbol is M_c. Each UEs channel encoder generates a code block with $Q \cdot M_c$ bits.

The code block generated by the j-th UE is separated in Q pieces: $x_1^{<j>}$, $x_2^{<j>}, \ldots, x_Q^{<j>}$ and transmitted o Q subcarriers, where $x_q^{<j>}$ is an $M_c \times 1$ vector of bits, $j = 1, 2, \ldots, M$ is the index of UE and $q = 1, 2, \ldots, Q$ is the index of subcarrier.

Given the q-th subcarrier, denote $s_q = [s_{q,1}, s_{q,2}, \ldots, s_{q,M}]^T$ as an $M \times 1$ vector representing constellation symbols transmitted by all UEs. The entries of s_q are chosen from some complex constellation $\mathcal{C}$ with 2^{M_c} points, e.g. $M_c = 2$ for quaternary phase-shift keying (QPSK). Constellation $\mathcal{C}$ is normalized as $E\left\{\|s_{q,j}\|^2\right\} = \frac{1}{M}$ so the total transmitted power is one.

The entries of s_q is determined by using mapping function $s_{q,j} = \mathtt{map}(x_q^{<j>})$ (e.g. gray mapping). The $M \cdot M_C \times 1$ vector $x_q = [x_{q,1}, x_{q,2}, \ldots, x_{q,M \cdot M_c}]^T$ representing the transmitted bits from all UE is obtained by stacking $x_q^{<1>}$, $x_q^{<2>}, \ldots, x_q^{<M>}$. The k-th bit of x_q equals the u-th bits transmitted by the j-th UE where

$$k = (j-1) \cdot M_c + u, u \in [1, M_c], k \in [1, M \cdot M_c] \tag{1}$$

In this paper, the logical zero for a bit is represented by amplitude level $x_{q,k} = -1$, and the logical one by $x_{q,k} = +1$, $k = 1, \ldots, M \cdot M_C$.

The vector of constellation symbols and the vector of transmitted bits is related as

$$s_q = \mathtt{vmap}(x_q) = [\mathtt{map}(x_q^{<1>}), \mathtt{map}(x_q^{<2>}), \ldots, \mathtt{map}(x_q^{<M>})]^T \tag{2}$$

At the q-th subcarrier the vector of received signals can be expressed by

$$y_q = H_q \cdot s_q + n_q \tag{3}$$

where H_q is a $N \times M$ complex CSI matrix representing the MIMO channel and n_q is a $N \times 1$ vector of independent zero-mean complex Gaussian noise with variance σ^2 per real component.

For convenience of describing per-antenna maximum likelihood detector, Eq. (3) can be reformulated as

$$y_q = \begin{bmatrix} y_{q,1} \\ y_{q,2} \\ \vdots \\ y_{q,N} \end{bmatrix} = \begin{bmatrix} h_{q,11} & h_{q,12} & \cdots & h_{q,1M} \\ h_{q,21} & h_{q,22} & \cdots & h_{q,2M} \\ \vdots & \vdots & \ddots & \vdots \\ h_{q,N1} & h_{q,N2} & \cdots & h_{q,NM} \end{bmatrix} \cdot s_q + n_q = \begin{bmatrix} h_{q,1} \\ h_{q,2} \\ \vdots \\ h_{q,N} \end{bmatrix} \cdot s_q + n_q \tag{4}$$

where $\boldsymbol{h}_{q,i}$ is a $1 \times M$ complex CSI vector representing the MIMO channel between the i-th antenna and all M uplink UEs at the q-th subcarrier, and $i = 1, 2, \ldots, N$ is the index of the receiving antenna.

The CSI vector $\boldsymbol{h}_{q,i}$ is obtained using the received pilots at the i-th antenna. The pilot from different UE distinguishes each other in frequency domain or code domain, e.g. ZC sequences in LTE systems. So the VN associated with the i-th antenna can be assumed to know $\boldsymbol{h}_{q,i}$.

3   Per-Antenna Maximum Likelihood Detector

Figure 1 gives a flowchart of the proposed PAML detector.

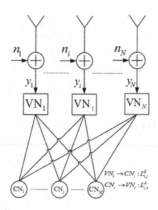

Fig. 1. The flowchart of PAML detector with factor graph based model

As Fig. 1 shown, PAML detector consists of N VNs and M CNs. Each VN associates with a receiving antenna. Each CN corresponds to an uplink UE. VNs and CNs are connected in fully meshed manner. Between VNs and CNs, LLR of each modulated bits are exchanged iteratively. VN sends extrinsic LLR to CN. CN sends *a priori* LLR to VN.

VN_i takes the received signals from the i-th antenna, and the *a priori* LLR from all CNs as its input. It extracts extrinsic LLR of bits transmitted by the j-th UE, denoted a s$\boldsymbol{L}_{i,j}^{E}$, and sends $\boldsymbol{L}_{i,j}^{E}$ to CN_j $(j = 1, 2, \ldots, M)$. $\boldsymbol{L}_{i,j}^{E}$ is a $M_c \times Q$ matrix. The q-th column of $\boldsymbol{L}_{i,j}^{E}$ contains LLR of the M_C bits transmitted at the q-th subcarrier by the j-th UE.

CN_j takes $\boldsymbol{L}_{i,j}^{E}$, $i = 1, 2, \ldots, N$ as its input. It combines all these LLR matrices, de-interleaves them, and passes them through the soft in/out channel decoder for the j-th UE. Channel decoders extrinsic LLR output is interleaved and sent to VNs as *a priori* LLR. These *a priori* LLR from CN_j to VN_i (interleaved version of the j-th channel decoders extrinsic output), denoted as $\boldsymbol{L}_{j,i}^{A}$, has same dimension and correspondence as $\boldsymbol{L}_{i,j}^{E}$. At first iteration, $\boldsymbol{L}_{j,i}^{A}$ is an all-zero matrix since no channel decoder has been called yet.

3.1 Per-antenna Maximum Likelihood Detection

VN_i stacks all of its *a priori* LLR inputs to be a global $M \cdot M_c \times Q$ *a priori* LLR matrix as

$$L^A = [l_1^A \; l_2^A \cdots l_Q^A] = \left[L_{1,i}^A{}^T \; L_{2,i}^A{}^T \cdots L_{M,i}^A{}^T\right]^T \tag{5}$$

where l_q^A is the q-th column of L^A. The k-th entry of l_q^A gives the *a priori* information of $x_{q,k}$ as

$$l_{q,k}^A = \log \frac{P(x_k = +1)}{P(x_k = -1)} \tag{6}$$

As described in [12], at the q-th subcarrier, extrinsic LLR of bit $x_{q,k}$ can be obtained using a scalar input $y_{q,i}$ as

$$l_{q,k}^E = \log \frac{\sum_{x_q \in \mathbb{X}_{+1}^k} p(y_{q,i} \mid x_q) \cdot \exp(0.5 \cdot x_{[k]}^T \cdot l_{q,[k]}^A)}{\sum_{x_q \in \mathbb{X}_{-1}^k} p(y_{q,i} \mid x_q) \cdot \exp(0.5 \cdot x_{[k]}^T \cdot l_{q,[k]}^A)} \tag{7}$$

where $\mathbb{X}_{+1}^k$ is the set of $2^{M \cdot M_c - 1}$ possible values of x_q having $x_{q,k} = +1$; $\mathbb{X}_{-1}^k$ is the set of $2^{M \cdot M_c - 1}$ possible values of x_q having $x_{q,k} = -1$; $x_{[k]}$ denotes the subvector of x_q obtained by omitting its k-th entry x_k; $l_{q,[k]}^A$ denotes the subvector of l_q^A also omitting its k-th entry $l_{q,k}^A$.

From (3) and (4) it is easily to found

$$p(y_{q,i} \mid x_q) = \frac{\exp(-\frac{1}{2\sigma^2} \cdot \|y_{q,i} - h_{q,i} \cdot s_q\|^2)}{2\pi\sigma^2} \tag{8}$$

where $s_q = \text{vmap}(x_q)$.

With approximation $\log(e^{a_1} + e^{a_2}) \approx \max(a_1, a_2)$, the extrinsic LLR of bit $x_{q,k}$ becomes

$$\begin{aligned}
l_{q,k}^E = &\frac{1}{2} \cdot \max_{x \in \mathbb{X}_{+1}^k} \left\{ -\frac{1}{\sigma^2} \cdot \|y_{q,i} - h_{q,i} \cdot s_q\|^2) + x_{[k]}^T \cdot l_{q,[k]}^A \right\} - \\
&\frac{1}{2} \cdot \max_{x \in \mathbb{X}_{-1}^k} \left\{ -\frac{1}{\sigma^2} \cdot \|y_{q,i} - h_{q,i} \cdot s_q\|^2) + x_{[k]}^T \cdot l_{q,[k]}^A \right\}
\end{aligned} \tag{9}$$

where $l_{q,k}^E$ is the u-th entry of the q-th column in VN_is output $L_{i,j}^E$. The indexes u and k obey the relation in (1).

In uplink MIMO, inter-UE interference and noise constrain system performance. Inter-UE interference is mitigated by ML detection described in (9). Averaging multiple observations, as the essential anti-noise method, cannot be carried out in VN since each VN has only one observation from the i-th antenna. To boost performance against noise, multi-antenna combination is introduced in CN.

3.2 Multi-antenna Combination and Iterative Detection

CN_j associates with the j-th UE. For the $M_C \times Q$ bits in j-th UE's code block, CN_j has N sets of LLR from N VNs, denoted as $\boldsymbol{L}_{i,j}^E$, $i = 1, 2, \ldots, N$. Using typical BP iteration, CN_j outputs the *a priori* LLR of these bits in code block to VN_i as

$$\boldsymbol{L}_{j,i}^A = \mathsf{dec}\Big(\sum_{1 \le i' \le N, i' \ne i} \boldsymbol{L}_{i',j}^E \Big) \tag{10}$$

where $\mathsf{dec}(\cdot)$ represents the procedure of de-interleaving, soft-in/out decoding and re-interleaving. Any soft-in soft-out channel decoding scheme is applicable, e.g. BahlCCockeCJelinekCRaviv (BCJR) algorithm.

Introduction of channel decoding in CN utilizes the diversity provided by channel code. Compared with the typical operations in CN, where simple synthesis of VN output is employed, the iteration number reduces significantly. The typical iteration number of iterative MIMO receiver is less than 10. On the other hand, we can see therere lots of girth-4 ring in PAML detectors factor graph from Fig. 1. With this issue no much improvement should be expected using typical BP algorithm with a huge iteration number.

With small iteration number, the accumulation of *a priori* information has negligible impact. So a simple procedure, described as

$$\boldsymbol{L}_{j,i}^A = \boldsymbol{L}_j^A = \mathsf{dec}\Big(\sum_{1 \le i' \le N} \boldsymbol{L}_{i',j}^E \Big) \tag{11}$$

can be used in CN. In this simple procedure, CN does not generate specific output for different VN. It combines LLR from all VN for channel decoding, and broadcasts a single version output to all VN.

3.3 Benefit to Parallel Processing

Because of per-antenna detection, a VN in PAML detector does not requires any information from other VNs. All VNs work independently so a full degree of parallelism, up to the huge number of receiving antenna N in massive MIMO, is obtained. High degree of parallelism conduces low latency processing. Similar independent processing is also obtained among CNs at per-UE level.

Introduction of channel decoding in CN converts the iteration between VN and CN into the iteration inside the channel decoder in CN. The significantly reduced iteration number between VN and CN benefits PAML detector with low latency detection and low intra-node communication load. Also a low complexity CN is obtained since the number of calling channel decoder reduces from N (once per VN) to 1 (once for the associated UE).

4 Simulation Results

In numerical simulations, two configurations are used: $N = 32$, $M = 2$ and $N = 64$, $M = 4$. Independent and identically distributed (i.i.d.) Rayleigh fading is used, and CSI is assumed to be known in receiver perfectly. For channel coding, we use the rate-1/2 LDPC code of MacKay in [13], which is based on a random regular factor graph with $d_s = 3$, $d_c = 6$. The length of code block is 4000. The BP iteration number for LDPC decoding in CN is 50. Four types of receivers are compared: MMSE, MLD, and the proposed PAML detector with one or two iterations between VN and CN. The simulation results are shown in Figs. 2 and 3.

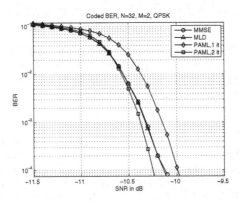

Fig. 2. Coded BER curves of massive MIMO with 32 receiving antennas and 2 concurrent uplink UEs using MMSE, MLD and PAML detector, QPSK

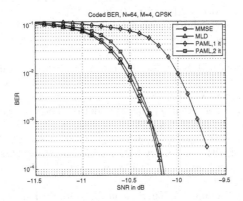

Fig. 3. Coded BER curves of massive MIMO with 64 receiving antennas and 4 concurrent uplink UEs using MMSE, MLD and PAML detector, QPSK

Figures 2 and 3 show that MMSE and MLD detector has almost same performance in massive MIMO, while PAML detector with one iteration approaches them with 0.2 0.5 dB gap. With two iterations, PAML detector slightly outperforms these two classical receivers.

5   Conclusion

In this paper, the per-antenna maximum likelihood (PAML) detector is proposed. PAML detector benefits low latency parallel processing for massive MIMO uplink receiver in terms of high degree of parallelism, low iteration number and low intra-node communication load. Simulation results show PAML detector slightly outperforms the classical MMSE and MLD detectors with two iterations. Further work will be directed towards BP-like detection for MIMO systems with short ring avoidance utilizing CSI feedback and its cooperation with channel codes.

Acknowledgment. This work is supported by the National Natural Science Foundation of China (No. 61171099), and 863 Program (No. 2015AA01A709).

The authors would also like to thank Mr. Sunny Zhang, the director of Intel Labs Chinas communication infrastructure research team, for his support.

References

1. Larsson, E.G., Tufvesson, F., Edfors, O., Marzetta, T.L.: Massive MIMO for next generation wireless systems. IEEE Commun. Mag. **52**(2), 186–195 (2014)
2. 3GPP TR 36.873 V12.2.0 (2014-09), Study on 3D channel model for LTE
3. 3GPP TR 36.897 V13.0.0 (2015-12), Study on Elevation Beamforming/ Full-Dimension (FD) MIMO for LTE
4. Marzetta, T.L.: Noncooperative cellular wireless with unlimited numbers of base station antennas. IEEE Trans. Wirel. Commun. **9**, 3590–3600 (2010)
5. Rusek, F., Persson, D., Lau, B.K., Larsson, E.G., Marzetta, T.L., Edfors, O., Tufvesson, F.: Scaling up MIMO: opportunities and challenges with very large arrays. IEEE Sig. Process. Mag. **30**, 40–46 (2013)
6. Lu, L., Li, G.Y., Swinlehurst, A.L., Ashikhmin, A., Zhang, R.: An overview of massive MIMO: benefits and challenges. IEEE J. Sel. Topics Sig. Process. **8**(5), 742–758 (2014)
7. Recommendation ITU-R M.2083 (2015-09), IMT Vision - Framework and overall objectives of the future development of IMT for 2020 and beyond
8. Dai, L., Gao, X., Su, X., Han, S., Chih-Lin, I., Wang, Z.: Low-complexity soft-output signal detection based on Gauss-Seidel method for uplink multiuser large-scale MIMO systems. IEEE Trans. Veh. Technol. **64**(99), 4839–4845 (2014)
9. Haroun, A., Nour, C.A., Arzel, M., Jego, C.: Symbolbased BP detection for MIMO systems associated with non-binary LDPC codes. In: Proceedings of IEEE Wireless Communications and Networking Conference (WCNC), Istanbul, Turkey, pp. 212–217, April 2014
10. Yang, J., Zhang, C., Liang, X., Xu, S., You, X.: Improved symbol-based belief propagationdetection for large-scale MIMO. In: IEEE Workshop on Signal Processing Systems (SiPS), October 2015
11. Lakshmi Narasimhan, T., Chockalingam, A.: Detection in large-scale multiuser SM-MIMO systems: algorithms and performance. In: IEEE 79th Vehicular Technology Conference (VTC Spring) (2014)
12. Hochwald, B.M., ten Brink, S.: Achieving near-capacity on a multiple-antenna channel. IEEE Trans. Commun. **51**(3), 389–399 (2003)
13. MacKay, D.J.C.: Online database of low-density parity-check codes. http://wol.ra.phy.cam.uk/mackay/codes/data.html

Joint User-Association and Resource-Allocation in Virtualized C-RAN

Xiaohong Zhang$^{(\boxtimes)}$, Yong Li, and Mugen Peng

The Key Laboratory of Universal Wireless Communication for Ministry of Education,
Beijing University of Posts and Telecommunications, Beijing 100876, China
zhangxh@bupt.edu.cn

Abstract. The Cloud Radio Access Network (C-RAN), which is a novel architecture, has been proposed as a promising solution to overcome the challenges of Next Generation (5G) cellular networks, in terms of efficiency, capacity, scalability, flexibility and sustainability in a cost-effective way. In this paper, we develop an efficient resource allocation scheme in the fronthaul-constrained C-RAN to support users of different slices (service providers). Multiple slices (service providers) share the resource of an InP, each slice has its own quality-of-service (QoS) requirement. In specific, we formulate an optimization problem for maximizing network throughput by joint subcarrier, power allocation and user-RRH association assignment in the downlink transmission of C-RAN. This problem is NP-hard, therefore, we introduce a two-step suboptimal algorithm to solve it. The original problem is decomposed into joint power and subcarrier allocation subproblem and user-RRH association assignment subproblem. Firstly, we solving the user-RRH association subproblem under the fronthaul capacity constraint by the binary search algorithm. Then the dual decomposition algorithm is used to solve the power and subcarrier allocation subproblem. Simulation results demonstrate the effectiveness of our proposed algorithm.

Keywords: Virtualized C-RAN · Fronthaul constrained
Joint subcarrier · Power and user-RRH association assignment

1 Introduction

Cloud radio access network (C-RAN) is a promising and cost-efficient mobile network architecture, which can improve network capacity and coverage to handle the ever-growing demand for mobile data transmission in 5G network [1]. The basic concept of C-RAN is to decouple traditional base station (BS) functions into two parts: the distributed installed remote radio heads (RRHs) and the baseband units (BBUs) clustered as a BBU pool in a centralized cloud server. As presented in the Fig. 1, a mobile user can be associated with one or multiple RRHs through wireless channel, and RRHs are connected to the BBU pool via the high-speed, low latency fiber transport link (fronthaul) [2,3]. Regardless of reducing the capital expenses (CAPEX) and operational expenses (OPEX)

© ICST Institute for Computer Sciences, Social Informatics and Telecommunications Engineering 2018
K. Long et al. (Eds.): 5GWN 2017, LNICST 211, pp. 265–275, 2018.
https://doi.org/10.1007/978-3-319-72823-0_26

that is achieved by C-RAN, a practical fronthaul is always capacity constrained, which will reduce C-RAN performance gain [4].

In C-RAN, supporting for resource sharing among multiple network slices is an important scenario. Network slicing consists of deploying multiple end-to-end logical networks in support of independent business operations. In contrast to deploying an independent network infrastructure, each slice should be possible to realize as a logical network corresponding to a shared infrastructure, which allows serving diverse service requirements and satisfy the traffic growing demand in 5G network [5,6]. For example, the radio resources of a network operator are shared among multiple service providers, which can serve their own users and can be considered as slices [7,8]. Each slice requires a minimum reserved rate representing its QoS requirement.

Resource management always has a significant impact on network performance. To achieve efficient network resource utilization, a network operator requires to dynamically allocate radio resources among service providers (slices). Previous studies have been performed on resource sharing in cellular networks. For example, in [8], a resource management scheme for jointing physical resource block (PRB) and power allocation in LTE system is studied, which schedules the slices based on a proportional fairness rule with the objective to maximize the sum rate. In [9], a resource virtualization scheme is studied by introducing two different types of slices, including rate based and resource-based slices, where the minimum rate and minimum network resources are preserved for each slice, respectively. Generally, these works have focused on analyzing resource virtualization in a single base station, which can't be directly extended to a C-RAN with densely deployed RRHs [10]. An efficient resource sharing mechanism to support multiple slices in a C-RAN can improve network performance and resource utilization efficiency. Therefore, we propose to study the combination of wireless resource virtualization and C-RAN to achieve efficient resource sharing.

Note that without the fronthaul capacity constraint, each user can be served by all RRHs, however, considering the practical fronthaul links are capacity constrained, it is beneficial to optimize the user-RRH association to improve the system performance in C-RAN [11]. Therefore, the main objective of this paper is to propose a new model that a number of slices share the C-RAN. Specifically, we aim to maximize the network throughput by joint optimizing the power, subcarrier allocation and user-RRH association assignment for different slices' users of C-RAN.

It is obvious that the optimization problem is NP-hard, in other words, it can't be optimally solved with large number of users and RRHs in C-RAN. Therefore, we introduce a two-step suboptimal algorithm to practically solve this problem, the optimization problem is decomposed into user-RRH association assignment subproblem and joint power and subcarrier allocation subproblem; the first subproblem can be solved by the binary search algorithm and the second one can be solved by the dual decomposition algorithm. This algorithm is proved to be effective by the simulation results.

The rest of the paper is organized as follows. Section 2 describes the system model and formalizes the problem. Section 3 proposes an algorithm for dynamic resource sharing of all slices' users. In Sect. 4, simulation results demonstrate that the algorithm is effective. Finally, this paper is concluded in Sect. 5.

2 System Model and Problem Formulation

2.1 System Model

As is shown in Fig. 1, we consider the downlink transmission of fronthaul-constrained C-RAN, where the coverage of a specific area is provided by N RRHs. It is assumed that each RRH n is connected to the BBU pool via a fronthaul link with a capacity of T_n. The total system bandwidth of B MHz is divided into C subcarriers and shared by users through orthogonal frequency-division multiple access (OFDMA). The bandwidth of each subcarrier i.e., $\mathcal{B}_c = B/C$ is assumed to be smaller compared to the coherent bandwidth of the wireless channel. Therefore the channel gain of user in each sub-carrier can be considered flat. The system serves a set of slices, $\mathcal{M} = \{1, \cdots, m, \cdots, M\}$, where the slice m has a set of users denoted by $\mathcal{K}_m = \{1, \cdots, k_m, \cdots, K_m\}$ and requests for a minimum reserved rate of R_m^{rsv} to guarantee a minimum acceptable service level for its users. Then the total number of users is $K = \sum_{m=1}^{M} K_m$.

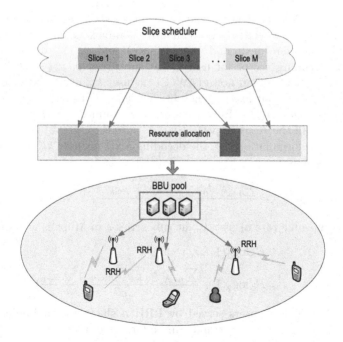

Fig. 1. System model of the downlink communication in C-RAN

Let p_{c,k_m} denotes the allocated power to user k_m on the subcarrier c, and h_{n,c,k_m} is the channel power gain of the wireless link between RRH n and user k_m of slice m over the subcarrier c, which represents the channel state information (CSI). The binary variables α_{c,k_m} and β_{n,k_m} represent the assignment of subcarrier and user-RRH association of user k_m, respectively, and where

$$\alpha_{c,k_m} = \begin{cases} 1 & \text{if subcarrier } c \text{ is allocated to user } k_m \\ 0 & \text{otherwise} \end{cases},$$

$$\beta_{n,k_m} = \begin{cases} 1 & \text{if RRH } n \text{ serves user } k_m \\ 0 & \text{otherwise} \end{cases}.$$

Due to the OFDMA limitation, one subcarrier must be allocated to exactly one user, it is required that $\sum_{m=1}^{M} \sum_{k=1}^{K_m} \alpha_{c,k_m} = 1$.

2.2 Optimization Problem Formulation

In the downlink of C-RAN, each user has a set of RRHs to provide service, the BBU pool sends the user messages to each serving RRH via its fronthaul link, then each serving RRH upconverts the user messages into wireless signals and sends them to the user [13]. Then the received equivalent baseband transmit signal of user k_m at subcarrier c can be expressed as

$$y_{c,k_m} = \sum_{n \in \mathcal{N}} \beta_{n,k_m} h_{n,c,k_m} w_{n,c,k_m} p_{c,k_m} x_{c,k_m} + z_{c,k_m} \tag{1}$$

where $x_{c,k_m} \sim CN(0,1)$ denotes the transmit message intended for user k_m (which is modeled as a circularly symmetric complex Gaussian (CSCG) random variable with zero-mean and unit-variance), and w_{n,c,k_m} denotes RRH n's normalized precoding vector for user k_m at subcarrier c. $z_{c,k_m} \sim CN(0,\sigma^2)$ is the additive white Gaussian noise (AWGN) at user k_m over subcarrier c, σ^2 is the noise power. Without loss of generality, consider σ^2 to be the same for users in all RRHs and subcarriers. In this paper, it is assumed that BBU pool knows the channels to all the K users perfectly.

According to formulation (1), the decoding SNR for user k_m at subcarrier c is thus expressed as

$$r_{c,k_m} = \frac{\sum_{n \in \mathcal{N}} \beta_{n,k_m} |h_{n,c,k_m}|^2 p_{c,k_m}}{\sigma^2} \qquad \forall c, k \tag{2}$$

Then, the achievable rate of user k_m at subcarrier c in Mbps is given by

$$R_{c,k_m} = B_c \log_2(1 + r_{c,k_m})$$

$$= B_c \log_2\left(1 + \frac{\sum_{n \in \mathcal{N}} \beta_{n,k_m} |h_{n,c,k_m}|^2 p_{c,k_m}}{\sigma^2}\right) \tag{3}$$

Considering that all users served by RRH n share its maximum transmit power P_n, then the power constraint can be formulated as:

$$C1: \sum_{m \in \mathcal{M}} \sum_{k \in \mathcal{K}_m} \sum_{c \in \mathcal{C}} \alpha_{c,k_m} \beta_{n,k_m} P_{c,k_m} \le P_n \qquad \forall n \tag{4}$$

If user k_m is served by RRH n, BBU pool will send the digital messages for user k_m to RRH n over its fronthaul link n at a rate of $R_{k_m,n}$, which is the transmitted rate of user k_m in all allocated subcarriers from RRH n. Therefore, take the fronthaul capacity constraint of RRH n into account, it can be expressed as :

$$C2: \quad \sum_{m \in \mathcal{M}} \sum_{k \in \mathcal{K}_m} \sum_{c \in \mathcal{C}} \alpha_{c,k_m} \beta_{n,k_m} R_{c,k_m} \leq T_n \quad \forall n \tag{5}$$

The required minimum reserve rate of slice m to guarantee its QoS requirement can be represented as:

$$C3: \quad \sum_{k \in \mathcal{K}_m} \sum_{c \in \mathcal{C}} \alpha_{c,k_m} R_{c,k_m} \geq R_m^{rsv} \quad \forall m \tag{6}$$

Next, the constraint of OFDMA in subcarriers allocation can be given below:

$$C4: \quad \sum_{m \in \mathcal{M}} \sum_{k \in \mathcal{K}_m} \alpha_{c,k_m} \leq 1 \quad \forall c \tag{7}$$

Hence, in order to achieve maximum network throughput of users of all slices, the joint power, subcarrier and RRH assignment for different slices' users in this system can be formulated as:

$$\max_{\{p,\alpha,\beta\}} \sum_{m \in \mathcal{M}} \sum_{k \in \mathcal{K}_m} \sum_{c \in \mathcal{C}} \alpha_{c,k_m} R_{c,k_m}$$
$$subject\,to: \quad C1, C2, C3 \ and \ C4 \tag{8}$$

3   Joint User-RRH Association and Resource Allocation

The optimization problem (8) is a non-convex mixed-integer problem, which has one continuous variable p and two binary variables α and β. Such an optimization problem is always NP hard [15], therefore, we propose an efficient two-step algorithm that is based on the decomposition of the original problem to the separate tasks of RRH assignment and joint subcarrier and power allocation, which obtains a suboptimal solution in general [14].

3.1   User-RRH Association Optimization Problem

Due to the fronthaul capacity is constrained, a user can't be served by all the RRHs, hence, we make attempt to optimize the user-RRH association for slices' users in C-RAN in problem (8). However, it is difficult to solve. In order to simplify the original problem (8), we separate the user-RRH association (fronthaul link) assignment problem from it, then propose a binary search method to allocate the fronthaul link by optimization maximizing the total rate gain over the active fronthaul links. Given the assumptions that average power distribution p_{k_m} and h_{n,k_m} is the path gain on link RRH n to user k_m without channel variations, the rate of user k_m transmitted by RRH n is

$$R_{n,k_m} = B \log 2(1 + \frac{|h_{n,k_m}|^2 p_{k_m}}{\sigma^2}) \tag{9}$$

Therefore, this optimization subproblem can be derived as :

$$\max_{\{\beta\}} \sum_{m \in \mathcal{M}} \sum_{k \in \mathcal{K}_m} \sum_{n \in \mathcal{N}} \beta_{n,k_m} R_{n,k_m}$$

$$s.t. \quad \sum_{n \in \mathcal{N}} \beta_{n,k_m} \leq S \quad \forall k$$

$$\sum_{m \in \mathcal{M}} \sum_{k \in \mathcal{K}_m} \beta_{n,k_m} R_{n,k_m} \leq T_n \quad \forall n \tag{10}$$

where the first constraint in problem (10) ensures each user can be connected with no more than s RRHs, so that to facilitate the simple binary search method to solve the allocation of fronthaul link. While the second constraint ensures that the sum-rate of users served by RRH n satisfies the capacity limitation of fronthaul link n. Then the fronthaul link allocation optimization problem can be solved by the binary search algorithm, it can be shown:

Algorithm 1. Binary-search algorithm

1: Initialization: $\boldsymbol{R}_{n,k_m} = \{R_{n,k_m}\} \in \mathbb{R}^{N \times K}$
   user-RRH association set: $\boldsymbol{\beta} \leftarrow \boldsymbol{0} \in \mathbb{R}^{N \times K}$
2: **for** $n = 1, 2, ..., N$
3: Initialize $R_n = 0$
4: Repeat
5:    **for** $k = 1, 2, ... k_m, ..., K$
6:    Find the user-RRH association:
         $(k_m^*, n^*) = \text{argmax}(R_{n,k_m})$
7:       **if** $R_n + R_{n^*,k_m^*} \leq T_n$ and $\sum_{n \in \mathcal{N}} \beta_{n,k_m} < S$
8:       **then:** $R_n \leftarrow R_n + R_{n^*,k_m^*}$
9:       $\beta(n^*, k_m^*) \leftarrow 1$
10:      $\boldsymbol{R}_{n,k_m} \leftarrow \boldsymbol{R}_{n,k_m} - \{R_{n^*,k_m^*}\}$
11:      **end if**
12:   **end for**
13: **end for**
14: Output β
15: Solve optimization problem (10).

3.2   Joint Subcarrier and Power Allocation Scheme

Given a feasible user-RRH association assignment, the value of β is determined, then the optimization problem of joint subcarrier and power allocation on different fronthaul links can be separated from problem (8) and expressed as:

$$\max_{\{p,\alpha\}} \sum_{m \in \mathcal{M}} \sum_{k \in \mathcal{K}_m} \sum_{c \in \mathcal{C}} \alpha_{c,k_m} R_{c,k_m}$$

$$s.t. \quad constraints \quad C1, C3, C4 \tag{11}$$

The problem (11) is still a mixed binary integer nonlinear programming problem, the decision variables α and p in the problem are binary variables and continuous variables, respectively. Such an optimization problem is generally hard to solve. Then the dual decomposition algorithm can be used to solve the problem effectively [15], since the duality gap between the primal problem and the dual problem in a multicarrier system is approximately zero for a large number of subcarriers [16].

First, we obtain the Lagrangian function of the original problem (11) as follows:

$$
\begin{aligned}
L(\boldsymbol{p}, \boldsymbol{\alpha}, \boldsymbol{\lambda}, \boldsymbol{\eta}) \\
= \sum_{m \in \mathcal{M}} \sum_{k \in \mathcal{K}_m} \sum_{c \in \mathcal{C}} \alpha_{c,k_m} R_{c,k_m} \\
- \sum_{n \in \mathcal{N}} \lambda_n \Big(\sum_{m \in \mathcal{M}} \sum_{k \in \mathcal{K}_m} \sum_{c \in \mathcal{C}} \alpha_{c,k_m} \beta_{n,k_m} p_{c,k_m} - P_n \Big) \\
+ \sum_{m \in \mathcal{M}} \eta_m \Big(\sum_{k \in \mathcal{K}_m} \sum_{c \in \mathcal{C}} \alpha_{c,k_m} R_{c,k_m} - R_m^{rsv} \Big)
\end{aligned}
\tag{12}
$$

where $\boldsymbol{\lambda} = [\lambda_1, \lambda_2, ..., \lambda_N]^T, \boldsymbol{\eta} = [\eta_1, \eta_2, ..., \eta_M]^T$ are dual variables. Thus, we can get the dual objective function of the original problem expressed as:

$$
g(\boldsymbol{\lambda}, \boldsymbol{\eta}) = \max_{\{\boldsymbol{p}, \boldsymbol{\alpha}\}} L(\boldsymbol{p}, \boldsymbol{\alpha}, \boldsymbol{\lambda}, \boldsymbol{\eta})
\tag{13}
$$

The dual problem of the original problem (11) can be expressed as follows:

$$
\min_{\{\boldsymbol{\lambda}, \boldsymbol{\eta}\}} \quad g(\boldsymbol{\lambda}, \boldsymbol{\eta})
$$
$$
s.t. \quad \boldsymbol{\lambda} \geq 0, \boldsymbol{\eta} \geq 0
\tag{14}
$$

Then the original problem is divided into one main problem and $C \times K$ subproblems by dual decomposition.

When the Lagrange multipliers are determined, $\sum_{n \in \mathcal{N}} \lambda_n P_n$ and $\sum_{m \in \mathcal{M}} \eta_m R_m^{rsv}$ are constants. For given $\boldsymbol{\alpha}$, we can first derive the optimal power allocation $\boldsymbol{P}^*$ from the subproblem below:

$$
\max_{\{\boldsymbol{p}\}} \quad (1 + \eta_m) R_{c,k_m} - \sum_{n \in \mathcal{N}} \lambda_n \beta_{n,k_m} p_{c,k_m}
$$
$$
s.t. \quad p_{c,k_m} \geq 0 \quad \forall c, k
\tag{15}
$$

Based on the optimal power allocation $\boldsymbol{P}^*$, we can obtain the rate set $\{R_{c,1}, ..., R_{c,K}\}$ of subcarrier c, therefore, the subcarriers $\boldsymbol{\alpha}^*$ are allocated according to the rule:

$$
\alpha_{c,k_m^*} = \begin{cases} 1 & k_m^* = \arg\max_{\{k\}} R_{c,k_m} \\ 0 & \text{otherwise} \end{cases}
\tag{16}
$$

In other word, the idea of this rule is to allocate subcarriers to users that have high performance gains. After solving above subcarrier assignment problems and $C \times K$ subproblems, the dual objective function $g(\boldsymbol{\lambda}, \boldsymbol{\eta})$ can be obtained.

With the help of sub-gradient method, the dual problem (14) to find the optimal values of dual variables can be solved. Based on the obtained power value P^*, subcarrier allocation value α^*_{c,k_m}, user-RRH association β_{n,k_m} and the initial $\boldsymbol{\lambda}_0$, $\boldsymbol{\eta}_0$, the dual variables at the $(t+1)$-th iteration can be updated as:

$$
\begin{aligned}
\lambda_n^{(t+1)} &= \left[\lambda_n^{(t)} - \delta_1^{(t)} (P_n - \sum_{k \in \mathcal{K}} \sum_{c \in \mathcal{C}} \alpha^*_{c,k_m} \beta^*_{n,k_m} P_{c,k_m}) \right]^+ \\
\eta_m^{(t+1)} &= \left[\eta_m^{(t)} - \delta_2^{(t)} (\sum_{k \in \mathcal{K}_m} \sum_{c \in \mathcal{C}} \alpha^*_{c,k_m} R_{c,k_m} - R_m^{rsv}) \right]^+
\end{aligned}
\tag{17}
$$

where $[x]^+ = \max\{0, x\}$, $\delta_1^{(t)}$ and $\delta_2^{(t)}$ are appropriate step size of the t-th iteration to guarantee the convergence of the sub-gradient method. In order to solve the problem (11), the allocated power P^* and subcarrier α^* should be recomputed under $\lambda(t)$ and $\eta(t)$. Once converged, the iteration will be stopped. Then the original optimization problem (8) for jointing power, subcarrier, and user-RRH association assignment for different slices' users in C-RAN can be solved.

3.3 Comparison Schemes

Besides two-step Algorithm 1 proposed above, we also consider the following benchmark schemes for network performance comparison.
○ Benchmark Scheme 1: Static resource sharing for different Slices (Algorithm 2). According to the service level agreement (SLA) between slices, different slices in system statically share radio resources and RRHs by a certain percentage. In this paper, we determine the resources allocation percentage based on the number of users served by different slices. Then each slice dynamically allocates the acquired resource to its users with the goal of maximizing the network throughput.
○ Benchmark Scheme 2: Average resource allocation algorithm (Algorithm 3). We distribute subcarrier, power and RRH equally to all users of different slices, regardless of the channel characteristics of the different subcarriers and the service level agreement (SLA) between slices.

4 Simulation Results

In this section, simulation results are provided to evaluate the performance of our proposed two-step algorithm for joint power and subcarrier and RRH assignment for users of different slices in C-RAN. Let's consider a virtualized C-RAN scenario with $N = 5$ RRHs serving M = 2 slices (service providers). Without loss of generality, the channels of different subcarriers are assumed to be independent of one another, and taken from i.i.d. complex Gaussian random variables with zero mean and unit variance. Each slice (service providers) serves a number of users. Furthermore, the minimum reserved rate R_m^{rsv} for each slice m is determined according to its QoS requirement. For all of our simulations, we assume

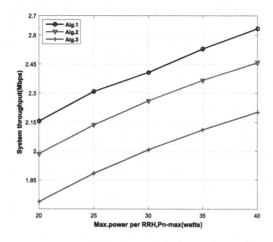

Fig. 2. Total throughput versus maximum transmit power of RRH

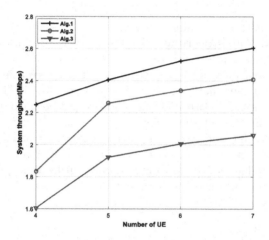

Fig. 3. Total throughput versus number of users, K

the fronthaul capacity T_n and the available power P_n are same for all RRH n, and $T_n = 1$ Mbps, each user could be served by no more than 3 RRHs.

Firstly, we evaluate and compare the total throughput achieved by Algorithm 1, Algorithm 2 and Algorithm 3 versus the maximum transmit power P_n and the number of users K in Figs. 2 and 3, respectively. Part of simulation parameters can be set to: in Fig. 2, $K = 5$, slice 1 has 3 users and the minimum reserved rate $R_1^{rsv} = 1$ Mbps, while slice 2 has 2 users and $R_2^{rsv} = 0.6$ Mbps. In Fig. 3, we evaluate the total throughput achieved for different number of users when $P_n = 30$ watts. The results in both Figs. 2 and 3 indicate that Algorithm 1 considerably outperforms Algorithm 2 and Algorithm 3 for different values of P_n and K.

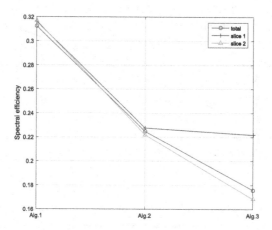

Fig. 4. Spectral efficiency

Then we evaluate and compare the spectral efficiency achieved by Algorithm 1, Algorithm 2 and Algorithm 3 for slice 1, slice 2 and the whole network. Where each slice has 3 users with the $P_n = 30$ watts, $R_1^{rsv} = R_2^{rsv} = 1$ Mbps. The results can be shown in Fig. 4 revealing that resource utilization achieved by Algorithm 1 is higher than Algorithm 2 and Algorithm 3. The resource allocation scheme based on Algorithm 1 and Algorithm 2 both can satisfy the SLA constraint between different slices, however, each slice assigns resources to its own users independently in Algorithm 2, hence, it can't achieve the dynamic sharing of resources between different slices. For Algorithm 3, lacking of flexibility in resource allocation leads to low resource utilization and can't achieve on-demand resources allocation for different slices.

5   Conclusion

In this paper, we considered a set of slices (service providers) in C-RAN, each of which serves its own users and requires a minimum reserved rate, then we formulate an NP-hard problem for jointing subcarrier and power allocation and RRH assignment for different slices' users. In order to solve it effectively, a two-step suboptimization algorithm is proposed. Numerical results confirm that the proposed algorithm is more efficient than other approaches. Furthermore, they show the algorithm can satisfy the QoS requirement of different slices' users and achieve better network performance in both throughput and spectral efficiency.

Acknowledgement. This work was supported in part by the National High Technology Research and Development Program (863 Program) of China under Grant No. 2014AA01A707.

References

1. Checko, A., Christiansen, H.L., Yan, Y., et al.: Cloud RAN for mobile networks a technology overview. IEEE Commun. Surv. Tutorials **17**(1), 405–426 (2015)
2. Peng, M., Wang, C., et al.: Fronthaul-constrained cloud radio access networks: insights and challenges. IEEE Wirel. Commun. **22**(2), 152–160 (2015)
3. Huang, J., Duan, R., Cui, C., Chih-Lin, I.: Overview of cloud RAN. In: Proceedings of URSI General Assembly and Scientific Symposium (URSI GASS), Beijing, pp. 1–4, April 2014
4. Sun, Y., Li, C., Huang, Y., Yang, L.: Energy-efficient resource allocation in C-RAN with fronthaul rate constraints. In: Proceedings of International Conference on Wireless Communications Signal Processing (WCSP), Yangzhou, pp. 1–6, August 2016
5. Yoo, T.: Network slicing architecture for 5G network. In: Proceedings of International Conference on Information and Communication Technology Convergence (ICTC), Jeju Island, South Korea, pp. 1010–1014, October 2016
6. Pries, R., Morper, H.J., Galambosi, N., Jarschel, M.: Network as a service - a demo on 5G network slicing. In: Proceedings of International Teletraffic Congress (ITC), Wrzburg, Germany, pp. 209–211, September 2016
7. Parsaeefard, S., Dawadi, R., Derakhshani, M., Le-Ngoc, T.: Joint user-association and resource-allocation in virtualized wireless networks. IEEE Access **4**, 2738–2750 (2016)
8. Kamel, M.I., Le, L.B., Girard, A.: LTE wireless network virtualization: dynamic slicing via flexible scheduling. In: Proceedings of IEEE, Vehicular Technology Conference (VTC), Vancouver, BC, pp. 1–5, September 2014
9. Feng, Z., Qiu, C., et al.: An effective approach to 5G: wireless network virtualization. IEEE Commun. Mag. **53**(12), 53–59 (2015)
10. Niu, B., Zhou, Y., Shah-Mansouri, H., et al.: A dynamic resource sharing mechanism for cloud radio access networks. IEEE Trans. Wirel. Commun. **15**(12), 8325–8338 (2016)
11. Liu, L., Zhang, R.: Downlink SINR balancing in C-RAN under limited fronthaul capacity. In: Proceedings of IEEE International Conference on Acoustics, Speech and Signal Processing (ICASSP), Shanghai, pp. 3506–3510, May 2016
12. Kokku, R., Mahindra, R., Zhang, H., Rangarajan, S.: NVS: a substrate for virtualizing wireless resources in cellular networks. IEEE ACM Trans. Netw. **20**(5), 1333–1346 (2012)
13. Liu, L., Bi, S., Zhang, R.: Joint power control and fronthaul rate allocation for throughput maximization in OFDMA-based cloud radio access network. IEEE Trans. Commun. **63**(11), 4097–4110 (2015)
14. Fallgren, M.: An optimization approach to joint cell, channel and power allocation in multicell relay networks. IEEE Trans. Wirel. Commun. **11**(8), 2868–2875 (2012)
15. Boyd, S., Vandenberghe, L.: Convex Optimization. Cambridge University Press, Cambridge (2004)
16. Yu, W., Liu, R.: Dual methods for nonconvex spectrum optimization of multicarrier systems. IEEE Trans. Commun. **54**(7), 1310–1322 (2006)

Adaptive Resource Allocation
for Device-to-Device Aided Cellular Systems

Xianxian Wang[1], Shaobo Lv[1], Xiaoyu Liang[1], Tong Liu[2(✉)], Hongwen Cheng[3],
and Zhongshan Zhang[1]

[1] Technology Research Center for Convergence Networks and Ubiquitous Services,
University of Science and Technology Beijing (USTB), Beijing 100083, China
zhangzs@ustb.edu.cn
[2] Department of Information and Communication Engineering,
Harbin Engineering University, 145 Nantong Street, Harbin, China
liutong@hrbeu.edu.cn
[3] China Unicom Huangshan Branch, Huangshan Road 170, Tunxi District,
Huangshan City, Anhui Provice, China
hongwencheng@chinaunicom.cn

Abstract. Resource allocation in device-to-device (D2D) aided cellular systems, in which the proximity users are allowed to communicate directly with each other without relying on the intervention of base stations (BSs), is investigated. A new uplink resource allocation policy is proposed for enabling the D2D user equipments (DUEs) to reuse the licensed spectrum, provided that the minimum signal-to-interference (SIR) requirement of conventional cellular user equipments (CUEs) is satisfied. Furthermore, the proposed resource-allocation problem can be formulated as "maximizing the number of simultaneously activated D2D pairs subject to the SIR constraints at both CUEs and DUEs". Numerical results relying on system-level simulation show that the proposed scheme is capable of substantially improving both the D2D-access probability and the network throughput without sacrificing the performance of conventional CUEs.

Keywords: Device-to-device · D2D-access probability
Network throughput

1 Introduction

With the rapid development of wireless communication techniques as well as the rapid popularity of smart terminals (e.g. ipad and iphone), the existing cellular networks are becoming increasingly difficult to meet the customers' exponentially growing data traffic demand [1–3]. Therefore, both wireless spectrum efficiency and network capacity need to be further enhanced [4–6]. Meanwhile, the base stations (BSs) may often operate at an overloaded state due to the existing BS-centric architecture of wireless access network (WAN), consequently resulting in a serious load imbalance over the whole WAN.

© ICST Institute for Computer Sciences, Social Informatics and Telecommunications Engineering 2018
K. Long et al. (Eds.): 5GWN 2017, LNICST 211, pp. 276–287, 2018.
https://doi.org/10.1007/978-3-319-72823-0_27

Device-to-Device (D2D) communication technology is regarded as one of the effective ways [7-9] for addressing the above-mentioned issues mainly based on the following benefits. On the one hand, proximity communication is capable of offering a higher channel quality between proximity-communication peers, corresponding to a higher channel capacity [10] as well as a lower power consumption [11]. On the other hand, a much lower delay than in conventional cellular communications can be guaranteed by implementing the scheme of direct transmission between users [12]. Furthermore, through reusing the licensed spectrum of conventional cellular user equipments (CUEs), the spectral efficiency of wireless networks can be substantially improved by activating D2D links [13,14].

However, activating the D2D links may impose a severe interference on the conventional CUEs, thus significantly eroding the performance of the latter [15]. To achieve a better overall system performance while guaranteeing the minimum Quality of Service (QoS) requirement of CUEs, an appropriate interference management technique (e.g., in terms of resource allocation, mode selection and power control) must be implemented in the activated D2D user equipments (DUEs).

Up to now, interference-management technologies for D2D aided cellular system have been widely studied in both academy and industry [15,16]. To coordinate the interference among CUEs and DUEs, the authors in [17] proposed a new technique for optimizing the sum data rate relying on power control schemes of different modes. Subject to a sum-rate constraint, a distributed power control algorithm relying on small-scale path losses has been proposed in [18] for minimizing the overall power consumption. Furthermore, a resource allocation scheme, in which the local awareness of the interference between CUEs and DUEs can be generated at the BSs, is proposed for minimizing the interference imposed on the CUEs [19]. In order to better combine the advantages of resource allocation and power control techniques, a jointly resource allocation and power control scheme has been proposed in [20] for maximizing the energy-efficiency (EE) of D2D aided underlaying cellular networks. In addition, a joint scheme by considering mode selection, channel assignment and power control simultaneously in D2D communications has been proposed in [21] for optimizing the overall system throughput while guaranteeing the SIR of both CUEs and DUEs.

Despite all this, most of the above-mentioned literatures mainly considered a relatively simple system model (e.g. comprising only a single CUE as well as D2D pair), in which the licensed spectrum of the objective CUE can be reused by at most one D2D pair. In this paper, resource allocation in D2D aided heterogeneous cellular systems is investigated by proposing a heuristic resource allocation algorithm for maximizing the number of simultaneously activated D2D pairs. The main contributions of this paper are reflected as follows:

1. The main objective of this paper is to maximize the number of simultaneously activated D2D pairs, while guaranteeing the minimum SIR of both CUEs and DUEs. Furthermore, a framework of resource allocation for D2D aided heterogeneous cellular systems is proposed, in which the licensed spectrum of a single CUE is allowed to be reused by more than one D2D pair.

2. Unlike [22], in the proposed system model, we assume that there exists an interference limited area (ILA) either for BSs or for D2D receivers, inside which the licensed spectrum is prohibited to be reused by DUEs.
3. By performing system-level simulations, it demonstrates that a significant performance improvement in terms of both the D2D access probability and the overall network throughput can be obtained, while without significantly sacrificing the performance of conventional CUEs.

The remainder of this paper is organized as follows. Section 2 gives out the system model. The proposed resource allocation strategy is discussed in Sect. 3, followed by evaluating the performance of the proposed algorithm using simulations in Sect. 4. Finally, Sect. 5 concludes this paper.

2   System Model

In this section, system model for the proposed D2D aided heterogeneous networks is first proposed, followed by analyzing the link SIR.

2.1   System Model for D2D Aided Heterogeneous Networks

In this paper, without loss of generality, licensed spectrum allocated to CUEs is allowed to be fully reused by DUEs, in which scenario a total of N_c CUEs are assumed to coexist with N_d D2D pairs. Meanwhile, multiple D2D pairs are allowed to reuse the licensed spectrum of a single CUE. However, an orthogonal spectrum is assumed to be allocated to an adjacent cell in order to avoid the inter-cell interference, and a fully-loaded spectrum allocation scenario with uplink resource sharing is considered in the proposed system model. Furthermore, To mitigate the D2D-induced interference inside a given cellular coverage, a circle guard zone, namely the ILA, is pre-set for both BSs and D2D receivers, inside which area the licensed spectrum is not prohibited to be reused by DUEs. In the following, the radius of the ILA is denoted by d.

2.2   SIR Analysis for Cellular and D2D Links

In this paper, without loss of generality, a typical Urban Micro (UMi) scenario is considered in the proposed system model. The performance erosion is assumed to be mainly induced by the impact of propagation and shadowing effects of wireless channels. Meanwhile, both the antenna gains of devices (i.e. including both BSs and CUEs/DUEs) and the feeder loss are taken into account. For convenience, we use $\mathcal{C} = \{1, 2, ..., N_c\}$ and $\mathcal{D} = \{1, 2, ..., N_d\}$ to denote the index sets of active CUEs and candidate D2D pairs, respectively, with N_c and N_d denoting the maximum number of CUEs and candidate D2D pairs, respectively. Furthermore, $\phi_i \subseteq \mathcal{D}$ is used to denote the set of admitted D2D pairs (i.e. the activated DUE pairs), which will reuse the spectrum allocated to the i-th CUE. In addition, parameters C_i and D_j are used to denote the i-th CUE and j-th D2D pair, respectively.

The Received SIR of the typical CUE-BS (i.e., C_i-BS) and D2D (i.e., D_j) links can be respectively represented as

$$\gamma_i^c = \frac{P_i^c g_{i,B}}{N_0 + \sum_{j \in \phi_i} P_j^d g_{j,B}}, \tag{1a}$$

$$\gamma_j^d = \frac{P_j^d g_j}{N_0 + \sum_{k \in \phi_i \setminus j} P_k^d g_{k,j} + P_i^c g_{i,j}}, \tag{1b}$$

where P_i^c and P_j^d stand for the transmit power of C_i and j-th D2D transmitter, respectively. Without loss of generality, we assume that $P_i^c = P_j^d = P_0$. Furthermore, $g_{i,B}$ denotes the channel gain between C_i and the corresponding BS, and $g_{j,B}$ denotes the channel gain between the j-th D2D transmitter and the associated BS. Thus, g_j can be used to denote the corresponding channel gain of D_j, with $g_{i,j}$ standing for the channel gain between C_i and the j-th D2D receiver. Finally, N_0 is used to denote the power of thermal noise. The sum throughput of the proposed D2D aided cellular systems can be expressed as

$$R_{\text{sum}} = \sum_{i \in \mathcal{C}} \left(\log\left(1 + \gamma_i^c\right) + \sum_{j \in \phi_i} \log\left(1 + \gamma_j^d\right) \right). \tag{2}$$

3   Resource Allocation Strategy for D2D Aided Cellular Systems

It has been shown that the activated D2D links may impose a severe interference on the CUEs and the interference induced by either CUEs or the geographically close-by D2D transmitters may also significantly erode the quality of a given activated D2D link during the uplink transmission periods. To mitigate the D2D-induced interference, a resource allocation strategy aiming at maximizing the number of simultaneously activated D2D pairs is proposed. For convenience of analysis, we can form a frequency reuse set comprising the objective CUE and its co-spectrum DUEs, provided that the minimum QoS (or in other words, minimum SIR) requirement of each user in this set can be guaranteed. Based on the above-mentioned principle, a resource-allocation framework can thus be formulated as:

$$\textbf{P1:} \quad \max_{\phi_1, \phi_2, \ldots, \phi_{N_c}} \quad T_D \tag{3}$$

$$\text{s.t.} \quad T_D = \sum_{i \in \mathcal{C}} |\phi_i|, \tag{3a}$$

$$T_D \leq N_d, \tag{3b}$$

$$\gamma_i^c \geq \gamma_{\min}^c, \forall i \in \mathcal{C}, \tag{3c}$$

$$\gamma_j^d \geq \gamma_{\min}^d, \forall j \in \mathcal{D}, \tag{3d}$$

$$\phi_p \cap \phi_q = \varnothing, \forall p, q \in \mathcal{C} \& p \neq q, \tag{3e}$$

$$d_{j,B} > d, d_{t,j} > d, \forall t \in \mathcal{C} || \mathcal{D} \setminus j, \forall j \in \mathcal{D}, \tag{3f}$$

where T_D denotes the total number of admitted D2D pairs in the whole system, ϕ_i represents the set of admitted D2D pairs reusing the spectrum of C_i, $\gamma_{\min}^c$ and $\gamma_{\min}^d$ stand for the minimum SIR requirement of C_i and D_j, respectively. $d_{j,B}$ denotes the distance between j-th D2D transmitter and BS, $d_{t,j}$ denotes the distance between interference transmitter (i.e. CUE or other D2D transmitter) and j-th D2D receiver. Furthermore, (3e) ensures that any single D2D pair can reuse the spectrum of one and only one CUE. In addition, (3f) is used to limit the D2D-induced interference imposed on both BSs and D2D receivers (i.e. corresponding to formulating the function of ILA).

According to (3c) and (3d), the maximum number of simultaneously activated D2D pairs can be expressed as

- when $\gamma_i^c \geq \gamma_{\min}^c$, $|\phi_i| \leqslant \frac{P_i^c g_{i,B}}{\gamma_{\min}^c \overline{I_i^c}} - \frac{N_0}{\overline{I_i^c}}$,
- when $\gamma_j^d \geq \gamma_{\min}^d$, $|\phi_i| \leqslant \frac{P_j^d g_j}{\gamma_{\min}^d \overline{I_j^d}} - \frac{N_0}{\overline{I_j^d}}$,

thus

$$|\phi_i| \leq \min\left(\frac{P_i^c g_{i,B}}{\gamma_{\min}^c \overline{I_i^c}} - \frac{N_0}{\overline{I_i^c}}, \frac{P_j^d g_j}{\gamma_{\min}^d \overline{I_j^d}} - \frac{N_0}{\overline{I_j^d}} \right), \tag{4}$$

where $\overline{I_i^c}$ and $\overline{I_j^d}$ denote the average interference ($\overline{I}$) imposed on C_i and D_j receivers, respectively. Since $I_i^c = P_j^d g_{j,B}$, and $I_j^d = P_t g_{t,j}, t \in \mathcal{C} || \mathcal{D} \setminus j$, we can identify the minimum-maximum value of $|\phi_i|$ when $g_{j,B} = g_{t,j} = g_{max}$, corresponding to the highest average interference level. From the definition of ILA, we can readily conclude that the maximum interference level may happen at the ILA boundary of the typical receivers, in which case the distance between the objective receivers and the interfering terminals would be very short. Therefore, the minimum-maximum value of any spectrum reuse set associated with the activated D2D pairs can be identified. When $\overline{I_i^c} = \overline{I_j^d} = \overline{I_{max}}$ satisfies, the minimum-maximum value can be expressed as

$$|\phi_i| = \begin{cases} \frac{g_{i,B}}{\gamma_{min}^c g_{max}} - \frac{N_0}{P_0 g_{max}}, & \frac{g_{i,B}}{\gamma_{min}^c} \leqslant \frac{g_j}{\gamma_{min}^d}, \\ \frac{g_j}{\gamma_{min}^d g_{max}} - \frac{N_0}{P_0 g_{max}}, & \text{otherwise.} \end{cases} \tag{5}$$

From (5), it is shown that the interference tolerance (IT)[1] of CUE is smaller than that of DUE, if $\frac{g_{i,B}}{\gamma_{min}^c} \leqslant \frac{g_j}{\gamma_{min}^d}$ is satisfied. Accordingly, the condition

---

[1] In this paper, the IT of a user is defined as $IT_k = |\phi_k| \overline{I}$, where $k = i, j$.

$g_{i,B} > \gamma^c_{min} g_{j,B}$ can be adopted as a criterion for identifying the candidate D2D pairs that can be activated in order to improve the D2D access ratio, while guaranteeing the SIR requirements of both CUEs and DUEs. Similarly, we can also employ the condition $g_j > \gamma^d_{min} g_{t,j}$ as a criterion for improving the D2D access ratio in the presence of $\frac{g_{i,B}}{\gamma^c_{min}} > \frac{g_j}{\gamma^d_{min}}$.

In summary, the D2D pairs having a better channel gain (i.e. g_j) will receive a higher activating priority, and the D2D access probability can be maximized by fully exploiting the channel gains of each candidate D2D pair, together with the inter-D2D-interference considered, as expressed as

$$\begin{cases} g_{i,B} > \gamma^c_{min} g_{j,B}, & \frac{g_{i,B}}{\gamma^c_{min}} \leqslant \frac{g_j}{\gamma^d_{min}}, \\ g_j > \gamma^d_{min} g_{t,j}, & \text{otherwise.} \end{cases} \tag{6}$$

From the above-mentioned analysis, the optimal conditions/constraints for improving the sum throughput of the proposed D2D aided cellular systems under the criteria of maximizing the activated D2D pairs can be derived as follows. Obviously, the sum throughput R_c in the traditional cellular network (i.e. without considering D2D communications) can be expressed as

$$R_c = \sum_{i \in C} \left(\log \left(1 + \xi^c_i \right) \right), \tag{7}$$

where $\xi^c_i = \frac{P^c_i g_{i,B}}{N_0}$. As compared to (4), the throughput gain brought about by employing D2D mode can be expressed as

$$\begin{aligned} R^G &= R_{\text{sum}} - R_c \\ &= \sum_{i \in C} \left(\log \left(\frac{(1 + \gamma^c_i) \prod\limits_{j \in \phi_i} \left(1 + \gamma^d_j \right)}{1 + \xi^c_i} \right) \right), \end{aligned} \tag{8}$$

leading to

$$\begin{cases} R^G \geq \sum\limits_{i \in C} \left(\log \left(\frac{1 + \gamma^c_i + \sum\limits_{j \in \phi_i} \gamma^d_j}{1 + \xi^c_i} \right) \right), \\ R^G \leq \sum\limits_{i \in C} \left(\log \left(\frac{\Upsilon}{1 + \xi^c_i} \right) \right), \end{cases} \tag{9}$$

where

$$\Upsilon = 1 + \left(\gamma^c_i + \sum_{j \in \phi_i} \gamma^d_j \right) + \frac{C^1_{m-1}}{2} \left(\gamma^c_i + \sum_{j \in \phi_i} \gamma^d_j \right)^2 + \cdots + \frac{C^{m-1}_{m-1}}{m} \left(\gamma^c_i + \sum_{j \in \phi_i} \gamma^d_j \right)^m, \tag{10}$$

with m denoting the size of spectrum reuse set. For conventional cellular systems, as a benchmark, it is easy to derive $R_{\text{sum}} = R_c$. However, for D2D aided cellular networks, it is shown that $R_{\text{sum}} > R_c$ can be met if $\gamma^c_i + \sum\limits_{j \in \phi_i} \gamma^d_j > \xi^c_i$ is satisfied.

Evidently, the sum throughput of the proposed D2D aided cellular systems (i.e. $\gamma_i^c + \sum_{j \in \phi_i} \gamma_j^d$) relying on the criteria of maximizing the number of simultaneously activated D2D pairs.

To maximize the number of simultaneously activated D2D pairs, we can readily make the following approximations, i.e. $\gamma_i^c \approx \gamma_{\min}^c$ and $\gamma_j^d \approx \gamma_{\min}^d$, thus leading to $\gamma_i^c + \sum_{j \in \phi_i} \gamma_j^d = \gamma_{\min}^c + \sum_{j \in \phi_i} \gamma_{\min}^d$. Without loss of generality, the maximum interference imposed on BS and D2D receivers can be denoted by $I_{\max}^c$ and $I_{\max}^d$, respectively. For any C_i sharing its spectrum with D2D pairs and inducing interferences $I_i^c = \sum_{j \in \phi_i} P_j^d g_{j,B} = I_{\max}^c$ and $I_j^d = \sum_{t \in \phi_i \setminus j || C_i} P_t g_{t,j} = I_{\max}^d$, the performance gain in terms of SIR can be expressed as

$$\gamma_{i,j}^G = \gamma_i^c + \sum_{j \in \phi_i} \gamma_j^d - \xi_i^c$$
$$= \frac{N_0 \Delta_1 + I_{\max}^c \Delta_2}{(N_0 + I_{\max}^d)(N_0 + I_{\max}^c)}, \tag{11}$$

where

$$\begin{cases} \Delta_1 = \sum_{j \in \phi_i} N_0 P_0 g_j - I_{\max}^c P_0 g_{i,B}, \\ \Delta_2 = \sum_{j \in \phi_i} N_0 P_0 g_j - I_{\max}^d P_0 g_{i,B}, \end{cases} \tag{12}$$

Evidently, $\gamma_{i,j}^G > 0$ (i.e. $R_{i,j}^G > 0$) holds if $\Delta_1 > 0$ and $\Delta_2 > 0$ are satisfied simultaneously, thus leading to

$$N_0 g_j > \max\left(p_j^d g_{j,B} g_{i,B}, p_t g_{t,j} g_{i,B}\right), \tag{13}$$

Consequently, **P1** can be heuristically rewritten as

$$\textbf{P2:} \quad \max_{\phi_1, \phi_2, \ldots, \phi_{N_c}} T_D \tag{14}$$

$$\text{s.t.} \quad (3a)-(3f),$$

$$g_{i,B} > \gamma_{\min}^c g_{j,B}, \text{if } \frac{g_{i,B}}{\gamma_{\min}^c} \leqslant \frac{g_j}{\gamma_{\min}^d}, \tag{14a}$$

$$g_j > \gamma_{\min}^d g_{t,j}, \quad \text{if } \frac{g_{i,B}}{\gamma_{\min}^c} > \frac{g_j}{\gamma_{\min}^d}, \tag{14b}$$

$$N_0 g_j > \begin{cases} p_j^d g_{j,B} g_{i,B}, \text{if } g_{j,B} > g_{t,j}, \\ p_t g_{t,j} g_{i,B}, \text{ if } g_{j,B} \leq g_{t,j}, \end{cases} \tag{14c}$$

where $i \in \mathcal{C}$, $j \in \mathcal{D}$ and $t \in \mathcal{C} || \mathcal{D} \setminus j$.

4 Numerical Analysis

In this section, numerical analysis for the proposed algorithm is performed relying on the proposed channel model to explore the attainable benefits brought about by the proposed algorithm. We consider a wrap-around system configuration comprising 19 sites (i.e. each comprising 3 cells). Without loss of generality, the minimum UE-to-BS distance is assumed to be 10 m, and the maximum distance between a pair of D2D peers is 50 m. In addition, the transmit power of BS and CUEs assumed to be 42 dBm and 24 dBm, respectively. Finally, the noise power spectrum density is assumed to be -174 dBm/Hz. The detailed parameter settings, which come from the standard [23], are elaborated on in Table 1.

Table 1. Parameter settings of the proposed system-level simulation

Parameters	Settings
Scenario environment	UMi
System bandwidth	10 MHz (TDD)
Carrier frequency	2.5 GHz
The min-distance of UE to BS	10 m
Antenna model of Macro BS	$A(\theta) = -\min\left[12(\frac{\theta}{\theta_{3\,\mathrm{dB}}})^2, A_m\right]$ $A_e(\phi) = -\min\left[12(\frac{\phi-\phi_{tilt}}{\phi_{3\,\mathrm{dB}}})^2, A_m\right]$ $-\min\left[-(A(\theta) + A_e(\phi)), A_m\right]$ $A_m = 20$ dB $\theta_{3\,\mathrm{dB}} = 70,\ \phi_{tilt} = 15$ $-180 \leq \theta \leq 180,\ -90 \leq \phi \leq 90$
Antenna model of UE	Omnidirectional
Traffic pattern	Full buffer
BS height	10 m
UE height	1.5 m
BSNoiseFigure	5 dB
UENoiseFigure	7 dB
BS transmit power	42 dBm
UE transmit power	24 dBm
Power level of thermal noise	-174 dBm/Hz

In Fig. 1, the performance of random spectrum allocation and proposed resource allocation algorithms in terms of the maximum number of simultaneously activated D2D pairs is performed by considering variant η values, with a single CUE considered. It is shown that the number of simultaneously activated D2D pairs decreases as η increases, because the interference tolerance of CUE decreases as the SIR threshold increases, thus requiring fewer D2D pairs to be activated simultaneously so as to impose a lower interference on CUE (i.e. to guarantee the minimum SIR requirement of the CUE). Anyway, the proposed algorithm is shown to always outperform the conventional random spectrum allocation scheme in terms of throughput, because the former is capable of coordinating the interference between CUEs and D2D pairs and optimizing the spectrum reuse set adaptively according to the instantaneous channel condition.

In Fig. 2, the impacts of ILA radius and CUE-SIR threshold on the number of simultaneously activated D2D pairs in a single-cellular scenario is investigated. It is shown that the access probability of the proposed algorithm is a monotonically decreasing function of η, because the interference tolerance of DUEs decreases as η increases. Meanwhile, it is also shown that the performance of proposed algorithm increases first, and then decreases as d increases. We can explain this observation as follows: when ILA radius is small, the interference imposed on signal receiver from one interference transmitter is more intensive compared with signal receiver power when the distance of interference link is bigger than D2D links. But when ILA radius is beyond the distance of D2D links, the probability of candidate D2D pairs access to network declines with the increase of d, as a result, the admitted D2D pairs decreases.

Figure 3 demonstrates the impact of ILA on the throughput as a function of η. Evidently, the throughput is a monotonically decreasing function of η, because the number of simultaneously activated D2D pairs decreases as the SIR threshold increases. Meanwhile, the performance of the proposed algorithm is also shown to increase firstly, and then decreases as d increases. This is because the interference is much more intensive when $d < 50$ (i.e. the maximum allowable distance of D2D links) compared with receiver signal power, and fewer D2D pairs can access to the network while guaranteeing the requirement of ILA radius, if ILA radius is beyond the distance of D2D links. Consequently, the sum throughput decreases.

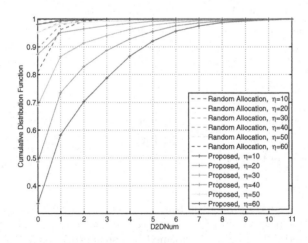

Fig. 1. Performance comparison of the proposed algorithm and the conventional random spectrum allocation scheme in terms of the maximum number of simultaneously activated D2D pairs for variant SIR thresholds, with a single CUE considered, where $N_c = 50$, $N_d = 300$ and $d = 50$.

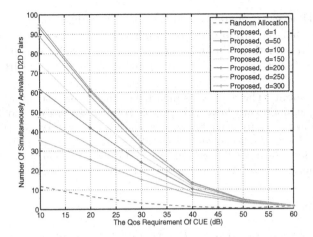

Fig. 2. The maximum number of simultaneously activated D2D pairs in the proposed system under different settings of SIR threshold, with a BS, where $N_c = 50, N_d = 300$.

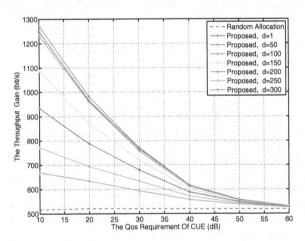

Fig. 3. Performance comparison of the proposed algorithm and the conventional random spectrum allocation scheme in terms of the sum throughput gain for variant radius of ILA, where $N_c = 50$ and $N_d = 300$.

5   Conclusions

In this paper, the problem of adaptive spectrum allocation was formulated as the maximization of the number of simultaneously activated D2D pairs in scenario of D2D reusing the uplink licensed spectrum, with a fully loaded cellular network considered. To maximize the number of simultaneously activated D2D pairs without eroding the SIRs of both CUEs and DUEs, a greedy heuristic algorithm was also implemented for finding the objective spectrum-reuse set. Numerical results showed that the proposed algorithm is capable of improving both the D2D-access probability and the sum throughput of the whole system. It was shown that the proposed algorithm is capable of increasing the admitted D2D pairs and sum throughput by about 800% and 80% as compared to the conventional random spectrum allocation algorithm when η=20 dB and $d = 50$.

Acknowledgement. This work was supported by the key project of the National Natural Science Foundation of China (No. 61431001), the open research fund of National Mobile Communications Research LaboratorySoutheast University (No. 2017D02), Key Laboratory of Cognitive Radio and Information Processing, Ministry of Education (Guilin University of Electronic Technology), and the Foundation of Beijing Engineering and Technology Center for Convergence Networks and Ubiquitous Services.

References

1. Zhang, Z., Long, K., Wang, J., Dressler, F.: On swarm intelligence inspired self-organized networking: its bionic mechanisms, designing principles and optimization approaches. IEEE Commun. Surv. Tutor. **16**(1), 513–537 (2014)
2. Zhang, Z., Long, K., Wang, J.: Self-organization paradigms and optimization approaches for cognitive radio technologies: a survey. IEEE Wirel. Commun. Mag. **20**(2), 36–42 (2013)
3. Dahlman, E., Parkvall, S., Skold, J.: 4G: LTE/LTE-Advanced for Mobile Broadband. Academic Press, Oxford (2013)
4. Zhang, Z., Chai, X., Long, K., Vasilakos, A.V., Hanzo, L.: Full duplex techniques for 5G networks: self-interference cancellation, protocol design, and relay selection. IEEE Commun. Mag. **53**(5), 128–137 (2015)
5. Zhang, Z., Long, K., Vasilakos, A.V., Hanzo, L.: Full-duplex wireless communications: challenges, solutions and future research directions. Proc. IEEE **104**(7), 1369–1409 (2016)
6. Wang, G., Liu, Q., He, R., Gao, F., Tellambura, C.: Acquisition of channel state information in heterogeneous cloud radio access networks: challenges and research directions. IEEE Wirel. Commun. **22**(3), 100–107 (2015)
7. Xiao, H., Ouyang, S.: Power allocation for a hybrid decodeamplify forward cooperative communication system with two sourcedestination pairs under outage probability constraint. IEEE Syst. J. **9**(3), 797–804 (2015)
8. Wang, G., Gao, F., Tellambura, C.: Ambient backscatter communication systems: detection and performance analysis. IEEE Trans. Commun. **64**, 4836–4846 (2016)
9. Zhang, H., Jiang, C., Mao, X., Chen, H.-H.: Interference-limit resource optimization in cognitive femtocells with fairness and imperfect spectrum sensing. IEEE Trans. Veh. Technol. **65**(3), 1761–1771 (2016)
10. Jnis, P., Yu, C.-H., Doppler, K., Ribeiro, C., Wijting, C., Hugl, K., Tirkkonen, O., Koivunen, V.: Device-to-device communication underlaying cellular communications systems. Int. J. Commun. Netw. Syst. Sci. **2**(3), 169 (2009)
11. Zhang, G., Yang, K., Liu, P., Du, Y.: Using full duplex relaying in device-to-device (D2D) based wireless multicast services: a two-user case. Sci. Chin. Inf. Sci. **58**(8), 1–7 (2015)
12. Ferrus, R., Sallent, O., Baldini, G., Goratti, L.: Lte: the technology driver for future public safety communications. IEEE Commun. Mag. **51**(10), 154–161 (2013)
13. Zhang, G., Liu, P., Yang, K., Du, Y., Hu, Y.: Orthogonal resource sharing scheme for device-to-device communication overlaying cellular networks: a cooperative relay based approach. Sci. China Inf. Sci. **58**(10), 1–9 (2015)

14. Zhang, H., Jiang, C., Beaulieu, N.C., Chu, X., Wen, X., Tao, M.: Resource allocation in spectrum-sharing OFDMA femtocells with heterogeneous services. IEEE Trans. Commun. **62**(7), 2366–2377 (2014)
15. Chai, X., Liu, T., Xing, C., Xiao, H., Zhang, Z.: Throughput improvement in cellular networks via full-duplex based device-to- device communications. IEEE Access **4**, 7645–7657 (2016)
16. Sun, J., Liu, T., Wang, X., Xing, C., Xiao, H., Vasilakos, A.V., Zhang, Z.: Optimal mode selection with uplink data rate maximization for D2D-aided underlaying cellular networks. IEEE Access **4**, 8844–8856 (2016)
17. Yu, C.-H., Tirkkonen, O., Doppler, K., Ribeiro, C.: Power optimization of device-to-device communication underlaying cellular communication. In: 2009 IEEE International Conference on Communications, pp. 1–5. IEEE (2009)
18. Fodor, G., Reider, N.: A distributed power control scheme for cellular network assisted D2D communications. In: 2011 IEEE Global Telecommunications Conference (GLOBECOM 2011), pp. 1–6. IEEE (2011)
19. Janis, P., Koivunen, V., Ribeiro, C., Korhonen, J., Doppler, K., Hugl, K., Interference-aware resource allocation for device-to-device radio under- laying cellular networks. In: IEEE 69th Vehicular Technology Conference: VTC Spring 2009, pp. 1–5. IEEE (2009)
20. Jiang, Y., Liu, Q., Zheng, F., Gao, X., You, X.: Energy efficient joint resource allocation and power control for D2D communications (2016)
21. Yu, G., Xu, L., Feng, D., Yin, R., Li, G.Y., Jiang, Y.: Joint mode selection and resource allocation for device-to-device communications. IEEE Trans. Commun. **62**(11), 3814–3824 (2014)
22. Min, H., Lee, J., Park, S., Hong, D.: Capacity enhancement using an interference limited area for device-to-device uplink underlaying cellular networks. IEEE Trans. Wirel. Commun. **10**(12), 3995–4000 (2011)
23. M Series: Guidelines for evaluation of radio interface technologies for IMT-advanced (2009)

A Utility-Based Resource Allocation in Virtualized Cloud Radio Access Network

Linna Chen[✉], Chunjing Hu, Yong Li, and Wenbo Wang

Wireless Signal Processing and Network Laboratory,
Key Laboratory of Universal Wireless Communications, Ministry of Education,
Beijing University of Posts and Telecommunications, Beijing 100876, China
chenlinna@bupt.edu.cn

Abstract. Network slicing is an emerging paradigm for 5G networks. Network slices are considered as different and independent virtualized end-to-end networks on a common physical infrastructure. Wireless resource virtualization is the key enabler to achieve high resource efficiency and meanwhile to isolate network slices from one another. In this paper, we propose a slice-specific utility-based resource allocation scheme in cloud radio access networks, where two sets of slices with different requirements are supported simultaneously. Every slice can determine its preference factor in utility function considering the trade-off between bandwidth gain and energy consumption. The objective is to maximize the sum utility of all slices taking the trade-off of all slices into account, which can be formulated as a mixed binary integer nonlinear programming problem. The Lagrange dual method is applied to solve the joint optimization problem. Finally, The performance of the proposed scheme is evaluated and the results show that the proposed scheme can meet different customized requirements of all slices, and enhance system performance when compared with other methods.

Keywords: Network slicing · Virtualization · Utility · Trade-off

1 Introduction

With rapid increase of traffic volumes and demand for a variety of services, the traditional one-size-fits-all network architecture is hard to adapt to the requirements of emerging use cases and changing subscriber demands. Network slicing is an emerging paradigm for 5G networks, which will enable operators to provide networks on an as-a-service basis and meet the wide range of use cases that the 2020 timeframe will demand. Each service provider (SP) can require its own logical network slice to support specific subscriber types and varying application usages on a shared physical infrastructure. In order to handle multiple slices in a robust way, radio access networks (RANs) shall provide radio resource management to efficiently multiplex traffics from multiple users in different network slice instances onto the available shared radio resources.

ⓒ ICST Institute for Computer Sciences, Social Informatics and Telecommunications Engineering 2018
K. Long et al. (Eds.): 5GWN 2017, LNICST 211, pp. 288–299, 2018.
https://doi.org/10.1007/978-3-319-72823-0_28

Wireless network virtualization is an effective means by which an infrastructure provider can partition the wireless and physical resources among SPs so that they can serve their subscribers, which facilitates new business models. Due to resource and infrastructure sharing, wireless network virtualization can reduce capital expenditure and operational expenditure, which leads to potential energy and capital savings [1]. Moreover, wireless network virtualization contributes to better resource utilization due to less unused resource.

The problem of wireless virtualization in LTE is addressed in many papers. The authors in [2] proposed a slicing scheme to allocate physical resources of LTE system to different SPs, in which fairness requirements of different SPs were considered. In [3], a centralized heuristic to allocate radio resource blocks in multi-cell LTE networks was proposed, which aimed to maximize the sum rate of the network. In [4,5], a resource allocation scheme was proposed by introducing two types of slices, including rate-based slices and resource-based slices. In [6], the authors introduced an idea of wireless virtualization into full-duplex relaying networks and proposed a virtual resource management architecture for virtualized networks. However, the wireless virtualization in cloud RAN (CRAN) has not been discussed adequately.

In this paper, we consider the joint subcarrier and power allocation problem in a CRAN downlink system, where two sets of slices with different requirements are supported simultaneously. Our main contribution is to introduce a slice-specific utility-based resource allocation scheme. The scheme aims at maximizing the sum utility of all slices under the service level agreement (SLA) and QoS requirement constrains, in which the specific preference requirements of different slices are considered. Every slice can determine a customized weighing factor in its utility function considering the trade-off between spectral efficiency and energy efficiency. The proposed allocation algorithm will take the preference requirements of all slices into account when assigning the subcarriers and power between different slices.

The rest of this paper is organized as follows. First, we present a description of the system model and the problem formulation in Sect. 2. The approach to solve the optimal problem is presented in Sect. 3. The simulation results and their discussions are given in Sect. 4. Finally, we conclude this paper in Sect. 5.

2   System Model and Problem Formulation

We consider the downlink of the CRAN architecture, where the coverage of a certain geographical area is provided by a cluster of RRHs, as illustrated in Fig. 1.

2.1   OFDMA-Based Wireless Transmission

We assume that OFDMA is used for downlink transmission. The total channel bandwidth is B Hz and is divided into N orthogonal subcarriers, thus the bandwidth of each subcarrier is B/N. The system consists of G slices, where each

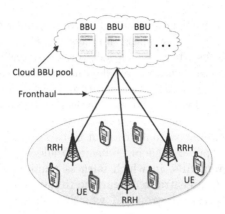

Fig. 1. System model.

slice g provides its service to K_g users, and each user is cooperatively served by its serving cluster of R RRHs.

Each RRH has a total transmit power of $P_{j,max}$ and let $p_{i,j,n}$ denote the power allocated to user i on subcarrier n at RRH j. The bandwidth of each subcarrier is assumed to be small compared with the coherent bandwidth of the wireless channel. Therefore, $h_{i,j,n}$ is the channel gain of the wireless link between RRH j and user i on subcarrier n which can be considered flat. Then the baseband complex symbol $y_{i,n}$ received by user i at subcarrier n can be expressed as

$$y_{i,n} = \sum_{j=1}^{R} h_{i,j,n} w_{i,j,n} \sqrt{p_{i,j,n}} s_{i,n} + z_{i,n}, \tag{1}$$

where $s_{i,n} \sim \mathcal{CN}(0,1)$ is the signal transmitted to UE i at subcarrier n, and $w_{i,j,n} = \frac{h_{i,j,n}^{*}}{|h_{i,j,n}|}$ denotes the complex precoding symbol, by which the phases of transmission signals from different RRHs could be rotated into the same direction as the phase of the initial transmission signal. Also $z_{i,n} \sim \mathcal{CN}(0,\sigma^2)$ denotes the received additive white Gaussian noise (AWGN), where σ^2 is the noise variance. Let $R_{i,n}$ denote the transmission rate of user i on subcarrier n, which can be calculated as

$$
\begin{aligned}
R_{i,n} &= \log_2\left(1 + \frac{|\sum_{j=1}^{R} h_{i,j,n} w_{i,j,n} \sqrt{p_{i,j,n}}|^2}{\sigma^2}\right) \\
&= \log_2\left(1 + \frac{|\sum_{j=1}^{R} (|h_{i,j,n}| \sqrt{p_{i,j,n}})|^2}{\sigma^2}\right).
\end{aligned}
\tag{2}
$$

2.2 Problem Formulation

The system provides services for two specific sets of slices: (1) One set with specific QoS requirements, the slice g in this set requires a minimum reserved rate $R_{g,min}$, $g = 1, 2, \ldots G1$; (2) The other set without QoS requirements, the traffic of slice g can be delivered in a best-effort manner, $g = G1 + 1, \ldots G$. Meanwhile, each slice must be assigned with a minimum amount of resources to guarantee the SLA, which can ensure isolation between slices to a certain extent. For example, when a slice is overloaded, the other slices could still obtain its certain amount of resources.

In this paper, a slice-specific utility-based resource allocation is proposed. Utility function varies across slices with different requirements considering the trade-off between the gain on throughput and the cost on power consumption, where ε_g denotes the preference coefficient. The preference coefficient reflects the specific need of the individual slice toward the above two types of aspects in the process of resource allocation. For example, with a higher ε_g, the slice needs to pay a higher cost for the allocated power, which means that the slice prefers to minimize the power consumption. Otherwise, the slice may be less concerned on power consumption but more concerned on the throughput gain. The scheduling policy would consider the preferences of all slices to allocate the resources between different slices properly. Let $x_{i,n} \in \{0, 1\}$ denote the subcarrier allocation binary variable, where $x_{i,n} = 1$ indicates that subcarrier n is assigned to user i, and otherwise $x_{i,n} = 0$. Thus the utility function of slice g is defined as follows

$$U_g = \sum_{i=1}^{K_g} \sum_{n=1}^{N} x_{i,n} R_{i,n} - \varepsilon_g \sum_{j=1}^{R} \sum_{i=1}^{K_g} \sum_{n=1}^{N} x_{i,n} p_{i,j,n}. \tag{3}$$

Therefore the problem we considered is to optimize the allocation of subcarriers and power jointly so as to maximize the total utility of all slices subject to the physical limitations and SLA of slices, which can be formulated as

$$\max_{\mathbf{x}, \mathbf{p}} \sum_{g=1}^{G} U_g$$

s.t.

$$C1 : \sum_{g=1}^{G} \sum_{i=1}^{K_g} x_{i,n} \leq 1, \forall n,$$

$$C2 : \sum_{g=1}^{G} \sum_{i=1}^{K_g} \sum_{n=1}^{N} x_{i,n} p_{i,j,n} \leq P_{j,max}, \forall j, \tag{4}$$

$$C3 : \sum_{i=1}^{K_g} \sum_{n=1}^{N} x_{i,n} R_{i,n} \geq R_{g,min}, \forall g = 1, 2 \ldots G1,$$

$$C4 : \sum_{i=1}^{K_g} \sum_{n=1}^{N} x_{i,n} \geq N \rho_{g,min}, \forall g = 1, 2 \ldots G,$$

where C1 represents the exclusive orthogonal constraint which ensures that each subcarrier is allowed to be assigned to one user at most, and C2 is the individual power constraint of each RRH, and C3 represents the minimum required rate of each slice g in the set with QoS requirements, and C4 ensures the isolation between slices such that each slice can access at least a certain number of sub-carriers to guarantee its SLA, where $\rho_{g,min}$ denotes the contracted minimum portion of resources assigned to slice g, $\rho_{g,min} \in [0,1], \forall g$ and $\sum_{g=1}^{G} \rho_{g,min} \leq 1$.

3   Problem Solution and Allocation Algorithm

3.1   Problem Solution

The objective function in (4) with its constraints can be classified as a mixed binary integer nonlinear programming problem, with the decision variables $x_{i,n}$ and $p_{i,j,n}$ being binary variable and continuous variable, respectively. The complexity of solving this problem is high, so we will propose an approach to make the problem tractable using the dual decomposition method, similar to the techniques used in [7–9]. Consequently, the Lagrange function of the above optimization problem is given by

$$
\begin{aligned}
L(\mathbf{x}, \mathbf{p}, \boldsymbol{\lambda}, \boldsymbol{\mu}, \boldsymbol{\nu}, \mathbf{u}) = & \sum_{g=1}^{G} \left[\sum_{i=1}^{K_g} \sum_{n=1}^{N} x_{i,n} R_{i,n} - \varepsilon_g \sum_{j=1}^{R} \sum_{i=1}^{K_g} \sum_{n=1}^{N} x_{i,n} p_{i,j,n} \right] \\
& + \sum_{n=1}^{N} \lambda_n (1 - \sum_{g=1}^{G} \sum_{i=1}^{K_g} x_{i,n}) \\
& + \sum_{j=1}^{R} \mu_j (P_{j,max} - \sum_{g=1}^{G} \sum_{i=1}^{K_g} \sum_{n=1}^{N} x_{i,n} p_{i,j,n}) \\
& + \sum_{g=1}^{G} \nu_g (\sum_{i=1}^{K_g} \sum_{n=1}^{N} x_{i,n} R_{i,n} - R_{g,min}) \\
& + \sum_{g=1}^{G} u_g (\sum_{i=1}^{K_g} \sum_{n=1}^{N} x_{i,n} - N \rho_{g,min}),
\end{aligned}
\tag{5}
$$

where $\boldsymbol{\lambda} = (\lambda_1, \ldots, \lambda_N)$, $\boldsymbol{\mu} = (\mu_1, \ldots, \mu_R)$, $\boldsymbol{\nu} = (\nu_1, \ldots, \nu_G)$, $\mathbf{u} = (u_1, \ldots, u_G)$ are the non-negative Lagrange multipliers for the constraints C1 - C4, respectively, and $\nu_g = \nu_g$ when $1 \leq g \leq G1$, or $\nu_g = 0$ when $G1 < g \leq G$. Herein, we can give the dual objective function as

$$
g(\boldsymbol{\lambda}, \boldsymbol{\mu}, \boldsymbol{\nu}, \mathbf{u}) = \max_{\mathbf{x}, \mathbf{p}} L(\mathbf{x}, \mathbf{p}, \boldsymbol{\lambda}, \boldsymbol{\mu}, \boldsymbol{\nu}, \mathbf{u}).
\tag{6}
$$

The dual optimization problem is then formulated as

$$
\begin{aligned}
\min_{\boldsymbol{\lambda}, \boldsymbol{\mu}, \boldsymbol{\nu}, \mathbf{u}} \quad & g(\boldsymbol{\lambda}, \boldsymbol{\mu}, \boldsymbol{\nu}, \mathbf{u}) \\
\text{s.t. } & \boldsymbol{\lambda} \succeq 0, \boldsymbol{\mu} \succeq 0, \boldsymbol{\nu} \succeq 0, \mathbf{u} \succeq 0.
\end{aligned}
\tag{7}
$$

To solve the dual problem, we can re-express the dual objective function as

$$g(\boldsymbol{\lambda}, \boldsymbol{\mu}, \boldsymbol{\nu}, \mathbf{u}) = \sum_{n=1}^{N} g_n(\boldsymbol{\lambda}, \boldsymbol{\mu}, \boldsymbol{\nu}, \mathbf{u}) + \sum_{n=1}^{N} \lambda_n + \sum_{j=1}^{R} \mu_g P_{j,max}$$
$$- \sum_{g=1}^{G} \nu_g R_{g,min} - \sum_{g=1}^{G} u_g N \rho_{g,min}, \tag{8}$$

where

$$g_n(\boldsymbol{\lambda}, \boldsymbol{\mu}, \boldsymbol{\nu}, \mathbf{u}) = \max_{\mathbf{x}, \mathbf{p}} \left[\sum_{g=1}^{G} \sum_{i=1}^{K_g} x_{i,n} g_{i,n}(\boldsymbol{\lambda}, \boldsymbol{\mu}, \boldsymbol{\nu}, \mathbf{u}) \right], \tag{9}$$

$$g_{i,n}(\boldsymbol{\lambda}, \boldsymbol{\mu}, \boldsymbol{\nu}, \mathbf{u}) = R_{i,n} - \varepsilon_g \sum_{j=1}^{R} p_{i,j,n} - \lambda_n - \sum_{j=1}^{R} \mu_j p_{i,j,n} + \nu_g R_{i,n} + u_g. \tag{10}$$

We have decomposed the dual function into the above N independent optimization sub-problems given by (9). By evaluating the Hessian matrix of $R_{i,n}$ at $p_{i,j,n}$ in (2), we can prove that the function in (2) is concave. Thus, the function in (10) is concave as any positive linear combination of concave functions is concave. Suppose subcarrier n is assigned to user i, the optimal $p^*_{i,j,n}$ that maximizes the object function in (10) for fixed Lagrange multipliers can be easily obtained. Then by comparing all possible user assignments of this subcarrier, we select user i for which $g_{i,n}(\boldsymbol{\lambda}, \boldsymbol{\mu}, \boldsymbol{\nu}, \mathbf{u})$ is maximized, and allocate subcarrier n to that user. The allocation of all N subcarriers can be obtained in the same way.

Once the optimal $\mathbf{x}^*$, $\mathbf{p}^*$ are obtained, we can use them to solve the dual problem in (7) to find the optimal values of dual variables. Note that the Lagrange function $L(\mathbf{x}, \mathbf{p}, \boldsymbol{\lambda}, \boldsymbol{\mu}, \boldsymbol{\nu}, \mathbf{u})$ is linear in $\boldsymbol{\lambda}$, $\boldsymbol{\mu}$, $\boldsymbol{\nu}$, $\mathbf{u}$ for fixed $\mathbf{x}^*$ and $\mathbf{p}^*$, and $g(\boldsymbol{\lambda}, \boldsymbol{\mu}, \boldsymbol{\nu}, \mathbf{u})$ is the maximum of these linear functions, so the dual problem in (7) is convex. With the help of the sub-gradient method, we can find the optimal values of dual variables, which can be given by

$$\mu_j^{t+1} = \left[\mu_j^t - \delta_j (P_{j,max} - \sum_{g=1}^{G} \sum_{i=1}^{K_g} \sum_{n=1}^{N} x^*_{i,n} p^*_{i,j,n}) \right]^+, \tag{11}$$

$$\nu_g^{t+1} = \left[\nu_g^t - \xi_g (\sum_{i=1}^{K_g} \sum_{n=1}^{N} x^*_{i,n} R^*_{i,n} - R_{g,min}) \right]^+, \tag{12}$$

$$u_g^{t+1} = \left[u_g^t - \zeta_g (\sum_{i=1}^{K_g} \sum_{n=1}^{N} x^*_{i,n} - N\rho_{g,min}) \right]^+, \tag{13}$$

where δ_j, ξ_g and ζ_g are the appropriate small step sizes to guarantee the convergence of the sub-gradient method. The iteration process will be stopped until certain criterion is fulfilled.

3.2   An Iterative Algorithm

The optimization problem is typically required to be decomposed into N sub-problems to reduce its complexity. After obtaining the optimal dual variables that minimize the dual function, it remains to find the optimal primal solutions $\mathbf{x}^*$, $\mathbf{p}^*$ that maximize the Lagrangian function and satisfy all constraints in the original problem (4). The final optimal solution would be achieved in such an iterative manner. Our proposed algorithm is proposed as follows:

1. Initialize the optimal variables $\mathbf{x}^0$, $\mathbf{p}^0$ and the dual variables $\boldsymbol{\lambda}^0$, $\boldsymbol{\mu}^0$, $\boldsymbol{\nu}^0$, $\mathbf{u}^0$.
2. For each iteration t, solve the N sub-problems in the following steps:
   (a) For the given dual variables, compute the optimal $p^*_{i,j,n}$ that maximizes the object function in (10).
   (b) Update the optimal $g^*_{i,n}$ for every user i.
   (c) Select $k = \arg\max g^*_{i,n}(\boldsymbol{\lambda}, \boldsymbol{\mu}, \boldsymbol{\nu}, \mathbf{u})$, and set $x_{k,n} = 1$, otherwise $x_{i,n} = 0$, for $i \neq k$.
   (d) Once the assignment problems are solved for all N subcarriers, the optimal variables $\mathbf{x}^*$, $\mathbf{p}^*$ can be obtained.
3. Update the $\boldsymbol{\lambda}^{t+1}$, $\boldsymbol{\mu}^{t+1}$, $\boldsymbol{\nu}^{t+1}$, $\mathbf{u}^{t+1}$ using the obtained $\mathbf{x}^*$ and $\mathbf{p}^*$ and let $t = t + 1$.
4. Continue to the next iteration in step (2) until convergence or the maximum iteration number t_{max} is reached.

3.3   Complexity of the Algorithm

The optimal solution to (10) can be obtained by using global searching, assuming that each $p_{i,j,n}$ takes discrete values and requires $\mathcal{O}(X)$ computational complexity. Thus, the optimal power allocation solution requires $\mathcal{O}(X^R)$ computational complexity. For the given dual variables, the complexity of updating $\mathbf{x}$ in each iteration is $\mathcal{O}(NGK_gX^R)$. Let L be the number of iterations needed to converge in the sub-gradient method. Therefore the total computation complexity of the proposed algorithm is $\mathcal{O}(LNGK_gX^R)$.

4   Numerical Results

4.1   System Setup

In this section, the performance evaluation for the proposed allocation algorithm is presented. There are 3 RRHs considered to cover a certain geographical area. Without loss of generality, the channels of different subcarriers are assumed to be independent of one another, which are taken from i.i.d. complex Gaussian random variables with zero mean and unit variance, and the noise variance is given as $\sigma^2 = 0.1$. The number of subcarriers is taken as 32. We assume that the system consists of two slices, each of which serves 10 subscribers. One slice (Slice 1) has QoS requirement that needs a minimum rate of 120 bit/Hz, and the other one (Slice 2) has no QoS requirement. Meanwhile, the contracted minimum resources of each slice is given as $\rho_{g,min} = 0.25$. For comparison, we use two baseline schemes. The first scheme is equal power allocation (EPA) algorithm where the total power is shared equally among subcarriers, and the second scheme is static sharing (SS) scheme, which statically assigns fixed subcarriers to each slice.

4.2   Results and Discussion

In Fig. 2, we present the total achievable system throughput of the proposed scheme, EPA scheme and SS scheme, respectively. In this case, the preference coefficient ε_g is set to zero for each slice, which means that both slices would like to maximize the bandwidth gain no matter how much power is consumed. We can see that, the maximum achievable throughput of all three schemes increases monotonically with P_{max}, and our proposed scheme outperforms all the other schemes. SS scheme offers the lowest throughput since users of each slice can only access their dedicated subcarriers, and have no chance to use underutilized resources that belong to other slice. Figure 3 depicts the impact of different QoS constraints of Slice 1 on sum utility of the system. In this case, the preference factors are set as $\varepsilon_1 = 0.6$ for Slice 1, and $\varepsilon_2 = 0.2$ for Slice 2. The results show that the sum utility decreases as the rate constraint of Slice 1 increases. This is because, by increasing R_{min}, more transmit power should be consumed to satisfy the QoS constraints. And the allocated subcarriers for users with best channel conditions in Slice 2 decreases when the Qos requirement of Slice 1 increases which leads to inefficient use of the resources hence lowering the sum utility. Thus the system can hold the strict rate constraint at the cost of sum utility. In addition, at the same R_{min}, the utility of the proposed scheme is larger than that of EPA scheme since our proposed scheme is a joint subcarrier and power allocation algorithm but EPA scheme is not.

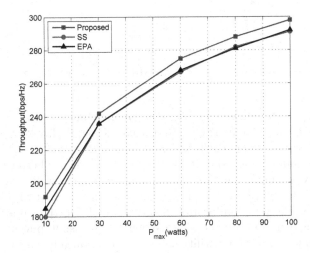

Fig. 2. Throughput of the system versus maximum transmit power P_{max}.

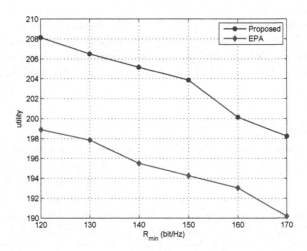

Fig. 3. The total utility of the system versus QoS constrain of Slice 1 R_{min}.

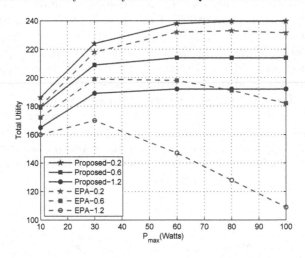

Fig. 4. Total utility versus P_{max} with different factor of Slice 1.

Figure 4 illustrates the impact of the maximum transmit power of each RRH on sum utility of the system. The preference coefficient of Slice 2 is given by $\varepsilon_2 = 0.2$, while Slice 1 has three coefficient sets, $\varepsilon_1 = 0.2$, $\varepsilon_1 = 0.6$ and $\varepsilon_1 = 1.2$ for comparison. It can be noticed that the proposed scheme has better performance than the EPA scheme in all three cases, and the system utility of a higher ε_1 is worse than that of a lower ε_1, since a higher ε_1 means that Slice 1 must pay much more for the power allocated in order to achieve the same throughput constraint. Further, we can see that, When the transmit power is relatively low, the maximum achievable utility increases monotonically with the increasing power in all schemes. The optimal utility can be achieved with a high power constraint P_{max}. In this case, the achievable utility of the proposed scheme no longer increases with the constraint P_{max} as no more power is consumed. However, the EPA scheme continues to allocate more power in the high P_{max} region, resulting in the system utility dropping dramatically, especially when the preference coefficient is higher. This is because, the system utility has a diminishing return with respect to the increase of the transmit power, higher power consumption counteracts the throughput gain.

To study the impact of different preference coefficients to the slice performance, we take "bit/Hz/Joule" as the metric for EE [10], and EE is defined as $\frac{R_g}{P_g}$ where R_g denotes the achieved throughput of the slice g, P_g denotes its consumed power. In this case, the preference factor of Slice 2 is fixed as $\varepsilon_2 = 0.2$, while the factor of Slice 1 has three options: $\varepsilon_1 = 0.2$, $\varepsilon_1 = 0.6$ or $\varepsilon_1 = 1.2$. From Fig. 5, we can observe that the higher ε_1 leads to higher slice-EE of Slice 1. This is because the higher ε_1 means that Slice 1 prefers to achieve the similar throughput in a more energy-efficient way, which can also easily explain why the EE of Slice 1 is much higher than that of Slice 2. In addition, it can be observed in Fig. 6 that the EE of Slice 2 is lower when the preference factor of Slice 1 is higher. Because Slice 1 is more concerned on power consumption than Slice 2 in such case, and the scheduling policy will consider the preference of both slices when allocating resources between slices in order to maximize the utility of whole system. Therefore the resource allocation is energy-efficient to Slice 1, while it may be opposite from the perspective of Slice 2. However, the two slices can only achieve very similar slice-EE in EPA scheme regardless of the preference coefficients they chose in their utility function, since the power allocation is unchanged in this scheme. Finally, Our proposed scheme can satisfy the different requirements of slices according to their trade-off between throughput gain and power consumption, which can achieve better system performance.

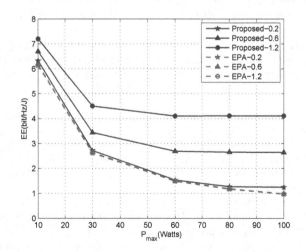

Fig. 5. EE of Slice 1 versus P_{max} for different factor of Slice 1.

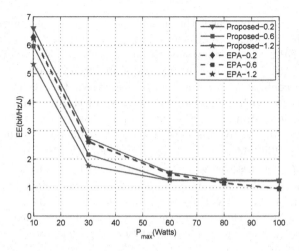

Fig. 6. EE of Slice 2 versus P_{max} for different factor of Slice 1.

5   Conclusions

In this paper, we studied slice-specific utility-based resource allocation in
CRANs. In the proposed resource allocation algorithm, each slice has a customized utility function taking their specific trade-off between spectral efficiency
and energy efficiency into account. The objective function is to maximize the sum
utility of all slices through joint subcarriers and power allocation under different
QoS requirement constraints of slices. Numerical results demonstrated that the
proposed algorithm significantly outperforms other candidates, which can satisfy
the customized preference of slices in terms of throughput gain and power cost.

Acknowledgement. The authors would like to thank DOCOMO Beijing Communications Laboratories Co., Ltd. for their support in this work. This work was supported
in part by the National High Technology Research and Development Program (863
Program) of China under Grant No. 2014AA01A707.

References

1. Kalil, M., Shami, A., Ye, Y.: Wireless resources virtualization in LTE systems. In:
Proceedings of IEEE INFOCOM Workshops 2014, Toronto, Ontario, Canada, pp.
363–368, April 2014
2. Kamel, M.I., Le, L.B., Girard, A.: LTE wireless network virtualization: dynamic
slicing via flexible scheduling. In: Proceedings of IEEE VTC Fall 2014, Vancouver,
British Columbia, Canada, pp. 1–5, September 2014
3. Kamel, M.I., Le, L.B., Girard, A.: LTE multi-cell dynamic resource allocation
for wireless network virtualization. In: Proceedings of IEEE WCNC 2015, New
Orleans, Louisiana, USA, pp. 966–971, March 2015

4. Kokku, R., Mahindra, R., Zhang, H., Rangarajan, S.: NVS: a substrate for virtualizing wireless resources in cellular networks. IEEE/ACM Trans. Netw. **20**(5), 1333–1346 (2012)
5. Parsaeefard, S., Jumba, V., Derakhshani, M., Le-Ngoc, T.: Joint resource provisioning and admission control in wireless virtualized networks. In: Proceedings of IEEE WCNC 2015, New Orleans, Louisiana, USA, pp. 2020–2025, March 2015
6. Liu, G., Yu, F.R., Ji, H., Leung, V.C.M.: Distributed resource allocation in virtualized full-duplex relaying networks. IEEE Trans. Veh. Technol. **65**(10), 8444–8460 (2016)
7. Palomar, D.P., Chiang, M.: A tutorial on decomposition methods for network utility maximization. IEEE J. Sel. Areas Commun. **24**(8), 1439–1451 (2006)
8. Yu, W., Lui, R.: Dual methods for nonconvex spectrum optimization of multicarrier systems. IEEE Trans. Commun. **54**(7), 1310–1322 (2006)
9. Palomar, D.P., Chiang, M.: Alternative decompositions for distributed maximization of network utility: framework and applications. In: Proceedings of IEEE INFOCOM 2006, Barcelona, Spain, pp. 1–13, April 2006
10. Zou, J., Xi, Q., Zhang, Q., He, C., Jiang, L., Ding, J.: QoS-aware energy-efficient radio resource allocation in heterogeneous wireless networks. In: Proceedings of IEEE ICCW 2015, London, UK, pp. 2781–2786, June 2015

Iterative Receiver with Gaussian and Mean-Field Approximation in Massive MIMO Systems

Sheng Wu[1], Linling Kuang[1(✉)], Xincong Lin[1], and Baosheng Sun[2]

[1] Tsinghua Space Center, Tsinghua University, Beijing 100084, China
{thuraya,kll}@tsinghua.edu.cn
[2] Beijing Space Information Relay and Transmission Technology Research Center, Beijing 100094, China

Abstract. In this paper, a computationally efficient message-passing receiver that performs joint channel estimation and decoding is proposed for massive multiple-input multiple-output (MIMO) systems with OFDM modulation. We combine the loopy belief propagation (LBP) with the mean-field approximation and Gaussian approximation to decouple frequency-domain channel taps and data symbols from noisy observations. Specifically, pair-wise joint belief of frequency-domain channel tap and symbol is obtained by soft interference cancellation, after which the marginal belief of frequency-domain channel tap and symbol are estimated from the pair-wise joint belief by the mean-field approximation. To estimate time-domain channel taps between each pair of antennas, a Gaussian message passing based estimator is applied. The whole scheme of joint channel estimation and decoding is assessed by Monte Carlo simulations, and the numerical results corroborate the superior performance of the proposed scheme and its superiority to the state of art.

Keywords: Belief propagation · Channel estimation · Decoding
Massive MIMO · Message passing · Mean-field approximation
Orthogonal frequency-division multiplexing (OFDM)

1 Introduction

Recently, massive MIMO systems with a large number of antennas at the basestation have gained great attention [1–6]. Accurate channel state information (CSI) is essential in massive MIMO systems, as high data rate and energy efficiency are achievable only when CSI is known. In TDD mode, the available training resources are limited by the channel coherence interval [7]. In contrast to conventional MIMO systems with a small number of antennas, the overhead required for channel estimation in massive MIMO systems may be overwhelming. Therefore, accurate channel estimation with reduced overhead is critical to massive MIMO systems.

This work was supported by the National Nature Science Foundation of China (Grant No. 91438206 and Grant No. 91638205).

© ICST Institute for Computer Sciences, Social Informatics and Telecommunications Engineering 2018
K. Long et al. (Eds.): 5GWN 2017, LNICST 211, pp. 300–316, 2018.
https://doi.org/10.1007/978-3-319-72823-0_29

A receiver that jointly estimates channel taps and data symbols can provide more accurate channel estimation with less pilot overhead [8–11]. Factor graph and loopy belief propagation (LBP) [12] have been used as a unified framework for iterative joint detection, estimation, interference cancellation, and decoding [13]. LBP algorithm combined with various approximate method has been proposed in [9,14–20]. Specifically, LBP combined with expectation-maximization (EM) was proposed in [16]; LBP combined with Gaussian approximation was studied in [9,16,17,21]. Riegler *et al.* merged LBP and the mean-field (MF) approximation (so called "BP-MF") in [19,22], and applied it to both single-input single-output OFDM systems and MIMO-OFDM systems [19,22,23]. However, the BP-MF has to learn the noise precision to take into count the interference from other users even when the noise power is exact known [24,25]. Moreover, the BP-MF in [22] requires high computational complexity and would only work in the case of few antennas and subcarriers, since large matrices need to be inverted to estimate channel coefficients. Although low-complexity BP-MF variants have been presented in [26,27], their performance are degraded.

In this paper, we consider the massive MIMO-OFDM system over frequency selective channels. In order to decouple frequency-domain channel taps and transmit symbols from noisy observations, we use the central-limit theorem to efficiently obtain the joint belief of each pair of frequency-domain channel tap and transmit symbol, and then employ the mean-field method to decouple them. Given messages of frequency-domain channel taps are extracted from observations, the time-domain channel taps between each pair of antennas is estimated by a Gaussian message passing estimator [20]. In addition, the computations at symbol variables are reduced by the expectation propagation [28–30].

The remainder of this paper is organized as follows. The system model is described in Sect. 2. Section 3 presents the proposed message passing algorithm and complexity analysis. Numerical results are presented in Sect. 4, followed by conclusions in Sect. 5.

Notation: Lowercase letters (e.g., x) denote scalars, bold lowercase letters (e.g., $\boldsymbol{x}$) denote column vectors, and bold uppercase letters (e.g., $\boldsymbol{X}$) denote matrices. The superscripts $(\cdot)^{\mathsf{T}}$, $(\cdot)^{\mathsf{H}}$ and $(\cdot)^*$ denote the transpose operation, Hermitian transpose operation, and complex conjugate operation, respectively. Also, $\boldsymbol{X} \otimes \boldsymbol{Y}$ denotes Kronecker product of $\boldsymbol{X}$ and $\boldsymbol{Y}$; $\boldsymbol{I}$ or $\boldsymbol{I}_d$ denotes an identity matrix of size $d \times d$, and $\ln(\cdot)$ denotes the natural logarithm. Furthermore, $\mathcal{N}_{\mathbb{C}}(x; \hat{x}, v_x) = (\pi v_x)^{-1} \exp\left(-|x - \hat{x}|^2 / v_x\right)$ denotes the Gaussian probability density function (PDF) of x with mean $\hat{x}$ and variance v, and $\mathsf{Gam}(\lambda; \alpha, \beta) = \beta^\alpha \lambda^{\alpha-1} \exp(-\beta\lambda) / \Gamma(\alpha)$ denotes the Gamma PDF of λ with shape parameter α and rate parameter β, where $\Gamma(\cdot)$ is the gamma function. Finally, $\propto$ denotes equality up to a constant scale factor; $\boldsymbol{x} \backslash x_{tnk}$ denotes all elements in $\boldsymbol{x}$ but x_{tnk}; and $\mathsf{E}_{p(x)}\cdot$ denotes expectation with respect to distribution $p(x)$.

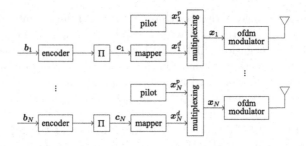

Fig. 1. Block-diagram representation of the transmitters.

2 System Model

We consider the up-link of a massive MIMO system with N users. Each user employs one transmit antenna, and the base station employs an array of $M \geq N$ antennas. Frequency-selective Rayleigh fading channels are assumed, and OFDM is employed to combat multipath interference. The transmitters for the users are shown in Fig. 1. For the nth user, the information bits $\boldsymbol{b}_n$ are encoded and interleaved, yielding a sequence of coded bits $\boldsymbol{c}_n$. Then each Q bits in $\boldsymbol{c}_n$ are mapped onto one modulation symbol, which is chosen from a 2^Q-ary constellation set $\mathcal{A}$, i.e., $|\mathcal{A}| = 2^Q$. The data symbols $\boldsymbol{x}_n^d$ are then multiplexed with pilot symbols $\boldsymbol{x}_n^p$, forming the transmitted symbols sequence $\boldsymbol{x}_n$. Pilot and data symbols are arranged in an OFDM frame of T OFDM symbols, each consisting of K subcarriers. More specifically, there are totally K_p pilot subcarriers in an OFDM frame and the pilot subcarriers are spaced $\lfloor K/(K_p - 1) \rfloor$ subcarriers apart. The pilot-subcarrier set of user n is denoted by $\mathcal{P}_n = \{(t, k) : x_{tnk} \text{ is pilot}\}$, $|\mathcal{P}_n| = T_p K_p$, and data-subcarrier set is denoted by $\mathcal{D} = \overline{\bigcup_n \mathcal{P}_n}$. Note that pilot-subcarrier sets belong to different users are mutual exclusive, i.e., $\bigcap_n \mathcal{P}_n = \emptyset$, and only one user actually transmits a pilot symbol at a given pilot subcarrier, whereas the other users keep silent, i.e., if $(t, k) \in \mathcal{P}_n$, then $x_{tn'k} = 0$, $\forall n' \neq n$. The frequency-domain symbols in the tth OFDM symbol transmitted by the nth user are denoted by $\boldsymbol{x}_{tn} = [x_{tn1}, \ldots, x_{tnK}]^\mathsf{T}$, where $x_{tnk} \in \mathcal{A}$ represents the symbol transmitted at the kth subcarrier. To modulate the OFDM symbol, a K-point inverse discrete Fourier transform (IDFT) is applied to the symbol sequence $\boldsymbol{x}_{tn}$, and then a cyclic prefix (CP) is added to it before transmission.

The OFDM symbols are transmitted through a wide-sense stationary uncorrelated scattering (WSSUS) channel. It is assumed that the time-domain channel taps keep static during one OFDM frame but vary from frame to frame. The time-domain channel taps from the nth user to the mth receive antenna are denoted by $\boldsymbol{h}_{mn} = [h_{mn1}, \ldots, h_{mnL}]^\mathsf{T}$, where h_{mnl} is the lth channel tap, and L is the maximum number of channel taps. Then, the frequency-domain tap w_{mnk} at the kth subcarrier from the nth user to the mth receiving antenna reads

$$w_{mnk} = \sum_{l=1}^{L} h_{mnl} \exp\left(-\frac{j2\pi lk}{K}\right). \tag{1}$$

At each receive antenna, the CP is first removed and the received signal is then converted into the frequency-domain through a K-point discrete Fourier transform (DFT). It is assumed that the N transmitters and the receiver are synchronized and the maximum delays are smaller than the duration of the CP, whereby the received signal for the tth OFDM symbol can be written as

$$y_{tmk} = \sum_{n=1}^{N} w_{mnk} x_{tnk} + \varpi_{tmk}, \tag{2}$$

where y_{tmk} denotes the received signal at the kth subcarrier on the mth receive antenna, ϖ_{tmk} denotes a circularly symmetric complex noise with zero mean and variance σ_{ϖ}^2. The received signal can be recast in a matrix-vector notation as

$$y = \sum_{n=1}^{N} W_n x_n + \varpi = W x + \varpi, \tag{3}$$

where $y = \begin{bmatrix} y_1^\mathsf{T} \cdots y_M^\mathsf{T} \end{bmatrix}^\mathsf{T}$ with $y_m = \begin{bmatrix} y_{1m1} \cdots y_{1mK} \cdots y_{Tm1} \cdots y_{TmK} \end{bmatrix}^\mathsf{T}$ denoting the received signal at the mth receive antenna for T OFDM symbols, $W_n = \begin{bmatrix} I_T \otimes \mathrm{diag}\{w_{1n\cdot}\} \cdots I_T \otimes \mathrm{diag}\{w_{Mn\cdot}\} \end{bmatrix}^\mathsf{T}$ with $w_{mn\cdot} = \begin{bmatrix} w_{mn1} \cdots w_{mnK} \end{bmatrix}^\mathsf{T}$ denoting the frequency-domain taps from the nth user to the mth antenna, $W = \begin{bmatrix} W_1 \cdots W_N \end{bmatrix}$, $x = \begin{bmatrix} x_1^\mathsf{T} \cdots x_N^\mathsf{T} \end{bmatrix}^\mathsf{T}$ with $x_n = \begin{bmatrix} x_{1n1} \cdots x_{1nK} \cdots x_{Tn1} \cdots x_{TnK} \end{bmatrix}^\mathsf{T}$ denoting the symbols transmitted by the nth user, and $\varpi = \begin{bmatrix} \varpi_1^\mathsf{T} \cdots \varpi_M^\mathsf{T} \end{bmatrix}^\mathsf{T}$ with $\varpi_m = \begin{bmatrix} \varpi_{1m1} \cdots \varpi_{1mK} \cdots \varpi_{Tm1} \cdots \varpi_{TmK} \end{bmatrix}^\mathsf{T}$ denoting the noise signal at the mth receive antenna.

3 Message Passing for Joint Detection and Decoding

We aim to jointly estimate the information bits $b = \begin{bmatrix} b_1^\mathsf{T} \cdots b_N^\mathsf{T} \end{bmatrix}$ and channel taps $h = \begin{bmatrix} h_{11\cdot}^\mathsf{T} \cdots h_{1N\cdot}^\mathsf{T} \cdots h_{M1\cdot}^\mathsf{T} \cdots h_{MN\cdot}^\mathsf{T} \end{bmatrix}^\mathsf{T}$ from the noisy observation y. The joint PDF of all involved random variables can be factorized as follows,

$$
\begin{aligned}
&p(b, c, x, y, W, h) \\
&= p(b)\,p(c \mid b)\,p(x \mid c)\,p(y \mid W, x)\,p(h, W) \\
&= p(b)\,p(c \mid b) \prod_{n=1}^{N} \prod_{(t,k)\in\mathcal{D}} \mathcal{M}_{tnk}(x_{tnk}, c_{tnk}) \prod_{t,m,k} f_{tmk}(x_{t\cdot k}, w_{tmk}) \\
&\quad \times \prod_{m,n,k} g_{mnk}(w_{mnk}, h_{mn\cdot}) \prod_{m,n,l} p(h_{mnl}), \tag{4}
\end{aligned}
$$

where $\mathcal{M}_{tnk}(x_{tnk}, c_{tnk}) = \delta\left(\varphi(c_{tnk}) - x_{tnk}\right)$ denotes the deterministic mapping $x_{tnk} = \varphi(c_{tnk})$, $\varphi(c_{tnk})$ denotes the symbol mapping function, and $\delta(\cdot)$ denotes the Kronecker delta function. The channel transition function $f_{tmk}(x_{t\cdot k}, w_{mnk})$ is given by

$$f_{tmk}(\boldsymbol{x}_{t\cdot k}, \boldsymbol{w}_{mnk}) = \mathcal{N}_{\mathbb{C}}\left(y_{tmk}; \sum_n w_{mnk} x_{mnk}, \sigma_{\varpi}^2\right). \tag{5}$$

As the frequency-domain channel taps w_{mnk} is the DFT (discrete Fourier transform) of time-domain taps $\boldsymbol{h}_{mn\cdot}$, we have

$$g_{mnk}(w_{mnk}, \boldsymbol{h}_{mn\cdot}) = \delta\left(w_{mnk} - \sum_{l=1}^{L} \phi_{kl} h_{mnl}\right), \tag{6}$$

where $\boldsymbol{\Phi} \in \mathbb{C}^{K \times L}$ denotes the DFT weighting matrix, and ϕ_{kl} denotes the entry in the kth row and lth column of DFT weighting matrix $\boldsymbol{\Phi}$. The probabilistic structure exposed by the factorization (4) can be represented with a factor graph, as depicted in Fig. 2. Due to high-dimensional integration, directly computing the marginal probability of information bit is computationally prohibitive. Hence, we resort to LBP to offer efficient solutions. As shown in Fig. 2, there exist two groups of loops, the group of detection-decoding-loops in the left and the group of the channel-estimation-loops in the right. Here, we choose to start passing messages at the channel transition nodes, then pass messages concurrently in both the detection-decoding-loop (the left loop) and the channel-estimation-loop (the right loop). Each of these full cycles of message passing will be referred to as a "turbo iteration".

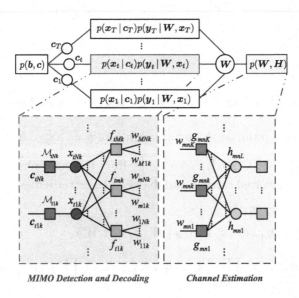

MIMO Detection and Decoding   **Channel Estimation**

Fig. 2. Factor graph of the Massive MIMO-OFDM system.

The presentation of message passing follows closely with the convention in [12]. All types of message are specified in Table 1. Applying the SPA to the factor graph in Fig. 2, the messages from the channel transition node f_{tmk} at the ith iteration are given by

Table 1. SPA message definitions at iteration $i \in \mathbb{Z}$.

$\mu_{tnk \leftarrow tmk}^{(i)}(\cdot)$	Message from node f_{tmk} to node x_{tnk}
$\mu_{tnk \leftarrow tnk}^{(i)}(\cdot)$	Message from node x_{tnk} to node $\mathcal{M}_{tnk}$
$\mu_{tnk \rightarrow tnk}^{(i)}(\cdot)$	Message from node $\mathcal{M}_{tnk}$ to node x_{tnk}
$\mu_{tnk \rightarrow tmk}^{(i)}(\cdot)$	Message from node x_{tnk} to node f_{tmk}
$\mu_{tmk \rightarrow mnk}^{(i)}(\cdot)$	Message from node f_{tmk} to node w_{mnk}
$\mu_{mnk \rightarrow mnk}^{(i)}(\cdot)$	Message from node w_{mnk} to node g_{mnk}
$\mu_{mnk \rightarrow mnl}^{(i)}(\cdot)$	Message from node g_{mnk} to node h_{mnl}
$\mu_{mnl \rightarrow mnk}^{(i)}(\cdot)$	Message from node h_{mnl} to node g_{mnk}
$\mu_{mnk \leftarrow mnk}^{(i)}(\cdot)$	Message from node g_{mnk} to node w_{mnk}
$\mu_{tmk \leftarrow mnk}^{(i)}(\cdot)$	Message from node w_{mnk} to node f_{tmk}
$\beta_{tnk}^{(i)}(\cdot)$	Belief of x_{tnk} at node x_{tnk}
$\beta_{mnk}^{(i)}(\cdot)$	Belief of w_{mnk} at node w_{mnk}

$$\mu_{tnk \leftarrow tmk}^{(i)}(x_{tnk}) = \sum_{\boldsymbol{x}_{t \cdot k} \backslash x_{tnk}} \int_{\boldsymbol{w}_{mk}} \Bigg(f_{tmk}(\boldsymbol{x}_{t \cdot k}, \boldsymbol{w}_{m \cdot k})$$
$$\times \prod_{n'=1}^{N} \mu_{tmk \leftarrow mn'k}^{(i-1)}(w_{mn'k}) \prod_{n'' \neq n}^{N} \mu_{tn''k \rightarrow tmk}^{(i-1)}(x_{tn''k}) \Bigg), \forall n, \tag{7}$$

$$\mu_{tmk \rightarrow mnk}^{(i)}(w_{mnk}) = \sum_{\boldsymbol{x}_{t \cdot k} \in \mathcal{A}^N} \int_{\boldsymbol{w}_{m \cdot k} \backslash w_{mnk}} \Bigg(f_{tmk}(\boldsymbol{x}_{t \cdot k}, \boldsymbol{w}_{m \cdot k})$$
$$\times \prod_{n' \neq n} \mu_{tmk \leftarrow mn'k}^{(i-1)}(w_{mn'k}) \prod_{n''} \mu_{tn''k \rightarrow tmk}^{(i-1)}(x_{tn''k}) \Bigg), \forall n. \tag{8}$$

As each symbol of $\boldsymbol{x}_{t \cdot k} \backslash x_{tnk} \in \mathcal{A}^{N-1}$ takes on values in the discrete set $\mathcal{A}$, the computations of $\mu_{tnk \leftarrow tmk}^{(i)}(x_{tnk})$ and $\mu_{tmk \rightarrow mnk}^{(i)}(w_{mnk})$ require exponential time to marginalize out the random vector $\boldsymbol{x}_{t \cdot k} \backslash x_{tnk}$, which are obviously intractable for the problem size of interests. Using (5), the messages with respect to known pilot symbol boil down to the following simple form

$$\mu_{tmk \rightarrow mnk}^{(i)}(w_{mnk}) \propto \mathcal{N}_{\mathbb{C}}\left(w_{mnk}; \frac{y_{tmk}}{x_{tnk}}, \frac{\sigma_{\varpi}^2}{|x_{tnk}|^2}\right), \forall (t,k) \in \mathcal{P}_n \tag{9}$$

$$\mu_{tmk \rightarrow mn'k}^{(i)}(w_{mn'k}) \propto \mathcal{N}_{\mathbb{C}}(w_{mn'k}; 0, \infty), \forall n' \neq n, \tag{10}$$

where we make use of the fact that other users keep silent on the pilot subcarriers $\mathcal{P}_n$.

3.1 LBP Combined with Gaussian Approximation and Mean-Field Approximation

Note that, to update the outgoing messages from the observation node f_{tmk}, the received signal in (2) can be rewritten as

$$y_{tmk} = w_{mnk}x_{tnk} + \sum_{n' \neq n}^{N} w_{mn'k}x_{tn'k} + \varpi_{tmk}, \forall n. \tag{11}$$

The interference term $\sum_{n' \neq n} w_{mn'k}x_{tn'k} + \varpi_{tmk}$ in (11) is considered as a Gaussian variable with mean $\tilde{z}_{tnk \leftarrow tmk}^{(i)}$ and variance $\tau_{tnk \leftarrow tmk}^{(i)}$,

$$\tilde{z}_{tnk \leftarrow tmk}^{(i)} = \sum_{n' \neq n} \hat{w}_{tmk \leftarrow mn'k}^{(i-1)} \hat{x}_{tn'k \rightarrow tmk}^{(i-1)},$$

$$\tau_{tnk \leftarrow tmk}^{(i)} = \sigma_{\varpi}^2 + \sum_{n' \neq n} \left(\left| \hat{w}_{tmk \leftarrow mn'k}^{(i-1)} \right|^2 \nu_{tn'k \rightarrow tmk}^{(i-1)} \right.$$

$$\left. + \left| \hat{x}_{tn'k \rightarrow tmk}^{(i-1)} \right|^2 \nu_{tmk \leftarrow mn'k}^{(i-1)} + \nu_{tn'k \rightarrow tmk}^{(i-1)} \nu_{tmk \leftarrow mn'k}^{(i-1)} \right). \tag{12}$$

where $\hat{w}_{tmk \leftarrow mn'k}^{(i-1)}$ and $\nu_{tmk \leftarrow mn'k}^{(i-1)}$ denote the mean and variance of variable x_{tnk} with respect to the message $\mu_{tmk \leftarrow mn'k}^{(i-1)}(w_{mnk})$, respectively; $\hat{x}_{tn'k \rightarrow tmk}^{(i-1)}$ and $\nu_{tn'k \rightarrow tmk}^{(i-1)}$ denote the mean and variance of variable w_{mnk} with respect to message $\mu_{tn'k \rightarrow tmk}^{(i-1)}(x_{tnk})$, respectively. As a result, the channel transition function f_{tmk} can be approximated as

$$f_{tmk}(\boldsymbol{x}_{t \cdot k}, \boldsymbol{w}_m^k) \approx \mathcal{N}_{\mathbb{C}}(w_{mnk}x_{tnk}; z_{tmk \rightarrow mnk}^{(i)}, \tau_{tmk \rightarrow mnk}^{(i)}), \forall n, \tag{13}$$

where $z_{tmk \rightarrow mnk}^{(i)} = y_{tmk} - \tilde{z}_{tnk \leftarrow tmk}^{(i)}$.

Using (13), a local joint belief of w_{mnk} and x_{tnk} is defined as

$$\beta_{tmk}^{(i)}(w_{mnk}, x_{tnk}) \propto \mathcal{N}_{\mathbb{C}}(x_{tnk}w_{mnk}; z_{tmk \rightarrow mnk}^{(i)}, \tau_{tmk \rightarrow mnk}^{(i)})$$

$$\times \mu_{tmk \leftarrow mnk}^{(i-1)}(w_{mnk}) \mu_{tnk \rightarrow tmk}^{(i-1)}(x_{tnk}), \tag{14}$$

In order to maintain the message passing analytically and efficiently, we project the joint belief $\beta_{tmk}^{(i)}(w_{mnk}, x_{tnk})$ onto a fully factorized belief $\tilde{\beta}_{tmk}^{(i)}(w_{mnk}, x_{tnk}) = \tilde{\beta}_{tmk}^{(i)}(x_{tnk}) \tilde{\beta}_{tmk}^{(i)}(w_{mnk})$, using the criterion of minimum inclusive KL divergence [31]

$$\min_{\tilde{\beta}_{tmk}^{(i)}(w_{mnk}, x_{tnk})} \mathrm{KL}\left(\tilde{\beta}_{tmk}^{(i)}(w_{mnk}, x_{tnk}) \, \| \, \beta_{tmk}^{(i)}(w_{mnk}, x_{tnk}) \right), \tag{15}$$

which amounts to the mean-field approximation in statistical physics. However, finding a global optimal solution to (15) is difficult, and hence, we instead resort to a local form of optimization. We use alternative measures to find the local beliefs $\tilde{\beta}_{tmk}^{(i)}(x_{tnk})$ and $\tilde{\beta}_{tmk}^{(i)}(w_{mnk})$ at the function node f_{tmk}

$$\mathsf{KL}\left(\tilde{\beta}_{tmk}^{(i)}\left(x_{tnk}\right)\tilde{\beta}_{tmk}^{(i-1)}\left(w_{mnk}\right)\parallel\beta_{tmk}^{(i)}\left(w_{mnk},x_{tnk}\right)\right),\tag{16}$$

$$\mathsf{KL}\left(\tilde{\beta}_{tmk}^{(i)}\left(w_{mnk}\right)\tilde{\beta}_{tmk}^{(i-1)}\left(x_{tnk}\right)\parallel\beta_{tmk}^{(i)}\left(w_{mnk},x_{tnk}\right)\right),\tag{17}$$

where the local beliefs $\tilde{\beta}_{tmk}^{(i-1)}\left(w_{mnk}\right)$ and $\tilde{\beta}_{tmk}^{(i-1)}\left(x_{tnk}\right)$ at variable nodes x_{tnk} and w_{mnk}, respectively, are defined later. Using variational calculus, $\tilde{\beta}_{tmk}^{(i)}\left(x_{tnk}\right)$ and $\tilde{\beta}_{tmk}^{(i)}\left(w_{mnk}\right)$ fulfill following updates[1]

$$\tilde{\beta}_{tmk}^{(i)}\left(x_{tnk}\right)=\exp\left(\mathsf{E}_{\beta_{mnk}^{(i-1)}\left(w_{mnk}\right)}\ln\beta_{tmk}^{(i)}\left(w_{mnk},x_{tnk}\right)\right),\tag{18}$$

$$\tilde{\beta}_{tmk}^{(i)}\left(w_{mnk}\right)=\exp\left(\mathsf{E}_{\beta_{tnk}^{(i-1)}\left(x_{tnk}\right)}\ln\beta_{tmk}^{(i)}\left(w_{mnk},x_{tnk}\right)\right).\tag{19}$$

According to the semantics of factor graph, the messages $\mu_{tnk\leftarrow tmk}^{(i)}\left(x_{tnk}\right),\forall n$ and $\mu_{tmk\rightarrow mnk}^{(i)}\left(w_{mnk}\right),\forall n$ then are updated as follows

$$\mu_{tnk\leftarrow tmk}^{(i)}\left(x_{tnk}\right)=\frac{\tilde{\beta}_{tmk}^{(i)}\left(x_{tnk}\right)}{\mu_{tnk\leftarrow tmk}^{(i-1)}\left(x_{tnk}\right)}\propto\mathcal{N}_{\mathbb{C}}\left(x_{tnk};\hat{x}_{tnk\leftarrow tmk}^{(i)},\nu_{tnk\leftarrow tmk}^{(i)}\right),$$

$$\mu_{tmk\rightarrow mnk}^{(i)}\left(w_{mnk}\right)=\frac{\tilde{\beta}_{tmk}^{(i)}\left(w_{mnk}\right)}{\mu_{tmk\leftarrow mnk}^{(i-1)}\left(w_{mnk}\right)}\propto\mathcal{N}_{\mathbb{C}}\left(w_{mnk};\hat{w}_{tmk\rightarrow mnk}^{(i)},\nu_{tmk\rightarrow mnk}^{(i)}\right),$$

$$\tag{20}$$

where

$$\nu_{tnk\leftarrow tmk}^{(i)}=\frac{\tau_{tmk\rightarrow mnk}^{(i)}}{\nu_{mnk}^{(i-1)}+\left|\hat{w}_{mnk}^{(i-1)}\right|^{2}},\tag{21}$$

$$\hat{x}_{tnk\leftarrow tmk}^{(i)}=\frac{\nu_{tnk\leftarrow tmk}^{(i)}}{\tau_{tmk\rightarrow mnk}^{(i)}}\hat{w}_{mnk}^{(i-1)*}z_{tnk\leftarrow tmk}^{(i)},\tag{22}$$

$$\nu_{tmk\rightarrow mnk}^{(i)}=\frac{\tau_{tmk\rightarrow mnk}^{(i)}}{\nu_{tnk}^{(i-1)}+\left|\hat{x}_{tnk}^{(i-1)}\right|^{2}},\tag{23}$$

$$\hat{w}_{tmk\rightarrow mnk}^{(i)}=\frac{\nu_{tmk\rightarrow mnk}^{(i)}}{\tau_{tmk\rightarrow mnk}^{(i)}}\hat{x}_{tnk}^{(i-1)*}z_{tmk\rightarrow mnk}^{(i)}.\tag{24}$$

with $z_{tnk\leftarrow tmk}^{(i)}$ and $\tau_{tmk\rightarrow mnk}^{(i)}$ having the same definitions as that of (12) and (12), respectively. Next, the local belief at the variable node x_{tnk} is updated by

---

[1] For the sake of efficient implementation, we consider to update all the beliefs concurrently in this paper.

$$\beta_{tnk}^{(i)}(x_{tnk}) = \frac{\mu_{tnk\to tnk}^{(i)}(x_{tnk}) \prod_m \mu_{tnk\gets tmk}^{(i)}(x_{tnk})}{\sum_{x_{tnk}\in\mathcal{A}} \mu_{tnk\to tnk}^{(i)}(x_{tnk}) \prod_m \mu_{tnk\gets tmk}^{(i)}(x_{tnk})}$$

$$= \frac{\mu_{tnk\to tnk}^{(i)}(x_{tnk})\, \mathcal{N}_{\mathbb{C}}(x_{tnk};\zeta_{tnk}^{(i)},\gamma_{tnk}^{(i)})}{\sum_{x_{tnk}\in\mathcal{A}} \mu_{tnk\to tnk}^{(i)}(x_{tnk})\, \mathcal{N}_{\mathbb{C}}(x_{tnk};\zeta_{tnk}^{(i)},\gamma_{tnk}^{(i)})}, \qquad (25)$$

where

$$\gamma_{tnk}^{(i)} = \frac{1}{\sum_{m=1}^{M} \frac{1}{\nu_{tnk\gets tmk}^{(i)}}}, \qquad (26)$$

$$\zeta_{tnk}^{(i)} = \gamma_{tnk}^{(i)} \sum_{m=1}^{M} \frac{\hat{x}_{tnk\gets tmk}^{(i)}}{\nu_{tnk\gets tmk}^{(i)}}. \qquad (27)$$

Then the message $\mu_{tnk\gets tnk}^{(i)}(x_{tnk})$ from the variable node x_{tnk} to the mapper node $\mathcal{M}_{tnk}$ is updated by

$$\mu_{tnk\gets tnk}^{(i)}(x_{tnk}) = \prod_{m=1}^{M} \mu_{tnk\gets tmk}^{(i)}(x_{tnk}) \propto \mathcal{N}_{\mathbb{C}}\left(x_{tnk};\zeta_{tnk}^{(i)},\gamma_{tnk}^{(i)}\right). \qquad (28)$$

With the message $\mu_{tnk\gets tnk}^{(i)}(x_{tnk})$ and the *a priori* LLRs $\left\{\lambda_{\mathsf{a}}^{(i-1)}(c_{tnk}^q),\forall q\right\}$ fed from decoder, the extrinsic LLRs $\{\lambda_{\mathsf{e}}^{(i)}(c_{tnk}^q),\forall q\}$ corresponding to the symbol x_{tnk} are obtained

$$\lambda_{\mathsf{e}}^{(i)}(c_{tnk}^q) = \ln\frac{\sum_{x_{tnk}\in\mathcal{A}_q^1} \mu_{tnk\to tnk}^{(i-1)}(x_{tnk})\, \mu_{tnk\gets tnk}^{(i)}(x_{tnk})}{\sum_{x_{tnk}\in\mathcal{A}_q^0} \mu_{tnk\to tnk}^{(i-1)}(x_{tnk})\, \mu_{tnk\gets tnk}^{(i)}(x_{tnk})} - \lambda_{\mathsf{a}}^{(i-1)}(c_{tnk}^q). \quad (29)$$

Once all the extrinsic LLRs $\{\lambda_{\mathsf{e}}^{(i)}(c_{tnk}^q),\forall t,\forall n,\forall k,\forall q\}$ are available, each channel decoder performs decoding and updates the *a priori* LLRs of coded bits. Then, the *a priori* LLRs $\left\{\lambda_{\mathsf{a}}^{(i)}(c_{tnk}^q)\right\}$ are interleaved and converted to the message

$$\mu_{tnk\to tnk}^{(i)}(x_{tnk}) = \prod_{q=1}^{Q} \frac{\exp\left(c_n^q \lambda_{\mathsf{a}}^{(i)}(c_{tnk}^q)\right)}{1 + \exp\left(\lambda_{\mathsf{a}}^{(i)}(c_{tnk}^q)\right)}. \qquad (30)$$

Direct evaluating $\left\{\hat{x}_{tnk\to tmk}^{(i)},\nu_{tnk\to tmk}^{(i)}\right\}$ via $\mu_{tnk\to tmk}^{(i)}(x_{tnk})$ is expensive, as the number of $\left\{\hat{x}_{tnk\to tmk}^{(i)},\nu_{tnk\to tmk}^{(i)},\forall t,\forall m,\forall n\right\}$ is up to TMN. Following the expectation propagation method proposed in [28], we can reduce the computational complexity of $\left\{\hat{\mu}_{tnk\to tmk}^{(i)}(x_{tnk})\right\}$. We consider every transmitted symbol x_{tnk} as a continuous random variable and will approximate its message $\mu_{tnk\to tmk}^{(i)}(x_{tnk})$ as a complex Gaussian PDF $\hat{\mu}_{tnk\to tmk}^{(i)}(x_{tnk}) = \mathcal{N}_{\mathbb{C}}\left(x_{tnk};\hat{x}_{tnk\to tmk}^{(i)},\nu_{tnk\to tmk}^{(i)}\right)$.

The symbol belief $\beta_{tnk}^{(i)}(x_{tnk})$ at the variable node is projected into a Gaussian PDF denoted by $\hat{\beta}_n^{(i)}(x_{tnk}) = \mathcal{N}_{\mathbb{C}}\left(x_{tnk}; \hat{x}_{tnk}^{(i)}, \nu_{tnk}^{(i)}\right)$, where

$$\hat{x}_{tnk}^{(i)} = \sum_{\alpha_s \in \mathcal{A}} \alpha_s \beta_{tnk}^{(i)}(x_{tnk} = \alpha_s), \tag{31}$$

$$\nu_{tnk}^{(i)} = \sum_{\alpha_s \in \mathcal{A}} |\alpha_s|^2 \beta_{tnk}^{(i)}(x_{tnk} = \alpha_s) - \left|\hat{x}_{tnk}^{(i)}\right|^2. \tag{32}$$

Then the approximate message $\hat{\mu}_{tnk \to tmk}^{(i)}(x_{tnk})$ is computed from the approximate symbol belief $\hat{\beta}_n^{(i)}(x_{tnk})$ as following

$$\hat{\mu}_{tnk \to tmk}^{(i)}(x_{tnk}) \approx \frac{\hat{\beta}_n^{(i)}(x_{tnk})}{\mu_{tnk \leftarrow tmk}^{(i)}(x_{tnk})} \propto \mathcal{N}_{\mathbb{C}}(x_{tnk}; \hat{x}_{tnk \to tmk}^{(i)}, \nu_{tnk \to tmk}^{(i)}), \tag{33}$$

where

$$\hat{x}_{tnk \to tmk}^{(i)} = \hat{x}_{tnk}^{(i)} + \nu_{tnk}^{(i)} \frac{\hat{x}_{tnk}^{(i)} - \hat{x}_{tnk \leftarrow tmk}^{(i)}}{\nu_{tnk \leftarrow tmk}^{(i)} - \nu_{tnk}^{(i)}}, \tag{34}$$

$$\nu_{tnk \to tmk}^{(i)} = \frac{\nu_{tnk}^{(i)} \nu_{tnk \leftarrow tmk}^{(i)}}{\nu_{tnk \leftarrow tmk}^{(i)} - \nu_{tnk}^{(i)}}. \tag{35}$$

We will refer to the proposed message passing as "BP-GMF", which is be summarized in Algorithm 1.

3.2 Complexity Comparisons

Table 2 shows the proposed scheme and other message-passing schemes. The computationally complexity of these scheme is compared in terms of floating-point operations (FLOPs) per iteration. For simplicity, the complexity of addition, subtraction, multiplication, and division is considered as being identical. Furthermore, we don't take the operations of $\exp(\cdot)$ and $\left\{\lambda_e^{(i)}(c_{tnk}^q)\right\}$ into accounted. Table 3 shows that the complexity of BP-MF-GMP, BP-GMF and BP-MF is $\mathcal{O}(T(M + Q|\mathcal{A}|)NK)$, and that of BP-GA is

Table 2. Receiver schemes and their component algorithms.

Receiver scheme	Channel estimation	Detection & decoding
BP-GA	GMP	BP-GA [32]
BP-GMF	GMP	BP-GMF
BP-MF	Algorithm in [22] using disjoint channel model	BP-MF [19,22]
BP-MF-M	Algorithm in [26] using markov channel model	BP-MF [19,22]
BP-MF-GAMP	GAMP	BP-MF [27]

Algorithm 1. The BP-GMF algorithm at the ith turbo iteration.

1: Initialization: $\hat{w}_{mnk\rightarrow tmk}^{(0)} = 0, \nu_{mnk\rightarrow tmk}^{(0)} =, \forall k, \forall l.$

2: **for** t, n, k, m **do**

3:    $z_{tnk\leftarrow tmk}^{(i)} = \sum_{n'\neq n} \hat{w}_{tmk\leftarrow mn'}^{(i-1)} \hat{x}_{tn'k\rightarrow tmk}^{(i-1)};$

4:    $\tau_{tnk\leftarrow tmk}^{(i)} = \sigma_\varpi^2 + \sum_{n'\neq n}\left[\left|\hat{w}_{tmk\leftarrow mn'}^{(i-1)}\right|^2 \nu_{tn'k\rightarrow tmk}^{(i-1)} + \left(\left|\hat{x}_{tn'k\rightarrow tmk}^{(i-1)}\right|^2 + \nu_{tn'k\rightarrow tmk}^{(i-1)}\right)\nu_{tmk\leftarrow mn'}^{(i-1)}\right]$

5:    $\nu_{tnk\leftarrow tmk}^{(i)} = \dfrac{\tau_{tnk\leftarrow tmk}^{(i)}}{\left|\hat{w}_{mnk}^{(i-1)}\right|^2 + \nu_{mnk}^{(i-1)}} \quad \nu_{tmk\rightarrow mnk}^{(i)} = \dfrac{\tau_{tnk\leftarrow tmk}^{(i)}}{\left|\hat{x}_{tnk}^{(i-1)}\right|^2 + \nu_{tnk}^{(i-1)}};$

6:    $\hat{x}_{tnk\leftarrow tmk}^{(i)} = \nu_{tnk\leftarrow tmk}^{(i)}\left(\hat{w}_{mn}^{(i-1)}\right)^* z_{tnk\leftarrow tmk}^{(i)}/\tau_{tnk\leftarrow tmk}^{(i)};$

7:    $\hat{w}_{tmk\rightarrow mnk}^{(i)} = \nu_{tnk\leftarrow tmk}^{(i)}\left(\hat{x}_{tnk}^{(i-1)}\right)^* z_{tnk\leftarrow tmk}^{(i)}/\tau_{tnk\leftarrow tmk}^{(i)};$

8: **end for**

9: **for** t, n, k **do**

10:    $\gamma_{tnk}^{(i)} = \left(\sum_m 1/\nu_{tnk\leftarrow tmk}^{(i)}\right)^{-1};$

11:    $\zeta_{tnk}^{(i)} = \gamma_{tnk}^{(i)} \sum_m \left(\hat{x}_{tnk\leftarrow tmk}^{(i)}/\nu_{tnk\leftarrow tmk}^{(i)}\right);$

12:    $\tilde{p}_{eq}^{(i)}(x_i) = \mu_{tnk\rightarrow tnk}^{(i-1)}(x_{tnk})\mathcal{N}_\mathbb{C}\left(x_{tnk}; \zeta_{tnk}^{(i)}, \gamma_{tnk}^{(i)}\right);$

13:    $\lambda_e^{(i)}\left(c_{tnk}^q\right) = \ln \dfrac{\sum_{x_{tnk}\in\mathcal{A}_q^1}\tilde{p}_{eq}^{(i)}(x_i)}{\sum_{x_{tnk}\in\mathcal{A}_q^0}\tilde{p}_{eq}^{(i)}(x_i)} - \lambda_a^{(i-1)}\left(c_{tnk}^q\right).$

14: **end for**

15: **for** n **do**

16:    Decode and generate LLRs $\{\lambda_a^{(i)}\left(c_{tnk}^q\right), \forall t, \forall k, \forall q\};$

17: **end for**

18: **for** t, n, k **do**

19:

20:    $\mu_{tnk\rightarrow tnk}^{(i)}(x_{tnk}) = \prod_q \exp\left(c_{tnk}^q\lambda_a^{(i)}\left(c_{tnk}^q\right)\right)/\left(1 + \exp\left(\lambda_a^{(i)}\left(c_{tnk}^q\right)\right)\right);$

21:    $\beta_{tnk}^{(i)}(x_{tnk}) = \dfrac{\mu_{tnk\rightarrow tnk}^{(i)}(x_{tnk})\mathcal{N}_\mathbb{C}\left(x_{tnk}; \zeta_{tnk}^{(i)}, \gamma_{tnk}^{(i)}\right)}{\sum_{x_{tnk}\in\mathcal{A}}\mu_{tnk\rightarrow tnk}^{(i)}(x_{tnk})\mathcal{N}_\mathbb{C}\left(x_{tnk}; \zeta_{tnk}^{(i)}, \gamma_{tnk}^{(i)}\right)};$

22:    $\hat{x}_{tnk}^{(i)} = \sum_{\alpha_s\in\mathcal{A}} \alpha_s\beta_{tnk}^{(i)}(x_{tnk} = \alpha_s);$

23:    $\nu_{tnk}^{(i)} = \sum_{\alpha_s\in\mathcal{A}} |\alpha_s|^2 \beta_{tnk}^{(i)}(x_{tnk} = \alpha_s) - |\hat{x}_{tnk}^{(i)}|^2;$

24:    $\nu_{tnk\rightarrow tmk}^{(i)} = \nu_{tnk}^{(i)}\nu_{tnk\leftarrow tmk}^{(i)}/(\nu_{tnk\leftarrow tmk}^{(i)} - \nu_{tnk}^{(i)}), \forall m;$

25:    $\hat{x}_{tnk\rightarrow tmk}^{(i)} = \hat{x}_{tnk}^{(i)} + \nu_{tnk}^{(i)}(\hat{x}_{tnk}^{(i)} - \hat{x}_{tnk\leftarrow tmk}^{(i)})/(\nu_{tnk\leftarrow tmk}^{(i)} - \nu_{tnk}^{(i)}), \forall m.$

26: **end for**

Table 3. Complexity of detection and decoding.

Receiver scheme	FLOPs per iteration
BP-GA	$(28\,|\mathcal{A}| + 33)\,TMNK + (2\,|\mathcal{A}| + 3Q\,|\mathcal{A}| + Q)\,TNK$
BP-GMF	$63TMNK + (23\,|\mathcal{A}| + 3Q\,|\mathcal{A}| + Q)\,TNK$
BP-MF [22]	$22TMNK + (11N + 4)\,M\,(K - K_\mathrm{p}) + (23\,|\mathcal{A}| + 3Q\,|\mathcal{A}| + Q)\,TNK$
BP-MF-M [26]	$33TMNK + (11N + 4)\,M\,(K - K_\mathrm{p}) + (23\,|\mathcal{A}| + 3Q\,|\mathcal{A}| + Q)\,TNK$
BP-MF-GMP	$33TMNK + (11N + 4)\,M\,(K - K_\mathrm{p}) + (23\,|\mathcal{A}| + 3Q\,|\mathcal{A}| + Q)\,TNK$

$\mathcal{O}\left(T(M\,|\mathcal{A}| + Q\,|\mathcal{A}|)NK\right)$. Table 4 shows the complexity of algorithms performing the task of channel estimation, where GMP is $\mathcal{O}\left(MNK\left(\log_2 K + T\right)\right)$, BP-MF is $\mathcal{O}\left(MNK^3\right)$, and BP-MF-M is $\mathcal{O}\left(MNKG^3\right)$.

Table 4. Complexity of channel estimation.

Receiver scheme	FLOPs per iteration
BP-GA	$MN \left(20K\log_2 K + 30TK + 11K - 26TK_p + 13K_p + 14L - 2\right)$
BP-GMF	
BP-MF-GAMP [27]	
BP-MF [22]	$MN \left(16K^3 + 12K^2 + 17TK - K\right) + 2TNK - 2NK - 2MN$
BP-MF-M [26]	$MN \left(118G^2 + 68G - 4\right) K - 112G^3 - 92G^3 + 5G$

4   Simulation Results

The proposed receiver algorithm BP-GMF is compared with the BP-GA [32], BP-MF variants, the MMSE, and the MFB-PCSI in terms of bit error rate (BER) and mean square error (MSE) of the channel estimation. A MIMO system with $N = 8$ single-antenna users is considered, each of which employs an OFDM with $K = 64$ subcarriers. We choose a $R = 1/2$ recursive systematic convolutional (RSC) code with generator polynomial $[G_1, G_2] = [117, 155]_{\text{oct}}$, followed by a random interleaver. For bit-to-symbol mapping, multilevel Gray-mapping is used. Each user employs $K_p = 8$ pilot subcarriers modulated with uniformly selected known BPSK symbols and uniformly placed in one selected OFDM symbol. The channel model in simulations is an 8-tap Rayleigh fading MIMO channel with equal tap power. At the receiver, the BCJR algorithm is used to decode the convolutional code. It is assumed that the transmit antennas from different users are spatially uncorrelated and that the receive antenna spacing is sufficient so that they are also spatially uncorrelated. The channels are block-static for the selected 8 transmitted OFDM symbols. For all simulation results, a minimum of 100 frame errors were counted. The energy per bit to noise power spectral density ratio E_b/N_0 is defined as [33]

$$\frac{E_b}{N_0} = \frac{E_s}{N_0} + 10\log_{10}\frac{M}{RNQ}, \tag{36}$$

where E_s/N is the average energy per transmitted symbol.

4.1   Channel-Tap NMSE Versus E_b/N_0

At the initial turbo iteration, only the pilots can be used for channel estimation. The BP-GMF, the BP-GA and the BP-MF-GAMP perform 5 inner iterations in the channel-estimation-loops during the initial turbo iteration and perform only 1 inner iteration during each subsequent turbo iterations. The channel estimator in the BP-MF is equivalent to the pilot-based LMMSE estimator at the initial turbo iteration and becomes the data-aided LMMSE estimator at subsequent turbo iterations. The channel estimation in the BP-MF-M is performed by the Kalman smoother proposed in [26], where the group-size of contiguous channel weights is set to $G = 4$. A maximum of 50 turbo iterations are used in all message-passing receivers, and the NMSE at the ith turbo iteration is calculated by

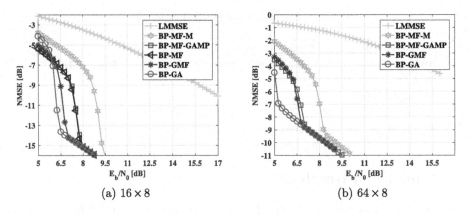

Fig. 3. NMSE of time-domain channel taps versus E_b/N_0.

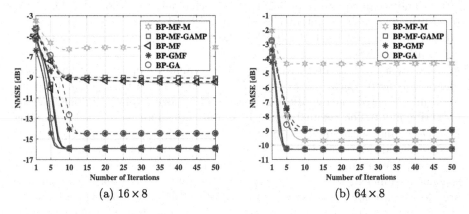

Fig. 4. NMSE of time-domain channel taps versus number of turbo iterations, under $E_b/N_0 = 7.25$ dB (dashed lines) and $E_b/N_0 = 8.75$ dB (solid lines).

$$\text{NMSE} = \frac{1}{\Theta} \sum_{\theta=1}^{\Theta} \frac{1}{MN} \sum_{m=1}^{M} \sum_{n=1}^{N} \frac{\sum_{l=1}^{L} \left| h_{mnl} - \hat{h}_{mnl}^{(i)} \right|^2}{\sum_{l=1}^{L} |h_{mnl}|^2}, \qquad (37)$$

where Θ is the number of Monte Carlo runs.

Figure 3 shows the normalized mean-squared error of the channel estimation versus E_b/N_0 in the 16×8 MIMO system and the 64×8 MIMO system, respectively. It is shown that the NMSE of the proposed BP-GMF outperforms the MMSE, the BP-MF-M, the BP-MF-GAMP and the BP-MF (which is evaluated only in the 16×8 MIMO system due to complexity issue) in both cases.

Figure 4 presents the NMSE performance versus the number of turbo iterations. Results indicate that the BP-GMF and BP-GA demonstrate almost the same convergency, and need less than 15 iterations to converge.

4.2 BER Versus E_b/N_0

Figure 5 shows the BER performance versus E_b/N_0 in the 16×8 MIMO system and the 64×8 system, respectively. The BP-GA algorithm and BP-GMF algorithm achieve the same performance that is about 0.8 dB away from the MFB-PCSI at BER $= 10^{-5}$; the BP-MF algorithm slightly outperforms the BP-MF-GMP algorithm, but its performance is about 1.3 dB away from the MFB-PCSI at BER $= 10^{-5}$.

Figure 6 presents the BER performance versus the number of turbo iterations. Results indicate that the BP-GMF and BP-GA demonstrate almost the same convergency, and need less than 15 iterations to converge.

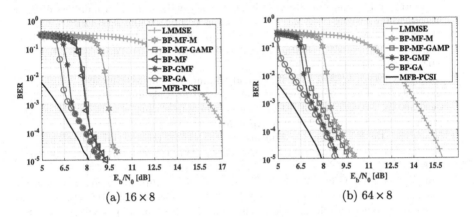

Fig. 5. BER versus E_b/N_0 in MIMO systems with 16QAM.

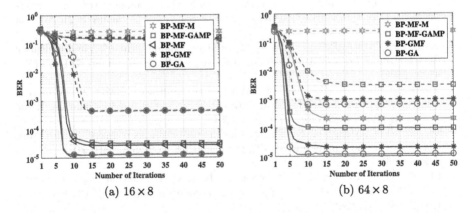

Fig. 6. BER versus number of turbo iterations, under $E_b/N_0 = 7.25$ dB (dashed lines) and $E_b/N_0 = 8.75$ dB (solid lines).

5 Conclusion

In this paper, a message-passing scheme combining LBP with Gaussian approximation and mean-field approximation is proposed for massive MIMO-OFDM systems. Simulation results show that the proposed scheme can achieve the performance of the BP-GA, within 0.8 dB of the known-channel bound in a 16×8 MIMO system and a 64×8 MIMO system, and outperforms the BP-MF and its low-complexity variants considerably.

References

1. Marzetta, T.L.: Noncooperative cellular wireless with unlimited numbers of base station antennas. IEEE Trans. Wirel. Commun. **9**(11), 3590–3600 (2010)
2. Wang, S., Li, Y., Zhao, M., Wang, J.: Energy efficient and low-complexity uplink transceiver for massive spatial modulation MIMO. IEEE Trans. Veh. Technol. **PP**(99), 1–1 (2014)
3. Wu, S., Kuang, L., Ni, Z., Lu, J., (David) Huang, D., Guo, Q.: Expectation propagation based iterative groupwise detection for large-scale multiuser MIMO-OFDM systems. In: Proceedings of IEEE Wireless Communications and Networking Conference (WCNC), pages 248–253, April 2014
4. Wang, S., Li, Y., Wang, J.: Multiuser detection in massive spatial modulation MIMO with low-resolution ADCs. IEEE Trans. Wirel. Commun. **14**(4), 2156–2168 (2015)
5. Liu, L., Yuen, C., Guan, Y.L., Li, Y., Su, Y.: A low-complexity Gaussian message passing iterative detector for massive MU-MIMO systems. In: 2015 10th International Conference on Information, Communications and Signal Processing (ICICS), pp. 1–5, December 2015
6. Liu, L., Yuen, C., Guan, Y.L., Li, Y., Su, Y.: Convergence analysis and assurance for Gaussian message passing iterative detector in massive MU-MIMO systems. IEEE Trans. Wirel. Commun. **15**(9), 6487–6501 (2016)
7. Dai, L., Wang, Z., Yang, Z.: Spectrally efficient time-frequency training OFDM for mobile large-scale MIMO systems. IEEE J. Sel. Areas Commun. **3**(2), 251–263 (2013)
8. Rossi, P.S., Müller, R.R.: Joint twofold-iterative channel estimation and multiuser detection for MIMO-OFDM systems. IEEE Trans. Wirel. Commun. **7**(11), 4719–4729 (2008)
9. Novak, C., Matz, G., Hlawatsch, F.: IDMA for the multiuser MIMO-OFDM uplink: a factor graph framework for joint data detection and channel estimation. IEEE Trans. Sig. Process. **61**(16), 4051–4066 (2013)
10. Wu, S., Ni, Z., Meng, X., Kuang, L.: Block expectation propagation for downlink channel estimation in massive MIMO systems. IEEE Commun. Lett. **20**(11), 2225–2228 (2016)
11. Lin, X., Wu, S., Kuang, L., Ni, Z., Meng, X., Jiang, C.: Estimation of sparse massive MIMO-OFDM channels with approximately common support. IEEE Commun. Lett. **PP**(99), 1 (2017)
12. Kschischang, F.R., Frey, B.J., Loeliger, H.-A.: Factor graphs and the sum-product algorithm. IEEE Trans. Inf. Theor. **47**(2), 498–519 (2001)
13. Worthen, A.P., Stark, W.E.: Unified design of iterative receivers using factor graphs. IEEE Trans. Inf. Theor. **47**(2), 843–849 (2001)

14. Liu, Y., Brunel, L., Boutros, J.J.: Joint channel estimation and decoding using Gaussian approximation in a factor graph over multipath channel. In: Proceedings of the International Symposium on Personal, Indoor and Mobile Radio Communication (PIMRC), pp. 3164–3168 (2009)
15. Kirkelund, G.E., Manchón, C.N., Christensen, L.P.B., Riegler, E., Fleury, B.H.: Variational message-passing for joint channel estimation and decoding in MIMO-OFDM. In: Proceedings of IEEE Global Telecommunications Conference (GLOBE-COM), pp. 1–6 (2010)
16. Guo, Q., (David) Huang, D.: EM-based joint channel estimation and detection for frequency selective channels using Gaussian message passing. IEEE Trans. Sig. Process. $59(8)$, 4030–4035 (2011)
17. Schniter, P.: A message-passing receiver for BICM-OFDM over unknown clustered-sparse channels. IEEE J. Sel. Top. Sig. Process. $5(8)$, 1462–1474 (2011)
18. Knievel, C., Hoeher, P.A., Tyrrell, A., Auer, G.: Multi-dimensional graph-based soft iterative receiver for MIMO-OFDM. IEEE Trans. Commun. $60(6)$, 1599–1609 (2012)
19. Riegler, E., Kirkelund, G.E., Manchón, C.N., Badiu, M.-A., Fleury, B.H.: Merging belief propagation and the mean field approximation: a free energy approach. IEEE Trans. Inf. Theor. $59(1)$, 588–602 (2013)
20. Wu, S., Kuang, L., Ni, Z., Lu, J., (David) Huang, D., Guo, Q.: Expectation propagation approach to joint channel estimation and decoding for OFDM systems. In: Proceedings of IEEE International Conference on Acoustics, Speech, and Signal Processing (ICASSP), pp. 1941–1945, May 2014
21. Schniter, P.: Joint estimation and decoding for sparse channels via relaxed belief propagation. In: Proceedings of the 44th Asilomar Conference on Signals, Systems and Computers (ASILOMAR), pp. 1055–1059. IEEE (2010)
22. Manchón, C.N., Kirkelund, G.E., Riegler, E., Christensen, L.P.B., Fleury, B.H.: Receiver architectures for MIMO-OFDM based on a combined VMP-SP algorithm. arXiv:1111.5848 (2011)
23. Badiu, M.-A., Kirkelund, G.E., Manchón, C.N., Riegler, E., Fleury, B.H.: Message-passing algorithms for channel estimation and decoding using approximate inference. In: Proceedings of IEEE International Symposium on Information Theory (ISIT), pp. 2376–2380 (2012)
24. Drémeau, A., Herzet, C., Daudet, L.: Boltzmann machine and mean-field approximation for structured sparse decompositions. IEEE Trans. Sig. Process. $60(7)$, 3425–3438 (2012)
25. Krzakala, F., Manoel, A., Tramel, E.W., Zdeborová, L.: Variational free energies for compressed sensing. In: Proceedings of IEEE International Symposium on Information Theory (ISIT), pp. 1499–1503, June 2014
26. Badiu, M.-A., Manchón, C.N., Fleury, B.H.: Message-passing receiver architecture with reduced-complexity channel estimation. IEEE Commun. Lett. $17(7)$, 1404–1407 (2013)
27. Yuan, Z., Zhang, C., Wang, Z., Guo, Q., Wu, S., Wang, X.: A low-complexity receiver using combined BP-MF for joint channel estimation and decoding in OFDM systems. CoRR, abs/1601.05856 (2016)
28. Wu, S., Kuang, L., Ni, Z., Lu, J., (David) Huang, D., Guo, Q.: Low-complexity iterative detection for large-scale multiuser MIMO-OFDM systems using approximate message passing. IEEE J. Sel. Top. Sig. Process. $8(5)$, 902–915 (2014)
29. Meng, X., Wu, S., Kuang, L., Ni, Z., Lu, J.: Expectation propagation based iterative multi-user detection for MIMO-IDMA systems. In: 2014 IEEE 79th Vehicular Technology Conference (VTC Spring), pp. 1–5, May 2014

30. Meng, X., Wu, S., Kuang, L., Lu, J.: An expectation propagation perspective on approximate message passing. IEEE Sig. Process. Lett. **22**(8), 1194–1197 (2015)
31. Minka, T.P.: Divergence measures and message passing. Technical report MSR-TR-2005-173, Microsoft Research Ltd., Cambridge, UK, December 2005
32. Wu, S., Kuang, L., Ni, Z., Huang, D., Guo, Q., Lu, J.: Message-passing receiver for joint channel estimation and decoding in 3D massive MIMO-OFDM systems. IEEE Trans. Wirel. Commun. **15**(12), 8122–8138 (2016)
33. Hochwald, B.M., ten Brink, S.: Achieving near-capacity on a multiple-antenna channel. IEEE Trans. Commun. **51**(3), 389–399 (2003)

Research and Application of Summer High Temperature Prediction Model Based on CART Algorithm

Yujie Guan[1], Wei Wang[2], Fengchang Xue[3(✉)], and Shoudong Liu[1]

[1] College of Applied Meteorology,
Nanjing University of Information Science and Technology,
Jiangsu 210044, China
[2] College of Atmospheric Sciences,
Nanjing University of Information Science and Technology,
Jiangsu 210044, China
[3] College of Geographic Information and Remote Sensing,
Nanjing University of Information Science and Technology,
Jiangsu 210044, China
xfc9800@126.com

Abstract. In this paper, the average summer high temperature effective accumulated for many years is used as a judge of the extent of the hot summer temperatures of standards. Based on data mining, the CART algorithm is applied to analyze the relationship between high temperature and some climatic factors such as the East Asian summer monsoon index, summer India Burma trough, the summer North Atlantic Oscillation (NAO), Equatorial Pacific sea surface temperature and so on. The high-temperature forecasting model is established with the setup of the high temperature prediction rules. The data of summer maximum temperature in summer in Zhangzhou, Fujian Province from 1955 to 2012 are selected to calculate the summer hot temperature of 58a. Then, multiple climatic factor data of the same period is given to the input variable, and 46 years of data is randomly selected to get 10 classifications of rule sets, resulting in the achievement of the accuracy rate to 91.49%. With the remaining data of 12a test, the accuracy rate reaches 91.67%. In general, the results of this paper validate the feasibility and validity of the high temperature prediction model, and provide a new idea for the study of the catastrophic weather model.

Keywords: CART · High temperature effective accumulated temperature
Summer high temperature forecast

1 Introduction

In recent years, China is facing more frequent and severs meteorological disasters under global climate warming and urbanization expansion. As one of the common meteorological disasters in summer, high temperature will not only affect the social and economic development, but also affect people's daily life and safety of life [1–5].

© ICST Institute for Computer Sciences, Social Informatics and Telecommunications Engineering 2018
K. Long et al. (Eds.): 5GWN 2017, LNICST 211, pp. 317–326, 2018.
https://doi.org/10.1007/978-3-319-72823-0_30

China Meteorological Administration provides the daily maximum temperature reached or exceeded 35 °C, known as high temperature. The occurrence of high-temperature events is the result of multi-factor and multi-system. At present, many factors have been studied on the influence factors of summer high temperature. Brabson et al. [5] studied the evolution of extreme temperatures in England and found that both cold winters and hot summer extreme temperatures were associated with changes in the lower atmospheric circulation; Lin et al. [6] and Yin et al. [7] found that summer high temperatures were associated with the West Pacific High anomalies; According to Sun [8], the extreme high temperature events in China and East Asia over the atmospheric circulation variation is consistent, and the role of low-level warm advection is rather important. Facing the high temperature caused by a variety of reasons, its influence cannot be underestimated. As a result, this calls for the establishment of high-temperature forecasting model.

In addition, the current high temperature of the degree of heat is no clear grade division. Some scholars use the 95th or 90th percentile of daily maximum temperature as a boundary [9, 10]. However, due to the climatic differences in regional level and people's long-term adaptation to local climate [11], the definition of the degree of hot does not only rely on the standard temperature, and the impact of high temperature on the human body or the extent of harm to develop should be taken into consideration. Therefore, according to the principle of high temperature warning and the impact of high temperature weather on the human body and crop hazards, high temperature effective accumulated temperature is adopted to distinguish the hot degree. The high temperature effective accumulated temperature (EAHT) is the sum of the difference between the daily maximum temperature and 35 °C. The larger the value is, the severe the hot event is, and the more harmful to human health, and vice versa. On this basis, the accumulated effective temperature can be calculated by month or year of high temperature to characterize the degree of hotness of the corresponding statistical period [12].

For the establishment of high-temperature forecasting model, an effective method of forecasting model is needed apart from the ideal high temperature index. Nowadays, there are mainly three modeling ideas [13]: The first is the statistical type. Through the statistical study of a large number of related data, we find the relationship between the climatic factors and the high temperature to establish the relationship model. And then use the change of factors to predict high temperature; The second is the theoretical analysis. Mainly through the basic principles of the weather science and other disciplines, use the numerical model to get the temperature of the forecast value and then forecast the high temperature [14, 15]. Even though the former is considered to be more comprehensive, the traditional methods of statistical analysis require numerous data and the process is too cumbersome and difficult to achieve the desired accuracy [16]. The latter can reflect the phenomenon of high temperature weather from a more essential level, but the parameters are not easy to obtain. Therefore, the third idea, which is, based on data mining methods, is used in the model.

The high temperature forecasting model based on climatic factors is established by using a large amount of relevant data. The data mining method has many categories, which can effectively and quickly extract effective information from a large number of related data to establish the model. Moreover, the operation is relatively simple, and the accuracy can reach a higher benchmark [17, 18] in the reasonable set of parameters.

The methods of data mining commonly used in meteorological forecasting model compose neural network, support vector machine and decision tree algorithm [13]. The decision tree algorithm is widely used because of its simple calculation, fast processing speed and easy explanation [13], which has a good application prospect in dealing with meteorological problems.

Therefore, in this paper, the classification regression tree algorithm (CART) is used to study the relationship between high temperature in summer and some climatic factors such as the East Asian summer monsoon index, summer India Burma trough, the summer North Atlantic Oscillation (NAO), Equatorial Pacific sea surface temperature, the landing typhoon, Nino3, Nion4, and Nino3.4 and so on. Then according to the obtained rule set, a high temperature forecast model based on climatic factors is established.

The following section will elaborate more on the data and analysis approaches and the results will be present in Sects. 3 and 4. In the last section, a brief discussion as well as the concluding remarks will be given.

2 Data and Methods

2.1 Data

The daily maximum temperature and daily mean temperature from the summer of 1955 to 2012 in Zhangzhou, Fujian Province were selected from the meteorological station data, and the missing data in the original data were excluded. (If no special instructions, the following research in this article are 6, 7 and 8 months for the study period)

The index data of the western Pacific subtropical high index, intensity index, west ridge point, ridge line position, north boundary position and Indo-Burmese trough index were derived from the National Climate Center of China from 1955 to 2012. And other climatic factors such as monthly mean sea surface temperature data for Nino1 + 2, Nino3, Nino4 and Nino 3.4 in 1955–2012 are obtained from NOAA website.

2.2 Research Methods

In this paper, high temperature effective accumulated temperature (EAHT) in summer is used to judge the hot degree of hot weather. The summer high temperature effective accumulated temperature is the sum of the daily maximum temperature and the difference of 35 °C in summer. The mean temperature of effective accumulated temperature in summer is −71.04 which is taken as the boundary of whether or not it is hot. This accumulated temperature considers the climate and physiology of the human body, which can better show that the high temperature hot degree.

Decision tree algorithm is an important classification method in data mining. It aims at obtaining decision-making steps, discovering rules, patterns and knowledge from archived databases [19]. The root node, the branch, and the leaf node are the necessary components of the decision tree. Where each interior node represents a detection on an attribute, each branch representing a detected output, and a leaf node of each tree represents a class or class distribution. In this paper, the classification and regression tree algorithm (CART) which is a classic decision tree algorithm [20] proposed by Breman et al. in 1984 is selected. The algorithm is a nonparametric statistical method for classifying discrete or continuous dependent variables.

CART is a supervised learning algorithm. Before CART is used to predict, the user must first provide a set of learning samples to build and evaluate CART. CART uses a learning sample set in the following structure:

$$L := \{X_1, X_2 \ldots X_m, Y\}$$
$$X_1 := (x_{11}, x_{12} \ldots x_{1t1}), \ldots, X_m := (x_{m1}, x_{m2} \ldots x_{mtn})$$
$$Y := (Y_1, Y_2 \ldots Y_k)$$

Where $X_1 \ldots X_m$ is called the attribute vectors, and its attributes can be ordered or discrete. Y is called the label vectors, and its attributes can be ordered or discrete. When Y is an ordered quantity, it is called a regression tree; when Y is a discrete value, it is called a classification tree [22]. Since the target variables of the high temperature prediction model are discrete, a classification decision tree is generated [21].

The criteria for variable classification in CART are the Gini Impurity Criterion and the Goal Dichotomy Criterion. Whether or not high temperature is a binary classification problem is a special case of multivariate classification. Given a node t, the estimated class probability p (j|t) represents the probability that the node belongs to class j (j = 1, 2, 3...J). The formula for determining the impurity of a given node is

$$i(t) = \phi[p(1/t), \ldots, p(J/t)]$$

Where Φ is the impurity function, the optimal partition is obtained when constructing the decision tree nodes, so that the impurity degree of each child node is the lowest. Impurity function is generally expressed as:

$$i(t) = \phi(p_1, p_1, \ldots, p_1) = -\sum_{j=1}^{J} p_j \log p_j$$

With the Gini diversity index, the form of the function is as follows

$$i(t) = \left[\sum_{j=1}^{J} p(j \mid t)\right]^2 - \sum_{j=1}^{J} p^2(j \mid t)$$

This paper discusses the binary classification problem; the index can be simplified as

$$i(t) = 2p(1 \mid t)p(2 \mid t)$$

At node t, randomly selected objects are assigned to class i according to probability p (i|t), and the estimated probability of the object actually belongs to class j is p (i|t). The estimated probability of misclassification under this rule is the Gini index,

$$Gini\ Index = \sum_{i \neq j} p(i \mid t)p(j \mid t) = 1 - \sum_{j=1}^{J} p_j^2$$

In the process of classifying the decision tree with high temperature, the optimal partitioning threshold and the best test variable are selected according to the Gini coefficient of the computing node. And the optimal decision tree is generated by recursive call until the end rule is satisfied.

3 Temporal Characteristics and Influencing Factors of Summer High Temperature

In this paper, data preprocessing in Zhangzhou area of Fujian Province was used to analyze the change trend of summer high temperature effective accumulated temperature. And the impact factors of summer high temperature were studied to determine their influence on high temperature trend.

3.1 Time Distribution of Summer High Temperature

As shown in Fig. 1, the effective accumulated temperature of high temperature in summer showed an upward trend during the period of 1955–2012. It is worth

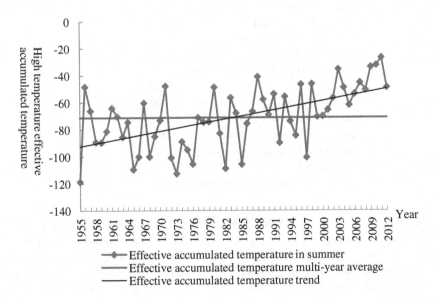

Fig. 1. The change trend of effective accumulated temperature in summer in Zhangzhou, Fujian

mentioning that the effective accumulated temperature in summer was higher than the average for many years after 2000, where the hot weather appeared.

When constructing a decision tree using CART algorithm, it is necessary to perform a preprocess analysis of the data set, which is the target variable and the input variable needed to be determined. In order to study the influence of climatic factors on this trend, we use the multi-year mean summer effective accumulated temperature (−71.04) as the target variable.

3.2   The Correlation Analysis of Summer High Temperature Index and Different Factors

Previous studies have found that there are significant correlations between the high temperature and some climatic factors, such as the western Pacific subtropical high, the intensity index, the west extension point, the landfall typhoon etc. In this paper, the correlations of summer high temperature effective accumulated temperature and the data of each factor in the same period in Zhangzhou, Fujian from 1955 to 2012 were analyzed. The results are as follows:

Table 1. 1955–2012 summer climatic factors and the summer high temperature effective accumulated temperature correlation coefficient set

Climatic factor	Correlation coefficient
Nino3	−0.023
Summer NAO	−0.331*
Nino4	0.079
Nino3.4	−0.037
Summer Western Pacific Subtropical High Strength Index	0.417**
Summer Western Pacific Subtropical High Area Index	0.413**
Summer Western Pacific Subtropical High West Stretch Point	−0.372**
Nino1+2	−0.026
Landing Typhoon	0.102
Summer East Asian Monsoon Index	−0.383**
Summer India Burma Trough	0.399**

Note: ** for the correlation coefficient through the $\alpha = 0.01$ significant test.
* for the correlation coefficient through the $\alpha = 0.05$ significant test.

It can be seen from Table 1 that Nino3, Nino3.4, summer NAO, summer western Pacific subtropical high west ridge point, Nino1+2 and East Asia summer monsoon index were negatively correlated with summer high temperature effective accumulated temperature; Besides, what is positively correlated is Nino4, summer western Pacific subtropical high Intensity index, the summer western Pacific subtropical high area index, landing typhoon, summer India and Myanmar and summer high temperature effective accumulated temperature. The correlation coefficients of summer western Pacific subtropical high intensity index, summer western Pacific subtropical high area index, summer western Pacific subtropical high west ridge point, East Asian summer monsoon index, summer Indian Burma trough and summer high temperature effective accumulated temperature were adopted $\alpha = 0.01$ significance test. The correlation coefficient between summer NAO and summer high temperature effective accumulated temperature was tested by $\alpha = 0.05$. The results showed that the summer high temperature is highly related to these, and other factors had some correlation with the summer high temperature. In this paper, these climatic factors are used as input variables when constructing decision tree using CART algorithm.

4 Construction and Application of High Temperature Forecast Model Based on CART Algorithm

Data mining methods (Fig. 2) are used in this research to identify and analyze the relation between summer temperatures effective accumulated temperature and climatic factors. The accessibility of the forecast data regarding climatic factors from air-sea coupled model forecasting together with the use of forecasted factors as input variables ensure the make prediction of the high temperature in summer.

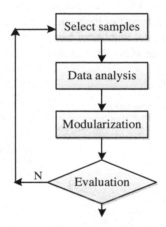

Fig. 2. Basic flow chart of data mining

4.1 Construction of Decision Tree Model Based on CART

In order to make the high temperature forecast more reasonable, this paper uses the multi-year average of summer high temperature effective accumulated temperature (−71.04) as the hot index, which is also the target variable when constructing the model.

The process of establishing a high temperature forecasting model based on the CART model is as follows: firstly, the input variable data is obtained (A number of climatic factor data, and pretreatment); secondly, using the temperature data, calculating the index of summer hot degree and judging whether it is hot in summer; then selecting some data randomly as training set, taking the climate data as the input variables and whether the summer high temperature as a target variable. Using the data mining software (IBM SPSS Modeler) and the CART algorithm to build the model, then obtain the forecast rule set. Finally, select the remaining data as the test set to verify the accuracy of the model.

4.2   Application of High Temperature Prediction Model

Taking Zhangzhou of Fujian Province as an example, the CART algorithm was selected by IBM SPSS Modeler to build a high temperature forecasting model.

The main contents of the decision tree are constructed by CART algorithm: the parent node recursively tests the random test variable and the segmentation threshold with the Gini coefficient until the best test variable and the segmentation threshold are generated. After entering the child node, the behavior of the parent node continued until the end condition is satisfied. The decision tree (Fig. 3) was obtained by using CART for a number of climatic factors during the summer of 1955–2000, and the accuracy of self-learning was 91.49% (Table 2). Each path from the root node to the child node represents a high-temperature prediction rule. The data in leaf nodes represent the high temperature, the total sample size and the number of misclassified samples respectively. Take "0 (1/0)" as an example: outside of the brackets represent non-high-temperature 0 (1 on behalf of high temperature), left side of the parentheses on behalf of a sample of the total number of brackets inside the right 0 represents the number of high-temperature samples. The difference, that is, $1 - 0 = 1$, represents the

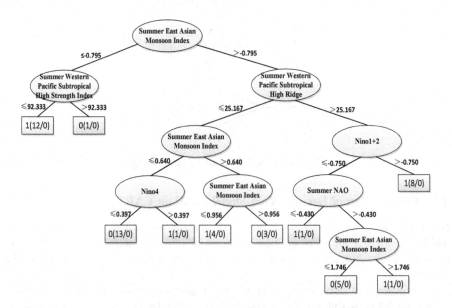

Fig. 3. The high temperature forecasting decision tree produced by CART algorithm

number of non-high temperature samples correctly classified. In order to further verify the reliability, the 2001–2010 climatic factor data was selected and the corresponding accuracy rate achieved 91.67% (Table 2).

Table 2. High temperature prediction model results table

	Training	Probability	Testing	Probability
Correct	43	91.49%	11	91.67%
Wrong	4	8.51%	1	8.33%
Total	47	100%	12	100%

With the high accuracy rate of 91.67%, the high temperature prediction model established by the data mining method can be considered valid and reliable. This also provides a new idea for the study of high temperature and other climate prediction.

5 Conclusion

This paper was based on the CART algorithm of data mining, and a high temperature climate prediction model was established. Taking Zhangzhou, Fujian as an example, and the following conclusions are obtained:

(1) The inter-annual variation of effective accumulated temperature of summer high temperature in Zhangzhou, Fujian is an upward trend, especially after 2000.
(2) There were significant correlations between summer NAO, summer western Pacific subtropical high intensity index, summer western Pacific subtropical high area index, summer western Pacific subtropical high west ridge point, East Asian summer monsoon index, summer Indian-Burmese trough and summer high temperature.
(3) Random selection of Zhangzhou from 1955 to 2012 of which 46 years of data, the establishment of classification decision tree to get the rule set, and classification accuracy rate of 91.49%. The remaining data for the inspection accuracy rate of 91.67%, indicating that the model has good reliability.

Although the prediction model established in this paper has reached certain accuracy, further studies are still needed. It is helpful to improve the accuracy of disaster prediction by discovering the potential information and laws concerning weather through the data mining method.

References

1. Eastcrling, D.R., Evans, J.L., Groisman, P.Y., et al.: Observed variability and trends in extreme climate events: brief review. Bull. Amerimete Soc. **81**(3), 417–425 (2000)
2. Changnon, S.A., Pielke, R.A., Changnon, D., et al.: Human factors explain the increased losses from weather and climate extremes. Bull. Amerimete Soc. **81**(3), 437–442 (2000)

3. Karl, T.R., Jones, P.D., Knighta, R.W., et al.: A new perspective on recent global warming: asymmetrie trends of daily maximum and minimum temperature. Bull. Am. Meteorol. Soc. **74**(6), 1007–1023 (1993)
4. Gruaz, G., et al.: Indictors of climate change for the Russian Federation. Clim. Chang. **42**, 219–242 (1999)
5. Brabson, B.B., Palutikof, J.P.: The evolution of extreme temperatures in the Central England temperature record. Geophys. Res. Lett. **29**(24), 2163–2166 (2002)
6. Lin, J., Bi, B., He, J.: Study on the variation of the western Pacific subtropical high and the formation mechanism of high temperature in Southern China in July 2003. Chin. J. Atmos. Sci. **29**(4), 594–599 (2005). (in Chinese)
7. Yin, J., Zhang, C., Zhang, C.: Analysis of rare high temperature climate in summer 2003 in Jiangxi Province. J. Nanjing Inst. Meteorol. **28**(6), 855–861 (2005). (in Chinese)
8. Sun, J., Wang, H., Yuan, W.: Decadal variability of the extreme hot event in China and its association with atmospheric circulations. Clim. Environ. Res. **16**(2), 199–208 (2011). (in Chinese)
9. Ding, T., Qian, W.H., Yan, Z.W.: Changes in hot days and heat waves in China during 1961–2007. Int. J. Climatol. **30**, 1452–1462 (2010)
10. He, S., Dai, E., Ge, Q., et al.: Spatiotemporal pattern prediction of high temperature disaster risk in China. J. Nat. Disasters **19**(2), 91–97 (2010). (in Chinese)
11. Ye, D., Yin, J., Chen, Z., et al.: Temporal and spatial characteristics of summer heat wave in China during 1961–2010. Chin. J. Clim. Chang. Res. **9**(1), 15–20 (2013). (in Chinese)
12. Chen, M., Geng, F., Ma, L., et al.: Analysis of high temperature heat wave in Shanghai area in recent 138 years. Plateau Meteorol. **32**(2), 597–607 (2013). https://doi.org/10.7522/j.issn. 1000-0534.2012.00058. (in Chinese)
13. Shi, D., Geng, H., Chen, J.I., et al.: Construction and application of road icing forecast model based on C4.5 decision tree algorithm. J. Meteorol. Sci. **35**(2), 204–209 (2015). (in Chinese)
14. Gao, X., Zhao, Z.: The experiment of extra seasonal prediction in China by OSU/NCC GCM for flood season. J. Appl. Meteorol. **11**(2), 180–188 (2000). (in Chinese)
15. Wang, Q., Feng, G., Zheng, Z., et al.: Study on objective and quantitative prediction of multi-factor combination for precipitation optimization in flood season of middle and lower reaches of Yangtze River. Chin. J. Atmos. Sci. **35**(2), 287–297 (2011). (in Chinese)
16. Wang, W., Xue, F., Shi, D., et al.: Research on summer drought prediction model based on CART algorithm. J. Meteorol. Sci. **36**(5) (2016). https://doi.org/10.3969/2015jms.0067. (in Chinese)
17. Zhang, W., Gao, S., Chen, B., et al.: The application of decision tree to intensity change classification of tropical cyclones in western North Pacific. Geophys. Res. Lett. **40**(9), 1883–1887 (2013)
18. Liu, Z., Du, Z., Chen, H., et al.: Study on the land use and cover classification of Zhengzhou based on decision tree. Meteorolog. Environ. Sci. **31**(3), 48–53 (2008). (in Chinese)
19. Friedl, M.A., Brodley, C.E.: Decision tree classification of land cover from remotely sensed data. Remote Sens. Environ. **61**(3), 399–409 (1997)
20. Zhao, P., Fu, Y., Zheng, L., et al.: Land use/cover classification of remote sensing images based on classification regression tree analysis. J. Remote Sens. **9**(6), 708–716 (2005). (in Chinese)
21. Zhang, W., Leung, Y., Chan, J.C.L.: The analysis of tropical cyclone tracks in the western North Pacific through data mining. Part I: tropical cyclone recurvature. J. Appl. Meteor. Climatol. **52**(6), 1394–1416 (2013)
22. Ying, T.: Remote Sensing Image Classification Based on Texture Information and CART Decision Tree Technology. Nanjing Forestry University (2008)

Research on Peak-to-Average Power Ratio Reduction for FBMC-Based 5G Transmission

Wenwan You, Junqi Guo$^{(\boxtimes)}$, Ke Shan, and Rongfang Bie

College of Information Science and Technology, Beijing Normal University,
Beijing 100875, China
youwenwan@mail.bnu.edu.cn, guojunqi@bnu.edu.cn

Abstract. The pursuit of high-quality modulation has become an inevitable trend along with a continuous evolution of mobile communication technologies. The filter-bank based multicarrier (FBMC) modulation, which has aroused wide concern recently for its higher spectral efficiency than orthogonal frequency division multiplexing (OFDM), is considered as a promising candidate solution to the air interface problem in the fifth-generation communication (5G). Since performance of multicarrier transmission is inevitably and largely affected by peak-to-average power ratio (PAPR), research on PAPR reduction methods is essential. After presenting the architecture of an FBMC transmission system and analyzing structural characteristics of FBMC signals, this paper studies several PAPR reduction methods which are previously used in OFDM transmission, and then attempts to apply them to an FBMC transmission environment by giving theoretical derivation. Computer simulation under different cases also verify their feasibility and effectiveness on PAPR reduction of FBMC signal waveform.

Keywords: Filter-bank based multicarrier (FBMC)
Peak-to-average power ratio (PAPR) reduction · 5G

1 Introduction

The fifth generation mobile communication system (5G) has attracted more and more attention recently. Under a 5G scenario, the more stringent requirements are put forward for the multicarrier multiple access transmission [1]. Therefore, analysis of multicarrier technology for 5G mobile communication is of great significance. orthogonal frequency division multiplexing (OFDM), which is one of the key technologies for the physical layer of the fourth generation mobile communication (4G), has been widely used for signal transmission over multi-path fading channels [2]. However, competitive power of OFDM in the 5G scenario proves to be weak due to its sensitivity to carrier frequency offset (CFO) and large peak-to-average power ratio (PAPR) [3]. Filter-bank based multicarrier (FBMC), which employs specially designed filter banks with small out-of-band attenuation in an architecture of multicarrier modulation, has been considered as a promising candidate solution to the 5G air interface problem [4]. Compared with OFDM, the FBMC modulation scheme has a lower spectrum leakage, which makes it very suitable for cognitive radio (CR) applications in a 5G scenario. However, FBMC signals still suffer from large PAPR due to

© ICST Institute for Computer Sciences, Social Informatics and Telecommunications Engineering 2018
K. Long et al. (Eds.): 5GWN 2017, LNICST 211, pp. 327–337, 2018.
https://doi.org/10.1007/978-3-319-72823-0_31

the superposition of multicarrier signals at the transmitter, which leads to performance degradation and attracts much research on PAPR reduction methods for FBMC-based 5G transmission. To the best of our knowledge, there are very few methods that can be effectively and actually employed for PAPR reduction in an FBMC transmission architecture. Some papers [2–4] introduce a tone reservation (TR) method and an overlapped selected mapping (SLM) technique, but they are not directly applicable to the FBMC scheme due to the fact that the overlap of time-domain symbols leads to a search with high computational complexity.

Based on the description of FBMC transmission architecture and analysis of structural characteristics of FBMC signals, this paper studies several PAPR reduction methods which are previously used in OFDM transmission, and then attempts to apply them to an FBMC transmission environment by giving detailed theoretical derivation. Computer simulation under different cases also verify feasibility and effectiveness of these PAPR reduction methods on the FBMC transmission scenario.

The organization of the paper is as follows. Section 2 briefly described the FBMC modulation and the structural characteristics of FBMC signals. In Sect. 3 traditional methods of reducing PAPR in an FBMC transmission system is introduced and improvement of the traditional algorithm is made. In Sect. 4 the algorithm mentioned in Sect. 3 is simulated. According to the simulation results, the performance of each algorithm is analyzed to find the algorithm which can reduce the PAPR effectively. Section 5 summarizes the results and concludes the paper with an overall evaluation of the discussed PAPR reduction schemes and next is the acknowledgement.

2 FBMC Transmission Architecture

2.1 System Principle

FBMC modulation is widely used in a multi-carrier modulation scheme. Similar to the OFDM system, multicarrier modulation is performed via IFFT, and then each sub-channel is filtered by a specially designed prototype filter which has a positive influence on the spectral characteristics of the transmitted signal. Through the analysis of FFT, a prototype filter which can be applied to FBMC system must have the following properties: (1) linear phase; (2) satisfies the Nyquist theorem to guarantee the mutual independence between the sub carriers; (3) small out-of-band attenuation. At present, many studies design a prototype filter based on an overlap factor [3]. The results show that this prototype filter under the conditions of the overlap factor $k = 4$ have better out-of-band attenuation performance than the FFT prototype filter [4].

In an FBMC system, the use of OQAM modulation is a good way to ensure the same code rate as the FFT filter bank. The cross-amplitude modulation signal is then transmitted in the system, in which there is a $T/2$ time delay between the imaginary and the real part of the input complex signal. Next, the imaginary part and the real part carry out the shift addition. The realization of the system block diagram is shown as below (Fig. 1).

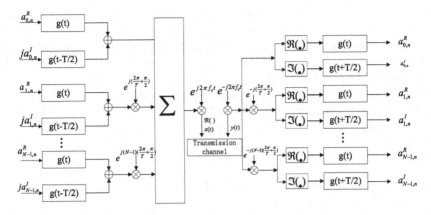

Fig. 1. The block diagram of realization of the system.

The structure of the FBMC system consists of a synthetic filter bank located at the transmitter and an analysis filter bank used by the receiver. The two filter banks are actually prototype filters after the shift. The status of the two filter banks in the system determines the unique nature of the FBMC signal. In the process of FBMC modulation, A prototype filter with a pulse response of P0 (represents the intensity of pulse response) and satisfying the Nyquist interval is applied to the sub carrier. Considering the superior performance of the prototype filter, the FBMC signal obviously has higher spectral efficiency than the OFDM signal. The following figure shows the basic architecture of the FBMC system (Fig. 2).

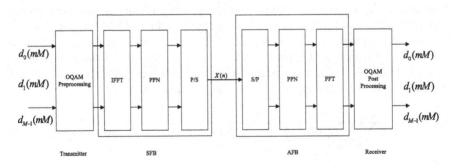

Fig. 2. The basic architecture of the FBMC system.

The figure shows that the FBMC system increases OQAM preprocessing module at the transmitter in order to separate the real and imaginary part of complex signals, then the synthetic filter bank, which includes IFFT processing module and PPN phase-multi structure, is employed to achieve frequency domain extension. Signals are then transmitted to the channel through the P/S transform. At the receiver, the received signal is first processed by the S/P transform. Next, the information flow is divided into multiplexed signals which then enter the analysis filter bank consisting of PPN phase-multi structure and FFT processing module. Finally, signals are demodulated through OQAM post-processing module. Since the carriers are orthogonal to each other in the system, the complete input signal can be restored at the receiver without being affected by subcarrier interference and inter-symbol interference.

The baseband signal $s[n]$ of discrete modulated in FBMC system can be expressed based on the complex modulation symbol $X_m[k]$ at the kth subcarrier during the mth time slot as follows:

$$s[n] = \sum_{m=-\infty}^{\infty} \sum_{k=0}^{N-1} (\theta_k \Re\{X_m[k]\} p_0[n - mN] + \theta_{k+1} \Re\{X_m[k]\} p_0[n - mN - \frac{\pi}{2}] e^{jk(n-mN)\frac{2\pi}{n}})$$

(1)

$$\theta_k = \begin{cases} 1, & k \text{ is even} \\ 0, & k \text{ is odd} \end{cases}$$

(2)

where: $j = \sqrt{-1}$ and N represent the number of available subcarriers. The overlapping ratio of continuous symbol is closely related to the length of the prototype filter. For simplicity, the filter is designed with an impulse response of length $K * N$, which means that the symbol duration is stretched and there are K symbols overlapping in time domain to avoid loss of data rate.

2.2   Structural Characteristics of FBMC Signals

In order to make a comprehensive understanding of the FBMC system, we construct the FBMC signal and study its structural characteristics. In the FBMC signal, there is a $T/2$ time delay in the time domain between the imaginary part and the real part of the signal, where T represents the symbol width. After the input signal is modulated by the prototype filter, the adjacent modulation signal frequency difference is $1/T$. The modulated signal can be expressed in time domain as follows:

$$\tilde{x}(t) = \sum_{n=0}^{N-1} \sum_{M=0}^{M-1} x_m^n(t) = \sum_{n=0}^{N-1} \sum_{M=0}^{M-1} [a_m^n h(t - mT) + jb_m^n h(t - mT - \frac{T}{2})] e^{jn\varphi_l}$$

(3)

where: N representing any positive integer. A_{mn} and B_{mn} respectively represent the real and imaginary parts of the signal input in the nth sub carrier of the mth data blocks. Obviously the impulse response of prototype filter is longer than T. Since the delay exists between the real and imaginary parts of the signal input, it will overlap between adjacent FBMC signal blocks.

In order to reflect signal PAPR more accurately, we oversample the signal with the sampling rate T/K, where $K = LN$ and L are over sampling coefficients. From the literature we know that when sampling coefficient $L = 4$, the sign changes can be described well [5]. The sampled signal can be expressed as follows:

$$x_m^n[k] = \begin{cases} (a_m^n h[k - mK] + jb_m^n h[k - mK - \frac{K}{2}])e^{jn(\frac{2\pi k}{TK} + \frac{\pi}{2})}, mK \le k \le mK + (A+1)K - 1 \\ 0, k < mK, k > mK + (A+1)K - 1 \end{cases} \quad (4)$$

where: A represents the number of overlapping data blocks with time domain signals $x_m[k]$; $h[k]$ represents the discrete time filters obtained by sampling, $h[k] = h[Tk/K]$.

3   PAPR Reduction for FBMC Transmission

This section will discuss methods of reducing PAPR in an FBMC transmission system. Through the study of some effective algorithms in a traditional OFDM system, we apply them to the FBMC environment and make some theoretical derivation.

3.1   Clipping

Note that the discrete amplitude of FBMC signals in time domain is limited to the threshold value $A_{\max}$. Clipping signal can be written as follows:

$$s^c[n] = \begin{cases} s[n], & |s[n]| \le A_{\max} \\ A_{\max}e^{j\varphi[s[n]]}, & |s[n]| > A_{\max} \end{cases} \quad (5)$$

where: $\varphi(s[n])$ is the phase of complex signal. The limiter is characterized by limiting ratio, which is defined as follows:

$$CR_{dB} = 10\log_{10}(\gamma) \quad (6)$$

where: $\gamma = A_{\max}/\sqrt{P_s}$; P_s is the average energy of the transmitted signal. The mathematical model of the limiting amplitude is derived from the derivation of the Bussgang theorem for the non-memory nonlinear Gauss input [6]. The limiting signal can be expressed as:

$$s^c[n] = \alpha s[n] + d[n] \quad (7)$$

where: α describes the attenuation; $d[n]$ is a limited range of noise which is also known as Bussgang noise. Attenuation factor can be calculated in the following way:

$$\alpha = 1 - e^{-\gamma^2} + \frac{\sqrt{\pi}}{2}\gamma erfc(\gamma) \quad (8)$$

The energy of clipping noise is then calculated as follows:

$$P_d = (1 - e^{-\gamma^2} - \alpha^2)P_s \tag{9}$$

Since some literatures study clipping iteration scheme and clipping combined with filtering scheme [6], we consider to combine the two schemes. Let it be able to reduce the system PAPR significantly and to reduce the nonlinear distortion of the system as far as possible. In accordance with this idea, an additional signal processing module is added before the transmitter transmits the signal, then FBMC modulation is performed on a conventional symbol X, after that the PAPR of the resulting signal $s[n]$ is measured. If it is less than a predetermined limit, it can be transmitted. If the amplitude is larger, apply clipping to it. After the amplitude is limited, the signal s^c is demodulated. The demodulation of the symbol X^c uses a special selection and processing algorithm. Then the new symbol X^{new} is modulated, and the PAPR of the signal s^{new} is measured. Repeat this process until the desired PRPR has been reached. The iterative signal is used to form an analog signal.

3.2   Partial Transmit Sequence (PTS)

The main idea of the traditional PTS methods applied in OFDM is given as follows [7]: First, the original input data is divided into several equal sub blocks of the combination; Next, each block is multiplied by the same rotation vector; Finally, signals with the smallest PAPR are selected to transfer. For the FBMC system, we choose to use a P-PTS method [7] based on a two-step optimization structure to reduce the PAPR. Due to the overlap of the FBMC signal structure, we should consider several overlapping data blocks when we study the reduction of peak power.

The first step of this method is similar to the traditional Selected Mapping (SLM) method [2] used in OFDM. The difference between these two methods is that optimization of the phase rotation sequence of current symbol is determined by the prior overlap of the FBMC-OQAM symbol. In other words, all of the symbols that overlap with the current symbol need to be considered when selecting the optimized phase rotation sequence. In addition, since each FBMC-OQAM symbol is not generated until the time FT, we should calculate the value of PAPR during $[0, FT]$ instead of $[0, T]$ to select the optimal rotation vector. The second step is similar to S-PTS which is mentioned in the reference [7], the main idea of which is to divide the FBMC-OQAM symbol into segments, and then the intersection of some blocks are separated and multiplied by the different phase rotation factors. However, as the PTS scheme exists a certain complexity itself, just using the PTS method to reduce FBMC PAPR will lead to high computational complexity.

3.3   PTS-Clipping

Here we consider a practical combination of the two methods above, which can achieve better performance of PAPR reduction for FBMC transmission. On the one hand, we know that the main idea of the PTS scheme is to divide the raw data into several disjoint sub blocks. Note that there are three main methods for the segmentation of data blocks, namely, the random method, the interleaving method and the adjacent method [8]. Through comparing the performance of the three methods, we find that the method of random segmentation reaches the most satisfying PAPR performance [9]. After the split, each sub data block is then multiplied by a corresponding phase rotation sequence, and the phase of the signal is adjusted by the phase rotation factor. Through finding the optimal phase factor combination we can minimize FBMC PAPR. On the other hand, the main idea of the clipping scheme is to set a threshold value. The signal exceeding the threshold value will be cut, while the one which does not exceed the threshold value will keep the same original value or be amplified by small amplitude, so that PAPR can be effectively reduced in this way. However, the scheme draws into the nonlinear distortion which leads to performance degradation. Now we consider the combination of the two methods. Generally, the signal has been selected which has the minimum limit noise after the original signal is processed by the PTS method, then we apply the clipping operation. In this way, the system error will be reduced and PAPR reduction can also be guaranteed.

The implementation steps of the combined method "PTS-Clipping" are given below:

(1) Block the input signal data, divided it into V sub blocks;
(2) The sub blocks generated by (1) are multiplied by the corresponding phase rotation factor, and the generated signal is used as an alternative;
(3) Calculation (2) clipping noise power of V road signal respectively.

$$\widehat{P}_{v,Clipping} = \frac{1}{N}\sum_{i=1}^{n}(|x_k| - T_h)^2, \quad 0 \le k \le N, 0 \le v \le V; \tag{10}$$

(4) The signal with the minimum limiting noise power is selected from the V road signal, then apply clipping to it.

$$\widehat{x}_k = \begin{cases} T_h e^{j\varphi(x_k')}, & |x_k'| > T_h \\ x_k', & |x_k'|| \le T_h \end{cases} \tag{11}$$

(5) Observe the PAPR performance and bit error rate (BER) performance of the signal after the above steps.

4   Simulation Results

Here we give some simulation results of the three algorithms above to verify their feasibility and effectiveness on FBMC PAPR reduction.

4.1   Simulation Result of Clipping

Firstly we need to set up the simulation parameters, number of subcarriers $M = 512$ and overlap factor $K = 4$, then the length of the prototype filter $h[k]$ is $L = M * N - 1$, the clipping ratio is set to 4, which is equivalent to 6 dB. Through the MATLAB programming and using the complementary cumulative distribution function to describe the system's PAPR performance, simulation results are shown as follows (Fig. 3):

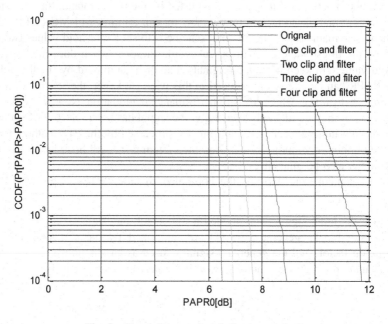

Fig. 3. Simulation results of clipping method

From the above figure, we can see the difference in the Complementary Cumulative Distribution Function (CCDF) curve between the signal PAPR after using the clipping method and the original signal PAPR. The PAPR performance of different clipping frequency is given, which demonstrates that clipping can effectively reduce PAPR. As the increase of the number of clipping, the performance of PAPR reduction is also improved.

4.2   Simulation Result of PTS

The simulation parameters are set as follows: the modulation mode is OQAM modulation, the number of sub carriers $M = 128$, the sub carriers are divided into 4 groups, the number of the rotation phase is 4, using random segmentation, simulation results are shown as follows (Fig. 4):

It can be seen from the above figure that the PTS is effective for reducing the peak-to-average power ratio of the FBMC system.

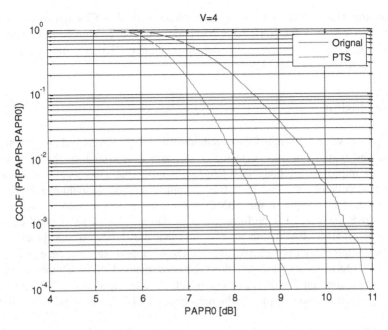

Fig. 4. Simulation results of PTS method

4.3 Simulation Result of PTS-Clipping

The simulation parameters are set as follows: number of subcarriers $M = 512$, the number of the rotation phase is 2, using 4 times oversampling. The simulation results are shown as below (Fig. 5):

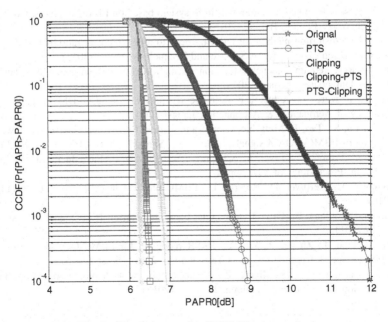

Fig. 5. Simulation result of PTS-Clipping method

From the figure we can see that using clipping method or PTS algorithm alone can only have a certain effect on PAPR reduction, but the combination algorithm has obviously better performance, which demonstrates that PTS-Clipping is a promising candidate solution to FBMC PAPR reduction.

5 Conclusion

In this paper, we have studied two methods for FBMC PAPR reduction which are clipping and partial transmit sequence (PTS), and then combined them together to present an improved method "PTS-Clipping". From the theoretical derivation and computer simulation, we find that: First, clipping method is undoubtedly the most simple method to operate in the FBMC system, but it will introduce nonlinear distortion which leads to BER performance degradation; Next, PTS method can effectively reduce FBMC PAPR, but we also find that the number of sub blocks greatly affect the computational complexity. Reduce the number of sub sequences will lead to poor PAPR performance; Finally, the combined method "PTS-Clipping" achieves better performance on PAPR reduction, which demonstrates that PTS-Clipping is a promising candidate solution to PAPR reduction for FBMC-based 5G transmission.

Acknowledgement. This research is sponsored by National Natural Science Foundation of China (No. 61401029), the Fundamental Research Funds for the Central Universities (No. 2012LYB46), Beijing Youth Excellence Program (YETP0296) and Beijing Advanced Innovation Center for Future Education (BJAICFE2016IR-004).

References

1. He, Z.: Research on key technology of ROF system based on FBMC. University of Science and Technology Beijing, Beijing (2015)
2. Lu, S.: Non distortion method for reducing peak to average power ratio of FBMC-OQAM signal. Huazhong University of Science and Technology, Hubei (2013)
3. He, X.: Research on channel estimation of multi-carrier system based on filter bank. Zhejiang University, Zhejiang (2013)
4. Guo, T.: Research on reducing peak-to-average power ratio in OFDM systems. Nanjing University of Aeronautics & Astronautics, Jiangsu (2007)
5. Qu, D., Lu, S., Tao, J.: Multi-block joint optimization for the peak-to-average power ratio reduction of FBMC-OQAM signals. IEEE Trans. Signal Process. **61**(7), 1605–1613 (2013)
6. Kollár, Z., Varga, L., Czimer, K.: Clipping-based iterative PAPR-reduction techniques for FBMC. In: Proceedings of VDE, pp. 1–7 (2012)
7. Bellanger, M., LeRuyet, D., Roviras, D.: FBMC physical layer: a prime. In: PHYDYAS (2010)
8. Farhang-Boroujeny, B.: OFDM versus filter bank multicarrier. IEEE Signal Process. **28**(3), 92–112 (2011)
9. Liu, K., Hou, J., Zhang, P., Liu, Y.: PAPR reduction for FBMC-OQAM systems using P-PTS scheme. J. China Univ. Posts Telecommun. **22**(6), 78–85 (2015)
10. Tao, Y., Liu, L., Liu, S., Zhang, Z.: A survey: several technologies of non-orthogonal transmission for 5G. China Commun. **12**, 1–15 (2015)

11. Zhuang, L., Weng, H.: Research on PAPR suppression algorithm for carrier aggregation in FBMC system. Sci. Technol. Engi. **16**(9), 221–225 (2016)
12. He, Y., Qu, D., Lu, S.: Sliding window tone reservation technique for the peak-to-average power ratio reduction of FBMC-OQAM signals. IEEE Wireless Commun. Lett. **1**(4), 268–271 (2012)

A Machine Learning Based Engine Error Detection Method

Xinsong Cheng[1], Liang Zhao[1(✉)], Na Lin[1], Changqing Gong[1],
and Ruiqing Wang[2]

[1] College of Computer Science, Shenyang Aerospace University,
Shenyang, China
18842458912@163.com,
{lzhao,linna,gongchangqing}@sau.edu.cn
[2] International School, Beijing University of Posts and Telecommunications,
Beijing, China
wrq@bupt.edu.cn

Abstract. Nowadays the fault of automobile engines climb due to the growth of automobiles. Traditional mechanical automobile testing is not efficient enough. In this paper, the Machine Learning based Engine Error Detection method (MLBED) is proposed for the complex nonlinear relation and operation parameters of automobile engine operating parameters such as large scale data, noise, fuzzy nonlinear etc. This method is a fault diagnosis and early warning method designed on the basis of self-organizing neural network, Elman neural network and probabilistic neural network. The experimental results show that MLBED has a great advantage in the current fault detection methods of automobile engine. The method improves the prediction accuracy and efficiency.

Keywords: Self-organizing neural network · Elman neural network
Probabilistic neural network · Engine fault

1 Introduction

At the moment, with the development of industry and the improvement of technology, the integration of automotive engine is very high. The most faults of automobiles is caused by the engine where the engine is the power source of an automobile. If an automobile is in a poor working condition, it is a very high possibility due to engine failure. The most common engine faults are as follows. Firstly, the fuel injection pressure of first cylinder is either too large or too small. Secondly, the needle valve of first cylinder injector is broken. Thirdly, abnormal fuel injection pressure of engine also can lead a direct impact on the engine's power efficiency, running stability and emission performance. Fourthly, oil path blockage anomaly can directly cause the engine fail. Therefore, it is necessary to monitor the working condition to avoid the failure of the engine [1, 2]. Early typical fault diagnosis methods are designed on the basis of the engine thermodynamic mathematical model [3, 4]. These methods can identify the performance loss of each component which detects multiple faults and quantifies the performance degradation of components. The fault diagnosis is to

K. Long et al. (Eds.): 5GWN 2017, LNICST 211, pp. 338–346, 2018.
https://doi.org/10.1007/978-3-319-72823-0_32

identify the pattern of the fault including both feature extraction and state identification. It is unnecessary to disassemble engine for measuring the shocking signal of engine cylinder. This is convenient and fast. The signal information of vibration and noise is abundant which can reflect the working condition of the engine in real-time [5, 6]. For a long time, there is still many shortcomings in the engine monitoring system such as the low frequency of engine examining and the poor reliability of data monitoring.

The rest of this paper is organized as follows. In Sect. 2, related engine fault diagnosis methods are reviewed. In Sect. 3, the proposed Machine Learning based Engine Error Detection method is introduced. The experimental results are shown in Sect. 4. And we conclude this paper and give the future research direction in the last section.

2 Related Work

There is a list of applications of Machine Learning Algorithms [7–13]. Ye et al. present a method for qualitative diagnosis of some prototype faults [7]. The Back Propagation Neural Network (BPNND) and the Probabilistic Neural Network (PNND) are applied in the qualitative diagnosis for some prototype faults of aero-engine. The proposed method solves the problem of the qualitative diagnosis of some prototype faults of aero-engine. The problem is that the collection of the measured data is not clear. This causes the further analysis cannot be taken based on data.

The adaptive fuzzy neural network is used by Ma et al. to engine fault diagnosis [8]. However, the measured parameters the authors are not collected clearly and a major process is missed to identify algorithm accurate.

Zhou et al. present a good method which obtains good results in the engine fault diagnosis [9]. The application of improved BP algorithm in engine fault diagnosis is studied while an example training process and test results are given. The shortcomings are basically caused by the structure characteristics of BP neural network. In the training of large samples and high precision, the network does not converge and easy to fall into the local optimal.

Gao et al. apply the Elman neural network in a engine performance fault identification and fault diagnosis model to prove the relationship between exhaust gas composition on engine performance [10]. However, the classification of engine operating conditions is insufficient, which is easy to cause the phenomenon of false positives.

A engine warning system is presented [11]. The patented system detects the moisture and sends out the warning signal to remind the user that the air filter is in the water and the automobile need to be stopped. The problem is the warning is only given when automobile engine is in bad condition, and there is no fault prediction.

3 Machine Learning Based Engine Error Detection

In view of the limitation and disadvantage of the automobile engine monitoring system, this paper proposes the Machine Learning based Engine Error Detection method (MLBED). Two major mechanisms are provided by MLBED methods. First, Component analysis is improved with extracting the method of feature values from the vibration signal and pressure signal parameters. The characteristic value preserves which establishes a comprehensive evaluation function. The characteristics of the comprehensive evaluation function are very related to the value of energy parameters, such as the kurtosis parameter, waveform parameters, margin parameters, pulse parameters and peak parameters. It allows the comprehensive evaluation value. The range of the experimental data obtained from the comprehensive evaluation value is from −4.78708 to 26.49655. Second, the SOM classifies operational parameter of engine and diagnoses its hitch. There are five types of faults as off-limits injection pressure of the first cylinder fuel, the broken needle valve of first cylinder injector, oil path blockage and exceeded fuel supply advance angle. Third, the Elman neural network is applied for find the characteristic value of the data to predict failure. In order to show that our results are valid and reliable, we classifies and diagnose them by using PNN and SOM. This method can predict, diagnosis and inspect of operating parameters of automobile engine.

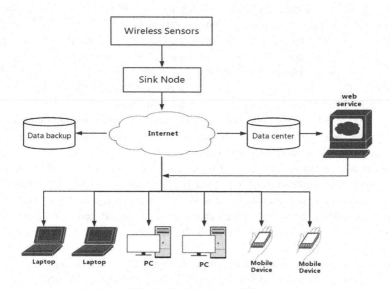

Fig. 1. Architecture module

Figure 1 is the structure of automobile engine warning system. Automobile engine early warning system includes wireless sensor device, background monitoring and early warning system. The following three components are shown.

(1) Wireless sensor data acquisition node is responsible for collecting the temperature, humidity, current, voltage, speed, torque and other data and transmit these data to the sink node.
(2) Sink node is responsible for receiving the data which sent from each monitoring sensor nodes and instantly transfer them to the monitoring background via wireless network.

(3) Wireless communication module is in charge of the whole network system. The network structure of wireless sensor network based on IEEE802.15 which can realize point to point communication between nodes in the network.

The backstage monitoring and warning system of automobile engine includes main data backup, data center (data storage), server (data pre-processing, data training and model building), feedback monitoring and early warning results.

3.1 Self-organizing Neural Network

As shown in Fig. 2, the engine analysis of Self-Organizing Neural network (SOM) structure schematic diagram can be classified into the field of artificial intelligence in unsupervised learning. Two dimensional SOM is called KFM (Feature Mapping Kohonen). The input network is a 6 dimensional vector $x = [x_1, x_2, x_3, x_4, x_5, x_6]$ of all 6 values while the output unit is two-dimensional array, the number of 6×6 species. The input layer and the output layer of each unit is fully connected where W indicates the connection weights. The KFM of the learning process is iterative learning of G sample vector and calculates the winning neuron. Until the change of weight W is less than a certain threshold or a certain number of iterations, the output units of the same sample vector belonging to the same class. Although KFM has a learning process, it can be seen that this kind of learning method is automatically acquired from all the samples.

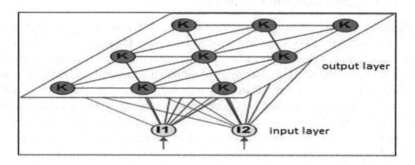

Fig. 2. SOM neural network structure

3.2 Elman Neural Network

A schematic diagram of automobile engine structure of Elman neural network is shown in Fig. 3. Elman neural network analysis can be classified into the field of artificial intelligence in supervised learning. The acquisition from operation parameters of automobile engine with 5 kinds of failure modes of vibration signal analysis of vibration waveform statistical processing including, energy parameters, kurtosis parameter, waveform parameters, margin parameters, pulse parameters and peak parameters. The prediction parameter values of the past parameters. Hence it is a problem of time series. If we want to solve problems by applying Elman neural network, one parameter is taken before this node N to predict a time node of the parameter value. The mapping function can be expressed as $x_n = f(x_{n-1}, x_{n-2}, \ldots, x_{n-N})$. The training samples and test samples are divided, and the Elman neural network is established.

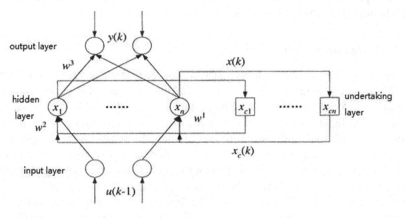

Fig. 3. Structure of Elman neural network

3.3 PNN Probabilistic Neural Network

A schematic structure of probabilistic neural network engine (PNN) is illustrated in Fig. 4. The analysis of PNN can be classified into the field of artificial intelligence in supervised learning. Acquisition of automobile engine normal operation and five kinds of failure modes of vibration signal analysis of vibration waveform statistical processing including energy parameters, kurtosis parameter, waveform parameters, margin parameters, pulse parameters and peak parameters. As a fault judgment training sample, twelve input samples, each sample is six dimensional vector $x = [x_1, x_2, x_3, x_4, x_5, x_6]$. Then the PNN is established for each of the samples, which is six dimensional vector and the classification model is six.

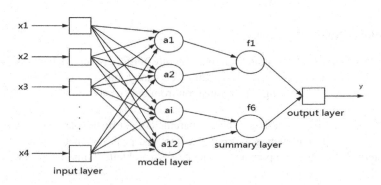

Fig. 4. Structure of PNN neural network

4 Simulation Results and Analysis

4.1 Improved Principal Component Analysis

Table 1 is SPSS results after the operation. The discriminant equation is obtained according to the coefficient of the non standardized discriminant equation:

$$D1 = 0.029 * EP + 0.05 * MP + 0.002 * PP1 + 0.009 * KP + (-0.017) * PP2 - 1.182$$

$$D2 = 0.045 * EP + (-0.029) * MP + (-0.001) * PP1 + 0.014 * KP + (-0.319) * PP2 - 0.583$$

$$D3 = 0.004 * WP + 0.012 * EP + 0.005 * MP + 0.011 * PP1 + (-0.004) * KP + 0.457 * PP2 - 2.009$$

Table 1. Canonical discriminant function coefficient

	Function		
	1	2	3
Waveform parameter (WP)	.000	.000	.004
Energy parameter (EP)	.029	.045	.012
Margin parameter (MP)	.050	−.029	.005
Peak parameters (PP1)	.002	−.001	.011
Kurtosis parameter (KP)	.009	.014	−.004
Pulse parameters (PP2)	−.017	−.319	.457
(constant)	−1.182	−.583	−2.009

4.2 Results of SOM Self Organizing Neural Network

Table 2 presents the results of Matlab operation. The application of SOM neural network presents the current operating state of the engine time node under time node from 1 to 4. The engine running state reflects the injector needle wear of first cylinder, low or high fuel injection pressure of the first cylinder, or the fuel supply advance angle before $5' \sim 6$.

Table 2. SOM output result

Time node	1	2	3	4	5
Running statement	Statement 2	Statement 1	Statement 1	Statement 2	Statement 2
Time node	6	7	8	9	10
Running statement	Statement 2	Statement 2	Statement 2	Statement 2	Statement 4
Time node	11	12	13	14	15
Running statement	Statement 4	Statement 4	Statement 2	Statement 3	Statement 4

4.3   Elman Neural Network Results

As shown in Fig. 5, the left figure is the prediction results of MLBED method, while the right figure is the prediction results by applying [11]. The prediction results are not good due to the small size of the sample, and the input dimension is high. Therefore for each input variable relative output characterization can be imprecise. However, if the sample data is large enough, the model is better.

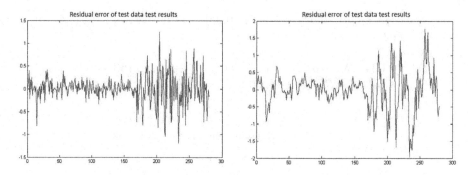

Fig. 5. Comparison of test results with other simulation results

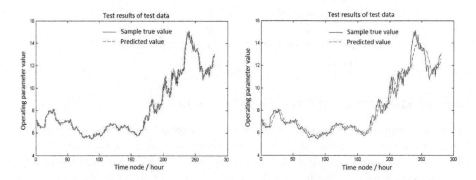

Fig. 6. Comparison of test results with other studies

As shown in Fig. 6, the left figure is the result of the MLBED method while the right figure is the residual error of applying [11]. Fine results of MLBED are shown in the vicinity of 0 of the residual fluctuations, it does not appear big deviation. However, compared to method of [11], you will find that the residuals are close to 0 near the convergence of data. If the forecast data is more than 170 of the time, the residual error appears larger fluctuations and the accuracy of the prediction is also high. Therefore the prediction of a certain range of data is still very accurate.

4.4   PNN Probabilistic Neural Network Results

Probabilistic neural network (PNN) is simple in structure and its training process. PNN model for the robust nonlinear classification capability. The fault sample space is mapped into the fault pattern space to form a fault diagnosis network system with strong fault tolerant capability and structure adaptive capability, which can improve the accuracy of fault diagnosis (Table 3).

Table 3. PNN output result

Sample	Actual	Judgement	True/False	Fault type
1	3	3	True	The broken needle valve of first cylinder
2	6	6	True	Normal
3	2	2	True	The first cylinder fuel injection pressure
4	5	5	True	Fuel supply advance angle exceeded
5	1	1	True	The first cylinder fuel injection pressure
6	4	6	True	Normal

5   Conclusion

In this paper, the early warning system is designed for automobile engine while the MLBED method is proposed on the basis of a data acquisition and machine learning method. It provides the classification of the automobile engine fault prediction. The experimental results show our proposed method provides accurate fault recognition and prediction.

Acknowledgment. This work is partially supported by the National Student's Platform for Innovation and Entrepreneurship Training Program (201610143022), the Research Project of Education Department of Liaoning Province (L201630) and the Doctoral Start-up Research Foundation of Shenyang Aerospace University (15YB03).

References

1. Zhou, Z.P.: Analysis and countermeasure of abnormal valve clearance of engine valve. Diesel Engine Des. Manuf. **18**(1), 52–56 (2012)
2. Saravanan, N., Siddab, S., Kumar, R.: A comparative study on classification of features by SVM and PSVM extracted using Morlet wavelet for fault diagnosis of spur bevel gear box. Expert Syst. Appl. **35**(3), 1351–1356 (2008)
3. Doel, D.L.: Temper—a gas-path analysis tool for commercial jet engines. J. Eng. Gas Turbines Power **116**(1), 82–89 (1994). J. Trans. ASME
4. Barwell, M.J.: Ground Based Engine Monitoring Program for General Application. R. SAE Technical Paper. No. 871734 (1987)
5. Shen, Z.X., Huang, X.Y., Ma, X.: Laugh EMD and support vector machine fault diagnosis of diesel engine. Vib. Test Diagn. **30**(1), 19–22 (2010)

6. Xu, Y.X., Yang, W.P., Lv, X.: Study on fault diagnosis of automobile engine based on support vector machine. Vib. Shock **32**(8), 143–146 (2013)
7. Xu, L.M., Wang, Q., Chen, J.P., Pan, Y.Z.: Prediction of debris flow average velocity based on BP neural network. Geol. Eng. Environ. Eng. **31**(2), 25–30 (2013)
8. Ye, Z.F., Sun, J.G.: Aeroengine fault diagnosis based on probabilistic neural network. J. Aeronaut. Sci. **23**(2), 155–157 (2002)
9. Ma, J.C., Si, J.P., Niu, J.H., Wang, E.M.: Engine fault diagnosis based on adaptive fuzzy neural network. Noise Vib. Control **35**(2), 165–174 (2015)
10. Qu, C.S., Lu, Y.Z., Tan, Y.: An improved empirical mode decomposition and its application in signal noise. J. Autom. **36**(1), 67–73 (2010)
11. Lian, Y., Feng, L.G., Wu, F.L., Zhao, Y.: Study on fault diagnosis of integrated navigation based on genetic PNN network. Foreign Electr. Meas. Technol. **33**(1), 120–126 (2012)
12. Xu, L., Chen, Y., Chai, K., Schormans, J., Cuthbert, L.: Self-organising cluster-based cooperative load balancing in OFDMA cellular networks. Wiley Wirel. Commun. Mob. Comput. **15**(7), 1171–1187 (2015)
13. Zhao, L., Li, Y., Meng, C., Gong, C., Tang, X.: A SVM based routing scheme in VANETs. In: 16th International Symposium on Communications and Information Technologies, Qingdao, pp. 380–383. IEEE Press (2016)
14. Xu, L., Luan, Y., Cheng, X., Xing, H., Liu, Y., Jiang, X., Chen, W., Chao, K.: Self-optimised joint traffic offloading in heterogeneous cellular networks. In: IEEE International Symposium on Communications and Information Technologies, Qingdao, pp. 263–267. IEEE Press (2016)
15. Xu, L., Chen, Y., Chai, K.K., Luan, Y., Liu, D.: Cooperative mobility load balancing in relay cellular networks. In: IEEE International Conference on Communication in China, Xi'an, pp. 141–146. IEEE Press (2013)

Beamforming Design for Physical Layer Security and Energy Efficiency Based on Base Station Cooperation

Wei Zhao$^{(\boxtimes)}$, Hao Zhang, Hui Bao, and Baogang Li

Department of Electronic and Communication Engineering,
North China Electric Power University (NCEPU), Baoding, China
andyzhaoster@gmail.com, winnerzhl991@163.com,
baohui20131228@126.com, baogangli@ncepu.edu.cn

Abstract. The balance problem between physical layer security and energy efficiency of legitimate users is jointly considered in this paper. After using the cooperation technology of macrocell base station and microcell base station as well as the derivation of convex optimization theory, we propose a cooperative beamforming scheme. From the perspective of secrecy energy efficiency and SINR, the simulation results show that the proposed algorithm can meet the requirements of the system security and energy efficiency.

Keywords: Physical layer security · Energy efficiency · Beamforming
Base station cooperation

1 Introduction

The rapid development of wireless communication makes the mobile communication users not only put forward higher requirements on the system security rate, but also request more harsh conditions for the energy consumption of the system. How to improve the energy efficiency while ensuring the physical layer security of is a hot issue in the field of wireless communication. As one of the key technologies in LTE-A, the base station cooperation technologyis an effective means to solve the aboveproblem [1–3]. This paper is organized as follows. In Sect. 2, we summarize the technology of base station cooperation in heterogeneous networks (HetNet). The system model in the downlink HetNet is proposed in Sect. 3, in which we introduce the user distribution in two-layer HetNet in detail. More importantly, the optimization algorithm is designed about the collaboration between multiple base stationsin Sect. 4 and simulation results

This work was supported by Beijing Natural Science Foundation (Grants No. 4164101), the Fundamental Research Funds for the Central Universities(Grants No. 2015MS95), National Natural Science Foundation of China (Grants No. 61501185), and Hebei Province Natural Science Foundation (Grants No. F2016502062).

show the effectivenessof the proposed algorithms in Sect. 5. Finally, concluding remarks are provided in Sect. 6.

2 Overview of Base Station Cooperative Technology

The basic idea of cooperative technology is to use the base stations, antennas, relays, users and other communication nodes in the network to establish a virtual antenna array, and then get space diversity or multiplexing gain. Figure 1 shows a schematic diagram of a typical base station cooperative communication [4–6]. Different from the traditional collaboration techniques, the cooperation between base stations can fully utilize each antenna to carry out joint signal detection or data transmission on the same frequency resource block and transform the interference signal between multiple base stations into the useful one. The technology can achieve multi-point cooperative transmission at the station level and obtain diversity gain at the receiving node at the same time.

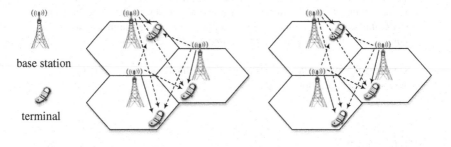

(a) The traditional collaboration techniques   (b) The cooperative network

Fig. 1. Base station cooperative communication

Note: in (a), the solid line indicates the message signal, and the broken line indicates the interference; in (b), the solid line represents the message signal, and the dashed line represents the available signal transmitted by the cooperative base station.

There are two main types of cooperative communication at the physical level: cooperative communication between different base stations and cooperative communication between base stations and terminals. One of the preconditions for base station collaboration is to exchange information and data between multiple cooperating base stations, which is one of the biggest problems for the traditional cellular network. However, under the LTE-Advanced standard, it's proposed that the base station can communicate with each other through the X2 interface, thus providing the possibility for the base station to cooperate.

The optimization of HetNet using base station collaboration technology has the following advantages:

(1) Increase capacity. In [7], the method of distributed compression is used to limit the uplink data rate of two users in HetNet with different backhaul rates. In this way, the cellular uplink capacity can greatly improve.
(2) Improve edge user performance. Since the user at the cell edge is farther from the central base station, the signal attenuation is more severe. It is possible to significantly improve the communication quality of the cell edge users by the space diversity gain caused by the cooperative transmission using a plurality of base stations [8].
(3) Saving energy. On the one hand, under the condition of a certain probability of outage, the transmission power of the system can be greatly reduced by the cooperative diversity transmission of multi-base stations [9]; on the other hand, by using the resource dynamic control strategy and the operational state switching policy between the base stations, the transfer between users can be realized, and thus achieve the purpose of energy-saving base station [10].

More importantly, the base station collaboration technology is not only applied to the inter-user performance improvement, but also be used to address the needs of energy saving. For instance, I. Ashraf et al. proposed a cooperative technology of different base stations to reduce the energy consumption of the system in the overlapping coverage area of the network [11].

It is worth mentioning that most of the research focused on the base station in the homogeneous network collaboration or only using the base station collaboration technology to implement the physical layer security or energy efficiency. Applying base station collaboration technology into HetNet is rarely studied, which is a big waste of system resources.

In order to make full use of the characteristics of HetNet, this paper designs a collaborative beamforming scheme in the two-layer HetNet by using the collaboration between the macro base station and the micro base station. What's more, the intentionally introduced CCI (co-channel interference) is employed. The security rate of the legitimate users in the micro-cell is combined with the system energy efficiency and the convex optimization theory is used to derive the algorithm. Finally, a power allocation scheme is obtained. The simulation results show the advantages of the proposed algorithm in improving system security and reducing energy consumption from the two aspects of security energy efficiency and SINR (the ratio of the power of the message signal to the interference power plus the noise power).

3 System Model

In the downlink of HetNet, there is one macrocell base station equipped with $N_M(N_M > M)$ antennas, which locates at the center of its coverage, and K microcell base stations equipped with $N_P(N_P > N)$ antennas. For the sake of convenience, it is assumed that the macrocell base station and the microcell base station all have a circular area as shown in the following figure. The number of legal users in macrocell and microcell are all single antenna users and each macro cell can cover M number of legitimate users, while the number of legitimate users can be N. A single antenna eavesdropper is within the coverage of the macrocelland attempts to eavesdrop on the $n(1 \leq n \leq N)$ microcell user located in the $k(1 \leq k \leq K)$ microcell. Assume that all channels are independent of each other and subject to Rayleigh flat fading. Figure 2 is the multi-cell system model diagram of HetNet in this paper.

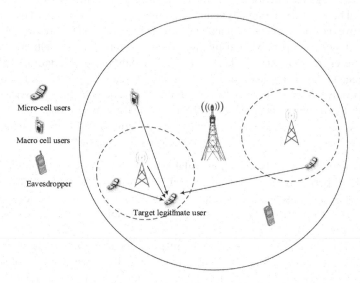

Fig. 2. System model

4   Optimization Algorithm Design

As can be seen from Fig. 2, the n-th legitimate user in the k-th microcell is listed as the reference object. Therefore, the desired message signal comes from the micro base station in the k-th microcell and the source of the interference includes other $N - 1$ legitimate micro-cell users in the same microcell with the target legitimate user, all $(k - 1) \cdot N$ legal microcell users in other $k - 1$ microcells, M legitimate macrocell users and eavesdropper in the macrocell. It is assumed that both the macro base station and the micro base station can obtain a complete CSI.

Suppose there are $K'(1 \leq K' \leq K - 1)$ cooperative microcell base stations can use CCI to interfere the eavesdroppers. Then according to the knowledge of information theory, the received signal of the target legitimate user can be expressed as:

$$y_{kn} = \underbrace{\mathbf{h}_{k,kn}\mathbf{w}_{kn}s_{kn}}_{\text{Useful signal}} + \underbrace{\sum_{\substack{a=1 \\ a \neq n}}^{N} \mathbf{h}_{k,kn}\mathbf{w}_{ka}s_{ka}}_{\substack{\text{Interference signals of other} \\ n-1 \text{ users under the same microcell}}} + \underbrace{\sum_{\substack{b=1 \\ b \neq k}}^{K}\sum_{c=1}^{N} \mathbf{h}_{b,kn}\mathbf{w}_{bc}s_{bc}}_{\substack{\text{Interference from all } (k-1)\cdot n \\ \text{micro-cell users under all other } k-1\text{microcells}}} + \underbrace{\sum_{m=1}^{M} \mathbf{h}_{kn}\mathbf{w}_m s_m + n_{kn}}_{\substack{\text{Interference from all} \\ \text{M macrocell users}}} \quad (1)$$

Now the meaning of the variables in the formula is explained as follows:

Variable	Definition
$\mathbf{h}_{k,kn}$	The channel vector from the k-th microcell base station to the target legitimate user
$\mathbf{w}_{kn}$	The beamforming vector for the target legitimate user
s_{kn}	The message signal intended for the target legitimate user; The essence of s_{kn} is a normalized vector, Satisfying $E\left(\|s_{kn}\|^2\right) = 1$
$\mathbf{w}_{ka}$	The beamforming vector for other $n - 1$ legitimate microcell users in the k-th microcell
s_{ka}	The message signal intended from the k-th microcell base station to other $n - 1$ legitimate microcell users in the k-th microcell
$\mathbf{h}_{b,kn}$	The channel vector from other $k - 1$ microcell base stations to the target legitimate user, $b \neq k$
$\mathbf{w}_{bc}$	The beamforming vector from other $k - 1$ microcell base stations to the legitimate microcell users inside
s_{bc}	The message signal intended from other $k - 1$ microcell base stations to the legitimate microcell users inside
$\mathbf{h}_{kn}$	The channel vector from the macrocell base station to the target legitimate user
$\mathbf{w}_m$	The beamforming vector from the macrocell users to the target legitimate user
s_m	The message signal intended from the macrocell base station to the target legitimate user
n_{kn}	n_{kn} obeying i.i.d. $CN \sim \left(0, \sigma_M^2\right)$

Similarly, the received signal at the eavesdropper is:

$$y_E = \mathbf{h}_E \mathbf{w}_{kn} s_{kn} + \sum_{\substack{a=1 \\ a \neq n}}^{N} \mathbf{h}_{n,E} \mathbf{w}_{ka} s_{ka} + \sum_{\substack{b=1 \\ b \neq k}}^{K} \sum_{c=1}^{N} \mathbf{h}_{b,kE} \mathbf{w}_{bc} s_{bc} + \sum_{m=1}^{M} \mathbf{h}_E \mathbf{w}_m s_m + n_{kn} \quad (2)$$

Suppose the user's CSI is known, according to the definition of SINR, the SINR of the target legitimate user is:

$$\mathbf{SINR}_{kn} = \frac{\left|\mathbf{h}_{k,kn} \mathbf{w}_{kn}\right|^2}{\sum_{\substack{a=1 \\ a \neq n}}^{N} \left|\mathbf{h}_{k,kn} \mathbf{w}_{ka}\right|^2 + \sum_{\substack{b=1 \\ b \neq k}}^{K} \sum_{a=1}^{N} \left|\mathbf{h}_{b,kn} \mathbf{w}_{ba}\right|^2 + \sum_{m=1}^{M} \left|\mathbf{h}_{kn} \mathbf{w}_m\right|^2 + \sigma_{kn}^2} \quad (3)$$

The SINR of the eavesdropper is:

$$\mathbf{SINR}_E = \frac{\left|\mathbf{h}_E \mathbf{w}_{kn}\right|^2}{\sum_{\substack{a=1 \\ a \neq n}}^{N} \left|\mathbf{h}_{n,E} \mathbf{w}_{ka}\right|^2 + \sum_{\substack{b=1 \\ b \neq k}}^{K} \sum_{a=1}^{N} \left|\mathbf{h}_{b,kE} \mathbf{w}_{ba}\right|^2 + \sum_{m=1}^{M} \left|\mathbf{h}_E \mathbf{w}_m\right|^2 + \sigma_E^2} \quad (4)$$

Then, according to the definition of confidential capacity, the confidential capacity of the target legitimate user is:

$$C_S = C_{kn} - C_E = B\log_2(1 + \mathbf{SINR}_{kn}) - B\log_2(1 + \mathbf{SINR}_E) \tag{5}$$

According to the definition of security energy efficiency [12], the confidential energy efficiency of the target legal user can be obtained as:

$$J_S = \frac{C_S}{\mathbf{P} + P_0} = \frac{B\log_2(1 + \mathbf{SINR}_{kn}) - B\log_2(1 + \mathbf{SINR}_E)}{\mathbf{P} + P_0} \tag{6}$$

In summary, the optimization problem of security energy-efficient beamforming can be summarizedas follows:

$$\max_{\substack{\{\mathbf{w}_m\}_{m=1'}^M \\ \{\{\mathbf{w}_{kn}\}_{n=1}^N\}_{k=1}^K}} \frac{log(1 + \mathbf{SINR}_{kn}) - log(1 + \mathbf{SINR}_E)}{\mathbf{P} + P_0} \tag{7}$$

$$s.t. \qquad \sum_{m=1}^M \|\mathbf{w}_m\|^2 \le P_M, m \in [1, \mathbf{M}] \tag{8}$$

$$\sum_{n=1}^N \|\mathbf{w}_{kn}\|^2 \le P_P, n \in [1, \mathbf{N}] \tag{9}$$

$$\mathbf{SINR}_m \ge \gamma_m \tag{10}$$

$$\mathbf{SINR}_{kn} \ge \gamma_{kn} \tag{11}$$

Next, we study the base station power optimization part.

The power amplifier is an important device in wireless communication system, the output power of which affects the transmission distance, thus affecting the entire coverage of macrocell. At the same time the power amplifier not only occupy a large weight in the wireless network static energy consumption, but alsoplay an important role in wireless network dynamic energy consumption. Therefore, from the base station side, through a reasonable power allocation to adjust the transmit power of base stationcan reduce the energy efficiency of the whole system.

Now optimize base station energy consumption. From the above description, wo can obtain the energy consumption of the system:

$$\mathbf{P} = \frac{\mathbf{P}_M}{\eta_M} + \sum_{n=1}^N \frac{\mathbf{P}_P^n}{\eta_p} + P_C \tag{12}$$

where $\mathbf{P}_M$, $\mathbf{P}_p$ is the transmit power of the power amplifier on the macrocell base station and the microcell base station side respectively; η_M, η_p is the effectiveness of the power amplifier; P_C is the total fixed circuit loss of the entire system.

Taking the target legitimate user as an example, we can get the transmit power of the macro base station as:

$$
\begin{aligned}
\mathbf{P}_M &= \sum_{n=1}^{N}\sum_{k=1}^{K}(\mathbf{w}_m)^{H}\mathrm{E}(|s_{kn}|^2)\mathbf{w}_m + \sum_{m=1}^{M}(\mathbf{w}_m)^{H}\mathrm{E}(|s_{kn}|^2)\mathbf{w}_m \\
&= \sum_{n=1}^{N}\sum_{k=1}^{K}(\mathbf{w}_m)^{H}\mathbf{w}_m + \sum_{m=1}^{M}(\mathbf{w}_m)^{H}\mathbf{w}_m
\end{aligned}
\tag{13}
$$

Similarly, the transmit power at the base station side is:

$$
\mathbf{P}_P = \sum_{n=1}^{N}\sum_{k=1}^{K}(\mathbf{w}_{kn})^{H}\mathbf{w}_{kn}
\tag{14}
$$

Through fractional programming, the above formula can be decomposed into the external part and the internal part. The external function can eventually be derived as:

$$
\max \quad \frac{1+G(\tau)}{1+\tau}
\tag{15}
$$
$$
s.t. \quad 0 \leq t \leq Tr(\mathbf{H}_1)P_{M\mathrm{max}}
$$

It can be seen that an external function can be solved using a one-dimensional linear search method. Among them, $G(\tau)$ is the internal function and can be optimized based on SDP optimization algorithm. The concrete optimization method is as follows:

$$
\max_{\substack{\{\mathbf{w}_m\}_{m=1'}^{M} \\ \{\{\mathbf{w}_{kn}\}_{n=1}^{N}\}_{k=1}^{K}}} \frac{Tr(\mathbf{H}_m\mathbf{W}_m)}{\sum_{m=1}^{M}Tr(\mathbf{H}_m\mathbf{W}_m) + \sum_{n=1}^{N}\sum_{k=1}^{K}Tr(\mathbf{H}_{n,m}\mathbf{W}_{kn})}
\tag{16}
$$

$$
s.t. \quad \sum_{m=1}^{M}Tr(\mathbf{X}_m) \leq P_{M\mathrm{max}}\zeta
\tag{17}
$$

$$
\sum_{n=1}^{N}\sum_{k=1}^{K}Tr(\mathbf{X}_{kn}) \leq P_{P\mathrm{max}}\zeta
\tag{18}
$$

$$
Tr(\mathbf{H}_m\mathbf{W}_m) \geq \gamma_m \left(\sum_{\substack{q=1 \\ q \neq m}}^{M}Tr(\mathbf{H}_m\mathbf{X}_q) + \sum_{n=1}^{N}\sum_{k=1}^{K}Tr(\mathbf{H}_{n,m}\mathbf{X}_{kn}) + \zeta \right)
\tag{19}
$$

$$Tr(\mathbf{H}_{n,kn}\mathbf{X}_{kn}) \geq \gamma_{kn}\left(\sum_{\substack{t=1\\t\neq k}}^{K} Tr(\mathbf{H}_{n,kn}\mathbf{X}_{tn}) + \sum_{\substack{p=1\\p\neq n}}^{N}\sum_{t=1}^{K} Tr(\mathbf{H}_{p,kn}\mathbf{X}_{tp}) + \sum_{m=1}^{M} Tr(\mathbf{H}_{kn}\mathbf{X}_{m}) + \zeta\right)$$

(20)

$$Tr(\mathbf{H}_E\mathbf{X}_1) \leq \tau\left(\sum_{m=1}^{M} Tr(\mathbf{H}_E\mathbf{X}_m) + \sum_{n=1}^{N}\sum_{k=1}^{K} Tr(\mathbf{H}_{n,E}\mathbf{X}_{kn}) + \zeta\right)$$

(21)

Where $H = h^H h$, $W = w^H w$, $W_m = \frac{\mathbf{X}_m}{\zeta}$, $W_{kn} = \frac{\mathbf{X}_{kn}}{\zeta}$ and X is the default auxiliary variable.

The optimization steps of the proposed algorithm can be summarized as follows:

Convex optimization method based on SDP:

1. Initial value: according to the simulation situation, give P_{Mmax}, P_{Pmax}, γ_m and γ_{kn} an initial value;

2. Compute $\tau_{max} = Tr(\mathbf{H}_1) \cdot P_{Mmax}$;

3. Get the optimal solution $G^*(\tau)$ by solving the internal SDP function, under τ_{max} ;

4. In the $[1, \tau_{max}]$ interval, after the one-dimensional linear search method to calculate the external function, we can get the optimal solution;

5. Through τ^* we can easily get (X_m^*, X_{kn}^*, ζ^*) ;

6. Based on $W_m = \frac{X_m}{\zeta}$, $W_{kn} = \frac{X_{kn}}{\zeta}$,the optimal solution of the beamforming vector W_m^* and

W_{kn}^* can be obtained

---

5 Simulation Analysis

In the actual simulation, the number of antennas is defined as follows: the antennas in the macro base station is $N_M = 10$, in the micro base station is $N_P = 4$, and in the macro cell is $M = 2$,

That is a legitimate users for macro cell, and an eavesdropping users. The number of legitimate microcell users in the microcell is $K = 1$, which is a microcell contains only one user. Otherwise, we also assuming that the number of the antenna in macrocell and in microcell, including the legitimate user and eavesdropping user is only one, and the channel of the system is Rayleigh fading channel. The simulation results are as follows (Fig. 3):

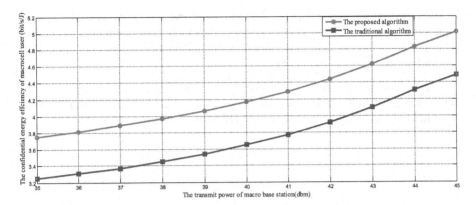

Fig. 3. The comparison of the traditional algorithm and the proposed algorithm on the security energy efficiency under different macro base station transmit power

The transmission power of the macro base station is not related to the cooperative interference between the micro base stations. However, according to the proposed algorithm, a significant improvement in security energy efficiency can be obtained (Fig. 4).

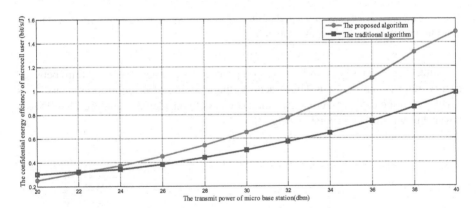

Fig. 4. The comparison of the traditional algorithm and the proposed algorithm on the security energy efficiency under different Micro base station transmit power

According to the simulation results, we can see that because of the cooperation between the micro base stations:

1. The transmission power is too small when the transmit power of micro-base station is less than 23 dbm, which leads to a large proportion of interference, therefore, it has a great influence on the security energy efficiency, so the proposed algorithm is slightly inferior to the traditional algorithm

2. The proposed algorithm is better than the traditional algorithm when the transmit power of micro-base station is exceed than 23 dbm. Because the transmitting power of the base station is increasing constantly, but the interference power is invariable, therefore, the curve is ascending.

Because of the presence of eavesdropping, the interference of the microcell increases larger than the legitimate signal along with the increase in transmission power at the macro base station, which causes the decreasing trend of SINR (Fig. 5).

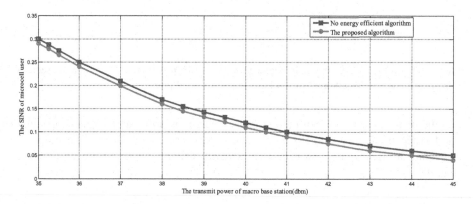

Fig. 5. Comparison of conventional algorithms and proposed algorithms in SINR at different transmit powers of the macro base station

Since the proposed algorithm is compromised optimization algorithm between energy-efficient and physical layer security, the resulting of beamforming vector W is smaller than the case where energy efficiency is not considered, therefore, the SINR is lower, but within an acceptable range (Fig. 6).

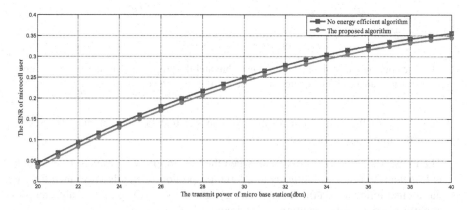

Fig. 6. Comparison of SINRs with traditional algorithms and proposed algorithms at different micro base station transmit powers

Different from the macro base station, the interference can be used as a means to interfering with the eavesdropping side. With the micro-base station transmission power increases, the SINR of micro-cell users also increases. But considering the energy efficiency and physical layer security, so the value is still slightly lower than the algorithm which the energy efficiency is not considered. Simultaneously, we also to know that with the cooperation of base stations between microcells and the effect of interference in microcell is larger than macrocell.

6   Concluding Remarks

This paper analyzes the tradeoff between physical layer security and energy efficiency of the legitimate users in HetNet. By using the CCI between cooperative micro-base stations, a cooperative beamforming scheme which conforms to the system model is designed; Combining the security rate of legitimate users in the microcell with the system energy efficiency, and using the convex optimization theory to derive the algorithm, a power allocation scheme is obtained. Finally, Simulation results show that, in the view of different macro base stations and micro-base station transmit power, a comparison chart between the traditional algorithm and the proposed algorithm is given. The results show that the proposed algorithm has the advantage of improving security and reducing energy consumption.

References

1. Zhang, H., Xing, H., Cheng, J., et al.: Secure resource allocation for OFDMA two-way relay wireless sensor networks without and with cooperative jamming. IEEE Trans. Industr. Inf. **12**(5), 1714–1725 (2016)
2. Zhao, J., Lu, Z., Wen, X., et al.: Resource management based on security satisfaction ratio with fairness-aware in two-way relay networks. Int. J. Distrib. Sens. Netw. **11**(7), 819195 (2015)
3. Zhang, H., Xing, H., Chu, X., et al.: Secure resource allocation for OFDMA two-way relay networks. In: 2012 IEEE Global Communications Conference (GLOBECOM), pp. 3649–3654. IEEE (2012)
4. Zhao, J., Zheng, W., Wen, X., Zhang, H., Lu, Z., Jing, W.: Research on the resource allocation of OFDMA relay network based on secrecy ratio. J. Electr. Inf. Technol. **36**(12), 2816–2821 (2014)
5. Zhang, H., Dong, Y., Cheng, J., et al.: Fronthauling for 5G LTE-U ultra dense cloud small cell networks. IEEE Wirel. Commun. **23**(6), 48–53 (2016)
6. Zhang, H., Liu, N., Chu, X., et al.: Network slicing based 5G and future mobile networks: mobility, resource management, and challenges. IEEE Commun. Mag. (2017)
7. Venturino, L., Prasad, N., Wang, X.: Coordinated scheduling and power allocation in downlink multicell OFDMA networks. IEEE Trans. Veh. Technol. **58**(6), 2835–2848 (2009)
8. Karakayali, M.K., Foschini, G.J., Valenzuela, R.A.: Network coordination for spectrally efficient communications in cellular systems. IEEE Wirel. Commun. **13**(4), 56–61 (2006)
9. Del Coso, A., Simoens, S.: Uplink rate region of a coordinated cellular network with distributed compression. In: 2008 IEEE International Symposium on Information Theory, pp. 2091–2095. IEEE (2008)

10. Jiang, C., Zhang, H., Ren, Y., et al.: Energy-efficient non-cooperative cognitive radio networks: micro, meso, and macro views. IEEE Commun. Mag. **52**(7), 14–20 (2014)
11. Shen, Y., Jiang, C., Quek, T.Q.S., et al.: Device-to-device cluster assisted downlink video sharing—a base station energy saving approach. In: 2014 IEEE Global Conference on Signal and Information Processing (GlobalSIP), pp. 108–112. IEEE (2014)
12. Liu, H., Zheng, W., Zhang, H., et al.: An iterative two-step algorithm for energy efficient resource allocation in multi-cell OFDMA networks. In: 2013 IEEE Wireless Communications and Networking Conference (WCNC), pp. 608–613. IEEE (2013)

A Survey on Big Data Analytics Technologies

Fei Su[1(✉)], Zhenya Wang[1], Shan Yang[1], Ke Li[1], Xin Lu[1], Yang Wu[1], and Yi Peng[2]

[1] China Unicom Network Technology Research Institute, Beijing, China
sufei@chinaunicom.cn
[2] National Satellite Meteorological Center, Beijing, China

Abstract. With the beginning of new era, data has grown rapidly in both the size and the variety. It becomes not only an important cornerstone of all walks of life, but also the national strategy. The big data collection, parsing, analysis, and applications are important issues to research. For different scenarios of big data applications, appropriate big data processing technologies are needed to complete the real-time and rapid data analysis. The objective of this paper is to analyze the typical big data analysis technologies, find out the characteristics and applicative scenarios, and then provide the reference for big data processing of all industries.

Keywords: Big data · Hadoop · Spark · NoSQL · Streaming · MPP database

1 Introduction

With the development of big data, a variety of data analysis technologies are arisen. These technologies are different from the traditional methods of data statistics and data mining. They have different characteristics and applicable scenarios. To research the characteristics of big data technologies is a key step to the deployment of big data strategy and data realization.

Traditional data warehouse architecture based on Oracle is no longer adapted to the current needs of big data analysis [1]. The open source data analysis architecture is the main stream. Currently, there are variety of big data analysis techniques [2]. Hadoop is an open-source software framework for distributed storage and distributed processing of very large data sets on computer clusters built from commodity hardware. All the modules in Hadoop are designed with a fundamental assumption that hardware failures are common and should be automatically handled by the framework. Spark is a fast and general engine for large-scale data processing. Its performance is better than Hadoop, because the calculation is processing in memory. Storm is a free and open source distributed real-time computation system. Storm makes it easy to reliably process unbounded streams of data, doing for real-time processing what Hadoop did for batch processing. Spark Streaming is an extension of the core Spark API that enables scalable, high-throughput, fault-tolerant stream processing of live data streams. Data can be ingested from many sources like Kafka, Flume, Twitter, ZeroMQ, Kinesis, or TCP sockets. Impala (incubating) is the open source, native analytic database for Apache Hadoop. HBase is an open-source, distributed, versioned, non-relational database

K. Long et al. (Eds.): 5GWN 2017, LNICST 211, pp. 359–370, 2018.
https://doi.org/10.1007/978-3-319-72823-0_34

modeled after Google's Bigtable: A Distributed Storage System for Structured Data by Chang et al. Just as Bigtable leverages the distributed data storage provided by the Google File System, Apache HBase provides Bigtable-like capabilities on top of Hadoop and HDFS.

How to effectively combine these big data techniques, and achieve the data's parsing, storage, and analysis for different industries is an important issue to research. The mainstream big data architecture usually adopts mixed style [3, 4]. Firstly, the HDFS [5, 6] is used to carry out the underlying storage. Secondly, the MR/SPARK is used to accomplish batch-processing. Finally, the resulting data set is stored in the traditional relational database, such as oracle. In this paper, we analyze the typical big data analysis technologies, find out the characteristics and applicative scenarios, and then provide the reference for big data processing of all industries.

2   Hadoop

Hadoop is an Apache open source framework written in java that allows distributed processing of large datasets across clusters of computers using simple programming models. As a result, we can easily write distributed programs which fully take advantage of the cluster power to do the computing and storage work without knowing the details of the lower-level of the distributed system. Compared with the other systems, Hadoop has several advantages [7, 8] such as higher reliability, higher extendibility, higher efficiency, higher fault-tolerance and lower cost, etc. (Fig. 1).

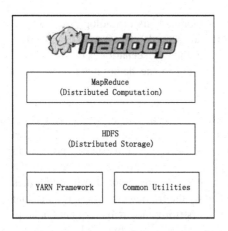

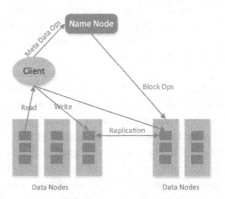

Fig. 1. Hadoop base framework   Fig. 2. HDFS architecture [9]

2.1   Hadoop Architecture

Hadoop framework mainly contains four modules:

- **MapReduce** is a YARN-based framework for parallel processing of large data sets in a reliable manner.

- **HDFS (Hadoop Distributed File System)** is a distributed file system that provides high-throughput access to application data.
- **Hadoop Common** contains Java libraries and utilities required by other Hadoop modules. These libraries include OS level abstractions and necessary files and scripts to start Hadoop.
- **YARN** is responsible for job scheduling and cluster resource management.

These four base modules provide base function of Hadoop system. We will focus on the HDFS and MapReduce in this section.

2.2   HDFS

As one of the top-level project in the Hadoop eco-system, HDFS is the fundamental of the distributed data storage system. It is based on the Google File System (GFS) and provides a distributed file system that is designed to run on large clusters of small computer machines in a reliable, fault-tolerant manner.

HDFS uses a master/slave architecture which is shown in Fig. 2. The master machine runs a NameNode software and is responsible for the management of the file system namespace and the regulation of the file access. The slave machines run a DataNodes software and perform read-write operation on the file systems according to the client requests, do block creation, deletion, and replication under the instructions of the NameNode. We should notice that there is no practical difference between master and slaver machines, they just run different software to perform different role in the HDFS system.

A file in an HDFS namespace is split into several blocks and those blocks are stored in a set of DataNodes. The NameNode determines the mapping of blocks to the DataNodes. The DataNodes takes care of read and write operation with the file system. They also take care of block creation, deletion and replication based on instruction given by NameNode (Fig. 3).

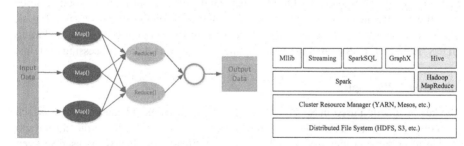

Fig. 3. Map and Reduce stage   **Fig. 4.** Typical Spark deployment plan

2.3   MapReduce

In 2004, Google proposed MapReduce as a parallel computation model in order to solve the calculation of the big data analysis problem. MapReduce module separates the parallel computation process into two stage: Map task and Reduce task [10]. Firstly, the set of data is collected and converts it into another set of data by map task. These data elements are broken down into key and value pairs. Secondly, the task reduction takes the output from a map as an input and combines those data tuples into a smaller set of tuples. Typically both the input and the output are stored in a file-system. The MapReduce framework takes care of scheduling tasks, monitoring them and re-executes the failed tasks.

By adopting MapReduce technique, it is much eases to scale data processing over multiple computing nodes: Decomposing a data processing application into mappers and reducers is normally a time-consuming work. However, once we write an application in the MapReduce form, scaling the application to run over hundreds, thousands, or even tens of thousands of machines in a cluster is merely a configuration change. This simple scalability is what has attracted many programmers to use the MapReduce model.

3 Spark

3.1 Spark Framework

Spark is an in-memory parallel computing framework which specialized in fast data analyzing on large-scale dataset. Thanks to its highly active open-source community, Spark contains several original libraries supporting structured data processing (SparkSQL), machine learning (MLlib), streaming (Spark Streaming) and graph-parallel computation (GraphX). It also supports various languages including Scala, Java, Python and R. Spark was first developed in UC Berkeley in 2009 and is currently hosted by Apache Software Foundation with over 1000 contributors worldwide.

As a data processing framework, Spark extends the MapReduce model to handle more complicated tasks, especially iterative computing and interactive analytics [11]. The former is commonly found in machine learning algorithms, and the latter is used in SQL queries on large datasets. On the other hand, Spark inherits those good features from the MapReduce model such as scalability and fault tolerance. As shown in Fig. 4, Spark is compatible with some core components of the Hadoop ecosystem including HDFS, Hive and YARN, making it one of the most universal data processing systems.

3.2 Spark Principles

The key abstraction used in Spark is called Resilient Distributed Dataset (RDD), which is a collection of partitioned data stored in memory across the nodes in the cluster and is able to be kept in memory for future reuse. A lineage mechanism is used to keep track of the data transformations to recovery from failure. In the typical cluster mode, a Spark application runs as the following procedures:

1. A SparkContext object is first created in the driver program, which acts as the controller of the entire application.

2. Next, the SparkContext contacts with the cluster resource manager, which assigns all the cores, memory and network IO required by the application.
3. Once connected, Spark acquires Executors on each worker node, which are collections of computation resources and the application code itself. Each application has a set of its own Executors.
4. Finally, the SparkContext sends different Tasks to each Executor to run the actual computation (Fig. 5).

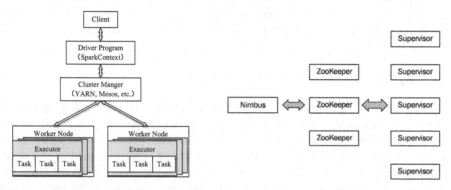

Fig. 5. Spark application running procedures   **Fig. 6.** Storm cluster architecture

The vanilla Spark supports more than 80 basic operators on RDDs, including map, filter, union, join, groupByKey, reduceByKey, etc. On top of RDD, a higher level data structure, DataFrame, is used in SparkSQL (and other modules as well) to deal with structured data processing. A DataFrame is similar to a table in a relational database, and can be created from either HDFS files or Hive tables. One can perform SQL queries directly on DataFrames, making it much easier analyzing data stored in an existing data platform. Likewise, Spark Streaming and MLlib also implement corresponding high-level APIs for real-time and machine learning applications.

3.3 Performance

According to an early research, native Spark runs 25× faster than Hadoop MapReduce on a Logistic Regression application. In another benchmark dealing with SQL queries, SparkSQL is generally competitive with Impala, an in-memory MPP database built on Hadoop [12]. Such result is remarkable considering Impala is written in C++ and is well-optimized for SQL queries, whereas Spark is a general data processing engine and runs in JVM. As for graph processing, Spark GraphX achieve a similar runtime performance compared with GraphLab and Giraph, and slightly better scaling performance than the latter two systems.

In general, Spark is a multi-functional data analyzing framework that excels in speed, scalability and reliability. It is compatible with Hadoop system and runs much faster than the MapReduce-based programs. Plus, Spark incorporates a series advanced APIs which significantly enhance the performance of big data applications such as streaming, SQL queries, machine learning and graph analysis.

4 Stream

Streaming data as a new form of large data more reflects the characteristics of high-speed and real-time processing. There are two ways to calculate large data: batch computing and stream computing. Streaming data is disordered and ineffective, so you can't store all data as in batch computing model. In the stream computing, streaming data is stored in memory for real-time computing. Existing streaming computing platforms are Storm, Spark streaming, Samza and so on, which are open-source distributed systems, with low latency, scalability and fault tolerance and many other advantages, allowing you to run the data stream code, tasks will be assigned to a series of fault-tolerant nodes on the parallel operation.

4.1 Storm

Apache Storm is a free and open source distributed real-time computation system for processing streams of data. Storm makes it easy to reliably process unbounded streams of data, doing for real-time processing what Hadoop did for batch processing. A stream is an unbounded sequence of tuples that is processed and created in parallel in a storm cluster. Every stream is given an id when declared. The work to process stream is delegated to different types of components that are each responsible for a simple specific processing task.

The input stream of a Storm cluster is handled by a component called a spout [13]. A spout is a source of streams in a topology. Generally spouts will read tuples from an external source and emit them into the topology. The spout passes the data to a component called a bolt, which transforms it in some way. Storm guarantees that every spout tuple will be fully processed by the topology. It does this by tracking the tree of tuples triggered by every spout tuple and determining when that tree of tuples has been successfully completed. Every topology has a "message timeout" associated with it. If Storm fails to detect that a spout tuple has been completed within that timeout, then it fails the tuple and replays it later.

A bolt either persists the data in some sort of storage, or passes it to some other bolt, which can do anything from filtering, functions, aggregations, joins, talking to databases, and more. Bolts can do simple stream transformations, while doing complex stream transformations often requires multiple steps and thus multiple bolts.

The logic for a real-time application is packaged into a Storm topology. A Storm topology is analogous to a MapReduce job. One key difference is that a MapReduce job eventually finishes, whereas a topology runs forever or until it is killed. A topology is a graph of spouts and bolts that are connected with stream groupings.

As Fig. 6 shows, in a Storm cluster [14], nodes are organized into a master node that runs continuously. There are two kind of nodes in a Storm cluster: master node and worker nodes. Master node run a daemon called Nimbus, which is responsible for distributing code around the cluster, assigning tasks to each worker node, and monitoring for failures. Worker nodes run a daemon called Supervisor, which executes a portion of a topology. A topology in Storm runs across many worker nodes on different machines. Since Storm keeps all cluster states either in Zookeeper or on local disk, the daemons are stateless and can fail or restart without affecting the health of the system.

The following are the features of storm [15]:

- Fast: Storm can process up to 1 million tuples per second per node.
- Horizontally scalable: being fast is a necessary feature to build a high volume/velocity data processing platform, but a single-node will have an upper limit on the number of events that it can process per second. Storm is linearly scalable. More nodes can be added to a Storm cluster to increase the processing capacity of applications.
- Fault tolerant: units of work are executed by worker processes in a Storm cluster. When a worker dies, Storm will restart that worker, and if the node on which the worker is running dies, Storm will restart that worker on some other node in the cluster.
- Guaranteed data processing: Storm provides strong guarantees that each message passed on to it to process will be processed at least once. In the event of failures, Storm will replay the lost tuples.
- Easy to operate: Storm is simple to deploy and manage. Once the cluster is deployed, it requires little maintenance.

4.2 Spark Streaming

Spark Streaming is an extension of the core Spark API that enables scalable, high-throughput, fault-tolerant stream processing of live data streams. Much like Spark is built on the concept of RDDs, Spark Streaming provides an abstraction called DStreams, which represents a continuous stream of data. Internally, each DStream is represented as a sequence of RDDs arriving at each time step. DStream can be created from various input sources, such as Flume [16], Kafka, HDFS, or by applying high-level operations on other DStreams.

Spark Streaming uses a "micro-batch" architecture, where the streaming computation is treated as a continuous series of batch computations on small batches of data. Spark Streaming receives data from various input sources and groups it into small batches. New batches are created at regular time intervals. At the beginning of each time interval a new batch is created. At the end of the time interval the batch is done growing. The size of the time intervals is determined by a parameter called the batch interval. The batch interval is typically between 500 ms and several seconds, as configured by the application developer. Each input batch forms an RDD, and is processed using Spark jobs to create other RDDs. The processed results are pushed out to external systems in batches. The high-level architecture is shown in Fig. 7.

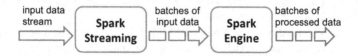

Fig. 7. Spark Streaming architecture

4.3   Samza

Apache Samza is a distributed stream processing framework. Samza processes streams, which should be composed of immutable messages of a similar type or category. A Samza job is code that performs a logical transformation on a set of input streams to append output messages to set of output streams. In order to scale the throughput of the stream processor, Samza chop streams and jobs up into smaller units of parallelism: partitions and tasks.

Each partition in the stream is a totally ordered sequence of messages. Each message in this sequence has an identifier called the offset, which is unique per partition. When a message is appended to a stream, it is appended to only one of the stream's partitions. The assignment of the message to its partition is done with a key chosen by the writer.

The task is the unit of parallelism of the job, just as the partition is to the stream. Each task consumes data from one partition for each of the job's input streams. A task processes messages from each of its input partitions sequentially, in the order of message offset. There is no defined ordering across partitions. This allows each task to operate independently. The YARN scheduler assigns each task to a machine, so the job as a whole can be distributed across many machines. The number of tasks in a job is determined by the number of input partitions.

As shown in Fig. 8 Samza is made up of three layers: a streaming layer, an execution layer, a processing layer. In streaming layer, it uses Apache Kafka for messaging. Samza can better leverage Kafka's unique architectural strengths. In execution layer, it uses Apache Hadoop YARN to provide fault tolerance, processor isolation, security, and resource management. In processing layer, Samaza API provide service. Both Samza's execution and streaming layer are pluggable, and allow developers to implement alternatives if they prefer.

Fig. 8. Samza architecture

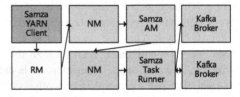

Fig. 9. Samza framework of yarn and kafka

Samza uses YARN and Kafka to provide a framework for stage-wise stream processing and partitioning. As shown in Fig. 9, everything put together, looks like this (different colors indicate different host machines).

The Samza client talks to the YARN RM when it wants to start a new Samza job. The YARN RM talks to a YARN NM to allocate space on the cluster for Samza's ApplicationMaster. Once the NM allocates space, it starts the Samza AM. After the Samza AM starts, it asks the YARN RM for one or more YARN containers to run SamzaContainers. Again, the RM works with NMs to allocate space for the containers. Once the space has been allocated, the NMs start the Samza containers.

The Samza client uses YARN to run a Samza job: YARN starts and supervises one or more SamzaContainers, and users processing code runs inside those containers. The input and output for the Samza StreamTasks come from Kafka brokers that are usually co-located on the same machines as the YARN NMs.

Samza's key features include:

- Managed state: Samza manages snapshotting and restoration of a stream processor's state. When the processor is restarted, Samza restores its state to a consistent snapshot. Samza can handle large amounts of state.
- Scalability: Samza is partitioned and distributed at every level. Kafka provides ordered, partitioned, repayable, fault-tolerant streams. YARN provides a distributed environment for Samza containers to run in.
- Fault tolerance: whenever a machine in the cluster fails, Samza works with YARN to transparently migrate your tasks to another machine.
- Durability: Samza uses Kafka to guarantee that messages are processed in the order they were written to a partition, and that no messages are ever lost.
- Processor isolation: Samza works with Apache YARN, which supports Hadoop's security model, and resource isolation through Linux CGroups (control groups).
- Pluggable: though Samza works out of the box with Kafka and YARN, Samza provides a pluggable API that lets users run Samza with other messaging systems and execution environments.

5 MPP Databases

Massive Parallel Processing (MPP) [17, 18] systems use share-nothing architecture with different computing modules coupling loosely. Unlike some other systems, MPP databases utilize a cluster of commercial x86 servers to achieve high performance, with a speed 10x or even 100x greater than traditional databases. Data are typically stored locally on each node and managed by a distributed file system. With a high compatibility with SQL, the ability to scale out and fault tolerance, MPP databases offer a cost efficient solution to big data technology.

Most MPP databases are commercial products, including Teradata, Vertica, Netezza, Amazon Redshift etc. Teradata targets high-end data warehouse and business decision-making system. However, with a rapid development of cloud computing and big data technology, the costly price of Teradata makes it less competitive today. Vertica is a column-based MPP database which offers high-speed, high-scalability and low-cost database technology. Netezza offers a warehouse solution, which combines storage, processing, database and analysis into one system. It is suitable for customers who intend to build high-level big data analysis with ready-to-use feature. As PB-level database, Amazon Redshift can easily coordinate with existing BI system. It utilizes columnar storage and data compression technology to enhance performance. Since Redshift is fully hosted at Amazon's cloud end, storage and computing resources can be assigned dynamically. Greenplum is a distributed relational database focused on

OLAP data engine. It consists of several independent small databases. Greenplum has been accepted as an open-source project by Apache Software Foundation and source code is currently hosed on GitHub.

6 NoSQL

NoSQL means "Not Only SQL", which generally refers to all non-relational databases. It is developed to handle large-scale structured, semi-structured and non-structured data brought by big data technology. NoSQL databases have several advantages such as open-source, high scalability, high concurrency, high performance, weak-transactional, and agility of development. In general, NoSQL databases can be categorized into four types, which are Key-Value type, Document-Oriented type, Column-Family Type and Graph type.

6.1 Key-Value

A Key-Value database is like a hash table used in many programming languages. One specific key is combined with one pointer, which points to some certain data. Thus, the key can be used to quickly add, query or delete data. Since data are accessed by a set of keys, such systems are able to achieve a high performance and high scalability. Redis, Memcached and other memory-based databases are normally used to in scenarios where high-speed cache on "hot data" is needed.

6.2 Document-Oriented

Document-oriented database store data as documents. Each document contains a data unit, which is a series of data collections. Each data unit contains a title and a corresponding value, which is either simple data type or complex data type. The minimum storage unit is a document. The document attribute stored in the same table can be diffident. Data can be stored as XML, JSON and JSONB, etc. MongoDB and CouchDB are the common document-oriented databases.

6.3 Column-Family

Columnar storage databases store data in column families. Frequently queried data are stored together in the same column family to handle massive data distributed on different machines. Column-Family databases typically store structured and semi-structured data. With aggressive compression technology, queries on certain columns have a great advantages on system IO. Cassandra, Hbase are the two major Column-Family databases and are used in social media websites and blogs which obtain a high volume of data in key-value type.

6.4 Graph-Oriented

Unlike other row-oriented or SQL-based databases, Graph-Oriented databases apply a more agile graph model and are able to scale out to multiple servers [19, 20]. Such systems store data in graph where entities are considered as vertices, and the relations between entities are considered as edges [21–23]. The prevalent Graph-Oriented database is Neo4J [24, 25], which is extremely suitable for strong-relationship data such as recommendation engines.

7 Conclusion

This paper studies the typical big data analysis techniques, such as Hadoop, Spark, Storm, MPP database, and NoSQL. These technologies all have their own application scenarios. They are for batch processing, fast memory calculations, real-time computing, fast OLAP, and unstructured data, respectively. The adoption of these technologies depend on different scenarios. We have put forth some of the challenges in big data processing techniques and the areas where a lot of work can be done in future. A lot of issues concerning data parsing and data sharing still remain challenging areas of research in big data.

References

1. Jie, Z., Yao, X., Han, G.J.: A survey of recent technologies and challenges in big data utilizations. In: International Conference on Information and Communication Technology Convergence, pp. 497–499 (2015)
2. Menon, S.P., Hegde, N.P.: A survey of tools and applications in big data. In: 9th IEEE International Conference on Intelligent Systems and Control, pp. 1–7 (2015)
3. Senbalci, C., Altuntas, S., Bozkus, Z.: Big data platform development with a domain specific language for telecom industries. In: High Capacity Optical Networks and Emerging/Enabling Technologies, pp. 116–120 (2013)
4. Cho, S.Y.: Fast memory and storage architectures for the big data era. In: IEEE Asian Solid-State Circuits Conference, pp. 1–4 (2015)
5. Tseng, J.-C., Tseng, H.C., Liu, C.W.: A successful application of big data storage techniques implemented to criminal investigation for telecom. In: 2013 15th Asia-Pacific Network Operations and Management Symposium, pp. 25–27 (2013)
6. Zhang, X.X., Xu, F.: Survey of research on big data storage. In: International Symposium on Distributed Computing and Applications to Business, Engineering & Science (DCABES), pp. 76–80 (2013)
7. Yan, X., Zhang, D.: Big data research. Comput. Technol. Dev., 1–5 (2013)
8. Meng, X., Ci, X.: Big data management: concepts, technology and challenges. J. Comput. Res. Dev. 50(1), 146–169 (2013)
9. Tan, X., Wang, H.: Big data analytics: competition and coexistence of RDBMS and MapReduce. J. Softw. 23(1), 32–45 (2012)
10. Arun, M., Vinod, K.V.: Apache Hadoop YARN–Moving Beyond MapReduce and Batch Processing with Apache Hadoop 2. Addison-Wesley Professional, Reading (2014)
11. Zaharia, M., Chowdhury, M., Franklin, M.J., Shenker, S., Stoica, I.: Spark: cluster computing with working sets. In: Usenix Conference on Hot Topics in Cloud Computing, vol. 15, p. 10. USENIX Association (2010)

12. Armbrust, M., Xin, R.S., Lian, C., Huai, Y., Liu, D., Bradley, J.K., Meng, X., Kaftan, T., Franklin, M.J., Ghodsi, A., Zaharia, M.: Spark SQL: relational data processing in spark. In: ACM SIGMOD International Conference on Management of Data, pp. 1383–1394. ACM (2015)
13. Leibiusky, J., Eisbruch, G., Simonassi, D.: Getting Started with Storm, pp. 29–37, 39–42. O'Reilly Media, Sebastopol (2012)
14. Taylor Goetz, P., O'Neill, B.: Storm blueprints: patterns for distributed real-time computation, pp. 36–37 (2014)
15. Jain, A., Nalya, A.: Learning Storm, pp. 8–9. Packt Publishing, Birmingham (2014)
16. Karau, H., Konwinski, A., Wendell, P., Zaharia, M.: Learning Spark, pp. 182–211. O'Reilly Media, Sebastopol (2015)
17. Babu, S., Herodotou, H.: Massively parallel databases and MapReduce systems. Found. Trends Databases **5**(1), 1–104 (2012)
18. Cheng, B., Guan, X., Wu, H.: A hypergraph based task scheduling strategy for massive parallel spatial data processing on master-slave platforms. In: 23rd International Conference on Geoinformatics, pp. 1–5 (2015)
19. Xu, L., Luan, Y., Cheng, X., Cao, X., Chao, K., Gao, J., Jia, Y., Wang, S.: WCDMA data based LTE site selection scheme in LTE deployment. In: International Conference on Signal and Information Processing, Networking and Computers, Beijing, pp. 249–260. CRC Press Taylor & Francis Group (2015)
20. Xu, L., Cheng, X., Liu, Y., Chen, W., Luan, Y., Chao, K., Yuan, M., Xu, B.: Mobility load balancing aware radio resource allocation scheme for LTE-advanced cellular networks. In: IEEE International Conference on Communication Technology, Hangzhou, pp. 806–812. IEEE Press (2015)
21. Xu, L., Chen, Y., Chai, K.K., Luan, Y., Liu, D.: Cooperative mobility load balancing in relay cellular networks. In: IEEE International Conference on Communication in China, Xi'an, pp. 141–146. IEEE Press (2013)
22. Cao, Y., Sun, Z., Wang, N., Riaz, M., Cruickshank, H., Liu, X.: Geographic-based spray-and-relay (GSaR): an efficient routing scheme for DTNs. IEEE Trans. Veh. Technol. **64**(4), 1548–1564 (2015)
23. Xu, L., Luan, Y., Cheng, X., Xing, H., Liu, Y., Jiang, X., Chen, W., Chao, K.: Self-optimised joint traffic offloading in heterogeneous cellular networks. In: IEEE International Symposium on Communications and Information Technologies, Qingdao, pp. 263–267. IEEE Press (2016)
24. Xu, L., Chen, Y., Gao, Y., Cuthbert, L.: A self-optimizing load balancing scheme for fixed relay cellular networks. In: IET International Conference on Communication Technology and Application, Beijing, pp. 306–311. IET Press (2011)
25. Cao, Y., Wang, N., Sun, Z., Cruickshank, H.: A reliable and efficient encounter-based routing framework for delay/disruption tolerant networks. IEEE Sens. J. **15**(7), 4004–4018 (2015)

Classification of Medical Consultation Text Using Mobile Agent System Based on Naïve Bayes Classifier

Xingyu Chen[1,4(✉)], Guangping Zeng[1,4], Qingchuan Zhang[2,4],
Liu Chen[1,4], and Zhuolin Wang[3]

[1] School of Computer and Communication Engineering,
University of Science and Technology Beijing, Beijing, China
cscserer@sina.com, zgp@ustb.edu.cn, chenliueve@163.com
[2] School of Computer and Information Engineering,
Beijing Technology and Business University, Beijing, China
zqc1982@126.com
[3] School of Humanities and Social Science,
University of Science and Technology Beijing, Beijing, China
zhuolinwang@yeah.net
[4] Beijing Key Laboratory of Knowledge Engineering for Materials Science,
Beijing, China

Abstract. Aiming at the interaction model of the Internet medical website, a classifier of medical text data based on Naive Bayes was proposed and realized in this paper. Once a user posed questions on the websites, this classifier would instantly classify the user's questions and enable accurate question delivery. Furthermore, a data service platform was realized by taking advantages of mobile agent technology. With the service platform, companies could avoid considering the security of data when conducting data analysis. Finally, experiments were conducted according to the process of data analysis in the service platform. The experimental results showed: the proposed service platform was feasible, and a medical consultation text classifier with high accuracy was realized to improve user experience of medical websites.

Keywords: Naive Bayes · Medical big data · Mobile agent
Artificial intelligence

1 Introduction

With the rapid development of the internet and the great enhancement of people's awareness of health, the internet is becoming an important channel to acquire medical information. By posing questions on medical websites, persons can get answers by professional doctors. After users having putting forward their questions, there would be doctors online to browse those questions. They will answer questions belonging to their special field and give their suggestions. Because most medical websites adopt a Q&A (Question and Answer) system with blackboard mechanism, the time effectiveness is poor. Users have to wait for doctors to answer them, while doctors have to spend time

© ICST Institute for Computer Sciences, Social Informatics and Telecommunications Engineering 2018
K. Long et al. (Eds.): 5GWN 2017, LNICST 211, pp. 371–384, 2018.
https://doi.org/10.1007/978-3-319-72823-0_35

browsing questions and deciding which and what to answer. In order to improve the experience for both users and doctors and increase the effectiveness of the system, data mining methods based on medical big data can be taken to analyze question texts [1]. With these methods, questions would be pushed prior to the doctors who are most likely to answer. Besides, users would be offered with reference materials before getting replied.

Medical big data plays an important role in the field of big data [2]. With the popularity of the mobile medical, internet medical, automatic analysis detectors, wearable devices, etc., all parties including patients, doctors, companies and the environments are becoming direct creators of data, generating mass medical data every day.

Compared with big data of other fields, medical big data have almost covered all the personal information of citizens, from the most private information of body and disease to the information of personal property, accommodation, medical insurance and so on. Therefore, when using medical big data, technical personnel should not only consider about security requirements from companies, hospitals and other providers, but also consider about the privacy of the data. Generally, there are two ways of conducting big data analysis: the first is that the companies which hold data provide technical supporters with data to carry out data analysis; the second is that the technical supporters appoint personnel to companies. In the first way, technical supporters have to insure the data security. In the second way, the results of data analysis are hard for promotion to create greater value. Because of the disadvantages of the ways mentioned above, what way should be taken to conduct data analysis has become a great concern of the companies and the academia. A reasonable way can not only reduce the cost of the enterprise, but also make the new technology produce more value.

In this paper, researchers have realized a text classifier based on Naive Bayes model with higher accuracy aiming at the process of the Q&A [3–5]. The classifier can help to quickly classify problem descriptions to different departments and to pre-diagnose the problems. Furthermore, the authors have designed a data analysis process based on mobile agent technology where a mobile agent data service platform has been realized [6, 7]. This service platform can make use of the mobility and self-determination characteristics of mobile agent. With this platform, the problems concerning the data security would be solved to some degree. What's more, the new data analysis technology would be used by more companies and clients.

2 Paper Preparation

2.1 Naïve Bayes

Naive Bayes classifier model is a kind of simple probability classifier applied in the independence assumption Bayes theorem. It assumes that each features are not related, depends on accurate natural probability models and enable to get very good classification effect in supervised learning sample sets. The classification process shows as follows:

(1) Using a dimensional feature vector $X = \{x_1, x_2, \cdots, x_n\}$ to represent each data sample, which separately describes n features $A_1, A_2, \cdots, A_n$ of samples.

(2) Assuming there are m classes $C_1, C_2, \cdots, C_n$. Given an unknown data sample X, the classification would predict that X belongs to the class with the Maximum a Posteriori (MAP) under the condition X. In other words, Naive Bayes classification would allocate the unknown sample X to class $C_i (1 \le i \le m)$, if and only if

$$P(C_i|X) > P(C_j|X), \; j = 1, 2, \cdots, m, \; j \ne i \tag{1}$$

Class C_i which would enable the Maximum a Posteriori $P(C_i|X)$ is called the Maximum a Posteriori Assumption. According to Bayes' theorem,

$$P(C_i|X) = \frac{P(X|C_i)P(C_i)}{P(X)} \tag{2}$$

(3) Because $P(X)$ is invariant, we just need to ensure the maximum $P(X|C_i)P(C_i)$. If the prior probability of class C_i is unknown, we generally assume that these classes are equiprobable, which is $P(C_1) = P(C_2) = \cdots = P(C_m)$. Therefore, the problem is converted to maximize $P(X|C_i)$. Otherwise, the prior probability of class C_i would be calculated by $P(C_i) = s_i/S$, where s_i is the number of training samples in class C_i while S is the total number of training samples.

(4) Given data sets with many features, we might cost too much to calculate $P(X|C_i)$. In order to lower the cost, we could assume that each features of samples are mutually of conditional independence, which means there is no dependency among each features, then

$$P(X|C_i) = \prod_{k=1}^{n} P(x_k|C_i) \tag{3}$$

The probability $P(X|C_i)$ can be estimated by training samples.

(5) This means that under the above independence assumptions, the conditional distribution over the class variable C is

$$P(C_i|X) = P(X|C_i)P(C_i) = P(C_i) \prod_{k=1}^{n} P(x_k|C_i) \tag{4}$$

And a Bayes classifier, is the function that assigns a class label $\hat{y} = C_i$ for some i as follow

$$\hat{y} = \underset{i \in \{1,\dots,m\}}{\operatorname{argmax}} P(C_i) \prod_{k=1}^{n} P(x_k|C_i) = \underset{y}{\operatorname{argmax}} P(y) \prod_{k=1}^{n} P(x_k|y) \tag{5}$$

A class's prior may be calculated by assuming equiprobable classes, or by calculating an estimate for the class probability from the training set. To estimate the parameters for a feature's distribution, one must assume a distribution or generate nonparametric models for the features from the training set [5]. The assumptions on distributions of features are called the event model of the Naive Bayes classifier.

2.2   Multinomial Event Model

With a multinomial event model [8], the distribution is parameterized by vectors multinomial $p_y = \{p_{y_1}, p_{y_2}, \cdots, p_{y_n}\}$ for each class y, where n is the number of features (in text classification, the size of the vocabulary) and p_{y_i} is the probability $P(x_i|y)$ of feature i appearing in a sample belonging to class y.

The parameters p_y is estimated by a smoothed version of maximum likelihood, i.e. relative frequency counting:

$$\hat{p}_{y_i} = \frac{f_{y_i} + \alpha}{f_y + n\alpha} \tag{6}$$

Where f_{y_i} is the eigenvalue of x_i, and f_y is the total count of all eigenvalue for class y.

The smoothing priors $\alpha \geq 0$ accounts for features not present in the learning samples and prevents zero probabilities in further computations.

2.3   TF-IDF

TF-IDF (Term Frequency–Inverse Document Frequency) is a numerical statistic that is intended to reflect how important a word is to a document in a collection or corpus [9]. It is often used as a weighting factor in information retrieval and text mining. The TF-IDF value increases proportionally to the number of times that a word appears in the document, but is offset by the frequency of the word in the corpus, which helps to adjust for the fact that some words appear more frequently in general.

Term Frequency is the number of times that a term w occurs in a document d. If we donate the number of times by $count(w, d)$ and the total number of word occurs in d by $size(d)$, then

$$TF(w, d) = \frac{count(w, d)}{size(d)} \tag{7}$$

The inverse document frequency is a measure of how much information the word provides, that is, whether the term is common or rare across all documents.

$$IDF(w) = log(\frac{n}{docs(w, D) + 1}) \tag{8}$$

$docs(w, D)$ is the count of documents that contain the word w. If the term is not in the corpus, this will lead to a division-by-zero. It is therefore common to adjust the denominator to $docs(w, D) + 1$.

Then $TFIDF(w, d)$ is calculated as

$$TFIDF(w, d) = TF(w, d) * IDF(w) \tag{9}$$

3 A Medical Consultation Text Classifier Based on Naive Bayes

With the rapid development on the Internet and the great enhancement on health awareness, using fence netting is becoming an important way to acquire medical information. People can put forward questions on medical websites and get answered by professional doctors. Their questions are generally posed as describing a series of symptoms to get disease diagnosed or seeking for notes and directions. For example,

(1) The cold is very afflictive wow! Rhinitis how should do?
(2) Darling 14 months, cold, have a fever, snorty, sleep to still be met shy, whats do not eat, how to do?

Those questions would be checked and answered by professional doctors sooner or later.

Through training analysis on the history Q&A data of medical websites, we have developed a classification method on medical consultation text – a smart consulting and diagnosing classifier. Once a user has submitted a question, this applied classifier would immediately deduce what possible disease the user wants to consult and which department he should turn to. That's to say, this classifier can not only quickly provide users with resources of related diseases, but also accurately recommend questions to experts in related fields.

3.1 Data Analysis

The hierarchical structure diagram of original data is shown as Fig. 1.

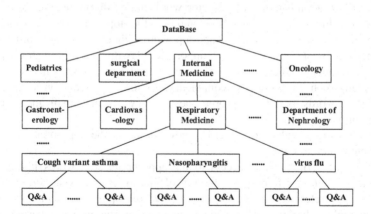

Fig. 1. The first layer is the total database. Each node of the second layer represents a comprehensive department. Each node of the third layer represents a specific department. Each node of the fourth floor represents a specific disease. Each node of the fifth floor represents a specific set of (Q&A).

According to requirements, we haven't carried out data analysis on comprehensive departments. It means that the nodes of the second layer have been excluded, and the nodes of specific departments have directly connected to the root node.

Classifying users' questions can be separated into two steps. The first step is to classify the departments corresponding to the questions. The second step is to classify the diseases under the charge of the departments. In this way, the training of the first-step classifier needs all the Q&A data, while the training of the second-step classifier just needs the Q&A data of a specific department. Therefore, the data sets used by the second-step classifier are the subsets of the first-step classifier. We have taken a data set of a specific department as the sample data. By analyzing the data set, we have implemented the function module which can figure out and generate classifier.

3.2   Data Pre-processing

In order to develop a dependable classifier, we have conducted data pre-processing during which we have acquired the terminology library and set the stop words library. Then we have conducted Chinese word segmentation and feature abstraction of text keywords. The terminology library refers to all the words and terms related to the medical field, which are the basic medical knowledge, including names of diseases, symptoms, body parts, medicines, and so on.

Setting up the terminology library makes contributions to better conducting Chinese word segmentation. Nouns of this part can be obtained from websites such as Medical Encyclopedia and Baidu Encyclopedia. Having considering that all the data of hospital departments are needed to design the processes of training classifiers, we have used web-crawler to access all the names of symptoms and diseases.

Setting up the appropriate stop words library can improve the accuracy of classifier. The specific operation is to identify the stop words library during feature abstraction of text keywords. In this way, the words belonging to the stop words library would not be included in the list of keywords. The stop words library contains words of high occurrence frequencies but of no prior supports for classification. Through sample data analysis, we conclude that some words with special parts of speech are useless in classification, such as pronouns, conjunctions, idioms, punctuation marks. If we identify these words as the stop words, the accuracy of our classification would be greatly improved.

The following pseudo-code describes how to access the appropriate stop words library before data training.

The algorithm of dynamic access to the appropriate stop words library. Input: $D = \{d_1, d_2, \cdots, d_n\}$, referring to the set of question text data; $stopProperty = \{p_1, p_2, \cdots, p_k\}$, referring to the set of parts of speech of stop words; $Dictionary$, referring to the terminology library used in Chinese word segmentation. Output: $stopWords = \{w_1, w_2, \cdots, w_m\}$, referring to the stop words library applied to D.

```
begin
  D = readTrainData()
  stopProperty = readStopProperty()
  Tool.load(Dictionary)
  stopWords = emptyList()
  wordPropertyListD = Tool.cut(D)
  foreach doc in wordPropertyListD
    foreach (word, prop) in doc
      if prop in stopProperty then
        stopWords.append(word)
  return stopWords
end
```

3.3   The Training Process of the Medical Consultation Text Classifier

The training algorithm process of the classifier based on Naive Bayes is as follows:

(1) Read out the Q&A data from database according to the classification.
(2) Upload the terminology library and the stop words library;
(3) Carry out word segmentation to all the question data. Because Q&A data are all in Chinese, Chinese word segmentation is needed;
(4) Calculate the TF-IDF eigenvector of the training data, and use an eigenvector to represent a question;
(5) Divide data into training data sets and testing data sets;
(6) Use multinomial Naive Bayes classifier model to get data training, and then get a multinomial Naive Bayes classifier based on TF-IDF;
(7) Use testing sets to test the accessed classifier.

This algorithm is described as the following pseudo-code:

The training algorithm of the classifier based on Naive Bayes. Input: $D = \{(d_1, t_1), (d_2, t_2), \cdots, (d_n, t_n)\}$, referring to the set of question text data with class identifiers; $stopWords = \{w_1, w_2, \cdots, w_m\}$, referring to the stop words library; $Dictionary$, referring to the terminology library used in Chinese word segmentation. Output: CLF, referring to the classifier; precision, referring to the accuracy of its tests.

```
begin
  D = readData ()
  stopWords = readStopWords()
  Tool.load(Dictionary)
  docs = Tool. chineseSplit(D)
  vec = vectorizer(docs, stopWords)
  (dataTrain, dataTest) = dataDivide(vec)
  CLF = MultinomialNB(dataTrain)
  precision = Test(CLF, dataTest)
  return CLF, precision
end
```

4 The Design of Medical Big Data Service Platform Based on Agent

With the application of mobile agent technology, the design of big data service platforms can better solve the security and privacy problems of data. A mobile agent is a program substituting for people or other program to perform certain tasks. It can move from a mobile agent environment (MAE) to another in the complex and heterogeneous network system. It can choose when and where to move to search for appropriate resources. It can be suspended according to requirements, and then restart or continue to execute. It also can take the advantage of being in the same host as the resources – processing or using these resources nearby, accomplishing specific tasks and returning results and messages in the end.

Mobility and autonomy are the two important characteristics of mobile agent. These two characteristics can be used to design a new solution which makes efficient use of distributed resources and the network.

A mobile agent system is made up of mobile agent and mobile agent service environment (the mobile agent platform). A common agent includes the security service module, environment interaction module, function library, internal state set, the routing policy, constraint condition and the task solving module, and these structures are mutually related. Generally, a mobile agent carries tasks, while the task solving module finally executes these tasks. During solving process, the task solving module should satisfy the constraint condition assigned by the builder.

4.1 The System Structure of the Medical Big Data Service Platform

The service platform in this paper is designed based on traditional mobile agent platform, and its system structure is shown as the following Fig. 2.

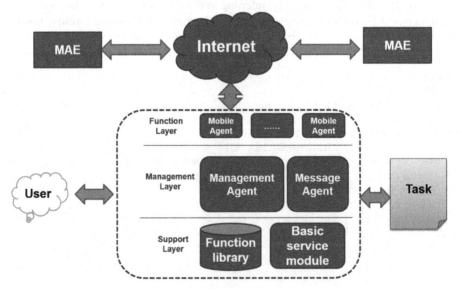

Fig. 2. The system structure of an agent platform is mainly made up of the following parts: message agent, management agent, task agent, function library and basic service module.

Message agent: in charge of receiving and sending messages between the platform and the outside, including: ① interacting with clients; ② receiving and sending messages of other agent platforms and task agent. The massage agent is only responsible for the interaction with the outside, while the management agent is responsible for understanding and processing messages.

Management agent: in charge of decision-making of the platform, including: ① setting up task agent by visiting function library; ② scheduling task agent, including executing and dispatching; ③ understanding and processing mutual information of message agent; ④ informing message agent to send messages or task agent to the outside.

Task agent: in charge of conducting specific tasks.

Function library: in charge of ① forming function modules; ② storing achievable and specific functions of task agent for management agent to schedule. The management agent can combine several function modules as a task solving module of the task agent.

Basic service module: in charge of providing necessary and basic service including directory services and security services.

The system structure of Client's agent platform and the data service platform are basically the same, but their difference lies in whether the function libraries of master station provide more function or not.

4.2   The Working Process of the Medical Big Data Service Platform

The working process is shown as the following Fig. 3.

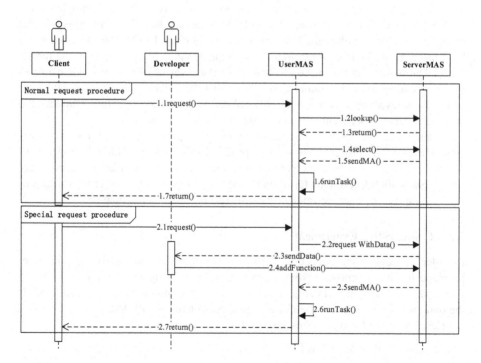

Fig. 3. Sequence diagram of working process on the medical big data service platform.

When Client need to take data analysis, he can conduct normal request procedure: Choose an existing function module of the service platform via his agent platform. The service platform only needs to put this function module into a task agent and then remove the task agent to the client's mobile agent platform. At last, practical data analysis and work would be accomplished.

If there is no suitable function module in the service platform, or if the client asks for special designing, technical personnel would write new function models according to the requirements of the client, as long as sample data and knowledge of the problem domain are given.

After accomplishing task solving, the task agent would return to service platform with results or execute operations such as instant death. Operations are determined by customer requirements and the specific situation.

5   The Experiment

5.1   Experimental Design

During the experiment, two computers with Linux system have been used to conduct the experiment. Consult texts provided by a large-scale Chinese medical consultation website have been taken as experimental examples. According to the provided data, the amount of texts reached 64060, related to 44 departments and 4801 kinds of diseases. Among them, 3950 kinds of diseases of 42 departments have texts under the catalogue. The 1553 texts of respiratory medicine department have been taken as sample data.

The classification experiment of sample data was conducted in a PC applied with mobile agent. With a multinomial Naive Bayes classifier based on TF-IDF, the conductors have taken the 1553 texts of respiratory medicine department as the data of the tuning model. During the experiment, conductors adopted the way of 10-fold cross-validation to get the accuracy of classification. Considering that the order of the data may affect the result of the classification and that the cross-validation on data segmentation is random, the average value of experiments have been used as the final result.

Sample data were used for parameter tuning of the generative process of the classification model. This process would be encapsulated into a task agent after the experiment and parameter tuning. Then, another platform turned to the service platform for the task agent, used 64060 Q&A texts for training and tested them by 10-fold cross-validation. With the above, the average value of experiments represented the final result.

5.2   Comparative Experiment

In order to validate the dialectical ability of the algorithm we used in the data set provided by the enterprise, several mature classification algorithms were selected to participate in testing experiments in this section. Using the classification results of all the data, we have compares the classification performances [10–14].

Here listed are the algorithms involved in the experiment:

(1) Decision Tree Algorithm [15]
(2) Random Forest Algorithm [16]

(3) k-Nearest Neighbor (KNN) [17]
(4) Support Vector Machine (SVM) [18]
(5) Naive Bayes with Multinomial event model using TF feature (MultinomialNB_TF)
(6) Naive Bayes with Bernoulli event model using TF-IDF feature (BernoulliNB)
(7) Naive Bayes with Multinomial event model using TF-IDF feature (MultinomialNB_TFIDF)

KNN algorithm has a key parameter k value need to be selected. The k value is the empirical parameter, which indicates the number of the selected neighbours. The selection of its value has a significant effect on the classification performance. In the experiment, the optimal value of k is not determined. We conducted the experiment using 1 to 20 as the k value, finding that with the k value increasing, the classification performance decrease. So we choose 1 as the k value.

During the whole experiment, the author used the same Chinese word segmentation tools, terminology library and stop word library.

5.3   The Classification Result

We have conducted 10-fold cross-validation many times on the sample data, expecting to get the comparatively stable process of generating the classifier. The results of the 5 times classification of respiration medicine department are shown as the following Table 1.

Table 1. The results of the 5 times classification of respiration medicine department

	1	2	3	4	5	6	7	8	9	10	Mean
1	86.5	82.7	86.5	83.2	88.4	88.4	88.4	87.7	89.0	87.1	86.8
2	87.8	87.8	81.4	85.2	87.1	89.0	86.5	87.7	85.8	87.7	86.6
3	89.1	89.1	87.2	86.5	85.8	90.3	84.5	87.1	86.5	90.3	87.6
4	90.4	88.5	87.8	82.6	84.5	83.9	89.7	89.7	89.0	88.4	87.5
5	88.5	82.1	86.5	85.8	87.1	84.5	90.3	85.2	87.7	84.5	86.2

Final result: 86.9%.

The classification results of all the data are shown as the following Table 2.

Table 2. The classification results of all the data

	1	2	3	4	5	6	7	8	9	10	Mean
1	86.4	86.0	85.0	86.2	85.8	85.2	86.2	85.4	86.0	85.6	85.8
2	86.0	85.7	86.8	85.8	85.5	86.0	85.2	86.2	85.3	86.0	85.9
3	85.5	85.6	86.3	85.9	85.8	85.7	86.6	85.9	86.2	85.2	85.9
4	86.2	85.2	85.8	86.2	85.4	85.7	84.9	86.0	86.3	85.9	85.8
5	85.5	85.5	85.4	86.1	86.3	85.5	85.5	85.5	86.5	85.3	85.7

Final result: 85.8%.

The results of pre-diagnosing diseases under each department are shown as the following Fig. 4.

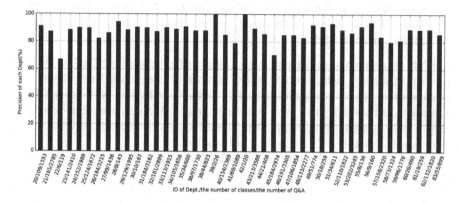

Fig. 4. The results of pre-diagnosing diseases under each department.

The experimental results of the comparative test are shown as following Fig. 5.

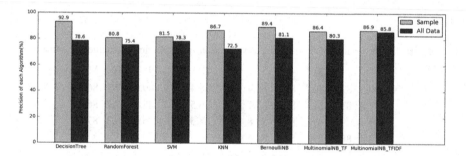

Fig. 5. The experimental results of the comparative test.

5.4 Experiment Analysis

The experiments above were carried out according to the data analysis process of the companies in the service platform. The results of the experiment can prove that the mobile agent data service platform proposed and implemented in this paper is feasible.

First of all, the data in Table 1 show that we have a classifier with the accuracy at 86.9% when experimenting with data from the Department of Respiratory Medicine. The data in Table 2 show that we can get a classifier with the accuracy at 85.8% for all data. These number means when the user publishes a new medical consultation question, the system will recommend the text to the doctors. There are average seventeen recommendations which are successful in twenty, other three recommendations need to be manually marked and re-pushed. And there are average fifteen people in twenty will get the right information as soon as possible, other five will get help after the question is reposted. And eventually they will get the guidance of doctors.

Secondly, by using the method of classifier generation for text classification in each department, the average classification accuracy is 87.7%.

At the last, through the comparison experiment, we can figure out that the Naive Bayesian algorithm using TF-IFD characteristic polynomial in this paper has good accuracy in the general data set. But through the comparison of the sample data, the accuracy rate of Decision Tree is as high as 92.9%, which indicates that Decision Tree is more accurate than Naive Bayes algorithm in pre-diagnosing disease under specified department. In order to confirm the conclusion, this paper uses Decision Tree to classify diseases in all departments. Result shows the average accuracy rate of Decision Tree algorithm is 93.1%. With the conclusion, those two algorithms can be combined to pre-diagnosing disease to get better performances.

6 Conclusion

The research of this paper is focused on the current research hotspot – medical big data. First of all, for the purpose of optimizing the user experience on the interaction process of this kind of websites, researchers have made deep understanding on a famous large-scale medical consultation website, and have conducted data analysis with the historical data. Secondly, with the analysis results, a classifier of medical text data based on Naive Bayes was proposed and realized to find out valuable medical logic knowledge. In addition, in order to meet the requirement for data confidentiality when doing outsourcing data analysis and to maximize the values of technology or models from data analysis, this paper has carried on the discussion on the issue. Finally, a prototype systems of data analysis service platform has been designed and realized using mobile agent technology based on Naive Bayes medical text classifier.

Through experiment and analysis, we have validated that the classifier based on the Naive Bayes can realize better classification of medical consultation texts and stability compared with other algorithms. Moreover, Decision Tree can better pre-diagnose the questions. The two algorithms can be combined to pre-diagnosing disease to get better performances in the reality.

Acknowledgements. Our work was supported by National High-tech R&D Program (863 Program No. 2015AA015403).

References

1. Russel, S.J., Norvig, P.: Artificial Intelligence - A Modern Approach. Prentice Hall, Upper Saddle River (2003)
2. Jee, K., Kim, G.H.: Potentiality of big data in the medical sector: focus on how to reshape the healthcare system. Healthc. Inf. Res. **19**(2), 79–85 (2013)
3. Zhang, H.: The optimality of Naive Bayes. In: Seventeenth International Florida Artificial Intelligence Research Society Conference, Miami Beach, Florida, USA (2005)

4. Metsis, V., Androutsopoulos, I., Paliouras, G.: Spam filtering with Naive Bayes - which Naive Bayes? In: CEAS 2006 - The Third Conference on Email and Anti-Spam, Mountain View, California, USA, 27–28 July 2006
5. John, G.H., Langley, P.: Estimating continuous distributions in Bayesian classifiers, pp. 338–345 (2013)
6. Essa, Y.M., Attiya, G., El-Sayed, A.: New framework for improving big data analysis using mobile agent. Int. J. Adv. Comput. Sci. Appl. **5**(3), 25–32 (2014)
7. Gray, R.S., Cybenko, G.: Agent TCL: a flexible and secure mobile-agent system. In: Proceedings of the 1996 TCL/TK Workshop, pp. 9–23 (1999)
8. Jin, X., Zhou, W., Bie, R.: Multinomial event naive Bayesian modeling for SAGE data classification. Comput. Stat. **22**(1), 133–143 (2007)
9. Robertson, S.: Understanding inverse document frequency: on theoretical arguments for IDF. J. Doc. **60**(5), 503–520 (2004)
10. Baker, L.D., McCallum, A.K.: Distributional clustering of words for text classification. In: International ACM SIGIR Conference on Research and Development in Information Retrieval, pp. 96–103 (2003)
11. Rogati, M., Yang, Y.: High-performing feature selection for text classification (2003)
12. Tong, S., Koller, D.: Support vector machine active learning with applications to text classification. J. Mach. Learn. Res. **2**(1), 45–66 (2002)
13. McCallum, A., Nigam, K.: A comparison of event models for Naive Bayes text classification. In: AAAI 1998 Workshop on Learning for Text Categorization, vol. 62(2), pp. 41–48 (2001)
14. Nigam, K.: Using maximum entropy for text classification. In: IJCAI 1999 Workshop on Machine Learning for Information Filtering, pp. 61–67 (1999)
15. Saad, M.K., Ashour, W.: Arabic text classification using decision trees. In: International Workshop on Computer Science and Information Technologies, CSIT 2010 (2010)
16. Bouaziz, A., Dartigues-Pallez, C., da Costa Pereira, C., Precioso, F., Lloret, P.: Short text classification using semantic random forest. In: Bellatreche, L., Mohania, M.K. (eds.) DaWaK 2014. LNCS, vol. 8646, pp. 288–299. Springer, Cham (2014). https://doi.org/10.1007/978-3-319-10160-6_26
17. Han, E.-H., Karypis, G., Kumar, V.: Text categorization using weight adjusted k-nearest neighbor classification. In: Cheung, D., Williams, G.J., Li, Q. (eds.) PAKDD 2001. LNCS (LNAI), vol. 2035, pp. 53–65. Springer, Heidelberg (2001). https://doi.org/10.1007/3-540-45357-1_9
18. Colas, F., Brazdil, P.: Comparison of SVM and some older classification algorithms in text classification tasks. In: Bramer, M. (ed.) Artificial Intelligence in Theory and Practice. IFIP AICT, vol. 217, pp. 169–178. Springer, Boston (2006). https://doi.org/10.1007/978-0-387-34747-9_18

Low-Complexity MMSE Signal Detection Based on the AOR Iterative Algorithm for Uplink Massive MIMO Systems

Zhenyu Zhang[1], Yuanyuan Dong[1], Zhongshan Zhang[1],
Xiyuan Wang[1], Xiaoming Dai[1(✉)], Linglong Dai[2],
and Haijun Zhang[1]

[1] University of Science and Technology Beijing, Beijing 100083, China
daixiaoming@ustb.edu.cn
[2] Tsinghua University, Beijing 100084, China

Abstract. Massive multiple-input multiple-output (MIMO) systems can substantially improve the spectral efficiency and system capacity by equipping a large number of antennas at the base station and it is envisaged to be one of the critical technologies in the next generation of wireless communication systems. However, the computational complexity of the signal detection in massive MIMO systems presents a significant challenge for practical hardware implementations. This work proposed a novel minimum mean square error (MMSE) signal detection method based on the accelerated overrelaxation (AOR) iterative algorithm. The proposed AOR-based method can reduce the overall complexity of the classical MMSE signal detection by an order of magnitude from $O(K^3)$ to $O(K^2)$, where K is the number of users. Numerical results illustrate that the proposed AOR-based algorithm can outperform the performance of the recently proposed Neumann series approximation-based algorithm and approach the conventional MMSE signal detection involving exact matrix inversion with significantly reduced complexity.

Keywords: Accelerated overrelaxation (AOR) · Iterative algorithm
Minimum mean square error (MMSE) · Convergence · Complexity

1 Introduction

Multiple-input multiple-output (MIMO) is widely acknowledged as a key technology for the fourth generation (4G) wireless communication systems [1, 2] due to the high diversity gain and system channel capacity. However, the exponential increase of mobile data traffic enabled by the wide proliferation of smartphones and tablet computers poses great challenges for the current 4G systems [3]. Massive MIMO systems which scale up the antennas at the base station (BS) by orders of magnitude contrasted to the current systems (e.g., 4 or 8 antennas in 4G system) [4] can serve multi-users on the same frequency band simultaneously [5]. Many research show that the large-scale antennas at the BS can effectively average out non-coherent interference and system noise. Massive MIMO system with large-scale antennas achieve significant enhancements in terms of spectral efficiency, multiplexing gains, and robustness compared to

© ICST Institute for Computer Sciences, Social Informatics and Telecommunications Engineering 2018
K. Long et al. (Eds.): 5GWN 2017, LNICST 211, pp. 385–394, 2018.
https://doi.org/10.1007/978-3-319-72823-0_36

the conventional MIMO systems [6], and it is envisaged to be the promising critical technology in the fifth generation (5G) wireless communication systems [7].

However, the promised gains on the multiplexing capability of massive MIMO systems come at the cost of the significant increase in signal detection complexity at both sides of the wireless communication links [1]. The optimal signal detection in MIMO systems is maximum likelihood (ML) signal detection in which the complexity increases exponentially with the number of transmitting antennas, which imposes an insurmountable cost for practical implementation in the massive MIMO systems [8]. The sphere decoding (SD) [9] can be utilized to simplify the hardware implementation of the ML signal detection; however, the complexity changes along with the channel condition and it is still quite high if the modulation order and/or the number of transmitting antennas is high. The K-best algorithm [10] with fixed complexity is also a popular method to simplify the ML detection, but the linear relationship between the critical path length and the number of antennas poses serious challenges for the large-scale MIMO systems. The linear signal detection such as the minimum mean square error (MMSE) signal detection [1] is utilized in massive MIMO systems to trade off the complexity and reliability; however, it incurs a complex matrix inversion operation whose complexity is immense especially for the large dimension of antennas. The Neumann series (NS) approximation-based algorithm has been proposed recently in [11, 12] to alleviate the complex matrix inversion operation in traditional MMSE signal detection, in which algorithm transforms the matrix inversion into a series of the matrix-vector multiplications and additions. However, the bit error ratio (BER) performance is unsatisfactory with small iteration numbers when the dimension of antennas is moderately large. Furthermore, the large iteration numbers incur even higher computational complexity compared to the classical MMSE signal detection. Hence, it is highly desirable to design low-complexity high-performance signal detection schemes that deliver acceptable BER performance and scale favorably to the high-dimensional signal detection problems.

In this paper, we propose a novel MMSE signal detection method based on the accelerated overrelaxation (AOR) iterative algorithm [13] for uplink massive MIMO systems. The proposed detection scheme reconstructs the transmitted signal without the complicated matrix inversion via an iterative operation. The symmetric positive definite property of the MMSE filtering matrix is amenable to the AOR-based approach. We provide a mathematical model of the AOR-based MMSE signal detection with a convergence and complexity analysis. Numerical results show that the proposed AOR-based algorithm can approach the BER performance of the classical MMSE method in a few iterations and outperform the NS-based approach with significantly reduced complexity.

The rest of the paper is structured as follows. In Sect. 2, the system model of the uplink massive MIMO system is described. In Sect. 3, the low-complexity MMSE signal detection based on the AOR iterative algorithm for uplink massive MIMO system is proposed. The convergence and complexity analysis are presented in the same section. In Sect. 4, the numerical results of the BER performance is specified. Finally, conclusions are drawn in Sect. 5.

Notation: Throughout the paper, upper-case boldface letters **S** and lower-case boldface letters **s** denote matrices and vectors, respectively; $\mathbf{S}^{-1}$, $\mathbf{S}^{T}$ and $\mathbf{S}^{H}$ refer to the matrix inversion, matrix transpose, and matrix conjugate transpose, respectively; $O(\cdot)$ and $E\{\cdot\}$ stand for the order of complexity and the expectation, respectively; $\Im\{\mathbf{s}\}$ and $\Re\{\mathbf{s}\}$ represent the imaginary part and real part of the complex number, respectively; s_i denotes the *ith* element of **s**; $s_{i,j}$ denotes the *ith* row and *jth* column entry of matrix **S**; Finally, $\mathbf{I}_K$ is the $K \times K$ identity matrix.

2 System Model

Consider a representative uplink multi-user massive MIMO system consisting of N antennas at the BS to serve K single-antenna users simultaneously [1], in which we normally have $N \gg K$. The transmitted encoded and interleaved bit streams are mapped to symbols by taking values from an energy-normalized quadrature amplitude modulation (QAM) constellation.

Let $\mathbf{x}_c \in \mathbb{C}^{K \times 1}$ denotes the complex-valued transmitted signal vector. The entries of the Rayleigh flat fading channel $\mathbf{H}_c \in \mathbb{C}^{N \times K}$ are independently and identically (i.i.d.) distributed and follow the complex Gaussian distribution $CN(0, 1)$ with zero mean and unit variance. $\mathbf{n}_c \in \mathbb{C}^{N \times 1}$ represents the additive white Gaussian noise (AWGN) vector whose entries are i.i.d. and follow the distribution $CN(0, \sigma^2)$. $\mathbf{y}_c \in \mathbb{C}^{N \times 1}$ denotes the received signal vector at the BS. Then the complex-valued uplink system model can be expressed as

$$\mathbf{y}_c = \mathbf{H}_c \mathbf{x}_c + \mathbf{n}_c. \tag{1}$$

For ease of representation, the complex-valued model can be converted into a corresponding real-valued one as

$$\begin{bmatrix} \Re\{\mathbf{y}_c\} \\ \Im\{\mathbf{y}_c\} \end{bmatrix} = \begin{bmatrix} \Re\{\mathbf{H}_c\} & -\Im\{\mathbf{H}_c\} \\ \Im\{\mathbf{H}_c\} & \Re\{\mathbf{H}_c\} \end{bmatrix} \begin{bmatrix} \Re\{\mathbf{x}_c\} \\ \Im\{\mathbf{x}_c\} \end{bmatrix} + \begin{bmatrix} \Re\{\mathbf{n}_c\} \\ \Im\{\mathbf{n}_c\} \end{bmatrix}. \tag{2}$$

Then the real-valued uplink system model can be described as

$$\mathbf{y} = \mathbf{H}\mathbf{x} + \mathbf{n}. \tag{3}$$

We assume the channel state information matrix **H** is known perfectly by receiver via the assigned training sequence [14, 15]. Then the transmitted signal can be reconstructed by the MMSE signal detector as

$$\hat{\mathbf{x}} = \left(\mathbf{H}^H \mathbf{H} + \sigma^2 \mathbf{I}_{2K}\right)^{-1} \mathbf{H}^H \mathbf{y} = \mathbf{W}^{-1} \hat{\mathbf{y}}, \tag{4}$$

where $\hat{\mathbf{x}}$ is the reconstructed signal vector, $\mathbf{W} = \mathbf{H}^H \mathbf{H} + \sigma^2 \mathbf{I}_{2K}$ represents the MMSE filtering matrix with a size of $2K \times 2K$, and $\hat{\mathbf{y}} = \mathbf{H}^H \mathbf{y}$ denotes the matched-filter output of **y**. It should be noted that the $\mathbf{W}^{-1}$ operation requires cubic computational complexity $O(K^3)$ and it is extremely high for the massive MIMO systems.

3 Proposed Low-Complexity MMSE Signal Detection Method

3.1 MMSE Signal Detection Based on the AOR Iterative Algorithm

Unlike the conventional MIMO systems, things that were random before and now start to look deterministic in large-scale MIMO systems [1]. Owing to the fact that the column vectors of **H** are asymptotically orthogonal [1], it is obvious that the MMSE filtering matrix **W** is symmetric positive definite in uplink massive MIMO systems. This property inspires us to employ the AOR iterative algorithm to solve (4). The AOR iterative algorithm [13] is a classical iterative scheme for the numerical solution of the linear system $\hat{\mathbf{x}} = \mathbf{W}^{-1}\hat{\mathbf{y}}$. Splitting **W** as $\mathbf{W} = \mathbf{D} - \mathbf{U} - \mathbf{L}$, where **D** denotes the diagonal element of **W**, **U** and **L** represent the negative of the strictly upper and lower triangular element of **W**, respectively. Then the transmitted signal reconstructs by the AOR scheme can be denoted as

$$\hat{\mathbf{x}}^{(n)} = (\mathbf{D} - r\mathbf{L})^{-1}\left\{[(1-\omega)\mathbf{D} + (\omega - r)\mathbf{L} + \omega\mathbf{U}]\hat{\mathbf{x}}^{(n-1)} + \omega\hat{\mathbf{y}}\right\}, \qquad (5)$$

where the coefficient ω and r represent the relaxation parameter and the acceleration parameter, respectively; and the superscript n denotes the iteration number. The initial iteration $\hat{\mathbf{x}}^{(0)}$ is set as a zero vector and the notation $\mathbf{L}_{r,\omega} = (\mathbf{D} - r\mathbf{L})^{-1}[(1-\omega)\mathbf{D} + (\omega - r)\mathbf{L} + \omega\mathbf{U}]$ denotes the iterative matrix.

3.2 Convergence Analysis

For uplink massive MIMO systems, the necessary and sufficient condition for the AOR-based MMSE signal detection algorithm being convergent is $\rho(\mathbf{L}_{r,\omega}) < 1$ [16], where the notation $\rho(\mathbf{L}_{r,\omega})$ denotes the spectral radius of the iterative matrix $\mathbf{L}_{r,\omega}$. The spectral radius is defined as $\rho(\mathbf{L}_{r,\omega}) = \max|\lambda_{r,\omega}|$, where $\lambda_{r,\omega}$ is the eigenvalue of $\mathbf{L}_{r,\omega}$. Then the convergence condition for the AOR iterative algorithm can be given as follows [17, 18]

$$\begin{aligned}
&(1)\, 0 < \omega \le r < 2\\
&(2)\, 0 < r < \omega < 2 \ (\min\lambda_{0,1} \ge 0)\\
&(3)\, \max\left(0, \omega + \frac{2-\omega}{\min\lambda_{0,1}}\right) < r < \omega < 2 \ (\min\lambda_{0,1} < 0),
\end{aligned} \qquad (6)$$

where $\min\lambda_{0,1}$ denotes the minimum eigenvalue of the Jacobi iteration matrix as $\mathbf{L}_{0,1} = \mathbf{D}^{-1}(\mathbf{L} + \mathbf{U})$.

3.3   Computational Complexity Analysis

In this subsection, we evaluate the complexity of the proposed AOR-based MMSE signal detection algorithm. The hardware complexity is mainly dominated by the multipliers, so we define the complexity as the number of multiplications. Rewrite (5) as

$$\hat{\mathbf{x}}^{(n)} = (1 - \omega)\hat{\mathbf{x}}^{(n-1)} + \omega \mathbf{D}^{-1}\left\{\hat{\mathbf{y}} + \frac{r}{\omega}\mathbf{L}\hat{\mathbf{x}}^{(n)} + \left[\left(1 - \frac{r}{\omega}\right)\mathbf{L} + \mathbf{U}\right]\hat{\mathbf{x}}^{(n-1)}\right\}. \quad (7)$$

Considering the definition of the matrix $\mathbf{D}$, $\mathbf{L}$ and $\mathbf{U}$, Eq. (7) can be expressed as

$$\hat{x}_i^{(n)} = (1 - \omega)\hat{x}_i^{(n-1)} + \frac{\omega}{w_{i,i}}\left(\hat{y}_i + \frac{r}{\omega}\sum_{j=1}^{i-1}w_{i,j}\hat{x}_j^{(n)} + \left(1 - \frac{r}{\omega}\right)\sum_{j=1}^{i-1}w_{i,j}\hat{x}_j^{(n-1)} + \sum_{j=i+1}^{2K}w_{i,j}\hat{x}_j^{(n-1)}\right). \quad (8)$$

where the parameter $\frac{r}{\omega}$ can be calculated separately. The number of multiplications required for computation of $(1 - \omega)\hat{x}_i^{(n-1)}$, $\frac{r}{\omega}\sum_{j=1}^{i-1}w_{i,j}\hat{x}_j^{(n)}$, $\sum_{j=i+1}^{2K}w_{i,j}\hat{x}_j^{(n-1)}$ and $\left(1 - \frac{r}{\omega}\right)\sum_{j=1}^{i-1}w_{i,j}\hat{x}_j^{(n-1)}$ are 1, i, $2K - i$ and i, respectively, so the required number of multiplications for $\hat{x}_i^{(n)}$ is $2K + i + 3$. Thus, the overall complexity for one iteration is $\sum_{i=1}^{2K}2K + i + 3 = 6K^2 + 7K$.

Table 1 compares the complexity of the proposed AOR-based algorithm with that of NS-based algorithm. The classical MMSE signal detection with exact matrix inversion operation has cubic computational complexity $O(K^3)$. Table 1 illustrates the complexity of the NS-based algorithm scales with $O(K^2)$ only for $n = 2$. However, the proposed AOR-based algorithm can decrease the complexity by an order of magnitude from $O(K^3)$ to $O(K^2)$.

Table 1. Computational complexity

Iteration number	NS-based algorithm	AOR-based algorithm
$n = 2$	$12K^2 - 2K$	$12K^2 + 14K$
$n = 3$	$8K^3 + 4K^2$	$18K^2 + 21K$
$n = 4$	$16K^3 - 4K^2 + 2K$	$24K^2 + 28K$

4   Simulation Results

To verify the validity of the proposed AOR-based MMSE signal detection, we evaluated the BER performance against the signal-to-noise ratio (SNR) and compared it with the recently proposed NS-based algorithm [11, 12]. The BER performance of the classical MMSE signal detection with exact matrix inversion was also given as the benchmark for comparison. A representative massive MIMO system scenario with $N \times K = 128 \times 16$ and the 64-QAM modulation scheme was adopted.

Figure 1 shows the BER performance of the proposed AOR-based MMSE signal detection versus the relaxation parameter ω and the acceleration parameter r in a three-dimensional way. The SNR is 15 dB and the iteration number is $n = 3$. The optimal parameters can achieve a faster convergence rate and a preferable performance. As shown in Fig. 1, the BER performance difference is negligible when the parameters are close to $\omega = 1.10$ and $r = 1.05$, indicating the robustness of the proposed method. So we chose the optimal relaxation and acceleration parameter as $\omega_{opt} = 1.10$ and $r_{opt} = 1.05$ in the following simulations.

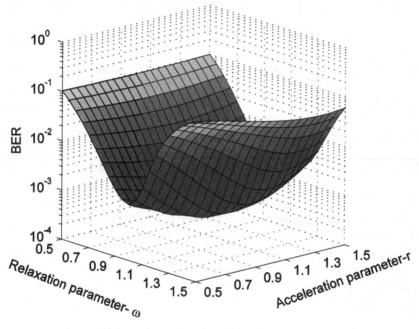

Fig. 1. BER performance of the AOR-based algorithm versus ω and r. The SNR is 15 dB and n is 3.

Next we evaluate the influence of the relaxation and acceleration parameters on the convergence rate. Figure 2 illustrates the BER performance of the proposed AOR-based MMSE signal detection versus the relaxation parameter ω with the acceleration parameter r being fixed. Figure 3 illustrates the BER performance of the proposed AOR-based MMSE signal detection versus the acceleration parameter r with the relaxation parameter ω being fixed. The BER curve behaves like a quadratic function curve. The BER performance initially improves with the value of ω up to approximately 1.10 and then starts to deteriorate for higher values. It is worth noting that the BER performance are extremely sensitive to the variation of the relaxation parameter with the fixed acceleration parameter. So we conclude that the relaxation parameter ω plays a dominant role in the convergence of the algorithm while the

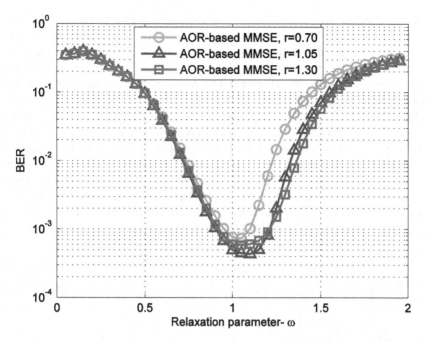

Fig. 2. BER performance of the AOR-based algorithm versus ω. The SNR is 15 dB and n is 3.

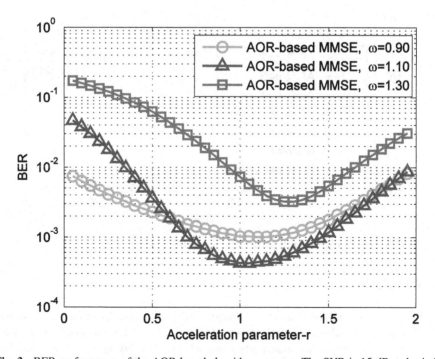

Fig. 3. BER performance of the AOR-based algorithm versus r. The SNR is 15 dB and n is 3.

acceleration parameter r can expedite the convergence rate to some extent in the proposed AOR-based MMSE signal detection. Based on this finding, a more robust system can be realized by selecting a proper acceleration parameter despite a small variation of the relaxation parameter. Numerical results show that the optimal relaxation parameter ω_{opt} can be set around 1.10 while the corresponding optimal acceleration parameter r_{opt} is close to ω_{opt}.

Figure 4 provides the BER performance comparison for different detection algorithms. It is apparent that the BER performance improves significantly with the increasing iteration number of the proposed algorithm. The BER performance of the AOR-based algorithm outperforms the NS-based algorithm with the same iteration number due to the faster convergence rate of the AOR iterative algorithm. For example, the proposed AOR-based method with n = 2 can even achieve similar performance levels as the NS-based method with n = 4. The BER performance of the AOR-based algorithm approaches the traditional MMSE method within 0.1 dB when the iteration number is n = 3 for the $N \times K = 128 \times 16$ massive MIMO systems.

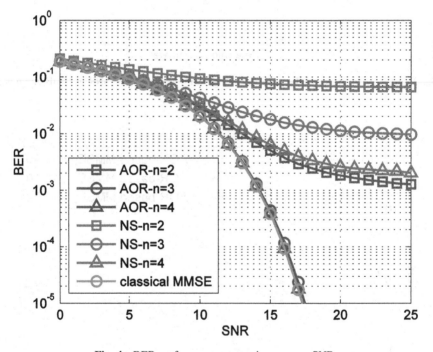

Fig. 4. BER performance comparison versus SNR.

5 Conclusions

In this paper, we proposed a low-complexity MMSE signal detection based on the AOR iterative algorithm for uplink massive MIMO systems. The proposed AOR-based algorithm reconstructs the transmitting signal via a relaxation and acceleration operation to refine the solution estimate in an iterative manner. Numerical results illustrate that the proposed AOR-based algorithm can obtain better BER performance than the recently proposed NS-based algorithm and approach the performance of the classical MMSE signal detection with a significantly reduced complexity. Owing to the superiority of the low-complexity AOR iteration algorithm, it can be utilized to solve other problems involving complicated matrix inversion operations such as the precoding technique in massive MIMO systems.

Acknowledgments. This work was supported by Huawei Innovation Research Program, the key project of the National Natural Science Foundation of China (No. 61431001), the 5G research program of China Mobile Research Institute (Grant No. [2015] 0615), the open research fund of National Mobile Communications Research Laboratory Southeast University (No. 2017D02), Key Laboratory of Cognitive Radio and Information Processing, Ministry of Education (Guilin University of Electronic Technology), the Foundation of Beijing Engineering and Technology Center for Convergence Networks and Ubiquitous Services, and Keysight.

References

1. Rusek, F., et al.: Scaling up MIMO: opportunities and challenges with very large arrays. IEEE Sig. Process. Mag. **30**(1), 40–60 (2013)
2. Zheng, L., Tse, D.N.C.: Diversity and multiplexing: a fundamental tradeoff in multiple-antenna channels. IEEE Trans. Inf. Theory **49**(5), 1073–1096 (2003)
3. Dai, X., et al.: Successive interference cancelation amenable multiple access (SAMA) for future wireless communications. In: 2014 IEEE International Conference on Communication Systems, Macau, pp. 222–226 (2014)
4. Marzetta, T.L.: Noncooperative cellular wireless with unlimited numbers of base station antennas. IEEE Trans. Wirel. Commun. **9**(11), 3590–3600 (2010)
5. Lu, L., Li, G.Y., Swindlehurst, A.L., Ashikhmin, A., Zhang, R.: An overview of massive MIMO: benefits and challenges. IEEE J. Sel. Top. Sig. Process. **8**(5), 742–758 (2014)
6. Xie, H., Gao, F., Zhang, S., Jin, S.: A unified transmission strategy for TDD/FDD massive MIMO systems with spatial basis expansion model. IEEE Trans. Veh. Technol. **66**(4), 3170–3184 (2017)
7. Boccardi, F., Heath, R.W., Lozano, A., Marzetta, T.L., Popovski, P.: Five disruptive technology directions for 5G. IEEE Commun. Mag. **52**(2), 74–80 (2014)
8. Artes, H., Seethaler, D., Hlawatsch, F.: Efficient detection algorithms for MIMO channels: a geometrical approach to approximate ML detection. IEEE Trans. Signal Process. **51**(11), 2808–2820 (2003)
9. Jalden, J., Ottersten, B.: On the complexity of sphere decoding in digital communications. IEEE Trans. Sig. Process. **53**(4), 1474–1484 (2005)
10. Bello, I.A., Halak, B., El-Hajjar, M., Zwolinski, M.: VLSI implementation of a scalable K-best MIMO detector. In: 2015 15th International Symposium on Communications and Information Technologies (ISCIT), Nara, pp. 281–286 (2015)
11. Wu, M., Yin, B., Wang, G., Dick, C., Cavallaro, J.R., Studer, C.: Large-scale MIMO detection for 3GPP LTE: algorithms and FPGA implementations. IEEE J. Sel. Top. Sig. Process. **8**(5), 916–929 (2014)
12. Zhu, D., Li, B., Liang, P.: On the matrix inversion approximation based on neumann series in massive MIMO systems. In: 2015 IEEE International Conference on Communications (ICC), London, pp. 1763–1769 (2015)

13. Hadjidimos, A.: Accelerated overrelaxation method. Math. Comput. **32**(141), 149–157 (1978)
14. Bölcskei, H.: Space-Time Wireless Systems: From Array Processing to MIMO Communications. Cambridge University Press, New York (2006)
15. Xie, H., Gao, F., Jin, S.: An overview of low-rank channel estimation for massive MIMO systems. IEEE Access **4**, 7313–7321 (2016)
16. Björck, Å.: Numerical Methods in Matrix Computations. TAM, vol. 59. Springer, Cham (2015). https://doi.org/10.1007/978-3-319-05089-8
17. Zeng, W.: On convergence of AOR method. Journal of Huqiao University (1985)
18. Chen, P.X.: Convergence of AOR Method. Mathematica Numerica Sinica (1983)

Outage Performance for IDF Relaying Mobile Cooperative Networks

Lingwei Xu[1(⊠)], Jingjing Wang[1], Yun Liu[1], Jie Yang[1],
Wei Shi[1], and T. Aaron Gulliver[2]

[1] Department of Information Science and Technology,
Qingdao University of Science and Technology, Qingdao 266061, China
gaomilaojia2009@163.com, kathyl003@163.com,
Lyun-1027@163.com, 463604226@qq.com,
shiwei6670595@126.com
[2] Department of Electrical and Computer Engineering,
University of Victoria, Victoria V8W 2Y2, Canada
agullive@ece.uvic.ca

Abstract. Cooperative communication has emerged as a key technique in fifth generation (5G) mobile wireless networks. In this paper, with incremental decode-and-forward (IDF) relaying and transmit antenna selection (TAS), we investigate the outage probability (OP) performance of mobile cooperative networks. Exact closed-form expressions for OP with optimal TAS are derived. These expressions are used to evaluate the impact of power allocation on OP performance. Then we verify the mathematical derivations using Monte Carlo simulations. The OP performance is influenced by power-allocation parameter.

Keywords: Mobile cooperative communication
Incremental decode-and-forward · Outage probability
Transmit antenna selection · Power allocation

1 Introduction

The tremendous growth in mobile data traffic has created significant interest in the development of fifth-generation (5G) wireless communication systems [1, 2]. Many new technologies are being proposed for 5G mobile communications to satisfy the demands, such as device-to-device (D2D), heterogeneous networks, ultra-dense networks, and massive multiple-input-multiple-output (MIMO) systems [3–5]. For example, in cognitive small cells, the authors used cooperative Nash bargaining game theory to investigate the power allocation problem in [5].

In 5G mobile wireless networks, cooperative communication is considered to be a key technology. The authors investigated average bit error probability (BEP) performance of threshold digital relaying, and incremental-selective decode-and-forward (DF) relaying in [6, 7]. In [8], the authors investigated the outage probability (OP) performance of incremental amplify-and-forward (AF) relaying.

The hardware complexity of MIMO systems increases with the number of antennas. Transmit antenna selection (TAS) has been proposed to reduce this complexity.

© ICST Institute for Computer Sciences, Social Informatics and Telecommunications Engineering 2018
K. Long et al. (Eds.): 5GWN 2017, LNICST 211, pp. 395–402, 2018.
https://doi.org/10.1007/978-3-319-72823-0_37

Using TAS, the authors investigated the OP performance of MIMO systems over Nakagami-m fading channels in [9]. The authors investigated symbol error rate (SER) performance of MIMO systems using TAS over η-μ fading channels in [10]. Further, using TAS and AF relaying, [11] provided new analysis results for OP and SER of MIMO systems over Rayleigh fading channels.

Although there are many results in the literature on TAS, the performance has been evaluated without considering the actual characteristics of a mobile communications channel. For example, the performance of TAS has only been investigated over Rayleigh, η-μ and Nakagami-m fading channels [9–11]. Recently, the N-Nakagami fading channel has been proposed to more accurately characterize mobile communications channels. Thus in this paper, TAS is considered for incremental delay-and-forward (IDF) relaying mobile cooperative networks over N-Nakagami fading channels. We investigate OP performance of optimal TAS, and the impact of the power allocation on OP performance is examined. In addition, these expressions are evaluated using Monte Carlo simulation, to verify the mathematical derivations.

The rest of the paper is organized as follows. Section 2 describes the mobile cooperative network model. We investigate the OP performance of the optimal TAS scheme in Sect. 3. Monte Carlo simulations are used to verify the mathematical derivations in Sect. 4. We give some conclusions in Sect. 5.

2   The System Model

The mobile cooperative model is shown in Fig. 1. With the help of L single-antenna mobile relay (MR) nodes, the mobile source (MS) node can communicate with the mobile destination (MD) node. MS has N_t antennas, while MD has N_r antennas.

$h = h_k, k \in \{h_{SDij}, h_{SRil}, h_{RDlj}\}$ represents the complex channel coefficients. h follows N-Nakagami distribution. The relative gain of the $MS_i \rightarrow MD_j$ link is $G_{SDij} = 1$, the relative gain of $MS_i \rightarrow MR_l$ is G_{SRil}, the relative gain of $MR_l \rightarrow MD_j$ is G_{RDlj}. MS and MR_l use the total energy E in the two time slots.

MS_i transmits the signal x in the first time slot. MD_j and MR_l receive the signals r_{SDij} and r_{SRil} as

$$r_{SDij} = \sqrt{KE}h_{SDij}x + n_{SDij} \qquad (1)$$

$$r_{SRil} = \sqrt{G_{SRil}KE}h_{SRil}x + n_{SRil} \qquad (2)$$

where K is the power allocation parameter, the mean and variance of n_{SRil} and n_{SDij} are 0 and $N_0/2$ [12].

The best MR compares γ_{SDij} to a threshold γ_T, and determines whether or not to use DF cooperation in the second time slot. The best MR is selected as follows

$$\gamma_{RDij} = \max_{1 \leq l \leq L}(\gamma_{RDlj}) \qquad (3)$$

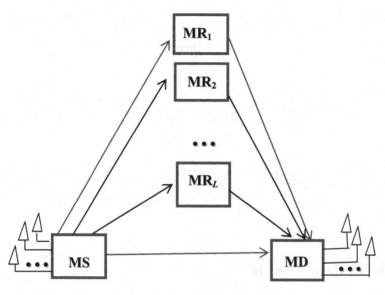

Fig. 1. The system model

where γ_{RDlj} represents the SNR of $MR_l \rightarrow MD_j$ link, and

$$\gamma_{RDlj} = \frac{(1-K)G_{RDlj}|h_{RDlj}|^2 E}{N_0} = (1-K)G_{RDlj}|h_{RDlj}|^2 \bar{\gamma} \tag{4}$$

If $\gamma_{SDij} > \gamma_T$, the best MR will not participate in cooperation. MD_j receives the SNR as

$$\gamma_{0ij} = \gamma_{SDij} \tag{5}$$

where

$$\gamma_{SDij} = \frac{K|h_{SDij}|^2 E}{N_0} = K|h_{SDij}|^2 \bar{\gamma} \tag{6}$$

If $\gamma_{SDij} < \gamma_T$, the best MR uses DF cooperation protocol. MD_j receives the signal as

$$r_{RDj} = \sqrt{(1-K)G_{RDj}E}h_{RDj}x_r + n_{RDj} \tag{7}$$

where the mean and variance of n_{RDj} are 0 and $N_0/2$.

MD_j uses the selection combining (SC) scheme, and receives the SNR as

$$\gamma_{SCij} = \max(\gamma_{SDij}, \gamma_{RDij}) \tag{8}$$

MD receives the SNR as

$$\gamma_{SC_i} = \max_{1 \leq j \leq N_r} (\gamma_{ij}) \tag{9}$$

where

$$\gamma_{ij} = \begin{cases} \gamma_{0ij}, & \gamma_{SDij} > \gamma_T \\ \gamma_{SCij}, & \gamma_{SDij} < \gamma_T \end{cases} \tag{10}$$

The transmit antenna w is selected as follows

$$w = \max_{1 \leq i \leq N_t} (\gamma_{SC_i}) = \max_{1 \leq i \leq N_t, 1 \leq j \leq N_r} (\gamma_{ij}) \tag{11}$$

3 The Optimal TAS OP

3.1 $\gamma_{th} > \gamma_T$

We obtain the OP as

$$\begin{aligned} F_{optimal} &= \Pr(\max_{1 \leq i \leq N_t, 1 \leq j \leq N_r} (\gamma_{ij}) < \gamma_{th}) = \\ &= (\Pr(\gamma_T < \gamma_{SD}, \gamma_0 < \gamma_{th}) + \Pr(\gamma_{SD} < \gamma_T, \gamma_{SC} < \gamma_{th}))^{N_t \times N_r} \\ &= (G_1 + G_2)^{N_t \times N_r} \end{aligned} \tag{12}$$

where γ_{th} is the threshold.

The G_1 is given as

$$G_1 = \frac{1}{\prod_{d=1}^{N} \Gamma(m_d)} G_{1,N+1}^{N,1} \left[\frac{\gamma_{th}}{\overline{\gamma}_{SD}} \prod_{d=1}^{N} \frac{m_d}{\Omega_d} \Big|_{m_1,\ldots,m_N,0}^{1} \right] -$$

$$\frac{1}{\prod_{d=1}^{N} \Gamma(m_d)} G_{1,N+1}^{N,1} \left[\frac{\gamma_T}{\overline{\gamma}_{SD}} \prod_{d=1}^{N} \frac{m_d}{\Omega_d} \Big|_{m_1,\ldots,m_N,0}^{1} \right] \tag{13}$$

$$\overline{\gamma}_{SD} = K\overline{\gamma} \tag{14}$$

where $G[\cdot]$ is the well-known Meijer's G-function, the fading coefficient is defined as m, and the scaling factor is defined as Ω [13].

The G_2 is given as

$$G_2 = \frac{1}{\prod\limits_{d=1}^{N} \Gamma(m_d)} G_{1,N+1}^{N,1} \left[\frac{\gamma_T}{\overline{\gamma}_{SD}} \prod_{d=1}^{N} \frac{m_d}{\Omega_d} \Big|_{m_1,\ldots,m_N,0}^{1} \right] \times$$

$$\left(\frac{1}{\prod\limits_{t=1}^{N} \Gamma(m_t)} G_{1,N+1}^{N,1} \left[\frac{\gamma_{th}}{\overline{\gamma}_{RD}} \prod_{t=1}^{N} \frac{m_t}{\Omega_t} \Big|_{m_1,\ldots,m_N,0}^{1} \right] \right)^{L} \quad (15)$$

$$\overline{\gamma}_{RD} = (1 - K) G_{RD} \overline{\gamma} \quad (16)$$

3.2 $\gamma_{th} < \gamma_T$

We obtain the OP as

$$\begin{aligned} F_{\text{optimal}} &= (\Pr(\gamma_{SD} < \gamma_T, \gamma_{SC} < \gamma_{th}))^{N_t \times N_r} \\ &= (\Pr(\gamma_{SD} < \gamma_{th}) \Pr(\gamma_{RD} < \gamma_{th}))^{N_t \times N_r} \quad (17) \\ &= (G_{11} G_{22})^{N_t \times N_r} \end{aligned}$$

The G_{11} is given as

$$\begin{aligned} G_{11} &= \Pr(\gamma_{SD} < \gamma_{th}) \\ &= \frac{1}{\prod\limits_{d=1}^{N} \Gamma(m_d)} G_{1,N+1}^{N,1} \left[\frac{\gamma_{th}}{\overline{\gamma}_{SD}} \prod_{d=1}^{N} \frac{m_d}{\Omega_d} \Big|_{m_1,\ldots,m_N,0}^{1} \right] \quad (18) \end{aligned}$$

The G_{22} is given as

$$\begin{aligned} G_{22} &= \Pr(\gamma_{RD} < \gamma_{th}) \\ &= \left(\frac{1}{\prod\limits_{t=1}^{N} \Gamma(m_t)} G_{1,N+1}^{N,1} \left[\frac{\gamma_{th}}{\overline{\gamma}_{RD}} \prod_{t=1}^{N} \frac{m_t}{\Omega_t} \Big|_{m_1,\ldots,m_N,0}^{1} \right] \right)^{L} \quad (19) \end{aligned}$$

4 Numerical Results

In this section, Monte Carlo simulations are used to verify the mathematical derivations. $E = 1$. We define $\mu = G_{SR}/G_{RD}$ (in decibels) as the relative geometrical gain.

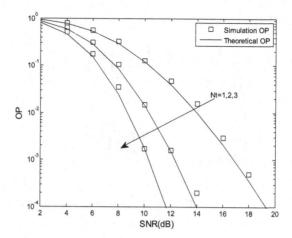

Fig. 2. The optimal TAS OP performance with $\gamma_{th} < \gamma_T$

Figure 2 presents the OP performance with $\gamma_{th} = 5$ dB, $\gamma_T = 6$ dB. Figure 3 presents the OP performance with $\gamma_{th} = 5$ dB, $\gamma_T = 2$ dB. The simulation parameters used are as follows: $N = 2$, $m = 2$, $K = 0.5$, $N_t = 1, 2, 3$, $L = 2$, $N_r = 1$, $\mu = 0$ dB. From Figs. 2 and 3, it is clear that Monte-Carlo simulation results and the analysis results match. Further, increasing N_t improves the OP performance. For example, when $\gamma_{th} = 5$ dB, $\gamma_T = 2$ dB, SNR = 10 dB, the OP is 2.9×10^{-1} with $N_t = 1$, 8.3×10^{-2} with $N_t = 2$, 2.4×10^{-2} with $N_t = 3$. With N_t fixed, increasing SNR decreases the OP.

The effect of K on OP performance is evaluated in Fig. 4. The simulation parameters used are as follows: $N = 2$, $m = 2$, $\mu = 0$ dB, $N_t = 2$, $L = 2$, $N_r = 2$, $\gamma_{th} = 5$ dB, $\gamma_T = 3$ dB. Simulation results show that increasing SNR improves the OP performance. For example, when $K = 0.7$, the OP is 2.8×10^{-1} with SNR = 5 dB,

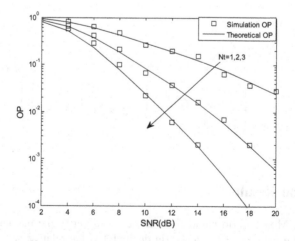

Fig. 3. The optimal TAS OP performance with $\gamma_{th} > \gamma_T$

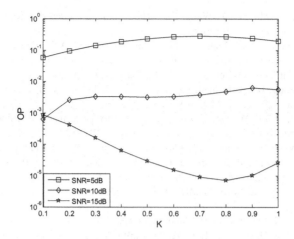

Fig. 4. The OP performance versus K

3.7×10^{-3} with SNR = 10 dB, 9.1×10^{-6} with SNR = 15 dB. When SNR = 5 dB, $K = 0.10$; SNR = 10 dB, $K = 0.10$; SNR = 15 dB, $K = 0.81$. We obtain that $K = 0.5$ is not the best choice. For most applications, we can store the optimum power allocation (OPA) values in a lookup table.

5 Conclusions

In this paper, with TAS, we investigate the OP performance of IDF relaying mobile cooperative networks. Monte Carlo simulation was used to verify these expressions, and to examine the effect of the power allocation on the OP performance. Future research will consider the impact of correlated channels on the performance.

Acknowledgments. This project was supported by the National Natural Science Foundation of China (No. 61671261, No. 61304222), Shandong Province Natural Science Foundation (No. ZR2017BF023), Open Research Fund from Shandong provincial Key Laboratory of Computer Networks (No. SDKLCN-2017-01), State Key Laboratory of Millimeter Waves (No. K201824), the Key Research and Development Program of Shandong Province (No. 2016GGX101007), and China Postdoctoral Science Foundation (No. 2017T100490, No. 2017M612223, No. 2014M551905).

References

1. Mumtaz, S., Huq, K.M.S., Rodriguez, J.: Direct mobile-to-mobile communication: paradigm for 5G. IEEE Wirel. Commun. **21**, 14–23 (2014)
2. Chen, S., Zhao, J.: The requirements, challenges and technologies for 5G of terrestrial mobile telecommunication. IEEE Commun. Mag. **52**, 36–43 (2014)
3. Zhang, H.J., Liu, H., Jiang, C.X., Nallanathan, A., Wen, X.M.: A practical semi-dynamic clustering scheme using affinity propagation in cooperative picocells. IEEE Trans. Veh. Technol. **64**, 4372–4377 (2015)

4. Ge, X.H., Tu, S., Mao, G.Q., Wang, C.X., Han, T.: 5G ultra-dense cellular networks. IEEE Wirel. Commun. **23**, 72–79 (2015)
5. Zhang, H.J., Jiang, C.X., Beaulieu, N.C., Chu, X.L., Wang, X.B., Quek, T.Q.S.: Resource allocation for cognitive small cell networks: a cooperative bargaining game theoretic approach. IEEE Trans. Wirel. Commun. **14**, 3481–3493 (2015)
6. Xu, L.W., Zhang, H.: Performance analysis of threshold digital relaying M2M cooperative networks. Wirel. Netw. **22**, 1595–1603 (2016)
7. Xu, L.W., Wang, J.J., Wang, H., Gulliver, T.A.: ABEP performance of ISDF relaying M2M cooperative networks. KSII Trans. Internet Inf. Syst. **10**, 5129–5148 (2016)
8. Xu, L.W., Wang, J.J., Zhang, H., Gulliver, T.A.: Performance analysis of IAF relaying mobile D2D cooperative networks. J. Franklin Inst. **354**, 902–916 (2017)
9. Yeoh, P.L., Elkashlan, M., Yang, N., Costa, D.B.D., Duong, T.Q.: Unified analysis of transmit antenna selection in MIMO multi-relay networks. IEEE Trans. Veh. Technol. **62**, 933–939 (2013)
10. Kumbhani, B., Kshetrimayum, R.: Analysis of TAS/MRC based MIMO Systems over $\eta - \mu$ Fading Channels. IETE Tech. Rev. **32**, 252–259 (2015)
11. Abdelnabi, A., Fawaz, A.Q., Shaqfeh, M., Ikki, S., Alnuweiri, H.: Performance analysis of MIMO multi-hop system with TAS/MRC in poisson field of interferers. IEEE Trans. Commun. **64**, 525–540 (2016)
12. Ochiai, H., Mitran, P., Tarokh, V.: Variable-rate two-phase collaborative communication protocols for wireless networks. IEEE Trans. Veh. Technol. **52**, 4299–4313 (2006)
13. Karagiannidis, G.K., Sagias, N.C., Mathiopoulos, P.T.: N*Nakagami: a novel stochastic model for cascaded fading channels. IEEE Trans. Commun. **55**, 1453–1458 (2007)

AES and SNOW 3G are Feasible Choices for a 5G Phone from Energy Perspective

Mohsin Khan[✉] and Valtteri Niemi

Department of Computer Science, University of Helsinki, P.O. Box 68,
Gustaf Hällströmin katu 2b, 00014 Helsinki, Finland
{mohsin.khan,valtteri.niemi}@helsinki.fi

Abstract. The aspirations for a 5th generation (5G) mobile network
are high. It has a vision of unprecedented data-rate and extremely pervasive connectivity. To cater such aspirations in a mobile phone, many
existing efficiency aspects of a mobile phone need to be reviewed. We
look into the matter of required energy to encrypt and decrypt the huge
amount of traffic that will leave from and enter into a 5G enabled mobile
phone. In this paper, we present an account of the power consumption
details of the efficient hardware implementations of AES and SNOW 3G.
We also present an account of the power consumption details of LTE
protocol stack on some cutting edge hardware platforms. Based on the
aforementioned two accounts, we argue that the energy requirement for
the current encryption systems AES and SNOW 3G will not impact the
battery-life of a 5G enabled mobile phone by any significant proportion.

Keywords: LTE · 5G · Cryptosystem · ASIC

1 Introduction

The aspirations of 5G network are reflected in the white papers published by the
leading telecommunication companies [22,24,25]. All of these white papers mention about the vision of more than 1 Gbps data rate. To facilitate our discussion,
we need to know what are the data that will be encrypted and decrypted in a
5G phone. We also need to know where and how many times the encryption and
decryption will take place across the protocol stack on the phone. But 5G is not
yet a reality and we do not have exact answers to these questions. So, we assume
things about a 5G network and argue on the basis of those assumptions. We
turn to the LTE (3GPP defined 4G network) network and different white papers
[23,26,27] published by the leading telecommunication companies to make the
assumptions. In an LTE phone, the data that leave and enter the phone can be
broadly classified into three categories.

1. The control signals in between the phone and the core network
2. The control signals in between the phone and the radio network
3. The user data sent and received at the phone's application layer

© ICST Institute for Computer Sciences, Social Informatics and Telecommunications Engineering 2018
K. Long et al. (Eds.): 5GWN 2017, LNICST 211, pp. 403–412, 2018.
https://doi.org/10.1007/978-3-319-72823-0_38

Both of the first two categories are confidentiality and integrity protected. For the third category, only the privacy is protected. Also note that, from the volume point of view, the major share of data belong to the third category. Comparing to the third category, the cryptographic computation required for the data of first and second categories is negligible. The user data in an LTE phone is only once encrypted and decrypted across the protocol stack in PDCP layer. For a 5G phone, we assume the following:

1. User data will remain as the major share of the total data leaving and entering the phone.
2. The cryptographic computational need for the total volume of control signals will be negligible in comparison with that of the user data.
3. The user data will only once be encrypted and decrypted somewhere across the protocol stack.
4. In order to have a pessimistic estimation of energy consumption, we assume that integrity protection of user data will be introduced in 5G.

Based on these assumptions, we will look into the cryptographic energy requirements and also the total energy requirements across the protocol stack of an LTE phone. Then we will scale up the data-rate from 100 Mbps to 1 Gbps and see how much extra pressure it puts on the battery of the phone in comparison with other energy hungry aspects of the phone like display and radio signalling.

The paper is organized by first giving a very short introduction to the architecture, the protocol stack and the cryptographic specifications of the LTE network in Sect. 2. In Sect. 3, we present the results found in the existing literature about the energy requirements of the two cryptosystems of interest, which are AES and SNOW 3G. In this section we also present the results about the energy consumption across the whole protocol stack of the link layer. In Sect. 4 we present the energy consumption distribution of the whole phone among its different functional modules and show that the energy needed for cryptographic computation is not a threat for the battery life of the phone.

2   LTE Specifications

An LTE network is comprised of broadly three components. The user equipment (UE), evolved radio network (E-UTRAN) known as radio network and evolved packet core (EPC) known as core network. The user equipment consists of a mobile equipment (ME) or a mobile phone for the context of this paper, and a universal integrated circuit card (UICC). The UICC hosts an application called subscriber identification module (SIM). In this paper when we refer to the user equipment, we mean it to be the mobile phone since the UICC does not have much functionality to consume a lot of energy (Fig. 1).

The UE is connected to the network via a radio link only with the radio network. The entity of the E-UTRAN that has the radio link with the UE is called eNodeB which is traditionally known as a base station. However, the UE also establishes a direct logical connection with an entity of the core network

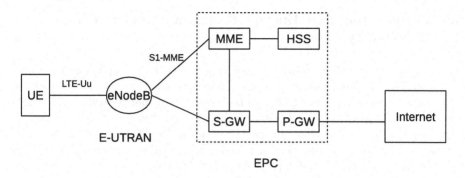

Fig. 1. LTE architecture

known as the mobility management entity (MME). This logical connection is used only for the control signals for the core network and hence we do not focus on it in this paper. The user data as mentioned in the introduction travels from the UE to the eNodeB. Figure 2 shows the protocol stack that the data travel across at the UE and at eNodeB. The L1 layer is the physical layer. We logically bundle the packet data convergence protocol (PDCP), radio link control (RLC), and medium access control (MAC) layers as layer 2 (L2). All the encryption and decryption takes place at the PDCP layer [1].

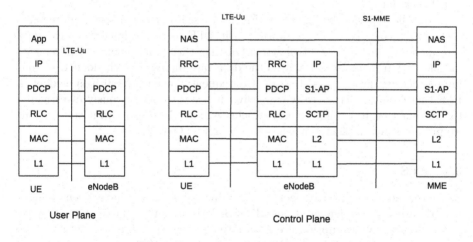

Fig. 2. Protocol stack in LTE network

According to [2], there are two mandatory sets of security algorithms in the 4th generation cellular network (LTE) developed by 3GPP. One is EEA1 in which the stream cipher SNOW 3G is used. The other is EEA2 in which the block cipher AES is used. The aspiration for the 5G networks is to obtain at least 1Gbps data-rate. The question arises if there are implementations of these two encryption systems that can achieve the required throughput and still be energy efficient enough to be used in a mobile phone.

3 Throughput and Energy Requirements of AES and SNOW 3G

In [12], the authors showed in their experiment that the computing power of a single embedded processor even at high clock frequency is not enough to cope with the L2 requirements of LTE and next generation mobile devices. The AES decryption was identified as the major time critical software algorithm, demanding half of the execution time of entire L2 of downlink (DL). So, advanced hardware acceleration methods were required while keeping the energy and area requirements at a reasonable level for a mobile phone.

In a study conducted on the L2 DL [14], the authors had shown that by a smart DMA (direct memory access) controller, the required throughput for LTE which is at most 100 Mbps can be achieved. They used Faraday's 90 nm CMOS technology, 128-bit data path and 11 round transformations for AES. However, to achieve this required throughput, the implementation consumed 9.5 mW of power whereas AES and SNOW 3G each required .5 and .57 mW of power respectively. So, the decryption consumes around 5% of the power budget of L2 DL. From energy point of view, it consumes 5.7 mJ of energy to decrypt 1 Gb of data. In [14, Fig. 6] the detailed comparison is presented. In Sect. 4, we will see that this is indeed a very small amount of energy when compared with total amount of energy consumed by the phone while exchanging bulk amount of network data.

From the experience of LTE [16, Fig. 9], we see that the energy requirements of radio interface technology (downlink) in LTE increases linearly as the data rate increases but with a small slope. On the other hand, energy requirements for encryption increases linearly as the data rate increases with slope 1. 5G has unprecedented data rate of 1 Gbps. Consequently, even though it is evident in LTE that ciphering is not very expensive, it needs to be rigorously investigated to conclude that it will not be very expensive in 5G. In the following sub-sections we present some implementations of AES and SNOW 3G.

3.1 AES

Since the adoption of Rijndael as AES by NIST, there have been a number of hardware implementations of AES. It is understandable that throughput and energy consumption are not mutually exclusive. In the beginning, the focus was completely on achieving high throughput. Over the time the need for high throughput, yet energy efficient implementations became more pressing and studies concerning the energy consumption of the implementations became available.

From Table 1, we find the implementations in [9–11] are potential candidates for using in 5G since they meet the required throughput of 5G and present their energy requirements which enable us to make a meaningful analysis. In [10], the authors present an implementation called SAME that achieves 114 Mbps throughput using 2 cores of the processor of a mobile phone. The implementation

Table 1. AES implementations

Year	Ref	Tech (nm CMOS)	TP (Gbps)	Gates (K)	Power (mW)	Energy (mJ/Gb)
2001	[4]	110	2.6	21.3	–	–
2001	[4]	110	0.311	5.4	–	–
2001	[5]	–	0.24	4	–	–
2006	[8]	180	0.570	–	20.34	35.68
2006	[8]	350	0.569	–	192.5	338.3
2007	[7]	180	0.384	21	–	–
2009	[6]	180	1.16	19.47	–	–
2009	[9]	90	1.00	38	0.78	.78
2011	[10]	–	0.114	–	.02	.24
2012	[11]	180	1.6	58.445	22.85	14.28

is based on slicing and merging the bytes of several data blocks to exploit processor's architecture width for multi-block encryption. According to [10, Fig. 8] the implementation is scalable with a speed up factor of 0.9; i.e., if the throughput achieved by 1 core is T, then $n > 1$ cores provide throughput $0.9nT$. According to [10, Fig. 9], the SAME implementation achieves 5.5 Mbps/μJ. Consequently, it spends 114/5.5 Mbps/(Mbps/μJ) = 20.72 μJ = .02 mJ to encrypt/decrypt 114 Mb. Now, by scaling up by 12 different 2-cores, it will achieve the throughput of $0.114 \cdot 12 \cdot 0.9 \approx 1$ Gbps while it will spend $0.02 \cdot 12 = 0.24$ mJ. Even though this implementation comes up as the most energy efficient in Table 1, it is still not practical choice in 5G because a mobile phone with 24 cores is a far fetched idea even for 5G. In [9], the authors present an application specific integrated circuit (ASIC) implementation based on Faraday's 90 nm CMOS technology. They do not provide the exact throughput but provide the time required for processing one byte and the power need to process at that rate. In LTE, to achieve 100 Mbps, 100 Kb of data is required to be processed by 0.6 ms. Similarly we assume that in 5G, to achieve 1 Gbps data rate, 1 Mb of data need to be processed in 0.6 ms. Consequently processing time of around 4 ns per byte is required to achieve 1 Gbps. In [9, Fig. 8] it is claimed that using one AES core with 128-bit data path, processing time of 4 ns per byte can be achieved while consuming 0.78 mJ of energy per second. In [9, Fig. 10], it is claimed that processing time of 4 ns per byte can be achieved using 2 AES core by using even less energy, 0.72 mJ per second. This implementation appears to be a very good candidate for a 5G phone. In [11], the implementation achieves the required throughput without any need of scaling up but it spends almost 30 times more energy than that of [9].

3.2 SNOW 3G

It appears that there have not been as many hardware implementations of SNOW 3G as there have been of AES. It may be attributed to the reason that AES is much more widely used in different protocols. As mentioned in Sect. 3, the implementation in [14] focuses on the throughput and energy efficiency of the whole L2 layer of LTE and doesn't give any account of the scalability of the SNOW 3G ciphering unit that can be used for much higher data rates than LTE. In [18], the authors present a parallel implementation of SNOW 3G by exploiting the multi-core processor of a smart phone that can provide the required throughput of LTE. The authors used voltage and frequency scaling (VFS) to reduce the energy consumption. It achieves the energy efficiency of 22 Mbps/μJ while providing throughput of 100 Mbps. So, it consumes 100/22 Mbps/(Mbps/μJ) = 4.5 μJ per second to achieve the throughput. If the technology was scalable to achieve the required throughput of 5G with a reasonable speed up factor, it would be an energy efficient solution. But the implementation depends on the cores of the processor of the phone to achieve the parallelism, and it seems it would take at least 10 times more cores than that of the phone used in the original implementation. As a result we do not find it as an appealing implementation for a 5G phone. There has been an ASIC implementation by Elliptic Semiconductor Inc. that achieves 2.5 Gbps throughput at 100 Mhz frequency and 15K gates as cited in [19]. In [19] the authors presented an ASIC implementation of SNOW 3G using the 130 nm CMOS library with 1.2 V core voltage and 25K gates. At 249 MHz they have been able to harness a throughput of 7.9 Gbps. Though both of the implementations provide much more than the throughput required in 5G, we can't argue anything with them as no concrete power figures are found. In [21], IP Cores Inc. presents two implementations of SNOW 3G called SNOW3G1 as shown in Table 2. They too do not provide any power/energy figures. Fortunately, in [20], the authors have used the SNOW3G implementation of IP Cores Inc. and have estimated that using 4 parallel blocks of SNOW3G1 with hard macro storage, a throughput of 30 Gbps is achievable at 1650 MHz while consuming 14.41 mJ of energy per second. We scale down the frequency by 30 times and expect the energy consumption per second will also be scaled down at the same proportion. According to that assumption, at 1650/30 MHz = 55 MHz, we should be able to harness the throughput of 1 Gbps by spending 14.41/30 mJ = 0.48 mJ of energy. The authors estimated the power consumption on a gate-level netlist by back-annotating the switching activity and using Synopsys Power Compiler tool.

Table 2. SNOW3G1 in [21]

Technology	Max frequency	Area/Resources	Throughput
TSMC 65 nm G+	302 MHz	7,475 gates	2.4 Gbps
TSMC 65 nm G+	943 MHz	8,964 gates	7.5 Gbps

4 Overall Comparison

The overall energy consumption of a phone depends on the usage pattern of the user of the phone. Radio activities of the cellular network, lighting up the screen, touch screen and CPU are the commonly considered as the most energy hungry aspects of a smart phone [15].

There are times when a smart phone remains idle and does nothing for a long duration of time. During this time it switches to a suspended state by transferring the state of the phone to the RAM. In suspended state the phone draws a minimal amount of energy from the battery to maintain the state in the memory and receive very limited control signals from the network to be able to receive the incoming traffic. In [15], the authors conducted an experiment on a 2.5G phone and two cutting edge 3G phones of the time. They showed that in suspended state, a 2.5G phone drew 103 mJ of energy per second whereas the 3G phones drew around 25 mJ per second. There is another state when the phone is awake but no application is running. This state is called the idle state. In [15], the authors showed on the same phones that during idle state the amount of energy drawn was less than 350 mJ per second.

Normally, the time duration a smart phone is in a suspended or idle state is much longer than that of when it remains active. So, the energy consumption of the phone during idle or suspended state is very critical for the battery life. However, during these times, the phone hardly encrypts or decrypts any data except the control signals which are mostly paging messages. The reason is that the attach procedure takes place only when the user switches on the phone and tracking area update takes place frequently only when the user is travelling on a vehicle. However, even though paging itself is a burden for the phone from energy point of view, the cryptographic energy requirement for paging message is insignificant. According to [17], even with traditional paging mechanism, there are 1000 paging messages for a phone in an hour, which is less than 1 in a second. According to [3], the paging message is no longer than hundreds of bytes. The energy requirements for AES for this tiny amount of data is very insignificant to the total need 25 mJ per second during the suspended state and of 300 mJ during the idle state.

To understand the energy expense of encryption, we need to focus on the total energy expense of the phone during the active states of the phone when encryption is also being performed. Such active states are phone call, web browsing, email, network data exchange (upload/download) and so on. We choose to focus on the case of network data exchange to argue our case. We assume that the phone would utilize its full download or upload capacity from the data volume point of view during the exchange. We will investigate this case for 2.5G, 3G and 4G phones to see the evolution the energy requirements.

In [15], the authors showed that the 2.5G phone consumed around 700 mJ of energy per second during the network data exchange. Around 640 mJ of this energy budget is spend for cellular network activities. We know in 2.5G, the maximum data rate can be 115 Kbps. At that rate the AES implementation in [9] would spend around 0.000078 mJ of energy per second which is of course very insignificant. The authors of [15] also showed that the 3G phones consumed a similar amount of total energy during data upload/download which is around 900 mJ per second. Considering the connection exchanged the data at its full capacity (7.2 Mbps), the energy share for encryption is around 0.005 mJ which is also very insignificant.

Both in the 2.5G and 3G phone the major energy share for network data exchange is attributed to the radio transmission. However, there has been a significant change in the LTE radio technology and has become even more expensive from energy consumption point of view. In LTE, there are different radio states and the phone promotes and demotes to different states to save energy. As a result even though LTE becomes less energy efficient than 3G for small data transfer, it remains as efficient as 3G in large size data transfer. Also, there is a significant difference in the energy consumption of LTE uplink and downlink. According to [16, Fig. 9], the LTE uplink consumes 3.2 J of energy per second while uploading at the rate of 5 Mbps. From the figure it appears that the energy consumption increases linearly with the uploading data rate with a factor of more than 1. Downloading on the other hand, is less energy expensive, consuming 2.1 J of energy per second at the rate of 19 Mbps. The energy consumption while downloading also increases almost linearly but with a very small factor after 10 Mbps. With screen off, the authors claimed that the energy was mostly consumed by the radio interfaces. The AES implementation in [10] consumes .78 mJ of energy per second providing throughput of 1 Gbps. In order to come up with a loose bound, let us consider that the LTE uplink and downlink would consume the same amount of energy even when the data rate is at the theoretical peak, which is 100 Mbps and around 90 Mbps downlink and uplink respectively. Then the energy share of encryption is still bounded by .04%. It should be noted here that the high energy requirements in LTE are mostly attributed to its radio interface technology. Nevertheless, the radio technology will be different in 5G than that of LTE. Let us consider that the LTE draws E_{lte} mJ of energy per second while transferring data at the theoretical maximum data rate. Let's assume that in 5G, the radio interface will draw E_{lte}/a mJ of energy while providing the throughput of 1 Gpps by using its new efficient radio technology. We know implementations of AES and SNOW 3G that take .78 and .48 mJ of energy per second to provide throughput of 1 Gbps. So, the energy share of encryption in 5G is $\frac{.78a}{E_{lte}} \times 100 = .04a$ percent for AES and $.03a$ percent for SNOW 3G. Considering that the integrity protection will also be incorporated for user data, the cryptographic effort will at most be doubled and hence they will be at most .08a and .06a percent for AES and SNOW 3G respectively.

However, we don't know the value of a for certain. Energy efficiency is a major concern for 5G network. Operators explicitly mention a reduction of total network energy consumption by 50% despite an expected 1,000-fold traffic increase [22]. In [23], it concludes that 5G systems with high energy performance should be built on two design principles. One is to only be active and transmit when needed and the other is to only be active and transmit where needed. In our above discussion the E_{lte} is considered as the energy only when data is being transmitted or received and doesn't include the energy when no data is being exchanged. We haven't found any account on how much more energy efficient 5G uplink and downlink will be. It is difficult to answer as there will be different radio interfaces involved. Search for a reasonably accepted value of a would be a further research question. Very optimistically even we consider the value of a to be 10, the cryptographic energy share still remains below 1%.

5 Conclusion

Number of energy efficient implementations of AES and SNOW 3G have been presented. Some of the implementations use the multiple cores of the CPU of the mobile phone while others use ASIC. We have found that the ASIC implementations can provide the required throughput of 5G. We made assumptions about a 5G network. Based on the assumptions and energy consumption related facts of LTE network available in the literature, we have shown that energy consumption for cryptographic computation is insignificant compared to the total energy need of the phone when bulk data transfer takes place. It should be noted that there might have other implementations of AES and SNOW 3G which are more energy efficient and provide the required throughput. But we did not look into any other implementations as it is evident that even with the implementations presented in this paper keeps the cryptographic energy share very low. However, as 3GPP advances on defining the 5G standards and more results on the energy consumption of the radio interfaces of 5G are published, the exact cryptographic energy share will be clearer.

Acknowledgement. Thanks to Kimmo Järvinen for his help to understand the ASIC implementations and to Jarno Alanko for proofreading.

References

1. 3GPP TS36.323. http://www.3gpp.org/ftp/specs/archive/36_series/36.323/
2. 3GPP TS33.401. http://www.3gpp.org/ftp/specs/archive/33_series/33.401/
3. 3GPP TS36.331. http://www.3gpp.org/ftp/specs/archive/36_series/36.331/
4. Satoh, A., Morioka, S., Takano, K., Munetoh, S.: A compact Rijndael hardware architecture with S-Box optimization. In: Boyd, C. (ed.) ASIACRYPT 2001. LNCS, vol. 2248, pp. 239–254. Springer, Heidelberg (2001). https://doi.org/10.1007/3-540-45682-1_15
5. Rudra, A., Dubey, P.K., Jutla, C.S., Kumar, V., Rao, J.R., Rohatgi, P.: Efficient Rijndael encryption implementation with composite field arithmetic. In: Koç, Ç.K., Naccache, D., Paar, C. (eds.) CHES 2001. LNCS, vol. 2162, pp. 171–184. Springer, Heidelberg (2001). https://doi.org/10.1007/3-540-44709-1_16
6. Cao, Q., Li, S.: A high-throughput cost-effective ASIC implementation of the AES algorithm. In: 2009 IEEE 8th International Conference on ASIC (2009)
7. Alam, M., Ray, S., Mukhopadhayay, D., Ghosh, S., RoyChowdhury, D., Sengupta, I.: Efficient Rijndael encryption implementation with composite field arithmetic. In: Proceedings of the Conference on Design, Automation and Test in Europe DATE 2007, pp. 1116–1121. Springer (2007)

8. Huang, Y.-J., Lin, Y.-S., Hung, K.-Y., Lin, K.-C.: Efficient implementation of AES IP. In: 2006 IEEE Asia Pacific Conference on Circuits and Systems (2006)
9. Hessel, S., Szczesny, D., Lohmann, N., Bilgic, A., Hausner, J.: Implementation and benchmarking of hardware accelerators for ciphering in LTE terminals. In: Global Telecommunications Conference, 2009 (2009)
10. Traboulsi, S., Sbeiti, M., Szczesny, D., Showk, A., Bilgic, A.: High-performance and energy-efficient sliced AES multi-block encryption for LTE mobile devices. In: 2011 IEEE 3rd International Conference on Communication Software and Networks (2001)
11. Sriniwas Shastry, P.V., Kulkarni, A., Sutaone, M.S.: ASIC implementation of AES. In: 2012 Annual IEEE India Conference (2012)
12. Szczesny, D., Showk, A., Hessel, S., Bilgic, A., Hildebrand, U., Frascolla, V.: Performance analysis of LTE protocol processing on an ARM based mobile platform. In: International Symposium on System-on-Chip, 2009 (2009)
13. Badawi, M., Hemani, A., Lu, Z.: Customizable coarse-grained energy-efficient reconfigurable packet processing architecture. In: 2014 IEEE 25th International Conference on Application-Specific Systems, Architectures and Processors (2014)
14. Hessel, S., Szczesny, D., Bruns, F., Bilgic, A., Hausner, J.: Architectural analysis of a smart DMA controller for protocol stack acceleration in LTE terminals. In: 2010 IEEE 72nd Vehicular Technology Conference Fall (VTC 2010-Fall) (2010)
15. Carroll, A., Heiser, G.: An analysis of power consumption in a smartphone. In: USENIXATC 2010, Proceedings of the 2010 USENIX Conference on USENIX Annual Technical Conference (2010)
16. Huang, J., Qian, F., Gerber, A., Morley Mao, Z., Sen, S., Spatscheckr, O.: A close examination of performance and power characteristics of 4G LTE networks. In: Proceedings of the 10th International Conference on Mobile Systems, Applications, and Services (2012)
17. Managing LTE Core Network Signaling Traffic by David Nowoswiat. https://insight.nokia.com/managing-lte-core-network-signaling-traffic
18. Traboulsi, S., Sbeiti, M., Bruns, F.: An optimized parallel and energy-efficient implementation of SNOW 3G for LTE mobile devices. In: 12th IEEE International Conference on Communication Technology (ICCT) (2010)
19. Kitsos, P., Koufopavlou, O.G.: High performance ASIC implementation of the SNOW 3G stream cipher. In: IFIP/IEEE VLSI-SOC08 - International Conference on Very Large Scale Integration, Greece (2008)
20. Gupta, S.S., Chattopadhyay, A., Khalid, A.: Designing integrated accelerator for stream ciphers with structural similarities. In: 15th International Conference on Cryptology in India (2014)
21. SNOW 3G Encryption Core. http://www.ipcores.com/Snow3G.htm. Accessed 13 Dec 2016
22. NGMN Alliance, February 2015, NGMN 5G White paper. https://www.ngmn.org/uploads/media/NGMN_5G_White_Paper_V1_0.pdf
23. Ericsson White Paper on 5G Energy Performance. https://www.ericsson.com/res/docs/whitepapers/wp-5g-energy-performance.pdf
24. 5G A Technology Vision. http://www.huawei.com/en/industry-insights/huawei-voices/white-papers
25. 5G radio access. https://www.ericsson.com/res/docs/whitepapers/wp-5g.pdf
26. 5G Nework Architecture Whitepaper. http://www.huawei.com/en/industry-insights/huawei-voices/white-papers
27. 5G Scenarios and Security Design. http://www.huawei.com/en/industry-insights/huawei-voices/white-papers

LR-RZF Pre-coding for Massive MIMO Systems Based on Truncated Polynomial Expansion

Chi Zhang[1(✉)], Zhengquan Li[1,2], Yaoyao Sun[1], Lianfeng Shen[1],
and Xinxin Ni[3]

[1] National Mobile Communications Research Laboratory,
Southeast University, Nanjing 210096, China
ci26zhang@163.com, {lzq722,220150799,
lfshen}@seu.edu.cn
[2] State Key Laboratory of Networking and Switching Technology,
Beijing University of Posts and Telecommunications, Beijing 100876, China
[3] School of Electronic Engineering of Tongda College,
Nanjing University of Posts and Telecommunications, Yangzhou 225127, China
2215798002@qq.com

Abstract. In order to effectively eliminate multi-user interference at the transmitter, the transmit signals are needed to be pre-processing, which is called pre-coding. Traditional linear pre-coding algorithms, especially regularized zero forcing (RZF) pre-coding, are famous for good performance and low computation complexity. However, they cause noise amplification which requires high transmit power to prevent. Lattice-reduction aided (LR-aided) technique is used to deal with the row/column of matrix, which can make the matrix orthogonality better. Therefore, to avoid noise amplification as well as effectively eliminate the multi-user interference, we propose a LR-RZF pre-coding algorithm which based on matrix truncated polynomial expansion (TPE) with J terms. TPE method can decrease the complexity of matrix inversion in RZF. Compared with RZF pre-coding, LR-RZF pre-coding has lower bit error rate.

Keywords: LR · RZF · TPE · Massive MIMO

1 Introduction

Massive MIMO systems is able to cope with the exponential growth in number of user terminals (UTs) and data traffic, so recently the deployment of massive MIMO has received a lot of attention. In this system, in order to effectively eliminate multi-user interference at the transmitter, the transmit signals are needed to be pre-processing, which is pre-coding. Pre-coding can be divided into linear and nonlinear pre-coding, where the nonlinear pre-coding mainly has the dirty paper pre-coding [1] and the constant envelope pre-coding [2, 3]. The basic idea of the dirty paper pre-coding is to process the signals at the transmitter, so that the receiver cannot think of the interference exiting between users in the receive signals, which can increase the total system capacity. While the basic idea of the constant envelope pre-coding is to pre-process the information symbols, so that the signal amplitudes are the same, and the receiver can recover the signals according to the signal phases. Unfortunately, the complexity of two nonlinearly pre-coding algorithms are very high. Therefore, some scholars proposed some low complexity pre-coding algorithms, in which the most famous is the regularized zero forcing (RZF) pre-coding algorithm. However, its complexity increases sharply when the number of antennas is large as it needs to compute matrix inversion. Therefore, scholars proposed to replace the matrix inversion with approximate algorithm. In [4, 5], authors used the matrix truncated polynomial expansion (TPE) to replace the matrix inverse operation in RZF pre-coding algorithm to reduce the computation complexity. But in this two references, only the sum of the mean square error is minimized and the optimal polynomial coefficients through optimization of power allocation is obtained, respectively. The coherence of the base station transmit antennas is considered [6, 7], in which the matrix TPE is used to carry out the linear pre-coding, so as to avoid the computation of matrix inverse in the RZF pre-coding algorithm.

Lattice-Reduction (LR) technology is a kind of mathematical processing method [8, 9]. The basic idea is that, the columns of a matrix A can be interpreted as the basis of a lattice. The aim of the lattice reduction is to transform a given basis A into a new basis consisting of roughly orthogonal basis vectors. For the channel matrix, because each row/column vector is not orthogonal, and after the lattice reduction technique processing, it can makes the row/column vector orthogonality better. In this paper, we propose a LR-RZF pre-coding algorithm based on matrix TPE. The channel matrix is handled by LR first and gets good orthogonality. Then it is applied in RZF and RZF based on the TPE pre-coding. Furthermore, we simulate the bit error rate of those pre-coding algorithms.

The paper is organized as follows. In Sect. 2, we describe the system model. The LR-RZF pre-coding algorithm based on matrix TPE is presented in Sect. 3. The simulation results are in Sect. 4. Some conclusions are made in Sect. 5.

2   System Model

We consider a downlink massive MIMO system in which a base station (BS), equipped with N transmit antennas, serves K single-antenna UTs, where $N \gg K$. Suppose $\mathbf{h}_k \sim CN(\mathbf{0}_{N \times 1}, \mathbf{\Phi}/K)$ represents the random channel vector between the transmit antennas at BS and the kth UT ($1 \leq k \leq K$), where $\mathbf{\Phi}$ is the channel covariance matrix with $N \times N$, and $\mathbf{0}_{N \times 1}$ is a zero vector. The signals needed by the K single-antenna UTs can be represented by $\mathbf{s} = [s_1,...,s_k,...,s_K]^T$, where s_k is the signal of the kth UT which satisfies $s_k \sim CN(0,1)$, and $(\cdot)^T$ denotes the transpose of a matrix. Suppose $\mathbf{G} = [\mathbf{g}_1,...,\mathbf{g}_k]$ is the pre-coding matrix with $N \times K$. The signal $\mathbf{s}$ is transmitted to the mobile UTs via the base station antennas after the pre-coding. So the received signal of the kth UT is

$$y_k = \mathbf{h}_k^H \mathbf{G} \mathbf{s} + n_k = \mathbf{h}_k^H \mathbf{g}_k s_k + \sum_{n=1,n \neq k}^{K} \mathbf{h}_k^H \mathbf{g}_n s_n + n_k \qquad (1)$$

where n_k is the additive circularly symmetric complex Gaussian noise at the kth UT, which satisfies $n_k \sim CN(0,\sigma^2)$, where σ^2 is the receiver noise variance. And $(\cdot)^H$ denotes the conjugate transpose of a matrix or a vector. Suppose that the total transmit power satisfies as follow

$$\frac{1}{K}\text{tr}(\mathbf{GG}^H) = P \tag{2}$$

where tr$(\cdot)$ is the trace of a matrix.

Then receive signal is detected as

$$\hat{\mathbf{s}} = G^{-1}\Omega(y_k) \tag{3}$$

where $\Omega(\bullet)$ is detection rule.

We suppose that the transmitter does not know the perfect instantaneous channel state information (CSI) $\hat{\mathbf{h}}_k$ of each mobile UT. Based on the model in [10, 11], we suppose that the instantaneous channel of the kth UT obey Gauss-Markov distribution. In other words, $\hat{\mathbf{h}}_k$ can be expressed as follow

$$\hat{\mathbf{h}}_k = \sqrt{1 - \tau^2}\mathbf{h}_k + \tau\mathbf{n}_k \tag{4}$$

where τ is a scalar parameter which indicates the quality of the instantaneous CSI, which satisfies $\tau \in [0, 1]$. We can get perfect instantaneous CSI and only statistical knowledge of channel for $\tau = 0$ and $\tau = 1$, respectively. Assuming that the joint imperfect channel matrix of all user channels can be denoted by $\hat{\mathbf{H}} = [\hat{\mathbf{h}}_1, \cdots, \hat{\mathbf{h}}_K]$, with $N \times K$.

3   LR-RZF Pre-coding Algorithm Based on the TPE

We conducted LR decomposition of the channel matrix $\hat{\mathbf{H}}$, assuming that the decomposition of the matrix $\hat{\mathbf{H}}$ into matrix $\tilde{\mathbf{H}}$, the two matrices are satisfied [8, 9]

$$\tilde{\mathbf{H}} = \hat{\mathbf{H}}\mathbf{T} \tag{5}$$

where $\mathbf{T}$ is a unimodular matrix with $K \times K$, it contains only Gaussian integers and det $(\mathbf{T}) = \pm 1$ or $\pm j$. The LR decomposition algorithm is listed in Algorithm 1.

Algorithm 1. LR algorithm

1. Initialize: T=I and $\tilde{\mathbf{H}} = \mathbf{H}$

2. Set $[\mathbf{S}]_{ij} = [\mathbf{H}^H\mathbf{H}]_{ij} = s_{ij}, [\mathbf{S'}]_{ij} = [(\mathbf{H}^H\mathbf{H})^{-1}]_{ij} = s'_{ij} \ \forall i, j$

3. for i=1 to K do

4. for j=1 to K do

5. $v_{ij} \leftarrow \dfrac{s'_{ji}}{2s'_{ii}} - \dfrac{s_{ji}}{2s_{jj}}$

6. $\lambda_{ij} \leftarrow \lfloor v_{ij} \rfloor$

7. $\Delta_{ij} \leftarrow 2s_{jj}s'_{ii}\{\text{real}(2\lambda_{ij}^* v_{ij} - |\lambda_{ij}|^2)\}$

8. end for

9. end for

10. $(n,l) \leftarrow \underset{(i,j)}{\arg\max}\, \Delta_{ij}$

11. $\mathbf{t}_n^u \leftarrow \mathbf{t}_n + \lambda_{n,l}\mathbf{t}_l$

12. $\mathbf{T} \leftarrow [\mathbf{t}_1, \cdots, \mathbf{t}_{n-1}, \mathbf{t}_n^u, \mathbf{t}_{n+1}, \cdots, \mathbf{t}_N]$

13. $\tilde{\mathbf{h}}_n^u \leftarrow \mathbf{h}_n + \lambda_{n,l}\tilde{\mathbf{h}}_l$

14. $\tilde{\mathbf{H}} \leftarrow [\tilde{\mathbf{h}}_1, \cdots, \tilde{\mathbf{h}}_{n-1}, \tilde{\mathbf{h}}_n^u, \tilde{\mathbf{h}}_{n+1}, \cdots, \tilde{\mathbf{h}}_N]$

15. Repeat 1 to 14, until all $\Delta_{ij} = 0$, we can get $\tilde{\mathbf{H}}$ and $\mathbf{T}$, which are the last $\tilde{\mathbf{H}}$ and the product of all $\mathbf{T}$, respectively.

Similar to [6, 11], we define LR-RZF pre-coding algorithm as

$$\mathbf{G}_{\text{LR-RZF}} = \beta\tilde{\mathbf{H}}\left(\tilde{\mathbf{H}}^H\tilde{\mathbf{H}} + \xi\mathbf{I}_K\right)^{-1} = \beta\left(\tilde{\mathbf{H}}\tilde{\mathbf{H}}^H + \xi\mathbf{I}_N\right)^{-1}\tilde{\mathbf{H}} \tag{6}$$

where β is the power normalization parameter, which is set such that the pre-coding matrix $\mathbf{G}_{\text{RZF}}$ satisfies the power constraint in (2). The parameter ξ depends on the total transmit power P, the noise variance σ^2, the scalar parameter τ affecting the instantaneous CSI, and system dimensions [11, 12].

Inspecting (6) shows that, when the base station antenna number N is very large, the complexity of the $N \times N$ matrix $\tilde{\mathbf{H}}\tilde{\mathbf{H}}^H + \xi\mathbf{I}_N$ inversion is very high. In order to reduce the computational complexity, the matrix inversion can be replaced by a matrix TPE. From [11] we know that for any positive definite Hermitian matrix $\mathbf{X}$, when the parameter α is selected such that $0 < \alpha < \frac{2}{\max_n \lambda_n(\mathbf{X})}$, the inverse of the matrix $\mathbf{X}$ can be expressed as

$$\mathbf{X}^{-1} = \alpha(\mathbf{I} - (\mathbf{I} - \alpha\mathbf{X}))^{-1} = \alpha \sum_{l=0}^{\infty} (\mathbf{I} - \alpha\mathbf{X})^{l} \tag{7}$$

By substituting (7) and the expression $(a+b)^{l} = \binom{l}{n} a^{l-n} b^{n}$ into (6), we can get the polynomial expansion of the pre-coding matrix $\mathbf{G}_{\text{LR-RZF}}$, and we just only consider the first J terms because of the low-order terms are the most influential ones. So we have

$$\mathbf{G}_{\text{LR-RZF}} = \beta \left(\tilde{\mathbf{H}} \tilde{\mathbf{H}}^{H} + \xi\mathbf{I}_{N} \right)^{-1} \tilde{\mathbf{H}} \approx \sum_{l=0}^{J-1} \omega_{l} \left(\tilde{\mathbf{H}} \tilde{\mathbf{H}}^{H} \right)^{l} \tilde{\mathbf{H}} \tag{8}$$

where ω_{l} is a scalar parameter, and its value is seen in [11].

4   Simulation results

In this section, we calculate the bit error rate performance of pre-coding algorithms, including RZF, LR-RZF, RZF based on the TPE and LR-RZF based on the TPE. The MIMO system has 8 transmit antennas in the BS and 8 antennas at receiver. The transmit symbols are modulated by BPSK and QPSK respectively. The detection method is MMSE.

According to Fig. 1, it can be seen that the BER performance of LR-RZF is better than RZF in the same condition using BPSK modulation. The channel matrix $\mathbf{H}$ is generated randomly which is independent and identically complex Gaussian random variables. When $\mathbf{H}$ is handled by LR algorithm, it is more orthogonal and the channel condition is improved. Therefore, at the target BER of 10^{-4}, LR-RZF gains about 4 dB transmit power compared with RZF which needs 25 dB SNR. What is more, LR-RZF can get 10^{-6} BER performance at 45 dB. However, the BER performance of RZF

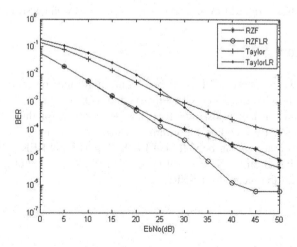

Fig. 1. BER performances of RZF pre-coding schemes with BPSK modulation

based on the TPE is worse than RZF because it estimates the matrix inversion with 3-order TPE. At low SNR, the performance of LR-RZF based on the 3-order TPE is worse than RZF based on the 3-order TPE. When SNR is 27 dB, two pre-coding has similar BER performance. With the increase of SNR, LR-RZF based on the 3-order TPE gains better performance. Besides, LR-RZF based on the 3-order TPE is able to get 10^{-5} BER performance at 50 dB.

According to Fig. 2, the transmit signal is modulated by QPSK. At the target BER of 10^{-3}, RZF needs about 28 dB SNR. LR-RZF gains about 3 dB transmit power compared with RZF. LR-RZF can get nearly 10^{-5} BER performance at 45 dB. At low SNR, LR-RZF based on 3-order TPE is not good. When SNR is 26 dB, LR-RZF based on 3-order TPE has similar performance compared with RZF based on the 3-order TPE. With the increase of SNR, LR-RZF based on 3-order TPE has better BER performance. At about 50 dB, it can get 10^{-5} BER performance.

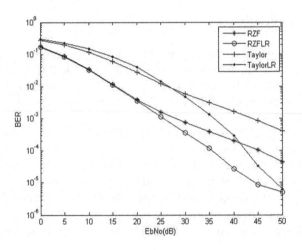

Fig. 2. BER performances of RZF pre-coding schemes with QPSK modulation

5   Conclusion

In this paper, we proposed a LR-RZF pre-coding algorithm based on the TPE. We apply LR algorithm to deal with channel matrix and make it more orthogonal. Then the improved channel matrix is used in RZF and RZF based on the TPE pre-coding. Therefore, improved pre-coding algorithm can decrease the noise amplification and multi-user interference. It can be seen that LR-RZF gets good BER performance than RZF. LR-RZF based on the TPE is not good when SNR is low, but gets better BER performance with the increase of SNR.

Acknowledgments. This work was supported in part by the National Natural Science Foundation of China (61571108), the Open Foundation of State key Laboratory of Networking and Switching Technology (Beijing University of Posts and Telecommunications) (SKLNST-2016-2-14), and the China Postdoctoral Science Foundation Funded Project (No. 2012M511175).

References

1. Peel, C.B.: On "Dirty-Paper coding". IEEE Signal Process. Mag. **20**(3), 112–113 (2003)
2. Mohammed, S.K., Larsson, E.G.: Per-antenna constant envelope precoding for large multi-user MIMO systems. IEEE Trans. Commun. **61**(3), 1059–1071 (2013)
3. Pan, J., Ma, W.K.: Constant envelope precoding for single-user large-scale MISO channels: efficient precoding and optimal designs. IEEE J. Sel. Top. Signal Proces. **8**(5), 982–995 (2014)
4. Zarei, S., Gerstacker, W., Muller, R.R., et al.: Low-complexity linear precoding for downlink large-scale MIMO systems. In: IEEE International Symposium on Personal Indoor and Mobile Radio Communications, pp. 1119–1124. IEEE (2013)
5. Zarei, S., Gerstacker, W., Schober, R.: A low-complexity linear precoding and power allocation scheme for downlink massive MIMO systems. In: Asilomar Conference on Signals, Systems and Computers, pp. 285–290 (2013)
6. Mueller, A., Kammoun, A., Björnson, E., et al.: Linear precoding based on polynomial expansion: reducing complexity in massive MIMO. EURASIP J. Wirel. Commun. and Netw. **2016**(1), 63 (2016)
7. Kammoun, A., Muller, A., Bjornson, E., et al.: Linear precoding based on polynomial expansion: large-scale multi-cell MIMO systems. IEEE J. Sel. Top. Signal Proces. **8**(5), 861–875 (2014)
8. Yao, H., Wornell, G.W.: Lattice-reduction-aided detectors for MIMO communication systems. In: Global Telecommunications Conference, GLOBECOM 2002, vol.1, pp. 424–428. IEEE (2002)
9. Chockalingam, A., Rajan, B.S.: Large MIMO Systems. Cambridge University Press, New York (2013). IEEE
10. Muller, A., Kammoun, A., Bjornson, E., et al.: Efficient linear precoding for massive MIMO systems using truncated polynomial expansion. In: Sensor Array and Multichannel Signal Processing Workshop. pp. 273–276. IEEE (2014)
11. Wagner, S., Couillet, R., Debbah, M., et al.: Large system analysis of linear precoding in correlated MISO broadcast channels under limited feedback. IEEE Trans. Inf. Theory **58**(7), 4509–4537 (2013)
12. Peel, C.B., Hochwald, B.M., Swindlehurst, A.L.: A vector-perturbation technique for near-capacity multiantenna multiuser communication, Part I: channel inversion and regularization. IEEE Trans. Commun. **53**(1), 195–202 (2005)

A Geographic Packet Forwarding Approach in 3D Mobile Ad Hoc Networks

Xiaolin Gao[1,3(✉)], Guiting Zhong[2], Jian Yan[2], and Jianhua Lu[1]

[1] Department of Electronic Engineering, Tsinghua University,
Beijing 100084, China
sgyybaby@126.com, lhh-dee@tsinghua.edu.cn
[2] Tsinghua Space Center, Tsinghua University, Beijing 100084, China
zhonggt12@mails.tsinghua.edu.cn,
yanjian_ee@tsinghua.edu.cn
[3] Beijing Aerospace Control Center, Beijing 100094, China

Abstract. In high dynamic 3D mobile ad hoc network, the mobility of node is the main factor that causes the topology change and the route instability. In this paper, we proposed a novel geographic forwarding approach based on node mobility features (FBMF) and selection of the relay node via distributed cooperation among receivers for highly dynamic 3D Ad hoc networks. Node mobility features are defined as the mobility factor which considers not only the individual node mobility but also the relative mobility of the other node. The proposed forwarding approach make use of node mobility features to select relay node. Simulation results show that compared with other methods, the proposed approach is more efficient in terms of packet delivery ratio and end-to-end delay, in other words, the stability of route is promoted in the highly dynamic mobile environment.

Keywords: 3D Ad hoc network · Geographic route · Greed forwarding
Random forwarding · Mobility factor

1 Introduction

In recent years, with the research and application of mobile Ad hoc networks, the application scenario has been extended from the traditional terrestrial 2D scene to the spatial 3D scene. Therefore, some new research areas have emerged, such as the Ad Hoc Network [8], UAV network [3], and underwater ad hoc network [2] and so on. The general characteristics of these networks are high-speed movement of nodes in 3D space, large-scale network distribution scenario and highly dynamic topology, which belong to 3D mobile Ad Hoc Networks (3D MANET). 3D MANET routing protocol is one of the important technologies to realize the out-of-sight transmission between network nodes, which has aroused the concern of researchers. The routing protocol based on geographical position information could realize the packet forwarding only by keeping the position information of the destination node. So the node does not maintain the end-to-end route, which is more suitable for such large-scale 3D MANET.

© ICST Institute for Computer Sciences, Social Informatics and Telecommunications Engineering 2018
K. Long et al. (Eds.): 5GWN 2017, LNICST 211, pp. 420–428, 2018.
https://doi.org/10.1007/978-3-319-72823-0_40

References [1, 4, 5, 7, 9] proposed a variety of routing protocol for 3D MANET based on the position information. This kind of routing protocol adopts the greedy forwarding approach. However, when a candidate node closer than the current relay node to the destination does not exist, a routing hole problem of the greedy forwarding approach would happen, which could degrade the protocol performance. In [6, 10], a random forwarding approach based on position information is proposed, which uses the distance between the relay node and the destination node as the route metrics to select next-hop node set (CNS). In this approach, the broadcast characteristics of the channel were used to realize multiple potential relay nodes to compete and decide whether to become the relay node autonomously. It improves the performance of the protocol.

However, the forwarding approach in the above-mentioned protocol only considers the static characteristics of the nodes. When selecting the relay nodes, the neighbor nodes are usually selected nearest to the destination nodes. This usually causes the selected relay nodes to be located near the communication radius of the source node. In the highly dynamic network such as 3D MANET, when the above-mentioned forwarding approach is used, the mobility of the node will cause the link to be switched on and off frequently. In this kind of network, the distance between nodes couldn't fully reflect the path quality, that is, the stability of the route is also affected by the link duration (lifetime) between relay nodes. Node mobility will affect the establishment of reliable routing, and thus affect the reliability of packet delivery performance and delay performance.

In this paper, we propose a geographic forwarding approach based on mobility features of the nodes (FBMF). In the selection of relay nodes, the mobility of nodes is taken into full account. The position information and the stability factor which is the function of the mobility of nodes and their neighbors are used as the routing metric to provide the basis for the selection of relay nodes. Because the mobility characteristics of the node are fully considered in the process of relay node determining, compared with the other geographic forwarding approach, the performance (which main parameters are the packet delivery ratio and the end-to-end delay) of the proposed forwarding approach have improved. Finally, the simulation results prove this point.

2   Positioning Service and Forwarding Policy

In this section, we define notations and terms used throughout this article. Then the proposed geographic packet forwarding approach is presented. We assume that:

1. Each node knows its geographic position.
2. Each node knows the geographic position of all other nodes, including the target node.

We further assume that the geographic position of each node is unique. In general, the geographic position of the node can be obtained by GPS or any other positioning algorithms. The position information of neighbor nodes is distributed by the beacon exchange between each other. The positioning service is essential to accomplish packet forwarding in the proposed geographic routing protocol.

We need to get the position information of the destination node through position service on account of the node mobility. With a focus on the impact of node mobility on packet forwarding performance, this work assumes that each node has implemented position service.

The relay node selection scheme is shown in Fig. 1. The communication radius of all nodes in the network is R. That is, when the distance between two nodes is less than R, the two-way communication link can be established. When the distance is larger than R, the link is broken. The nodes are moving at constant speed V. The direction of the node is unchanged during the move; The movement speed and direction of nodes are independent of each other.

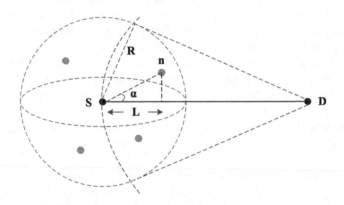

Fig. 1. Illustrations of the scheme used to select neighbors as forwarders

As shown in Fig. 1, P_s is the position information of the source node S, which is represented as (x_s, y_s, z_s). The position information of the destination node D is P_d, which is represented as (x_d, y_d, z_d). N is defined as the neighbor nodes set of source node, which is represented as $N = \{n_1, n_2, \ldots, n_m\}$.

N' is defined as candidate next-hop node set

$$N' = \{n_i : L_{min} \leq L_i \leq R\}, \tag{1}$$

and $N' \subset N$. L_{min} is defined as the minimum advance value, which is the condition to select the relay node set. L_i is the distance from the source node S to the destination node D when the node n_i is chosen as the relay node, which is represented as

$$L_i = \sqrt{(x_s - x_{n_i})^2 + (y_s - y_{n_i})^2 + (z_s - z_{n_i})^2} \cdot \cos \alpha. \tag{2}$$

In order to avoid repeating forward, the candidate next hop nodes that received a packet wait for a back-off time before forwarding the packet. $T_f^{n_i}$ is the back-off time of node n_i, which is computed on the position of node n_i, source node position, destination node position and the metrics M_{n_i}, following Eq. (3)

$$T_f^{n_i} = k \cdot \max_{n_i \in N'} \left\{ \frac{1}{d(P_s, P_d) - d(P_{n_i}, P_d)} - \frac{1}{d(P_{n_i}, P_s)} \right\} \cdot M_{n_i}. \qquad (3)$$

The triangle inequality asserts that candidate next-hop nodes could hear packet forwarding each other. The metrics M_{n_i} is determined by the stability factor and the distance information. The short back-off time should mean good position advancement and high relatively stable.

FBMF Forwarding Process

- The source node S selects the candidate next-hop node set N', according to the position information P_d of the destination node D.
- Sending the packet to the candidate next-hop node set, which includes the *ID* of the source node S, the *ID* of the destination node D, the position information and the speed information.
- The node that received the packet calculates the back-off time according to the position information and the metrics in the received packet. Equation (3) shows that the shorter the back-off time, the higher the probability that the node will be selected as the relay node, which could cooperate with the other relay nodes to decide the forwarding order/priority. The metrics information is determined by the stability factor and the distance information, the calculation method of metrics information is shown in the following section.

In this forwarding approach, when the candidate relay node receives the packet, it sends it in the order of the back-off time. Obviously, a node with a short back-off time has high priority than a node with a long back-off time. After the other candidate relay node has heard the packet has been forwarded, it discards the local corresponding packet. When the candidate relay node does not detect that the packet is forwarded within a certain period of time, it thinks the packet fails to be forwarded, and then forwards the packet automatically. Therefore, this method does not require message loss recovery mechanism. Compared to the greedy forwarding strategy, it could reduce the feedback information. On the other hand, this method is easier to extend than the GeRaF approach [10], which is based on the handshake mechanism of MAC protocol to cooperative between the candidate relay nodes' order/priority.

3 Calculation of Metrics

The selection of the candidate next-hop node set is the key factor which would affect the performance of the forwarding protocol. The node based on GeRaF [10] measures the geographical distance, and it only needs to know the position of neighboring nodes and the destination node. It uses the distance from each neighbor to the destination node as a measure to select the set of relay nodes. The proposed method uses a static factor S and distance parameter L as the standard of metrics M calculation. The great value of the node-static factors and the close to the destination node would mean the node is in the high the forwarding priority, and the node is more likely to be selected as a relay node. The metrics M takes into account the mobility of the nodes and the group mobility of their neighbors (represented by the static factor S), and the distance parameter L_d, which is a function of both. The following is a detailed calculation process.

3.1   Static Factor

The three velocity components of a node n_i in the relay node set N' are v_{ix}, v_{iy}, v_{iz}, respectively.

The different between the average speed of the node n_i and the average speed of the source node S are

$$\Delta v_{2i} = \sqrt{(v_{ix} - v_{sx})^2 + (v_{iy} - v_{sy})^2 + (v_{iz} - v_{sz})^2} \tag{4}$$

The average velocity components of the group of neighbor nodes of node n_i are v_x, v_y, v_z, respectively.

And

$$v_x = \frac{1}{m}\sum_{i \in I} v_{ix}, v_y = \frac{1}{m}\sum_{i \in I} v_{iy}, v_z = \frac{1}{m}\sum_{i \in I} v_{iz},$$

where I is the neighbor nodes set of node n_i, and m is the number of the neighbor nodes.

The difference between the average speed of the node n_i and the neighbor group is

$$\Delta v_{1i} = \sqrt{(v_{ix} - v_x)^2 + (v_{iy} - v_y)^2 + (v_{iz} - v_z)^2} \tag{5}$$

The static factor S_i is defined as follows

$$S_i = \frac{\Delta v_{1i} + \Delta v_{2i}}{2|V|} \tag{6}$$

It represents the relative motion stability of a single node n_i relative to the source node and its neighbor node set.

From the Eq. (6), the small the relative speed of the source node, and the small the dynamics of the whole neighbor group, would mean the node n_i is relatively stable.

3.2   Calculation of Routing Metrics

The metrics M_i of the node n_i takes into account the static factor S_i and the distance parameter L_{d_i}.

The formula is:

$$M_{n_i} = (S_i + 1)^{L''_{di}} \tag{7}$$

L''_{d_i} is the normalized distance, which is defined as:

$$L''_{d_i} = \frac{L_{d_i}}{L_{sd} - L_{min}} \tag{8}$$

The influence of the static factor S and the distance parameter L_d on the metrics parameters is shown in Fig. 2. As it can be seen from Fig. 2, the great the static factor S and the great the distance result to the great the metrics. According to Eq. (3) the node has the longer back-off time, which would have the lower forwarding priority. Since node only calculates their own metrics M, it may determine the forwarding order/priority in a distributed manner.

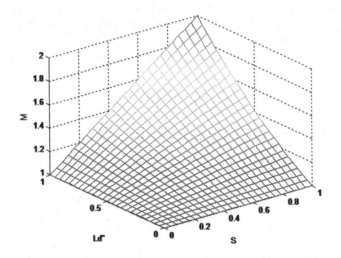

Fig. 2. Influence of S and L''_{d_i} on M

From the calculation process of the metric M, the algorithm actually weighs the mobility and position characteristics of the nodes and chooses the node with low mobility and near to the destination node as the relay nodes.

4   Simulation Results

Comparison of three methods of 3D Greedy forwarding (3DGF), 3D random forwarding (3DRAF) and the forwarding approach based on mobility features (FBMF) proposed in this paper are carried out. The simulation environment is as follows: 50 nodes are randomly distributed in the $\sqrt{L^2 + H^2/2} \times \sqrt{L^2 + H^2/2}$ 3D space. L is the maximum length and width of the node distribution range, the value is 15 km. H is the maximum height of the node distribution range, the value is 10 km. The node's velocity component is given by $(-V, +V)$, and V is the maximum velocity of the node movement. After the node reaches the boundary of the region, it returned to the simulation area at the original speed. The bounce angle is randomly selected between $[0, 2\pi]$. Since 3DRAF forwards based strategy of RTS/CTS, the simulation using the

IEEE 802.11 MAC protocols, the data transfer rate is 2 Mbit/s. Traffic model is the continuous bit rate (CBR), traffic packet length is 1024 bits, packet interval is 0.1 s. Each source node randomly selects the nodes in the simulation region as the destination node.

Figure 3 shows the results of the packet delivery ratio of three forwarding approaches under different moving speeds. When the node speed is 0, the network is a static, and the packet delivery ratio of the three methods is all higher than 85%. Due that 3DRAF and FBMF methods take into account the broadcast characteristics of the wireless channel and adopt the relay node cooperation mechanism, they achieved higher packet delivery ratio than 3DGF method. With the increase of the node's moving speeds, the dynamic of the network increases gradually, then the packet delivery ratio of 3DGF and 3DRAF decreases obviously. However, FBMF considers the mobility of the nodes in the selection of relay nodes, the node with low relative mobility (high stability) is selected as the relay node, thus maintaining a stable high packet delivery ratio.

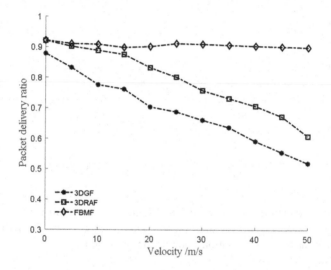

Fig. 3. Packet delivery ratio

Figure 4 shows the comparison of average end-to-end delay. Since FBMF chooses a node that is close to the destination node and with a smaller relative mobility (high stability) as the next-hop forwarding node, it reduces the possibility of routing holes (no next-hop nodes) which would increase the number of forwarding. Therefore, under dynamic network conditions compared to the other two forwarding approaches to get a lower average end to end delay.

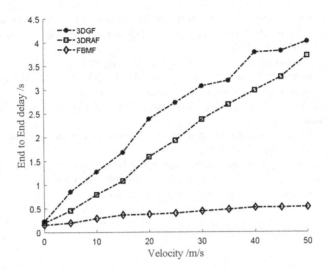

Fig. 4. End to end delay

5 Conclusions

In high dynamic 3D mobile ad hoc network, the mobility of node is the main factor that causes the topology change and affects the route stability. Therefore, taking node mobility into consideration in the process of relay node selection and path maintenance can improve the performance of routing algorithm. In this paper, we proposed a routing metrics based on node mobility, then presented a forwarding strategy make use of the routing metrics. The simulation results show that the packet delivery and end-to-end delay are better than the other two types of forwarding approaches when the node moves at high speed. Therefore, the performance of this approach under high dynamic conditions has obvious advantages.

Acknowledgment. This work is partially supported by Natural Science Foundation of China under Grant No. 91338108, 91438206.

References

1. Cadger, F., Curran, K., Santos, J., Moffett, S.: A survey of geographical routing in wireless Ad-hoc networks. IEEE Commun. Surv. Tutor. **15**(2), 621–653 (2013)
2. Foo, K., Atkins, P., Collins, T., Pointer, S., Tiltman, C.: Sea trials of an underwater, Ad-hoc, acoustic network with stationary assets. IET Radar Sonar Navig. **4**(1), 2–16 (2010)
3. Frew, E., Brown, T.: Airborne communication networks for small unmanned aircraft systems. Proc. IEEE **96**(12), 2008–2027 (2008)
4. Liu, C., Wu, J.: Efficient geometric routing in three dimensional Ad-hoc networks. IEEE INFOCOM **2009**, 2751–2755 (2009)

5. Liu, S., Fevens, T., Abdallah, A.E.: Hybrid position-based routing algorithms for 3D mobile ad hoc networks. In: 2008 The 4th International Conference on Mobile Ad-hoc and Sensor Networks, pp. 177–186, December 2008
6. Odorizzi, A., Mazzini, G.: M-GeRaF: a reliable random forwarding geographic routing protocol in multisink Ad-hoc and sensor networks. In: 2007 International Symposium on Intelligent Signal Processing and Communication Systems, pp. 416–419, November 2007
7. Tahan, A.M.A., Watfa, M.K.: A position-based routing algorithm in 3D sensor networks. Wirel. Commun. Mob. Comput. 12(1), 33–52 (2010)
8. Zheng, B., Zhang, H., Huang, G., Ren, Q.: Status and development of aeronautical Ad-hoc networks. Telecommun. Sci. 27(5), 38–47 (2011)
9. Zhou, J., Chen, Y., Leong, B., Sundaramoorthy, P.S.: Practical 3D geographic routing for wireless sensor networks. In: Proceedings of the 8th ACM Conference on Embedded Networked Sensor Systems, pp. 337–350. ACM (2010)
10. Zorzi, M., Rao, R.: Geographic random forwarding (GeRaF) for Ad-hoc and sensor networks: energy and latency performance. IEEE Trans. Mob. Comput. 2(4), 349–365 (2003)

Probabilistic Caching in Wireless Device to Device Networks with Contention Based Multimedia Delivery

Xiaoshi Song[✉], Yuting Geng, Xiangbo Meng, Ning Ye, Jun Liu, and Weimin Lei

Northeastern University, Shenyang 110819, China
songxiaoshi@cse.neu.edu.cn

Abstract. This paper studies the optimal probabilistic caching placement in large-scale cache-enabled D2D networks to maximize the cache hit performance, which is defined as the probability that a random user request can be served by mobile helpers (MHs) in the vicinity. To avoid collisions of the concurrent transmissions, a contention based multimedia delivery protocol is proposed, under which a MH is allowed to transmit only if its back-off timer is the smallest among its associated contenders. By applying tools from stochastic geometry, the optimal caching probability is derived and analyzed. It is shown that the optimal solution of the probabilistic caching placement depends on the density of MHs, the D2D communication range, and the user request distribution. With the derived optimal caching probabilities, we further characterize the transmission probability of MHs and thereby the successful content delivery probability of the cache-enabled D2D network. Simulations are provided to validate our analysis.

Keywords: Cache-enabled D2D networks
Contention based multimedia delivery protocol
Optimal probabilistic caching strategy · Stochastic geometry
Transmission probability · Cache hit probability
Successful content delivery probability

1 Introduction

The proliferation of smart mobile devices has triggered an explosive increase of data traffic over recent years, mainly driven by the ever-growing demand of bandwidth-intensive multimedia services. Predicted by Cisco [1], the mobile data traffic is expected to reach 30.6 exabytes per month by 2020, an eightfold increase over 2015, in which more than 80% would be contributed by multimedia streaming. Facing such an unprecedented growth of multimedia data traffic over the air, it is crucial for mobile operators to seek and leverage more advanced techniques to facilitate the content-centric design of next generation wireless networks [2–4].

The emerging cache-enabled device-to-device (D2D) communication paradigm is considered to be an effective approach to tackle the mobile data tsunami induced by massive demands on multimedia content delivery [5–9]. Particulary, with caching abilities enabled at the proximate mobile devices (helpers), the D2D communication

© ICST Institute for Computer Sciences, Social Informatics and Telecommunications Engineering 2018
K. Long et al. (Eds.): 5GWN 2017, LNICST 211, pp. 429–444, 2018.
https://doi.org/10.1007/978-3-319-72823-0_41

can cost-effectively bring the multimedia contents closer to users, and simultaneously exploit the spatial recuse and (coded or uncoded) multicasting opportunities in data dissemination to relieve the heavy burden of the fast growing traffic.

Existing works on the modeling and analysis of cache-enabled D2D communication has taken two main directions. The first line of work [10, 11] focuses on the theoretical analysis of asymptotic scaling laws for cache-enabled D2D networks under the classic protocol model, where the reception of a data packet from source u to destination v is assumed to be successful only if their transmission distance $d(u, v)$ is less than or equal to a predefined collaboration range r, and no other concurrent transmissions is within distance $(1 + \Delta)r$ from destination v for $\Delta > 0$. Particularly, in [10], Ji et al. characterized the optimal throughput-outage tradeoff for cache-enabled D2D networks in terms of scaling laws, under the assumption that both the number of users n and the library size m grow to infinity. With decentralized random caching and unicast delivery, it was shown in [10] that, for arbitrary outage probability $\rho \in (0, 1)$, the per-user throughput of the cache-enabled D2D networks can achieve a bit rate of order $\frac{M}{m}$, where M denotes the caching capacity of each device and $M \gg \frac{M}{m}$. Based on [10], in [11], Ji et al. further characterized the scaling laws of the same cache-enabled D2D network by applying both spatial reuse and coded multicasting. Interestingly and somehow counterintuitively, it was shown in [11] that the gain of spatial reuse and the gain of the coded multicasting do not accumulate in the order sense.

The second line of work [12–17] considers the physical model, where the successful communication between two nodes is based on the received signal-to-interference ratio (SIR) or signal-to-interference-plus-noise ratio (SINR). Tools from stochastic geometry have been widely applied in this category for tractable characterization of key network performance metrics, such as coverage, rate, and spatial throughput. Particularly, in [12], Jarray et al. studied the hit performance of caching in D2D networks for different degrees of node mobility. In [13], Malak et al. developed the optimal spatially-independent content caching strategies that aim to maximize the average density of successful receptions under different fading distributions. In [14], Malak et al. further investigated the optimal geographic content placement problem for D2D networks, and proposed spatially correlated caching strategies to maximize the D2D cache hit probability. In [15], Afshang et al. characterized the performance of cluster-centric content placement in a cache-enabled D2D network by developing a comprehensive analytical framework with foundations in stochastic geometry. In [16], Chen et al. provided analytical and numerical results to compare the performance of caching at mobile devices and caching at small cells, in terms of the cache hit probability, the density of cache-served requests and average power consumption. In [17], Chen et al. studied the optimal caching probabilities with numerical optimization by analyzing a closed-form approximation of cache-aided throughput, which measures the density of successfully served requests by local device caches.

Interference management is of critical importance in the design of cache-enabled D2D networks. With elaborate interference management schemes, the effective spatial reuse and thereby the overall performance of cache-enabled D2D networks can be significantly improved. It is worth noting that in the above prior works [10–17], the interference management issue of cache-enabled D2D networks has not been well addressed.

Particularly, in [10, 11], the studied protocol model and the corresponding guard-zone based interference avoidance strategy failed to capture the effect of small-scale fading and aggregate interference on the performance of successful reception. While in [12–17], though tractable analytical results on network performance were characterized under the physical model, the interference management problem was not discussed. As such, the benefits of advanced interference management mechanisms in enhancing the performance of cache-enabled D2D networks remain to be explored.

In this paper, we investigate the optimal probabilistic caching strategy in large-scale cache-enabled D2D networks under the physical model to maximize the cache hit performance, which is defined as the probability that a random user request can be served by mobile helpers (MHs) in the vicinity. Different from that in [12–17], a contention based multimedia delivery protocol is proposed to tackle the interference management issue, which is described as follows.

Contention based Multimedia Delivery Protocol: In the content delivery phase, to avoid collisions among the concurrent transmissions, the MHs under requests are assumed to each start with a random back-off timer, which is uniformly distributed on [0, 1]. By monitoring the medium, a MH then makes decision to initiate its transmission if no contender with contention threshold N_d is detected prior to the expiration of its back-offer timer, while otherwise it defers. In other words, in the content delivery phase, under the proposed contention based multimedia delivery protocol, a MH under request is allowed to transmit only if it has the minimal back-off timer among its contenders with contention threshold N_d.

It is worth noting that under the proposed contention based multimedia delivery protocol, due to the interactions among the concurrent transmissions, the positions of the active MHs are in general dependent. As a result, how to effectively characterize the dependencies among the active MHs is the major challenge to be tackled in this paper.

The remainder of this paper is organized as follows. The system model and performance metrics are described in Sect. 2. The optimal probabilistic caching placement is characterized in Sect. 3. The transmission probability of MHs is derived in Sect. 4. The successful content delivery probability of the cache-enabled D2D networks is analyzed in Sects. 5. Simulation results are presented in Sect. 6. Finally, we conclude the paper in Sect. 7.

2 Model and Metrics

2.1 System Model

We consider a large-scale cache-enabled D2D network formed by dedicated MHs, intended UEs, and a library of multimedia files $\mathcal{F} := \{1, 2, \cdots, F\}$ on $\mathbb{R}^2$ as illustrated in Fig. 1. The locations of MHs and UEs are modeled as two independent HPPPs with density λ_m and λ_u, respectively. To simplify the analysis, it is assumed that the files in library $\mathcal{F}$ are of the same size, and each MH has a cache memory of $M = 1$ file. A decentralized probabilistic caching strategy is investigated in this paper, under which the MH randomly caches the f-th file in $\mathcal{F}$ with probability c_f. We further assume that the popularity of the f-th file in $\mathcal{F}$ follows the Zipf distribution as

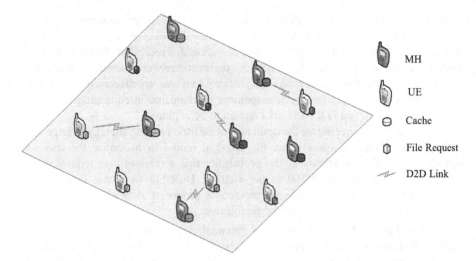

Fig. 1. Cache-enabled D2D network formed by dedicated MHs, intended UEs, and a library of multimedia files $\mathcal{F}$.

$$pf = \frac{1/f^{\gamma}}{\Sigma_{j=1}^{F} 1/j^{\gamma}}, \tag{1}$$

where $0 < \gamma < 1$ denotes the Zipf parameter.

The propagation channel is modeled as the combination of the small-scale Rayleigh fading and the large-scale path-loss given by

$$g(d) = hd^{-\alpha}, \tag{2}$$

where h denotes the exponentially distributed power coefficient with unit mean, d denotes the propagation distance, and α denotes the path-loss exponent. The transmit power of MHs is denoted by P_d. For the sake of simplicity, we ignore the thermal noise in the regime of interest and simply focus on the received signal-to-interference ratio (SIR). Let R_d denote the collaboration distance of D2D transmission between MH and UE. We further denote θ_d as the SIR target for successful data receptions under D2D communication.

To avoid collisions among the concurrent transmissions, a contention based multimedia delivery protocol with contention threshold N_d is proposed, under which a content request from the UE can be served iff:

1. The requested file is available at the MHs (denoted by eligible MHs) within a distance of R_d.
2. At least one of the eligible MHs has the minimal back-off timer among its contenders[1] with contention threshold N_d.

Upon finding the eligible MHs, the UEs then associate with the nearest ones for data transmission.

2.2   Performance Metric

The performance metrics studied in this paper are specified as follows.

Transmission Probability: The transmission probability of MH, denoted by q_d, is defined as the probability that a MH is eligible to launch the transmission.

Cache Hit Probability: The cache hit probability, denoted by ξ_d, is defined as the probability that a randomly requested file can be found at the caches of eligible MHs which are able to launch the transmissions within a distance of R_d Let ξ_f denote the conditional cache hit probability for the f-th file in $\mathcal{F}$. Then, the cache hit probability ξ_d of the cache-enabled D2D network is given by

$$\xi_d = \sum_{f=1}^{F} p_f \cdot \xi_f. \tag{3}$$

Coverage Probability: The coverage probability of a randomly requested file is defined as the probability that a UE succeeds in decoding the received data packets of the file from its associated MH. In particular, for the f-th file in $\mathcal{F}$, given the received SIR SIR_f, and the SIR target θ_d, the coverage probability C_f is defined as

$$c_f = \Pr\left(\text{SIR}_f \geq \theta_d\right). \tag{4}$$

Successful Content Delivery Probability: The successful content delivery probability in cache-enabled D2D networks, denoted by τ_d, is defined as the probability that a random UE request is successfully served by MHs within a distance of R_d. In particular, for the f-th file in $\mathcal{F}$, given the conditional cache hit probability ξ_f, and the coverage probability C_f, the successful content delivery probability τ_d of the cache-enabled D2D network is defined as

$$\tau_d = \sum_{f=1}^{F} p_f \cdot \xi_f \cdot C_f \tag{5}$$

---

[1] For two eligible MHs located at $\mathbf{x}$ and $\mathbf{y}$, we say $\mathbf{y}$ is a contender of $\mathbf{x}$ with contention threshold N_d if $P_d h |\mathbf{y} - \mathbf{x}|^{-\alpha} \geq N_d$.

3 Optimal Probabilistic Caching Placement

In this section, we derive the optimal probabilistic caching placement to maximize the cache hit performance. We first obtain the following lemma.

Lemma 1. *The cache hit probability of the studied large-scale cache-enabled D2D network is given by*

$$\rho_d = 1 - \sum_{f=1}^{F} p_f e^{-\lambda_m c_f \pi R_d^2}, \tag{6}$$

where F denotes the size of library $\mathcal{F}$

Proof. Given p_f, c_f, and R_d, (6) can be immediately obtained by characterizing the void probability that none of the MHs within a distance of R_d caches the requested file. This thus completes the proof of Lemma 1.

Based on (6), the optimization problem for maximizing the cache hit probability is defined as

$$\max_{cf} \rho d \tag{7}$$

$$s.t. \ c_f \geq 0, \tag{8}$$

$$\sum_{f=1}^{F} c_f = 1. \tag{9}$$

It is worth noting that the second order derivative of the objective function (7) is strictly negative over the feasible set of c_f. As such, ρ_d is a concave function with respect to c_f. By introducing the Lagrangian multipliers γ_f and v on (8) and (9), respectively, we obtain the Lagrangian function of (7) as

$$L = -\rho_d - \sum_{f=1}^{F} \gamma_f c_f + v \left(\sum_{f=1}^{F} c_f - 1 \right), \tag{10}$$

which leads to the following Karush-Kuhn-Tucker (KKT) optimality conditions [18]

$$-\lambda_m p_f \pi R_d^2 . e^{-\lambda_m c_f \pi R_d^2} - \gamma_f + v = 0, \forall f, \tag{11}$$

$$\sum_{f=1}^{F} c_f - 1 = 0, \tag{12}$$

$$\gamma_f . c_f = 0, \forall f, \tag{13}$$

$$c_f \geq 0, \forall f, \qquad (14)$$

$$\gamma_f \geq 0, \forall f. \qquad (15)$$

Further, with (11), (13) and (15), it can be easily verified that

$$v - \lambda_m p_f \pi R_d^2 . e^{-\lambda_m c_f \pi R_d^2} \geq 0, \forall f, \qquad (16)$$

and

$$(v - \lambda_m p_f \pi R_d^2 . e^{-\lambda_m c_f \pi R_d^2}).c_f = 0, \forall f, \qquad (17)$$

respectively.

It is worth noting that for $v < \lambda_m p_f \pi R_d^2$, (16) holds only if $c_f > 0$. As such, based on (17), we have

$$c_f = -\frac{1}{\lambda_m \pi R_d^2} \ln \left(\frac{v}{\lambda_m p_f \pi R_d^2} \right), \qquad (18)$$

for $v < \lambda_m p_f \pi R_d^2$. On the other hand, for $v \geq \lambda_m p_f \pi R_d^2$, it can be easily verified from (17) that

$$c_f = 0. \qquad (19)$$

By combining the results derived in (18) and (19), we then obtain that

$$c_f = \left(-\frac{1}{\lambda_m \pi R_d^2} \ln \left(\frac{v}{\lambda_m p_f \pi R_d^2} \right) \right)^+, \qquad (20)$$

where $(z)^+ = \max \{0, z\}$. To characterize the optimal solutions of c_f, we substitute (20) for c_f into (12) and obtain that

$$\sum_{f=1}^{F} \left(-\frac{1}{\lambda_m \pi R_d^2} \ln \left(\frac{v}{\lambda_m p_f \pi R_d^2} \right) \right)^+ = 1. \qquad (21)$$

Then, based on (21), by applying a computational procedure, the optimal value of c_f, which is denoted by c_f^*, is readily obtained.

Remark 3.1. It can be observed from the analysis that the optimal solution c_f^*, depends on the density of MHs λ_m, the D2D communication range R_d, and the user request distribution p_f.

4 Transmission Probability

In this section, we characterize the transmission probability of MHs in large-scale cache-enabled D2D networks under the proposed contention based multimedia delivery protocol. Particularly, let ζ_d denote the probability that a MH is under request. We first derive ζ_d in the following lemma.

Lemma 2. *For large-scale cache-enabled D2D networks, the probability that a MH is under request is given by*

$$\zeta_d \sum_{f=1}^{F} c_f \cdot \left(1 - e^{-\lambda_u p_f \pi R_d^2} \right). \tag{22}$$

Proof. Given p_f, c_f, and R_d, (22) can be immediately obtained by considering the void probability that there is no UE request of the file cached at the tagged MH within a distance of R_d. This thus completes the proof of Lemma 2.

Let Ψ_m^r be the point process formed by the MHs under request and let λ_m^r be the corresponding density. Then, based on Lemma 2, we obtain the following corollary.

Corollary 1. *For large-scale cache-enabled D2D networks, the density of Ψ_m^r is given by*

$$\lambda_m^r = \lambda_m \cdot \zeta_d. \tag{23}$$

It is worth noting that for MHs within a distance of R_d, the requests of UEs are spatially correlated. As such, Ψ_m^r does not follow a HPPP. Furthermore, since the higher order statistics of Ψ_m^r are intractable, the transmission probability of MHs, which depends on the probability generating functional (PGFL) [19] of Ψ_m^r is difficult to be characterized exactly. To tackle this difficulty, similar to [20–22], we make the following approximation on Ψ_m^r, which will be verified later by simulations in Sect. 6.

Assumption 1. *For large-scale cache-enabled D2D networks, Ψ_m^r follows a HPPP with density λ_m^r*

With (22) and (23), based on Assumption 1, we are ready to evaluate the transmission probability of MHs under the proposed contention based multimedia delivery protocol, as given by following theorem.

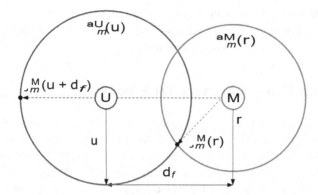

Fig. 2. Conditional distribution of active MH under the proposed contention based multimedia delivery protocol.

Theorem 1. *For large-scale cache-enabled D2D networks, under the proposed contention based multimedia delivery protocol, based on Assumption 1, the transmission probability of MHs is given by*

$$qd = \zeta d \cdot \vartheta d, \tag{24}$$

where ϑ_d denotes the probability that a MH in Ψ^r_m is eventually allowed to launch the transmission as

$$\vartheta_d = \frac{1 - e^{-\pi \lambda^r_m \Gamma \left(1 + \frac{2}{\alpha}\right)\left(\frac{N_d}{p_d}\right)^{-\frac{2}{\alpha}}}}{\pi \lambda^r_m \Gamma \left(1 + \frac{2}{\alpha}\right)\left(\frac{N_d}{p_d}\right)^{-\frac{2}{\alpha}}}. \tag{25}$$

Proof. The proof of Theorem 1 is omitted due to space limitation.

Remark 4.1. It can be easily verified from Theorem 1 that $\xi_d < 1$ and thereby $q_d < \zeta_d$.

Let Ψ^a_m be the point process formed by active MHs under the proposed contention based multimedia delivery protocol and let λ^a_m be the corresponding density. Based on Theorem 1, we obtain the following corollary

Corollary 2. *For large-scale cache-enabled D2D networks, under the proposed contention based multimedia delivery protocol, based on Assumption 1, the density of Ψ^a_m is given by*

$$\lambda^a_m = \lambda_m \cdot q_d. \tag{26}$$

In the following section, with Theorem 1, we characterize the successful content delivery probability of large-scale cache-enabled D2D networks under the proposed contention based multimedia delivery protocol.

5 Successful Content Delivery Probability

To analyze the successful content delivery probability of the studied large-scale cache-enabled D2D networks, thanks to the stationarity of the point processes formed by the MHs and UEs, we focus on a typical UE at the origin denoted by **U** with its associated MH at a random distance of d_f away denoted by **M**. Let $\Psi_m^U(u)$ and $\Psi_m^M(u)$ be the point processes formed by the active MHs on a circle of radius u centered at **U** and **M**, respectively, as illustrated in Fig. 2. Further, let $\lambda_m^U(u)$ and $\lambda_m^M(u)$ be the average density of $\Psi_m^U(u)$ and $\Psi_M^M(u)$, respectively.

In the following, we first characterize the distributions of $\Psi_m^U(u)$ and $\Psi_m^M(u)$, respectively, and then derive the successful content delivery probability of the large-scale cache-enabled D2D network.

Lemma 3. *Under the proposed contention based multimedia delivery protocol, based on Assumption 1, conditioned on a typical UE at the origin, $\Psi_m^M(u)$ is isotropic[2] with respect to **M** with density $\lambda_m^M(u)$ given by*

$$\lambda_m^M(u) = \lambda_m^a \left(1 - e^{-\frac{N_d u^\alpha}{P_d}} \right). \tag{27}$$

Proof. Conditioned on a typical UE at the origin, under Assumption 1, the probability that a MH on a circle of radius u centered at **M** is active is given by $q_d \cdot \Pr\left(h \le \frac{N_d u^\alpha}{P_d} \right)$, where h denotes an exponentially distributed random variable with unit mean. Based on this result, it can be easily verified that $\Psi_m^M(u)$ is isotropic around **M** with density $\lambda_m^M(u)$ given by (27). This thus completes the proof of Lemma 3.

It is worth noting that due to the contentions among the MHs, even under Assumption 1, $\Psi_m^M(u)$ does not follow a HPPP. As a result, with only the first-order moment measures (average densities) of $\Psi_m^M(u)$ being obtained, the successful content delivery probability of the studied large-scale cache-enabled D2D network is difficult to be characterized exactly. To tackle this difficulty, we make the following approximation on the conditional distribution of the active MHs, which will be verified later by simulations in Sect. 6.

Assumption 2. *Under the proposed contention based multimedia delivery protocol, based on Assumption 2, conditioned on a typical UE at the origin, $\Psi_m^M(u)$ follows a HPPP with density $\lambda_m^M(u)$.*

---

[2] A point process $\mathcal{N}$ is isotropic if its characteristics are invariant under rotation [24].

Based on Lemma 3 and Assumption 2, we characterize the distribution of $\Psi_m^U(u)$ in the following two lemmas.

Lemma 4. *Under the proposed contention based multimedia delivery protocol, conditioned on a typical UE at the origin, an upper bound on $\lambda_m^U(u)$ is given by*

$$\lambda_m^U(u) \leq \lambda_m^a \cdot \left(1 - e^{-\frac{N_d(u+d_f)^\alpha}{P_d}}\right). \tag{28}$$

Proof. The proof immediately follows from Fig. 2 by observing that the highest density of $\Psi_m^U(u)$ is $\lambda_m^M(u+d_f)$.

Lemma 5. *Under the proposed contention based multimedia delivery protocol, based on Assumption 2, conditioned on a typical UE at the origin, the following inequality on $\lambda_m^U(u)$ holds:*

$$\int_0^\infty \frac{\lambda_m^U(u)}{1 + \frac{u^\alpha}{\theta_d d_f^\alpha}} u \, du \geq \int_0^\infty \frac{\lambda_m^M(u)}{1 + \frac{u^\alpha}{\theta_d d_f^\alpha}} u \, du. \tag{29}$$

Proof. The proof of Lemma 5 is omitted due to space limitation.

With Lemmas 4 and 5, we are ready to evaluate the successful content delivery probability of this D2D network, as given by the following theorem.

Theorem 2. *For large-scale cache-enabled D2D networks, under the proposed contention based multimedia delivery protocol, based on Assumption 2, the successful content delivery probability is lower-bounded and upper-bounded, respectively, by*

$$\tau_d \geq \sum_{f=1}^F p_f \int_0^{R_d} \exp\left\{-(1-c_f)\int_0^\infty \eta(u+d_f) u \, du\right\}$$
$$\times \exp\left\{-c_f \int_{d_f}^\infty \eta(u+d_f) u \, du\right\} \cdot \varpi_f(d_f) \, dd_f, \tag{30}$$

$$\tau_d \leq \sum_{f=1}^F p_f \int_0^{R_d} \exp\left\{-(1-c_f)\int_0^\infty \eta(u) u \, du\right\}$$
$$\times \exp\left\{-c_f \int_{d_f}^\infty \eta(u-d_f) u \, du\right\} \cdot \varpi_f(d_f) \, dd_f, \tag{31}$$

where $\eta(x)$ is given by

$$\eta(x) = 2\pi\lambda_m^a \cdot \frac{\left(1 - e^{-\frac{N_d x^\alpha}{P_d}}\right)}{1 + \frac{u^\alpha}{\theta_d d_f^\alpha}},\tag{32}$$

and $\varpi_f(d_f)$ is given by

$$\varpi_f(d_f) = 2\lambda_m^a c_f \pi d_f \cdot e^{-\lambda_m^a c_f \pi d_f^2}.\tag{33}$$

Proof. The proof of Thereom 2 is omitted due to space limitation.

6   Numerical Results

In this section, we present simulation results on the performance of the cache-enabled D2D network to validate our analytical results. Throughout this section, unless specified otherwise, we set up $P_d = 10, P_d/N_d = 5, \theta_d = 2, R_d = 25, \gamma = 1$, and $\alpha = 4$.

6.1   Cache Hit Probability

Figure 3 shows the cache hit probability ρ_d versus the number of files in library F when $\lambda_m = 0.05$ and 0.01, respectively. It is observed in Fig. 3 that cache hit probability is a decreasing function of F and λ_m. We also compare the proposed optimal probabilistic caching strategy with the random caching strategy in terms of the cache hit performance. It is also observed that the proposed optimal probabilistic caching strategy outperforms the Zipf-like random caching strategy.

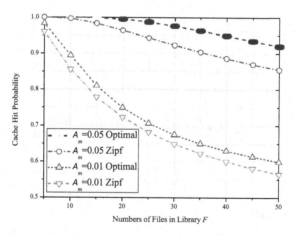

Fig. 3. Cache hit probability ρ_d versus the number of files in library F.

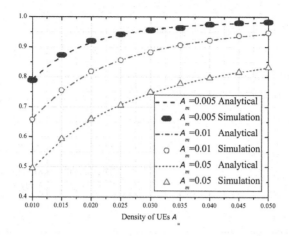

Fig. 4. Transmission probability q_d versus the density of UEs λ_u.

6.2 Transmission Probability

Figure 4 shows the analytical and simulated results on the transmission probability q_d versus the density of UEs λ_u when $\lambda_m = 0.005$, 0.01, and 0.05, respectively, with $F = 20$. It is observed that the transmission probability in the cache-enabled D2D network is an increasing function of λ_u, while a decreasing function of λ_m, which are intuitively expected according to Theorem 4.1. It is also observed that the simulation results fit closely to our analytical results.

6.3 Successful Content Delivery Probability

Figure 5 compares the analytical and simulated results on the successful content delivery probability τ_d versus the transmission probability λ_u, when $\lambda_m = 0.005$, and 0.01, respectively. It is observed that the simulated successful content delivery probability of the cache-enabled D2D network falls between the upper and lower bounds derived in Theorem 5.1 as expected. It is also observed that the successful content delivery probability τ_d is an increasing function of the density of UEs λ_u.

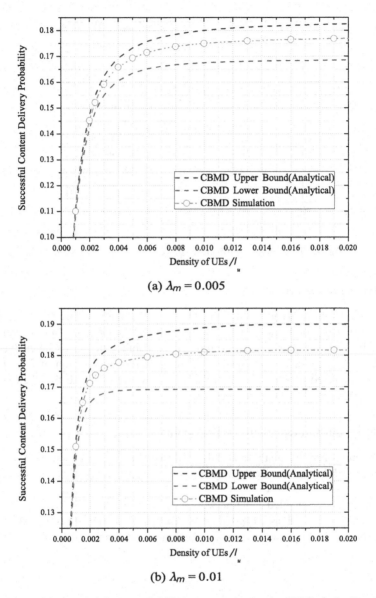

Fig. 5. Successful content delivery probability τ_d versus the density of UEs λ_u for $F = 5$, where CBMD stands for the contention based multimedia delivery protocol.

7 Conclusion

This paper has studied the performance of large-scale cache-enabled D2D networks with contention based multimedia delivery protocol. By applying tools from stochastic geometry, the optimal caching probability is derived and analyzed. It is shown in the analytical results that the optimal solution of the probabilistic caching placement depends on the density of MHs, the D2D communication range, and the user request distribution. With the derived optimal caching probabilities, we further characterize the transmission probability of MHs and thereby the successful content delivery probability of the cache-enabled D2D network. Simulations are provided to validate our analysis. It is hoped that the results in this paper will provide new insights to the optimal design of large-scale cache-enabled D2D networks.

Acknowledgements. This work was supported in part by Fundamental Research Funds for the Central Universities under Grant No. N150403001, the National Natural Science Foundation of China under Grant 61671141, U14331156, 1151002, 61401079, 61501038, and the Major Research Plan of the National Natural Science Foundation of China under Grant 91438117,91538202.

References

1. Cisco: Cisco visual networking index: global mobile data traffic forecast update, 2015–2020, Whitepaper, June 2016
2. Liu, H., Chen, Z., Tian, X., Wang, X., Tao, M.: On content-centric wireless delivery networks. IEEE Wirel. Commun. **21**(6), 118–125 (2014)
3. Liu, H., Chen, Z., Qian, L.: The three primary colors of mobile systems. arXiv preprint arXiv:1603.03551 (2016)
4. Zhao, Z., Peng, M., Ding, Z., Wang, W., Poor, H.V.: Cluster content caching: an energy-efficient approach to improve quality of service in cloud radio access networks. IEEE J. Sel. Areas Commun. **34**(5), 1 (2016)
5. Ji, M., Caire, G., Molisch, A.F.: Wireless device-to-device caching networks: basic principles and system performance. IEEE J. Sel. Areas Commun. **34**(1), 176–189 (2016)
6. Sheng, M., Xu, C., Liu, J., Song, J.: Enhancement for content delivery with proximity communications in caching enabled wireless networks: architecture and challenges. IEEE Commun. Mag. **54**(8), 70–76 (2016)
7. Bai, B., Wang, L., Han, Z., Chen, W., Svensson, T.: Caching based socially-aware D2D communications in wireless content delivery networks: a hypergraph framework. IEEE Wirel. Commun. **23**(4), 74–81 (2016)
8. Liu, D., Chen, B., Yang, C., Molisch, A.F.: Caching at the wireless edge: design aspects, challenges, and future directions. IEEE Commun. Mag. **54**(9), 22–28 (2016)
9. Golrezaei, N., Molisch, A.F., Dimakis, A.G., Caire, G.: Femtocaching and device-to-device collaboration: a new architecture for wireless video distribution. IEEE Commun. Mag. **51**(4), 142–149 (2013)
10. Ji, M., Caire, G., Molisch, A.F.: The throughput-outage tradeoff of wireless one-hop caching networks. In: 2013 IEEE International Symposium on Information Theory Proceedings (ISIT), pp. 1461–1465. IEEE (2013)
11. Ji, M., Caire, G., Molisch, A.F.: Fundamental limits of caching in wireless D2D networks. IEEE Trans. Inf. Theory **62**(2), 849–869 (2014)
12. Chedia, J., Giovanidis, A.: The effects of mobility on the hit performance of cached D2D networks. Spatial Stochastic Models for Wireless Networks (2016)
13. Derya, M., Al-Shalash, M., Andrews, J.G.: Optimizing the spatial content caching distribution for device-to-device communications. In: IEEE International Symposium on Information Theory (2016)

14. Derya, M., Al-Shalash, M., Andrews, J.G.: Spatially correlated content caching for device-to-device communications. arXiv preprint arXiv:1609.00419 (2016)
15. Afshang, M., Dhillon, H.S., Chong, P.H.J.: Fundamentals of cluster-centric content placement in cache-enabled device-to-device networks. IEEE Trans. Commun. **64**(6), 2511–2526 (2015)
16. Chen, Z., Kountouris, M.: D2D caching vs. small cell caching: where to cache content in a wireless network? In: IEEE International Workshop on Signal Processing Advances in Wireless Communications (2016)
17. Chen, Z., Pappas, N., Kountouris, M.: Probabilistic caching in Wireless D2D Networks: Cache Hit Optimal vs. Throughput Optimal. arXiv preprint arXiv:1611.03016 (2016)
18. Boyd, S., Vandenberghe, L.: Convex Optimization. Cambridge University Press, Cambridge (2003)
19. Haenggi, M., Ganti, R.K.: Interference in Large Wireless Networks. Foundations and Trends in Networking. NOW, Hanover (2009)
20. Lee, C., Haenggi, M.: Interference and outage in Poisson cognitive networks. IEEE Trans. Wirel. Commun. **11**(4), 1392–1401 (2012)
21. Song, X., Yin, C., Liu, D., Zhang, R.: Spatial throughput characterization in cognitive radio networks with threshold-based opportunistic spectrum access. IEEEJ. Sel. Areas Commun. **32**(11), 2190–2204 (2014)
22. Nguyen, T., Baccelli, F.: A probabilistic model of carrier sensing based cognitive radio. In: Proceedings of IEEE Symposium on New Frontiers in Dynamic Spectrum Access Networks, Singapore, April 2010
23. Kingman, J.F.C.: Poisson Processes. Oxford University Press, New York (1993)
24. Stoyan, D., Kendall, W., Mecke, J.: Stochastic Geometry and Its Applications, 2nd edn. Wiley, New York (1996)

Eigenvalue and Capacity Analysis Based on Measurement of Massive MIMO System at 3.5 GHZ

Ruijie Xu[✉], Jianhua Zhang, and Jie Xi

Key Lab of Universal Wireless Communications, State Key Lab of Networking
and Switching Technology, Ministry of Education,
Beijing University of Posts and Telecommunications,
P.O. Box 92, Beijing 100876, China
{superjerry1992,jhzhang,xijie}@bupt.edu.cn

Abstract. This paper mainly focus on the analysis of the eigenvalues and capacity for massive multiple-input multiple-output (MIMO) systems based on the channel measurements conducted at 3.5 GHz with 200 MHz. The measurements are conducted under three typical deployment scenarios: the Outdoor to Indoor (O2I), the Urban Macro cell (UMa) and the Urban Micro cell (UMi). Then we investigate the results of the normalized eigenvalues of the channel correlation matrix and angular spread (AS) for both azimuth and elevation direction. Under the line of sight (LoS) condition, the cumulative density function (CDF) of the normalized eigenvalues under O2I has the most uniform distribution followed by UMi, and UMa in the last. The eigenvalues and the orthogonality between sub-channels are affected by the angular spread. The AS of both azimuth and elevation arrival angle under UMi scenario are the biggest, and smallest under UMa. Finally, ergodic capacity for all scenarios is investigated and the advantages of the Massive MIMO system are highlighted. With same signal to noise ratio (SNR), the largest capacity is achieved under UMi in non-line of sight (NLoS) condition.

1 Introduction

Multiple input multiple output (MIMO) has been used in downlink transmission as a must-option in long term evolution (LTE) system. However, with the limits of MIMO channels, to achieve higher data rates is particularly challenging for systems that are power, bandwidth, and complexity limited [1]. Massive MIMO has drawn concern since the concept was firstly introduced by Marzetta [2]. Massive MIMO system takes advantage of multiple transmit and receive antennas, another way significantly increase channel capacity. The basic idea behind massive MIMO is to achieve all the benefits of conventional MIMO on a much larger antenna number scale. Massive MIMO scales conventional MIMO by an order or two in magnitude [3], and extra antennas help by focusing energy into ever smaller regions of space to transmit the signal to desired users and bring

© ICST Institute for Computer Sciences, Social Informatics and Telecommunications Engineering 2018
K. Long et al. (Eds.): 5GWN 2017, LNICST 211, pp. 445–458, 2018.
https://doi.org/10.1007/978-3-319-72823-0_42

huge improvements in throughput and radiated energy efficiency by reducing intra-cell interference. Other advantages include extensive use of inexpensive low-power components, reduced latency, simplification of the MAC layer, and robustness against intentional jamming [4].

There has been researches about the massive MIMO system with measurements conducted at 2.6 GHz with 50 MHz [5], the effects on the singular value and capacity of uniform cylindrical array (UCA) and uniform linear array (ULA) antennas at base station (BS) are presented. Some other measurements are conducted at 5.8 GHz with 100 MHz [6] and the analysis mainly focuses on the effect of antenna aperture on frequency dependence. So the propagation characteristics, changing along with the frequency of electromagnetic wave and surrounding environment, play important roles for the performance of the wireless communication systems [7]. One problem worthy of study is that how the massive MIMO system performs under different scenarios at another frequency. Considering 3.5 GHz being a test frequency for the 5th generation wireless communication, we conduct a series of field measurements at 3.5 GHz with 200 MHz. And besides analysing eigenvalues and capacity of the system, we furthermore relate them to the AS.

The distribution of eigenvalues is the most basic property of the channel correlation matrix. It directly represents the spatial correlation of the channel, the number of parallel independent sub-channels that can be used, the multiplexing gain and maximum beam forming gain of massive MIMO system. So another problem worthy of attention is that how the correlation of the subchannels changes with the number of antennas at BS or mobile station (MS) side changes. With the help of the normalized eigenvalues and the direct observation of the correlation matrix, we will have a more profound understanding. The mean value of the angular spread (AS) shows the degree of freedom (DOF) in the propagation and affects the spatial correlation between the sub-channels. Also the reciprocal of the angular spread is the coherence distance. Finally to evaluate the performance of Massive MIMO system, the capacity results calculated from the real measurement data are compared to the capacity results of simulation for independent identically distributed (i.i.d) channel.

This paper is organized as follows. In Sect. 2, there is the description of both the measurement and the scenarios. The illustration of the data post processing in Sect. 3. Then the analysis of the parameters is given in Sect. 4. Finally, the conclusions are drawn in Sect. 5.

2   Measurement

2.1   Measurement Description

The channel measurements are conducted in Beijing University of Post and Telecommunications, China, utilizing the Elektrobit Propsound Sounder described. Three measurements scenarios are the O2I scenario, the UMa scenario and the UMi scenario. The massive MIMO system considered is that of 128 antenna elements at the BS side and 32 antenna elements at the MS side.

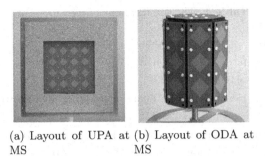

(a) Layout of UPA at MS   (b) Layout of ODA at MS

Fig. 1. Layout of antennas

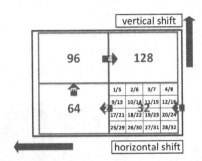

Fig. 2. Illustration of the virtual uniform planar array

At the BS side, the inter element spacing is defined as d and it is fixed on $\lambda/2$ (λ refers to the wave length) for both the horizonal and elevational direction. In the literature [8], it is shown that mutual coupling among antenna elements will have an impact on the system capacity when $d \leq 0.2\lambda$ (Fig. 2).

The layout of the antenna arrays at BS and MS side is illustrated in Fig. 1. Two dual-polarized omnidirectional array (ODA) consisting of 16 antenna elements with 8 adjacent sides and a top surface were used at the MS side. At the BS side, there is a dual-polarized uniform planar array (UPA) with 32 antenna elements. In order to meet the requirement, the UPA is moved to four different position to form a virtual uniform planar array with 128 antenna elements. The rationality of the virtual measurement was proved in [9]. The configuration of the antenna arrays along with other measurement parameters are shown in Table. 1.

2.2   Scenario Description

For the UMi scenario, a residential quarter inside the campus is chosen, a typical one. The concrete scenario is illustrated in Fig. 3. The UPA is set on a building with a height of 14.4 m as shown in Fig. 3(a). The mobile MS is located on nine positions of the streets around the building, which are shown in Fig. 3(b), covering both the line of sight (LoS) and non line of sight (NLoS) conditions. When it comes to the UMa scenario, the UPA is set on the rooftop of the main teaching building with 71 m height. The positions for MS are chosen around the

Table 1. The specifications of measurement

Parameter		Value	
Antenna type		ODA (MS)	UPA (BS)
Number of antenna ports		32	32
Number of elements		8 dual polarized	16 dual polarized
Polarized		±45°	±45°
Angle range	Azimuth	−180° ∼ 180°	−70° ∼ 70°
	Elevation	−70° ∼ 90°	−70° ∼ 70°
Center frequency		3.5 GHz	
Band width		200 MHz	
TX power	UMi	32.1 dBm	
	O2I	31.1 dBm	
	UMa	32.8 dBm	
PN sequence		127 chips (UMi, O2I), 255 chips (UMa)	

(a) BS Position for UMi   (b) MS Position for UMi

Fig. 3. Illustration of UMi scenario

(a) BS Position for UMa   (b) MS Position for UMa

Fig. 4. Illustration of UMa scenario

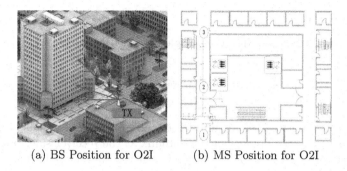

(a) BS Position for O2I   (b) MS Position for O2I

Fig. 5. Illustration of O2I scenario

building right in front of the main teaching building to cover both the LoS and NLoS conditions. Figure 4 is for the illustration. Finally, for the O2I scenario, the UPA is on the rooftop of the no. 1 teaching building of a height of 13.4m. The MS are planned to be on the 4th floor with a height of 14.4 m and 7th floor with a height of 26 m in the building shown in Fig. 5(a). The floor plan display is shown in Fig. 5(b). Detailed values of the scenarios are shown in Table. 2.

Table 2. The specifications of scenario

Scenario	UMi	UMa	O2I 4th floor	O2I 7th floor
Height of UPA (m)	14.4	71	13.4	13.4
Height of ODA (m)	1.9	1.9	14.4	26.0
Parameter	Horizontal distance (m) BS to MS			
Pos1	28	58	28	28
Pos2	27.5	97	28	28
Pos3	51	154	28	28
Pos4	74.5	78	-	-
Pos5	75	101	-	-
Pos6	72.5	149	-	-
Pos7	29	172	-	-
Pos8	48	167	-	-
Pos9	58	-	-	-

3   Data Processing

Measurement data acquired using Elektrobit Propsound sounder [10] enables us to analyze how the massive MIMO system performs. After getting the channel impulse response (CIR) from the original data, the frequency response can be acquired.

3.1 Eigenvalue

$H(j,k)_{M,N}$ is defined as a discrete sample of the CIR matrix $H(t,f)_{M,N}$, which can be written as

$$H_{M,N}(j,k) = H_{M,N}(t,f)|_{t=j\cdot\Delta t, f=k\cdot\Delta f}$$
$$= H(j\cdot\Delta t, k\cdot\Delta f) \tag{1}$$

where the row number M is the number of the transmitter antenna and the column number N is the number of the antenna at the receiver side. And Δt and Δf respectively represent discrete interval in the time domain and frequency domain. $H(j,k)_{M,N}$ is the form of the CIR matrix after fast fourier transformation (FFT). To the CIR matrix at moment j and frequency point k, the singular value decomposition (SVD) of it can be written as

$$H(j,k) = U_{SVD}(j,k)\sum(j,k)V_{SVD}^T(j,k)$$
$$= \sum_{i=1}^{r}\xi_i(j,k)u_i(j,k)v_i(j,k) \tag{2}$$

$1 \leq r \leq \min(M,N)$ refers to the rank of the channel impulse response matrix at moment j and frequency point k. ξ_i is the ith biggest singular value of matrix $H(j,k)$. The distribution of eigenvalues of channel correlation matrix plays a very important role for the performance analysis of MIMO transmission systems. When calculating the channel correlation matrix from the BS side, it is defined as

$$R(j) = E\left\{H(j,k)_{M,N}H^T(j,k)_{M,N}\right\} = E\left\{R(j,k)\right\} \tag{3}$$

$R(j)$ is the average of all the correlation matrix $R(j,k)$ by dimension k.

$$R(j) = U\Lambda U^T \tag{4}$$

So $\xi_i = \sqrt{\lambda(i)}$, $\lambda(i)$ is the ith biggest eigenvalue of the channel correlation matrix. Then CDF of the normalized eigenvalues can be written by

$$F(l) = \sum_{1\leq l\leq i}\lambda(l) \setminus \sum_{1\leq l\leq rank(h(t,f)_{M,N})}\lambda(l) \tag{5}$$
$$(i = 1,2,...,rank(H(j,k)_{M,N}))$$

3.2 Angular Spread (AS)

Root mean square angle spread σ_{AS} can reflect the dispersion of the propagation path gain in the spatial domain, that is, the two order statistics. The mean angle spread μ and the circular angle spread (CAS) σ_{AS} can be calculated by [11]. The concept of CAS is adopted to avoid the angle ambiguity problem.

$$\mu(\Delta) = \frac{\sum_{m=1}^{M}\phi_m(\Delta)P_m}{\sum_{m=1}^{M}P_m} \tag{6}$$

$$\sigma_{AS} = \sqrt{\frac{\sum_{m=1}^{M} (\phi_m - \mu(\Delta))^2 P_m}{\sum_{m=1}^{M} P_m}} \tag{7}$$

$$\phi_m(\Delta) = \phi_m + \Delta \tag{8}$$

$$\phi_m = \begin{cases} 2\pi + \phi_m & \phi_m < -\pi \\ \phi_m & |\phi_m| \leq \pi \\ 2\pi - \phi_m & \phi_m > \pi \end{cases} \tag{9}$$

where M, P_m, and $\phi_m(\Delta)$ denote the number of paths, the power of the mth path and the angle of the mth path adding a shifted angle which denotes a certain angular shift. To get the angular spread, the CIR is processed with the SAGE algorithm [12] to extract the above parameters. Then the angular spread σ_{AS} can be calculated by Eq. 6.

3.3 Capacity

Channel capacity of the jth time index can be caculated by [13]

$$C(j) = \frac{1}{K} \sum_{k=1}^{K} \log_2 \det \left(I_N + \frac{\rho}{\beta M} H_{M,N}(j;k) H_{M,N}{}^H(j;k) \right) \tag{10}$$

where ρ is the signal-to-noise ratio (SNR) and β is a common normalization factor to remove the effects of pathloss, defined by

$$E\left[\frac{1}{\beta} \|H_{M,N}(j;k)\|_F^2\right] = M \cdot N \tag{11}$$

4   Analysis of the Measurement Results

4.1   Eigenvalues

The antenna number of the BS side is denoted as N_{bs} and $N_{bs} = 128$. The antenna number of the mobile station is denoted as N_{ms}. We study the normalized eigenvalues of one mobile station for two cases: case1-$N_{ms} = 4$ and case2-$N_{ms} = 16$. And we display the result with the LoS condition under the UMi scenario in Fig. 6. So for the case2, the number of the sub-carrier are definitely more than that of case1. The main eigenvalues are emphatically focused, especially the largest eigenvalue. Taking 0.5 CDF value as an example, the largest eigenvalue of case2 is smaller than that of case1 by 0.1 for sum ratio. The distribution of main eigenvalues is also more concentrated. From Fig. 6, we can see that for case1 the first two eigenvalues count for over 90% of the whole, while for case2 seven eigenvalues count the same. The largest eigenvalue referred to the path with the best transmitting ability and the main eigenvalues referred to the paths that make a major contribution in the Massive MIMO system performance. As the transmitting power staying unchanged, the main eigenvalues

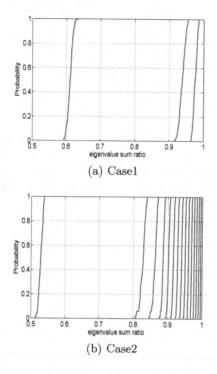

Fig. 6. The normalized eigenvalues of different antenna numbers of one MS

decrease as the power is more evenly allocated to each sub channel and more paths are contributing. Thus in the picture the level of dispersion grows, however, the speed of growth gets slower as the number of MS antennas growing from 8 to 128.

Then the comparison for the orthogonality of the antennas at the MS side is displayed in Fig. 7. Here, we define the orthogonality of the mobile stations as $O_{ant1,ant2}$:

$$O_{ant1,ant2} = \frac{1}{\rho_{ant1,ant2}} \tag{12}$$

$\rho_{ant1,ant2}$ denotes the correlation between the antennas at the MS side, $ant1, ant2$ refers to the antenna index. As mentioned in Sect. 2, there are two ODAs each with 16 antennas as two mobile stations. One ODA has antennas with the indices from 1 to 16 and connected to the ports with the same indices on the ODA. Another ODA with antenna indices from 17 to 32 also has the antennas connected to ports from 1 to 16. For the two ODA, the antenna pair consisting of antenna 1 and 2 or antenna 17 and 18 facing directly to the UPA, which means that these antennas correspond to the main sub-channels when under LoS condition. The two mobile stations are placed at symmetric positions to the receiver with a interval-$d_{ms} = 20\lambda$. The examples in Fig. 7(a) and (b) show the orthogonality between the antennas with indices: 1, 2, 17, 18 with the LoS

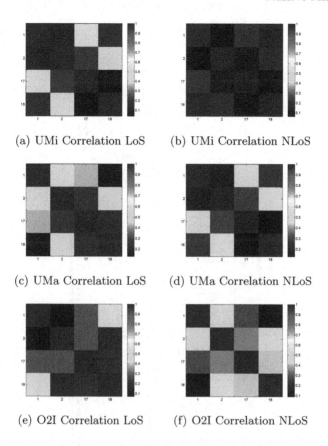

(a) UMi Correlation LoS   (b) UMi Correlation NLoS

(c) UMa Correlation LoS   (d) UMa Correlation NLoS

(e) O2I Correlation LoS   (f) O2I Correlation NLoS

Fig. 7. Correlation of the users

condition and NLoS condition under the UMi scenario. In Fig. 7(c) and (d) the corresponding results under the UMa scenario are shown. For the LoS condition under the UMi scenario, the orthogonality between antenna1 and antenna 17 is the lowest than that of other antenna combination of antenna1 or antenna17, with $O_{1,17} = 1.8$, while the highest orthogonality woulde be $O_{17,18} > 10$. Then as a comparison, with NLoS condition, $O_{ant1,ant2} > 5$ for any two antennas. A similar phenomenon that can be observed for the UMa scenario. So orthogonality between antennas increases when changing from LoS condition to NLoS condition. However, when it comes to the O2I scenario, the results shown in Fig. 7(e) and (f) become irregular due to the shadow fading which leads to a random scattering environment. So considering the narrow space, the affect of space interval between the two ODAs counts more when compared to other scenarios.

Then considering case3-N_{bs} changes and the receive antenna number remains fixed. Four antenna elements of one mobile station are chosen. For all scenarios, we picked the measurment location with the LoS condition and results of a configuration with three kind of BS antenna element numbers are shown in Fig. 8.

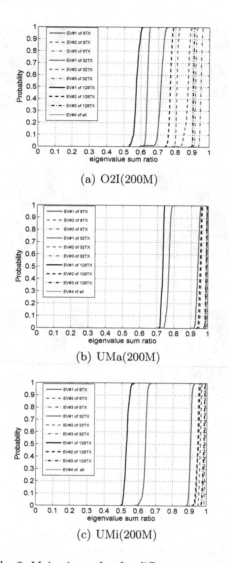

(a) O2I(200M)

(b) UMa(200M)

(c) UMi(200M)

Fig. 8. Main eigenvalue for different scenarios

In case3, as N_{bs} grows, similar law appears in the CDF of the normalized eigenvalues as N_{ms} grows. Besides, we can see the difference between the CDF of the normalized eigenvalues under different scenarios. The largest eigenvalue under the UMa scenario is the biggest among the three scenarios and the eigenvalue distribution is also the most dispersed. Then for UMi and O2I scenario, when $N_{bs} = 32/128$, the largest eigenvalues are almost the same meaning that the power of LoS path for the two scenarios are close. However, the O2I scenario have other three resolvable paths while the UMi scenario have another strong path, thus the power allocation is more uniform under the O2I scenario.

But when $N_{bs} = 8$, there is mainly one LoS path for both UMi and UMa as only 8 antennas take use of part of the space. With more antennas at the BS side, the size of the antenna array is larger and makes better use of the space.

Comparing the results of cases with antenna numbers changing whether at the BS side or the MS side, the main eigenvalue distribution of the less antenna numbers is relatively dispersed, which indicates that most of the energy of the channel is mainly distributed in one sub channel. Because the energy of other sub channels is weak, the data transmission ability is poor and unstable to interference. In this way, the multiplexing gain of the whole channel is limited and the spatial correlation of the channel is relatively high. One testification has been drawn from the result that no mater how large the number of antennas grows, the largest 2–4 eigenvalues occupy more than 60% of the whole.

4.2 Angular Spread (AS)

From the values of the azimuth angle spread of arrival (AASA) shown in Table 3, azimuth angle spread of departure (AASD), elevation angle spread of arrival (EASA), elevation angle spread of departure (EASD), we can see that UMa scenario gets the smallest AASA and EASA with LoS condition, while the UMi scenario gets the largest. To explain this, we go to the illustration picture Fig. 4, we can see that under the UMa scenario, due to a broad space and geographical location in the suburbs, there is not much scatterers such as: pedestrians, vehicles between the UPA and ODA, only some of the sparse distributed tall buildings. Then compared to the UMa scenario, the UMi scenario gets densely distributed pedestrians, vehicles and tall buildings around on, as a result, the mobile stations face a much richer scattering environment. Due to a richer scattering environment, the degree of dispersion of energy increases and brings bigger AS, so the AS of arrival for both horizon and elevation plane under UMi scenario are the largest. With bigger AS, there is a bigger DOF [14] meaning lower spatial correlation for the sub-channels. Then we have more concentrated eigenvalue as Fig. 8 displays.

Table 3. AS ($N_{bs} = 32$) for LoS condition under all scenarios

Scenario	Variable	UMi	UMa	O2I
AASA(lg(°))	μ_σ	1.7524	0.76616	1.54042
	ε_σ	0.0473	0.1643	0.0412
AASD(lg(°))	μ_σ	1.12561	1.37954	1.38654
	ε_σ	0.0818	0.0394	0.0536
EASA(lg(°))	μ_σ	1.59731	1.06604	1.33906
	ε_σ	0.0243	0.0616	0.0698
EASD(lg(°))	μ_σ	1.46058	1.42876	1.418
	ε_σ	0.0445	0.0161	0.0256

As for the O2I scenario, the MSs are placed indoor and on different floors. Walls, doors, rooms and other objects in the building on the specific floor contribute as the scatters. Compared to the UMi scenario, the distribution of the scatterer for the MS mainly changes on the elevation direction. Thus, with the LoS condition, there is the LoS path directly from the BS to the antenna of the MS facing to the UPA dominating the channel. The power of the strongest sub-channel depends on the propagation distance. And we pcik the measurement data of position2 of the UMi scenario and position1 on the 4th floor of the O2I scenario to analysis. Figure 3(b) shows the concrete scene for position2 of the UMi scenario. The horizontal distances are both 28 m and the propagation distances are very close. So as Fig. 8 shows, the largest eigenvalue are almost the same. However, the distribution of the 2th, 3rd, 4th eigenvalue is more uniform than that of the UMi scenario. As an explanation, we can see that the 1st and 2nd strongest paths can directly arrive at the MS side under the UMi scenario, so compared to other paths, the power of the 1st, 2nd paths are much stronger. But under the O2I scenario, the 1st stongest path can pass through the windows, while the 2nd, 3rd, 4th paths pass through walls, rooms and doors and get weaker.

4.3   Capacity

Capacity for different scenarios with a configuration of 128 antennas at the BS side and 32 antennas at the MS side and for the i.i.d channel is shown in Fig. 9. From the picture, we can see that under one scenario, capacity for NLoS condition is bigger than that for LoS condition and better SNR improve more capacity for NLoS condition than LoS condition. The capacity for i.i.d channel with an antenna configuration of 128 transmitting antennas and 32 receiving antennas and another antenna configuration of 8 transmitting antennas and 8 receiving antennas as a typical conventional MIMO system are displayed. Taking SNR = 15 dB, the capacity under UMi scenario and NLoS condition, C = 100 bps/Hz,

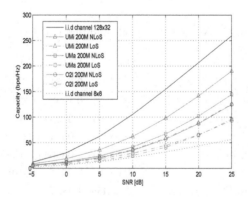

Fig. 9. Capacity

approaches that of the 128×32 i.i.d channel the most closely. However, the difference is still impressive as the capacity gap is almost 50 bps/Hz. So increasing the number of BS or MS antenna elements can still help improve the practical capacity of the multiuser MIMO system [15]. But over all, the performance of the massive MIMO system is even better than the ideally achieved capacity of the conventional MIMO system.

5   Conclusion

Based on the measurement data, we study that how the distribution of eigenvalues changes for three cases. Case1: a growing receiving antenna number. From result, it can be seen that orthogonality between the users increased. So distinguishing the user will be easier. Case2: the growing number at the BS side. And we see that more transmitting antennas will bring bigger multiplexing gain and deteriorative spatial correlation between the sub-channels. Case3: different propagation characteristics. We see that a richer scattering environment can also reduce the spatial correlation and improve the system performance.

After getting the result of AS, it is explained by analyzing the scenarios. So the AS can reflect the effect of propagation characteristics on spatial correlation. Finally, we display the real capacity under different scenarios and comparison to the i.i.d channels. According to the result of performance, the massive MIMO system do have its advantages at the frequency 3.5 GHz, but the gap to ideal channel performance shows us there is still a lot of work to do to accomplish the 5G goal of providing higher capacity.

Acknowledgment. This research is supported in part by National Science and Technology Major Project of the Ministry of Science and Technology (2015ZX03002008), and in part by MOE-CMCC 1-5, and in part by National Natural Science Foundation of China (61322110, 61461136002), and by 863 Program (2015AA01A703) and Doctoral Fund of Ministry of Education (20130005110001). The authors would also like to thank the support from the Huawei Technologies Co., Ltd.

References

1. Goldsmith, A., Jafar, S.A., Jindal, N., et al.: Capacity limits of MIMO channels. IEEE J. Sel. Areas Commun. **21**(5), 684–702 (2006)
2. Marzetta, T.L.: Noncooperative cellular wireless with unlimited numbers of base station antennas. IEEE Trans. Wirel. Commun. **9**(11), 3590–3600 (2010)
3. Rusek, F., Persson, D., Lau, B.K., et al.: Scaling up MIMO: opportunities and challenges with very large arrays. IEEE Sign. Process. Mag. **30**(1), 40–60 (2012)
4. Larsson, E., Edfors, O., Tufvesson, F., et al.: Massive MIMO for next generation wireless systems. IEEE Commun. Mag. **52**(2), 186–195 (2014)
5. Gao, X., Edfors, O., Rusek, F., et al.: Massive MIMO performance evaluation based on measured propagation data. IEEE Trans. Wirel. Commun. **14**(7), 1–1 (2015)
6. Martinez, A.O., Carvalho, E.D., Nielsen, J.O., et al.: Frequency dependence of measured massive MIMO channel properties. In: IEEE Vehicular Technology Conference (2016)

7. Goldsmith, A.: Wireless Communications. Stanford University, California (2008)
8. Liu, X., Bialkowski, M.E.: Effect of antenna mutual coupling on MIMO channel estimation and capacity. Int. J. Antennas Propag. **2010**(6), 252–260 (2010)
9. Yu, H., Zhang, J.H., Zheng, Q., et al.: The rationality analysis of massive MIMO virtual measurement at 3.5 GHz. In: IEEE/CIC International Conference on Communications in China (2016)
10. Zhang, J.H.: Review of wideband MIMO channel measurement and modeling for IMT-advanced systems. Sci. Bullet. **57**(19), 2387–2400 (2012)
11. Rappaport, T.S.: Wireless Communications: Principles and Practice, 2nd edn. Prentice Hall, Upper Saddle River (2001)
12. Fleury, B.H., Tschudin, M., Heddergott, R., et al.: Channel parameter estimation in mobile radio environments using the SAGE algorithm. IEEE J. Sel. Areas Commun. **17**(3), 434–450 (1999)
13. Heath, R.W., Paulraj, A.J.: Switching between diversity and multiplexing in MIMO systems[J]. IEEE Trans. Commun. **53**(6), 962–968 (2005)
14. Gesbert, D., Kountouris, M., Heath, R.W., et al.: Shifting the MIMO paradigm. IEEE Sign. Process. Mag. **24**(5), 36–46 (2007)
15. Zhang, J.H., Pan, C., Pei, F., et al.: Three-dimensional fading channel models: a survey of elevation angle research. IEEE Commun. Mag. **52**(6), 218–226 (2014)

Power Allocation for Downlink of Non-orthogonal Multiple Access System via Genetic Algorithm

Xinli Ma[1], Juan Wu[1], Zhenyu Zhang[1], Zhongshan Zhang[1],
Xiyuan Wang[1], Xiaomeng Chai[1], Linglong Dai[2],
and Xiaoming Dai[1(✉)]

[1] Technology Research Center for Convergence Networks
and Ubiquitous Services, University of Science and Technology Beijing (USTB),
Beijing 100083, China
dxmsjtu@sohu.com
[2] Department of Electronic Engineering, Tsinghua University,
Room 709, Tsinghua-Rohm EE Hall, Beijing 100084, China
dail1@tsinghua.edu.cn

Abstract. Non-orthogonal multiple access (NOMA) is a promising technology in future communication systems due to high spectral efficiency. In this paper, we propose an efficient power allocation method based on the genetic algorithm (GA) to solve the non-linear optimization problem for maximizing the achievable sum rate under a total power constraint and the users' quality of service (QoS) in the downlink NOMA systems. Different power allocation coefficients can be obtained with different objective functions and optimization criteria. Simulation results demonstrate that the NOMA systems with power allocation using GA can achieve better performance than the orthogonal multiple access (OMA) systems in terms of the achievable sum rate.

Keywords: Non-orthogonal multiple access (NOMA)
Quality of service (QoS) · Power allocation · Genetic algorithm

1 Introduction

Along with the development of wireless communication technology, spectral scarcity has become a serious problem [1]. Spectrum efficiency has ignited great interest from both academia and industry. The traditional mobile communication systems are faced with drastic changes and enormous challenges, including the explosive growth of mobile data services and massive machine-type communications. The 5th generation of communication systems (5G) will support high data rate communications, massive device connections, ultra-low latency, high reliability, and so on [2]. But the conventional multiple access technique-orthogonal multiple access (OMA) schemes, for instance, frequency division multiple access (FDMA), time division multiple access (TDMA), and code division multiple access (CDMA), will hardly meet those

© ICST Institute for Computer Sciences, Social Informatics and Telecommunications Engineering 2018
K. Long et al. (Eds.): 5GWN 2017, LNICST 211, pp. 459–470, 2018.
https://doi.org/10.1007/978-3-319-72823-0_43

requirements and challenges in 5G. Non-orthogonal multiple access (NOMA) is a promising multiple access technique for 5G communication systems with utilizing superposition coding (SC) at the transmitter and successive interference cancellation (SIC) [3] at the receiver. Compared to the conventional OMA, NOMA can be able to support multi-users to share the same time-frequency resources [4]. In essence, the NOMA systems achieve high spectral efficiency at the cost of increased receiver complexity.

Power allocation in OFDMA has been well studied in [5, 6], however, power allocation in the NOMA systems is still a challenging open problem and important for optimizing the achievable sum rate under a total power constraint in the NOMA downlink systems. Many previous works have already focused on power allocation for the NOMA systems. In [7], a minorization-maximization algorithm (MMA) was applied to maximize the downlink sum rate and the nonconvex optimization problem was converted into a convex optimization problem. In [8], Choi proposed an approach to optimize the sum capacity of multiple-input multiple output NOMA (MIMO-NOMA) systems with layered transmissions which allocated power to multiple layers and used the alternating maximization (AM) algorithm that can be regarded as a two-block Gauss-Seidel method. In [9], the mutual information was chosen as the optimal objective function to optimize power allocation for the maximum achievable rate. In [10], Liu demonstrated that the performance of MIMO-NOMA is better than MIMO-OMA in terms of the sum channel capacity (except for the case in which there is only one user being communicated to).

The existing works about NOMA power allocation under the users' QoS constraints are mostly analyzed for two users. In [11], a bisection search algorithm was proposed along with a low complexity suboptimal algorithm to optimize two users' ergodic capacity of MIMO-NOMA system under the total transmission power constraint and the minimum achievable rate constraint of the weak user. In [12], Wang utilized the Karush–Kuhn–Tucker (KKT) conditions to obtain closed-form solutions for maximizing the channel capacity in terms of two users' power allocation under a total power constraint and the QoS constraints of each user, and moreover extended the solutions to a MIMO scenario. In [13], Oviedo proposed a Fair-NOMA that means the two users are capable of achieving higher capacity in the NOMA systems than the OMA systems. In [14], Choi proposed proportional fairness scheduling (PFS) to obtain two users' optimal power allocation with different criteria in the downlink NOMA systems.

In this paper, we analyze the multi-user NOMA power allocation under a total power constraint and the users' QoS constraints, regardless of the user selection criteria, and utilize the effective methods based on the genetic algorithm (GA) to solve the nonconvex optimal problem. The rest of the paper is organized as follows. The system model is outlined in Sect. 2. Section 3 formulates an optimization problem of power allocation in the NOMA systems. Section 4 introduces the genetic algorithm. The simulation results are presented and discussed in Sect. 5. Finally, the conclusions are given in Sect. 6.

2   System Model

Consider a downlink communication scenario, with a base station $\mathcal{B}$ equipped with a single antenna and N users each equipped with a receive antenna; the base station $\mathcal{B}$ transmits signal data to each user and the total transmitted total power is P; $\alpha_i (i = 1, 2...N)$ are the fractions of the total power allocated to the i-th user. The 1st user is the weakest user (the furthest from the base station $\mathcal{B}$), and the N-th user is the strongest user (the nearest from the base station $\mathcal{B}$). The channel fading coefficients $h_i (i = 1, 2...N)$ satisfy the Gaussian distribution with zero mean and variance $\sigma_{h_n}^2$. The channels are sorted as $0 \leq |h_1|^2 \leq |h_2|^2 ... \leq |h_N|^2$. The additive white Gaussian noise (AWGN) is assumed to be normalized with zero mean and variance σ_n^2. According to the NOMA principle, the system will allocate more power to the users with weak channel conditions and less power to the users with strong channel conditions. The users' power allocation coefficients are ordered as: $\alpha_1 \geq \alpha_2 \geq ... \geq \alpha_N$. The weak user decodes its signal information, and perceives the signal information from the strong user as interference due to its less power. The strong user utilizes the SIC at the receiver and decodes its own signal information after decoding and removing the reference induced by the weak user.

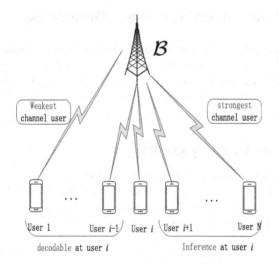

Fig. 1. Multiuser downlink system topology.

The multi-user NOMA scheme is shown as Fig. 1. It is shown that the i-th user can decode and remove the m-th (when $m < i$) user's signal information and perceive the signal information from the k-th (when $k > i$) users as interference since they are negligible to the i-th user. In this way, the achievable rate for the i-th $(i = 1, 2, \cdots, N - 1)$ user is formulated as follows:

$$R_i = log_2 \left(1 + \frac{\alpha_i P |h_i|^2}{P |h_i|^2 \sum_{k=i+1}^{N} \alpha_k + \sigma_n^2} \right) \tag{1}$$

The *N-th* user can decode and remove all the other users' signal information. Thus, the achievable rate of the *N-th* user is formulated as follows:

$$R_N = log_2 \left(1 + \frac{\alpha_N P |h_N|^2}{\sigma_n^2} \right) \tag{2}$$

Therefore, the system achievable sum rate is formulated as follows:

$$R_{sum} = \sum_{i=1}^{N-1} log_2(1 + SINR_i) + log_2 \left(1 + \frac{\alpha_N P |h_N|^2}{\sigma_n^2} \right) \tag{3}$$

where $SINR_i = \frac{\alpha_i P |h_i|^2}{P |h_i|^2 \sum_{k=i+1}^{N} \alpha_k + \sigma_n^2}, i = 1, 2, \cdots, N - 1.$

3 NOMA Power Allocation Problem Formulation

The different optimization power allocation coefficients can be obtained with different optimization criteria, and the following describes two different optimization criteria. One is to maximize the achievable sum rate to get the optimal power allocation; the other is to maximize the weighted sum rate for obtaining the power allocation coefficients to calculate the capacity.

3.1 Maximize the Achievable Sum Rate

The optimal capacity is obtained by maximizing the achievable sum rate when each user meets its quality of service (QoS) that refers to the minimum rate requirement. For instance, the *i-th* user has to satisfy the inequality $SINR_i \geq \gamma_i$, and the optimization problem can be formulated as follows:

$$\begin{aligned} &\max_{\alpha_i} R_{sum} \\ &\text{s.t. } (i) \sum_{i=1}^{N} \alpha_i = 1 \\ &\quad (ii) \, 0 \leq \alpha_i \leq 1 \\ &\quad (iii) \, \alpha_1 \geq \alpha_2 \geq \ldots \geq \alpha_N \\ &\quad (iv) \, SINR_i \geq \gamma_i, i = 1, 2, \cdots N \end{aligned} \tag{4}$$

where $(4, i)$ represents the sum of all the users' power is P; $(4, ii)$ represents that the lower bound and the upper bound of all the users' power allocation coefficients; $(4, iii)$ represents the NOMA principle that power allocated to the weaker user must be more than that of the stronger user; and $(4, iv)$ expresses the constraints that the SINR of each user must meet the targeted SINR γ_i to guarantee the QoS.

Subsequently, the constraint $(4, iv)$ is analyzed and can be described in detail as (5).

$$\begin{cases} \dfrac{\alpha_i P |h_i|^2}{P|h_i|^2 \sum_{k=i+1}^{N} \alpha_k + \sigma_n^2} \geq \gamma_i, (i = 2, 3, \ldots, N-1) \\ \dfrac{\alpha_N P |h_N|^2}{\sigma_n^2} \geq \gamma_N \end{cases} \tag{5}$$

The bound of the power allocation coefficients α can be obtained and formulated as follows:

$$\begin{cases} 1 \geq \alpha_i \geq \dfrac{\gamma_i \left(|h_i|^2 \theta + \frac{1}{\rho} \right)}{(1 + \gamma_i)|h_i|^2}, (i = 1, 2, \ldots, N-1) \\ 1 \geq \alpha_N \geq \dfrac{\gamma_N}{\rho |h_N|^2} \end{cases} \tag{6}$$

where ρ is the transmission SNR, $\rho = \frac{P}{\sigma_n^2}$, set $\alpha_0 = 0$, and get $\theta = 1 - \sum_{k=0}^{i-1} \alpha_k$, $(0 \leq \theta \leq 1)$. The inequalities in (6) show the constraints between the users' power allocation coefficients induced by the users' QoS constraints. The lower bound of $\alpha_i (i = 1, 2, \ldots, N)$ are denoted as $\beta_i (i = 1, 2, \ldots, N)$. If $\beta_i \geq 1, (i = 1, 2, \ldots, N)$, it means that the i-th user can't be supported to meet the QoS, even if the BS allocates the total power to the user.

We utilize 4 users to analyze the problem in detail as follows:

$$\max \sum_{i=1}^{3} log_2(1 + SINR_i) + log_2\left(1 + \frac{\alpha_4 P |h_4|^2}{\sigma_n^2}\right)$$
$$s.t. \ (i) \ \alpha_1 + \alpha_2 + \alpha_3 + \alpha_4 = 1$$
$$(ii) \ 0 \leq \alpha_1 \leq 1, 0 \leq \alpha_2 \leq 1, 0 \leq \alpha_3 \leq 1, 0 \leq \alpha_4 \leq 1$$
$$(iii) - \alpha_1 + \alpha_2 \leq 0, -\alpha_2 + \alpha_3 \leq 0, -\alpha_3 + \alpha_4 \leq 0 \tag{7}$$
$$(iv) - \alpha_1 \leq - \eta_1,$$
$$-\lambda_2 \alpha_1 - \alpha_2 \leq - \eta_2,$$
$$-\lambda_3 \alpha_1 - \lambda_3 \alpha_2 - \alpha_3 \leq - \eta_3,$$
$$-\alpha_4 \leq - \frac{\gamma_4}{\rho |h_4|^2}$$

where $\lambda_i = \frac{\gamma_i}{1 + \gamma_i}$, $\eta_i = \frac{\gamma_i \left(|h_i|^2 + \frac{1}{\rho} \right)}{(1 + \gamma_i)|h_i|^2}$, and the constraints in (7) correspond to that in (4) respectively.

3.2 Maximize the Weighted Sum Rate

We consider the weighted sum rate as the optimization objective function to allocate power for multi-users and the objective function is shown as (8):

$$\max_{\alpha_i} R_{weighted\_sum} = \sum_{i=1}^{N} \frac{R_{i-NOMA}}{R_{i-OMA}} \tag{8}$$

where R_{i-NOMA} equals to R_i shown as Eqs. (1) and (2), $R_{i-OMA} = log_2\left(1 + P|h_i|^2/\sigma_n^2\right)$ represents the users' OMA capacity. The constraints of the problem (8) are the same as (4). The optimal power allocation coefficients are obtained by optimizing the problem (8) and substituted into (3) to obtain the optimal achievable sum rate.

In general, there is no analytical solutions for the multivariable optimization problem, and the GA function in MTLAB can be used to obtain optimal power allocation coefficients, but the computational process of the genetic algorithm is complex and time-consuming.

4   Genetic Algorithm

Genetic algorithm is an optimization method inspired by the process of natural selection that belongs to the evolutionary algorithms [15]. Traditionally, a population is represented in binary as strings of 0s and 1s. In the genetic algorithm, a population of candidate solutions to an optimization problem evolves towards to better solutions. The solutions selected based on their fitness will be mutated and altered, and offspring will be used to form a new population. The new population will be better than the old one. The process will be repeated until there's a solution satisfied.

The genetic algorithm process is as follows [16] and the flowchart of the algorithm is shown as Fig. 2.

Step 1: Represent the problem domain as a chromosome of fixed length and determine the number of chromosomes, generations, and mutation rate and crossover rate value;

Step 2: Choose the initial population;

Step 3: Evaluate the fitness of each individual chromosome by calculating the objective function;

Step 4: Select a pair of chromosomes from the current population for mating, based on their fitness scores (the better fitness, the bigger chance to be selected);

Step 5: Crossover from those parents to create a pair of offspring chromosomes;

Step 6: Mutation (maintain genetic diversity from one generation of a population to the next);

Step 7: Return to Step3 and repeat the process until the termination (or optimization) criterion is met;

Step 8: Get the solution.

The general iterative algorithm can easily fall into the local minimum, But GA is a good way to overcome the drawback due to its good global search capabilities that can find the best possible solution with a high probability. Compared with the traditional optimization methods (enumeration, heuristic, etc.), GA has a good convergence and high explorative ability. In addition, GA is widely used to solve function optimization problems, combinatorial optimization problems, production scheduling problems, adaptive control, robotics, image processing, genetic programming, data mining, robotic learning, and artificial life. Although the genetic algorithm is applied in various fields, it has its own shortcomings, for example, the local search ability and

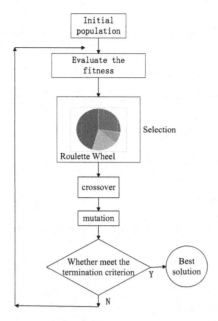

Fig. 2. The flowchart of genetic algorithm.

convergence is poor, and it takes a long time to find the optimal solution. The primary problem is to improve the search ability and the convergence speed of the algorithm.

5 Numerical Results

In this section, the performance of the downlink NOMA systems with power allocation using genetic algorithm is compared to that achieved by the OMA systems. For a given downlink NOMA scheme with a base station and N users, the channel gains are generated as $h_i = \sqrt{d_i^{-\mu}} g_i$, where $g_i \sim CN(0,1)$ (i.e. $\sigma_{h_n}^2 = d^{-\mu}$), μ is the pass-loss exponent $\mu = 2$, and the distances between the base station and the users are fixed and uniformly distributed between 1 and D. The noise power for each user is normalized to $\sigma_n^2 = 1$. The i-th user's OMA capacity is given as: $Coma_i = (1/N)log_2(1 + \left(P|h_i|^2\right)/\sigma_n^2)$, $(i = 1, 2, \ldots, N)$.

Figures 3 and 4 show the capacity of a user and the sum capacity versus P (dB) for the NOMA schemes with power allocation using genetic algorithm and for the OMA schemes.

Figure 3 compares three users' achievable rate and the maximum sum rate of the NOMA scheme acquired by maximizing the sum rate to that of the OMA scheme. Simulation parameters for performance evaluation are given as follows. We will take D = 11 and the distance vector between the three users and the base station is $d' = [11, 6, 1]$ meters. The vector of the users' QoS is $\gamma' = [-20, -15, -5]$ dB. The channels

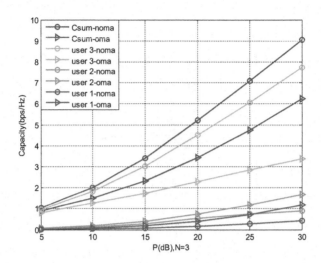

Fig. 3. Three users' capacity analysis of NOMA and OMA by maximizing the sum rate.

need to satisfy the order of $|h_1|^2 \leq |h_2|^2 \leq |h_3|^2$ to ensure that the users' signal information can be decoded. The sum capacity and the third user's capacity of the NOMA system is higher than the capacity of the OMA system. The NOMA capacity of the first user and the second user is lower than the OMA capacity.

Figure 4 depicts the four users' capacity and the sum capacity for the NOMA and OMA systems, and the NOMA power allocation is optimized by maximizing the sum rate. Simulation parameters are set as follows. The distance vector is $d'' = [11, 7.67, 4.33, 1]$ meters and the users' QoS vector is $\gamma'' = [-30, -25, -20, -10]$ dB. The channels need to satisfy the order of $|h_1|^2 \leq |h_2|^2 \leq |h_3|^2 \leq |h_4|^2$. The sum capacity and the fourth user's capacity of the NOMA system are higher than the capacity of the OMA system while the others are lower than the capacity of the OMA system respectively.

Figures 5 and 6 depict the achievable rate of 3 users and 4 users with power allocation obtained by maximizing the weighted sum rate under the same simulation parameters as Figs. 3 and 4, respectively. In both Figs. 5 and 6, the sum capacity of the NOMA system is higher than the capacity of the OMA system. In Fig. 5, the NOMA capacity of the first user and the third user is higher than the OMA capacity while the second user's capacity of the NOMA system is lower than the capacity of the OMA system. In the Fig. 6, the NOMA capacity of the first user and the fourth user is higher than the OMA capacity while the NOMA capacity of the second user and the third user is lower than the OMA capacity.

Figure 7 compares the NOMA sum capacity optimized by maximizing sum rate and weighted sum rate for three users and four users. The sum capacity obtained by maximizing the weighted sum rate is lower than that obtained by maximizing the sum rate for both three users and four users.

For the maximizing sum rate scenario, only the strongest user's capacity and the sum capacity of the NOMA system are higher than the capacity of the OMA system,

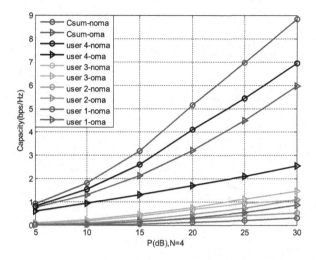

Fig. 4. Four users' capacity analysis of NOMA and OMA by maximizing the sum rate.

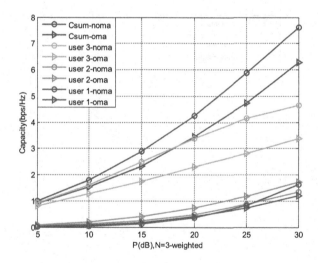

Fig. 5. Three users' capacity analysis of NOMA and OMA by maximizing the weighted sum rate.

respectively, while the other users' capacity of the NOMA system is lower than that of the OMA system, grows slowly and only satisfy the required SNR. For the maximizing weighted sum rate scenario, except for the strongest user, the weakest user's NOMA capacity is also higher than the OMA capacity at the cost of the reduction of the sum capacity shown as Fig. 7. Different optimal criteria will lead to different results, but the NOMA systems is better than the OMA systems in terms of the sum capacity whatever criteria is chosen.

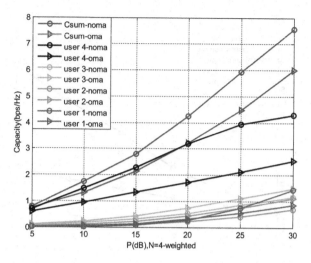

Fig. 6. Four users' capacity analysis of NOMA and OMA by maximizing the weighted sum rate.

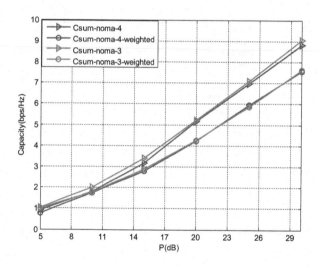

Fig. 7. The comparison of NOMA capacity optimized by maximizing the sum rate and weighted sum rate.

6 Conclusion

In this paper, we studied the capacity maximization problem under a total power constraint and users' QoS constraints for power allocation by utilizing GA in NOMA downlink systems. We derived the optimal power allocation and obtained the optimal capacity by maximizing the sum rate and the weighted sum rate. The simulation results show that the performance of the NOMA system based on GA can achieve higher gain than the traditional OMA schemes when the channel state information is available to the transmitters and different optimization criteria will induce different results. The values of the users' QoS is fixed in this paper and the dynamic QoS will be considered in the future work. On the other hand, the solution obtained by a simple genetic algorithm is time-consuming and the genetic algorithm is prone to premature convergence in practical application. Therefore, the combination of genetic algorithm and other algorithms will be studied in the future work.

Acknowledgements. This work was supported by Huawei Innovation Research Program, the key project of the National Natural Science Foundation of China (No. 61431001), the 5G research program of China Mobile Research Institute (Grant No. [2015] 0615), the open research fund of National Mobile Communications Research Laboratory Southeast University (No. 2017D02), Key Laboratory of Cognitive Radio and Information Processing, Ministry of Education (Guilin University of Electronic Technology), the Foundation of Beijing Engineering and Technology Center for Convergence Networks and Ubiquitous Services, and Keysight. The Corresponding author is Dr. Xiaoming Dai.

References

1. Dai, L., Wang, B., Yuan, Y., et al.: Non-orthogonal multiple access for 5G: solutions, challenges, opportunities, and future research trends. IEEE Commun. Mag. **53**(9), 74–81 (2015)
2. Vision IMT: Framework and overall objectives of the future development of IMT for 2020 and beyond. Working document toward preliminary draft new recommendation ITU-R M [IMT. Vision] (2014)
3. Dai, X., Chen, S., Sun, S., Kang, S., Wang, Y., Shen, Z., Xu, J.: Successive interference cancelation amenable multiple access (SAMA) for future wireless communications. In: Proceedings of IEEE ICCS 2014, pp. 1–5, November 2014
4. Benjebbour, A., Saito, Y., Kishiyama, Y., et al.: Concept and practical considerations of non-orthogonal multiple access (NOMA) for future radio access. In: 2013 International Symposium on Intelligent Signal Processing and Communications Systems (ISPACS), pp. 770–774. IEEE (2013)
5. Zhang, H., Nie, Y., Cheng, J., Leung, V.C.M., Nallanathan, A.: Sensing time optimization and power control for energy efficient cognitive small cell with imperfect hybrid spectrum sensing. IEEE Trans. Wirel. Commun. **16**(2), 730–743 (2017)
6. Zhang, H., Jiang, C., Beaulieu, N.C., Chu, X., Wen, X., Tao, M.: Resource allocation in spectrum -sharing OFDMA femtocells with heterogeneous services. IEEE Trans. Commun. **62**(7), 2366–2377 (2014)
7. Hanif, M.F., Ding, Z., Ratnarajah, T., et al.: A minorization-maximization method for optimizing sum rate in the downlink of non-orthogonal multiple access systems. IEEE Trans. Sig. Process. **64**(1), 76–88 (2016)
8. Choi, J.: On the power allocation for MIMO-NOMA systems with layered transmissions. IEEE Trans. Wirel. Commun. **15**(5), 3226–3237 (2016)
9. Choi, J.: On the power allocation for a practical multiuser superposition scheme in NOMA systems. IEEE Commun. Lett. **20**(3), 438–441 (2016)
10. Liu, Y., Pan, G., Zhang, H., et al.: On the capacity comparison between MIMO-NOMA and MIMO-OMA. IEEE Access **4**, 2123–2129 (2016)

11. Sun, Q., Han, S., Chin-Lin, I., et al.: On the ergodic capacity of MIMO NOMA systems. IEEE Wirel. Commun, Lett. **4**(4), 405–408 (2015)
12. Wang, C.L., Chen, J.Y., Chen, Y.J.: Power allocation for a downlink non-orthogonal multiple access system. IEEE Wirel. Commun. Lett. **5**(5), 532–535 (2016)
13. Oviedo, J.A., Sadjadpour, H.R.: A new NOMA approach for fair power allocation. In: 2016 IEEE Conference on IEEE Computer Communications Workshops (INFOCOM WKSHPS), pp. 843–847 (2016)
14. Choi, J.: Power allocation for max-sum rate and max-min rate proportional fairness in NOMA. IEEE Commun. Lett. **20**(10), 2055 (2016)
15. Sivanandam, S.N., Deepa, S.N.: Introduction to Genetic Algorithms. Springer, Heidelberg (2007). https://doi.org/10.1007/978-3-540-73190-0
16. Gen, M., Cheng, R.: Genetic Algorithms and Engineering Design. Wiley, New York (1997)

Research on the Interference and Coexistence of CBTC in 1.8 GHz Band

Ruichen Xu[✉], Xiao Peng, Xiaobo Wang, Ji Fang, and Bo Yuan

The State Radio Monitoring Center Testing Center, Beijing 100041, China
{xuruichen,pengxiao,wangxiaobo,fangji,
yuanbo}@srtc.org.cn

Abstract. The current Communication Based Train Control (CBTC) system is assigned to 2.4 GHz unlicensed band, which can be easily interfered. To enhance safety, the state radio regulatory commission assigned 1785 MHz–1805 MHz band to CBTC system. However, under the interference of first use telecommunication system in identical and adjacent frequency, it's a problem to guarantee the safety isolation distance between interfere and interfered party, so that to improve CBTC system safety. To solve this problem, this paper firstly analyzes relative domestic frequency assignment situation to determine interfere party, and then finds out study scenario based on field testing data. Afterward, obtain isolation distance between interfere and interfered party by ACIR modeling and deterministic calculations. Based on the research above, the advice that CBTC system should be assigned in 1790 MHz–1800 MHz band is given.

Keywords: 1.8 GHz · TDD-LTE · CBTC · Interference · Isolation distance

1 Introduction

Communication Based Train Control (CBTC) [1] system realizes bi-directional train ground communication, which makes the train break through from fixed blocked system to moving blocked system. And the ability of carrying capacity of a section is increasing by adding in-train entertainment information service, which has widely application prospect. However, China assigned CBTC system in 2.4 GHz unlicensed frequency band, which can be easily interfered by hand-held WiFi hot spot devices. As a result, several subway emergency brake accidents were caused in Shenzhen and Beijing. Security risks are brought out. To solve above issue, MIIT [2015] No. 65 document is published by China radio regulatory, which indicated that 1785 MHz–1805 MHz private band is assigned to TDD-LTE CBTC system, to enhance security of train transit. Besides that, CBTC system may apply 5G communication technology [3, 4] in forseeable future, which has higher spectrum efficiency.

However, under the interference of 3 kinds of first use telecommunication systems [5–7] in identical and adjacent frequency, it's a problem that guarantee the safety isolation distance between interfere and interfered party, so that to improve CBTC system safety. Reference [8–10] study on the overall framework, system function and interface specification of TD-LTE based CBTC system, respectively.

© ICST Institute for Computer Sciences, Social Informatics and Telecommunications Engineering 2018
K. Long et al. (Eds.): 5GWN 2017, LNICST 211, pp. 471–483, 2018.
https://doi.org/10.1007/978-3-319-72823-0_44

Base on reference review of this paper, there is only 1 reference [11] focused on interference and coexistence of radio access system in 1785 MHz–1805 MHz frequency band, which includes CBTC system. Reference [11] applies deterministic calculations to study on interference and coexistence problem of 1785 MHz–1805 MHz radio access system base station and adjacent band IMT system base station. The security isolation between interfered and interfere base station is given, but radio access system downlink system interference is not take into consider.

Therefore, based on analysis on frequency distribution situation on 1785 MHz–1805 MHz, according to test and deterministic calculation methodology, this paper obtains the safety isolation distance between CBTC system and the other 4 interfere parties.

2 Frequency Assignment Situation in 1785 MHz–1805 MHz

2.1 Adjacent Frequency Assignment Situation in 1785 MHz–1805 MHz

According to reference [11] and [12], IMT spectrum assignment around 1.8 GHz in China is shown in Fig. 1. From Fig. 1 and reference [12], 1785 MHz–1805 MHz adjacent frequency is used for LTE FDD uplink in 1765 MHz–1785 MHz and GSM downlink in 1805 MHz–1820 MHz. GSM and FDDLTE network has wide coverage, especially in the city where CBTC has greater density. Therefore, it's necessary to study the interference of GSM downlink and FDDLTE uplink to CBTC terminal.

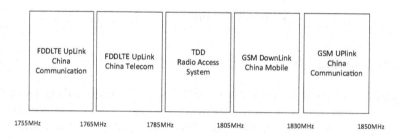

Fig. 1. Domestic frequency allocation situation in 1.8 GHz

2.2 Frequency Assignment Situation in 1785 MHz–1805 MHz

According to reference [2], 1785 MHz–1805 MHz is assigned to city rail transportation, electric, fuel and telecommunication industries. Currently, McWill broadband wireless access system has been deployed in this band. According to the data of The State Radio Monitoring Center,McWill system, which works in 1785 MHz–1805 MHz, is widely used in urban wireless access, heavy haul rail, petroleum fields, harbours, airports and other fields. The deployed McWill system has covered the entire 20 MHz band of 1785 MHz–1805 MHz. Single base station bandwidth range is [1 MHz–5 MHz], transmit power range is [1 W, 3 W], which is deployed over the ground. As the city wireless access systems, airports and other areas may overlap with the CBTC system operating area, it is necessary to study the interference of the McWill system to the CBTC train terminal.

3 Interference Scenarios

This section analyzes interference scenario requirement from systematic perspective. Afterwards, study scenario is determined from field test data.

As shown in Fig. 2, the interference source of interfered CBTC train is LTE FDD uplink, GSM downlink and McWill uplink and downlink. Therefore, interference from GSM base station, McWill base station, McWill terminal and LTE FDD terminal to CBTC train should be taken into consideration.

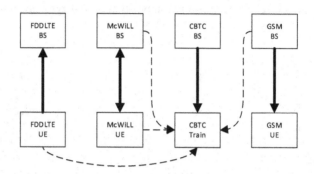

Fig. 2. Analysis on interference source to CBTC train

After determination of interference source, study scenario need to be found out. CBTC system can be divided to underground subway and over ground rail. The propagation environment is quite different. So test method is applied to determine CBTC train interference scenario.

To analyze scenario, by using test method in Beijing subway line 2, line 5 and line 13 underground and over ground respectively, the power level of 1710 MHz–1785 MHz, 1785 MHz–1805 MHz and 1805 MHz–1880 MHz can be obtained. The test settings can be found in Table 1, and test instrument and attachment list is shown in Table 2.

Table 1. Test setting

Setting	Value
Test frequency	1710 MHz–1785 MHz; 1785 MHz–1805 MHz; 1805 MHz–1880 MHz
Scan method	Clear Write
Internal attenuation	0 dB
Reference level	−10 dBm
VBW	1 MHz
RBW	1 MHz
Scan type	Auto
Pre-release state	OFF
Detection mode	Max Hold

Table 2. Test instruments and accessories

Device name	Version	Manufacturer
Spectrum analyzer	N9344C	Agilent
Lazer range finder	LRB5000	FeiXunDianZi
LapTop	X230	ThinkPad
Log periodic antenna	LM1250	FeiChuang

As shown in Fig. 3, test section of line 2 is underground, test section of line 13 is over ground, and test section of line 5 is combination of underground and over ground.

Beijing Line 2 Test Section   Beijing Line 13 Test Section   Beijing Line 5 Test Section

Fig. 3. Test section of CBTC

The test screen print for Beijing subway line 2, line 5 and line 13 can be found in Fig. 4. The test result of line 2 is shown in Table 3, line 13 in Table 4, and line 5 in Table 5.

As indicated in Table 3, when the train is underground, the power spectrum density stays stable and nearly identical. Since there is no McWill base station underground, −75 dBm/MHz– −74 dBm/MHz is almost underground electromagnetic environment background noise. This power spectrum density (PSD) matches the test result of line 5 underground part.

From Tables 4 and 5, we know when the train is over ground, the PSD of 3 test frequency band changes significant. 1710 MHz–1785 MHz over ground PSD is 35 dB higher than underground. And the result changes on various test interval, which is affect by uplink assignment and different population densities, like PSD in Xizhimen section is larger than other sections. The average value of 1785 MHz–1805 MHz over-ground is about −50 dBm/MHz, which changes on different test interval. For example, the PSD value of line 13 is larger than the one of line 5, which is related to McWill base station assignment density. According to in use radio station data from The State Radio Monitoring Center, Mcwill base station density along line 13 is higher than line 5, which matches test data. The average PSD of 1805 MHz–1880 MHz

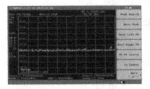

Beijing Line 2, Test section from ChongWen to Qian Men, Reception Lever in 1710MHz-1785MHz

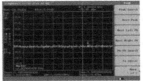

Beijing Line 2, Test section from ChongWen to Qian Men, Reception Lever in 1785MHz-1805MHz

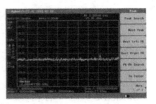

Beijing Line 2, Test section from ChongWen to Qian Men, Reception Lever in 1805MHz-1880MHz

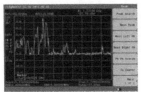

Beijing Line 13, Test section from Xizhimen to Dazhongsi, Reception Lever in 1710MHz-1785MHz

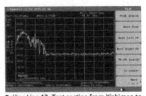

Beijing Line 13, Test section from Xizhimen to Dazhongsi, Reception Lever in 1785MHz-1805MHz

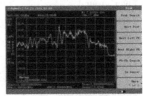

Beijing Line 13, Test section from Xizhimen to Dazhongsi, Reception Lever in 1805MHz-1880MHz

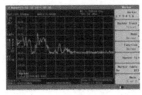

Beijing Line 5, Test section from Lishuiqiao to Lishuiqiaonan, Reception Lever in 1710MHz-1785MHz

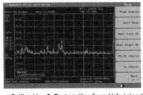

Beijing Line 5, Test section from Lishuiqiao to Lishuiqiaonan, Reception Lever in 1785MHz-1805MHz

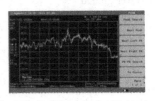

Beijing Line 5, Test section from Lishuiqiao to Lishuiqiaonan, Reception Lever in 1805MHz-1880MHz

Fig. 4. The test screen print for Beijing subway line 2, line 5 and line 13

Table 3. Reception level testing result of Beijing line 2

Testing frequency band	1710 MHz–1785 MHz (dBm/MHz)	1785 MHz–1805 MHz (dBm/MHz)	1805 MHz–1880 MHz (dBm/MHz)
Section 1 Under ground	−75.92	−75.45	−76.36
Section 2 Under ground	−75.47	−74.98	−75.51
Section 3 Under ground	−75.62	−75.70	−74.72
Section 4 Under ground	−75.76	−75.18	−71.71
Section 5 Under ground	−76.36	−75.55	−74.82
Section 6 Under ground	−75.23	−75.76	−75.00
Section 7 Under ground	−76.24	−75.31	−75.88
Section 8 Under ground	−75.79	−79.68	−75.69
Average	−75.81	−75.95	−74.96

Table 4. Reception level testing result of Beijing line 13

Testing frequency band	1710 MHz–1785 MHz (dBm/MHz)	1785 MHz–1805 MHz (dBm/MHz)	1805 MHz–1880 MHz (dBm/MHz)
Section 1 Over ground	−27.70	−44.61	−36.71
Section 2 Over ground	−41.67	−56.22	−36.17
Section 3 Over ground	−35.74	−44.39	−33.96
Section 4 Over ground	−41.22	−43.76	−35.80
Section 5 Over ground	−49.36	−52.73	−34.21
Section 6 Over ground	−44.19	−56.33	−36.87
Section 7 Over ground	−49.36	−41.18	−38.40
Section 8 Over ground	−41.30	−61.17	−37.18
Average	−41.30	−50.04	−36.18

Table 5. Reception level testing result of Beijing line 5

Testing frequency band	1710 MHz–1785 MHz (dBm/MHz)	1785 MHz–1805 MHz (dBm/MHz)	1805 MHz–1880 MHz (dBm/MHz)
Section 1 Over ground	−51.16	−66.18	−36.22
Section 2 Over ground	−52.51	−61.40	−36.87
Section 3 Over ground	−53.91	−65.07	−39.08
Section 4 Over ground	−48.71	−64.41	−34.21
Section 5 Under ground	−75.45	−76.26	−76.19
Section 6 Under ground	−76.87	−76.11	−76.86
Section 7 Under ground	−75.98	−76.58	−76.79
Section 8 Under ground	−77.17	−75.54	−75.83
Average	−63.97	−70.19	−56.51

over-ground is about −36 dBm/MHz, and changes little in different sections, which is GSM downlink and related to stable density of GSM BS assignment. Moreover, the PSD of 1785 MHz–1805 MHz is smaller than other 2 bands, since Mcwill base station transmitting power is 6 dB smaller than GSM, and the number of public network UE is huge, etc.

According to above analysis, the CBTC downlink interfered scenario is chosen to be over-ground scenario. The upcoming scenario setting, parameter setting and propagation model should be set up as over-ground scenario.

4 Safety Isolation and Safety Isolation Distance

This section firstly introduces interfere and interfered RF parameters. Then ACIR of different situation can be obtained by calculation of interfere side's ACLR and interfered side's ACS. The secured isolation distance between CBTC train side and interfere side can be got from backward deduction of propagation model.

4.1 RF Parameters of Interfered and Interfere Sides

The system parameters [11, 12] of 4 kinds of interfere side can be found as Table 6. The RF parameters of CBTC system [10] can be found as Table 7.

Table 6. System parameters of 4 kinds of interfere side

System parameters	GSM BS	LTE FDD UE	McWill BS	McWill UE
Frequency band	1805 MHz–1820 MHz	1765 MHz–1785 MHz	1785 MHz–1805 MHz	1785 MHz–1805 MHz
Carrier bandwidth	200 kHz	5 MHz	5 MHz	5 MHz
Maximum transmit power	46 dBm	23 dBm	40 dBm	30 dBm
Thermal noise power spectral density	−174 dBm/Hz	−174 dBm/Hz	−174 dBm/Hz	−174 dBm/Hz
Noise figure	5 dB	9 dB	5 dB	9 dB
Cell radius	250 m	–	250 m	
Maximum antenna gain (including feeder loss)	15 dB	0 dB	15 dB	0 dB
Antenna height	30 m	1.5 m	30 m	1.5 m

Table 7. System parameters of CBTC system

System parameters	CBTC BS	CBTC Train
Frequency band	1785 MHz–1805 MHz	1785 MHz–1805 MHz
Bandwidth	5 MHz/10 MHz	5 MHz/10 MHz
Maximum transmit power	40 dBm/43 dBm	30 dBm/33 dBm
Noise figure	5 dB	9 dB
Maximum antenna gain(including feeder loss)	15 dB	0 dB
Antenna height	20 m	5 m
Protection criterion(I/N)	−6 dB	−6 dB
Receiving sensitivity	–	−93 dBm

4.2 ACIR Analysis and Calculation

It's identical frequency interference that McWill system interferes CBTC system. And LTE FDD and GSM to CBTC system is adjacent frequency interference. 4 kinds of interference scenarios are taken into account in this paper: (1) The bandwidth of CBTC system is 5 MHz, which has 5 MHz frequency isolation with adjacent interfere system; (2) The bandwidth of CBTC system is 10 MHz, which has 5 MHz frequency isolation with adjacent interfere system; (3) The bandwidth of CBTC system is 5 MHz, which adjoin adjacent interfere system; (4) The bandwidth of CBTC system is 10 MHz, which adjoin adjacent interfere system. Since the modulation feature of GSMK, there is 200 kHz isolate bandwidth between adjoin GSM and CBTC system. To begin with, ACIR calculation model is introduced. Then, ACIR value of different interference situation is determined depending on the calculation of ACLR and ACS.

ACIR can be obtained by Eq. (1), where dB is applied as unit, and ACS is Adjacent Channel Selectivity, unit is dB.

$$ACIR = 10 \lg\left(1/\left(1/10^{ACLR/10} + 1/10^{ACS/10}\right)\right) \tag{1}$$

Based on reference [13], Spectrum Emission Mask of LTE FDD can be found as Table 8.

According to different frequency interval and data in Table 8, subsection integration is applied to get the power leakage P(mW) from LTE FDD side to CBTC side. Then ACLR of different frequency isolation can be obtained by Eq. (2) as Table 9, where P_T is transmitting power of LTE FDD terminal, whose unit is dBm.

$$ACLR = P_T - 10\log(P) \tag{2}$$

Table 8. Spectrum emission mask of LTE FDD

Δf_{OOB} (MHz)	1.4 MHz	3.0 MHz	5 MHz	10 MHz	15 MHz	20 MHz	Measurement bandwidth
±0–1	−10	−13	−15	−18	−20	−21	30 kHz
±1–2.5	−10	−10	−10	−10	−10	−10	1 MHz
±2.5–2.8	−25	−10	−10	−10	−10	−10	1 MHz
±2.8–5		−10	−10	−10	−10	−10	1 MHz
±5–6		−25	−13	−13	−13	−13	1 MHz
±6–10			−25	−13	−13	−13	1 MHz
±10–15				−25	−13	−13	1 MHz
± 15–20					−25	−13	1 MHz
± 20–25						−25	1 MHz

Table 9. ACLR from LTE FDD side to CBTC side in different frequency isolation

Case	Adjoin adjacent interfere/5 MHz bandwidth	Adjoin adjacent interfere/10 MHz bandwidth	5 MHz frequency isolation/5 MHz bandwidth	5 MHz frequency isolation/10 MHz bandwidth
ACLR(dB)	21.37	21.19	35.02	35.02

The ACLR model that GSM base station interferes CBTC Train is shown as Fig. 5.

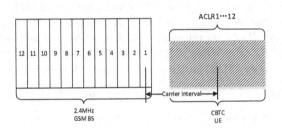

Fig. 5. The ACLR model that GSM base station interferes CBTC train

Based on reference [14], the spectrum emission mask of GSM base station can be found as Table 10. And according to reference [14] Sect. 4.2.1.1, subsection integration is applied on the specified measurement bandwidth and data in Table 10, to get the power leakage P(mW) from GSM base station to CBTC Train. Then ACLR that GSM base station interferes CBTC Train, in different frequency isolation can be obtained by Eq. (2) as Table 11.

CBTC train terminal belongs to TD-LTE terminal. Depending on reference [11], the ACS of CBTC train side can be obtained by Eq. (3).

$$ACS = P_{Interfer} - N - 10 * log10(10^{M/10} - 1) \qquad (3)$$

Table 10. Spectrum emission mask of GSM base station

Power level	100	200	250	400	≥ 600	≥ 1 800	≥ 3 000	≥ 6 000
≥ 39	+0,5	−30	−33	−60	−66	−69	−71	−77
37	+0,5	−30	−33	−60	−64	−67	−69	−75
35	+0,5	−30	−33	−60	−62	−65	−67	−73
≤ 33	+0,5	−30	−33	−60*	−60	−63	−65	−71

Table 11. ACLR from GSM side to CBTC side in different isolation cases

Case	200 kHz frequency isolation/5 MHz bandwidth	200 kHz frequency isolation/10 MHz bandwidth	5 MHz frequency isolation/5 MHz bandwidth	5 MHz frequency isolation/10 MHz bandwidth
ACLR(dB)	21.26	21.25	57.97	54.97

where $P_{Interfer}$ stands for in band blocking, whose unit is dBm. and N is noise floor, whose unit is dBm. M stands for uplift measure of noise floor whose unit is dB.

(1) ACS calculation of CBTC terminal interfered by GSM base station

According to reference [14], it's narrow band signal interference that GSM base station interferes CBTC terminal. However, the B/2 bandwidth narrow out band blocking limit is not given. Where B stands for system bandwidth of CBTC. To be more strictly, assume that $P_{Interfer}$ is identical between CBTC and GSM isolation 5 MHz or 10 MHz. Based on reference [14] Table 7.6.3.1–1 and reference [12], we know $P_{Interfer} = -55$ dBm. When CBTC bandwidth is 5 MHz, $N = -98.01$ dBm, $M = 13$ dB. And when CBTC bandwidth is 10 MHz, $N = -95$ dBm, $M = 10$ dB.

(2) ACS calculation of CBTC terminal interfered by LTE FDD terminal

Depending on reference [13], when the frequency interval between CBTC terminal and LTE FDD terminal is under 15 MHz, then it belongs to in band blocking. As a result, $P_{Interfer}$ is identical in situation 5 MHz and 10 MHz isolation between CBTC and LTE FDD system. Based on reference [13] Table 7.6.1.1–1, it can be found that $P_{Interfer} = -44$ dBm. When bandwidth of CBTC is 5 MHz, $N = -98.01$ dBm, $M = 6$ dB. And when bandwidth of CBTC is 10 MHz, $N = -95$ dBm, M = 6 dB.

The above calculation parameters are taken into Eq. (3). Then ACS of CBTC train side in different condition can be found in Table 12.

Table 12. The ACS of CBTC train side in different condition

Case	GSM interfere CBTC/Bandwidth of CBTC is 5 MHz	GSM interfere CBTC/Bandwidth of CBTC is 10 MHz	FDD LTE interfere CBTC/Bandwidth of CBTC is 5 MHz	FDD LTE interfere CBTC/Bandwidth of CBTC is 10 MHz
ACS(dB)	30.23	30.45	49.26	46.25

The ACLR and ACS obtained are taken into Eq. 1. The ACIR of 4 categories CBTC train interfered by interference system can be found as Table 13.

Table 13. The ACS of CBTC train side in different condition

Case	Adjoin adjacent interfere/5 MHz bandwidth		Adjoin adjacent interfere/10 MHz bandwidth		5 MHz frequency isolation/5 MHz bandwidth		5 MHz frequency isolation/10 MHz bandwidth	
Interfere side	GSM	FDDLTE	GSM	FDDLTE	GSM	FDDLTE	GSM	FDDLTE
ACIR(dB)	20.74	21.36	20.75	21.17	30.22	34.85	30.43	34.70

4.3 Calculation of Safety Isolation Distance

Safety isolation can be obtained by Eq. (4).

$$L_P = P_T + G_T + G_R - L_T - L_R - ACIR - I \qquad (4)$$

P_T stands for maximum transmit interfere power, whose unit is dBm. And G_T is antenna gain of interfere system, whose unit is dB. G_R stands for antenna gain of interfered system, whose unit is dB. L_T stands for feed line loss of interfere system, whose unit is dB. And L_R stands for feed line loss of interfered system, whose unit is dB. $ACIR$ is adjacent channel interference power ratio, whose unit is dB. I stands for maximum interference signal power of interfered system, whose unit is dBm, which can be obtained by protection principle of interfered system $I/N = -6$ dB.

Vehicle environment model [15] of UMTS is applied as BS to terminal path loss, which can be described as Eq. (5), where d is distance, unit is km, f is carrier frequency, unit is MHz, H is height of antenna, unit is m, h is benchmark roof height, which is set to be 15 m, and s is log normal distribution, which is set to be 5 dB.

$$L_P = 40 \cdot (1 - 4 \times 10^{-3} \cdot (H - h)) \lg(d) - 18 \lg(H - h) + 21 \cdot \lg(f) + 80 + s \quad (5)$$

PCS micro cell model [16] is applied as terminal to terminal path loss, which can be described as (6), where n_1 and n_2 are path loss index, which are valued 2.3 and 3.1 respectively, λ is wavelength, d is distance between transmit and receive antenna, whose unit is m, d_f is distance of first Fresnel zone, whose unit is m, s is transit path loss of 1 m, which can be obtained by free space model, whose unit is dB, ht and hr stand for antenna height of transmitter and receiver respectively, whose unit is m.

$$\begin{aligned} L_P &= 10 n_1 \lg(d) + s & 1 < d < d_f \\ L_P &= 10 n_1 \lg(d/d_f) + 10 n_2 \lg(d_f) + s & d > d_f \\ d_f &= \tfrac{1}{\lambda} \sqrt{16 h_t^2 h_r^2 - \lambda^2 (h_t^2 + h_r^2) + \lambda^4/16} \end{aligned} \qquad (6)$$

By taking data of Tables 6, 7 and 13 into Eqs. (5) and (6), the safety isolation and isolation distance between CBTC train side and interfere system can be found in Table 14.

Table 14. Isolation and isolation distance between CBTC train and interferes in different condition

Case	Adjoin adjacent interfere/5 MHz bandwidth		Adjoin adjacent interfere/10 MHz bandwidth		5 MHz frequency isolation/5 MHz bandwidth		5 MHz frequency isolation/10 MHz bandwidth	
Interfere side	GSM	FDD LTE	GSM	FDD LTE	GSM	FDD LTE	GSM	FDD LTE
Safety Isolation (dB)	138	102	135	100	128	89	125	86
Isolation distance (km)	1.427	0.384	1.187	0.331	0.773	0.146	0.643	0.117

Case	Same frequency band/5 MHz bandwidth		Same frequency band/10 MHz bandwidth					
Interfere side	McWill BS	McWill UE	McWill BS	McWill UE				
Safety Isolation (dB)	156	128	153	131				
Isolation distance (km)	4.297	2.64	3.576	3.31				

From above analysis, the isolation distance between GSM base station, LTE FDD terminal, McWill base station, McWill terminal and CBTC train side is quite long. It is inappropriate to deploy CBTC system in the area where McWill system exists. The method that assigns CBTC system in 1790 MHz–1800 MHz can be used to realize minimum isolation distance between CBTC system and interfere systems. However, only apply isolation distance measures is not enough. For example, when CBTC system works in 1790 MHz–1800 MHz band, safety isolation between CBTC train and GSM base station is 0.643 km. The cell radius of GSM is 250 m, which can not fulfill isolation distance requirement. Hence, additional isolation measures are needed to guarantee that GSM base station and LTE FDD terminal do not cause harmful interference to CBTC system.

5 Conclusion

To solve 1785 MHz–1805 MHz CBTC downlink interference problem, this paper firstly analyzes domestic identical and adjacent frequency band assignment situation. Then this paper finds out study scenario based on field testing data. Afterward, this paper calculates isolation distance between interfere and interfered party by ACIR modeling and deterministic calculations. Depending on the research results mentioned above, the advice is given that CBTC system should be assigned to 1790 MHz–1800 MHz.

References

1. Wan, Y., Wang, D., Mei, M., Waterman, M.S.: Composable modeling method for generic test platform for CBTC system based on the port. J. Int. J. Adv. Comput. Sci. Appl. 12(6) (2015)
2. MIIT No. 65 Document (2015)
3. Zhang, H., Dong, Y., Cheng, J., Hossain, Md.J., Leung, V.C.M.: Fronthauling for 5G LTE-U Ultra Dense Cloud Small Cell Networks. IEEE Wirel. Commun. 23(6), 48–53 (2016)
4. Zhang, H., Liu, N., Chu, X., Long, K., Aghvami, A., Leung, V.: Network slicing based 5G and future mobile networks: mobility, resource management, and challenges. IEEE Commun. Mag. 55(8), 138–145 (2017)
5. Wang, C.Y., Wei, H.Y., Chen, W.T.: Resource block allocation with carrier-aggregation: a strategy-proof auction design. J. IEEE Trans. Mob. Comput. 15(12), 3142–3155 (2016)
6. Cui, Y., Yang, L., Liu, B., Li, R.: Multiband planar antenna for LTE/GSM/UMTS and WLAN/WiMAX handsets. J. IET Microwaves Antennas Propag. 10(5), 502–506 (2016)
7. Zhu, G.: McWill and its applications in power communication system. [J]. Telecommunications for Electric Power System (2009)
8. Terminal Equipment Specification for LTE-M. http://www.camet.org.cn
9. General System Architecture and Function Specification for LTE-M. http://www.camet.org.cn
10. LTE-M Interface Specification for CBTC. http://www.camet.org.cn
11. Jingdi, L., Jian, F., Ge, M.: Research on Interference and Coexistence between Radio Access System in 1785 MHz–1805 MHz Band and Adjacent IMT System. Technical report, CCSA TC5 WG8 82th Meeting, Chang Sha (2016)
12. Liyan, Y., Jian, J.: Research on Interference and Coexistence between GSM in 900/1800 MHz Band and LTE(FDD/TDD). Technical Report, CCSA TC5 WG8 63th Meeting, Zhang Jia Jie (2013)
13. 3GPP TS 36.101 V13.5.0(2016-09). http://www.3gpp.org/DynaReport/36-series.htm
14. 3GPP TS 45.005 V13.2.1(2016-09). http://www.3gpp.org/DynaReport/45-series.htm
15. 3GPP TR 36.942 V13.0.0(2016-01). http://www.3gpp.org/DynaReport/36-series.htm
16. Propagation Model. http://wenku.baidu.com

Joint C-V-BLAST and DS-NOMA for Massive MIMO

Khawla A. Alnajjar[1(✉)] and Mohamed El-Tarhuni[2]

[1] Department of Electrical and Computer Engineering, University of Sharjah,
Sharjah, United Arab Emirates
kalnajjar@sharjah.ac.ae
[2] Department of Electrical Engineering, American University of Sharjah,
Sharjah, United Arab Emirates
mtarhuni@aus.edu

Abstract. We investigate the performance of modified non orthogonal multiple access (NOMA) which uses the modified low complexity Vertical Bell Laboratories Layered Space Time (C-V-BLAST) in an uplink massive multiple-input-multiple-output (MIMO) deployment with distributed single-antenna users and a large base-station array. Unlike previous work which assumes no spreading, we focus on the scenario where signal spreading is included by using the Gold Code family. It is shown that the proposed scheme provides a significant performance improvement over the conventional V-BLAST system for a large MIMO deployment when the number of transmit and receive antennas are comparable by exploiting the extra dimension added by the spreading to mitigate the interference. However, for a massive MIMO system, both schemes provide similar performance. We also show that the proposed scheme has a much better performance when the average received power for the users is the same, a scenario that the C-V-BLAST scheme struggles with due to its dependence on the ordering of users according to their power levels.

Keywords: Gold code · Massive MIMO · MRC
Non Orthogonal Multiple Access (NOMA) · V-BLAST

1 Introduction

It has been shown that massive multi-input multi-output (MIMO) systems increase throughput, the degrees of freedom, energy efficiency and reliability of wireless systems [1,2]. Hence, massive MIMO is one of the key proposed technologies for fifth generation (5G) systems. Due to the large number of base station (BS) antennas, finding the right tradeoff between system performance and receiver complexity is a critical concern.

One of the most successful receiver strategies for traditional MIMO is the Vertical Bell Laboratories Layered Space Time (V-BLAST) method. It is a multi-layer symbol detection scheme. It combines linear (interference suppression) and

© ICST Institute for Computer Sciences, Social Informatics and Telecommunications Engineering 2018
K. Long et al. (Eds.): 5GWN 2017, LNICST 211, pp. 484–492, 2018.
https://doi.org/10.1007/978-3-319-72823-0_45

nonlinear algorithms (serial cancellation). The majority of works on traditional V-BLAST consider the use of minimum-mean-square-error (MMSE) or zero forcing (ZF) detection. Therefore, conventional V-BLAST is too computationally intensive for massive MIMO. In [3], a modified V-BLAST scheme was proposed by replacing ZF or MMSE receivers with maximal ratio combining (MRC) and using a one-shot ordering method based on channel norms. This scheme, which is denoted as C-V-BLAST, has similar performance to linear ZF detection, but lower complexity. Both MRC and the single ordering technique were needed in [3] to obtain the reduction in complexity.

Non-Orthogonal Multiple Access (NOMA) techniques introduce redundancy by coding/spreading to facilitate the users signals separation at the receiver. In NOMA, multiple users are encouraged to transmit at the same time, code and frequency, but with different power levels. In fact, NOMA allocates less power to the users with better channel conditions, and these users can decode their own information by applying successive interference cancellation. Conventional V-BLAST with code division multiple access (CDMA) has been studied in [4–6]. NOMA for 5G has been studied such as in [7–10].

To the best of our knowledge, the performance of NOMA with C-V-BLAST in the context of massive MIMO has not been investigated. Thus, in this paper, our contribution is that we proposed a modified NOMA algorithm to investigate massive MIMO system performance. Instead of applying successive interference cancellation at each stage, we use the idea of C-V-BLAST by sorting the users once and this will reduce the receiver complexity. Each user data is spread using a Gold Code to provide further separation among the users resulting in an improved performance of the C-V-BLAST scheme with minor increase in complexity. We study the effect of power distribution of users and system size.

The rest of the paper is organized as follows. Section 2 introduces the system model. Section 3 gives an overview of receiver structures used in this work. Simulation results are provided in Sect. 4, and finally our conclusions are in Sect. 5.

2   System Model

We consider an uplink system with N_t single antenna user equipments (UEs) and a base station (BS) with N_r receive antennas. The vector, $\mathbf{s}$, of size $N_t \times 1$ is $\mathbf{s} = [s_1, s_2, \ldots s_{N_t}]^T$, where s_j is the data symbol of UE j drawn form a finite alphabet. The spreading code matrix $\mathbf{C}_c = [\mathbf{c}_1, \mathbf{c}_2, \ldots \mathbf{c}_{N_t}]$ and has a size of $N_t \times L_c$, where L_c is the code length. Note that $\mathbf{c}_j$ is vector of size $L_c \times 1$ representing the code of user j. In this paper we consider Gold Code for with $L_c = 127$. Suppose the transmitted data symbol matrix $\mathbf{X} = [\mathbf{x}_1, \mathbf{x}_2, \ldots, \mathbf{x}_{N_t}]$ where, $\mathbf{x}_j = s_j \mathbf{c}_j$, $s_j = \{-1, 1\}$ and $j = 1, \ldots, N_t$. The channel matrix of size $N_r \times N_t$ is $\mathbf{H} = [\mathbf{h}_1 \cdots \mathbf{h}_{N_t}]$, where $\mathbf{h}_i = [h_{i1} h_{i2} \ldots h_{iN_r}]^T$. The noise matrix, $\mathbf{N}$, of size $N_r \times L_c$ has independent and identically distributed (i.i.d.) complex Gaussian elements, i.e., $n_i \sim \mathcal{CN}(0, \sigma^2)$. The received signal, $\mathbf{Y}$ of size $N_r \times L_c$, is given by

$$\mathbf{Y} = \mathbf{HX} + \mathbf{N} = \mathbf{Hs}\mathbf{C}_c^T + \mathbf{N}. \tag{1}$$

The transmitted signal power is $e[|x_j|^2] = E_s = 1$ and the noise power is $e[|n_i|^2] = \sigma^2$. When there is no spreading, $C = 1$ and $L_c = 1$.

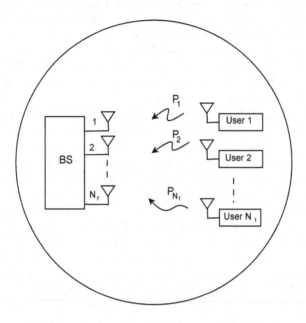

Fig. 1. System diagram where UEs are located randomly in a circular coverage area.

The channel matrix is given by

$$H = UP^{\frac{1}{2}}. \tag{2}$$

The channel coefficient, h_{ij}, from UE j to receive antenna i has a link gain $e[|h_{ij}|^2] = P_j$. The elements of U are i.i.d. $\mathcal{CN}(0,1)$, and the link gain matrix is $P = \mathrm{diag}(P_1, P_2, \ldots, P_{N_t})$ where P_j is the link gain of user j, which accounts for path loss, shadowing, etc. We utilize a simple model [11] so that the link gain of the jth user can be calculated as $P_j = \mathcal{A}\beta^{j-1}$, where β controls the rate of decay of the link gains ($0 < \beta \leq 1$), and $\mathcal{A}$ is the link gain of the strongest UE. This model gives ordered link gains of the users such that $P_1 > P_2 > \cdots > P_{N_t}$. This has no effect on the generality of the results because the user order is arbitrary. As $\beta \to 0$ the link gains are dominated by one strong UE, while as $\beta \to 1$ the link gains become equal. This simple model is used in order to control the P_j's with a single parameter, β, which has a physical interpretation. Additionally, this model is useful because of the importance of the decay rate in V-BLAST, which is heavily dependent on the differences between the link gains.

3   Receivers

In this paper, we focus on MRC within a low complexity V-BLAST structure (C-V-BLAST) [3]. The simplest linear combiner, MRC, of the form, $H^H Y$, where H^H represents the complex conjugate transpose of H. The linear zero forcing combiner in general performs better than MRC. The combining matrix of ZF is calculated by $W = H(H^H H)^{-1}$. Note that ZF combiner involves matrix inversion which may be undesirable in massive MIMO because of stability and complexity issues.

The C-V-BLAST method [3] utilizes V-BLAST combined with MRC detection and a single ordering based upon instantaneous channel norms. This technique provides results similar to V-BLAST combined with linear ZF [3] while avoiding the computational bottlenecks of conventional V-BLAST. Assume ordered set $S^{(C)} = \{k_1^{(C)}, k_2^{(C)}, \ldots, k_{N_t}^{(C)}\}$ be a permutation of $\{1, 2, \ldots, N_t\}$, which decides the detecting order of x. The ordering for C-V-BLAST is calculated by [3]

$$k_i^{(C)} = \underset{j \notin \{k_1, k_2, \ldots, k_{i-1}\}}{\arg \max} \ ||h_j||^2. \tag{3}$$

We used the same receiver structure as the C-V-BLAST scheme but with an additional operation that processes the baseband received spread message for each user and de-spread it with its corresponding Gold Code. The output of the de-spreading block is applied to the C-V-BLAST detector for normal processing. Algorithm 1 shows the pseudo-code algorithm of the proposed (Gold C-V-BLAST) scheme. The de-spreading operation is relatively simple to implement with a total number of additional $N_t L_c$ complex multiplications.

In terms of the number of complex multiplications, the complexity of C-V-BLAST is $O(N_r N_t)$, but that of ZF is $O(N_r N_t^2)$ [3]. Table 1 shows a comparison of the implementation complexity of the proposed scheme to the ZF and C-V-BLAST.

Table 1. Complexity comparison

Technique	Complexity
ZF	$O(N_r N_t^2)$
C-V-BLAST	$O(N_r N_t)$
Gold C-V-BLAST	$O(N_r N_t + N_t L_c)$

4 Simulation Results

In this section, we use numerical simulations to investigate the performance of massive MIMO receivers.

Performance is measured by the symbol error rate (SER) assuming quadrature phase shift keying (QPSK) modulation. The results were averaged over the users and 10,000 independent channel realizations. In the figures, the SNR is the SNR of the strongest UE, given by $\frac{A}{\sigma^2}$, where $A = 1$ without loss of generality.

The C-V-BLAST receiver is used with and without spreading. Gold Code is used for spreading but other types of codes might be used as well. In this paper,

Algorithm 1. Gold C-V-BLAST Algorithm

1) Initialization:	
$i = 1$	i is the iteration number.
$\mathbf{c}$	$\mathbf{c}$ is the code matrix.
$\mathbf{y}$	$\mathbf{y}$ is the received signal.
$\mathbf{H}$	$\mathbf{H}$ is the channel matrix.
$\mathbf{k}$	Sort decently based on k_i.
	$k_i = \underset{j \notin \{k_1, k_2, \dots, k_{i-1}\}}{\arg\max} \ \|\mathbf{h}_j\|^2.$
2) Iterative Process:	
$\mathbf{W} = \mathbf{H}$	Calculate the MRC linear combiner.
$\mathbf{G} = \mathbf{W}^H$	Find the Hermitian of the linear combiner, $\mathbf{W}$.
$\mathbf{m}_{k_i} = (\mathbf{G}_i)_{k_i}.$	$\mathbf{m}_{\mathbf{k_i}}$ is the ith row of $\mathbf{G}$.
$\tilde{x}_i = \mathbf{m}_{k_i}\mathbf{y}$	Calculate the estimated input signal $\tilde{x}_i$.
$\hat{x}_i = \hat{Q}[\sum_{i=1}^{L_c} \tilde{x}_i \mathbf{c}_{k_i}]$	$\hat{Q}(.)$ is the quantization (slicing) operation appropriate to the constellation in use.
$\mathbf{y}_{i+1} = \mathbf{y}_i - \mathbf{h}_{k_i}(x_{\hat{k}_i}\mathbf{c}_{k_i})$	The interference due to $x_{\hat{k}_i}\mathbf{c}_{k_i}$ is canceled.
$\mathbf{H}_{i+1} = \mathbf{H}_i^{\bar{k}_i}$	Update $\mathbf{H}$ at iteration i by zeroing the k_i column.
	This is denoted by $\mathbf{H}_i^{\bar{k}_i}$.
$i = i + 1$	Update i,.
$k_i = \mathbf{k}(i).$	Update k_i index.

we consider the length of Gold Code with $L_c = 127$. We use [1 0 0 0 1 0 0] and [1 0 0 0 1 1 1] as the preferred polynomials for length 127 code generation [12]. We assume that the code is fixed for each user.

The baseline parameters are: $\beta = 0.7, N_t = 10, N_r = 100$ and the modified NOMA which C-V-BLAST uses Gold Code with length 127 (Gold C-V-BLAST 127). Where other parameters are used, they are given in the figure captions.

Figure 2 shows the SER performance of C-V-BLAST and Gold C-V-BLAST 127 vs SNR with $N_t = 10$, $\beta = 0.7$, $N_r \in \{10, 50, 100\}$. We notice that as N_r decreases and approaches N_t, spreading becomes beneficial since the C-V-BLAST system cannot cope with the high interference with the small number of antennas and the extra dimension added by the spreading is exploited to mitigate the interference. Note that when $N_r > N_t$, spatial diversity will improve the C-V-BLAST system performance and there is no gain from using the spreading scheme.

Figure 3 shows the SER performance of C-V-BLAST and Gold C-V-BLAST 127 vs SNR with $N_r = 10$, $\beta = 0.7$, $N_t \in \{10, 50, 100\}$. As N_t exceeds N_r with larger size, C-V-BLAST performance is already poor and hence spreading will not help much. When the ratio $N_r/N_t = 1$, coding becomes beneficial when the system size is small, i.e. small number of base station antennas.

Figure 4 shows the SER performance of C-V-BLAST and Gold C-V-BLAST 127 vs SNR with $N_r = 100$, $\beta = 0.7$, $N_t \in \{10, 50, 100\}$. It is observed that as Nt increases, the performance of both schemes improve but there is no performance difference with or without spreading. We have noticed that for systems with a large size (i.e. N_r/N_t exceeds 10), spreading is not beneficial.

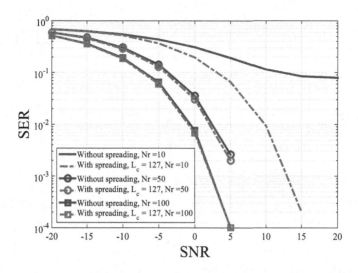

Fig. 2. SER versus SNR for C-V-BLAST (without spreading) and Gold C-V-BLAST 127 (with spreading). $N_t = 10$, $\beta = 0.7$, $N_r \in \{10, 50, 100\}$.

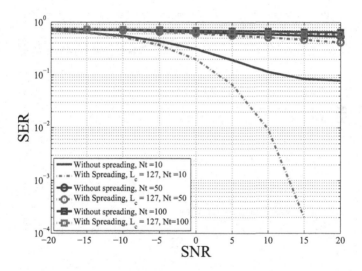

Fig. 3. SER versus SNR for C-V-BLAST (without spreading) and Gold C-V-BLAST 127 (with spreading). $N_r = 10$, $\beta = 0.7$, $N_t \in \{10, 50, 100\}$.

Figure 5 shows the SER performance of C-V-BLAST and Gold C-V-BLAST 127 with $N_t = 10, N_r = 10$, $\beta \in \{0.5, 0.9, 0.7\}$. The system performance is strongly affected by β. As β increases, the proposed scheme provides more improvement over the C-V-BLAST scheme, which suffers from poor performance when the channel link gain are not widely distinctive.

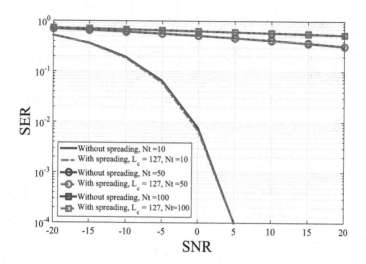

Fig. 4. SER versus SNR for C-V-BLAST (without spreading) and Gold C-V-BLAST 127 (with spreading). $N_r = 100$, $\beta = 0.7$, $N_t \in \{10, 50, 100\}$.

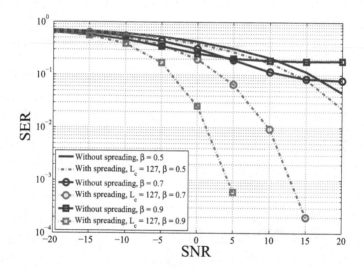

Fig. 5. SER versus SNR for C-V-BLAST (without spreading) and Gold C-V-BLAST 127 (with spreading). $N_t = 10, N_r = 10$, $\beta \in \{0.5, 0.9, 0.7\}$.

For more clarification of Fig. 5, the SER performance of C-V-BLAST and Gold C-V-BLAST 127 vs β with $N_t = \{10, 100\}, N_r = \{10, 100\}$ at SNR = 0 dB is presented in Fig. 6. It is noted that as β increases, the SER performance degrades. This is because C-V-BLAST works best when there is a wide difference among the users' powers but fails to perform adequately when the channel links have similar power levels. However, spreading the users' data using the Gold Codes results in good performance when the users have almost equal powers.

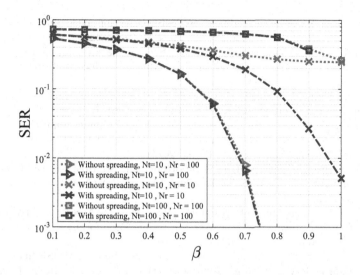

Fig. 6. SER versus β for C-V-BLAST (without spreading) and Gold C-V-BLAST 127 (with spreading). $N_t = \{10, 100\}, N_r = \{10, 100\}$ and SNR = 0 dB.

5   Conclusions

In this paper, we propose a modified NOMA scheme for uplink massive MIMO applications. The user data is spread using a Gold Code prior to transmission and a reduced complexity receiver based on C-V-BLAST structure is used. It is shown that spreading results in improved symbol error rate performance for large size MIMO system. However, for a massive MIMO system with a large number of receive antennas, there is no gain from spreading. Finally, the impact of the link gain difference among the users is investigated.

Acknowledgment. This research was supported in part by the Distributed and Networked Systems Research Group Operating Grant number 150410, University of Sharjah, and Seed Grant No. 1602040224-P.

References

1. Ngo, H.Q., Larsson, E.G., Marzetta, T.: Energy and spectral efficiency of very large multiuser MIMO systems. IEEE Trans. Commun. **61**(4), 1436–1449 (2013)
2. Rusek, F., Persson, D., Kiong, B.L., Larsson, E., Marzetta, T.L., Edfors, O., Tufvesson, F.: Scaling up MIMO: Opportunities and challenges with very large arrays. IEEE Signal Process. Mag. **30**(1), 40–60 (2013)
3. Alnajjar, K.A., Smith, P.J., Woodward, G.K.: Low complexity V-BLAST for massive MIMO. In: Proceedings of Australian Communications Theory Workshop (AusCTW), pp. 22–26. IEEE (2014)
4. Zhao, J., Li, X.: A novel iterative equalization algorithm for multicode CDMA system with V-BLAST architecture. In: Proceedings of Consumer Communications and Networking (CCNC), pp. 211–214. IEEE (2005)

5. Fu, H., Tao, Y.: A novel nonlinear precoding detection algorithm for VBLAST in MIMO-MC-CDMA downlink system. Phys. Procedia **24**, 1133–1139 (2012)
6. Samardzija, D., Wolniansky, P., Ling, J.: Performance evaluation of the VBLAST algorithm in W-CDMA systems. In: Proceedings of Vehicular Technology (VTC), vol. 2, pp. 723–727 (2001)
7. Ding, Z., Peng, M., Poor, H.V.: Cooperative non-orthogonal multiple access in 5G systems. IEEE Commun. Lett. **19**(8), 1462–1465 (2015)
8. Al-Imari, M., Xiao, P., Imran, M.A., Tafazolli, R.: Uplink non-orthogonal multiple access for 5G wireless networks. In: Proceedings of Wireless Communications Systems (ISWCS), pp. 781–785. IEEE (2014)
9. Lei, L.: From Orthogonal to Non-orthogonal Multiple Access: Energy-and Spectrum-Efficient Resource Allocation. Linkoping University Electronic Press, Linkoping (2016)
10. Ali, M.S., Hossain, Kim, D.I.: Non-Orthogonal Multiple Access (NOMA) for Downlink Multiuser MIMO Systems: User Clustering, Beamforming, and Power Allocation. arXiv preprint arXiv:1611.07425 (2016)
11. Gao, H., Smith, P.J., Clark, M.V.: Theoretical reliability of MMSE linear diversity combining in Rayleigh-fading additive interference channels. IEEE Trans. Commun. **46**(5), 666–672 (1998)
12. Peterson, W.W., Weldon, E.J.: Error-Correcting Codes. MIT press, Cambridge (1972)

Low-Complexity Equalization of Continuous Phase Modulation Using Message Passing

Jian Zhang[1(✉)], Zuyao Ni[2], Sheng Wu[2], and Linling Kuang[2]

[1] Department of Electronic Engineering, Tsinghua University, Beijing, China
jian-zha14@mails.tsinghua.edu.cn
[2] Tsinghua Space Center, Tsinghua University, Beijing, China
{nzy, thuraya, kll}@tsinghua.edu.cn

Abstract. In this paper, based on factor graphs and Laurent decompositions, we propose an iterative receiver of CPM signals over interference (ISI) channels. We adopt the Gaussian message passing to simplify the message passing in factor graphs. Compared with the conventional receivers with the minimum mean squared error (MMSE) frequency domain equalization (FDE) and the BCJR demodulator, the proposed algorithm has advantages in terms of complexity. And the proposed algorithm can achieve better performance with the convolutional code.

Keywords: Continuous phase modulation · Iterative receivers
Factor graphs · ISI

1 Introduction

Continuous phase modulation (CPM) is a nonlinear modulation in which the phase is a continuous function of time [1]. CPM is attractive for its good spectral efficiency and constant envelope. However, the optimal receiver of CPM using maximum-likelihood sequence detection (MLSD) is consists of a filter bank followed by a Viterbi decoder. As a consequence, the optimal receiver of M-ary CPM signals requires a bank of $2M^L$ matched filters and a trellis diagram with pM^{L-1} states, where L is the memory of the CPM pulse and p is the number of phase states.

Considering the practical applications of CPM, several methods have been proposed in the literature to reduce the complexity of the receiver, such as Rimoldi decomposition [2], Walsh decomposition [3] and Laurent decomposition (LD) [4]. In [4], by Laurent decomposition (LD), the binary CPM signal is decomposed into a sum of pulse amplitude modulation (PAM) signals. Moreover, Mengali and Morelli extend the LD from binary CPM signals to M-ary CPM signals [5]. The LD can significantly reduce both the number of matched filters and the number of states in trellis diagram, and is more popular used than the other methods. Such as, a reduced-complexity suboptimal detection of CPM signals is proposed based on the extended Laurent representation in [6].

To mitigate the inter-symbol interference (ISI) caused by multipath environments, the equalization is necessary at the receiver to mitigate the ISI for CPM. The optimum receiver of CPM with ISI is a kind of maximum likelihood sequence estimation

© ICST Institute for Computer Sciences, Social Informatics and Telecommunications Engineering 2018
K. Long et al. (Eds.): 5GWN 2017, LNICST 211, pp. 493–505, 2018.
https://doi.org/10.1007/978-3-319-72823-0_46

(MLSE) receiver in the time domain. The complexity of this receiver is effected by both the memory of CPM signals and the delay spread of the multipath channel. As the complexity grows exponentially with the length of the spread, the MLSE receiver is unfeasible for the channel with long delay multipath taps. To solve this problem, the frequency domain equalization (FDE) approach is extended to the CPM scenarios. A series of literature concerned on the study of FDE in CPM receivers appears since 2000s. In 2005, Tan and Stuber study the application of linear single-carrier frequency-domain equalization (SC-FDE) to CPM [7]. Their method can provide better BER performance and lower complexity cost than the optimal receivers for multipath channels having long delay components. A year later, Pancaldi and Vitetta combined the frequency-domain equalization and iterative information exchange [8]. In [9], a frequency domain double turbo equalizer of CPM is proposed by combining the soft-input soft-output (SISO) FDE, the SISO CPM demodulator and the SISO decoder.

Iterative receivers based on factor graphs (FG) and the sum-product algorithm (SPA) have been widely used in linear modulation scenarios to solve the problem of the inter-symbol interference. Moreover, various approximate inference algorithms have been proposed to reduce the complexity of message passing in graphical models, such as the Gaussian message passing (GMP) [10], the expectation propagation [11–13]. However, less attention has been devoted to the application of this method to CPM scenario. In [14], the FG and SPA is used in the detection of CPM signals over channel affected by phase noise.

In this paper, we consider the equalization and detection of CPM signals over multipath channels based on factor graphs and the SPA. By using the Laurent decomposition and the Gaussian message passing, we proposed a kind of low-complexity time-domain turbo equalization of CPM signals. It will be shown that the designed receivers have similar performance with respect to the optimal detectors regardless of the code part. Considering the convolutional code, it has better performance than the MMSE-FDE and optimal detectors.

The paper is organized as follows. In Sect. 2, we describe the system model including the signal model of CPM based on the Laurent decomposition and the model of received signals after multipath channel. The system model is used in Sect. 3 to realize the low-complexity turbo equalization. Section 4 shows the simulation results and conclusions are drawn in Sect. 5 finally.

2   Signal Model

In this paper, only single modulation index CPM is considered. In general, a CPM signal can be expressed as [1]:

$$s(t, \vec{a}) = \sqrt{\frac{2E_s}{T}} \exp\{j2\pi h \sum_n a_n q(t - nT)\} \tag{1}$$

where E_s is the energy per symbol, T is the symbol period, $h = r/p$ is the modulation index (r and p are relatively prime integers), $\{a_n\}$ are the transmitted information symbols, $a_n \in \{\pm 1, \pm 3, \ldots, \pm M - 1\}$, $n = 0, \ldots, N - 1$. The function $q(t)$ is the phase response and has the form as:

$$q(t) = \begin{cases} 0, & \text{if } t \leq 0 \\ \int_0^t g(\tau) d\tau, & \text{if } 0 < t < LT \\ 1/2, & \text{if } t \geq LT \end{cases} \tag{2}$$

where the $g(\tau)$ is the frequency pulse defined over a finite time interval $0 \leq t \leq LT$.

Exploiting the extended Laurent decomposition [4, 5], the CPM signals can be expressed as a sum of linearly modulated signals:

$$s(t, \vec{a}) = \sum_{k=0}^{K-1} \sum_n \alpha_{k,n} p_k(t - nT) \tag{3}$$

in which $K \leq Q^{\log_2 M}(M - 1)$, $Q = 2^{L-1}$ and $p_k(t)$ is the k th PAM component and the symbols $\{\alpha_{k,n}\}$ are the function of the transmitted information symbols $\{a_n\}$. The Laurent decomposition in (3) can exactly express the CPM signals when $K = Q^{\log_2 M}(M - 1)$. Considering most of the signal power is concentrated on the first $M - 1$ PAM components, a value of $K = M - 1$ is usually be used to attain a good tradeoff between the complexity of the system and the approximation quality of Laurent decomposition. In this paper, we only consider the first PAM component to further reduce the complexity of the receiver. As a consequence, we obtain an approximation of $s(t, \vec{a})$:

$$s(t, \vec{a}) \approx \sum_n \alpha_{0,n} p_0(t - nT). \tag{4}$$

As shown in [6], the symbol $\alpha_{0,n}$ can be expressed as a function of $\alpha_{0,n-1}$ and a_n:

$$\alpha_{0,n} = \alpha_{0,n-1} e^{j\pi h a_n}. \tag{5}$$

Furthermore, we employ an equivalent representation of information symbols:

$$\overline{a_n} = \frac{a_n + (M - 1)}{2} \tag{6}$$

in which $\overline{a_n} \in \{0, 1, \ldots, M - 1\}$. Substituting (6) into (5), we can get a new expression about $\alpha_{0,n}$:

$$\alpha_{0,n} = e^{-j\pi h(M-1)(n+1)} e^{j2\pi h \phi_n} \tag{7}$$

$$\phi_n = [\phi_{n-1} + \overline{a_n}]_p \tag{8}$$

where ϕ_n is the accumulation of phase, $\phi_n \in \{0, 1, \ldots, p - 1\}$ and $[\cdot]_p$ denotes the "modulo p" operator.

Considering the multipath channels, the received signals can be expressed as:

$$r(t) = \sum_{l=0}^{N_L-1} h_l s(t - \tau_l T) + w(t) \tag{9}$$

where h_l and τ_l ($\{\tau_l\}$ are positive integers in this paper) are the gain and the symbol number of the propagation delay for the lth path and N_L is the number of channel paths. The function $w(t)$ is complex-valued Additive White Gaussian Noise(AWGN) with variance σ_w^2. Exploiting the Laurent decomposition of CPM signals, a discrete-time expression of received signals can be written as:

$$r_n = \sum_{l=0}^{N_L-1} h_l s_{n-\tau_l} + w_n \tag{10}$$

$$r_n \triangleq \int r(t) p_0(t - nT) dt \tag{11}$$

$$s_n \triangleq \int s(t) p_0(t - nT) dt = \sum_{m=0}^{N-1} \int p_0(t - mT) p_0(t - nT) dt \alpha_{0,m} \tag{12}$$

where w_n is assumed to be independent identical distributed Gaussian sequence with variance σ_n^2. As shown in [5], $p_0(t)$ is the first component of pulse amplitude modulation (PAM) signals. The integral value of $\int p_0(t - mT) p_0(t - nT) dt$ varies with the value of $|m - n|$ which is maximum when $|m - n|$ is zero and takes zero when $|m - n|$ is big enough. Based on this property, we can further simplify the expression (12):

$$s_n \approx \sum_{m=n-L_m}^{n+L_m} \int p_0(t - mT) p_0(t - nT) dt \alpha_{0,m} = \sum_{m=n-L_m}^{n+L_m} P_{|m-n|} \alpha_{0,m} \tag{13}$$

where L_m is an integer associated with M and L.

3   The Proposed Algorithm

Based on the signal model mentioned in Sect. 2, we derive the factor graph based receiver of CPM signals in this section. Our goal is to restore the transmitted information bits $\mathbf{b}$ from the received signals $\mathbf{r}$. Generally, we use the Maximum a Posteriori (MAP) strategy to estimate the information sequence:

$$\widehat{b}_i = \arg \max_{b_i} p(b_i|\mathbf{r}) \tag{14}$$

where b_i denotes the i th information bit and $p(b_i|\mathbf{r})$ is the marginal probability mass function of the joint posterior probability distribution $p(\mathbf{b}|\mathbf{r})$. According to the Bayesian rule, $p(\mathbf{b}|\mathbf{r})$ can be expressed as:

$$p(\mathbf{b}|\mathbf{r}) \propto p(\mathbf{r}|\mathbf{s})p(\mathbf{s}|\boldsymbol{\alpha})p(\boldsymbol{\alpha}|\boldsymbol{\phi})p(\boldsymbol{\phi}|\mathbf{a})p(\mathbf{a}|\mathbf{c})p(\mathbf{c}|\mathbf{b})p(\mathbf{b}) \tag{15}$$

where $\propto$ denotes proportionality and $\mathbf{c}$ is the code bits. The element c_n^q denotes the q th information bit of the n th symbol a_n. Using (10) in Sect. 2, the conditional probability $p(\mathbf{r}|\mathbf{s})$ can be factorized into:

$$p(\mathbf{r}|\mathbf{s}) = \prod_n f_n(r_n|\mathbf{s}) = \prod_n \exp\left\{ -\frac{\left(r_n - \sum_{l=0}^{N_L-1} h_l s_{n-\tau_l}\right)^2}{\sigma_n^2} \right\} \tag{16}$$

in which $n = 0, 1, \ldots, N-1$ and we assumed the channel is already known to the receiver – in other words, the h_l and τ_l are already known. Similarly, we can get the factorization of the conditional probabilities $p(\mathbf{s}|\boldsymbol{\alpha}),p(\boldsymbol{\alpha}|\boldsymbol{\phi})$ and $p(\boldsymbol{\phi}|\mathbf{a})$ using Eqs. (13), (7) and (8)

$$p(\mathbf{s}|\boldsymbol{\alpha}) = \prod_n g_n(s_n, \boldsymbol{\alpha}) = \prod_n \delta\left(s_n - \sum_{m=n-L_m}^{n+L_m} P_{|m-n|}\alpha_{0,m} \right) \tag{17}$$

$$p(\boldsymbol{\alpha}|\boldsymbol{\phi}) = \prod_n I_n(\alpha_{0,n}, \phi_n) = \prod_n \delta\left(\alpha_{0,n} - e^{-j\pi h(M-1)(n+1)} e^{j2\pi h\phi_n} \right) \tag{18}$$

$$p(\boldsymbol{\phi}|\mathbf{a}) = \prod_n J_n(a_n, \phi_n, \phi_{n-1}) \tag{19}$$

in which $g_n(\cdot)$, $I_n(\cdot)$ and $J_n(\cdot)$ are the indicator functions and $\{a_n\}$ are assumed to be unipolar symbols, $a_n \in \{0, 1, \ldots, M-1\}$. The conditional probability $p(\mathbf{a}|\mathbf{c})$ in (15) can be factorized into

$$p(\mathbf{a}|\mathbf{c}) = \prod_n p(a_n|\mathbf{c_n}) = \prod_n \delta(a_n - \varphi(\mathbf{c_n})) \tag{20}$$

where $\delta(\cdot)$ is the Kronecker delta function and $\varphi(\mathbf{c_n})$ is the mapping function and $\mathbf{c_n}$ is comprised of $\{c_n^q, \forall q\}$, $q = 0, 1, \ldots, Q, Q = \log_2 M - 1$.

According to the factorization (16)–(20), we can get the factor graph representation of the receiver, as depicted in Fig. 1. In Fig. 1, f_n denotes the channel transition function $f_n(r_n|\mathbf{s})$, g_n denotes the Laurent decomposition constraint $g_n(s_n, \boldsymbol{\alpha})$, M_n denotes the mapping constraint $p(a_n|\mathbf{c_n})$, $P(\phi_{-1})$ and $P(\phi_{N-1})$ denotes the initial probabilities of the variables ϕ_{-1} and ϕ_{N-1}, $P(\phi_{-1}) = P(\phi_{N-1}) = 1/p$.

Given the factor graph representation, the marginals can be computed exactly by message passing. Before study the detailed message computation, we introduce the representation of messages that follows. The messages passing between the function nodes A and variable nodes B of the ith iteration are denoted as $\mu_{A \to B}^i(B)$ and $\mu_{B \to A}^i(B)$. For example, the messages passing between the nodes $\{f_n\}$ and $\{s_n\}$ are denoted as $\mu_{f_n \to s_k}^i(s_k)$ and $\mu_{s_n \to f_t}^i(s_n)$ respectively, $k = n - \tau_l$, $t = n + \tau_l$, $l = 0, \ldots, N_L - 1$, $n = 0, \ldots, N-1$.

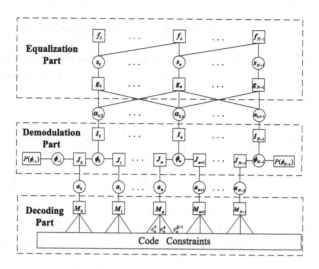

Fig. 1. Factor graph representation.

Firstly, we focus on the equalization part of the factor graph. By applying the updating rules of the SPA in the factor graph, messages $\mu_{f_n \to s_k}^i(s_k)$ and $\mu_{s_n \to f_t}^i(s_n)$ can be calculated by

$$\mu_{s_n \to f_t}^i(s_n) = \prod_{t' \neq t} \mu_{f_{t'} \to s_n}^{i-1}(s_n) \mu_{g_n \to s_n}^i(s_n) \tag{21}$$

$$\mu_{f_n \to s_k}^i(s_k) = \int_{\vec{s}/s_k} f_n(\vec{s}) \prod_{k' \neq k} \mu_{s_{k'} \to f_n}^i(s_{k'}). \tag{22}$$

However, a direct computation of Eqs. (21) and (22) is intractable for high-dimensional integral. Hence, we derive the reduced-complexity receiver based on the Gaussian message passing method.

Considering the practical application scenarios, we can assume that s_n is a continuous complex Gaussian random variable. According to the Eq. (10), w_n is a Gaussian variable, and then $(r_n - \sum_{l=0}^{N_L-1} h_l s_{n-\tau_l})$ is also a Gaussian variable. We can reasonably assume that the messages $\mu_{f_n \to s_k}^i(s_k)$ and $\mu_{s_n \to f_m}^i(s_n)$ are approximated as Gaussian density function:

$$\mu_{s_n \to f_t}^i(s_n) = N_C(s_n; x_{s_n \to f_t}^i, v_{s_n \to f_t}^i) \tag{23}$$

$$\mu_{f_n \to s_k}^i(s_k) = N_C(h_l s_k; x_{f_n \to s_k}^i, v_{f_n \to s_k}^i) \tag{24}$$

where $x_{s_n \to f_t}^i$ and $v_{s_n \to f_t}^i$ respectively denote the mean and the variance of the variable s_n with respect to the message $\mu_{s_n \to f_t}^i(s_n)$, $x_{f_n \to s_k}^i$ and $v_{f_n \to s_k}^i$ denote the mean and the variance of the variable $h_l s_k$ with respect to the message $\mu_{f_n \to s_k}^i(s_k)$. According to

Eqs. (13) and (17), considering the linear relationship between variables s_n and $\alpha_{0,n}$, we can assume $\alpha_{0,n}$ is a continuous complex Gaussian random variable too. According to SPA, the messages passing between nodes s_n and g_n can be express as:

$$\mu^i_{s_n \to g_n}(s_n) = N_C(s_n; x^i_{s_n \to g_n}, v^i_{s_n \to g_n}) \tag{25}$$

$$\mu^i_{g_n \to s_n}(s_n) = N_C(s_n; x^i_{g_n \to s_n}, v^i_{g_n \to s_n}). \tag{26}$$

Similarly, the messages passing between nodes $\alpha_{0,n}$ and g_n can be express as:

$$\mu^i_{\alpha_{0,n} \to g_j}(\alpha_{0,n}) = N_C(\alpha_{0,n}; x^i_{\alpha_{0,n} \to g_j}, v^i_{\alpha_{0,n} \to g_j}) \tag{27}$$

$$\mu^i_{g_n \to \alpha_{0,m}}(\alpha_{0,m}) = N_C(p_{|m-n|}\alpha_{0,m}; x^i_{g_n \to \alpha_{0,m}}, v^i_{g_n \to \alpha_{0,m}}) \tag{28}$$

where $n = 0, \ldots, N-1$, $n - L_m \leq j \leq n + L_m$, $n - L_m \leq m \leq n + L_m$.

According to the properties of Gaussian distribution and the rules of SPA, the means and the variances mentioned above can be exactly calculated as:

$$x^i_{f_n \to s_k} = r_n - \sum_{l' \neq l} h_{l'} x^i_{s_{n-\tau_{l'}} \to f_n}, \quad v^i_{f_n \to s_k} = \sigma^2_n + \sum_{l' \neq l} |h_{l'}|^2 v^i_{s_{n-\tau_{l'}} \to f_n} \tag{29}$$

$$v^i_{s_n \to f_t} = \left(\frac{1}{u^i_{g_n \to s_n}} + \sum_{l' \neq l} \frac{|h_{l'}|^2}{v^{i-1}_{f_{n+\tau_{l'}} \to s_n}} \right)^{-1}, \quad x^i_{s_n \to f_t} = v^i_{s_n \to f_t} \left(\frac{x^i_{g_n \to s_n}}{v^i_{g_n \to s_n}} + \sum_{l' \neq l} \frac{|h_{l'}| x^{i-1}_{f_{n+\tau_{l'}} \to s_n}}{v^{i-1}_{f_{n+\tau_{l'}} \to s_n}} \right) \tag{30}$$

$$v^i_{s_n \to g_n} = \left(\sum_l \frac{|h_l|^2}{v^i_{f_{n+\tau_l} \to s_n}} \right)^{-1}, \quad x^i_{s_n \to g_n} = v^i_{s_n \to g_n} \sum_l \frac{h_l x^i_{f_{n+\tau_l} \to s_n}}{v^i_{f_{n+\tau_l} \to s_n}} \tag{31}$$

$$x^i_{g_n \to s_n} = \sum_{m=n-L_m}^{n+L_m} p_{|m-n|} x^i_{\alpha_{0,m} \to g_n}, \quad v^i_{g_n \to s_n} = \sum_{m=n-L_m}^{n+L_m} |p_{|m-n|}|^2 v^i_{\alpha_{0,m} \to g_n} \tag{32}$$

$$x^i_{g_n \to \alpha_{0,m}} = x^i_{s_n \to g_n} - \sum_{m' \neq m} p_{|m'-n|} y^{i-1}_{\alpha_{0,m'} \to g_n}, \quad v^i_{g_n \to \alpha_{0,m}} = v^i_{s_n \to g_n} + \sum_{m' \neq m} |p_{|m'-n|}|^2 v^{i-1}_{\alpha_{0,m'} \to g_n} \tag{33}$$

$$v^i_{\alpha_{0,n} \to g_j} = \left(\frac{1}{v^i_{I_n \to \alpha_{0,n}}} + \sum_{j' \neq j} \frac{|p_{|j'-n|}|^2}{v^i_{g_{j'} \to \alpha_{0,n}}} \right)^{-1}, \quad x^i_{\alpha_{0,n} \to g_j} = v^i_{\alpha_{0,n} \to g_j} \left(\frac{x^i_{I_n \to \alpha_{0,n}}}{v^i_{I_n \to \alpha_{0,n}}} + \sum_{j' \neq j} \frac{p_{|j'-n|} x^i_{g_{j'} \to \alpha_{0,n}}}{v^i_{g_{j'} \to \alpha_{0,n}}} \right) \tag{34}$$

where $p_{|m-n|} \triangleq \int p_0(t - mT) p_0(t - nT) dt$.

Next we study the demodulation part of the factor graph in Fig. 1. By applying the rules of SPA continually, the message $\mu^i_{\alpha_{0,n} \to I_n}(\alpha_{0,n})$ can be computed:

$$\mu^i_{\alpha_{0,n} \to I_n}(\alpha_{0,n}) = \prod_j \mu^i_{g_j \to \alpha_{0,n}}(\alpha_{0,n}). \tag{35}$$

Considering the equations in (34), we can further compute the message $\mu^i_{\alpha_{0,n} \to I_n}(\alpha_{0,n})$ as:

$$v^i_{\alpha_{0,n} \to I_n} = \left(\sum_j \frac{|p_{|j-n|}|^2}{v^i_{g_j \to \alpha_{0,n}}} \right)^{-1}, \quad x^i_{\alpha_{0,n} \to I_n} = v^i_{\alpha_{0,n} \to I_n} \left(\sum_j \frac{p_{|j-n|} x^i_{g_j \to \alpha_{0,n}}}{v^i_{g_j \to \alpha_{0,n}}} \right) \tag{36}$$

where $x^i_{\alpha_{0,n} \to I_n}$ and $v^i_{\alpha_{0,n} \to I_n}$ are the mean and the variance of the message $\mu^i_{\alpha_{0,n} \to I_n}(\alpha_{0,n})$.

Before computing the message $\mu^i_{\phi_n \to I_n}(\phi_n)$, we focus on the value of the variable $\alpha_{0,n}$. According to the Eq. (7), $\alpha_{0,n}$ is actually a discrete random variable with p values. The probability distribution of $\alpha_{0,n}$ can be calculated by

$$P_\downarrow(\alpha_{0,n}) = \frac{N_C(\alpha_{0,n}; x^i_{\alpha_{0,n} \to I_n}, v^i_{\alpha_{0,n} \to I_n})}{\sum_{\alpha_{0,n}} N_C(\alpha_{0,n}; x^i_{\alpha_{0,n} \to I_n}, v^i_{\alpha_{0,n} \to I_n})}. \tag{37}$$

By applying the updating rules of the SPA, messages with reference to the demodulation part can be recursively computed as:

$$\mu^i_{I_n \to \phi_n}(\phi_n) = \sum_{\alpha_{0,n}} I_n(\alpha_{0,n}, \phi_n) \mu^i_{\alpha_{0,n} \to I_n}(\alpha_{0,n}) \tag{38}$$

$$\mu^i_{\phi_n \to I_n}(\phi_n) = \mu^i_{J_n \to \phi_n}(\phi_n) \mu^i_{J_{n+1} \to \phi_n}(\phi_n) \tag{39}$$

$$\mu^i_{I_n \to \alpha_{0,n}}(\alpha_{0,n}) = \sum_{\phi_n} I_n(\alpha_{0,n}, \phi_n) \mu^i_{\phi_n \to I_n}(\phi_n) \tag{40}$$

$$\mu^i_{J_n \to \phi_n}(\phi_n) = \sum_{a_n} \sum_{\phi_{n-1}} J_n(a_n, \phi_n, \phi_{n-1}) \mu^{i-1}_{a_n \to J_n}(a_n) \mu^i_{\phi_{n-1} \to J_n}(\phi_{n-1}) \tag{41}$$

$$\mu^i_{\phi_n \to J_{n+1}}(\phi_n) = \mu^i_{J_n \to \phi_n}(\phi_n) \mu^i_{I_n \to \phi_n}(\phi_n) \tag{42}$$

$$\mu^i_{J_n \to \phi_{n-1}}(\phi_{n-1}) = \sum_{a_n} \sum_{\phi_n} J_n(a_n, \phi_n, \phi_{n-1}) \mu^{i-1}_{a_n \to J_n}(a_n) \mu^i_{\phi_n \to J_n}(\phi_n) \tag{43}$$

$$\mu^i_{\phi_n \to J_n}(\phi_n) = \mu^i_{J_{n+1} \to \phi_n}(\phi_n) \mu^i_{I_n \to \phi_n}(\phi_n) \tag{44}$$

$$\mu^i_{J_n \to a_n}(a_n) = \sum_{\phi_n} \sum_{\phi_{n-1}} J_n(a_n, \phi_n, \phi_{n-1}) \mu^i_{\phi_n \to J_n}(\phi_n) \mu^i_{\phi_{n-1} \to J_n}(\phi_{n-1}) \tag{45}$$

In Eqs. (41) and (44), the messages $\mu^i_{\phi_{n-1} \rightarrow J_n}(\phi_{n-1})$ and $\mu^i_{J_{n+1} \rightarrow \phi_n}(\phi_n)$ have the following initial conditions:

$$\mu^i_{\phi_{-1} \rightarrow J_0}(\phi_{-1}) = \mu^i_{J_N \rightarrow \phi_{N-1}}(\phi_{N-1}) = 1/p. \tag{46}$$

In Eq. (38), the message $\mu^i_{I_n \rightarrow \phi_n}(\phi_n)$ is a discrete probability distribution function about the variable ϕ_n and can be computed just like the means in Eq. (37). As for the message $\mu^i_{I_n \rightarrow \alpha_{0,n}}(\alpha_{0,n})$ in Eq. (40), it can be approximated as Gaussian density function and can be computed using the message $\mu^i_{\phi_n \rightarrow I_n}(\phi_n)$:

$$\mu^i_{I_n \rightarrow \alpha_{0,n}}(\alpha_{0,n}) = N_C(\alpha_{0,n}; x^i_{I_n \rightarrow \alpha_{0,n}}, v^i_{I_n \rightarrow \alpha_{0,n}}) \tag{47}$$

$$P_\uparrow(\alpha_{0,n}) = P(\phi_n) = \mu^i_{\phi_n \rightarrow I_n}(\phi_n) \tag{48}$$

$$x^i_{I_n \rightarrow \alpha_{0,n}} = E_{P_\uparrow(\alpha_{0,n})}[\alpha_{0,n}], \quad v^i_{I_n \rightarrow \alpha_{0,n}} = E_{P_\uparrow(\alpha_{0,n})}[|\alpha_{0,n}|^2] - |x^i_{I_n \rightarrow \alpha_{0,n}}|^2. \tag{49}$$

Finally, we focus on the decoder part of the factor graph in Fig. 1. A soft-input-soft-output (SISO) decoder is used to implement the turbo iteration with the demodulation part. According to the rules of SPA, the message $\mu^i_{a_n \rightarrow M_n}(a_n)$ can be updated by

$$\mu^i_{a_n \rightarrow M_n}(a_n) = \mu^i_{J_n \rightarrow a_n}(a_n). \tag{50}$$

Using the message $\mu^i_{a_n \rightarrow M_n}(a_n)$ in Eq. (50) and the a priori logarithm likelihood ratios (LLRs) $\{\lambda^{i-1}_a(c^q_n), \forall q\}$ fed back from the SISO decoder at previous turbo iteration, the extrinsic LLRs $\{\lambda^i_e(c^q_n), \forall q\}$ which are the input of the SISO decoder can be obtained as follows:

$$\lambda^i_e(c^q_n) = \ln \frac{\sum_{a_n \in A^1_q} \mu^i_{a_n \rightarrow M_n}(a_n)}{\sum_{a_n \in A^0_q} \mu^i_{a_n \rightarrow M_n}(a_n)} - \lambda^{i-1}_a(c^q_n). \tag{51}$$

Once the extrinsic LLRs $\{\lambda^i_e(c^q_n), \forall q\}$ are available, the decoder performs decoding and feeds back the a priori logarithm likelihood ratios (LLRs) $\{\lambda^i_a(c^q_n), \forall q\}$ which can be used to compute the message $\mu^i_{M_n \rightarrow a_n}(a_n)$.

$$\beta(a_n) = \prod_q \frac{\exp\{c^q_n \lambda^i_a(c^q_n)\}}{1 + \exp\{c^q_n \lambda^i_a(c^q_n)\}} \tag{52}$$

$$\mu^i_{M_n \rightarrow a_n}(a_n) = \frac{\beta(a_n)}{\sum_{a_n} \beta(a_n)}. \tag{53}$$

In Eq. (53), $\mu^i_{M_n \to a_n}(a_n)$ is a discrete probability distribution function about the discrete random variable a_n. By applying the updating rules of SPA, the message $\mu^i_{a_n \to J_n}(a_n)$ can be expressed as:

$$\mu^i_{a_n \to J_n}(a_n) = \mu^i_{M_n \to a_n}(a_n). \tag{54}$$

In summary, the messages passing in one turbo iteration are exactly derived as the equations in this section shown. Because of the factor graph in Fig. 1 is loopy, we consider a message passing form the bottom to the top and then back again as one turbo iteration. At the beginning of the first turbo iteration, we set $\mu^0_{\phi_n \to I_n}(\phi_n) = 1/p$, $\forall n$, $\lambda^0_a(c^q_n) = 0$, $\forall q$, $\forall n$.

4   Simulation Results

In this section, we present the simulation results for the proposed algorithm. The performance of the proposed algorithm is assessed in terms of bit error rate (BER) versus E_b/N_0. For each considered channel, we compare the proposed algorithm with the conditional receiver of the CPM signals which uses the minimum mean squared error (MMSE) frequency domain equalization (FDE) and the optimal BCJR demodulator. In both receivers, we consider the $1/2 - rate$ convolutional code with generators $G_1 = 91$ and $G_2 = 121$ (octal notation) and the encoding length is 1024.

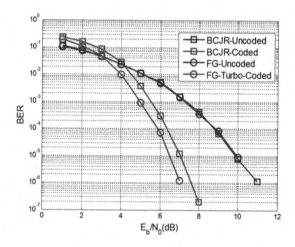

Fig. 2. 1RC modulation with h = 1/2 and M = 2 for AWGN channel.

In Fig. 2, we consider a relatively simple scenario, AWGN channel, to verify the performance of the algorithm proposed in Sect. 3. A binary CPM signal with frequency pulse of duration $L = 1$ symbol interval and the modulation index $h = 1/2$ is considered. When using the proposed algorithm, we set the parameters as follows $N_L = 1$ and $L_m = 1$. As shown in Fig. 2, we compare the BER performance of the proposed algorithm and the BCJR method with and without the convolutional code respectively. The performance of the two algorithms is similar in the scenario without the convolutional code. When we consider the convolutional code in both systems, the performance of the proposed algorithm using the turbo iteration is better than the BCJR demodulation.

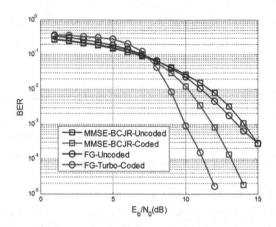

Fig. 3. 1RC modulation with h = 1/4 and M = 4 for Channel I

In Fig. 3, we consider an ISI channel (channel I) characterized by $N_L = 2$ and

$$\boldsymbol{h} = [0.8165 \ 0.5773], \ \boldsymbol{\tau} = [0 \ 20] \tag{55}$$

in which the vector $\boldsymbol{h}$ denotes the gain of each path of the channel and the vector $\boldsymbol{\tau}$ denotes the symbol number of the propagation delay for each path of the channel. A quaternary CPM signal with frequency pulse of duration $L = 1$ symbol interval and the modulation index $h = 1/4$ is considered. We set the parameters of the proposed algorithm $N_L = 2$ and $L_m = 2$. The length of FFT in the MMSE-FDE method is 1024. In this scenario, the receiver with the MMSE-FDE and the BCJR demodulator and the receiver using the proposed algorithm are considered. Similar to Fig. 2, we compare the BER performance of the two methods with and without the convolutional code respectively. As shown in Fig. 3, the performance of the two methods is similar without the convolutional code. When take the convolutional code into account, the performance of the proposed algorithm is better than the MMSE-FDE-BCJR receiver.

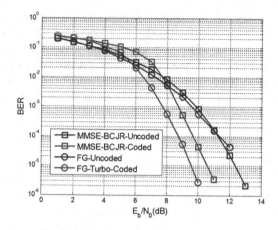

Fig. 4. 1RC modulation with h = 1/4 and M = 4 for Channel II.

In Fig. 4, we consider an ISI channel (channel II) characterized by $N_L = 5$ and

$$\boldsymbol{h} = [0.7\ 0.2\ 0.05\ 0.03\ 0.02], \tau = [0\ 5\ 10\ 15\ 20] \tag{56}$$

where the vector $\boldsymbol{h}$ denotes the gain of each path of the channel and the vector τ denotes the symbol number of the propagation delay for each path of the channel. A quaternary CPM signal with frequency pulse of duration $L = 1$ symbol interval and the modulation index $h = 1/4$ is considered. The parameters of the proposed algorithm are set as $N_L = 5$, $L_m = 2$. As shown in Fig. 4, the performance of the two methods is similar without the convolutional code. And the performance of the proposed algorithm is better than the MMSE-BCJR receiver with the convolutional code.

In terms of computational complexity, we point out that the decode parts in both receivers is the same. They differ in the equalization part and the demodulation part. For the equalization part, the computational complexity of the MMSE-FDE is $O(N \log_2 N)$ and that of the proposed algorithm is $O(NN_L)$ which is associated with the number of the path of the channel. For the demodulation part, the computational complexity of the BCJR algorithm is $O(pM^L N)$ while that of the proposed algorithm is $O(p(N+1))$.

5 Conclusion

Based on the Laurent decomposition and the Gaussian message passing, we presented a low-complexity turbo iterative receiver of CPM signals. According the simulations of different scenarios as shown in Sect. 4, the performance of the proposed algorithm is similar to the receiver with the MMSE-FDE and the BCJR demodulator in uncoded systems. When take the coding module into account, the proposed algorithm can achieve better performance. Moreover, the proposed algorithm has lower computational complexity than the receiver with the MMSE-FDE and the BCJR demodulator.

Acknowledgments. This work was supported by the National Natural Science Foundation of China under Grant Nos. 91438206.

References

1. Anderson, J.B., Aulin, T., Sundberg, C.E.: Digital Phase Modulation. Springer Science & Business Media, New York (2013). https://doi.org/10.1007/978-1-4899-2031-7
2. Rimoldi, B.E.: A decomposition approach to CPM. IEEE Trans. Inf. Theory **34**(2), 260–270 (1988)
3. Tang, W., Shwedyk, E.: A quasi-optimum receiver for continuous phase modulation. IEEE Trans. Commun. **48**(7), 1087–1090 (2000)
4. Laurent, P.: Exact and approximate construction of digital phase modulations by superposition of amplitude modulated pulses (AMP). IEEE Trans. Commun. **34**(2), 150–160 (2003)
5. Mengali, U., Morelli, M.: Decomposition of M-ary CPM signals into PAM waveforms. IEEE Trans. Inf. Theory **41**(5), 1265–1275 (1995)
6. Colavolpe, G., Raheli, R.: Reduced-complexity detection and phase synchronization of CPM signals. IEEE Trans. Commun. **45**(9), 1070–1079 (1997)
7. Tan, J., Stuber, G.L.: Frequency-domain equalization for continuous phase modulation. IEEE Trans. Wireless Commun. **4**(5), 2479–2490 (2005)
8. Pancaldi, F., Vitetta, G.M.: Equalization algorithms in the frequency domain for continuous phase modulations. IEEE Trans. Commun. **54**(4), 648–658 (2006)
9. Ozgul, B., Koca, M., Deliç, H.: Double turbo equalization of continuous phase modulation with frequency domain processing. IEEE Trans. Commun. **57**(2), 423–429 (2009)
10. Guo, Q., Huang, D.: GMP-based channel estimation for single-carrier transmissions over doubly selective channels. IEEE Sig. Process. Lett. **17**(1), 8–11 (2010)
11. Wu, S., Kuang, L., Ni, Z., Lu, J., Huang, D., Guo, Q.: Low-complexity iterative detection for large-scale multiuser MIMO-OFDM systems using approximate message passing. IEEE J. Sel. Top. Sig. Process. **8**(5), 902–915 (2014)
12. Wu, S., Kuang, L., Ni, Z., Huang, D., Guo, Q., Lu, J.: Message-passing receiver for joint channel estimation and decoding in 3D massive MIMO-OFDM systems. IEEE Trans. Wirel. Commun. **15**(12), 8122–8138 (2016)
13. Wu, S., Kuang, L., Ni, Z.: Expectation propagation based iterative group wise detection for large-scale multiuser MIMO-OFDM systems. In: 2014 IEEE Wireless Communications and Networking Conference (WCNC) (2014)
14. Barbieri, A., Colavolpe, G.: Simplified soft-output detection of CPM signals over coherent and phase noise channels. IEEE Trans. Wirel. Commun. **6**(7), 2486–2496 (2007)

Range-Difference Based Resource Allocation Scheme for D2D-Aided Heterogeneous Networks

Shaobo Lv[1], Xianxian Wang[1], Hongwen Cheng[2], and Zhongshan Zhang[1(✉)]

[1] Beijing Engineering and Technology Research Center for Convergence Networks and Ubiquitous Services, University of Science and Technology Beijing (USTB), Beijing, China
zhangzs@ustb.edu.cn
[2] China Unicom, Huangshan Branch, Huangshan Road 170, Tunxi District, Huangshan City, Anhui Province, China

Abstract. In this paper, the resource allocation issues in Device-to-Device (D2D) aided heterogeneous networks are investigated, with successive interference cancellation (SIC) capabilities enabled in base stations (BSs). The problem of maximizing the sum throughput of whole network by considering real-time transmissions is formulated. After that, the globally optimal power control is carried out relying on both the *enumeration* and *Kuhn-Munkres* methods. To both guarantee the successful transmission probability (STP) of cellular users (CUEs) and reduce the system's management overhead, a range-difference based resource allocation scheme is proposed. Numerical results show that the average throughput of CUEs can be substantially improved without sacrificing the performance of CUEs by invoking the proposed resource allocation scheme.

Keywords: Heterogeneous network · Device-to-Device (D2D)
Resource allocation · Successive Interference Cancellation (SIC)
Range-difference

1 Introduction

With the rapid development of mobile communication technologies, the telecom operators are struggling to meet the customers' exponentially increasing demand of mobile data traffic, thus requiring both spectral efficiency and throughput of the wireless networks to be substantially improved [1–3]. Furthermore, the existing wireless access networks (WANs) architecture is based on the centralized control of base stations (BSs), which have often been operating at overload state, it is highly required to offload the mobile traffics from the BS side to the mobile terminal side [4, 5].

Device-to-Device (D2D) communications mode, which enables the geographically close-by user equipments (UEs) to form D2D pairs by creating a direct wireless link between them (i.e. without relying on the intervention of BSs),

K. Long et al. (Eds.): 5GWN 2017, LNICST 211, pp. 506–516, 2018.
https://doi.org/10.1007/978-3-319-72823-0_47

has been regarded as a promising traffic-offloading technique [6,7]. Note that either half-duplex mode or full-duplex [8–10] mode can be implemented in D2D devices. Meanwhile, in light of the fact that the negative effect of large-scale power loss due to the relatively longer BS-to-UE distance in conventional cellular networks can be effectively relieved by implementing D2D mode, the power efficiency as well as spectral efficiency of the wireless networks can be substantially improved [11]. Thus, the underlaying cellular networks that support both the conventional cellular communications and the D2D mode can be implemented for both substantially improving the network throughput and effectively enhancing the load balance capability of the whole networks.

Despite of the promising benefits in terms of spectral/power efficiencies offered by D2D-aided heterogeneous networks, the potential performance gains may still be degraded due to the frequency reuse between these two tiers. Thus, a reasonable resource allocation strategy must be implemented for effectively mitigating the impact of D2D induced interference [12].

A variety of works associated with intelligent power control and resource allocation strategies have been carried out for facilitating the D2D-induced interference coordination and management [13–16]. For instance, in [13], a pricing-based mechanism is proposed for managing the interference imposed on the cellular users (CUEs) by D2D users (DUEs) through controlling the prices on the corresponding sub-channels. Combining with a non-cooperative Nash game among D2D pairs, the quality of service (QoS) of both CUEs and DUEs can be guaranteed in the pricing-based mechanism. Furthermore, in [16], a centralized power control strategy is proposed to guarantee a sufficiently high coverage probability of CUEs by limiting the D2D-induced interference (while scheduling as many D2D links as possible). In addition, advanced signal processing techniques can also be employed for performing interference cancellation in D2D-aided heterogeneous networks [17,18]. Relying on the successive interference cancellation (SIC) capabilities [19,20] of both BSs and DUEs, authors in [18] attempted to adjust both transmit power and data rate for managing the interference between cellular and D2D tiers, whereas the authors in [17] mainly analyzed the successful transmission probability (STP) of the multi-cell networks by using stochastic geometry method.

While most of the existing resource allocation algorithms are carried out by solving complicated optimization or game problems, both of which generally require accurate channel state information (CSI), the system's management overhead will thus be significantly increased. Besides the above-mentioned algorithms, guard zone based interference management schemes have also been widely investigated [21,22] for offering innovated resource allocation strategies. In this paper, we mainly focus our attention on maximizing the (real-time) sum throughput, with a range-difference based scheme proposed for the D2D-aided heterogeneous networks. The main contributions of this paper are reflected in the following aspects:

1. The resource allocation problem for D2D-aided underlaying cellular networks is formulated, with SIC capabilities considered in terminals.

2. The optimization model of maximizing the (real-time) sum throughput of the whole network is provided.
3. The globally optimal solution of the proposed algorithm is derived relying on the *enumeration* and *Kuhn-Munkres* methods.
4. A range-difference based resource allocation scheme is proposed for simultaneously improving the average STP of CUEs and reducing the system's management overhead.

The remainder of this paper is organized as follows. Section 2 describes the system model for D2D-aided heterogeneous networks, together with the formulation of the problem of sum throughput maximization. In Sect. 3, a range-difference based resources allocation scheme is proposed. After that, the numerical results are given out in Sect. 4. Finally, Sect. 5 concludes this paper.

2   System Model and Problem Formulation

In this section, we first describe the system model for the proposed D2D aided heterogeneous networks, followed by formulating the resource allocation problem of the proposed system, with SIC capabilities enabled in the devices. After that, we derive the globally optimal solution of the above-mentioned optimization problem relying on the *enumeration* and *Kuhn-Munkres* methods.

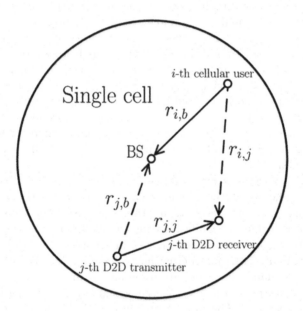

Fig. 1. D2D aided heterogeneous network, in which the uplink licensed spectrum is assumed to be reused by DUEs.

2.1 System Model for D2D-Aided Heterogeneous Networks

In this paper, we consider the D2D-aided underlaying cellular networks, in which the uplink licensed spectrum is allowed to be reused by D2D pairs, as illustrated in Fig. 1. To ease our analysis, we consider the scenario in which a total of N CUEs share spectrum resources with N D2D pairs simultaneously. Meanwhile, we assume that the i-th CUE operates at transmit power P_i^c, where $i \in \{1, 2, \cdots, N\}$. Without loss of generality, the transmit power of j-th DT is assumed to be $P_j^d = \beta_{i,j} P_i^c$, where the coefficient $\beta_{i,j}$ is no less than 0 for any $i, j \in \{1, 2, \cdots, N\}$. Furthermore, the radius of the cell is denoted by R. Distances associated with the i-th CUE-to-BS link and the j-th DT-to-BS link are represented by $r_{i,b}$ and $r_{j,b}$, respectively. Meanwhile, the distance between i-th CUE and j-th D2D receiver (DR) is denoted by $r_{i,j}$. Similarly, r_{jj} denotes the distance between the peers of the j-th D2D pair. In addition, both CUEs and DTs are assumed to be distributed randomly and uniformly within the cellular coverage, with DRs uniformly located within the radius-50 m circle area that is centered by the corresponding DTs.

At the BS side, the received signal power from CUE and DT can be denoted by $P_{i,b}^c = h_{i,b} r_{i,b}^{-\alpha} P_i^c$ and $P_{j,b}^d = h_{j,b} r_{j,b}^{-\alpha} P_i^d$, respectively, under assumption of Rayleigh fading channels with small scale fading coefficients $h_{i,b}, h_{j,b} \sim \exp(1)$, where $h_{i,b}$ and $h_{j,b}$ denote the corresponding channel attenuations, and $\alpha > 2$ denotes the path-loss exponent. According to the aforementioned uniform-distribution properties of both CUEs and DTs, the probability density function (pdf) of $r_{i,b}$ and $r_{j,b}$ can be represented by $f(r_{i,b}) = 2r_{i,b}/R^2$ and $f(r_{j,b}) = 2r_{j,b}/R^2$, respectively. Furthermore, through sample variable substitutions, we can readily derive both $P_{i,b}^c \sim \exp(r_{i,b}^\alpha/P_i^c)$ and $P_{j,b}^d \sim \exp(r_{j,b}^\alpha/\beta_{i,j}/P_i^c)$.

2.2 Problem Formulation

In this paper, we aim to maximize the network's sum throughput relying an appropriately designed resource allocation algorithm as

$$\textbf{P1: } \max \sum_{i \in \mathcal{C}, j \in \mathcal{D}} \alpha_{i,j} R_{i,j} \tag{1}$$

$$\text{s.t.} \quad \sum_{i \in \mathcal{C}} \alpha_{i,j} = 1, \tag{1a}$$

$$\sum_{j \in \mathcal{D}} \alpha_{i,j} = 1, \tag{1b}$$

$$\alpha_{i,j} = \{0, 1\}, \quad \forall i \in \mathcal{C}, j \in \mathcal{D}, \tag{1c}$$

where $\mathcal{C}$ and $\mathcal{D}$ denote the index sets of CUEs and D2D paris, respectively, $R_{i,j}$ is the aggregative rates of i-th CUE (i.e. R_i^c) and j-th D2D pairs (i.e. R_j^d), i.e. $R_{i,j} = R_i^c + R_j^d$, $\alpha_{i,j}$ denotes the resource sharing relationship between i-th CUE and j-th D2D pair, and $\alpha_{i,j} = 1$ when the i-th CUE and j-th D2D pair share the same spectrum resource (otherwise $\alpha_{i,j} = 0$). On one hand, constraints in (1a) and (1b) guarantee the one-to-one correspondence between CUEs and D2D pairs, requiring that any single D2D pair must reuse the spectrum of one and only one CUE. On the other hand, any individual CUE must coexist with one and only one D2D pair. We can readily show that **P1** is identical to a maximum weighted bipartite matching problem that can be faultlessly solved out via *Kuhn-Munkres* method [23], where CUE and D2D pair are the bipartite vertexes, $R_{i,j}$ stands for the weight.

In the following, we will focus on mitigating the D2D-induced interference, thus enhancing the sum throughput of the network. Without loss of generality, we assume that the BSs are capable of implementing SIC. From information theory, the desired signal from CUE in the SIC-enabled BS receiver side will not be deteriorated by the DT-induced interference, and consequently we have $R_i^c = \log_2\left(1 + \frac{P_i^c g_{i,b}}{\Gamma N_0}\right)$ if $R_j^d \le \log_2\left(1 + \frac{P_j^d g_{j,b}}{\Gamma\left(P_i^c g_{i,b} + N_0\right)}\right)$ can be satisfied[1]. Otherwise, the interference caused by DT cannot be totally eliminated, thus leading to $R_i^c = \log_2\left(1 + \frac{P_i^c g_{i,b}}{\Gamma\left(P_j^d g_{j,b} + N_0\right)}\right)$, where Γ denotes the signal-to-interference-plus-noise ratio (SINR) gap [24] that is set to be $\Gamma = 8.8$ dB in this paper. The problem of $R_{i,j}$-maximization can thus be rewritten as

$$\textbf{P2: } \max R_i^c + R_j^d \tag{2}$$

$$\text{s.t. } R_i^c = A\log_2\left(1 + \frac{P_i^c g_{i,b}}{\Gamma\left(P_j^d g_{j,b} + N_0\right)}\right) \tag{2a}$$
$$+ (1-A)\log_2\left(1 + \frac{P_i^c g_{i,b}}{\Gamma N_0}\right),$$

$$R_j^d = \log_2\left(1 + \frac{P_j^d g_{j,j}}{\Gamma\left(P_i^c g_{i,j} + N_0\right)}\right), \tag{2b}$$

$$A = \mathbb{1}\left\{R_j^d > \log_2\left(1 + \frac{P_j^d g_{j,b}}{\Gamma\left(P_i^c g_{i,b} + N_0\right)}\right)\right\}, \tag{2c}$$

$$P_c^{th} \le P_i^c \le P_c^{max}, \tag{2d}$$

---

[1] In other words, the transmission rate of DT is not beyond its channel capacity, therefore the interference caused by DT can be cancelled completely in theory.

$$P_d^{th} \leq P_j^d \leq P_d^{max}, \tag{2e}$$

where (P_c^{th}, P_c^{max}) and (P_d^{th}, P_d^{max}) are the minimum and maximum values of transmit power of CUE and DT, respectively. Denoting $f\left(P_i^c, P_j^d\right) = R_{i,j} = R_i^c + R_j^d$, it has been shown in [25], $f(\lambda P_i^c, \lambda P_j^d) > f(P_i^c, P_j^d)$ will always hold that in the interior of the feasible space when $\lambda > 1$. Thus, $f(P_i^c, P_j^d)$ would reach its maximum if either of the following conditions, i.e. $P_i^c = P_c^{max}$ and $P_j^d = P_d^{max}$, can be satisfied. Furthermore, it has also been proved in [25] that $f\left(P_i^c, P_j^d\right)$ would be a convex function of P_i^c (or P_j^d) if $P_j^d = P_d^{max}$ (or $P_i^c = P_c^{max}$) is satisfied. Evidently, the maximum of $f\left(P_i^c, P_j^d\right)$ must be reachable at one of the extreme points of the feasible space.

By substituting (2b) into (2c), we can readily derive that $A = 0$ if

$$\frac{g_{j,j}}{P_i^c g_{i,j} + N_0} \leq \frac{g_{j,b}}{P_i^c g_{i,b} + N_0} \tag{3}$$

is satisfied. Otherwise, we have $A = 1$ when

$$\frac{g_{j,j}}{P_i^c g_{i,j} + N_0} > \frac{g_{j,b}}{P_i^c g_{i,b} + N_0}. \tag{4}$$

If $A = 0$ is met, we can readily conclude that the extreme points of P_i^c (denoted by $P_{i,0}^c$) are just happened at the apexes of the intersection of (2d) and (3). Similarly, when $A = 1$ is met, we can obtain the extreme points $P_{i,1}^c$, which correspond to the apexes of the intersection of (2d) and (4). In addition, we will get the optimal solution of problem **P2** relying on the *enumeration* method, with the optimal power pair (P_i^{c*}, P_j^{d*}) represented by

$$(P_i^{c*}, P_j^{d*}) = \underset{(P_i^c, P_j^d) \in U_0 \cup U_1 \cup U}{\arg\max} R_{i,j}, \tag{5}$$

where $U_0 = (P_i^c \in P_{i,0}^c, P_d^{max})$, $U_1 = (P_i^c \in P_{i,1}^c, P_d^{max})$, and $U = (P_c^{max}, P_d^{th}) \cup (P_c^{max}, P_d^{max})$.

Following the above-mentioned derivations, we can always derive the maximum $R_{i,j}$ for any $i \in \mathcal{C}$ and $j \in \mathcal{D}$ settings, which will be saved as the weight of the edges between bipartite vertexes $\mathcal{C}$ and $\mathcal{D}$. Eventually, the maximum sum throughput can be obtained.

3   Range-Difference Based Resource Allocation

In this section, a heuristic range-difference based resource allocation strategy is proposed for reducing the system complexity. At the SIC-enabled BS side, the desired signal from CUE will be decoded correctly, if $P_{i,b}^c > P_{j,b}^d$ is satisfied. Otherwise, if $P_{j,b}^d > P_{i,b}^c$ is met, the signal of interfering DT will be firstly decoded and eliminated from the received superposition signal, followed by decoding the

CUE's message from the interference-free signal. For a given decoding threshold η, the CUE's STP as a function of $(\eta, r_{i,b}, r_{j,b})$ can be expressed as

$$P_{\text{STP}}(\eta, r_{i,b}, r_{j,b}) = \text{Pr}\left[\frac{P_{i,b}^c}{N_0} \geq \eta, \frac{P_{j,b}^d}{P_{i,b}^c + N_0} \geq \eta, P_{j,b}^d > P_{i,b}^c\right]$$
$$+ \text{Pr}\left[\frac{P_{i,b}^c}{P_{j,b}^d + N_0} \geq \eta, P_{i,b}^c \geq P_{j,b}^d\right]. \tag{6}$$

It has been shown in [21] that $P_{\text{SIC}}(\eta, r_{i,b}, r_{j,b}) = \text{Pr}\left(P_{j,b}^d > P_{i,b}^c\right) + \text{Pr}\left(P_{j,b}^d \leq P_{i,b}^c\right) = 1$ will be met in interference-limited networks (i.e. $N_0 \rightarrow 0$), if $\eta < 1$ is satisfied. Otherwise, when $\eta \geq 1$, $P_{\text{SIC}}(\eta, r_{i,b}, r_{j,b})$ is shown to be a convex function of $r_{j,b}$, with its minimum value attainable at $r_{j,b} = r_{i,b}\beta_{i,j}^{1/\alpha}$.

As inspired by the aforementioned results, we should try to prevent CUE and D2D pair with special properties (i.e. $r_{j,b} \approx r_{i,b}\beta_{i,j}^{1/\alpha}$) from sharing the same spectrum, when we perform resource allocation. Heuristically speaking, we aim to maximize the distance between CUEs and DTs, thus proposing the range-difference based resource allocation optimization model as

$$\textbf{P3}: \max \sum_{i \in \mathcal{C}, j \in \mathcal{D}} \alpha_{i,j} d_{i,j} \tag{7}$$

$$\text{s.t.} (2a) - (2c),$$

$$P_i^c = P_c^{max}, \tag{7a}$$

$$P_j^d = \beta P_i^c = P_d^{max}, \tag{7b}$$

where $d_{i,j} = |r_{j,b} - r_{i,b}\beta^{1/\alpha}|$. Similarly, **P3** can also be viewed as a maximum weighted bipartite matching problem, which can be successfully solved by using *Kuhn-Munkres* algorithm. Compared with the power control strategy in **P1**, scheme in **P3** does not require accurate channel state information (CSI) and has ah lower computational complexity.

4   Numerical Results

In this section, we will numerically validate the proposed analysis as well as evaluate the performance of the proposed scheme. We consider the scenario comprising 100 geographically randomly and uniformly distributed CUEs that coexist with 100 D2D pairs inside a single-cell coverage having a radius of 500 m. The distributions of both DTs and DRs are shown in Sect. 2. Furthermore, the maximum distance between a D2D pair is assumed to be 100 m. The path loss exponent α is set to be 4, with rayleigh fading channels assumed in each link. Meanwhile, the SINR gap is set to 8.8 dB. In addition, the maximum transmit powers of CUEs and DTs are assumed to be $P_c^{max} = 30$ dBm and $P_d^{max} = 21$ dBm, respectively, corresponding to twice the minimum transmit powers, i.e. $P_c^{th} = 1/2P_c^{max}$ and $P_d^{th} = 1/2P_d^{max}$. Finally, the noise power density is assumed to be $-174\,\mathrm{dBm/Hz}$.

In Fig. 2, the CUE's STP as a function of $r_{j,b}$ is evaluated under variant $r_{i,b}$ and decoding thresholds η. For a given set of parameters, the CUE's STP will first decrease and then increase as $r_{j,b}$ increases, implying that there always exists an attainable minimum value.

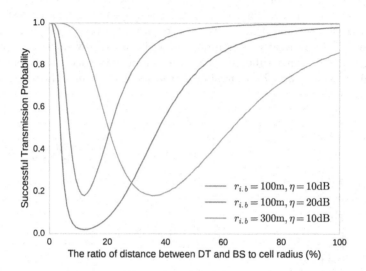

Fig. 2. Successful transmission probability of CUE as a function of the distance between DT and BS $r_{j,b}$ under variant CUE-to-BS distances $r_{i,b}$ and decoding thresholds η.

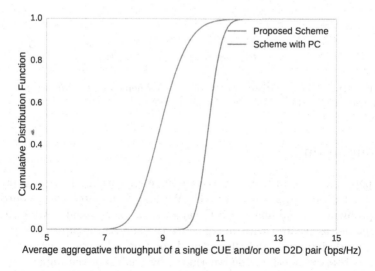

Fig. 3. Performance comparisons of the proposed scheme and scheme with power control in terms of CDF of the average aggregative throughput of a single CUE and/or D2D pair.

In Fig. 3, the cumulative distribution function (CDF) of the average aggregative throughput of one CUE/D2D pair is evaluated. As a performance benchmark, numerical results associated with scheme using power control are also provided. It is obvious that the maximum possible throughput of the two schemes are reasonably identical. Furthermore, it is shown that the sum throughput of the proposed scheme is slightly lower than that using power control aided scheme.

In Fig. 4, the CDF of the average throughput of CUE is evaluated. For comparing and analyzing the impact of the proposed scheme, numerical results associated with the scheme using power control are also presented. It is observed that the CUE's average throughput will be improved by using the proposed scheme, since the range-difference based technique will successfully prevent the geographically specific UEs from sharing the same spectrum, thus guaranteeing the QoS of CUEs.

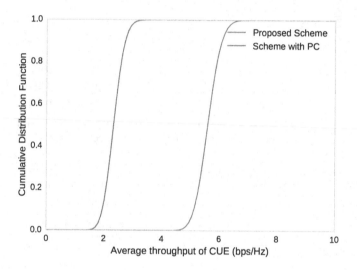

Fig. 4. Performance comparisons of the proposed scheme and scheme with power control in terms of CDF of the average throughput of CUE.

5   Conclusion

In this paper, a range-difference based resource allocation scheme was proposed for D2D-aided heterogeneous networks. We first formulated the resource allocation problem by enabling the SIC capabilities in terminals. After that, the system model associated with maximizing the sum throughput was provided, followed by deriving the globally optimal solution relying on the *enumeration* and *Kuhn-Munkres* methods. Furthermore, by analyzing the impacting factors of CUEs' STP, a range-difference based resource allocation scheme was proposed for both guaranteeing the QoS of CUEs and reducing the system's management overhead. Numerical results validated the proposed analysis, showing that the average throughput of CUEs can be substantially improved by invoking the proposed range-difference based resource allocation scheme.

Acknowledgement. This work was supported by the key project of the National Natural Science Foundation of China (No. 61431001), the open research fund of National Mobile Communications Research Laboratory Southeast University (No. 2017D02), Key Laboratory of Cognitive Radio and Information Processing, Ministry of Education (Guilin University of Electronic Technology), and the Foundation of Beijing Engineering and Technology Center for Convergence Networks and Ubiquitous Services. (Corresponding author: Zhongshan Zhang).

References

1. Chen, S., Zhao, J.: The requirements, challenges, and technologies for 5G of terrestrial mobile telecommunication. IEEE Commun. Mag. **52**(5), 36–43 (2014)
2. Zhang, Z., Long, K., Wang, J., Dressler, F.: On swarm intelligence inspired self-organized networking: its bionic mechanisms, designing principles and optimization approaches. IEEE Commun. Surv. Tuts. **16**(1), 513–537 (2014). First Quarter
3. Zhang, Z., Long, K., Wang, J.: Self-organization paradigms and optimization approaches for cognitive radio technologies: a survey. IEEE Wirel. Commun. Mag. **20**(2), 36–42 (2013)
4. Zhang, H., Jiang, C., Beaulieu, N.C., Chu, X., Wen, X., Tao, M.: Resource allocation in spectrum-sharing OFDMA femtocells with heterogeneous services. IEEE Trans. Commun. **62**(7), 2366–2377 (2014)
5. Zhang, H., Jiang, C., Mao, X., Chen, H.-H.: Interference-limited resource optimization in cognitive femtocells with fairness and imperfect spectrum sensing. IEEE Trans. Veh. Technol **65**(3), 1761–1771 (2016)
6. Doppler, K., Rinne, M., Wijting, C., Ribeiro, C.B., Hugl, K.: Device-to-device communication as an underlay to LTE-advanced networks. IEEE Commun. Mag. **47**(12), 42–49 (2009)
7. Feng, D., Lu, L., Yuan-Wu, Y., Li, G., Li, S., Feng, G.: Device-to-device communications in cellular networks. IEEE Commun. Mag. **52**(4), 49–55 (2014)
8. Zhang, Z., Chai, X., Long, K., Vasilakos, A.V., Hanzo, L.: Full duplex techniques for 5G networks: self-interference cancellation, protocol design, and relay selection. IEEE Commun. Mag. **53**(5), 128–137 (2015)
9. Zhang, Z., Long, K., Vasilakos, A.V., Hanzo, L.: Full-duplex wireless communications: challenges, solutions and future research directions. Proc. IEEE **104**(7), 1369–1409 (2016)
10. Chai, X., Liu, T., Xing, C., Xiao, H., Zhang, Z.: Throughput improvement in cellular networks via full-duplex based device-to-device communications. IEEE Access **4**, 7645–7657 (2016)
11. Asadi, A., Wang, Q., Mancuso, V.: A survey on device-to-device communication in cellular networks. IEEE Commun. Surv. Tuts. **16**(4), 1801–1819 (2014)
12. Phunchongharn, P., Hossain, E., Kim, D.I.: Resource allocation for device-to-device communications underlaying LTE-advanced networks. IEEE Wirel. Commun. **20**(4), 91–100 (2013)
13. Yin, R., Yu, G., Zhang, H., Zhang, Z., Li, G.Y.: Pricing-based interference coordination for D2D communications in cellular networks. IEEE Trans. Wirel. Commun. **14**(3), 1519–1532 (2015)

14. Yin, R., Zhong, C., Yu, G., Zhang, Z., Wong, K.K., Chen, X.: Joint spectrum and power allocation for D2D communications underlaying cellular networks. IEEE Trans. Veh. Technol. **65**(4), 2182–2195 (2016)
15. Sun, J., Liu, T., Wang, X., Xing, C., Xiao, H., Vasilakos, A.V., Zhang, Z.: Optimal mode selection with uplink data rate maximization for D2D-aided underlaying cellular networks. IEEE Access **4**, 8844–8856 (2016)
16. Lee, N., Lin, X., Andrews, J.G., Heath, R.: Power control for D2D underlaid cellular networks: modeling, algorithms, and analysis. IEEE J. Sel. Areas Commun. **33**(1), 1–13 (2015)
17. Ma, C., Wu, W., Cui, Y., Wang, X.: On the performance of successive interference cancellation in D2D-enabled cellular networks. In: 2015 IEEE Conference on Computer Communications (INFOCOM), pp. 37–45, April 2015
18. Song, H., Ryu, J.Y., Choi, W., Schober, R.: Joint power and rate control for device-to-device communications in cellular systems. IEEE Trans. Wirel. Commun. **14**(10), 5750–5762 (2015)
19. Saito, Y., Kishiyama, Y., Benjebbour, A., Nakamura, T., Li, A., Higuchi, K.: Nonorthogonal multiple access (NOMA) for cellular future radio access. In: Proceedings of IEEE Vehicular Technology Conference (VTC Spring), pp. 1–5, June 2013
20. Sen, S., Santhapuri, N., Choudhury, R.R., Nelakuditi, S.: Successive interference cancellation: carving out MAC layer opportunities. IEEE Trans. Mob. Comput. **12**(2), 346–357 (2013)
21. Lv, S., Xing, C., Zhang, Z., Long, K.: Guard zone based interference management for D2D-aided underlaying cellular networks. IEEE Trans. Veh. Technol. **66**(6), 5466–5471 (2016)
22. Chen, Z., Kountouris, M.: Guard zone based D2D underlaid cellular networks with two-tier dependence. In: IEEE International Conference on Communication Workshop (ICCW), pp. 222–227 (2015)
23. Kuhn, H.W.: The Hungarian method for the assignment problem. Naval Res. Logistics Q. **2**(1–2), 83–97 (1955)
24. Garcia-Armada, A.: SNR gap approximation for M-PSK-based bit loading. IEEE Trans. Wirel. Commun. **5**(1), 57–60 (2006)
25. Gjendemsjo, A., Gesbert, D., Oien, G.E., Kiani, S.G.: Optimal power allocation and scheduling for two-cell capacity maximization. In: Proceedings of 2006 IEEE International Symposium on Modeling and Optimization in Mobile, Ad Hoc and Wireless Networks, pp. 1–6 (2006)

LTE-WLAN Integrated Virtualization Network Architecture

Fenglin Dai[✉], Qixun Zhang, Yuhang Sun, and Mengyuan Liu

Beijing University of Posts and Telecommunications, Beijing 100876,
People's Republic of China
{dfl2011212800,zhangqixun,SunYuhang613,lmy19931117}@bupt.edu.cn

Abstract. Heterogeneous network is an inevitable trend for the fifth generation wireless communications (5G). The existing scheme for the interworking of the Long Term Evolution (LTE) system and Wireless Local Area Network (WLAN) system is achieved by Packet Data Network Gateway (PGW) at the core network. However, it is not efficient enough since 5G may bring in signaling storm for some increasing popular scenarios, such us instant messaging, device-to-device communications. In this paper, we propose a new LTE-WLAN integrated architecture. This architecture is designed based on Software Defined Mobile Network (SDMN) and network virtualization. A new entity called Macrocell Integrated Controller (Ma-IC) is introduced in the new architecture. It can shield the differences of the two systems for core network to simplify the management procedure and minimize the change of the core network to be adaptive to this proposed architecture. In addition, some control functions originally in core network are immigrated into Ma-IC, which can help save some backhaul signaling overhead. Another main function of Ma-IC is to coordinate the LTE system and WLAN system to provide user equipment (UE) more available resources. Besides, a new mechanism of handover for UE is designed based on this proposed architecture, and the simulation shows that handover signaling can be reduced by 29.8% compared with existing mechanism defined in 3GPP standards.

Keywords: LTE · WLAN · Architecture · Handover

1 Introduction

Recently, enormous multi-media equipment rushes into the market. The demand of high-speed wireless communications is increased [1]. Many advanced technologies, such as Orthogonal Frequency Division Multiplexing (OFDM) and Multiple-Input Multiple-Output (MIMO), are adopted to improve the user experience. However, in the traditional network architecture, interaction among base station (BS) is unable to support a unified resource scheduling and high performance mobility management. To some extent, the architecture is a bottleneck to the development of the wireless network. A more intelligent architecture is the key of the research in 5G. Moreover, the diversity of the user services and

© ICST Institute for Computer Sciences, Social Informatics and Telecommunications Engineering 2018
K. Long et al. (Eds.): 5GWN 2017, LNICST 211, pp. 517–528, 2018.
https://doi.org/10.1007/978-3-319-72823-0_48

the explode of the traffic pose a huge challenge to the LTE network since the spectrum resource has already been extremely scarce [2,3]. Meanwhile, WLAN can use the unlicensed frequency band to provide high-speed data transmission service, so it forms a great advantage in resource utilization. Besides, as a low-cost, easy-deployment wireless access network, WLAN has been wildly used. So converge LTE and WLAN is an effective way to alleviate the shortage of resource.

Except from different modes, 5G will also converge base stations that with different coverages [4], different powers and different service bearing capabilities to constitute a complex heterogeneous network. Heterogeneous network can increase the density of the access networks in an area [5], so how to manage and coordinate these networks to make full advantage of every one of them is another problem. The proposal of the SDMN [6] provides a new thought to this problem. SDMN is an extension of SDN, which is used to be applied in computer field. One of the core concepts of SDN is to decouple the control plane and the data plane [7,8]. In SDMN, a centralized control plane can dispatch different access networks for users, thus realize the network virtualization. And some network equipment only takes charge of data plane, and forward data according to the signaling from centralized control plane. Ijaz Ahmad et al. [2] do a survey about SDMN, but they give no technical details. In this paper, we conduct a thorough study about SDMN and apply it to a new wireless network architecture. LTE network and WLAN network are integrated in this architecture, to realize the effective utilization of different frequency bands and take full advantages of multi modes access network. Except from different modes, the coverages of access points are also different. With control-service split technology [10], the control signaling and service data are decoupled, and are respectively forwarded by access points in macrocells and microcells. The employment of SDMN facilitates the management of heterogeneous networks and also reduces the service response time. Meanwhile, frequent handover caused by dense deployment is reduced, which help avoid extra signaling overhead and negative effect on user experience.

The rest of the paper is organized as follows. Section 1 introduces the background information and some related work is described in Sect. 2. Then, the proposed architecture is presented in Sect. 3. After that, Sect. 4 is about the new mechanism of handover and Sect. 5 is the simulation results. Finally, a conclusion is given in Sect. 6.

2   Related Work

The existing system in Fig. 1 integrates LTE and WLAN at the PGW in core network [11], and the high throughput may make it a bottleneck to the performance of the whole network. Besides, instant messaging is wildly used, and in the existing network, every short message has to go through the backhaul to core network, which may cause a severe signaling overhead.

In [12], the author proposes three different LTE-WLAN integration architectures. In the first one, the Mobility Management Entity (MME) serves as the

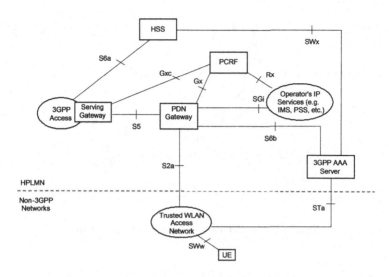

Fig. 1. Existing integrated network [11]

control plane integration point while the Serving Gateway (S-GW) serves as the user plane integration point. The second one integrates LTE and WLAN system. The integration point is moved out of the EPC to a proposed ISW Gateway. In the third architecture, an enhanced X2 interface is proposed directly between the WLAN AP and the HeNB. However, all these networks give no consideration to the coordination of all these densely-deployed access networks. And the modification of the existing network is significant, which will cause a great expense to adopt this architecture.

To address these problems, an optimized architecture is proposed in this paper and the details are described in the following sections.

3 Controller-Based Converged Architecture

The Controller-Based Converged Architecture (CBCA) is deployed as Fig. 2. Ma-IC, a new added entity, mainly takes charge of control signaling, and the data forwarding is accomplished by Microcell Connection Point (MiCP): Microcell Wi-Fi Access Point (Mi-WAP) and Microcell LTE Base Station (Mi-LBS). To realize the above functions, the protocol stack of CBCA network is designed as Fig. 3, which demonstrates an obvious control-service split design. UE sends control signaling to Ma-IC, after processing, it is sent to MME in core network. As for service data, multi-mode UE send them through two individual link: Mi-LBS and Mi-WAP, and are both received by SGW.

3.1 Ma-IC

Ma-IC is the core entity of CBCA. It can implement basic function of a base station, but with a larger coverage. And there are some enhancements in the

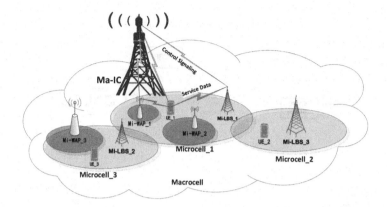

Fig. 2. Controller-based converged architecture

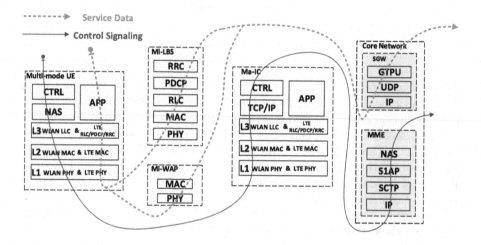

Fig. 3. Protocol stack of CBCA

control plane. The current core network gateway devices, such as MME and S-GW, forward both service data and control signaling, which are coupled together. However, Ma-IC adopts the idea of SDN, that is, decoupling control plane from data plane. The relevant control functions in core network gateways and base stations are extracted into Ma-IC to achieve a centralized control.

Since Ma-IC has the ability to communicate with both cellular network and WLAN network, so the entire WLAN protocol is added to the original LTE protocol. The PHY layer, MAC layer and LLC layer in WLAN protocol, corresponding to the PHY layer, MAC layer, RLC layer, PDCP layer and RRC layer in LTE protocol are stay unchanged. Above these layers and below the TCP/IP layer of LTE protocol, a new layer called CTRL layer is added. And there are mainly three function modules in this layer:

1. Data Processing Module

   When communicate with MiCP, this module demultiplexes signaling from upper layer, and encapsulates them respectively into LTE and WLAN format, then send them down to the corresponding lower layers, and then to the corresponding MiCP. And when Ma-IC responds to Mi-WAPs' request, it can transform packets from WLAN LLC into LTE format and integrate them with those from LTE lower protocol, then send the complete packets to upper layer to be processed. By this way, the differences of access networks can be shielded from the core network, and WLAN network can be easily integrated into the LTE system. In this design, UE is a dual-link device, and it can simultaneously connect with Mi-LBS and Mi-WAP to receive data. So the protocol stack of UE also integrates both LTE and WLAN protocol. But when interact with Mi-IC, to streamline the process, only LTE protocol is used.

2. Information Management Module

   By broadcast channel, every Ma-IC establishes a RAN Table. This table tracks the location information, configuration information, and connection status of Mi-WAPs, Mi-LBSs as well as UEs that are connected to that Ma-IC. This can help Ma-IC have an overall view about the entire network. And when there are some changes in those connected Mi-WAPs, Mi-LBSs or UEs, Ma-IC will update these RAN Table. In addition, information about Ma-IC itself is also recorded in the table to decide whether there is enough resource for another connection. Furthermore, Home Subscriber Server (HSS) in core network can also obtain information from RAN Table.

3. Connection Control Module

   Ma-IC executes access procedure when there are some new Mi-WAPs, Mi-LBSs or UEs. Two different sets of access process are executed correspondingly for LTE system and WLAN system, which are the same as the existing standard process for users. So users can arrange their own microcell access networks based on requirement. And the Ma-IC can dynamically adjust the resource allocation according to user demand and network traffic statistical characteristic. Besides, the handover process of the access equipment is also executed by this module. And the details will be described in Sect. 4.

3.2 Mi-CP

The features of Mi-WAP and Mi-LBS are dense deployment and high-speed transmission. Work principle is still in accordance with the 3GPP standards. However, since UE can simultaneously connect to a Mi-WAP and a Mi-LBS to receive packets, so every packets will be labeled in order to be rearranged by UE. And when a packet needs to be retransmitted, the only information that needs to be feedback is the label. It can help reduce the signaling overhead.

With the change of the architecture, the interaction among network entities is also changed. Take a basic data request scenario for example to illustrate how Mi-CP works. As shown in Fig. 4:

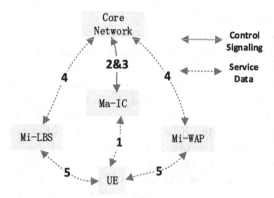

Fig. 4. Interaction among entities in CBCA

Step 1 UE sends data request to Ma-IC.

Step 2 Ma-IC obtains UE connection status from the RAN Table and calculates a Distribution Ratio (DR). RAN Table keeps records about the configuration information, available resources, network status of the Mi-CPs under the coverage of that Ma-IC. It also keeps real-time updates of UEs connection status of Mi-CPs.

Step 3 Ma-IC send DR and data request together to core network, which informs core network to split downlink data transmission to the corresponding access network according to DR.

Step 4 Core network encapsulates data and send them to Mi-LBS and Mi-WAP respectively.

Step 5 Then Mi-CPs forward data to UE.

4   Handover Scenario

There are two scenarios: Microcell Handover (MiHO) and Macrocell Handover (MaHO). As in Fig. 5, MiHO occurs when UE handovers between two microcells while the Ma-IC stay connected; MaHO occurs when UE handovers between two macrocells, both Ma-IC and MiCP need to be reselected.

The detailed procedure of MiHO is:

Step 1 Ma-IC checks for real time update of RAN Table, and when strength of signal UE receives from Source MiCP is smaller than a threshold, Ma-IC trigger the Mi-HO and send Handover Preparation signaling to UE, including relevant information of optimal Target MiCP selected from RAN Table.

Step 2 UE sends Handover ACK back to Ma-IC.

Step 3 Ma-IC then sends the same information of Target MiCP to Core Network., in order to inform core network to send the data packet to both source MiCP and Target MiCP.

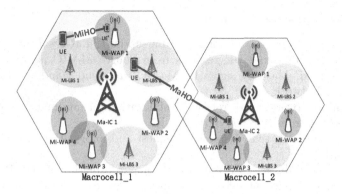

Fig. 5. MiHO and MaHO

Step 4 Ma-IC sends Handover Request to Target MiCP to prepare it for UE's access.

Step 5 UE sends synchronization information to Target MiCP, receive acknowledgement information and execute access procedure. After successful access, UE begins to receive packets from Target MiCP that prepared in step (3).

Step 6 Target MiCP send successful handover ACK back to Ma-IC.

Step 7 Ma-IC send Resource Release to Source MiCP and Core Network, so UE disconnects with Source MiCP and Core Network stops to send data packets to Source MiCP (Fig. 6).

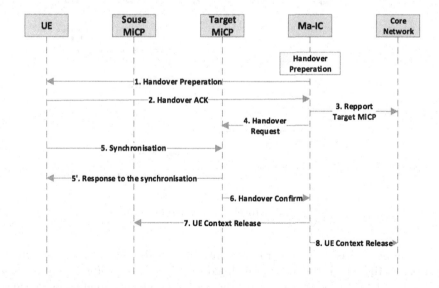

Fig. 6. Microcell handover procedure

The Detail procedure of MaHO is:

Step 1 Source Ma-IC checks for real time update of RAN Table, and when strength of signal UE receives from Source MA-IC is smaller than a threshold, Ma-IC trigger the Ma-HO and send Handover Decision to Core Network.

Step 2 Core Network send relevant information of optimal Target Ma-IC selected from HSS to Source Ma-IC.

Step 3 Source Ma-IC send Handover Request and information of UE to Target Ma-IC.

Step 4 Target Ma-IC select Target MiCP using information of local RAN Table, then send relevant information and handover acknowledgement back to Source Ma-IC.

Step 5 Source Ma-IC then sends the information of Target MiCP and Target Ma-IC to Core Network and UE, in order to inform core network to send the data packet to both source MiCP and Target MiCP.

Step 6 UE sends synchronization information to Target MiCP, receive acknowledgement information and execute access procedure. After successful access, UE begins to receive packets from Target MiCP that prepared in Step 5.

Step 7 Target Ma-IC send successful handover ACK back to Source Ma-IC.

Step 8 Source Ma-IC send Resource Release to Source MiCP and Core Network, so UE disconnects with Source MiCP and Core Network stops to send data packets to Source MiCP (Fig. 7).

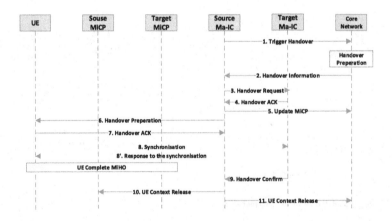

Fig. 7. Macrocell handover procedure

It can be noticed that the procedure of MiHO is simplified to a great extent, and both MiHO and MaHO are soft handover. Under the wide area of an Ma-IC, only MiHO will be triggered. So, the overall handover signaling overhead is reduced.

5   Simulation Results and Analysis

In order to testify the performance of the CBCA, a simulation is performed using OPNET. OPNET is a fully functional network simulation platform, and it has the complete network entity modules with standard configuration. Based on these modules, we reprogram to realize the Ma-IC and the corresponding UE.

5.1   Simulation Setup

The simulation parameter is set as Table 1. Contrast network is the network that used in the present LTE system, in which the UE can only access one network and handover procedure is hard handover.

Table 1. Simulation parameter

Parameter	CBCA network			Contrast network	
	Ma-IC	Mi-LBS	Mi-WAP	Mi-LBS	Mi-WAP
Quantity	1	3	1	3	1
Quantity of UE	12	3	3	3	3
Effective UE	3 in Mi-LBS2				
Transmission power	46 dbm	30 dbm	17 dbm	30 dbm	17 dbm
Radius of coverage	100 m	50 m	10 m	50 m	10 m
Cell selection metric	RSRQ	RAN table	RAN table	RSRQ	RSRQ
Service	Video Conference				

The CBCA is deployed as in Fig. 8, and the contrast architecture is deployed as in Fig. 9.

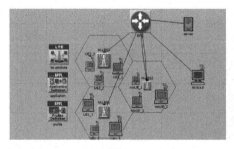
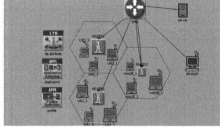

Fig. 8.   Controller-based   converged architecture deployment

Fig. 9. Contrast network deployment

The mixUE in CBCA deployment is a new developed entity, which can access to LTE and WLAN simultaneously. Its protocol is designed in accordance with

Fig. 3, and the process of UE is shown in Fig. 10. The lower layer protocol of WLAN is added into the original LTE protocol. So mixUE can receive data from both LTE port and WLAN port, then integrate them at CTRL layer and forward to upper layer.

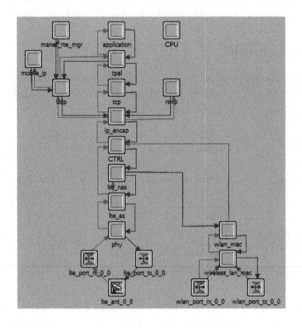

Fig. 10. Process of UE

As for the Ma-IC, to simplify the programming, we put the code of it in core network (EPC in figure), as shown in Fig. 11. The modules in the green square is used for interaction with WLAN network.

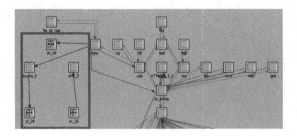

Fig. 11. Ma-IC in core network (Color figure online)

In contrast network, due to the limitation of OPNET, we split a UE into two part to simulate the UE that can only access one network during the handover:

one part can access LTE system and the other one can only access WLAN network. For example, UE2-1 and STA1-1 forms a complete UE handovering from LTE to WLAN network.

5.2 Simulation Results

When simulation starts, mixUE in CBCA firstly execute the access procedure to Mi-LBS2, that is, LTE system. And then when the handover is triggered, mixUE connect to WLAN AP without breaking the connection with eNB2 as described in Sect. 4. The throughput of mixUE is shown in Fig. 12. We can see that the soft handover is achieved since the data transmission is successive during the handover.

And in contrast network, take UE2-1 and STA1-1 as an example again. When simulation starts, UE2-1 initiate the access procedure to Mi-LBS2, that is, LTE system. And then when the handover is triggered, STA1-1 access to Mi-WAP and then UE2-1 disconnects with Mi-LBS2, simulating the hard handover. From Fig. 13, we can see that there is a break-off of the data transmission when handover to the WLAN network.

Three hundred simulation is performed, and the average handover signaling overhead in CBCA network is 73 entries and in contrast network is 104 entries. By contrast, the signaling overhead in CBCA network is reduced by 29.8%.

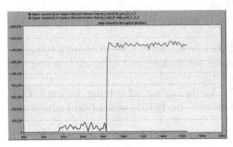   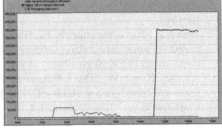

Fig. 12. MixUE throughput   **Fig. 13.** Existing UE throughput

6 Conclusion

In this paper, we have proposed a new integrated architecture and a corresponding handover mechanism to improve the current interworking between LTE system and WLAN system. A centralized controller which includes data processing module, information management module and connection control module has been employed. It possesses the ability to flexibly dispatch resources among Mi-CPs and also it has a global view of the attached entities to maintain a RAN table, which can be utilized to control the network. The simulation results show that the performance of handover mechanism is enhanced by decoupling the control signaling and service data, since that the control procedure is simplified and thus release more spectrum occupation. In summary, the controller-based integrated architecture satisfied the trend of 5G.

Acknowledgment. This work was supported by the National High-Tech R&D Program (863 Program 2015AA01A705), the National Natural Science Foundation of China (No. 61601055).

References

1. Gupta, A., Jha, R.K.: A survey of 5G network: architecture and emerging technologies. IEEE Access **3**, 1206–1232 (2015)
2. Zhang, H., Chu, X., Guo, W., Wang, S.: Coexistence of Wi-Fi and heterogeneous small cell networks sharing unlicensed spectrum. IEEE Commun. Mag. **53**(3), 158–164 (2015)
3. Abinader, F.M., Almeida, E.P., Chaves, F.S., Cavalcante, A.M., Vieira, R.D., Paiva, R.C., Sousa, V.A.: Enabling the coexistence of LTE and Wi-Fi in unlicensed bands. IEEE Commun. Mag. **52**(11), 54–61 (2014)
4. Ling, J., Kanugovi, S., Vasudevan, S., Pramod, A.K.: Enhanced capacity and coverage by Wi-Fi LTE integration. IEEE Commun. Mag. **53**(3), 165–171 (2015)
5. Kim, D.S., Noishiki, Y., Kitatsuji, Y., Yokota, H.: Efficient ANDSF-assisted Wi-Fi control for mobile data offloading. In: International Wireless Communications and Mobile Computing Conference (IWCMC), pp. 343–348 (2013)
6. Chen, T., Matinmikko, M., Chen, X., Zhou, X.: Software defined mobile networks: concept, survey, and research directions. Commun. Mag. IEEE **53**(11), 126–133 (2015)
7. Wood, T., Ramakrishnan, K.K., Hwang, J., Liu, G., Zhang, W.: Toward a software-based network: integrating software defined networking and network function virtualization. IEEE Netw. **29**(3), 36–41 (2015)
8. An, X., Kiess, W., Perez-Caparros, D.: Virtualization of cellular network EPC gateways based on a scalable SDN architecture. In: IEEE Global Communications Conference, pp. 2295–2301 (2014)
9. Ahmad, I., Liyanage, M., Namal, S., Ylianttila, M.: New concepts for traffic, resource and mobility management in software-defined mobile networks. In: Conference on Wireless On-Demand Network Systems and Services, pp. 1–8 (2016)
10. Jha, S.C., Sivanesan, K., Vannithamby, R., Koc, A.T.: Dual connectivity in LTE small cell networks. In: IEEE Globecom Workshops (GC Wkshps), pp. 1205–1210 (2014)
11. 3GPP TS 23.402: Architecture Enhancements for Non-3GPP Accesses (2016)
12. Tomici, J., Starsinic, M., Mohamed, A.S.I., Li, Q.: Integrated small cell and Wi-Fi networks. In: IEEE Wireless Communications and Networking Conference (WCNC), pp. 1261–1266 (2015)

A Phase Difference Based Cooperative Spectrum Sensing Scheme for Cognitive Radio Network

Zheng Xie[✉], Sai Huang, Yifan Zhang, and Zhiyong Feng

Key Laboratory of Universal Wireless Communications, Ministry of Education,
Wireless Technology Innovation Institute (WTI), Beijing University of Posts
and Telecommunications, Beijing 100876, People's Republic of China
xiexiaozheng@bupt.edu.cn

Abstract. The increasing scarcity of spectrum resources is one of the most challenging issues to cognitive radio systems in 5G era. Traditional schemes fail to gain the balance between accuracy and complexity, which are the two of the most significant parameters to evaluate the performance of the spectrum sensing. In this paper, in order to improve the sensing accuracy and reduce the computation complexity, we propose a novel cooperative spectrum sensing scheme based on phase difference is proposed. By using the mean of Phase Difference (PD) as the test statistics, the proposed PD mean detection is formulated for efficient spectrum sensing and its performance is analyzed under Rayleigh fading channel and Gaussian noise, which has a low complexity of $O(K)$ and is immune to the noise uncertainty in contrast to the energy detection scheme. Moreover, to improve performance of the sensing scheme based on phase difference by a single CR, we consider the cooperative scenario with multiple CR nodes. Simulation verifies that our scheme obtains 3–4 dB gains comparing with energy detection.

Keywords: Cognitive radio · Spectrum sensing · Means
Phase difference · Fading · Cooperative sensing

1 Introduction

In 4G era, the mobile telecommunication pursues 1 Gb/s for fixed or low mobility and 100 Mb/s for high mobility with regard to user data rate, but this has not been satisfied due to the dramatically increasing numbers of mobile devices nowadays. With the approaching of the 5G which is being promoted by various organization, the mobile telecommunication needs more frequency to satisfied those needs. But with the spectrum resources become more and more scarce, some measurement shows the average utilization rate of current spectrum below 3 GHz is merely 5.2%, which unveils that the spectrum resources are heavily under utilized [1]. To improve the spectrum utilization greatly, we can allow a secondary user to access licensed band when the primary user (PU) is absent. In 3GPP Release 13, Long Term Evolution-Unlicensed (LTE-U) [2] is newly

© ICST Institute for Computer Sciences, Social Informatics and Telecommunications Engineering 2018
K. Long et al. (Eds.): 5GWN 2017, LNICST 211, pp. 529–543, 2018.
https://doi.org/10.1007/978-3-319-72823-0_49

proposed to struggle for performance in unlicensed bands. LTE-U adopts carrier aggregation (CA) technology and operates on unlicensed frequency bands in 5 GHz, aiming to achieve higher data rate by eliminating interference from the industrial, scientific, and medical (ISM) bands. Therefore, Cognitive Radio (CR) is playing a key role in working out the circumstance of scarce spectrum and promoting the 5G. Cognitive radio, as an agile radio technology, has been proposed to promote the efficient use of the spectrum [3]. Cognitive radio is booming technology which has the capacity to deal with the stringent requirement and scarcity of the radio spectrum. The evolution of this technology has revealed a phenomenon that the design of wireless systems will consider more and more about the ability of radio spectrum sensing, self-adaptation, and dynamic spectrum sharing. The above considerations are nothing more than to achieve higher spectral efficiency. Cooperative communications and networking is another new communication technology paradigm that allows distributed terminals in a wireless network to collaborate through some distributed transmission or signal processing so as to realize a new form of space diversity to combat the detrimental effects of fading channels.

The essence of cognitive radio technology is that the SU (secondary user) share the spectrum with the primary user (PU) and will not interference the PU. Thus it is crucial to obtain the status of PU for CR in a way. As an essential way to obtain the status of PU, spectrum sensing is the basis for efficient spectrum utilization in CR [4]. Energy detection (ED) [5], matched filtering [6] and cyclostationary detection [7] are three most widely used spectrum sensing methods. All of these methods have their own advantages and disadvantages [8]. The Matched Filtering scheme maximizes the SNR of the received signal and needs less time to achieve high processing gain but the prior information must be known. Energy detection can be implemented without prior information but it has poor performance under low SNR environment. Cyclostationary Detection still has better sensing performance under low SNR circumstance but this scheme needs high algorithm complexity and prior information still needs. Traditional spectrum sensing schemes fail to resolve the contradiction between accuracy and complexity. And they focus on the amplitude of signal, which is extremely sensitive to the noise uncertainty and multi-path fading such as Rayleigh fading. Therefore, it is important to design a new scheme to sense the spectrum.

In [9–11], Pawula and Adachi derived the distribution of phase difference (PD) of the noise-perturbed signal. These promote us to use the phase difference of received signal to design the spectrum sensing scheme. Through careful analysis, it is noticed that there is an obvious difference in the PD's distributions between Gaussian noise and noise-perturbed signal. Besides, this difference still exist in Rayleigh Fading channel and we will prove this regular by formulas. We take advantage this PD's character and set test statistics in order to sense the status of PU with low complexity. All the scheme above implemented by one CR, but a signal CR will face more problems such as blocking by buildings thus this paper will let more CRs to join the scheme to further improve the accuracy.

The rest of this paper is organized as follows. Section 2 introduces the system model and the definition of PD, analyzes the distribution of signal's PD. Section 3 formulates the test statistics and analyzes the scheme's performance for a signal CR, the last part of this section put more attention on analyzing the performance of cooperative detection for multi CRs. Simulation analysis is provided in Sect. 4. Finally, the paper is concluded in Sect. 5.

2   System Model and Phase Difference

2.1   System Model

The spectrum sensing problem can be considered as a binary hypothesis test problem and two hypotheses can be formulated as follows:

$$
\begin{aligned}
H_0^i &: r_i(n) = w_i(n) & n = 1, 2, ..., N & \quad i = 1, 2, ...N_c \\
H_1^i &: r_i(n) = w_i(n) + h_i s(n) & n = 1, 2, ..., N & \quad i = 1, 2, ...N_c
\end{aligned}
\tag{1}
$$

where $r_i(n)$ is the nth sample of received signal from the ith CR, h_i is the instantaneous channel gain between PU and the ith CR, $w(n)$ is the Additive White Gaussian Noise (AWGN) samples and $s(n)$ is the PU signal. H_0^i is the hypothesis stating that only noise is present and PU is absent, while H_1^i indicates that PU is present and all the hypothesis are made from the ith CR decision. N represents the length of signal samples and also denotes that our scheme handles finite length samples. N_c represents the number of CRs. In the ideal situation, the ith CR will make false alarm decision H_1^i when the PU is present, while make the opposite decision H_0^i when the PU is not present by our scheme. However, the CRs sometimes make wrong decisions because of the AWGN and Rayleigh fading. Therefore, to evaluate the performance of our scheme, we made P_d^i presents the detection probability and P_f^i presents false alarm probability for the ith CR, P_d^i and P_f^i can be formulated as follows:

$$
\begin{aligned}
P_d^i &= P(H_1^i | H_1) \\
P_f^i &= P(H_1^i | H_0)
\end{aligned}
\tag{2}
$$

P_d^i represents the detection probability that the ith CR makes correctly decision when the PU is presents and larger P_d^i indicates that the CRs has little interference to PU. P_f^i represents the probability that the ith CR makes wrong decision when the PU is not present and lower P_f^i indicates more access opportunity. So an excellent scheme means lower P_f and higher P_d. However, there is a trade-off between P_f and P_d for most sensing schemes, which makes it impossible to improve P_d and reduce P_f at the same time. Thus receiver operating characteristic (ROC) curve (P_f vs P_d) is usually used as the performance metric of sensing schemes. Next, we will discuss the phase difference on the case of single CR. Moreover, the case of more CRs is same as the case of signal CR, thus the following discussion is under one CR case.

2.2   Definition of Phase Difference

The received signal can be formulated as follows:

$$r(n) = [s(nT)e^{j2\pi f_c nT}]h(nT) + w(nT) \tag{3}$$

where, T is the sampling interval, and $s(nT)$ is the instantaneous value of PU signal, f_c represents the residual carrier frequency after down conversion, $h(nT)$ is channel impulse responses, $w(nT)$ is Gaussian noise. The phase θ of received data sample, $r(n)$ can be calculated through following formula:

$$\theta_n' = \begin{cases} \arctan(\dfrac{Im(r(n))}{Re(r(n))}) & (Re(r(n)) \geq 0) \\ (\arctan(\dfrac{Im(r(n))}{Re(r(n))}) + \pi) & (Re(r(n)) < 0) \end{cases} \tag{4}$$

$$\theta_n = \theta_n' \ mod \ 2\pi$$

where, $Re(r(n))$ and $Im(r(n))$ represent the real and imaginary part respectively of the received data sample. Where needs paying special attention is that we introduce the modulo 2π operation to ensure phase θ_n is in the range of $[0, 2\pi]$. Then, the phase difference φ_n between two adjacent samples is defined as follows:

$$\varphi_n = (\theta_{n+1} - \theta_n) \ mod \ 2\pi \tag{5}$$

2.3   PD Distribution of Gaussian Noise

We all know that the instantaneous phase θ_n of Gaussian noise follows a uniform distribution in $[0, 2\pi]$, which means $\theta_n \sim U(0, 2\pi)$. According to the nature of Gaussian noise, the two adjacent phases are completely irrelevant and in other words, the two adjacent phases are completely independently identically distributed. Thus, $\varphi_n' = \theta_{n+1} - \theta_n$ follow a triangular distribution from -2π to 2π which can be expressed as:

$$P_{\varphi_n'} = \begin{cases} \dfrac{1}{2\pi} + \dfrac{\varphi_n'}{4\pi^2} & -2\pi \leq \varphi_n' < 0 \\ \dfrac{1}{2\pi} - \dfrac{\varphi_n'}{4\pi^2} & 0 \leq \varphi_n' \leq 2\pi \end{cases} \tag{6}$$

Considering that the φ_n' is in the range of $[0, 2\pi]$, then we make $\varphi_n = \varphi_n' \ mod \ (2\pi)$. When the φ_n' is in the range $[-2\pi, 0]$, $\varphi_n = \varphi_n' \ mod \ (2\pi)$. So the distribution of the φ_n can be expressed as follows:

$$P_{\varphi_n} = P_{\varphi_n'}(\varphi_n) + P_{\varphi_n'}(\varphi_n - 2\pi) = \tfrac{1}{2\pi} \tag{7}$$

We can conclude that the PD φ_n of Gaussian noise complying with a uniformly distributed in $[0, 2\pi]$ based the above analysis. Therefore, according to the nature of uniformly distributed, it is easy to obtain the mean and variance value of PD of Gaussian noise by the following formula and the mean and variance are π and $\frac{\pi^2}{3}$ respectively.

$$\mu_\varphi = \int_0^{2\pi} \varphi P_\varphi d\varphi \tag{8}$$

$$\sigma_\varphi^2 = \int_0^{2\pi} (\varphi - \mu_\varphi)^2 P_\varphi d\varphi \tag{9}$$

There is no signal component in our analysis under this circumstance, i.e. hypothesis H_0 and all the results are about noise. Then, in the next section, we will pay more attention to the PD distribution of signal perturbed by Gaussian noise. Besides, that problem will be discussed in two different channel conditions, the first channel condition is AWGN channel without fading, and kind channel condition is AWGN channel with Rayleigh fading which is more in line with the actual scenarios.

2.4 PD Distribution of Signal Perturbed by Gaussian Noise (AWGN Channel)

Regard to the noise-perturbed signal, papers [9–11] has already derived formulas that illustrate the characteristics of PD distribution. Thus, in this paper, we are not doing a detailed derivation for that and the formula of CDF is as following:

$$F_{\varphi_n}(\varphi_n) = \frac{1}{4\pi} \int_{-\frac{\pi}{2}}^{\frac{\pi}{2}} e^{-E} \left[\frac{W \sin(\Delta\omega)}{E} + \xi \right] dt \tag{10}$$

where

$$E = U - V \sin t - W \cos \Delta\omega \cos t \tag{11}$$
$$U = (SNR_{n+1} - SNR_n)/2 \tag{12}$$
$$V = (SNR_{n+1} + SNR_n)/2 \tag{13}$$
$$W = \sqrt{SNR_{n+1}SNR_n} = \sqrt{U^2 - V^2} \tag{14}$$
$$\xi = \frac{\alpha \sin \varphi_n - \beta \cos \varphi_n}{1 - (\alpha \cos \varphi_n + \beta \sin \varphi_n) \cos t} \tag{15}$$
$$\Delta\omega = \phi_n - \varphi_n \tag{16}$$

in which, SNR_n and SNR_{n+1} are the instantaneous SNR of the nth and the $n+$1th sampling point respectively, φ_n is phase difference between the nth sampling point and the $n+1$th sampling point of PU signal without noise and Rayleigh fading. It's worthy to noted that $\alpha + \beta j$ represents the complex correlation of the sum of Rayleigh fading signal and noise and $\xi = 0$ because of AWGN channel. Continuous wave only be considered here, so the SNR_n will be equal to SNR_{n+1}, and we can assume the $SNR_{n+1} = SNR_n = \gamma$. And then, after substituting and derivation of CDF, the formula of PDF is as follows:

$$P_{\varphi_n}(\varphi_n) = [1 + 2\gamma - \gamma(1 - \cos \Delta\omega \cos t)]e^{-\gamma(1 - \cos \Delta\omega \cos t)} \tag{17}$$

2.5 PD Distribution of Signal Perturbed by Gaussian Noise and Rayleigh Fading

In this section, we consider the PU signal's PD distribution which perturbed by Gaussian noise and Rayleigh fading. Thus, the complex correlation of the sum of Rayleigh fading signal and noise cannot be neglect and it can be expressed as $\alpha + \beta j$. Similarly, only continuous wave be considered, so we can still assume the $SNR_{n+1} = SNR_n = \gamma$. According to the condition $\alpha + \beta j$ and $SNR_{n+1} = SNR_n = \gamma$, we can obtain the following formula:

$$\alpha + \beta j = \sqrt{\alpha^2 + \beta^2}e^{j\phi_n} = \frac{\gamma e^{j\phi_n}}{\gamma+1} \tag{18}$$

As our spectrum detect scheme work under low SNR condition, so the term approximate to constant one. Thus, the CDF of PD distribution can be expressed as following:

$$
\begin{aligned}
F_{\varphi_n}(\varphi_n) \\
= \frac{1}{4\pi} \int_{-\pi/2}^{\pi/2} [\frac{\sin \Delta\omega}{1 - \cos \Delta\omega \cos t} + \frac{\gamma \sin \Delta\omega}{\gamma(1 - \cos \Delta\omega \cos t) + 1}]dt \\
= \frac{\sin \Delta\omega}{\pi |\sin \Delta\omega|} \arctan \left| \cot \frac{\Delta\omega}{2} \right| \\
+ \frac{\sin \Delta\omega}{\pi\sqrt{(1 + 1/\gamma)^2 - \cos^2 \Delta\omega}} \arctan \sqrt{\frac{(\gamma + 1) + \gamma \cos \Delta\omega}{(\gamma + 1) - \gamma \cos \Delta\omega}}
\end{aligned}
\tag{19}
$$

and the distribution of $\Delta\omega$ can be described as following:

$$F_{\Delta\omega}(\Delta\omega) = \begin{cases} F_{\varphi_n}(\Delta\omega) - F_{\varphi_n}(-\pi) & \Delta\omega \le 0 \\ F_{\varphi_n}(\Delta\omega) - F_{\varphi_n}(-\pi) + 1 & \Delta\omega > 0 \end{cases} \tag{20}$$

After transformation of the terms *arctan*, a simplified form of $F_{\Delta\omega}(\Delta\omega)$ can be expressed by following formula:

$$F_{\Delta\omega}(\Delta\omega) = 1/2 + \Delta\omega/2\pi + \frac{\sin \Delta\omega T(\Delta\omega)}{2\pi Q(\Delta\omega)} \tag{21}$$

where

$$T(\Delta\omega) = \frac{\pi}{2} + \arcsin \frac{\gamma \cos \Delta\omega}{\gamma + 1} \tag{22}$$

$$Q(\Delta\omega) = \sqrt{(1 + \frac{1}{\gamma})^2 - \cos^2 \Delta\omega} \tag{23}$$

and as $\Delta\omega = \phi_n - \varphi_n$, so

$$f_{\varphi_n}(\varphi_n) = f_{\Delta\omega}(\phi_n - \varphi_n) = F'_{\Delta\omega}(\phi_n - \varphi_n) \tag{24}$$

Thus, after the derivation, the PDF of PD can be represents by following:

$$f_{\varphi_n}(\varphi_n) = \frac{1}{2\pi} + \frac{\cos \Delta\omega T(\Delta\omega)}{2\pi Q(\Delta\omega)}$$
$$- \frac{\cos \Delta\omega \sin^2 \Delta\omega T(\Delta\omega)}{2Q(\Delta\omega)}$$
$$- \frac{\gamma \sin^2 \Delta\omega}{2\pi(\gamma + 1)Q(\Delta\omega)\sqrt{1 - \frac{\gamma^2 \cos^2 \Delta\omega}{(\gamma+1)^2}}} \tag{25}$$

3 Test Statistics and Cooperative Sensing

3.1 Test Statistics

After the derivation above, we can easily obtain the conclusion that the mean and variance of signal perturbed by noise are very different from the Gaussian noise. Thus, every CR can take advantage those characteristic to sense the status of PU. So, in this paper, we design a scheme that every CR makes the mean of PD as test statistics and the mean of PD is:

$$S_\theta^i = \frac{1}{N} \sum_{i=1}^{N} \varphi_n^i \tag{26}$$

where the S_θ^i is test statistic calculated by the ith CR, N represents the number of PDs, and the φ_n^i is the PD between the nth sampling point and the $(n+1)$th sampling point of the receive signal from ith CR, calculated by formula (3) (4) (5). When the mean of PD S_θ^i falls in the range of $\left[\pi - \varphi_0^i, \pi - \varphi_0^i\right]$, the ith CR will make the decision that the PU in not present and the ith CR's decision model is expressed as follows:

$$D_i = \begin{cases} H_0^i & \left|S_\theta^i - \pi\right| \leq \varphi_0^i \\ H_1^i & \left|S_\theta^i - \pi\right| > \varphi_0^i \end{cases} \tag{27}$$

where, D_i is the ith CR's decision and φ_0^i is the decision threshold.

3.2 Threshold Setting

If the number of φ_n^i is large enough, the test statistics S_θ^i can be approximated as a Gaussian distribution according to the central limit theorem, whose mean and variance are π and $\frac{\pi^2}{3N}$ respectively. Thus, the PDF of test statistics S_θ^i can be expressed as follows:

$$f(S_\theta^i|H_0) = \frac{1}{\sqrt{2\pi^3/3N}} e^{-\frac{(S_\theta^i - \pi)^2}{2\pi^2/3N}} \tag{28}$$

We can easily obtain the false alarm probability P_f^i by following formula:

$$P_f^i = 1 - \int_{\pi-\varphi_0^i}^{\pi+\varphi_0^i} \frac{1}{\sqrt{2\pi^3/3N}} e^{-\frac{(S_\theta^i-\pi)^2}{2\pi^2/3N}} dS_\theta^i$$

$$= erfc(\frac{S_\theta^i}{\sqrt{2\pi^2/3N}})$$

(29)

In practice, the threshold is usually chosen according to a fixed false alarm probability, which can be expressed as follows:

$$\varphi_0^i = \sqrt{2\pi^2/3N} erfc^{-1}(P_f)$$

(30)

As the case the PU is presents, we can easily obtain the value of mean μ_i and the variance σ_i^2 by formulas (17) or (25). For the case H_1, according to the central limit theorem, the PDF of test statistics S_θ^i can be expressed as follows:

$$f(S_\theta^i|H_1) = \frac{1}{\sqrt{2\pi\sigma_i^2/N}} e^{-\frac{(S_\theta^i-\mu_i)^2}{2\sigma_i^2/N}}$$

(31)

Thus, the detection probability P_d^i of the ith CR can be expressed as follows:

$$P_d^i = 1 - \int_{\pi-\varphi_0^i}^{\pi+\varphi_0^i} \frac{1}{\sqrt{2\pi\sigma_i^2}} e^{-\frac{(S_\theta^i-\mu^i)^2}{2\sigma_i^2}} dS_\theta^i$$

$$= erfc(\frac{S_\theta^i}{\sqrt{2\sigma_i^2}})$$

(32)

3.3   Cooperative Sensing

In an actual scenario, the hidden terminal problem which occurs when the CR is sheltered by giant buildings especially in urban area and that become an urgent issue to tackle. In this case, the CR cannot detect the existence of PU, and will access the spectrum which the PU is occupying. Thus certainly caused a series severe interference to the PU. In our sensing scheme, we deploy more CRs to collaborate [12]. The cooperative spectrum structure is illustrated in the Fig. 1, the overall process works like this: Firstly, every CR performs their local spectrum sensing scheme based on PD independently and make a local decision on whether the PU is present or not. And then, every CR forward their local decisions to the fusion center. Finally, the fusion center fuses the all CR's decisions by fusion algorithm and makes the final decision of the status of PU. There are mainly two fusion algorithms, which are decision fusion and data fusion respectively. In decision fusion case, fusion center receive all one-bit binary decisions from CRs, and fused together according to an OR logic. Instead,

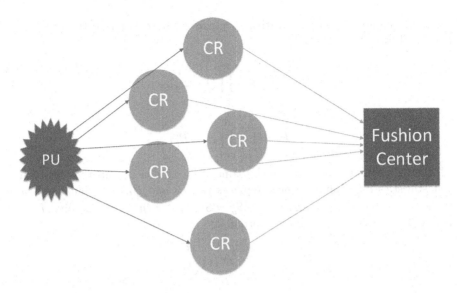

Fig. 1. Cooperative spectrum sensing structure

in data fusion case, fusion center not receive one-bit binary decisions but receive the observation value from all CRs. In our scheme, decision fusion algorithm is employed as CRs transmit less amount of data [13,14]. In this paper, we use the number 0 to denote the decision H_0^i and number 1 to denote the decision H_1^i from the ith CR. So the decision from the ith CR D_i has only two values, 0 or 1, which can be expressed by $D_i \in \{0,1\}$. On one side of the fusion center, all decisions from the CRs are fused together according to the following logic:

$$D = \sum_{i=1}^{K} D_i \begin{cases} \geq n, H_1 \\ < n, H_0 \end{cases} \tag{33}$$

where, H_1 and H_0 represent the final decision of status of PU from the fusion center. If the fusion center makes the decision, i.e. H_1, there must be at least n out of K CRs making decision H_1^i and transmit 1s to the fusion center, vice versa. It is worthy to noted that when the n is set to be 1, this logic can be seen as OR rule and this logic rule can be seen as AND logic rule when the n is K. Under the circumstance of OR rule, the fusion center makes the decision that the PU is presence when at least one CR make the local decision H_1.

The OR logic can be seen as a kind of conservative logic when the CR access the spectrum and OR logic will lower the interference to the PU because of higher P_d. For the AND logic rule, it can be seen as more radical logic and improve the utilization ratio of spectrum, but at the cost of higher collision probability with the PU. In this paper, we discuss only two basic fusion algorithms, there are also many more fusion algorithms that can be studied and different algorithms are suitable for different actual scenes. The final detection probability P_d and false alarm probability P_f of cooperative spectrum sensing based on the OR rule is presented by following formulas:

$$P_d = 1 - \prod_{i=1}^{K}(1 - P_d^i) \tag{34}$$

$$P_f = 1 - \prod_{i=1}^{K}(1 - P_f^i) \tag{35}$$

All the CRs can be considered in the same radio condition, thus they have same test statistics distribute. So here replaces the P_d^i and P_f^i by formula (32) and formula (29) respectively and makes $S_\theta^i = S_\theta$, $\sigma_i = \sigma$, $\mu^i = \mu$. The final P_d and P_f can be expressed by following formulas:

$$P_d = 1 - (1 - erfc(\frac{S_\theta}{\sqrt{2\sigma^2}}))^K \tag{36}$$

$$P_f = 1 - (1 - erfc(\frac{S_\theta}{\sqrt{2\pi^2/3N}}))^K \tag{37}$$

And for the AND logic rule, the final detection probability P_d and false alarm probability P_f of cooperative spectrum sensing can be expressed by following formulas:

$$P_d = \prod_{i=1}^{K} P_d^i = (erfc(\frac{S_\theta}{\sqrt{2\sigma^2}}))^K \tag{38}$$

$$P_f = \prod_{i=1}^{K} P_f^i = (erfc(\frac{S_\theta}{\sqrt{2\pi^2/3N}}))^K \tag{39}$$

3.4   Performance Analysis

According to the nature of our scheme, only $N + 1$ sampling points need to be store for every CR and the computational complexity is $O(N)$. To be contrasted with the other more sophisticated schemes such as sensing scheme based on cyclostationary feature, our sensing cost every CR's lower computing resource.

4   Simulation Analysis

In this section, the method of Monte Carlo Simulation is applied in our simulation to offset the random error, thus improving the accuracy of our simulation and simulation times is set to 1000. According to the analysis above, the performance of our scheme is related to many factors, such as the length of sample points, the number of CRs, the fusion logic rules and channel condition. All of the simulations are implemented under the Rayleigh fading channel condition as it is more similar to the practical radio environment.

Figure 2 compares the detection probability P_d of our scheme with the detection probability P_d that of scheme by energy detection for several basic modulation signals, when the $N = 1000$, $P_f = 0.01$ and the number of CR is set to $8(K = 8)$. With the SNR increasing, detection probability P_d is also increasing, so those curves are accord with the general regular. We can observe that our scheme obtains 3–4 dB gains when the P_d is above 90% comparing with the scheme based on energy detection. The overlapping of curves in most parts prove that our scheme is robust to modulation mode which is similarly as energy detection. The curves in small parts are not overlapping and detection probability of sine wave signal is higher than signals modulated by other modulation in those parts, that is because the phase of sine wave signal is more continuous than the others.

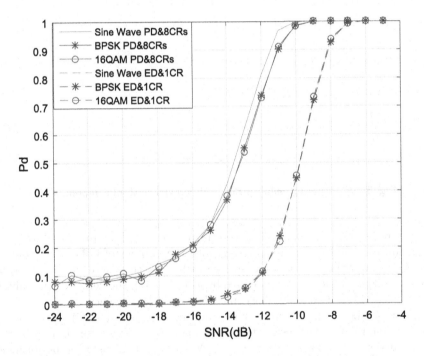

Fig. 2. Detection probability for different ways of modulation

Figure 3 shows the detection probability versus signal length N, when the P_f is set to 0.01 and the number of CRs is set to 8. According to the Fig. 3, we can obtained the regular that when three curves reached the same level of P_d, the curve whose length of sample data is longer needs the lower SNR. This regular can be explained by the reason that the length of sample data is longer, the test statistics, i.e. the mean of PD will converge to mathematical expectation according to the law of large numbers.

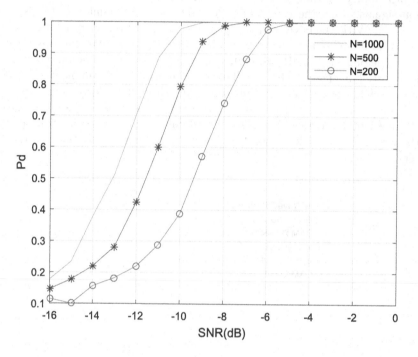

Fig. 3. Detection probability Pd for different length of sampling points

Figure 4 shows the relation between the number of CRs represented by K and detection probability. We can get that with the number of CRs increasing, the detection probability P_d is increasing too when all the curves are in the same SNR condition. That can be explained by formula (34), the detection probability P_d is less to 1, so the larger K become, the larger P_d becomes.

Figure 5 shows the receiver operating characteristic (ROC) curves which describe the relation between detection probability P_d and false alarm probability P_f under the condition that $K = 8$, $N = 1000$. That lists the performance results of cooperative spectrum sensing for different fusion rules and the case of ED over Rayleigh fading channels with the $SNR = -14$ dB. With the false alarm probability P_f increasing, detection probability P_d of three curves increase too, but in the area of lower P_f, the P_d of our scheme based on OR fusion logic rule increases sharply. So the OR rule is the better rule than the AND rule, and our scheme based on OR fusion logic rule have the best performance than others.

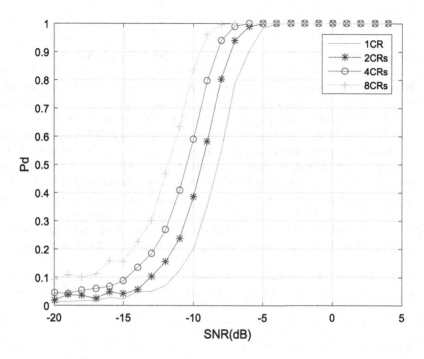

Fig. 4. Detection probability Pd for different number of CRs

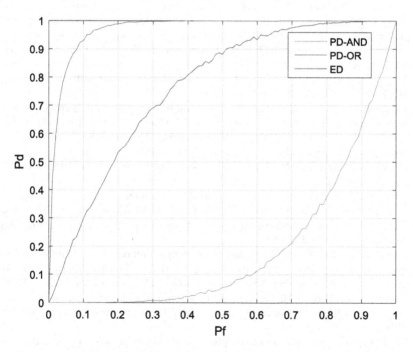

Fig. 5. ROC curves at $-14\,\mathrm{dB}$

5   Conclusion

In this paper we proposed a novel cooperative spectrum scheme based on phase difference which can improve the spectrum sensing performance compared with traditional sensing scheme. Firstly, we analyze the distributions of the phase difference between two adjacent samples under the condition of Gaussian noise, the signal perturbed by noise and the signal perturbed by Rayleigh fade, and find that the mean and variance of those signal are very different as the their distributions are very different. On that basis, we select the mean of PD as test statistics, which follows Gaussian distribution and needs lower computer resource. According to the analysing above, we obtain the threshold of detection. Cooperative spectrum sensing was then considered and shown to be a powerful method for dealing with the hidden terminal problem. Simulation shows that our scheme has best performance compared to energy detection under the Rayleigh Faded channel and OR rules has better performance than AND performance.

Acknowledgment. This work was supported by the National Natural Science Foundation of China (61227801), the National Key Technology R&D Program of China (2015ZX03002008-002).

References

1. August, P., Mchenry, M.A.: NSF spectrum occupancy measurements project summary (2005)
2. Al-Dulaimi, A., Al-Rubaye, S., Ni, Q., Sousa, E.: 5G communications race: pursuit of more capacity triggers LTE in unlicensed band. IEEE Veh. Technol. Mag. **10**(1), 43–51 (2015)
3. Mitola, J., Maguire, G.Q.: Cognitive radio: making software radios more personal. IEEE Pers. Commun. **6**(4), 13–18 (1999)
4. Ghasemi, A., Sousa, E.S.: Spectrum sensing in cognitive radio networks: requirements, challenges and design trade-offs. IEEE Commun. Mag. **46**(4), 32–39 (2008)
5. Zhao, Y., Li, S., Zhao, N., Wu, Z.: A novel energy detection algorithm for spectrum sensing in cognitive radio. Inf. Technol. J. **9**(8), 1659–1664 (2010)
6. Price, R., Abramson, N.: Part 4: detection theory. Inf. Theor. IRE Trans. **7**(3), 135–139 (1961)
7. Kim, K., Akbar, I.A., Bae, K.K., Um, J.S., Spooner, C.M., Reed, J.H.: Cyclostationary approaches to signal detection and classification in cognitive radio. In: IEEE International Symposium on New Frontiers in Dynamic Spectrum Access Networks, pp. 212–215 (2007)
8. Bhargavi, D., Murthy, C.R.: Performance comparison of energy, matched-filter and cyclostationarity-based spectrum sensing. In: IEEE Eleventh International Workshop on Signal Processing Advances in Wireless Communications, pp. 1–5 (2010)
9. Pawula, R.F., Rice, S.O., Roberts, J.: Distribution of the phase angle between two vectors perturbed by Gaussian noise. IEEE Trans. Commun. **30**(8), 1828–1841 (1982)
10. Pawula, R.F.: Distribution of the phase angle between two vectors perturbed by Gaussian noise II. IEEE Trans. Veh. Technol. **50**(2), 576–583 (2001)

11. Adachi, F., Tjhung, T.T.: Distribution of phase angle between two Rayleigh vectors perturbed by Gaussian noise. Electr. Lett. **28**(10), 923–925 (1992)
12. Cabric, D., Mishra, S.M., Brodersen, R.W.: Implementation issues in spectrum sensing for cognitive radios. In: Conference Record of the Thirty-Eighth Asilomar Conference on Signals, Systems and Computers, vol. 1, pp. 772–776 (2004)
13. Letaief, K., Zhang, W.: Cooperative communications for cognitive radio. Proc. IEEE **97**(5), 878–893 (2009)
14. Chen, X., Chen, H.H., Meng, W.: Cooperative communications for cognitive radio networks from theory to applications. IEEE Commun. Surv. Tutorials **16**(3), 1180–1192 (2014)

Power Allocation for NOMA System via Dual Sub-gradient Descent

Juan Wu[1], Xinli Ma[1], Zhenyu Zhang[1], Zhongshan Zhang[1],
Xiyuan Wang[1], Xiaomeng Chai[1], Linglong Dai[2],
and Xiaoming Dai[1(✉)]

[1] Technology Research Center for Convergence
Networks and Ubiquitous Services, University of Science and Technology
Beijing (USTB), Beijing 100083, China
dxmsjtu@sohu.com, daixiaoming@ustb.edu.cn
[2] Tsinghua-Rohm EE Hall, Department of Electronic Engineering,
Tsinghua University, Beijing 100084, China
dail1@tsinghua.edu.cn

Abstract. Non-orthogonal multiple access (NOMA) has attracted great attention as a promising downlink multiple access technique for the next generation cellular networks (5G) due to its superior spectral efficiency. Power allocation of multi-user scenario in NOMA is a challenging issue and most of existing works focus on two-user scenario. In this work, we develop a dual sub-gradient descent algorithm based on Lagrange dual function to optimize multi-user power allocation for the multiple-input single-output (MISO) downlink NOMA system. The objective function is a non-convex optimization problem and we can solve it with a log-convex method and an approximation based approach. Numerical results demonstrate that the proposing scheme is able to achieve higher capacity performance for a NOMA transmission system compared with the traditional orthogonal multiple access (OMA) with a few iterations.

Keywords: Non-orthogonal multiple access · Power allocation
Log-convex · Dual sub-gradient descent

1 Introduction

The power domain based NOMA utilizes superposition coding (SC) [1] at transmitter and successive interference cancellation (SIC) [2] at the receiver to achieve a higher spectral efficiency. Compared with the contemporary orthogonal multiple access approaches, non-orthogonal communication techniques have more advantages, such as larger system capacity, higher spectral efficiency and reduced latency, making NOMA an attractive option for implementation in future wireless standards.

There are two key techniques contained in NOMA: (1) NOMA utilizes SIC to process the received signals on the user equipment where users are sorted based on their effective channel gains. At the receiving terminal, the stronger user can eliminate interference imposed by the weaker user through SIC operation. (2) NOMA is a multiplexing scheme which is applied in power domain. User de-multiplexing is

© ICST Institute for Computer Sciences, Social Informatics and Telecommunications Engineering 2018
K. Long et al. (Eds.): 5GWN 2017, LNICST 211, pp. 544–555, 2018.
https://doi.org/10.1007/978-3-319-72823-0_50

ensured by large power difference between paired users. Theoretically, pairing the user having the worst channel gain with the user having the best channel gain in each cluster can obtain a better channel capacity. In a word, employing SC and SIC in NOMA can achieve a better system performance [3].

NOMA applying non-orthogonal transmission technique between the sub-channels, thus there is no apparent near-far effect and multiple access interference (MAI) compared with the traditional CDMA and OFDMA in 3G. However, it would be rather complex than other receivers as a non-orthogonal transmission receiver and the power-domain multiplexing is still on the researching stage, NOMA is facing some challenges in technical implementation, and there is still much of work to do.

Power allocation in NOMA has been studied in many existing works and has been extended to various systems and different schemes. In [4], a power allocation approach named Fair-NOMA is introduced. The key idea of Fair-NOMA is that the capacity of two mobile users has the opportunity to always achieve that of the OMA system. According to the Shannon capacity equation, if the capacity of NOMA is greater than or equal to OMA, a reasonable power allocation coefficient can be derived. In both single-input single-output (SISO) and multiple-input multiple-output (MIMO) scenarios, two optimal power allocation solutions with closed form based on the Karush-Kuhn-Tucker (KKT) condition have been studied in [5]. For MIMO-NOMA with layered transmission, Choi [6] explored an approach based on alternating maximization (AM) algorithm and showed that the sum rate optimization problem is concave in allocated powers to multiple layers of users. Energy efficient (EE) resource allocation problem has not been well studied for NOMA system until [7], where the author proposed a low-complexity suboptimal matching scheme for sub-channel assignment (SOMSA) algorithm to maximize the system energy efficiency and numerical simulation results in this work have shown that NOMA has much better sum rate and superior EE performance compared with OMA.

In [8] Ding utilized an approximation of the original non-convex optimization problem with a minorization-maximization algorithm (MMA) in downlink MISO-NOMA system. In each step of the MMA, the author utilized a second-order cone program to get a subset of the feasibility set of the original problem and the algorithm is numerically shown to converge within a few iterations. Finally, a linear multiuser superposition transmission (MUST) scheme is studied in [9], in which a Monte Carlo simulations based approach is devised to maximizing the total mutual information with a reasonable power allocation scheme.

Compared to the previous power allocation schemes in NOMA system, our main contributions can be summarized as follows:

(i)   The prior studies of power allocation about NOMA have focused on two-user scenarios. In this paper, we will investigate multi-users power allocation problems in the downlink of a MISO-NOMA system. Furthermore, constraints are also included to guarantee the capacity of the weaker users fulfilling their target data rates and it should be noted that this power allocation scheme is not quality-of-service (QoS) guaranteed for the strong user because the minimum rate requirement of the strong user is always accessibility in our algorithm.

(ii) Using the log-convex concept, and combined with the Lagrange dual function, we develop a dual sub-gradient descent algorithm that solves the NOMA sum capacity maximization problems. We also show that the proposed algorithm is convergent in a few iterations.

(iii) We present an approximation to the original optimization problem to reduce the complexity of the proposed method. To provide more insight, we perform this approximation specifically designed for the characteristics of log-convex. Finally, numerical examples are presented to show the validity of the proposed algorithm.

The rest of the paper is organized as follows: The system model for downlink MISO-NOMA is outlined in Sect. 2. The based approach for the optimal power allocation to maximize the sum capacity is investigated in Sect. 3. Simulation results are presented in Sect. 4. Finally, Sect. 5 concludes the paper with some remarks and discussed the future works to be considered.

2 System Model

In this section, we present a multiple-input single-output (MISO) downlink NOMA transmission system. We consider that the base station (BS) in a cellular system is equipped with N antennas and K single antenna users. The channel gain between the k-th user and the BS is denoted by h_k. It is assumed that $h_k = d_k^{-\theta} g_k$, with d_k being the distance from the BS to the k-th user, where $g_k \sim CN(0, 1)$ and θ is the pass loss exponent. Furthermore, we assume that the distances from the users to the BS are fixed and users are equally spaced in the cellular system. We allocate powers for each user based on their channel state information (CSI) and user who have better channel gain will obtain lower power. Thus, the stronger users can detect the weaker users according to SIC at the receiving terminals. Generally, the distances are sorted as $d_1 \geq \ldots \geq d_k$. The channel gains of each user are sorted as $|h_1|^2 \leq \ldots \leq |h_k|^2$ and the powers of them are then allocated as $p_1 \geq \ldots \geq p_k$, accordingly. Based on NOMA transmission protocol, the BS will send $\sum_{k=1}^{K} \sqrt{p_k s_k}$ to each user, where the message for the k-th user is s_k, and p_k is the transmission power for user k. Therefore, the received signal at the k-th user is given as:

$$y_k = h_k \sum_{k=1}^{K} \sqrt{p_k} s_k + n_k, \tag{1}$$

Here n_k denotes the additive noise and $n_k \sim CN(0, \sigma^2)$. The k-th user signal to interference plus noise ratio (SINR) is

$$SINR_k = \frac{|h_k|^2 p_k}{|h_k|^2 \sum_{i=k+1}^{K} p_i + \sigma^2}, \tag{2}$$

The SINR of the K-th user is

$$SINR_K = \frac{|h_K|^2 p_K}{\sigma^2}. \tag{3}$$

The target rate for each user will be set as to achieve an acceptable QoS requirement. Therefore, for user k, we can define

$$\log_2(1 + SINR_k) \geq R_{target}. \tag{4}$$

This constraint provides a guarantee that all users can meet their QoS requirements.

3 Problem Formulation

In this section, a dual sub-gradient descent algorithm based on Lagrange dual function is used to maximize the sum capacity of NOMA system. Firstly, we express the optimization function as:

$$\sum_{k=1}^{K} R_k = \sum_{k=1}^{K} \log_2(1 + SINR_k) \tag{5}$$

To solve the optimization problem (5), a mathematical model is developed according to standardized Lagrange dual function as follows:

$$\max \sum_{k=1}^{K} R_k$$
$$s.t. \begin{cases} C1 : R_k \geq R_{target} \\ C2 : 0 \leq p_k \leq P, \ k = 1, 2..., K \\ C3 : \sum_{k=1}^{K} p_k = P \end{cases} \tag{6}$$

In this optimization problem, constraint C1 represents the fact that the capacity of each user must meet their corresponding QoS requirement, and constraint C2 reflects the NOMA principle that the power allocation of the weak user must be greater than that of the strong user. By defining A_k as the upper bound of interference plus noise, we can define that

$$|h_k|^2 \sum_{i=k+1}^{K} p_i + \sigma^2 = A_k. \tag{7}$$

In NOMA, power allocation is of importance to enhance the achievable capacity of each user and it is a non-convex optimization problem. Inspired from the results presented in [10, 11], we devise a new power allocation algorithm named dual sub-gradient descent in the NOMA system based on Lagrange dual function. The core idea of Lagrange function is to embed constraint conditions into the objective function, adding weighted sum of the constraint conditions to obtain an augmented objective function. The Lagrange dual function is the minimum value of Lagrange function.

Even though the Lagrange function has no lower bound on x, the value of dual function is $-\infty$ [12]. The dual function is a kind of affine function on x, so even if the original question is non-convex, the dual function is still a concave function. Thus, on account of using log-convex algorithm, it is obvious that maximizing the sum capacity in (5) is equivalent to maximizing the objective function in (8).

$$\max \sum_{k=1}^{K} \ln(|h_k|^2 p_k A_k^{-1}) \tag{8}$$

Through logarithm transformation, we can define $p_k = e^{x_k}$, $A_k = e^{y_k}$ and substitute (8) into (6), then the mathematical model in (6) can be rewritten as:

$$\max \sum_{k=1}^{K} \ln(e^{x_k - y_k + \ln(|h_k|^2)})$$
$$s.t. \begin{cases} C1 : |h_k|^{-2} e^{y_k - x_k} (2^{R_{target}} - 1) - 1 \leq 0 \\ C2 : e^{x_k} P^{-1} - 1 \leq 0, k = 1, 2 \dots, K \\ C3 : P^{-1} \sum_{k=1}^{K} e^{x_k} - 1 = 0 \end{cases} \tag{9}$$

Algorithm 1 Power Allocation with Dual Sub-gradient Descent Function

---

1:Niter:the iteration number
2:Unum:the total number of users
3:**Initialization**
4:Set $\lambda_0 = 0$, $\mu_0 = 0$, $\gamma_0 = 0$;
   Set $P_1 \geq P_2 \geq P_3$.
5: **for** $n = 1$ to Niter **do**
6:    **for** $k = 1$ to Unum **do**
7:        Set $x_k = P_k$ and $y_k = |h_k|^2 \cdot sum(P_{k+1} : P_3) + \sigma^2$;
8:        $\lambda_{n+1} = \{\lambda_n + \alpha(\partial L(v) / \partial \lambda)\}^+$;
9:        where α is the update step.
10:       $\mu_{n+1} = \{\mu_n + \alpha(\partial L(v) / \partial \mu)\}^+$;
11:       $\gamma_{n+1} = \{\gamma_n + \alpha(\partial L(v) / \partial \gamma)\}^+$;
12:       where $\{z\}^+ = max(0, z)$.
13:       $x_{n+1} = min\{x_{n+1} - \alpha(\partial L(v) / \partial x), x_{n,max}\}$;
14:       $y_{n+1} = y_{n+1} - \alpha(\partial L(v) / \partial y)$;
15:    **end for**
16: **end for**
17:    $R_k = \log_2 \{1 + |h_k|^2 \exp(x_{Niter}) / \exp(y_{Niter})\}$.
       where h_k is the effective channel gain.
18:**end procedure**

Proving the optimization model in (9) is a convex optimization problem, amounts to proving the objective function is being a convex function and all of the constraint inequalities are being the convex set of these optimization variables. Since the left side of these constraint inequalities in (9) are the sum of exponential functions after transformation, we can conclude that these constraint inequalities are the convex sets of optimization variables x and y. Meanwhile, the logarithmic function is a kind of monotone increasing function and the objective function after variable substitution is a convex function on x and y. Therefore, we can prove that the problem in (9) is a convex optimization problem.

To solve the above-mentioned problem, we adopt the convex optimization algorithm to obtain the globally optimal solution of this log-convex problem. Combined with the characteristics of NOMA system, we draw Lagrange multipliers into each communication link and assume that λ, μ, γ denote the Lagrange dual variables of formulae C1, C2 and C3, respectively. The corresponding Lagrange dual function is shown as follows:

$$
\begin{aligned}
L(x, y, \lambda, \mu, \gamma) = & -\sum_{k=1}^{K} \ln(e^{x_k - y_k + \ln(|h_k|^2)}) \\
& + \lambda_k[|h_k|^{-2} e^{y_k - x_k}(2^{R_{target}} - 1) - 1] \\
& + \mu_k(P^{-1} e^{x_k} - 1) + \gamma_k(P^{-1} \sum_{i=1}^{K} e^{x_k} - 1)
\end{aligned}
\tag{10}
$$

Defining $v = \{x, y, \lambda, \mu, \gamma\}$ to express the optimization variables and Lagrange dual variables, we use grad $\nabla L(v)$ to iterate and update them until the algorithm converges. Detailed steps are given in Algorithm 1.

In Algorithm 1, we fix the total power of users and allocate it to each user according to their CSI by defining $x_k = p_k$, $y_k = |h_k|^2 \sum_{i=k+1}^{K} p_i + \sigma^2$ to initialize x_k and y_k, where $k = 1, 2, \ldots, K$. After the algorithm converges, we can obtain the optimal value of each user's power p_k and interference plus noise A_k through inverse the transformation. Finally, we use the Shannon Formula to compute each user's capacity.

4 Simulation Results

In this section, we investigate the performance of the proposed method to the NOMA power allocation problem. It should be noted that in simulations the user distances are fixed, we adopt the common path-loss model with pass-loss exponent $\theta = 2$ for a fading channel, where the mean value of each user's channel is 0 and whose variance is taken to be unity.

For comparison, we also consider OMA transmission as a reference scheme. In [13], we studied a kind of power allocation scheme in the TDMA system which requires K time slots to support K users, while NOMA can support K users during a single time slot. Thus, the achievable rate of user k in OMA system is given as

$$R_{k,OMA} = a(k)\log_2(1 + \frac{b(k)P|h_k|^2}{a(k)\sigma^2})$$ (11)

where $a(k)$ and $b(k)$ are the time division weighting coefficient and power allocation coefficient for user k, respectively, P is the total power of all users and $|h_k|^2$ is the k-th user effective channel gain. Then we assume that $a(k) = b(k)$, which yields a modified format as

$$R_{k,OMA} = a(k)\log_2(1 + \frac{P|h_k|^2}{\sigma^2})$$ (12)

The sum rate of OMA system is obtained via full search to meet the user rate requirements as well as to maximize the system capacity.

4.1 Convergence Verification

In [5], the KKT algorithm needs $2N_RN_T + 4$ and $2N_RN_T + 8$ iterations to calculate the value of minimum and maximum power coefficients in two users scenario, where N_R and N_T are the numbers of antennas equipped at the BS and mobile users, respectively. In this paper, we set that $N_T = 3$ and $N_R = 1$, thus the iteration number is 24 with KKT algorithm. In the proposed method, the calculation of the Lagrange dual variables λ, μ, γ, results of power allocation and rate for each user using less than 50 iterations for the three users' scenario. The results are shown in Figs. 1, 2, 3, 4 and 5, where the update step $\alpha = 0.1$.

Figures 1, 2 and 3 depict the convergence features of Lagrange dual variables λ, μ, γ. In Fig. 1, the value of lamda3 is always be zero due to which always being smaller than or equal to zero. In Fig. 3, the value of γ in each communication link is the same because γ is the dual variable of formula C3 in (9), which is a constraint of sum transmit power and is unrelated to an individual user power.

Figure 4 provides the characteristics of the convergent power allocation, where UE1 is the weakest user and UE3 is the strongest user, and it is clearly depicting that UE1 gets more power than others. UE 3 is allocated the lowest power, simultaneously. In Fig. 5, it is shown that UE1 has the lowest user rate because it is the weakest user and UE3 has the highest rate. Both of the power allocation and user rate have good convergent property.

In Fig. 6, the solid lines give the shapes of the target function R_k, where Capacity1 represents user one's capacity, and the remaining are the same. The dotted lines express the value of dual function for each user, where Lower Bound 1 represents the lower bound of dual function for user one. Since dual function gives the lowest bound of Lagrange function, which is always smaller than the target function R_k. Therefore, we can conclude that the solutions of our target function are in the feasibility region.

Furthermore, after those Lagrange dual variables λ, μ, γ converging, we substituted them into the original optimal model (9) and proved that all constraints are satisfied, which means that the algorithm we proposed is exact in calculation.

4.2   Comparison with OMA

In this subsection, we provide some simulation results to evaluate the system performance of the proposed power allocation algorithm. All the simulations are conducted by averaging 10^5 channel realizations to guarantee the accuracy of the proposed algorithm.

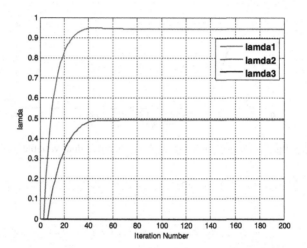

Fig. 1. Convergence behavior of Lagrange dual variable λ

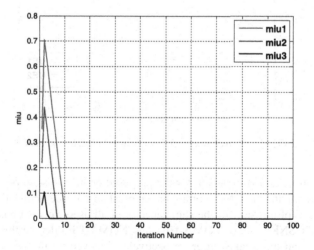

Fig. 2. Convergence behavior of Lagrange dual variable μ

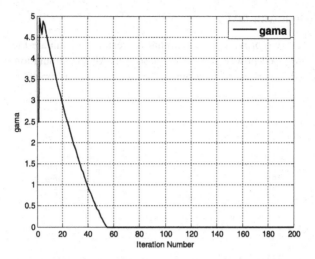

Fig. 3. Convergence behavior of Lagrange dual variable γ

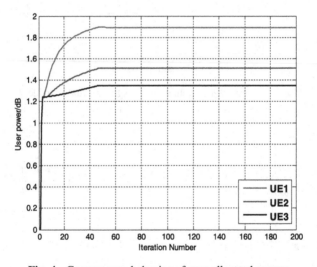

Fig. 4. Convergence behavior of user allocated powers

Figure 7 provides a comparison for the proposed NOMA system power allocation algorithm and traditional OMA communication scheme by depicting the achievable ergodic capacity of one user or the sum capacity of all users versus transmit signal to noise ratio (TX-SNR), where NOMA-UE1 and NOMA-UE3 denote the capacities of strongest user and the weakest user, respectively, achieved by the proposed NOMA. Similarly, OMA-UE1 and OMA-UE3 represent those for the OMA system; where NOMA Sum-Capacity and OMA Sum-Capacity represent the sum capacity in NOMA and OMA system, respectively. Figure 7 demonstrates that the performance of the NOMA system is better than the performance of an OMA system.

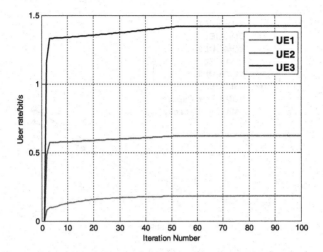

Fig. 5. Convergence behavior of user rates

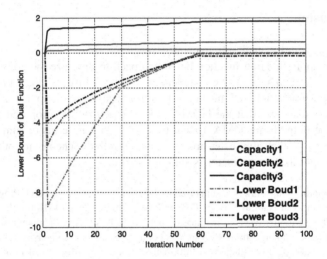

Fig. 6. The lower bound of dual function compared with target function R_k.

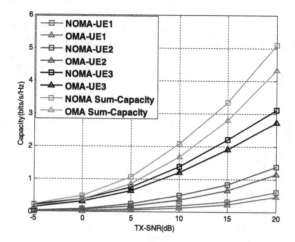

Fig. 7. The ergodic capacity of one user or the sum capacity versus TX-SNR for the proposed NOMA scheme compared with the OMA scheme.

5   Conclusions

This work proposed a dual sub-gradient descent algorithm based on Lagrange dual function and approximation-function based approach to optimize the power allocation for downlink NOMA systems. Numerical results illustrate that the proposed approximation-function based method can significantly speed up the convergence. Simulation results show that the NOMA system based on the proposed power allocation scheme outperforms OMA system by 20% – 25% in terms of sum capacity. It must be stressed that the extension of this proposed scheme to other difficult non-convex optimization problems is straightforward.

Acknowledgment. This work was supported by Huawei Innovation Research Program, the key project of the National Natural Science Foundation of China (No. 61431001), the 5G research program of China Mobile Research Institute (Grant No. [2015] 0615), the open research fund of National Mobile Communications Research Laboratory Southeast University (No. 2017D02), Key Laboratory of Cognitive Radio and Information Processing, Ministry of Education (Guilin University of Electronic Technology), the Foundation of Beijing Engineering and Technology Center for Convergence Networks and Ubiquitous Services, and Keysight. The Corresponding author is Dr. Xiaoming Dai.

References

1. Cover, T.M., Thomas, J.A.: Elements of Information Theory, pp. 155–183. Wiley, Tsinghua University Press, New York, Beijing (1990)
2. Dai, X., Chen, S., Sun, S., et al.: Successive interference cancelation amenable multiple access (SAMA) for future wireless communications. In: 2014 IEEE International Conference on Communication Systems (ICCS), pp. 222–226. IEEE (2014)

3. Dai, L., Wang, B., Yuan, Y., et al.: Non-orthogonal multiple access for 5G: solutions, challenges, opportunities, and future research trends. IEEE Commun. Mag. **53**(9), 74–81 (2015)
4. Oviedo, J.A., Sadjadpour, H.R.: A New NOMA approach for fair power allocation (2016). arXiv preprint arXiv:1605.00390
5. Wang, C.L., Chen, J.Y., Chen, Y.J.: Power allocation for a downlink non-orthogonal multiple access system. IEEE Wirel. Commun. Lett. **5**(5), 532–535 (2016)
6. Choi, J.: On the power allocation for MIMO-NOMA systems with layered transmissions. IEEE Trans. Wirel. Commun. **15**(5), 3226–3237 (2016)
7. Fang, F., Zhang, H., Cheng, J., et al.: Energy efficiency of resource scheduling for non-orthogonal multiple access (NOMA) wireless network. In: 2016 IEEE International Conference on Communications, ICC 2016, pp. 1–5. IEEE (2016)
8. Hanif, M.F., Ding, Z., Ratnarajah, T., et al.: A minorization-maximization method for optimizing sum rate in the downlink of non-orthogonal multiple access systems. IEEE Trans. Signal Process. **64**(1), 76–88 (2016)
9. Choi, J.: On the power allocation for a practical multiuser superposition scheme in NOMA systems. IEEE Commun. Lett. **20**(3), 438–441 (2016)
10. Tu, H.U., Jing, Z.H., Zhang, L., et al.: Power control algorithm based on convex optimization in cognitive ad hoc networks. J. Air Force Eng. Univ. (2012)
11. Zhang, H., Jiang, C., Mao, X., et al.: Interference-limited resource optimization in cognitive femtocells with fairness and imperfect spectrum sensing. IEEE Trans. Veh. Technol. **65**(3), 1 (2015)
12. Boyd, S., Vandenberghe, L.: Convex Optimization. Cambridge University Press, New York (2004)
13. Shariatpanahi, S.P., Khalaj, B.H., et al.: Power allocation scheme in time division multiple access distributed multiple-input multiple-output interference channels. IET Commun. **7**(5), 391–396 (2013)

A Differential QAM Scheme for Uplink Massive MIMO Systems

Peng Zhang[1(✉)], Shuaishuai Guo[2], and Haixia Zhang[2]

[1] School of Computer Engineering, Weifang University,
Weifang, People's Republic of China
sduzhangp@163.com
[2] School of Information Science and Engineering,
Shandong University, Jinan, People's Republic of China
guoshuai@mail.sdu.edu.cn, haixia.zhang@sdu.edu.cn

Abstract. An uplink massive MIMO system with a single antenna transmitter and a single receiver with a large number of antennas is considered. For this system we propose one new differential QAM scheme based on the division operation. Specially, by designing one looking-up table, we provide the transmitted differential QAM symbol generating process and the non-coherent detection method, which is only based on two adjacent received signals, while not using any instantaneous channel state information. At last the bit error rate (BER) performance is simulated and the simulation results have shown that the new proposed differential QAM scheme achieves much better performance than the other differential QAM or differential amplitude phase shift keying (DAPSK) schemes in uplink massive MIMO systems, especially for higher dimensional modulation constellations.

Keywords: Differential modulation · QAM · Massive MIMO

1 Introduction

Recently, in order to improve the transmission performance and spectrum efficiency, an increasing number of antennas are being used in the transmitter and receiver of wireless communications. In fact, massive multiple input multiple output (MIMO) has become the preferred technology for the development of 5G communications. By using hundreds of antennas, a significant antenna array gain can be achieved [1–4]. However, in massive MIMO systems, channel estimation is really one challenging problem. Because, the huge number of antennas greatly increases the complexity of the channel estimation algorithms. Furthermore, if using pilots to perform channel estimation, there may be no enough orthogonal pilot sequences available for use, and the pilot overhead will also become an important issue. Aiming at the channel estimation problem, there are two main research branches. One is trying to find the channel estimation algorithms with reduced pilot overhead, such as the recent literatures [5–7]. The other is to adopt non-coherence detection approaches, such as [8–12].

© ICST Institute for Computer Sciences, Social Informatics and Telecommunications Engineering 2018
K. Long et al. (Eds.): 5GWN 2017, LNICST 211, pp. 556–567, 2018.
https://doi.org/10.1007/978-3-319-72823-0_51

In this paper, we only focus on the non-coherence schemes for the uplink massive MIMO systems. Hereafter, let's give a brief overview of the research results in this area. In [8, 9], one non-coherent detection method for massive MIMO systems is proposed based on the concept of autocorrelation-based detection by using differential M-ary PSK constellation. In [10, 11], the non-coherent detection for uplink multi-users massive MIMO systems is proposed based on the received average signal energy, which need that the signal constellation for each user is different and should be further designed. Obviously, these studies of [8–11] did not involve the cases of QAM modulation. As we have known, in order to pursue higher spectrum efficiency, M-ary QAM constellation is often used. Especially, for the uplink massive MIMO Systems, the combined signal to noise ratio will be good enough to use QAM constellation. Therefore, it is of great significance to study the differential schemes based on QAM constellation for uplink massive MIMO systems. The latest research in [12] has addressed differential non-coherence detections in uplink massive MIMO systems by utilizing the channel statistics information, wherein the differential quadrature amplitude modulation (QAM) based on the finite group theory of [13] is adopted. But it is really regrettable that there exists the detection performance floor, especially when the number of receive antennas is not large enough, or higher dimensional QAM constellation is adopted.

In order to overcome the shortcomings of the current schemes for uplink massive MIMO systems, we proposed one new differential QAM scheme based on the division operation. At the transmitter, the transmit symbol is derived from the QAM constellation, and the next transmit symbol are generated by looking up one table based on the last transmit symbol and current input source information. At the receiver, the differential non-coherence detection is only based on two adjacent received signals while without considering any channel state information. The simulation results have shown that the new proposed differential QAM scheme achieves much better performance than the previous differential QAM scheme in [12] and other differential amplitude phase shift keying (DAPSK) [13].

In this paper, the following notations are adopted. Upper and lower bold face letters denote matrices and vectors, respectively. The superscripts T and H stand for the transpose and Hermitian operators, respectively. x with the top mark $-$, i.e., $\bar{x}$, denotes the conjugate of x. $j = \sqrt{-1}$. The capital letter of the Greek alphabet accounts for the symbol set.

2 System Model and Differential Design for Uplink Massive MIMO Systems

2.1 System Model

Here, the uplink massive MIMO system is considered which contains only one transmit antenna at the mobile station and a large number of receive antennas at the base station. In the following, N denotes the number of receive antennas. The transmitted symbols are generated from one M-ary QAM constellation, which denoted as $\mathbb{C}_M$. h_{it} denotes the channel gain between the transmit antenna and the i-th receive antenna at the t-th time instant, which is supposed to be independent and identically distributed, and satisfy the complex normal distribution with zero mean and one variance, i.e., $h_{it} \sim CN(0,1)$. And the channel vector at the t-th time instant is defined as $\mathbf{h}_t = [h_{1t}, h_{2t}, \ldots, h_{Nt}]$.

At the receiver, the received signals at two adjacent t-th and $(t+1)$-th time instants could be written as

$$\mathbf{y}_t = s_t \mathbf{h}_t + \mathbf{n}_t \tag{1}$$

$$\mathbf{y}_{t+1} = s_{t+1} \mathbf{h}_{t+1} + \mathbf{n}_{t+1} \tag{2}$$

where $s_t \in \mathbb{C}_M$ and $s_{t+1} \in \mathbb{C}_M$ denote the transmit modulation symbols at the t-th and $(t+1)$-th time instant, respectively; $\mathbf{y}_t = [y_{1t}, y_{2t}, \ldots, y_{Nt}]$, $\mathbf{y}_{t+1} = [y_{1t+1}, y_{2t+1}, \ldots, y_{Nt+1}]$ with $y_{it}, y_{it+1}, i = 1, 2, \ldots, N$ denoting the received signal from the i-th receive antenna at the t-th and $(t+1)$-th time instant, respectively; $\mathbf{n}_t = [n_{1t}, n_{2t}, \ldots, n_{Nt}]$, $\mathbf{n}_{t+1} = [n_{1t+1}, n_{2t+1}, \ldots, n_{Nt+1}]$ with $n_{it}, n_{it+1}, i = 1, 2, \ldots, N$ denoting the additive white Gaussian noise (AWGN) with mean zero and variance σ^2 received from the i-th receive antenna at the t-th and $(t+1)$-th time instant, respectively. In order to achieve the non-coherent signal detection without the need of channel estimation, here we assume that the channel remains unchanged at the two adjacent time instants, i.e., $\mathbf{h}_t = \mathbf{h}_{t+1}$.

2.2 Differential Design for Uplink Massive MIMO Systems

From (1) and (2), we have

$$
\begin{aligned}
\frac{\mathbf{y}_{t+1}\mathbf{y}_{t+1}^H}{\mathbf{y}_t\mathbf{y}_{t+1}^H} &= \frac{(s_{t+1}\mathbf{h}_{t+1} + \mathbf{n}_{t+1})(s_{t+1}\mathbf{h}_{t+1} + \mathbf{n}_{t+1})^H}{(s_t\mathbf{h}_t + \mathbf{n}_t)(s_{t+1}\mathbf{h}_{t+1} + \mathbf{n}_{t+1})^H} \\
&= \frac{s_{t+1}\bar{s}_{t+1}\mathbf{h}_{t+1}\mathbf{h}_{t+1}^H + s_{t+1}\mathbf{h}_{t+1}\mathbf{n}_{t+1}^H + \bar{s}_{t+1}\mathbf{n}_{t+1}\mathbf{h}_{t+1}^H + \mathbf{n}_{t+1}\mathbf{n}_{t+1}^H}{s_t\bar{s}_{t+1}\mathbf{h}_t\mathbf{h}_{t+1}^H + s_t\mathbf{h}_t\mathbf{n}_{t+1}^H + \bar{s}_{t+1}\mathbf{n}_t\mathbf{h}_{t+1}^H + \mathbf{n}_t\mathbf{n}_{t+1}^H}
\end{aligned}
\tag{3}
$$

Note that, when the number of receive antennas is very large, it could be obtained that

$$\lim_{N \to \infty} \frac{s_t\mathbf{h}_t\mathbf{n}_{t+1}^H + \bar{s}_{t+1}\mathbf{n}_t\mathbf{h}_{t+1}^H + \mathbf{n}_t\mathbf{n}_{t+1}^H}{N} = 0 \tag{4}$$

$$\lim_{N \to \infty} \frac{s_{t+1}\mathbf{h}_{t+1}\mathbf{n}_{t+1}^H + \bar{s}_{t+1}\mathbf{n}_{t+1}\mathbf{h}_{t+1}^H}{N} = 0 \tag{5}$$

$$\lim_{N \to \infty} \frac{\mathbf{n}_{t+1}\mathbf{n}_{t+1}^H}{N} = \sigma^2 \tag{6}$$

Then, with the massive receive antennas as well as $\mathbf{h}_t = \mathbf{h}_{t+1}$ (3) can be approximately rewritten as

$$\frac{\mathbf{y}_{t+1}\mathbf{y}_{t+1}^H - N\sigma^2}{\mathbf{y}_t\mathbf{y}_{t+1}^H} \approx \frac{s_{t+1}\bar{s}_{t+1}\mathbf{h}_{t+1}\mathbf{h}_{t+1}^H}{s_t\bar{s}_{t+1}\mathbf{h}_t\mathbf{h}_{t+1}^H} = \frac{s_{t+1}}{s_t} \tag{7}$$

According to the received signals (1) and (2), (7) has given one non-coherent signal detection method. In fact, there is another non-coherent signal detection method as follows.

$$\frac{\mathbf{y}_{t+1}\mathbf{y}_t^H}{\mathbf{y}_t\mathbf{y}_t^H - N\sigma^2} \approx \frac{s_{t+1}\bar{s}_t\mathbf{h}_t\mathbf{h}_t^H}{s_t\bar{s}_t\mathbf{h}_t\mathbf{h}_t^H} = \frac{s_{t+1}}{s_t} \tag{8}$$

Here, the transmitted differential constellation is denoted as $\mathbb{C}_M$ with $s_t \in \mathbb{C}_M$ and $s_{t+1} \in \mathbb{C}_M$. For simplicity, we use a special mapping operator $F[\bullet]$ to denote differential operation. Specially, $s_{t+1} = F[d_t, s_t]$ with $d_t \in \mathbb{C}_M$ denoting the transmit source symbol, which carries the source information bits. On the basis of (7), our hope is to find one differential operator $F[\bullet]$ to achieve the source information detection directly only based on two adjacent receive signals y_t and y_{t+1} while without considering any channel state information. That is to say, for the differential operator $s_{t+1} = F[d_t, s_t]$, it should have one corresponding reverse differential operator denoted as $d_t = F^{-1}[s_{t+1}, s_t]$. According to (7), the reverse differential operator $d_t = F^{-1}[s_{t+1}, s_t]$ should be based on the division operation $\frac{s_{t+1}}{s_t}$, i.e., the transmit source symbol d_t should be only determined by the division $\frac{s_{t+1}}{s_t}$. For the sake of clarity, we define the reverse differential operation as $d_t = F^{-1}[s_{t+1}, s_t] = F^{-1}\left[\frac{s_{t+1}}{s_t}\right]$.

It must be noted that for the traditional differential M-ary PSK constellation [8, 9], $s_{t+1} = F[d_t, s_t] = d_t \cdot s_t$. However, for the new differential QAM constellation $s_{t+1} = F[d_t, s_t]$ will represent a more general mapping operation instead of the multiplication operation.

In order to ensure the correct detection, the operation $d_t = F^{-1}[s_{t+1}, s_t] = F^{-1}\left[\frac{s_{t+1}}{s_t}\right]$ should satisfy the following properties for any complex modulation symbols $s_t \in \mathbb{C}_M$, $s_t' \in \mathbb{C}_M$, $s_{t+1} \in \mathbb{C}_M$ and $s_{t+1}' \in \mathbb{C}_M$.

$$\text{If } \frac{s_{t+1}}{s_t} = \frac{s_{t+1}'}{s_t'}, F^{-1}\left[\frac{s_{t+1}}{s_t}\right] = F^{-1}\left[\frac{s_{t+1}'}{s_t'}\right]. \tag{9}$$

$$\text{If } s_{t+1} \neq s_{t+1}', F^{-1}\left[\frac{s_{t+1}}{s_t}\right] \neq F^{-1}\left[\frac{s_{t+1}'}{s_t}\right]. \tag{10}$$

(9) means that the same division results will generate the same differential detection results. While (10) expresses that with the same t-th transmit symbol s_t, different input source symbols will produce different $(t + 1)$-th transmit symbols. At this point, as long as we can find a mapping operator $s_{t+1} = F[d_t, s_t]$ to meet (9) and (10), then we can achieve the non-coherent detection on the base of (7).

In the following section, we will present the detailed differential QAM design process based on (7), (9) and (10).

3 Differential QAM Design for Uplink Massive MIMO Systems

3.1 Differential QAM Design

For the sake of clarity, M-ary QAM constellation $\mathbb{C}_M$ are listed as $\mathbb{C}_M = \{g_1, g_2, \ldots, g_M\}$. Furthermore, one looking-up table T_M with M rows and M columns is constructed to express the differential operation with the properties of (9) and (10), and $T_M(u, v)$ stands for the element of the u-th, $u = 1, 2, \ldots, M$ row and the v-th, $v = 1, 2, \ldots, M$ column of T_M. And then, the reverse differential operator $d_t = F^{-1}\left[\frac{s_{t+1}}{s_t}\right]$ could be represented by $T_M(u, v) = g_x$ with $s_{t+1} = g_u$, $s_t = g_v$ and $d_t = g_x$, i.e., $g_x = F^{-1}\left[\frac{g_u}{g_v}\right]$. With the help of such definitions, the differential properties (7), (9) and (10) could be further rewritten as

$$T_M(u, v) = i, \text{ if } F^{-1}\left[\frac{g_u}{g_v}\right] = g_i \tag{11}$$

$$T_M(u, v) = T_M(u', v'), \text{if } \frac{g_u}{g_v} = \frac{g_{u'}}{g_{v'}} \tag{12}$$

$$T_M(u, v) \neq T_M(u', v), \text{ if } g_u \neq g_{u'} \tag{13}$$

According to (13), we could know that each symbol of $\mathbb{C}_M = \{g_1, g_2, \ldots, g_M\}$ will appear in each column of T_M and will appear only once. Therefore, for given g_i, there are a total of M different combinations of $\{g_u, g_v\}$ satisfying $F^{-1}\left[\frac{g_u}{g_v}\right] = g_i$. Obviously, these M different divisions should be as close as possible in order to combat the incorporated noise interference in the transmission process. In other words, if the two different while very close divisions mapped to different source symbols, the result is very small noise pollution may cause the demodulation error. We define this design idea as the nearest group theory.

In order to facilitate the practical design process, a heuristic algorithm is designed based on the nearest group theory. Firstly, define one set containing all the division elements $\frac{g_u}{g_v}$, i.e., $\mathbb{Q} = \left\{\frac{g_u}{g_v} \middle| g_u \in \mathbb{C}_M, g_v \in \mathbb{C}_M\right\}$. It should be noted that for two different pairs $\{g_u, g_v\}$ and $\{g_{u'}, g_{v'}\}$ with the same division result, i.e., $\frac{g_u}{g_v} = \frac{g_{u'}}{g_{v'}}$, they will be consider one element in $\mathbb{Q}$. Correspondingly, one counting number set is define as $\mathbb{N} = \{n(g_u/g_v) | g_u \in \mathbb{C}_M, g_v \in \mathbb{C}_M\}$ with its element $n(g_u/g_v)$ denoting the total number of $\{g_u, g_v\}$ with the same division result. We further define one counting vector $\mathbf{c} = [c_1, c_2, \ldots, c_n]$ with $c_i, i = 1, 2, \ldots, M$ denoting the number of $T_M(u, v) = i$ in the looking-up table T_M, which will be equal to M after finishing the construction of T_M.

Define the group set $\Omega_{g_i} = \left\{ \frac{g_u}{g_v} \middle| F^{-1}\left[\frac{g_u}{g_v}\right] = g_i, g_u \in \mathbb{C}_M, g_v \in \mathbb{C}_M \right\}$.

Without loss of generality and for simplicity, we define $g_1 = \varepsilon = 1$, and then the heuristic algorithm to design the reverse differential table T_M corresponding to (11) is presented as follows.

Step 1: Set $c_i = 0$ and $\Omega_{g_i} = \emptyset$, $i = 1, 2, \ldots, M$ with $\emptyset$ denoting empty set. Let $T_M(u, v) = 0$ with 0 denoting an invalid symbol; $F^{-1}\left[\frac{g_u}{g_v}\right] = 0$ denotes that the division $\frac{g_u}{g_v}$ has not been assign one valid differential symbol.

Step 2: Examine symbol pair $\{g_u, g_v\}$ one by one. If $\frac{g_u}{g_v} = g_i$, let $T_M(u, v) = i$, $c_i = c_i + 1$ and $\Omega_{g_i} = \Omega_{g_i} \cup \{g_i\}$, i.e., $F^{-1}\left[\frac{g_u}{g_v}\right] = g_i$.

Step 3: Find one valid $\frac{g_{u'}}{g_{v'}}$ and its nearest group set Ω_{g_i}, do differential symbol assignment for $\frac{g_{u'}}{g_{v'}} \neq g_i$.

(A) Divide the division set $\mathbb{Q} = \left\{ \frac{g_u}{g_v} \middle| g_u \in \mathbb{C}_M, g_v \in \mathbb{C}_M \right\}$ into two subset, one is $\mathbb{Q}_Y$ with its elements having been assigned one differential symbol successfully, the other is $\mathbb{Q}_N$ with its elements having not completed assignment. Correspondingly, the number set $\mathbb{N} = \{n(g_u/g_v) | g_u \in \mathbb{C}_M, g_v \in \mathbb{C}_M\}$ is also divided into two subsets with $\mathbb{N}_Y$ and $\mathbb{N}_N$ corresponding to $\mathbb{Q}_Y$ and $\mathbb{Q}_N$, respectively.

(B) For each $\frac{g_u}{g_v} \in \mathbb{Q}_N$, determine the nearest group set Ω_{g_i} close to $\frac{g_u}{g_v}$, and calculate the minimum distance between $\frac{g_u}{g_v}$ and the nearest group set Ω_{g_i} as follows:

$$\Omega_{g_i} = \arg \min_{g_x \in \mathbb{C}_M M - c_x \geq n(g_u/g_v)} \left(\min_{a_y \in \Omega_{g_x}} \left| \frac{g_u}{g_v} - a_y \right| \right) \tag{14}$$

$$d\left(\frac{g_u}{g_v}\right) = \min_{g_x \in \mathbb{C}_M M - c_x \geq n(g_u/g_v)} \left(\min_{a_y \in \Omega_{g_x}} \left| \frac{g_u}{g_v} - a_y \right| \right) \tag{15}$$

In (14), the condition $M - c_x \geq n(g_u/g_v)$ means that the total number of $\{g_u, g_v\}$ with the same division result $(n(g_u/g_v))$ should be no more than the number of symbol pair $\{g_u, g_v\}$ that can be accepted by $\Omega_{g_x}(M - c_x)$.

(C) Find one valid $\frac{g_{u'}}{g_{v'}} \in \mathbb{Q}_N$ and its nearest group set Ω_{g_i} by examining (14) and (15), specially,

$$\left[\frac{g_{u'}}{g_{v'}}, \Omega_{g_i}\right] = \arg \min_{\frac{g_u}{g_v} \in \mathbb{Q}_N} \left(\min_{g_x \in \mathbb{C}_M M - c_x \geq n(g_u/g_v)} \left(\min_{d_y \in \Omega_{g_x}} \left| \frac{g_u}{g_v} - d_y \right| \right) \right) \tag{16}$$

Which further satisfy the following condition (17).

Define $\mathbf{c}' = [c_1', c_2', \ldots, c_n'] = \mathbf{c} = [c_1, c_2, \ldots, c_n]$, and update $c_i' = c_i + n(g_{u'}/g_{v'})$. Define $\mathbb{N}_N' = \mathbb{N}_N \setminus \{n(g_{u'}/g_{v'})\}$, i.e., $\mathbb{N}_N'$ is formed by deleting element $n(g_{u'}/g_{v'})$ from $\mathbb{N}_N$. And then, for all elements $n_p \in \mathbb{N}_N'$, $p = 1, 2, \ldots, P_N$ with P_N denoting the total element number of $\mathbb{N}_N'$, we should be able to find P_N elements $\check{c}_p, p = 1, 2, \ldots, P_N$ in $\mathbf{c}' = \begin{bmatrix} c_1', c_2', \ldots, c_n' \end{bmatrix}$ to satisfy

$$M - \check{c}_p \geq n_p \tag{17}$$

Condition (17) can ensure the convergence of the algorithm.

(D) For the valid selection $\left[\frac{g_{u'}}{g_{v'}}, \Omega_{g_i} \right]$, by examining symbol pair $\{g_u, g_v\}$ one by one, if $\frac{g_u}{g_v} = \frac{g_{u'}}{g_{v'}}$, let $T_M(u, v) = i$, i.e., $F^{-1} \left[\frac{g_u}{g_v} \right] = g_i$. After finishing assignment, update $c_i = c_i + n(g_{u'}/g_{v'})$ and $\Omega_{g_i} = \Omega_{g_i} \cup \left\{ \frac{g_{u'}}{g_{v'}} \right\}$.

Return to step 3 to re-execute until all elements of table T_M are assigned successfully.

3.2   Simplified Differential Design for Square QAM

In this sub-section, we mainly consider a square M-ary QAM constellation with $M = 2^m$, just because square M-ary QAM constellation has a wide range of practical applications, and has very good symmetrical properties. From the above analysis of the nearest group theory we will conclude that these symmetrical properties are of great significance to simplify the differential operation design.

As we have known, for a square M-ary QAM constellation with $M = 2^m$, if $g_x \in \mathbb{C}_M$, we have $jg_x \in \mathbb{C}_M$, $-g_x \in \mathbb{C}_M$ and $-jg_x \in \mathbb{C}_M$. It is not difficult to know that the division $\frac{g_u}{g_v}$ also have these symmetrical properties. Therefore, it is reasonable to assume that the differential operation also have these symmetrical properties, specifically, we have

$$
\begin{aligned}
F^{-1} \left[\frac{g_u}{g_v} \right] = g_x, \quad F^{-1} \left[j \frac{g_u}{g_v} \right] = jg_x, \\
F^{-1} \left[-\frac{g_u}{g_v} \right] = -g_x, \quad F^{-1} \left[-j \frac{g_u}{g_v} \right] = -jg_x
\end{aligned}
\tag{18}
$$

Therefore, in the heuristic algorithm to design the differential table T_M, we could only focus on a quarter of division elements to complete all division elements assignment. More details could be found in the following design examples.

3.3   Differential 16QAM Design Example

Here, the 16QAM constellation set $\mathbb{C}_{16}$ is defined as

$$
\begin{aligned}
\mathbb{C}_{16} = \{ & g_1 = \varepsilon = 1, \quad g_2 = 3, \quad\; g_3 = 2 + 1j, \; g_4 = 2 - 1j, \\
& g_5 = jg_1, \quad g_6 = jg_2, \quad g_7 = jg_3, \quad g_8 = jg_4, \\
& g_9 = -g_1, \quad g_A = -g_2, \quad g_B = -g_3, \quad g_C = -g_4, \\
& g_D = -jg_1, \; g_E = -jg_2, \; g_F = -jg_3, \; g_G = -jg_4 \}
\end{aligned}
\tag{19}
$$

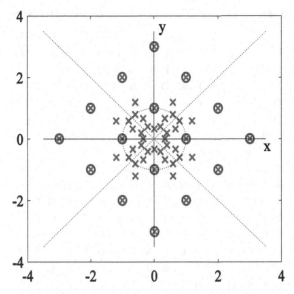

Fig. 1. 16QAM constellation ("○") and $\frac{g_u}{g_v}$ results ("×")

herein, A = 10, B = 11, C = 12, D = 13, E = 14, F = 15, G = 16 .

As shown in Fig. 1, the mark "○" denotes the symbols of 16QAM set $\mathbb{C}_{16}$, and the mark "×" accounts for the division results of $\frac{g_u}{g_v}$ with $g_u \in \mathbb{C}_{16}, g_v \in \mathbb{C}_{16}$.

Based on symmetrical properties of Fig. 1, we only focus on a quarter of plane located between the two straight lines $y = \pm x$ with $x > 0$. In which there are only 4 baseband 16QAM symbols $\{g_1 = \varepsilon = 1, g_2 = 3, g_3 = 2 + 1j, g_4 = 2 - 1j\}$ and 13 division symbols. And hereby the design complexity is really very small. Once one division symbol in the focus area has completed assignment, we could use (18) to realize the other symmetric division symbols' assignment.

By carry out the heuristic algorithm presented in sub-Sect. 3.1, the reverse differential looking-up table T_{16} is constructed, as demonstrated in Table 1.

It should be noted that Table 1 is the reverse differential looking-up table corresponding to $F^{-1}\left[\frac{g_u}{g_v}\right] = g_x$. In the practical applications one differential looking-up table corresponding to $s_{t+1} = F[d_t, s_t]$ could be also constructed according to $F^{-1}\left[\frac{g_u}{g_v}\right] = g_x$, which will be used to accelerate the transmitted differential symbols generation.

3.4 Differential 64QAM Design Example

Here, the 64QAM constellation set $\mathbb{C}_{64}$ is defined as

$$\mathbb{C}_{64} = \{\mathbb{C}_{16}^1, j * \mathbb{C}_{16}^1, -1 * \mathbb{C}_{16}^1, -j * \mathbb{C}_{16}^1\} \tag{20}$$

Table 1. Reverse differential looking-up Table (16QAM).

	1	2	3	4	5	6	7	8	9	A	B	C	D	E	F	G
1	1	4	2	2	D	G	E	E	9	C	A	A	5	8	6	6
2	2	1	3	3	E	D	F	F	A	9	B	B	6	5	7	7
3	3	2	1	8	F	E	D	4	B	A	9	G	7	6	5	C
4	4	3	G	1	G	F	C	D	C	B	8	9	8	7	4	5
5	5	8	6	6	1	4	2	2	D	G	E	E	9	C	A	A
6	6	5	7	7	2	1	3	3	E	D	F	F	A	9	B	B
7	7	6	5	C	3	2	1	8	F	E	D	4	B	A	9	G
8	8	7	4	5	4	3	G	1	G	F	C	D	C	B	8	9
9	9	C	A	A	5	8	6	6	1	4	2	2	D	G	E	E
A	A	9	B	B	6	5	7	7	2	1	3	3	E	D	F	F
B	B	A	9	G	7	6	5	C	3	2	1	8	F	E	D	4
C	C	B	8	9	8	7	4	5	4	3	G	1	G	F	C	D
D	D	G	E	E	9	C	A	A	5	8	6	6	1	4	2	2
E	E	D	F	F	A	9	B	B	6	5	7	7	2	1	3	3
F	F	E	D	4	B	A	9	G	7	6	5	C	3	2	1	8
G	G	F	C	D	C	B	8	9	8	7	4	5	4	3	G	1

with

$$\mathbb{C}_{16}^1 = \{g_1 = \varepsilon = 1, \ g_2 = 3, \ g_3 = 5, \ g_4 = 7,$$
$$g_5 = 2 + 1j, g_6 = 2 - 1j, g_7 = 4 + 1j, g_8 = 4 - 1j,$$
$$g_9 = 6 + 1j, g_A = 6 - 1j, g_B = 3 + 2j, g_C = 3 - 2j,$$
$$g_D = 5 + 2j, g_E = 5 - 2j, \ g_F = 4 + 3j, g_G = 4 - 3j\} \tag{21}$$

The reverse differential looking-up table for 64QAM is constructed as shown in Table 2. It should be noted that Table 2 only provides a part of elements, just because other elements could be derived from these elements according to (18). For example,

$$F^{-1}\begin{bmatrix} g_{40} \\ g_{18} \end{bmatrix} = F^{-1}\begin{bmatrix} -1 * g_8 \\ j * g_2 \end{bmatrix} = F^{-1}\begin{bmatrix} j\dfrac{g_8}{g_2} \end{bmatrix} = jF^{-1}\begin{bmatrix} g_8 \\ g_2 \end{bmatrix}.$$

4 Simulation Results

In this section, the BER (Bit Error Rate) performances of the new differential 16QAM and 64QAM are simulated over Rayleigh fading channels. Gray mapping is adopted for the transmitted 16QAM and 64QAM constellations. The simulation results are shown in Figs. 2 and 3, in which N denotes the number of receive antennas. "Old DQAM", "New DQAM" and "DAPSK" represent the differential QAM schemes provided in [12], the new proposed differential QAM schemes and the differential amplitude phase shift keying (DAPSK) schemes [12, 14], respectively.

Table 2. Part of reverse differential looking-up Table (64QAM).

	1	2	3	4	5	6	7	8	9	A	B	C	D	E	F	G
1	1	11	16	16	12	13	14	14	16	16	13	13	16	16	12	13
2	2	1	7	9	2	2	2	2	11	11	7	7	7	7	10	10
3	3	12	1	4	6	5	3	3	3	3	14	14	5	5	14	15
4	4	8	6	1	11	11	10	10	2	2	2	2	9	9	15	14
5	5	4	13	14	1	30	6	11	12	15	3	25	12	30	7	28
6	6	5	12	15	63	1	11	6	15	12	57	3	62	12	61	7
7	7	2	2	7	3	3	1	7	5	7	4	32	2	10	6	27
8	8	3	3	8	4	4	7	1	7	5	64	4	10	2	59	6
9	9	13	4	2	7	16	9	12	1	6	8	15	4	13	8	32
A	10	15	5	3	16	7	12	9	6	1	15	8	13	4	64	8
B	11	9	10	12	13	24	4	29	10	13	1	21	6	27	2	21
C	12	10	11	13	56	12	61	4	13	10	53	1	59	6	53	2
D	13	6	8	5	14	25	5	15	4	9	11	28	1	15	3	25
E	14	7	9	6	57	15	15	5	9	4	60	11	15	1	57	3
F	15	14	15	10	10	22	8	32	8	30	6	26	3	24	1	20
G	16	16	14	11	53	10	64	8	62	8	58	6	56	3	52	1

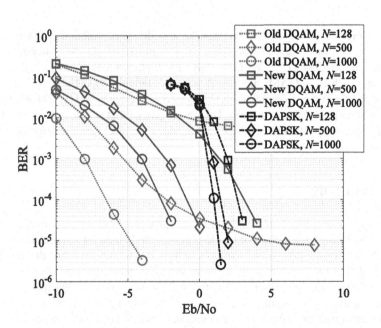

Fig. 2. BER performance of differential 16QAM and 16DAPSK

From Fig. 2 we could know that new designed differential 16QAM is superior to DAPSK schemes [12, 14]. Furthermore, our design method could be easily extend to higher dimensional modulation constellations, such as 64QAM, which is really difficult for the traditional DAPSK schemes.

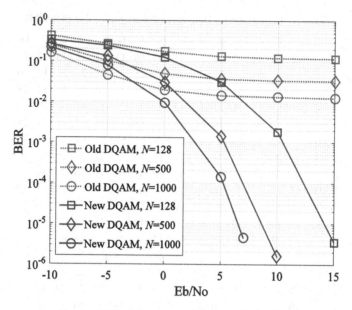

Fig. 3. BER performance of differential 64QAM.

From Figs. 2 and 3, we also see that the new designed differential QAM schemes completely eliminates the performance floor compared with the differential QAM schemes provided in [12, 13]. Especially, for higher dimensional modulation constellations, such as 64QAM, the new designed differential QAM schemes are greatly superior to that of the differential 64QAM schemes presented in [12, 13] and the latter has very serious performance floor. This result proves that the new differential QAM schemes are very suitable for the applications in the next generation wireless communications.

5   Conclusions

In this paper, a new differential QAM scheme is proposed for the uplink massive MIMO systems. Specially, one looking-up table is constructed based on the division operation between two transmitted QAM symbols, which is used to generate the transmitted differential QAM symbols at the transmitter and to carry out the non-coherent detection at the receiver. The new differential detector only uses two adjacent received signals without requiring any channel state information. And hereby, there is no so-called phenomena of performance floor, while the performance floor really exists and may by very harmful for the newly presented differential QAM schemes in [12]. Furthermore, the new differential QAM schemes provides a better flexibility compared with the traditional DAPSK schemes, especially for higher dimensional constellations. Taken together, the new differential QAM schemes are especially suitable for massive MIMO systems to achieve great performance while without the requirement of large amounts of pilots and complicated channel estimations.

Acknowledgment. This research was supported by National Natural Science Foundation of China (No. 61471269, 61622111, 61671278, 61501461, 61601269), Doctoral Scientific Research Fund Project of Weifang University (No. 2014BS12), Weifang Science and Technology Development Plan Project (No. 2014GX021), and Shangdong Province Young and Middle-Aged Scientists Research Awards Fund (No. BS2013DX040).

References

1. Xiang, G., Edfors, O., Rusek, F., Tufvesson, F.: Massive MIMO performance evaluation based on measured propagation data. IEEE Trans. Wirel. Commun. **14**(7), 3899–3911 (2015). IEEE Press, New York
2. Jin, S., Liang, X., Wong, K.-K., Gao, X., Zhu, Q.: Ergodic rate analysis for multipair massive MIMO two-way relay networks. IEEE Trans. Wirel. Commun. **14**(3), 1480–1491 (2015). IEEE Press, New York
3. Lu, L., Li, G., Swindlehurst, A.L., Ashikhmin, A., Zhang, R.: An overview of massive MIMO: benefits and challenges. IEEE J. Sel. Top. Sig. Process. **8**(5), 742–758 (2014). IEEE Press, New York
4. Bogale, T.E., Le, L.B.: Massive MIMO and Millimeter Wave for 5G Wireless HetNet: Potentials and Challenges. IEEE Vehicular Technology Magazine (to appear)
5. Wen, C.K., Jin, S., Wong, K.K., Chen, J.C.: Channel estimation for massive MIMO using gaussian-mixture Bayesian learning. IEEE Trans. Wirel. Commun. **14**(3), 1356–1368 (2015). IEEE Press, New York
6. Ngo, B.Q., Larsson, E.G.: EVD-based channel estimation in multicell multiuser MIMO systems with very large antenna arrays. In: IEEE International Conference on Acoustics, Speech and Signal Processing, pp. 3249–3252. IEEE Press, New York (2012)
7. Wang, R., Chen, Y., Tan, H.: Data-assisted channel estimation for uplink massive MIMO systems. In: IEEE Global Communications Conference, pp. 3766–3771. IEEE Press, New York (2014)
8. Schenk, A., Fischer, R.F.H.: Noncoherent detection in massive MIMO systems. In: International ITG Workshop on Smart Antennas, pp. 1–8. IEEE Press, New York (2013)
9. Yammine, G., Fischer, R.F.H.: Soft-decision decoding in noncoherent massive MIMO systems. In: International ITG Workshop on Smart Antennas, pp. 53–59. IEEE Press, New York (2016)
10. Manolakos, A., Chowdhury, M., Goldsmith, A.J.: Constellation design in noncoherent massive SIMO systems. In: IEEE Global Communications Conference, pp. 3690–3695. IEEE Press, New York (2014)
11. Chowdhury, M., Manolakos, A., Goldsmith, A.J.: Design and Performance of Noncoherent Massive SIMO Systems. In: Annual Conference on Information Sciences and Systems, pp. 1–6. IEEE Press, New York (2014)
12. Kong, D., Xia, X.-G., Jiang, T.: A differential QAM detection in uplink massive MIMO systems. IEEE Trans. Wirel. Commun. **15**(9), 6371–6383 (2016)
13. Egri, R.G., Homgan, F.A.: A finite group of complex integers and its application to differentially coherent detection of QAM signals. IEEE Trans. Inf. Theory **40**(1), 216–219 (1994). IEEE Press, New York
14. Adachi, F., Sawahashi, M.: Decision feedback differential detection of differentially encoded 16APSK signals. IEEE Trans. Commun. **44**(4), 416–418 (1996). IEEE Press, New York

REFF: REliable and Fast Forwarding in Vehicular Ad-hoc Network

Daxin Tian[1,4,5,6(✉)], Ziyi Dai[1,4], Kunxian Zheng[1,4], Jianshan Zhou[1,4],
Xuting Duan[1,4], Peng Guo[2], Hui Rong[2], Wenyang Wang[2],
and Haijun Zhang[3]

[1] Beijing Advanced Innovation Center for Big Data and Brain Computing,
Beihang University, XueYuan Road No. 37, Beijing 100191, China
dtian@buaa.edu.cn
[2] China Automotive Technology and Research Center,
Automotive Engineering Research Institute,
East Xianfeng Road No. 68, Tianjin 300300, China
[3] School of Computer and Communication Engineering,
University of Science and Technology Beijing,
XueYuan Road No. 30, Beijing 100083, China
[4] Beijing Key Laboratory for Cooperative Vehicle Infrastructure Systems
and Safety Control, School of Transportation Science and Engineering,
Beihang University, XueYuan Road No. 37, Beijing 100191, China
[5] Jiangsu Province Collaborative Innovation Center of Modern Urban
Traffic Technologies, Si Pai Lou. 2, Nanjing 210096, China
[6] Key Lab of Urban ITS Technology Optimization and Integration,
The Ministry of Public Security of China, Hefei 230088, China

Abstract. Vehicular Ad-Hoc Network (VANET) has emerged as an increasingly dominant technology for future connected vehicle and vehicular networks, where the focus of the development of VANET lies in the standardization of message transmission and dissemination via multi-hop broadcasting. However, the current communication protocols concerning VANET face many challenges, including data flooding and collision, transmission delay and other problems. Most of the challenges are closely related to next-hop selection. Therefore, this paper proposes a new routing protocol named REliable and Fast Forwarding (REFF) to optimize the selection of nodes in VANET. In this protocol, node filtering and node evaluation are two main steps. Distance between previous node and candidate node, relative velocity between previous node and candidate nodes, included angle between direction of target node's velocity and candidate node's velocity and transmission power of candidate node are adopted as indexes to help select a specific node as the next hop using Technique for Order of Preference by Similarity to Ideal Solution (TOPSIS). By using this technique, the number of candidates as next-hop is largely reduced, avoiding the data flooding and resulting transmission relay. In addition, simulations based on experiments are done to verify the feasibility. The results show that message achieves a faster and more reliable transmission using REFF.

Keywords: VANET · Multi-hop broadcasting · Next-hop selection · TOPSIS

© ICST Institute for Computer Sciences, Social Informatics and Telecommunications Engineering 2018
K. Long et al. (Eds.): 5GWN 2017, LNICST 211, pp. 568–580, 2018.
https://doi.org/10.1007/978-3-319-72823-0_52

1 Introduction

Fifth Generation Mobile Networks (5G) has emerged as a more advanced way in telecommunications with faster speed, broader coverage and higher capacity. In recent years, 5G have also extended its use in the field of connected vehicles [4]. 5G serve as an important kind of networking wireless technology in Vehicular Ad-hoc Network (VANET). Cooperative transmission is an effective approach for vehicular networks to improve wireless transmission capacity and reliability in the fifth-generation small-cells networks, as denser and smaller cells are expected to provide a higher transmission rate for users [6, 19]. 5G technologies also propose a device-to-device (D2D) approach for direct and short-range communications between vehicles since the data transmission is easily influenced by surrounding environment. D2D communications can also enhance the communication capacity by allowing nearby devices to establish links, thusly accommodating a large number of data-heavy mobile devices and multiapplication services to face the challenge of dealing with an ever-increasing demand of mobile traffic [18]. Therefore, 5G can be adopted as a critical network technology supporting VANET.

Vehicular Ad-hoc Network (VANET) is an embranchment of Mobile Ad-hoc Network (MANET), which is the spontaneous establishment of a wireless network for the purpose of real-time data transmission and exchange in the fields of vehicle networks. In recent years, Vehicular Ad-hoc Network (VANET) has become an increasingly important component in Connected Vehicle in Intelligent Transportation System (ITS). Communication in ITS consists of two parts, the Vehicle-to-Vehicle (V2V) communication and the Vehicle-to-Infrastructure (V2I) communication. VANET is mainly adopted as the paradigm in V2V communication. In the future, V2V, V2I and D2D network are expected to be interworking as the integrated network so as to support Intelligent Transportation Space (ITSP) and Intelligent Transportation System-Smart Grid (ITS-SG) [14].

In order to realize the real-time transmission of data and information in VANET, two essential conditions are required in V2V network; firstly, every vehicle is required to be equipped with on-board wireless network devices and multiple sensors, such as GPS, Bluetooth, monocular camera and radar, secondly, one type of networking wireless technology is needed as the basis for VANET. One type of prominent technology is Dedicated Short Range Communication (DSRC), under which 75 MHz in 5.9 GHz band in IEEE 802.11p is allocated to the fields of vehicular network. In addition, cellular technologies can also be used as the basis, both the Long-term Evolution Vehicle (LTE-V) and Fifth Generation Mobile Networks (5G) are promoted, while 5G achieves a faster speed, broader coverage, higher capacity and reduced latency [1].

With the V2V technology, a safer and well-organized traffic environment is presumed. Several specific scenarios and applications have been proposed, including reliable traffic density estimation and the detection and avoidance of forward obstacle and approaching emergency vehicle warning [7]. Vehicle chain cooperative collision avoidance (CCA) systems or cooperative adaptive cruise control (CACC) are typical safety applications of inter-vehicle communications (IVC) [15]. As VANET develops, some non-safety applications are also expected, mostly aiming at the optimization of traffic flow like platooning and some additional entertainment.

In VANET, the most noticeable characteristic is its high changeability and insta-bility, which make it different from the traditional MANET. The velocity of nodes in VANET can achieve up to 40 [m/s] while the average velocity of nodes in traditional MANET is 5 [m/s] [10]. Due to the high mobility of vehicles in VANET, the topology network is highly active and changing all the time [20]. And in a typical vehicular environment, the number of vehicles is always huge, which can lead to congestion in traffic environment, making the data transmission and rebroadcasting even more complex [2]. In addition, the vehicular networks may not have connections all the time. Furthermore, large numbers of vehicles are usually restricted to a certain spatial pattern. These reasons lead to the failing of some protocols in MANET to be applied in VANET [16]. Thusly, the study and performance evaluation of routing protocols in vehicular networks are of great importance [11]. Among many aspects, the study of VANET performance is critical in evaluating the performance in V2V communication; experts and professionals have also proposed a series of methods working on vehicular networks such as stochastic learning model, environment-specific propagation model and etc. [5, 8, 9, 21].

In VANET, multi-hop broadcasting is adopted as a primary method to realize the transmission of messages. Since the messages in the domain of vehicular network are mostly related to safety fields, it is required that the transmission of messages to related vehicles has to be punctual and allows little delay and few mistakes. Considering the process of message transmission, next-hop selection is a key section. However, the current routing protocols of VANET still face many problems in next-hop selection. The most prominent one is that due to the large number and high density of vehicles within an area, the nodes for rebroadcasting messages can be plentiful, which can cause several undesirable scenarios, i.e. (i) data flooding, which will lead to the chaotic collisions in data transmission and further lead to the delay and latency of safety-related messages, (ii) repetition of message transmission; a node is likely to implement an unnecessary repeated transmission while a neighboring node has already received and subsequently rebroadcasted the message and (iii) instability in rebroadcasting; stability and reliability are compromised in message transmission in VANET in order to realize the longest distance of a single transmission, connectivity is less stable as the distance between two nodes increases. Other problems are related to the different level of network capacity and transmission power in each vehicle.

In this paper, we bring forward a new routing protocol named *REliable and Fast Forwarding* (REFF), targeting at solving the redundancy of nodes as next hop and increasing the level of stability in message rebroadcasting in VANET. This routing protocol optimizes the total multi-hop broadcasting process by reducing the nodes in message transmission, therefore avoiding the data flooding and collision. Before a vehicle initiates its message transmission to the next hop, two steps are proceeded. A node-filtering step and a calculation step are proceeded by the vehicle to wipe out redundant unnecessary nodes and evaluate the suitability of the rest potential node to be chosen as the next hop. Then the suitability of every potential node as the next hop is ranked in descending order, and the node that ranks the top will be finally selected as the exclusive next-hop in the vicinity, thusly reducing the number of nodes used in a complete message transmission from the original node to the target node. We name this type of node as the Optimal Node (ON). This preliminary work is indeed a decision-making process, which plays an essential role in the relay selection in cooperative communication considering the selfish and greedy behavior of users in reality [13].

We organize this paper as follows. In Sect. 2, we introduce *REliable and Fast Forwarding* (REFF), containing the two major phases in next-hop selection, indexes we choose as evaluation criteria and the process of evaluation using TOPSIS. In Sect. 3, we present and assess the performance of REFF by adopting it in different traffic scenarios; both the simulation environment and simulation results are shown, confirming the feasibility and advancement of this routing protocol. In Sects. 4, conclusions are drawn and outlooks are put forward.

2 REliable and Fast Forwarding

In a real traffic environment, there are multiple scenarios in which sudden change in the velocity of traffic flow can happen. Assume a situation where an accident happened in the front of a traffic flow, due to hindrance of drivers' eyesight in the rear,message notifying the occurrence of the traffic accident in the front should reach vehicles in the back in time to function in these two way, i.e., (i) to remind drivers in the rear to decelerate the vehicle to avert severe brakes and collisions and (ii) to notify drivers in the rear of the accident to spare them some time to choose and change to an alternative path to avoid heavier congestion in the accident spot. By adopting the REFF method, situations like this can be efficaciously assuaged.

In REFF, we leverage on several preconditions, i.e. (i) vehicles driving in the lanes come in a Poisson Distribution, (ii) all the vehicles have a constant transmission range and (iii) all vehicles are installed with GPS and sensors to acquire basic information about positions and routes.

2.1 Node Filtering

In a common situation where a vehicle needs to transmit the Cooperative Awareness Message (CAM) to designated vehicles, the transmission is unidirectional in most cases. Since the transmission range of vehicles is circular, nodes that are unnecessary in this unidirectional transmission should be filtered out primarily, this step can effectively prevent data flooding and redundant transmission, which also help to save some network capacity. We filter these redundant nodes out by drawing two circles, i.e. (i) circle A with the position of the original vehicle (which is ready to rebroadcast the message to the next node) as the center and its transmission length as the radius, and (ii) circle B with the position of the target vehicle as the center and distance between the original vehicle and the target vehicle as the radius. Then the overlapping range of these two circles are determined and chosen, we define this overlapping range as *valid vicinity* (VV) in this paper. Every node in the valid vicinity qualifies as a potential next hop for the rebroadcasting of messages. We define these nodes as *candidate node* (CN). A further next-hop selection and decision is based on the completion of this node-filtering phase. After a vehicle finishes one next-hop selection, the node selected becomes the new 'original' vehicle, initiating a new round of next-hop selection by using the same node-filtering method, drawing circles with new center and new radius and determining new valid vicinity.

In a typical two-way four-lane highway as shown in Fig. 1, we assume the source node (where the message transmission initiates) and destination node (where the message transmission terminates) of a complete transmission to be fixed in our simulation environment. The vehicle in blue is a message carrier, preparing to select its next hop and rebroadcast the message to it. By using node-filtering method, we can draw the cross range of these two circles and define it as valid vicinity (VV) in this paper. Vehicles inside this valid vicinity (which are in red) are identified as candidate nodes. After a next-hop selection by using TOPSIS, optimal node can be determined and message can be rebroadcasted to the target node.

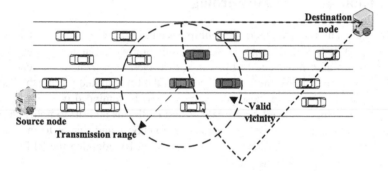

Fig. 1. Two-way four-lane road map. (Color figure online)

2.2   Next-Hop Selection Using TOPSIS

After the primary node-filtering phase, the original vehicle will firstly send a Request-To-Broadcast (RTB) message to all candidate nodes and establish a link with all candidate nodes in the valid vicinity, so that basic information about the candidate nodes can be achieved to make further evaluation and comparison. At this time, cooperative awareness message (CAM) packets are at state of readiness to be transmitted. But the original vehicle preparing to rebroadcast CAM is required to execute a calculating process firstly to evaluate the suitability of every candidate node for potential rebroadcasting, then the matching degree and performance level of every node are ranked in descending order. Finally, the node that performs the best is selected as the only candidate for next hop, sending back a Clear-To-Broadcast message to the original vehicle, then realizing a reliable and fast forwarding.

To execute the calculation process, several indexes are picked to form a comprehensive evaluating system.

Notation: Throughout this paper, we use boldface letter to denote vectors, which are all column vectors. We use regular font letters to denote random quantities (such as D_i, θ_i). We use $\|\cdot\|_2$ to denote operator of Euclidean norm (norm-2). The original node is denoted as o in the subscript, candidate node is denoted as i in the subscript and target node (which is ready to receive message from candidate node) is denoted as t.

- Distance between candidate node and original node D_i:

$$D_i = \|\boldsymbol{p}_i - \boldsymbol{p}_o\|_2 \tag{1}$$

A longer distance between the candidate node and original node ensures a longer broadcasting length, reducing the number of nodes used in a single complete transmission and precipitating the transmission.

- Relative velocity between candidate node and original node ΔV_i:

$$\Delta V_i = \|\boldsymbol{v}_i - \boldsymbol{v}_o\|_2 \tag{2}$$

A lower relative velocity improves the stability between these two nodes, preventing the candidate node from suddenly leaving the valid vicinity and improving the reliability of forwarding.

- Angle-related criteria C_i: we use the Sigmoid function to calculate the criteria related to the included angle θ_i between velocity direction of candidate node and velocity direction of target node:

$$\theta_i = arccos \left\| \frac{\boldsymbol{v}_i \cdot \boldsymbol{v}_t}{|\boldsymbol{v}_i| \times |\boldsymbol{v}_t|} \right\|_2 \tag{3}$$

If $0° \leq \theta_i \leq 90°$, a smaller included angle between the direction of v_i and v_t is preferred because it ensures a more reliable and stable transmission, while a larger angle implies a larger probability to disconnect.

If $90° < \theta_i \leq 180°$, a larger included angle between the direction of v_i and v_t is preferred because it ensures a faster and more robust transmission, while a smaller angle implies a larger probability to disconnect.

Thusly,

$$C_i(\theta) = \begin{cases} \frac{1}{1+exp\left(\frac{4a}{\pi}\theta_i - a\right)} & \left(0 \leq \theta_i \leq \frac{\pi}{2}\right) \\ \frac{1}{1+exp\left(-\frac{4a}{\pi}\theta_i + 3a\right)} & \left(\frac{\pi}{2} < \theta_i \leq \pi\right) \end{cases} \tag{4}$$

in this equation, a is used as the calibration parameter. A larger C_i brings about a more stable and faster transmission (Fig. 2).

Results of C_i are shown in a different variation degree as we change the calibration parameter a. But a general variation tendency is sure in these two ways, i.e., (i) if θ_i is near $0°$ or $180°$, C_i will appear near 1, which is the best condition and (ii) if θ_i is near $90°$, C_i will appear near 0, which is the worst condition.

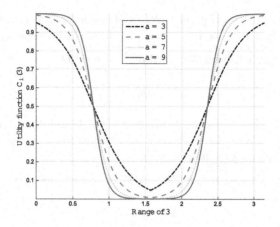

Fig. 2. Variation trend of C_i with different value of parameter a

- Transmission power of the candidate node P_i: an increase in the transmission power improves the probability of successful data transmissions if the link reliability is below a certain threshold. With a higher transmission power, the physical layer can use modulation and coding schemes with a higher bit ratio, increasing the bandwidth under heavy workloads [3].

Considering the conflicting characteristics in these indexes, we adopt the Technique for Order of Performance by Similarity to Ideal Solution (TOPSIS) as the calculating principle in consideration of its compensatory property that one poor result in one criterion can be negated by a good result in another criterion. Then an optimal candidate node can be confirmed and selected. The calculation is conducted in the following way:

- Step 1. Creating an evaluation matrix consisting of m CNs and 4 indexes

$$X_{ij} = \begin{pmatrix} x_{1,1} & \cdots & x_{1,4} \\ \vdots & \ddots & \vdots \\ x_{m,1} & \cdots & x_{m,4} \end{pmatrix} \tag{5}$$

- Step 2. Normalizing the matrix considering incongruous dimensions of four indexes

$$R = (r_{ij})_{m \times 4} \tag{6}$$

by using the normalization method, $r_{ij} = \dfrac{X_{ij}}{\sqrt{\sum_{i=1}^{m} X_{ij}^2}} (i = 1, 2, \cdots, m; j = 1, 2, 3, 4)$.

- Step 3. Calculating the weighted normalized decision matrix

$$t_{ij} = r_{ij} \times w_j (i = 1, 2, \cdots, m; \ j = 1, 2, 3, 4) \tag{7}$$

where $w_j = W_j / \sum_{j=1}^{4} W_j (j = 1, 2, 3, 4)$, so that $\sum_{j=1}^{4} w_j = 1$; w_j is the original weight assigned to each index.

- Step 4. Determining the worst candidate C_w and the best candidate C_b

$$C_w = \left\{ \langle max t_{ij} | j \in J_- \rangle, \langle min t_{ij} | j \in J_+ \rangle \right\} \equiv \{ t_{wj} | j = 1, 2, 3, 4 \} \tag{8}$$

$$C_b = \left\{ \langle min t_{ij} | j \in J_- \rangle, \langle max t_{ij} | j \in J_+ \rangle \right\} \equiv \{ t_{wj} | j = 1, 2, 3, 4 \} \tag{9}$$

where,

$J_+ = \{ j = 1, 2, 3, 4 | j$ associated with the index having a positive impact;
$J_- = \{ j = 1, 2, 3, 4 | j$ associated with the index having a negative impact.

- Step 5. Calculating the L2-distance between candidate nodes to the worst condition C_w and best condition C_b

$$d_{iw} = \sqrt{\sum_{j=1}^{4} \left(t_{ij} - t_{wj} \right)^2} (i = 1, 2, \cdots, m) \tag{10}$$

$$d_{ib} = \sqrt{\sum_{j=1}^{4} \left(t_{ij} - t_{bj} \right)^2} (i = 1, 2, \cdots, m) \tag{11}$$

where d_{iw} and d_{ib} are Euclidean norm (norm-2) distances from the candidate node i to the worst and best conditions, respectively.

- Step 6. Calculating the similarity to the worst conditions

$$s_{iw} = \frac{d_{iw}}{d_{iw} + d_{ib}} (i = 1, 2, \cdots, m) \tag{12}$$

where $0 \le s_{iw} \le 1$,

$s_{iw} = 1$ if and only if the candidate node meets the best condition;
$s_{iw} = 0$ if and only if the candidate node meets the worst condition.

- Step 7. Rank m candidate nodes according to their s_{iw} in descending order $(i = 1, 2, \cdots, m)$.

Finally, after the original vehicle acquires a list of all candidate nodes ranking on basis of their s_{iw} in descending order, the one that ranks the top is determined as the optimal node and then selected as the next hop for message rebroadcasting. At this time, the original vehicle will release its link with other candidate nodes and transmit CAM to the optimal node to continue message transmission. If a message transmission needs multiple rebroadcasting in VANET, the same technique is adopted every time to select the next hop.

3 Performance Evaluation

3.1 Simulation Settings

We conduct our simulation based on a real traffic scenario that vehicles arrive according to Poisson distribution in a two-way four-lane road. To evaluate the performance of REFF in such traffic scenarios, we set some factors as quantitative and some indexes as variables, comparing the final performance as indexes change and drawing the variation tendency corresponding to each index. We list the simulation environment parameters in Table 1:

Table 1. Simulation environment parameters

Simulation parameter	Value
Length of lane	3 km
Width of lane	3.75 m
Number of lane	4
Transmission range	300 m
Duration	100 s
Vehicle density	[10,60] veh/km

In a highly mobile and dense traffic environment, cooperation is affected by the constant addition and deletion of nodes [12]. And in such an environment, a node's position and velocity are influenced by its vicinity structure, which means that the dynamics of a node's position and velocity are denoted by the move of the node in front of it. Hence, we assume all nodes in the simulation environment moves according to the Intelligent Driver Model (IDM), which is a time-continuous car-following model. For vehicle i, X_i denotes its position and V_i denotes its velocity at time t. Furthermore, l_i denotes the length of vehicle. Net distance and velocity difference are also defined as $s_i = x_{i-1} - x_i - l_{i-1}$ and $\Delta v_i = v_i - v_{i-1}$, in which $i-1$ refers to the vehicle directly in front of vehicle i. Thusly, the dynamics of vehicle i can be described in these two ordinary differential equations:

$$\dot{x}_i = \frac{dx_i}{dt} = v_i \tag{13}$$

$$\dot{v}_i = \frac{dv_i}{dt} = a\left(1 - \left(\frac{v_i}{v_0}\right)^\sigma - \left(\frac{s^*(v_i, \Delta v_i)}{s_i}\right)^2\right) \tag{14}$$

with $s^*(v_i, \Delta v_i) = s_0 + v_i \times T + \frac{v_i \times \Delta v_i}{2\sqrt{ab}}$.

v_0, s_0, T, a and b are model parameters that have the following meaning, i.e., (i) desired velocity v_0: the velocity the vehicle could drive at in free traffic, (ii) minimum spacing s_0: a minimum desired net distance. A car cannot move if the distance from the car in the front is not at least s_0, (iii) desired time headway T: the desired time headway to the vehicle in the front, (iv) acceleration a: the maximum vehicle acceleration and (v) comfortable braking deceleration b: a positive number. The exponential σ is usually set to 4.

3.2 Simulation Results

In evaluating the performance of message transmission in VANET, an important metric is the average transmission delay from one node to the next node. A longer transmission delay has a negative impact on the total performance of V2V communication considering the significance of timeliness in communication. Thusly, we comparing the average delay in message rebroadcasting from hop to hop under two different routing techniques: REliable and Fast Protocol (REFF) as a type of unicast routing and Epidemic Routing as a common type of broadcast routing.

In Fig. 3(a) the variation trend of average delay is shown with traffic density changing. As expected, the average transmission delay decreases as traffic density increases because a denser traffic environment ensures a larger number of nodes to rebroadcast messages and more stable transmission. When compared with Epidemic Routing, REFF displays a sharply decrease in average transmission delay from one node to the next. The average transmission delay under REFF is 2.41 [s] while the transmission delay under Epidemic Routing is 2.41 [s]. With initial speed of vehicles remaining constant at 25 [m/s] and as traffic density varies from 10 [veh/km] to 60 [veh/km], a 49.3% decrease in average transmission delay is seen in REFF when compared to Epidemic Routing on average. A lower traffic density experiences a larger difference in average delay between REFF and Epidemic Routing.

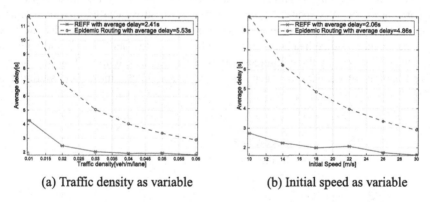

(a) Traffic density as variable   (b) Initial speed as variable

Fig. 3. Average transmission delay under two routing protocols

In Fig. 3(b) the variation trend of average delay is shown with average vehicle velocity changing. As expected, the average transmission delay decreases as initial speed of vehicles increases because a faster speed ensures a more stable link and a faster transmission. When compared with Epidemic Routing, REFF displays an evident decrease in average transmission delay from one node to the next. The average transmission delay in REFF is 2.06 [s] while the average transmission delay is 4.86 [s]. With traffic density remaining constant at 60 [veh/km] and as initial speed of vehicles varies from 10 [m/s] to 30 [m/s], a 56.95% decrease in average transmission delay is seen in REFF when compared to the performance of Epidemic Routing. A slower speed experiences a larger difference in average delay between REFF and Epidemic Routing.

When we compare the performance of REFF and Epidemic Routing in message rebroadcasting, another important fact that we cannot ignore is the collision phenomena in broadcast routing. Data collision can lead to the failure of message being transmitted to the destination vehicle.

In a complex traffic environment, due to the large number and high density of vehicles, the transmission of one node has the probability to collide with the transmission of another node if waiting time difference between them is short. Thusly, we calculate the collision probability (CP) of one node with another node under the flooding-based routing protocol by using the formula introduced in RObust and Fast Forwarding (ROFF) routing protocol [17]:

$$CP = P(Range \cdot \frac{minDiff}{MaxWT} > (d_{f_N} - d_{f_{N-1}})) \tag{15}$$

In this equation, CP is equal to the probability that $Range \cdot \frac{minDiff}{MaxWT}$ is bigger than the space headway of vehicle f_N and f_{N-1}, where $Range$ is the transmission range of node, $minDiff$ is the minimum waiting time difference between vehicle f_N and f_{N-1}, $MaxWT$ is the maximum waiting time and d_{f_i} is the distance between f_i and previous node.

We calculate collision probability of Epidemic Routing as traffic density varies from 10 [veh/km] to 60 [veh/k], which corresponds to different traffic scenarios. In measuring the collision probability, different maximum waiting time is a critical influencing factor. As expected, from the variation trend we can tell that the collision probability when rebroadcasting a message increases as the traffic density increases because smaller vehicle headway on the road can lead to data flooding and collision. Moreover, as shown by three different curves, a smaller maximum waiting time adds to the probability of collision between nodes because a smaller maximum waiting time

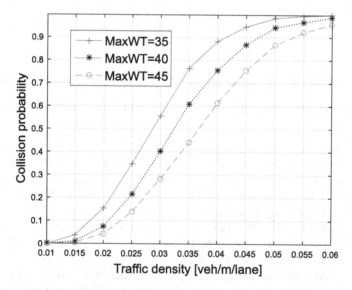

Fig. 4. Collision probability under different value of *MaxWT*

results in a smaller minimum waiting time difference between nodes in the vicinity. The result concerning collision probability is shown in Fig. 4. On the contrast, unicast routing usually displays zero probability in collision. Thusly, the REFF we propose which belongs to unicast routing outperforms Epidemic Routing when taking collision probability into account.

4 Conclusions

Aiming at solving the data flooding problem and transmission delay in VANET supported by 5G, LTE-V, DSRC and etc. in V2V communication, we introduce the REliable and Fast Forwarding (REFF) in this paper. In REFF, two phases are essential before rebroadcasting the message from one node to the next, which are node filtering and next-hop selection using TOPSIS. These two steps targets at eliminating the redundant node and determine the only optimal candidate node for rebroadcasting the message. By adopting this technique, the number of nodes in a complete message transmission is largely reduced and a more reliable and faster transmission is thusly guaranteed. Compared with some other routing protocols, REFF performs better at transmission delay and it is not disturbed by the problem of data collision. In the future, how to more effectively merging the REFF technique with cross-layer technique will be our main focus.

Acknowledgments. This research was supported in part by no. Beijing Science and Technology Program no. D171100000317003 and the National Natural Science Foundation of China under Grant nos. 61672082, U1564212.

References

1. Chen, S., Hu, J., Shi, Y., Zhao, L.: LTE-V: A TD-LTE based V2X solution for future vehicular network. IEEE Internet Things J. **3**(6), 997–1005 (2016)
2. Chen, S., Zhao, J.: The requirements, challenges and technologies for 5G of terrestrial mobile telecommunication. IEEE Commun. Mag. **52**(5), 36–43 (2014)
3. Correia, L.H.A., Macedo, D.F., Dos Santos, A.L., Loureiro, A.A.F., Nogueira, J., Marcos, S.: Transmission power control techniques for wireless sensor networks. Comput. Netw. **51**(17), 4765–4779 (2007)
4. Cortéspolo, D., Callecancho, J., Carmonamurillo, J., Gonzálezsánchez, J.: Future trends in mobile-fixed integration for next generation networks: classification and analysis. Int. J. Veh. Telematics Infotain. Syst. (IJVTIS) **1**(1), 33–53 (2017)
5. Gaamel, A.M., Maratha, B.P., Sheltami, T.R., Shakshuki, E.M.: Fault-tolerance evaluation of VANET under different data dissemination models. Int. J. Veh. Telematics Infotain. Syst. (IJVTIS) **1**(1), 54–68 (2017)
6. Ge, X., Cheng, H., Mao, G., Yang, Y.: Vehicular communication for 5G cooperative small cell networks. IEEE Trans. Veh. Technol. **65**, 1 (2016)
7. Huang, Y., Wang, J., Jiang, C., Zhang, H., Leung, V.C.M.: Vehicular network based reliable traffic density estimation. In: Proceedings of the IEEE Vehicular Technology Conference (VTC), Nanjing, 15–18 May 2016

8. Jiang, C., Zhang, H., Han, Z., Cheng, J., Ren, Y., Hanzo, L.: On the outage probability of information sharing in cognitive vehicular networks. In: Proceedings of IEEE International Conference on Communications (ICC), Kuala Lampur, Malaysia, 23–27 May 2016
9. Mir, Z.H., Filali, F.: A simulation-based study on the environment-specific propagation model for vehicular communications. Int. J. Veh. Telematics Infotain. Syst. (IJVTIS) 1(1), 15–32 (2017)
10. Mostafa, A., Vegni, A.M., Agrawal, D.P.: Review article: A probabilistic routing by using multi-hop retransmission forecast with packet collision-aware constraints in vehicular networks. Ad Hoc Netw. 14(3), 118–129 (2014)
11. Pressas, A., Özpolat, M., Sheng, Z., Ali, F.: Performance evaluation of networking protocols for connected vehicles. Int. J. Veh. Telematics Infotain. Syst. (IJVTIS) 1(1), 1–14 (2017)
12. Shivshankar, S., Jamalipour, A.: An evolutionary game theory-based approach to cooperation in vanets under different network conditions. IEEE Trans. Veh. Technol. 64(5), 2015–2022 (2015)
13. Tian, D., Zhou, J., Sheng, Z., Ni, Q.: Learning to be energy-efficient in cooperative networks. IEEE Commun. Lett. 20(12), 2518–2521 (2016)
14. Tian, D., Zhou, J., Wang, Y., Lu, Y.: A dynamic and self-adaptive network selection method for multimode communications in heterogeneous vehicular telematics. IEEE Trans. Intell. Transp. Syst. 16(6), 1–17 (2015)
15. Tian, D., Zhou, J., Wang, Y., Sheng, Z., Xia, H., Yi, Z.: Modeling chain collisions in vehicular networks with variable penetration rates. Transp. Res. Part C Emerg. Technol. 69, 36–59 (2016)
16. Tian, D., Zhou, J., Wang, Y., Zhang, G., Xia, H.: An adaptive vehicular epidemic routing method based on attractor selection model. Ad Hoc Netw. 36(P2), 465481 (2015)
17. Yoo, H., Kim, D.: Roff: Robust and fast forwarding in vehicular ad-hoc networks. IEEE Trans. Mobile Comput. 14(7), 1490–1502 (2015)
18. Yu, R., Ding, J., Huang, X., Zhou, M.T.: Optimal resource sharing in 5G-enabled vehicular networks: A matrix game approach. IEEE Trans. Veh. Technol. 65(10), 1 (2016)
19. Zhang, H., Dong, Y., Cheng, J., Leung, V.C.M.: Fronthauling for 5G LTE-U ultra dense cloud small cell networks. IEEE Wirel. Commun. 23(6), 48–53 (2016)
20. Zhang, H., Liu, N., Chu, X., Long, K., Aghvami, A.H., Leung, V.C.M.: Network slicing based 5G and future mobile networks: mobility, resource management, and challenges. IEEE Commun. Mag. 55(8), 138–145 (2017)
21. Zheng, Q., Zheng, K., Zhang, H., Leung, V.C.M.: Delay-optimal virtualized radio resource scheduling in software-defined vehicular networks via stochastic learning. IEEE Trans. Veh. Technol. 65(12), 9479–9492 (2016)

A Novel Intrusion Detection System Based on Advanced Naive Bayesian Classification

Yunpeng Wang[1,4,5,6], Yuzhou Li[1,4], Daxin Tian[1,4(✉)],
Congyu Wang[1,4], Wenyang Wang[2], Rong Hui[2], Peng Guo[2],
and Haijun Zhang[3]

[1] Beijing Advanced Innovation Center for Big Data and Brain Computing,
Beihang University, XueYuan Road No. 37, Beijing 100191, China
dtian@buaa.edu.cn
[2] China Automotive Technology and Research Center,
Automotive Engineering Research Institute,
East Xianfeng Road No. 68, Tianjin 300300, China
[3] School of Computer and Communication Engineering,
University of Science and Technology Beijing,
XueYuan Road No. 30, Beijing 100083, China
[4] Beijing Key Laboratory for Cooperative Vehicle Infrastructure Systems
and Safety Control, School of Transportation Science and Engineering,
Beihang University, XueYuan Road No. 37, Beijing 100191, China
[5] Jiangsu Province Collaborative Innovation Center of Modern Urban
Traffic Technologies, Si Pai Lou. 2, Nanjing 210096, China
[6] Key Lab of Urban ITS Technology Optimization and Integration,
The Ministry of Public Security of China, Hefei 230088, China

Abstract. Intrusion Detection System is a pattern recognition task whose aim is to detect and report the occurrence of abnormal or unknown network behaviors in a given network system being monitored. In this paper, we propose a machine learning model, advanced Naive Bayesian Classification (NBC-A) which is based on NBC and ReliefF algorithm, to be used in the novel IDS. We use ReliefF algorithm to give every attribute of network behavior in KDD'99 dataset a weight that reflects the relationship between attributes and final class for better classification results. The novel IDS has a higher True Positive (TP) rate and a lower False Positive (FP) rate in detection performance.

Keywords: IDS · Information security · NBC · ReliefF
Detection performance · KDD'99

1 Introduction

Network in a profound impact on people's lives and ways of working at the same time, it also brings a lot of security risks and threats. A variety of viruses, security vulnerabilities, attacks have caused the loss of users, enterprise, government, even national security. With increasing network security incidents in recent years, people have a strong sense of security and privacy protection. Therefore, the well-designed security system is a very

© ICST Institute for Computer Sciences, Social Informatics and Telecommunications Engineering 2018
K. Long et al. (Eds.): 5GWN 2017, LNICST 211, pp. 581–588, 2018.
https://doi.org/10.1007/978-3-319-72823-0_53

important and urgent problem in the field of network information security especially in next generation networks (5G) [1, 2] with great security challenges.

At present, the network information security protection measures are divided into passive security and active security. Passive security includes data encryption [3, 4], security authentication [5], firewall [6] and other measures and these Active security is a technology represented by Intrusion Detection System (IDS) [7] which detect possible intrusion by collecting network datasets or information, and sending alerts and responding before an intrusion occurs, or before a hazard occurs. With the development of IDS, even that it could replace the traditional network security measures.

In recent years, with the rise of machine learning (ML)-related models [8], it is becoming a trend to apply machine learning methods into intrusion detection system. In the field of machine learning, Naive Bayesian Classification (NBC) [9] is widely used as the most classical learning algorithm with good classification accuracy. However, the NBC is based on the independence of event attributes, which is difficult to achieve in realistic network behaviors especially in future networks (such as 5G) with great complexity [10]. In response to this shortage, many scholars have put forth an improved method which is based on different attribute weights. Paper [11] propose a weighted BNC model based on Rough Set, it could performance well in small data sets and could do some changes in original information. Paper [12] use the value of every attribute to be as weights, but the attributes attribute are more, each weighted coefficients are small, it cannot play its role in real complex networks. Paper [13] propose a weighted NBC based on correlation coefficient, and it could improve the classification ability of the Bayesian, but the current measure formula is not described accurately for all conditions.

In this paper, we propose a novel IDS based on machine learning an advanced Naive Bayesian Classification (NBC-A) which we give every attributes a weight to reflect the relations between attributes and final classification results. We use the ReliefF [14] algorithm that is robust [15] and can deal with incomplete and noisy data to estimate weights and we get a higher True Positive (TP) rate and a lower False Positive (FP) rate [16] in detection performance that means it has better performance than NBC.

In this paper, we introduce some network information security related works and machine learning works in Sect. 2; we proposed the IDS based on NBC-A in Sect. 2.1; detection performance based on dataset KDD'99 and analysis is in Sect. 3; conclusion and outlook are in Sect. 4.

2 Advanced Naive Bayesian Classification (NBC-A) Model in Intrusion Detection System (IDS)

The method of intrusion detection is to design a network behavior classifier to distinguish the normal and abnormal data in the dataset, simulation or realistic network, so as to realize the alarm function of the attacking behavior. At the same time, intrusion detection by IDS is an uncertain behavior, and Naive Bayes theory is suitable for uncertain probabilistic events. Therefore, the introduction of intrusion detection technology based on NBC in IDS research design is completely reasonable.

2.1   Naive Bayesian Classification (NBC)

The Bayesian decision-making theory provides a probabilistic approach to reasoning. It assumes that the variables to be investigated follow certain probability distributions and can reason from these probabilities and observed data to make optimal decisions. Naive Bayesian Classification (NBC) model based on Bayesian decision-making theory [17], is a simplified Bayesian probability model. The classification model is simple in implementation, fast in classification and high in accuracy. It is one of the most widely used classification models in machine learning.

Given a data set of K attributes and assumed that the values of the K attributes are discrete, the purpose of classification is to predict the type of every case in the test set which is a part of dataset (the other part is train set whose task is to make the NBC's train). We can give a specific example, whose attributes are from a_1 to a_k. The probability of the example belonging to class C_i is $P(C = c_i | A_1 = a_1, \ldots, A_k = a_k)$. Obviously, according to Bayesian decision-making theory:

$$P(C = c_i | A_1 = a_1, \ldots, A_k = a_k) = \frac{P(A_1 = a_1, \ldots, A_k = a_k | C = c_i) P(C = c_i)}{P(A_1 = a_1, \ldots, A_k = a_k)} \quad (1)$$

Here, $P(C = c_i)$ is a prior probability and can be easily calculated from train set. In data set, $P(A_1 = a_1, \ldots, A_k = a_k)$ is same to every class c_i and it assumes that the values of attributes are independent, we can know:

$$P(A_1 = a_1, \ldots, A_k = a_k) = 1 \quad (2)$$

$$P(A_1 = a_1, \ldots, A_k = a_k | C = c_i) = P(A_1 = a_1 | C = c_i) \ldots P(A_k = a_k | C = c_i) \quad (3)$$

Putting Formula (2) and (3) in to Formula (1), we can get the method used by Naive Bayesian Classification, that is:

$$V_{NBC}(x) = \arg \max P(C = c_i) \prod P(A_j = a_j | C = c_i) \quad (4)$$

Here $V_{NBC}(x)$ is indicated the target value out by NBC indicated that the output target. In theory, NBC has the minimum misclassification rate, compared with all the other classification algorithms and it is suitable to be used in IDS to find abnormal behaviors in network.

2.2   Attribute Weighted Naive Bayesian Classification

However, the independence assumption is difficult to meet in the real network behaviors, each network behavior has its own attributes, which have complex relationships and can directly affect the results of intrusion detection judgments. Paper [18] established an attribute weighted NBC, is assigned to give different weights to each attribute to make these relationships effect on NBC:

$$V_{wNBC}(x) = \arg \max P(C = c_i) \prod P(A_j = a_j | C = c_i)^{W_j} \tag{5}$$

Here, W_j is the weight of A_j. Different W_j has different inferences on NBC, great W_j makes great impacts on IDS. The key of NBC in IDS is how to determine the weights of different attributes.

2.3   The W_j Determined by ReliefF Algorithm

In the next generation network (such as 5G), the network behavior of the relationship will be far more complex than the current network. However, the algorithm for determining w_j are focusing on relations among on attributes instead of class C_i, these algorithms be very difficult to play a role because of the high complexity. Therefore, we propose to use ReliefF algorithm, which directly focuses on the relationship between attribute and final classification (class C_i) results rather than the relationship between attribute and attribute. The ReliefF algorithm as follows:

ReliefF algorithm is a multi-class attribute selection algorithm proposed by Kononenko. Its basic idea is to assign a weight value to each attribute in the attribute set, assign a higher weight to the attribute which could has direct and high relation to final classification (class C_i). For that purpose, given a randomly selected network behavior X_i (line 3), ReliefF searches for its two nearest neighbors: one from the same class, called nearest hit H, and the other from the different classes (class C_i, $o \neq i$), called nearest miss M (line 4). Function $diff(A, I_1, I_2)$ (line 6) calculates the difference between the values of the attribute A for two network behaviors I_1 and I_2. The whole process is repeated for m (line 2) times, where m is a user-defined parameter. i, j, o and k are count constants.

ReliefF Algorithm for determining W_j:

Input: for each behavior X_i in train set attributes $A(A_1 = a_1, \ldots, A_j = a_j, \ldots, A_k = a_k)$ values and the class C_i.

Output: the vector $W(W_1 = w_1, \ldots, W_j = w_j, \ldots, W_k = w_k)$ of weights of the qualities of attributes A.

Step1 set all W as an initial value $W_j = 0$;
Step2 for $i := 1$ to m do begin
Step3 randomly select a network behavior X_i;
Step4 find nearest $H_s(s = 1, 2, \ldots, q)$ in hit H and nearest $M_s(s = 1, 2, \ldots, q)$ in miss M;
Step5 for $j := 1$ to k do
Step6 $W_j := W_j - \sum_{s=1}^{q} \frac{diff(A, X_i, H_s)}{mq}$

$\qquad + \sum_{\substack{Y \neq class\, C_i \\ Y = class\, C_{io}}} \left[\frac{P(Y)}{1 - P(classC_i)} \sum_{s=1}^{q} diff(A, X_i, M_s) \right] / (mq);$

Step7 end;

ReliefF Algorithm does not set the value range of W_j, it may be negative, in order to avoid this situation, the proposed standardized operation [19] of W_j, the formula is as follows:

$$W'_j = \frac{W_j - min_W}{max_W - min_W} \tag{6}$$

Here W'_j is the standard W_j, min_W is the minimum value of W and max_W is the maximum one.

2.4 The Processes of the Novel IDS Based on Model NBC-A

Combining 3.1–3.3, we get the advanced NBC (NBC-A) which be used in the novel IDS proposed in this paper is:

$$V_{NBC-A}(x) = \arg \max P(C = c_i) \prod P\left(A_j = a_j | C = c_i\right)^{W'_j} \tag{7}$$

$$W'_j = \frac{W_j - min_W}{max_W - min_W} \tag{8}$$

$$W_j := W_j - \sum_{s=1}^{q} diff(A, X_i, H_s)/(mq)$$
$$+ \sum_{\substack{Y \neq class\,C_i \\ Y = class\,C_{io}}} \left[\frac{P(Y)}{1 - P(classC_i)} \sum_{s=1}^{q} diff(A, X_i, M_s)\right]/(mq) \tag{9}$$

We divide the IDS into two processes: in the train process, the Train Set includes the known network behavior data and the marked classes, and then Preprocesses: discretization and feature selection. Finally, we use the ReliefF algorithm to weight the feature to get NBC-A; in the test process, the Test Set includes unknown network behavior data, and then discretization, and finally the use of NBC-A to get behavior classification results. The processes of the novel IDS as follows (Fig. 1):

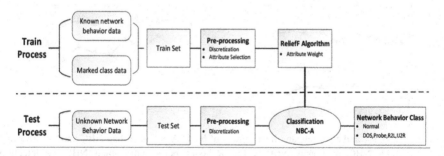

Fig. 1. The whole process is divided into 2 parts: Train Process and Test process, the model NBC-A based on NBC and ReliefF algorithm is used to get the network behavior class in Test Process.

3   Detection Performance and Analysis

3.1   Dataset KDD'99 for Detection Performance

We utilize dataset KDD Cup 1999 (KDD'99) [20] to be as the data for detection performance. KDD'99 is the standard dataset of intrusion detection and consists of two parts: 7 weeks of train data set, about 5,000,000 network connections; 2 weeks of test data set, about 2,000,000 network connections. Each network connection record is marked as normal (Normal) or abnormal (Anomaly), abnormal type is divided into 4 categories of 39 kinds of attack types. For time saving and computer performance, we utilize 10% KDD'99 to be the performance data. The distribution of data as follows (Table 1):

Table 1.   The distribution of intrusion types in 10% KDD'99

Type	Train examples	Test examples	10% KDD'99 Train distribution	10% KDD'99 Test distribution
Normal	97,278	60,593	19.69%	19.48%
Probe	4,107	4,166	0.83%	1.34%
DOS	391458	229,853	79.24%	73.90%
U2R	52	228	0.01%	0.07%
R2L	1,126	16,189	0.23%	5.20%
Total	497,021	31,1029	100%	100%

3.2   Performance Analysis

In detection performance, the experimental platform environment is: Operation System: Windows 7 ultimate, CPU 3.00 GHz, RAM 8 GB, Hard Disk 500G; Programming tools: Spyder (Python 2.7), Dataset: 10% KDD'99 (80% Train Set and 20% Test Set), the detection performance results as follows:

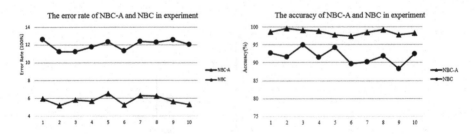

Fig. 2.   Accuracy and error rate are the accuracy of NBC-A is higher than NBC and the error rate is lower than NBC, it means NBC-A has a better performance than NBC in detection performance.

(1) From Fig. 2, we could find that the accuracy of NBC-A is greatly higher than NBC one, and the error rate of NBC-A is lower than the NBC in intrusion detection performance. Actually, the average of NBC-A accuracy is 98.50% and NBC is 91.73%. The average of NBC-A error rate is 5.79% and the NBC is 11.98%. It means that model NBC-A can performance greatly better than in NBC in data mining by using ReliefF algorithm.

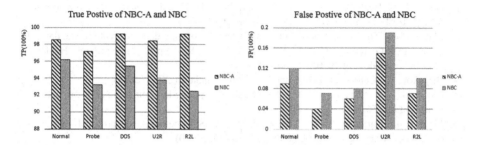

Fig. 3. TP of NBC-A is high than NBC and FP of NBC-A is lower, that means novel IDS based on NBC-A is more secure and useful the NBC one.

(2) From Fig. 3, for different types of intrusion attacks, the TP of NBC-A is generally higher than that of NBC and the FP of NBC-A is much lower than that of NBC. This means the novel IDS we propose in this paper, uses ReliefF algorithm to weight the class attributes to obtain a good effect, can effectively detect the intrusion behaviors in the networks, to ensure the safety of the system.

4 Conclusion and Outlook

Aiming at the massive and complex network attacks on the current Internet or next generation network 5G (the more massive and complex), it is reasonable to apply the NBC of Naive Bayes decision theory to IDS. We propose a novel IDS based on NBC-A which makes improvements on the NBC. The novel IDS we propose in this paper utilizes ReliefF algorithm to estimate attribute. Compared with other algorithm, Relief is more robust and efficient, it directly reflects the relationship between attributes and final class results. Model NBC-A is more suitable for large-scale and high-complexity networks. The detection performance shows that we get a higher TP rate and a lower FP rate in detection performance that means that NBC-A has better performance than NBC and practical application significance.

In this novel IDS, we have a lot of improvement in the performance of classifier space, in the future work, how to more effectively combine ReliefF algorithm and relationship of attributes between attributes, and other machine learning classification algorithm, which can further enhance the classifier's ability of intrusion detection for complex network.

Acknowledgments. This research was supported by the National Key Research and Development Program of China (2016YFB0100902).

References

1. Rappaport, T.S., Sun, S., Mayzus, R., Zhao, H.: Millimeter wave mobile communications for 5G cellular: it will work! IEEE Access **1**(1), 335–349 (2013)
2. Boccardi, F., Heath, R.W., Lozano, A., Marzetta, T.L.: Five disruptive technology directions for 5G. IEEE Commun. Mag. **52**(2), 74–80 (2013)
3. Matsui, M.: The first experimental cryptanalysis of the data encryption standard. In: Desmedt, Y.G. (ed.) CRYPTO 1994. LNCS, vol. 839, pp. 1–11. Springer, Heidelberg (1994). https://doi.org/10.1007/3-540-48658-5_1
4. Biryukov, A., Cannière, C.D.: Data encryption standard (DES) (2005)
5. Lowe, G.: An attack on the Needham-Schroeder public-key authentication protocol. Inf. Process. Lett. **56**(3), 131–133 (1995)
6. Manner, J., Karagiannis, G., Mcdonald, A.: NSIS signaling layer protocol (NSLP) for quality-of-service signaling. IETF **31**(2), 152–160 (2010)
7. Huang, M.Y., Jasper, R.J., Wicks, T.M.: A large scale distributed intrusion detection framework based on attack strategy analysis. Comput. Netw. **31**(23–24), 2465–2475 (1998)
8. Bache, K., Lichman, M.: UCI Machine Learning Repository (2013)
9. Flach, P.A., Lachiche, N.: Naive Bayesian classification of structured data. Mach. Learn. **57** (3), 233–269 (2004)
10. Muirhead, D., Imran, M.A., Arshad, K.: Insights and approaches for low-complexity 5G small-cell base-station design for indoor dense networks. IEEE Access **3**, 1562–1572 (2015)
11. Deng, W., Wang, G., Wang, Y.: Weighted Naive Bayes classification algorithm based on rough set. Comput. Sci. **34**(2), 204–205 (2007)
12. Cheng, K., Zhang, C.: Feature-based weighted Naive Bayesian classifier (2006)
13. Yao, S., Li, L.: Weighted Naïve Bayesian classification algorithm based on correlation coefficients. Int. J. Adv. Comput. Technol. **4**(20), 29–35 (2012)
14. Robnikšikonja, M., Kononenko, I.: Theoretical and empirical analysis of ReliefF and RReliefF. Mach. Learn. **53**(1), 23–69 (2003)
15. Deng, Z., Chung, F.L., Wang, S.: Robust relief-feature weighting, margin maximization, and fuzzy optimization. IEEE Trans. Fuzzy Syst. **18**(4), 726–744 (2010)
16. Hamid, Y., Sugumaran, M., Journaux, L.: Machine learning techniques for intrusion detection: a comparative analysis. In: International Conference on Informatics and Analytics (2016)
17. Fei, Z., Guo, J., Wan, P., Yang, W.: Fast automatic image segmentation based on Bayesian decision-making theory. In: International Conference on Information and Automation (2009)
18. Zhang, C., Wang, J.: Attribute weighted Naive Bayesian classification algorithm. Microcomputer Information, pp. 27–30 (2010)
19. Han, J., Kamber, M., Pei, J.: Data Mining: Concepts and Techniques, 2nd edn. (The Morgan Kaufmann Series in Data Management Systems) (2006)
20. Pfahringer, B.: Winning the KDD99 classification cup: bagged boosting. ACM SIGKDD Explor. Newsl. **1**(2), 65–66 (2000)

Power Allocation in One-Way Untrusted AF Relay System with Friendly Jamming

Ronghua Luo[1(✉)], Chao Meng[1], Guobing Hu[2], and Hua Shi[1]

[1] School of Networks and Telecommunications Engineering
in Jinling Institute of Technology, Nanjing, China
{lrh,mengchao,shihuawindy}@jit.edu.cn
[2] School of Electronical and Information Engineering
in Jinling Institute of Technology, Nanjing, China
s0304152@jit.edu.cn

Abstract. In this paper, the physical layer security in one-way untrusted AF relay system is considered. For improving the physical layer security, external friendly jammers offer help through transmitting interference signal to the untrusted relay. It is indicated that a nonzero secrecy rate is achievable in one-way untrusted AF relay system with the help of friendly jammers. The source optimization problem is further formulated. In this optimization problem, in order to increasing the secrecy rate, the source must pay the jammers for exchanging their service of jamming. Finally, an optimal transmit power allocation of all the nodes is provided for the system. And simulation results verify the properties.

Keywords: Physical layer security · Secrecy rate · Friendly jammer
Source optimization problem · Power allocation

1 Introduction

Recently, physical layer based security attracting much attention due to the broadcasting nature of wireless communication. The theoretical foundation to study the secure communication at the physical layer is the wiretap channel and the information-theoretic notion of secrecy introduced by Wyner [1]. It has been proved that if the main channel condition is worse than the wiretap channel, the secrecy capacity will be zero [2], in order to overcoming this limitation, cooperative relaying [3, 4] and cooperative jamming [5, 6] has been proposed in wireless communication networks. And, physical layer security is also very important in 5G networks, such as ultra dense networks [7], LTE-U [8], and network slicing [9].

When the channel between the source and destination is worst, the relay node must be utilized to forward the information of source. However, in some cases, the relay node is untrusted. For example, the relay has a lower sense of security, and so, it does not trust the confidential messages it is relaying. How to communicate securely with the untrusted relay has been studied in [10, 11]. In [12], the destination can perform cooperative jamming, and which disable the untrusted relay from deciphering what it relaying. And recently, considering physical layer security in two-way untrusted relay

© ICST Institute for Computer Sciences, Social Informatics and Telecommunications Engineering 2018
K. Long et al. (Eds.): 5GWN 2017, LNICST 211, pp. 589–596, 2018.
https://doi.org/10.1007/978-3-319-72823-0_54

system was also studied in [13]. In this paper, with the help of friendly jammers, the secrecy rate of the sources can be effectively improved.

In this paper, the physical layer security of AF untrusted one-way relay system with friendly jamming is investigated. Because there is no direct communication link between the source and the destination, an essential relay is needed, meanwhile, this relay is also a malicious eavesdropper. In [14], it is indicated that the secrecy rate is zero. Because that the untrusted relay can decipher the confidential message from the source. Therefore, the destination can only receive the signals from the untrusted relay who knows all the confidential message the destination knows. And then, it is impossible to make the source-destination pairs keeping secret from the untrusted relay. So, in this paper, we utilize the jammers as helpers that confusing the eavesdropping relay. After more analysis, it is indicated that a non-zero secrecy rate is indeed available by utilizing proper jamming power from the friendly jammers. The source optimization problem is further formulated. In the optimization problem, in order to improve the secrecy rate, the source must pay the jammers for interfering the malicious relay. The friendly jammers charge the sources with a certain price for their service of jamming. And the simulation results verify the properties.

The paper is organized as follows. Section 2 presents the channel model, two-phase protocol that utilizes cooperative jamming and the secrecy rate for the destination is defined. In Sect. 3, we formulate the source optimization problem and analyze the optimizing problem of physical layer security with jammers. In Sect. 4, simulation results are presented. And main conclusions are drawn in Sect. 5.

2 System Model

As shown in Fig. 1, we consider a one-way AF relay network consisting of one source node, one untrusted relay node, one destination and N friendly jammer nodes, which are denoted by S, R, D and FJ_i, $i = 1, 2, ..., N$, respectively. It is assumed that all nodes are half-duplex and there includes two phases, called phase one and phase two respectively. In phase one, the source transmits signal X_s with power p_s. At the same time, the jammer nodes transmit jamming signals X_{J_i} with $p_i^J, j = 1, 2, ..., N$ for confusing the relay node. We define the received signal at the relay in phase one as X_R

$$X_R = \sqrt{p_s}X_s h_{S,R} + \sum_{i=1}^{N} \sqrt{p_i^J}X_{J_i}h_{J_i,R} + Z_1 \tag{1}$$

Where Z_1 is an additive white Gaussian noise (AWGN), the mean is zero and variance is σ^2.

In phase two, the relay node amplifies and forward (AF) the received signal X_R with a factor β. And β is defined as

$$\beta = (p_s|h_{S,R}|^2 + \sum_{i=1}^{N} p_i^J |h_{J_i,R}|^2 + \sigma^2)^{-1/2} \tag{2}$$

The received signal at the destination in phase two is defined as Y_D, which is expressed as

$$Y_D = \beta\sqrt{p_r}X_R h_{R,D} + \sum_{i=1}^{N}\sqrt{p_i^J}X_{J_i}h_{J_i,D} + Z_2 \tag{3}$$

Where Z_2 is also an AWGN with zero-mean and variance of σ^2. Assuming that the signal X_{J_i} is known to the destination. After calculation, Y_D can be given as

$$Y_D = \beta\sqrt{p_s p_r}X_s h_{S,R}h_{R,D} + \beta\sqrt{p_r}h_{R,D}Z_1 + Z_2 \tag{4}$$

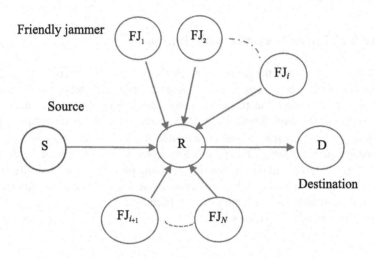

Fig. 1. System model of the one-way relay network

Then, the corresponding SINR (signal-to-interference-and-noise ratio) at the relay, defined as γ_R, can be given by

$$\gamma_R = \frac{p_s|h_{S,R}|^2}{\sigma^2 + \sum_{i=1}^{N}p_i^J|h_{J_i,R}|^2} \tag{5}$$

The corresponding SINR at the destination defined as γ_D, can be given by

$$\gamma_D = \frac{p_r p_s|h_{S,R}|^2|h_{R,D}|^2}{\sigma^2(p_s|h_{S,R}|^2 + \sum_{i=1}^{N}p_i^J|h_{J_i,R}|^2 + \sigma^2 + p_r|h_{R,D}|^2)} \tag{6}$$

And then, the untrusted relay node has the capacity as

$$C_R = \frac{W}{2} \log_2(1 + \gamma_R) \tag{7}$$

The destination has the capacity as

$$C_D = \frac{W}{2} \log_2(1 + \gamma_D) \tag{8}$$

Then, the secrecy rate for the destination can be defined as

$$C_D^s = (C_D - C_R)^+ \tag{9}$$

Where $(x)^+$ denotes $\max\{x, 0\}$.

3 Physical Layer Security with Jammers

From [14], we know that the secrecy rate of the destination is zero without friendly jammers. However, when using friendly jammers, these jammers can transmit interference signal to confuse the malicious relay, meanwhile, the interference signal is known for the destination. Then, a non-zero secrecy rate of the destination with the help of friendly jammers may be indeed available at some power vectors of (p_s, p_r, p_i^J). In this section, after further analyzing, it is found that the secrecy rate of the destination can be effectively improved through buying jamming power from the friendly jammers. And then, the problem comes to how to optimize the secrecy rate of the destination by allocating the jamming power from different friendly jammers.

From (7), (8) and (9), we have

$$C_D^s = \frac{W}{2} \left[\log_2 \left(1 + \frac{p_r p_s |h_{S,R}|^2 |h_{R,D}|^2}{\sigma^2 (p_s |h_{S,R}|^2 + \sum_{i=1}^{N} p_i^J |h_{J_i,R}|^2 + \sigma^2 + p_r |h_{R,D}|^2)} \right) \\ - \log_2 \left(1 + \frac{p_s |h_{S,R}|^2}{\sigma^2 + \sum_{i=1}^{N} p_i^J |h_{J_i,R}|^2} \right) \right]^+ \tag{10}$$

From (10), we can find that if $\frac{\sigma^2}{p_r |h_{R,D}|^2} < 1$, in some region of the jamming power p_i^J, the secrecy rate will be positive, which implies that the secrecy rate can be improved with friendly jammers' help compared to the secrecy rate without friendly jammers.

And $\frac{\partial C_D^s}{\partial p_r} > 0$ is always hold, which means that C_D^s is a monotonically increasing function of p_r. Thus, when $p_r = p_{max}$, the secrecy rate C_D^s reaches the maximum, where p_{max} denotes the optimal relay power. In this paper, our main interested thing is how to optimize the utility value of the source by allocating the jamming power, and meanwhile, all the nodes transmit with independent power, we can consider the source power p_s as a constant. If the source wants to improve the secrecy rate with the help of jammers, they must pay the cost to the jammers. So, in this paper, the utility function of the source is defined as

$$U_s = \alpha C_D^s - M \tag{11}$$

Where the constant $\alpha > 0$ is a factor that converts utility units to currency. M is the cost to pay for the jammers, which is defined as

$$M = \sum_{i=1}^{N} \lambda_i p_i^J \tag{12}$$

Where λ_i is the price per unit power charged by the friendly jammer i.

So, subject to the secrecy rate constraint and individual power constraint, the source optimization problem can be formulated as

$$\begin{aligned} \max \quad & U_s = \alpha C_D^s - M \\ st. \quad & C_D^s > 0 \\ & 0 \le p_i^J \le p_{\max}, fixed \quad p_r, p_s \end{aligned} \tag{13}$$

For maximizing the optimization problem, we can calculate the first derivative of U_s, we have

$$\frac{\partial U_s}{\partial p_i^J} = \frac{\alpha W}{2 \ln 2} \left[\frac{A |h_{J_i,R}|^2}{(B + \sum_{i=1}^{N} p_i^J |h_{J_i,R}|^2 + A)(B + \sum_{i=1}^{N} p_i^J |h_{J_i,R}|^2)} - \frac{p_s |h_{S,R}|^2 |h_{J_i,R}|^2}{(\sigma^2 + \sum_{i=1}^{N} p_i^J |h_{J_i,R}|^2 + p_s |h_{S,R}|^2)(\sigma^2 + \sum_{i=1}^{N} p_i^J |h_{J_i,R}|^2)} \right] - \lambda_i \tag{14}$$

Where $A = p_r p_s |h_{S,R}|^2 |h_{R,D}|^2$, $B = p_s |h_{S,R}|^2 + p_r |h_{R,D}|^2 + \sigma^2$. When $\partial U_s / \partial p_i^J = 0$, we can obtain the forth-order polynomial equation as

$$(p_i^J)^4 + C_{i,3} (p_i^J)^3 + C_{i,2} (p_i^J)^2 + C_{i,1} p_i^J + C_{i,0} = 0 \tag{15}$$

Where $C_{i,n}, n = 0, 1, 2, 3$ are formulas of A, B, λ_i and p_i^J. Because that the solutions of the forth-order polynomial equation are very complex and not necessary for our following work, so our main interest is the parameters that affect these optimalsolutions. Then, the optimal power solutions of the friendly jammer i can be denoted as

$$p_i^{J^*} = p_i^{J^*}(A, B, \{P_j^J\}_{j \neq i}, \lambda_i) \tag{16}$$

Further, subject to the constraints, the optimal jamming power can be denoted as

$$p_{i\_opt}^J = \min(\max(p_i^{J^*}, 0), p_{\max}) \tag{17}$$

4 Simulation Results

The proposed scheme has been simulated numerically using MATLAB software. In the simulation, we consider a one-way AF relay network with one source, one relay, one destination which are located at $(-1, 0)$, $(0, 0)$ and $(1, 0)$ respectively. The other parameters are defined as: $p_{\max} = 10$, the transmission bandwidth $W = 1$, the noise variance $\sigma^2 = 0.01$,the path loss factor is 2, and $\alpha = 1$.

When only one friendly jammer helps to the source, the two friendly jammer locations are considered as $(0.3, 0.4)$ and $(0.6, 0.8)$. In Fig. 2, the power of source is set up to $p_{\max} = 10$ and $\lambda = 0.1$, we can find that the utility of source can be maximized, when the jammers power is 2 and 4 respectively. And we can see, if the friendly jammer is close to the untrusted relay, the utility function can be improved more effectively. Figure 3 shows that the optimal jamming power is decreased with the asking price creasing, and it is foreseeable that the jamming power which buys from the jammer will be zero. So, when setting the price λ, a tradeoff must be considered for the friendly jammer.

In Fig. 4, two different scenarios are considered in simulations. On the one hand, there is no sufficiently effective friendly jammer, which implies that maximum secrecy rate cannot be achieved with the help of only one friendly jammer. And meanwhile, in this scenario, the secrecy rate increases with the number of friendly jammers. When the

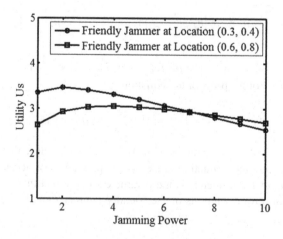

Fig. 2. The source's utility versus the jamming power

number of friendly jammers is 20, the secrecy rate can reach the maximum. However, on the other hand, when there is at least one sufficiently effective friendly jammer, which means that multiple friendly jammers can offer sufficiently effective help, we can see that the secrecy rate remains unchanged with the number of friendly jammers increasing.

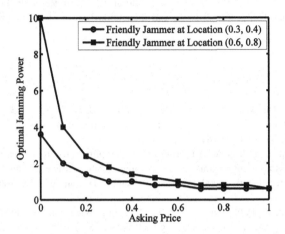

Fig. 3. The optimal jamming power versus asking price

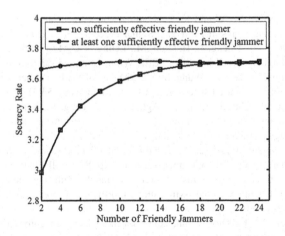

Fig. 4. Secrecy rate versus the number of friendly jammers

5   Conclusions

In this paper, we have investigated the one-way untrusted relay communications with friendly jammers. The source optimization problem is defined, and the optimal solution of jammer power is obtained. Simulation results show that the utility function of the source can be improved with friendly jammers' help. And there exists a tradeoff for the price of jammers, otherwise, the source will not select the jammers as cooperators.

Acknowledgement. This work was supported by the Natural Science Foundation of Jiangsu Province (Grants No. BK20161104), The Scientific Research Fund Project of JIT (2016 incentive program, jit-2016-jlxm-24), the Natural Science Foundation of the Jiangsu Higher Education Institutions of China (16KJB510011), the Doctoral Scientific Research Foundation of JIT (jit-b-201409, jit-b-201408, jit-b-201633) and Incubation Project of Science Foundation of JIT (jit-fhxm-201605).

References

1. Wyner, A.D.: The wire-tap channel. Bell Syst. Tech. J. **54**(8), 1355–1387 (1975)
2. Csiszar, I., Korner, J.: Broadcast channels with confidential messages. IEEE Trans. Inf. Theory **24**(3), 339–348 (1978)
3. Dong, L., Han, Z., Petropulu, A.P., Poor, H.V.: Amplify-and-forward based cooperation for secure wireless communications. In: Proceedings of the IEEE International Conference on Acoustics, Speech and Signal Processing, Taipei, Taiwan, pp. 2613–2616. IEEE Press (2009)
4. Dong, L., Han, Z., Petropulu, A.P., Poor, H.V.: Improving wireless physical layer security via cooperating relays. IEEE Trans. Signal Process. **58**(3), 1875–1888 (2010)
5. Tekin, E., Yener, A.: The general gaussian multiple-access and two-way wiretap channels: achievable rates and cooperative jamming. IEEE Trans. Inf. Theory **54**(6), 2735–2751 (2008)
6. Zheng, G., Choo, L.-C., Wong, K.-K.: Optimal cooperative jamming to enhance physical layer security using relays. IEEE Trans. Signal Process. **59**(3), 1317–1322 (2011)
7. Zhang, H., Dong, Y., Cheng, J., Hossain, M., Leung, V.C.M.: Fronthauling for 5G LTE-U ultra dense cloud small cell networks. IEEE Wirel. Commun. **23**(6), 48–56 (2016)
8. Zhang, H., Chu, X., Guo, W., Wang, S.: Coexistence of Wi-Fi and heterogeneous small cell networks sharing unlicensed spectrum. IEEE Commun. Mag. **53**(3), 158–164 (2015)
9. Zhang, H., Liu, N., Chu, X., Long, K., Aghvami, A., Leung, V.: Network slicing based 5G and future mobile networks: mobility, resource management, and challenges. IEEE Commun. Magazine **55**(8), 138–145 (2017)
10. Oohama, Y.: Coding for relay channels with confidential messages. In: Proceedings of IEEE Information Theory Workshop, Caims, Australia, pp. 87–89. IEEE Press (2001)
11. Oohama, Y.: Capacity theorems for relay channels with confidential messages. In: Proceedings IEEE International Symposium Information Theory, Nice, France, pp. 926–930. IEEE Press (2007)
12. He, X., Yener, A.: Two-hop secure communication using an untrusted relay: a case for cooperative jamming. In: Proceedings of IEEE Global Communications Conference, New Orleans, LA, pp. 1–5. IEEE Press (2008)
13. Zhang, R., Song, L., Han, Z., Jiao, B., Debbah, M.: Physical layer security for two-way untrusted relaying with friendly jammers. IEEE Trans. Veh. Technol. **61**(8), 3693–3703 (2012)
14. He, X., Yener, A.: Cooperation with untrusted relay: a secrecy perspective. IEEE Trans. Inf. Theory **56**(8), 3807–3827 (2010)

A Vehicular Positioning Enhancement with Connected Vehicle Assistance Using Extended Kalman Filtering

Daxin Tian[1,4,5,6(✉)], Wenhao Liu[1,4], Xuting Duan[1,4], Hui Rong[2],
Peng Guo[2], Wenyang Wang[2], and Haijun Zhang[3]

[1] Beijing Advanced Innovation Center for Big Data and Brain Computing,
Beihang University, XueYuan Road No. 37, Beijing 100191, China
dtian@buaa.edu.cn

[2] China Automotive Technology and Research Center, Automotive Engineering
Research Institute, East Xianfeng Road No. 68, Tianjin 300300, China

[3] School of Computer and Communication Engineering, University of Science
and Technology Beijing, XueYuan Road No. 30, Beijing 100083, China

[4] Beijing Key Laboratory for Cooperative Vehicle Infrastructure Systems
and Safety Control, School of Transportation Science and Engineering, Beihang
University, XueYuan Road No. 37, Beijing 100191, China

[5] Jiangsu Province Collaborative Innovation Center of Modern
Urban Traffic Technologies, Si Pai Lou. 2, Nanjing 210096, China

[6] Key Lab of Urban ITS Technology Optimization and Integration,
The Ministry of Public Security of China, Hefei 230088, China

Abstract. In this paper, we consider the problem of vehicular positioning enhancement with emerging connected vehicles (CV) technologies. In order to actually describe the scenario, the Interacting Multiple Model (IMM) filter is used for depicting varies of observation models. A CV-enhanced IMM filtering approach is proposed to locate a vehicle by data fusion from both coarse GPS data and the Doppler frequency shifts (DFS) measured from dedicated short-range communications (DSRC) radio signals. Simulation results state the effectiveness of the proposed approach called CV-IMM-EKF.

Keywords: Vehicular positioning enhancement · Target vehicle (TV)
GPS · CV-IMM-EKF

1 Introduction

Due to the development of the fifth-generation (5G) mobile communications, this new communicated method attracts more and more attention because of its faster transfer speed, high adaptability and better end-to-end performance [2, 3]. And the more transfer technologies such like the ultra dense cloud small cell network (UDCSNet) [1] are used in the construction of vehicular network. About applications, some of the communications problems in the society have been resolved such as LTE-V systematic and integrated V2X solution [4], software-defined heterogeneous vehicular network (SERVICE) [5], credible RTI sharing mechanism [6], traffic density estimation [7] and

© ICST Institute for Computer Sciences, Social Informatics and Telecommunications Engineering 2018
K. Long et al. (Eds.): 5GWN 2017, LNICST 211, pp. 597–608, 2018.
https://doi.org/10.1007/978-3-319-72823-0_55

the physical layer outage performance of information sharing [8], and the effectiveness in the application has improved greatly [9–11].

The availability of high-accuracy location-awareness is essential for a diverse set of vehicular applications including intelligent transportation systems, location-based services (LBS), navigation, as well as a couple of emerging cooperative vehicle-infrastructure systems (CVIS) [12]. Typically, as an important technique, the real-time vehicle positioning system has drawn great attention in the fields of transportation and mobile communications [13]. However, it still faces a big challenge in the areas with inconsistent availability of satellite networks, especially in dense urban areas where the standalone global navigation satellite systems (GNSSs) (e.g., GPS). Even the high precision GNSS equipment associated with a high cost (e.g., DGPS), sometimes provides serious outliers caused by non-line-of-sight (NLOS) (e.g., buildings, walls, trees, vehicles, and more obstructions) and severe multipath issues [14].

The accurate positioning with sub-meter error is significant for vehicles in vehicle ad-hoc networks (VANETs). Because any vehicle with this capability and wireless communications would be able to sense others accurately and simply, which is an extremely essential factor for vehicular collision avoidance, lane change assistance and so on [15, 16]. In [14, 18, 19], the fundamental techniques in positioning systems have been presented based on the real-time measurements of time of arrival (TOA), time difference of arrival (TDOA), direction of arrival (DOA), received signal strength indicator (RSSI), Doppler frequency shift (DFS), fingerprinting, and wireless channel state information (CSI) techniques and so on. Especially, cloud-based wireless network proposed in [20] is expected to provide flexible virtualized network functions for vehicular positioning. Recent researches indicate that these measurements are challenged by some drawbacks varying from complexities of the time synchronization, occupations of the high-bandwidth, to huge costs on the implementations [14]. Although there already exist some location systems, such as those presented in [17], which can achieve lane-level location performance, these systems require the accurate detection on unique driving events through smart phones or the deployment of lane anchors.

To tackle the aforementioned problems, a new class of cooperative positioning (CP) methods that relies on vehicle-to-vehicle (V2V) communications and data fusion filtering [20–22] has been presented in recent years, which can further improve the accuracy of positioning. Actually, such concern raised in CP is the reliability of the localization approaches in heavy multipath and NLOS scenarios, which is similar to that in indoor environment [19, 20].

Because of the low speed of vehicles, the DFS is too difficult to be extracted from noise, and thus for DFS vehicular positioning methods, the standard deviation (STD) of positioning error increases as the relative speed between the target vehicle and the other vehicles decreases. So we will investigate the method to overcome this problem. In this paper, We will focus on the scenario that the neighbor vehicles travel in the opposite direction of the target vehicle (TV), for this case can provide obviously detectable Doppler Effect.

In this paper, we design a CV-enhanced Interacting Multiple Model Extended Kalman filter (CV-IMM-EKF) for vehicular positioning. Firstly a first-order Tylor series expansion is used to transform a nonlinear problem to a linear problem.

Secondly, a multiple-model is used to describe the variation of the DFS measurements. Finally, IMM-EKF is used to estimate the target vehicle's state. The next, we integrate the GPS measurements from both a target vehicle and its neighbors into a vehicular positioning filter and set a relatively conservative number of neighbors for the basic set, which can reduce the dispensable computation complexity. And the information fusion provides a great enhancement compared with GPS-only localization from the simulation results.

The problem to be solved and the analytical models are presented in Sect. 2, the CV-IMM-EKF steps are described in detail in Sect. 3, and the simulation results are revealed and compared in Sect. 4. Finally, Sect. 5 concludes this paper.

2 Problem Statement

The problem to be solved is to estimate the position of a TV moving on a 2-D road, where there are many other neighbors around the TV. All of the vehicles are able to know their own state information, including position, velocity, etc., provided by coarse GPS receiver and they can know the neighbors' state information via vehicular communications as well. Consequently, this case can be treated as a simple but practical CV scenario. A TV is considered as a research object for positioning enhancement based on CV, and a neighbor is considered as the vehicle who is within a certain communication range to the TV and travel in the opposite direction of the TV. Each vehicle is assumed to be with an OBU providing both the DSRC and the DFS measurements [24].

Considering the ith moving vehicle at time instant k with a state vector $\theta_k^i = \left[p_{x,k}^i, p_{y,k}^i, v_{x,k}^i, v_{y,k}^i \right]^T$, $i = 1, \ldots, n_p$, where the $(p_{x,k}^i, p_{y,k}^i)$ and $\left(v_{x,k}^i, v_{y,k}^i \right)$ denote the ith vehicle's position and velocity, respectively, and n_p is the total number of the vehicles driving on the road, and T is a transpose operator. The dynamic state can be modeled by the following system:

$$\theta_k^i = F_{k-1}^i \theta_{k-1}^i + G_{k-1}^i \left(u_{k-1}^i + w_{k-1}^i \right) \tag{1}$$

where F_{k-1}^i is the state transition matrix, and G_{k-1}^i is the noise distribution matrix. u_{k-1}^i is the control vector and w_{k-1}^i is zero-mean white Gaussian noise with covariance matrix Q_{k-1}^i.

For the dynamic model presented by (1), the following observation model can be defined:

$$\Psi_k = h(\theta_k) + \Upsilon_k(r_e) \tag{2}$$

where $h = \left[p_{x,k}^i, p_{y,k}^i, v_{x,k}^i, v_{y,k}^i, \omega_k^1, \ldots, \omega_k^j \right]^T$ is a nonlinear observation vector in terms of θ_k. ω_k^j is the DFS of the received signal from the jth neighbor, $j = 1, \ldots, n_k, n_k < n_p$, and n_k is the total number of the neighbors on the road. $\Upsilon_k(r_e)$ is the observation noise that can be used to describe the M types of observation errors by assuming a set of another covariance matrixes. The transition among M types of the errors is generally modeled as a first-order M-state homogeneous Markov chain r_e, $e = 1, 2, \ldots, M$.

Specifically, assuming that the DFS measurements from the OBU can be modeled in a derivative form of the DSRC carrier frequency, f, as follows:

$$\omega_k^j = -\frac{f}{c}\nabla_t\left(d_k^j + \vartheta_k^j r_e\right) \tag{3}$$

$$d_k^j = \sqrt{\left(p_{x,k} - p_{x,k}^j\right)^2 + \left(p_{y,k} - p_{y,k}^j\right)^2} \tag{4}$$

where c is the speed of light, d_k^j is the relative distance between the TV and its neighbor j, and ϑ_k^j is the DFS observation noise of neighbor j. Substituting (4) into (3) yields

$$\omega_k^j = -\frac{f}{c}\left[\frac{\left(p_{x,k} - p_{x,k}^j\right)\left(v_{x,k} - v_{x,k}^j\right) + \left(p_{y,k} - p_{y,k}^j\right)\left(v_{y,k} - v_{y,k}^j\right)}{\sqrt{\left(p_{x,k} - p_{x,k}^j\right)^2 + \left(p_{y,k} - p_{y,k}^j\right)^2}}\right] + \Upsilon_k(r_e) \tag{5}$$

where $(p_{x,k}^j, p_{y,k}^j)$ and $\left(v_{x,k}^j, v_{y,k}^j\right)$ is the position and velocity vector of the neighbor j. To solve this nonlinear observation function, with the first-order Taylor expansion of (5) around an arbitrary state vector, h can be transformed to a fixed form of matrix, in which all of the components are supposed to obtain from both the GPS and OBU. As a result, the observation model of the TV can be reformulated as a linear one:

$$Z_k = H_k\theta_k + \Upsilon_k(r_e) \tag{6}$$

and with the observation transition matrix:

$$H_k = \begin{bmatrix} 1 & 0 & 0 & 0 \\ 0 & 1 & 0 & 0 \\ 0 & 0 & 1 & 0 \\ 0 & 0 & 0 & 1 \\ h_k^{11} & h_k^{12} & h_k^{13} & h_k^{14} \\ \vdots & \vdots & \vdots & \vdots \\ h_k^{j1} & h_k^{j2} & h_k^{j3} & h_k^{j4} \end{bmatrix} \tag{7}$$

where

$$h_k^{j1} = \nabla_{p_{x,k}}\left(\omega_k^j\right) = -\frac{f}{c}\frac{\left(p_{y,k} - p_{y,k}^j\right)}{\left(d_k^j\right)^3} \tag{8}$$

$$\left[\left(p_{y,k} - p_{y,k}^j\right)\left(v_{x,k} - v_{x,k}^j\right) + \left(p_{x,k} - p_{x,k}^j\right)\left(v_{y,k} - v_{y,k}^j\right)\right]$$

$$h_k^{j2} = \nabla_{p_{y,k}}(\omega_k^j) = -\frac{f}{c} \frac{\left(p_{x,k} - p_{x,k}^j\right)}{\left(d_k^j\right)^3}$$

$$\left[\left(p_{x,k} - p_{x,k}^j\right)\left(v_{y,k} - v_{y,k}^j\right) + \left(p_{y,k} - p_{y,k}^j\right)\left(v_{x,k} - v_{x,k}^j\right)\right] \qquad (9)$$

$$h_k^{j3} = \nabla_{v_{x,k}}(\omega_k^j) = -\frac{f}{c} \frac{\left(p_{x,k} - p_{x,k}^j\right)}{d_k^j} \qquad (10)$$

$$h_k^{j4} = \nabla_{v_{y,k}}(\omega_k^j) = -\frac{f}{c} \frac{\left(p_{y,k} - p_{y,k}^j\right)}{d_k^j} \qquad (11)$$

Based on the aforementioned models from (1) and (6), it is reasonable to assume that F_{k-1}^i and G_{k-1}^i in the system model are invariable at both each time instant and vehicle. Therefore, the position estimation of the TV can be formulated as the problem of linear filtering for M-state jump Markov systems and the model can be simplified as:

$$\begin{cases} \theta_k^i = F\theta_{k-1}^i + G\left(u_{k-1}^i + w_{k-1}^i\right) \\ Z_k = H_k\theta_k + \Upsilon_k(r_e) \end{cases} \qquad (12)$$

Because H_k can be estimated by data fusion from both the GPS and OBU at each time instant k, a CV-enhanced Interacting Multiple Model Extended Kalman filter (IMM-EKF) can be deployed.

3   Connected Vehicles-Enhanced Interacting Multiple Model Extended Kalman Filtering for Vehicular Positioning

In this section, we adopt the IMM approach to propose a vehicular positioning enhancement algorithm based on CV. The structure of the vehicular positioning system is illustrated in Fig. 1.

And the steps of this algorithm is as followed:

Step (1) Mixing Probabilities and State Estimates

$$\mu_{k+1,s|t} = \pi_{st}\mu_{k,s}/c_t \qquad (13)$$

where $\mu_{k+1,s|t}$ is known as the mixing probability in the IMM estimator, $\mu_{k,s}$ is the probability of the event that the sth motion model is in effect at time step k, $s, t = 1, 2, \ldots, M$, correspond to the s, tth mode of the Markov chain r_e, and

$$c_t = \sum_{s=1}^{M} \pi_{st}\mu_{k,s} \qquad (14)$$

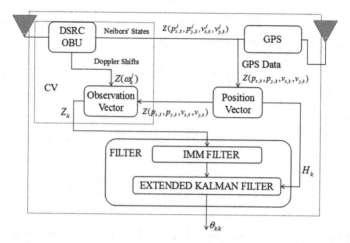

Fig. 1. Vehicular positioning system with information fusion of the DFS and GPS measurements from both itself and the other neighbors

where c_t is a normalization constant and

$$\theta_{k|k,t}^0 = \sum_{s=1}^{M} \mu_{k+1,s|t} \theta_{k|k,t}^{0,0} \tag{15}$$

$$P_{k|k,t}^0 = \sum_{s=1}^{M} \mu_{k+1,s|t} \times \left\{ P_{k|k,t}^{0,0} + \left[\theta_{k|k,t}^{0,0} - \theta_{k|k,t}^0 \right] \left[\theta_{k|k,t}^{0,0} - \theta_{k|k,t}^0 \right]^T \right\} \tag{16}$$

Step (2) Mode Update and Prediction Steps

Calculate $h_k^{j1}, h_k^{j2}, h_k^{j3}, h_k^{j4}$, according to the Eqs. (8)–(11) and then update the observation transition matrix H_k defined in (7).

The CV-IMM-EKF advanced prediction is given by

$$\theta_{k|k-1,t} \approx F_k \theta_{k-1|k-1,t} = F \theta_{k-1|k-1,t} \tag{17}$$

and the State prediction error covariance matrix is as follows:

$$P_{k|k-1,t} \approx F_k P_{k-1|k-1,t} (F_k)^T + Q_{k-1} = F P_{k-1|k-1,t} F^T + Q_{k-1} \tag{18}$$

From the previous data, the CV-IMM-EKF gain is given by

$$K_k = P_{k|k-1,t} H_k^T (\varphi_k(N)) \\ \times \left\{ H_k(\varphi_k(N)) P_{k|k-1,t} H_k^T(\varphi_k(N)) + R_k(r_e(N)) \right\}^{-1} \tag{19}$$

where $\varphi_k(N)$ and $r_e(N)$ are functions of N and can change the dimension of the observation transition matrix H_k and the covariance matrix R_k, respectively.

The CV-IMM-EKF update steps are given by

$$\theta^0_{k|k,t} = \theta^0_{k|k-1,t} + K_k\left\{Z_k - H_k(\varphi_k(N))\theta^0_{k|k-1,t}\right\} \tag{20}$$

$$P^0_{k|k,t} = P^0_{k|k-1,t} - K_k\left\{Z_k - H_k(\varphi_k(N))\theta^0_{k|k-1,t} + R_k(r_e(N))\right\}K_k^T \tag{21}$$

The CV-IMM-EKF prediction steps are given by

$$\theta^0_{k+1|k,t} = F\theta^0_{k|k,t} + G\mu_{k,t} \tag{22}$$

$$P^0_{k+1|k,t} = F\theta^0_{k|k,t}F^T + GQG^T \tag{23}$$

The likelihood function $\Lambda_{k,t}$ and predicted mode probability $\mu_{k,t}$ are given by

$$\Lambda_{k,t} = \mathcal{N}\left(\begin{matrix} Z_k - H_k(\varphi_k(N))\theta^0_{k|k-1,t}; \\ 0, H_k(\varphi_k(N))P^0_{k|k-1,t}H_k^T(\varphi_k(N)) + R_k(r_e(N)) \end{matrix}\right) \tag{24}$$

$$\mu_{k,t} = \Lambda_{k,t}c_t/c \tag{25}$$

where c is a normalizing constant defined as follows:

$$c = \sum\nolimits_{t=1}^{M} \Lambda_{k,t}c_t \tag{26}$$

Step (3) Estimates Combination

$$\theta_{k|k} = \sum\nolimits_{t=1}^{M} \mu_{k,t}\theta_{k|k,t} \tag{27}$$

$$P_{k|k} = \sum\nolimits_{t=1}^{M} \mu_{k,t} \times \left\{P_{k|k,t} + \left[\theta_{k|k,t} - \theta_{k|k}\right]\left[\theta_{k|k,t} - \theta_{k|k}\right]^T\right\} \tag{28}$$

4 Numerical Study

4.1 Simulation Scenario

A basic set with N neighbors for the TV can be formed through Algorithm CV-IMM-EKF. Considering a section of urban roads, which is with a width of four lanes (each one is 3.5 m wide) and a length of one kilometer. It is assumed that the traffic density of the road section is 20 vehicles/km and the average speed of traffic is generated stochastically in duration from 50 km/h to 60 km/h following a uniform distribution. The initial positions of the neighbors are generated stochastically on the road following a uniform distribution as well. The vehicle dynamics described in (12) is with

$$F = \begin{bmatrix} I & \Delta t I \\ O & I \end{bmatrix}, G = \begin{bmatrix} \frac{1}{2} \Delta t^2 I \\ \Delta t I \end{bmatrix} \tag{29}$$

where I is a 2×2 identity matrix, O is a 2×2 zero matrix, and Δt is the sampling period. The control vector in (12) is $u^i = [0\ 0.01]^T$. The noise vector $w_{k-1}^i = [\sigma_{ax,k-1}, \sigma_{ay,k-1}]^T \sim \mathcal{N}(0, Q)$, with covariance matrix $Q = diag\left[\sigma_{ax}^2, \sigma_{ay}^2\right]$, where the elements $\sigma_{ax,k-1} = \sqrt{0.99/2}$ and $\sigma_{ay,k-1} = \sqrt{0.01/2}$ are the acceleration noises along the X and Y-axis, respectively, with standard deviation (STD) in m/s^2. The covariance matrix $R(r_e)$ of observation noise $\Upsilon_k(r_e) \sim \mathcal{N}(0, R(r_e))$ is described as a first-order Markov chain switching between two models $R(r_1) = diag\left[\sigma_{px}^2, \sigma_{py}^2, \sigma_{vx}^2, \sigma_{vy}^2, \sigma_{\omega 1}^2(r_1), \ldots, \sigma_{\omega N}^2(r_1)\right]$ and $R(r_2) = diag\left[\sigma_{px}^2, \sigma_{py}^2, \sigma_{vx}^2, \sigma_{vy}^2, \sigma_{\omega 1}^2(r_2), \ldots, \sigma_{\omega N}^2(r_2)\right]$, of which the elements are with STDs in units of m, m/s^2 and Hz. The transition probability for this Markov chain is $\pi_{r_1 r_2} = \begin{bmatrix} 0.9 & 0.1 \\ 0.1 & 0.9 \end{bmatrix}$ and their initial probability is $\mu_0 = [0.5\ 0.5]$. According to the achievable performance discussed in [12, 19], as the number of the neighbors is increasing, the performance enhancement can be less obvious and lead to more additionally computational burden. Therefore, we set $N = 4$, which is a relatively conservative number of the neighbors for the basic set, which is mentioned in Algorithm CV-IMM-EKF.

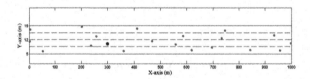

Fig. 2. Initial scenario (Color figure online)

The vehicles that start at the first two lanes from the bottom move towards the positive direction of the X-axis in Fig. 2. On the contrary, the vehicles that start at the first two lanes from the top move towards the negative direction of the X-axis. The 'black dot' and 'red note' denote the initial positions of the TV and the neighbors, respectively. The TV starts at position (300,5) in m, with the initial velocity vector (60,0) in m/s^2. However, because of the system noise and control vector set in the dynamics model, the actual velocity is changing slightly over the sampling period.

In the simulations, the sampling period and length are taken to be 0.2 s and 100, respectively, and the communication range of the DSRC is 300 m. As the DFS measurements presented in [19, 22], the Probability Density Function (PDF) of the DFS is approximately zero-mean asymmetric Gaussian with the left and right STDs of 100 Hz and 120 Hz, when the vehicles travel at the speed of 60 km/h, broadcasting the DSRC packets with a frequency of 5.89 GHz and a rate of 100 packets/s. It is worth noting that the PDF of the DFS remains a fairly consistent estimation from LOS to NLOS.

Considering the noise of the DFS measurements as zero-mean Gaussian with two states of STDs: $\sigma_{wN}(r_1) = 100\,\text{Hz}$ and $\sigma_{wN}(r_2) = 120\,\text{Hz}$. Specifically, the state of the observation noise remains unchanged in r_1 between 0 to 6 s, and changes in the following 10 s to r_2. Finally, the state changes back to r_1 for another 4 s. The position and velocity measured by GPS are assumed to be added noise with the variance $\left(\sigma_{px} = \sqrt{200/2}m, \sigma_{py} = \sqrt{200/2}m\right)$ and $\left(\sigma_{vx} = \sqrt{15/2}m, \sigma_{vy} = \sqrt{15/2}m\right)$, respectively.

4.2   Simulation Results

From the Fig. 3, the Mean-CV-EKF has a higher order of magnitude than the Mean-CV-IMM-KF and the Mean-GPS, and change curve fluctuates greatly. So the interacting multiple model is necessary and we should ignore the huge error on numerical value and put the next two in the Fig. 4 to compare the errors.

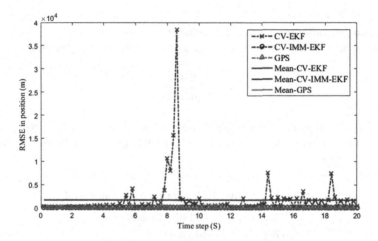

Fig. 3. CV-EKF, CV-IMM-EKF and GPS performance in positioning error

To quantify the performance of the proposed approach, the root mean square error (RMSE) of vehicular positioning is calculated to assess the closeness of the estimated trajectory $\left(\hat{p}_{x,k}, \hat{p}_{y,k}\right)$ to the true trajectory $\left(p_{x,k}, p_{y,k}\right)$ at each time instant over $N_m = 500$ Monte Carlo simulations. In (28), $\left(\hat{p}_{x,k}(m), \hat{p}_{y,k}(m)\right)$ denotes the estimated position vector in the mth Monte Carlo run at the kth step.

$$RMSE = \sqrt{\frac{1}{N_m}\sum_{m=1}^{N_m}\left[\left(\hat{p}_{x,k}(m) - p_{x,k}\right)^2 + \left(\hat{p}_{y,k}(m) - p_{y,k}\right)^2\right]} \qquad (30)$$

The performance comparison between the proposed CV-IMM-EKF and the GPS-only approach is shown in Fig. 3 with respect to the RMSE in distance. It is obvious that the proposed CV-IMM-EKF method outperforms the GPS alone

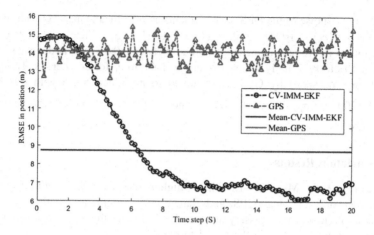

Fig. 4. CV-IMM-EKF and GPS performance in positioning error

localization. In order to indicate the enhancement of vehicular positioning of the proposed approach, the enhancement indicator μ is calculated as follows:

$$\mu = \left(1 - \frac{A\_RMSE}{B\_RMSE}\right) \times 100\% \tag{31}$$

The enhancement of vehicular positioning is shown in Table 1. Compared to the GPS-based localization, the proposed CV-IMM-EKF approach achieves the enhancement of $\mu = 40.15\%$.

Table 1. CV-IMM-EKF and GPS error comparison

Method	RMSE	Enhancement
GPS	14.3268	N/A
CV-IMM-EKF	8.5032	40.15%

If A_RMSE is better than B_RMSE, μ will be greater than zero. And the increase of μ is link to the good performance of A_RMSE. By describing the transition of the measurement noise as a first-order M-state jump Markov chain, the proposed CV-IMM-EKF approach has been proved to achieve better performance in a scenario that is similar to a practical one.

5 Conclusion

In this paper, a vehicular positioning algorithm has been proposed. The observation transition matrix and the covariance matrix of observation noise are updated by the fusion data at each time instant with the assistance of CV, which provide additional useful information compared to the traditional filtering approach. Finally, the simulation results show that the proposed approach outperforms the GPS-based localization.

Acknowledgments. This research was supported in part by no. Beijing Science and Technology Program no. D171100000317003 and the National Natural Science Foundation of China under Grant nos. 61672082, U1564212.

References

1. Chen, S., Hu, J., Shi, Y., Zhao, L.: LTE-V: A TD-LTE based V2X solution for future vehicular network. IEEE Internet Things J. **3**(6), 997–1005 (2016)
2. Chen, S., Zhao, J.: The requirements, challenges and technologies for 5G of terrestrial mobile telecommunication. IEEE Commun. Mag. **52**(5), 36–43 (2014)
3. Cortéspolo, D., Callecancho, J., Carmonamurillo, J., Gonzálezsánchez, J.: Future trends in mobile-fixed integration for next generation networks: classification and analysis. Int. J. Veh. Telematics Infotain. Syst. (IJVTIS) **1**(1), 33–53 (2017)
4. Gaamel, A.M., Maratha, B.P., Sheltami, T.R., Shakshuki, E.M.: Fault-tolerance evaluation of VANET under different data dissemination models. Int. J. Veh. Telematics Infotain. Syst. (IJVTIS) **1**(1), 54–68 (2017)
5. Huang, Y., Wang, J., Jiang, C., Zhang, H., Leung, V.C.M.: Vehicular network based reliable traffic density estimation. In: Proceedings of the IEEE Vehicular Technology Conference (VTC), Nanjing, 15–18 May 2016
6. Jiang, C., Zhang, H., Han, Z., Cheng, J., Ren, Y., Hanzo, L.: On the outage probability of information sharing in cognitive vehicular networks. In: Proceedings of IEEE International Conference on Communications (ICC), Kuala Lampur, Malaysia, 23–27 May 2016
7. Mir, Z.H., Filali, F.: A simulation-based study on the environment-specific propagation model for vehicular communications. Int. J. Veh. Telematics Infotain. Syst. (IJVTIS) **1**(1), 1–18 (2017)
8. Pressas, A., Özpolat, M., Sheng, Z., Ali, F.: Performance evaluation of networking protocols for connected vehicles. Int. J. Veh. Telematics Infotain. Syst. (IJVTIS) **1**(1), 1–14 (2017)
9. Zhang, H., Dong, Y., Cheng, J., Leung, V.C.M.: Fronthauling for 5G LTE-U ultra dense cloud small cell networks. IEEE Wirel. Commun. **23**(6), 48–53 (2016)
10. Zhang, H., Liu, N., Chu, X., Long, K., Aghvami, A.H., Leung, V.C.M.: Network slicing based 5G and future mobile networks: mobility, resource management, and challenges. IEEE Commun. Mag. **55**(8), 138–145 (2017)
11. Zheng, Q., Zheng, K., Zhang, H., Leung, V.C.M.: Delay-optimal virtualized radio resource scheduling in software-defined vehicular networks via stochastic learning. IEEE Trans. Veh. Technol. **65**(12), 9479–9492 (2016)
12. Alam, N., Dempster, A.G.: Cooperative positioning for vehicular networks: facts and future. IEEE Trans. Intell. Transp. Syst. **14**, 1708–1717 (2013)
13. Rappaport, T.S., Reed, J.H., Woerner, B.D.: Position location using wireless communications on highways of the future. IEEE Commun. Mag. **34**, 33–41 (1996)
14. Zekavat, R., Buehrer, R.M.: Handbook of Position Location: Theory, Practice and Advances, vol. 27. Wiley, Hoboken (2011)
15. Jiang, S., Ji, Y.: Artificial fish swarm algorithm for solving road network equilibrium traffic assignment problem. Comput. Simul. (2011). ISSN 1006-9348, 06-0326-04

16. Sengupta, R., Rezaei, S., Shladover, S.E., Cody, D., Dickey, S., Krishnan, H.: Cooperative collision warning systems: concept definition and experimental implementation. J. Intell. Transp. Syst. **11**, 143–155 (2007)
17. Shladover, S.E., Tan, S.-K.: Analysis of vehicle positioning accuracy requirements for communication-based cooperative collision warning. J. Intell. Transp. Syst. **10**(3), 131–140 (2006). http://www.tandfonline.com/doi/abs/10.1080/15472450600793610
18. Alam, N., Balaei, A.T., Dempster, A.G.: A DSRC Doppler-based cooperative positioning enhancement for vehicular networks with GPS availability. IEEE Trans. Veh. Technol. **60**, 4462–4470 (2011)
19. Tian, D., Zhu, K.: Swarm model for cooperative multi-vehicle mobility with inter-vehicle communications. J. IET Intell. Transp. Syst. **9**, 887–896 (2015)
20. Sayed, A.H., Tarighat, A., Khajehnouri, N.: Network-based wireless location: challenges faced in developing techniques for accurate wireless location information. IEEE Sig. Process. Mag. **22**, 24–40 (2005)
21. Duan, X., Wang, Y., Tian, D., et al.: A vehicular positioning enhancement with connected vehicle assistance. In: IEEE Vehicular Technology Conference, pp. 1–5. IEEE (2015)
22. Schmidl, T.M., Cox, D.C.: Robust frequency and timing synchronization for OFDM. IEEE Trans. Commun. **45**, 1613–1621 (1997)

A Multi-queue Aggregation Framework for M2M Traffic in LTE-A and Beyond Networks

Wen Feng, Hongjia Li[(⊠)], Ding Tang[(⊠)], Liming Wang, and Zhen Xu

State Key Laboratory of Information Security, Institute of Information Engineering,
Chinese Academy of Sciences, Beijing 100093, China
{lihongjia,tangding}@iie.ac.cn

Abstract. Traffic aggregation has been considered as an effective app-roach to improve the radio resource utilization for M2M communication in LTE-A and beyond networks. In the LTE-A specification, the Relay Node (RN) is recommended to aggregate uplink M2M small-sized pack-ets. However, the delay brought by the packets aggregation is inevitably increased, which is a vital metric for M2M packets with low delay require-ment, such as emergency alerting. In this paper, we propose a new frame-work for optimal aggregation implemented in the PDCP of RN, which features balancing a tradeoff between QoS requirements of packets and the utilization efficiency of Physical Radio Blocks (PRBs). Specifically, (1) the RN dispatches the new arrival M2M packets into correspond-ing virtual queues according to their priorities set by M2M devices. Then, an Optimal Aggregating Scheme (OAS) is designed to minimize the PRB usage in condition satisfying the specific restriction of waiting time of packets in virtual queues. (2) The optimal aggregating problem is proved to be a NP-hard problem, which is solved by the Priority Branch and Bound Algorithm (PBBA) and the Priority Aggregating Heuristic. Numerical results illustrate that OAS achieves a tradeoff of QoS and PRB utilization efficiency in comparison with four existing schemes.

Keywords: M2M · Quality of service · Packet aggregation · LTE-A

1 Introduction

Massive Machine-to-Machine (M2M) communication is considered as the poten-tial important research direction in 5G networks. M2M communication is a pat-tern which identifies the evolving paradigm of interconnected devices communi-cating with each other without or with limited human interaction. The applica-tion domain of M2M traffic includes smart metering, e-health, surveillance and security, intelligent transportation, city automation, smart monitoring and many more. M2M traffic patterns vary in diverse application domains and in most of the applications, and especially some M2M devices mainly are small packets that consist of a few bytes. Because the payload of the data packets associated with

© ICST Institute for Computer Sciences, Social Informatics and Telecommunications Engineering 2018
K. Long et al. (Eds.): 5GWN 2017, LNICST 211, pp. 609–621, 2018.
https://doi.org/10.1007/978-3-319-72823-0_56

M2M applications is usually smaller than a Physical Resource Block (PRB) [1]. Thus, M2M traffic is supposed to degrade the utilization of radio spectrum. In addition, M2M devices can have different delay tolerances based on their applications, ranging from a few milliseconds (ms) to several minutes or even hours, e.g., emergency alerting may need to provide a very stringent low delay, while temperature monitoring can owe a great delay tolerance [2]. Therefore, it is a significant problem for the evolution of M2M communication to improve the utilization of radio spectrum and satisfy delay requirement.

Packets or traffic aggregation, which collects and accumulates data packets from multiple nodes before transmitting to the next hop, is supposed to effectively improve the utilization of radio spectrum for M2M traffic in future 5G networks because of reducing the extra overhead and adding the size of data in a PRB. For example, packets aggregation significantly improves the PRB utilization compared to the conventional without multiplexing approach [3]. However, packets aggregation inevitably results in the delay increasing of M2M application. Because the incoming packets can be transmitted only when certain aggregation conditions are satisfied. Therefore, it is a fundamental problem to obtain a tradeoff between Quality-of-Service (QoS) requirements of packets and the utilization efficiency of Physical Radio Blocks (PRBs).

Some efforts have been separately made to improve radio spectrum utilization and reduce time delay of M2M communication. For instance, in [4], the authors propose a data aggregation scheme which aggregates uplink M2M traffic by sharing the PRBs to increase the number of M2M packet in a PRB. Reference [5] efficiently integrates M2M traffic into cellular networks to take advantage of uplink transmission time slot and reduce resource wastage at both the network and device. Authors in [6] propose an optimal aggregation for multirate WLANs to minimize overall transmission time. In [7], a packet chunking is introduced which need multiple buffers and then classifies the arrival packets to one buffer based on their acceptable waiting time to take the best use of the core router's forwarding capacity. However, few arts have delved into the combination of improving radio spectrum utilization and reducing time delay of M2M packets.

Thus motivated, we propose a new framework for optimal aggregation, which features balancing a tradeoff between QoS requirements of packets and the utilization efficiency of PRBs. For this purpose, a Relay Node (RN) of LTE-A are introduced to aggregate uplink M2M traffic. The main contributions are summarized below. (1) The RN dispatches the new arrival M2M packets into corresponding virtual queues according to their priorities set by the M2M devices. Then, an Optimal Aggregating Scheme (OAS) is designed to minimize the PRB usage in condition satisfying the specific restriction of waiting time of packets in virtual queues. (2) In order to solve the optimal aggregating problem which is proved to be a NP-hard problem, we propose a Priority Branch and Bound Algorithm (PBBA). Due to the low computational efficiency of PBBA, the Priority Aggregating Heuristic is introduced.

The rest of this paper is organized as follows. Section 2 overviews the framework of optimal traffic aggregation. Section 3 presents the optimal aggregating problem formulation and the solution algorithms. Section 4 evaluates the performance of our proposed algorithms. Finally, Sect. 5 concludes the paper.

2   The Framework of Optimal Traffic Aggregation

2.1   System Framework

In this part, we propose a new framework for optimal aggregation implemented in the Packet Data Convergence Protocol (PDCP) of RN as shown in Figs. 1 and 2. Traffic from M2M devices located in the proximity of an RN is accumulated at the RN. According to 3GPP specification [8], the access link (Uu) and the backhaul link (Un) antennas of the RN are assumed to be well separated in order to avoid self-interference. We have made two changes in RN. First, in order to satisfy delay requirement of diverse applications, multiple queues are introduced in the PDCP of RN, which are used to distinguish various applications. Second, the operation of de-multiplexes is made in the GPRS Tunnelling Protocol (GTP) of Public Data Network GateWay (P-GW) to reduce the additional overheads.

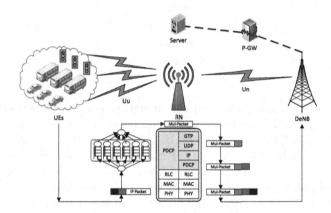

Fig. 1. An illustration of M2M packet flow with the packets aggregation in from UE to DeNB.

We consider an uplink priority aggregated scenario in RN. As shown in Fig. 1, packets of User Equipment (UE) are aggregated by the RN, and then are transited to DeNB. Packets are aggregated at the PDCP layer of RN in order to maximize the multiplexing gain. The main functionalities and services of PDCP layer for the user plane include header compression and decomposition, user data transfer, delivery of upper layer packet data units (PDUs) in sequence, as well as retransmission of the lost PDCP service data units (SDUs), etc. On the other hand, the control plane services include ciphering and integrity protection and transfer of control plane data.

When arriving at the PDCP layer of RN, the incoming data packet is scheduled to one of six virtual queues which are mapping six priority levels as $p \in \{1, 2, 3, 4, 5, 6\}$. We assume that $p = 1$ (resp. $p = 6$) corresponds to the highest (resp. lowest) priority level. The six virtual queues are used to distinguish six services as shown in Table 1. According to 3GPP TS 36.107 [9], the typical Human-to-Human (H2H) services are divided into four different QoS classes, namely conversational, streaming, interactive and background, in which the differentiation have mainly considered the delay requirement. However, some of M2M applications cannot be properly mapped to the four QoS classes, especially emergency alerting and some applications of delay tolerant as shown in [10]. Thus, we extend the typical H2H services classification scheme. An indicative classification scheme, adding two service classes (i.e. emergency alerting and time tolerant), is shown in Table 1.

Table 1. M2M applications classification

Priority level	Service classes	Waiting time
1	Emergency Alerting	0 ms
2	Conversational	10 ms
3	Streaming	100 ms
4	Interactive	1 s
5	Background	10 s
6	Time Tolerant	100 s

By scheduling, some packets in six virtual queues are aggregated and sent to GTP. Then, the RN adds the additional overheads such as the GTP, User Datagram Protocol/Internet Protocol (UDP/IP), PDCP and Radio Link Control (RLC), and sends to P-GW via a GTP tunnel. A GTP option is added before packet is sent to P-GW, which can provide the needed information for extracting the original small packets in the aggregated packet. The aggregated packet flow from RN to P-GW when adding the GTP option is given in Fig. 2.

When receiving the aggregated packet, the P-GW de-multiplexes and extracts the original transmitted standalone packets according to the GTP option information, and then sends them to Public Data Network (PDN). Finally, the original small packets are sent to the application servers. The P-GW also serves the regular LTE-A traffic. If the packets are received from regular users, then the P-GW directly forwards them to PDN. On the other hand, if the aggregated packet are received from the RN, the original small packets are extracted by P-GW, and then sent to PDN.

2.2   Optimal Aggregating Scheme (OAS)

In this part, an Optimal Aggregating Scheme (OAS) is designed, which minimize the PRB usage in condition satisfying the specific restriction of waiting time of

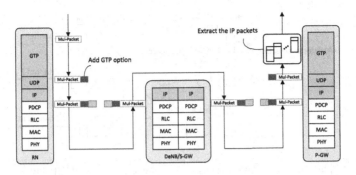

Fig. 2. The aggregated packet flow from RN to P-GW when adding the GTP option.

packets in virtual queues. Here, we denote L as the total size of all the packets in the virtual queues, and L_{max} as the maximum size that RN can aggregates the incoming M2M packets according to the size of available transport block - RN Un protocol overhead, see Fig. 1. The size of available transport block is determined by the number of PRB allocated by DeNB in a transmission time interval (TTI). According to [11], The minimum scheduling resource unit in LTE that are allocated to a single UE is a PRB in a TTI. A PRB can transmit several hundred bits under favorable channel conditions [12]. For example, 712 bits are sent in a TTI with an Modulation and Coding Scheme (MCS) of 26 when a PRB allocated by DeNB. The RN Un protocol overhead is 46 bytes: 12 bytes for GTP, 8 bytes for UDP, 20 bytes for IP, 1 byte for PDCP, 2 bytes for RLC, and 3 bytes for the MAC overhead. The payload of the data packets associated with M2M applications is IP packet. it will increases when the GTP option is added.

Priority Classification when arriving at the PDCP layer of RN, the incoming data packet is scheduled as shown in Step A of Fig. 3, which dispatchs it to one of the virtual queues according to its priority level. Before sent to RN, the packet's priority level p would be set at the Type of Service (ToS) segment of IP header by M2M devices. In the Transmission Control Protocol/Internet Protocol (TCP/IP), ToS segment of IP header has three bits that indicate six priority levels as shown by Table 1.

Packets Scheduling after priority classification, the M2M packet is placed into the tail of the corresponding virtual queue as shown in Step B of Fig. 3. Each arrival packet starts a waiting timer when in the virtual queue, which records the waiting time t of the incoming packet. The waiting time t is the time that the packet stay in PDCP of RN. Due to different delay requirements for the virtual queues, a waiting time T is introduced for the virtual queues, which denote the current waiting time of the virtual queues and is equal to the waiting time of head-of-line packet in that virtual queue. Without loss of generality, let T_{max} denotes the maximum waiting time of the virtual queues.

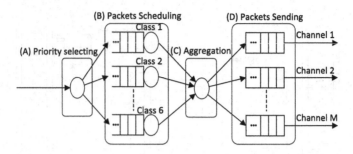

Fig. 3. The M2M schedule procession of packets at the PDCP layer of RN.

Aggregation when some aggregating conditions are satisfied, a optimal aggregating sequence of M2M packets is selected and aggregated into a large aggregated packet as shown in Step C of Fig. 3. We set two aggregating conditions: (a) The total size L exceed the maximum aggregated size of RN L_{max}; (b) The waiting time T_p ($p \in \{1, 2, 3, 4, 5, 6\}$) is greater than the maximum waiting time T^p_{max}. T_{max} is set a suitable value for six virtual queues according to characteristic of M2M packets in virtual queue. For example, the packet of the highest priority will be served immediately when incoming, and the packet of the lowest priority can be set a high value due to delay tolerance.

Packets Sending the aggregated packet is sent through one of M channels that are mapping the size of transport block allocated by DeNB, as shown in Step D of Fig. 3. Which channels are selected is determined by the number of PRB allocated by DeNB.

3   Optimal Aggregating Problem Formulation and Solution Algorithm

3.1   Optimal Aggregating Problem Formulation

We denote the set of all the packets in the PDCP of RN as I with integer index $i \in \{1, 2, 3, ...\}$, and each packet has two attributes: the priority p_i and the length l_i. We assume that 0-1 decision variable ρ_i indicate whether the data packet i is selected by RN, which is defined as

$$\rho_i = \begin{cases} 1, & \text{if the packet } i \text{ is selected} \\ 0, & \text{else} \end{cases}. \tag{1}$$

Meanwhile, the weight value of each UE's packet i in virtual queues, denoted by v_i, is defined as follows

$$v_i = \frac{t_i}{p_i}, \tag{2}$$

where p_i and t_i separately are the priority level and the waiting time of the packet i, and v_i represents the weight value of the packet i that is a significant parameter that distinct priority packets can be treated differently. v_i has two main purposes: let the high priority packet can be served faster than the low, and increase the probability that the low priority packets are served.

The goal of the following formulated problem is to obtain the optimal aggregating sequence of M2M packets such that the total weight value $\mathcal{P}(\rho)$ is maximized at any TTI.

$$\begin{aligned} \max_{\rho} \quad & \mathcal{P}(\rho) = \sum_{i=1}^{n} v_i \rho_i, \\ s.t. \quad & \sum_{i=1}^{n} l_i \rho_i \leq L_{max}, (A) \\ & \rho_i \in \{0,1\}, \forall i \in I, (B) \end{aligned} \qquad (3)$$

where $\rho = \{\rho_i, i \in I\}$ is the set of decision variables for the UE's packet in the PDCP of RN, and n is the total number of all UE's packets in the virtual queues. Due to constraint (B), this problem has been well proved NP-hard in [13].

3.2   Priority Branch and Bound Algorithm

In order to solve the proposed optimal aggregating problem in (3), we propose a priority branch and bound algorithm (PBBA) as given in Algorithm 1. Branch and bound algorithm (BBA) has the attractive feature to reach the optimal solution, it is sufficient to enumerate only some of the possible by branching and bounding strategies. Specifically, the proposed algorithm consists of two stages: the waiting stage and the aggregating stage. In the waiting stage, the proposed algorithm distributes the incoming packet to one of the virtual queues, and checks the aggregating conditions. If satisfying the aggregating condition, it comes into the aggregating stage. If not, it go to the next cycle. In the aggregating stage, it sorts packets descending order by the weight value, and then get the aggregated packet with ρ by BBA. Finally it send the aggregated packet to DeNB.

The principle behind BBA is perform a systematic enumeration of candidate solutions. The search process is done in a tree structure manner, which starts at the root node and goes down in the tree. Taking problem (3) as the root problem, we denote the optimal variables as $\rho_i^{*(0)}$ and its optimal solution as $\mathcal{P}^{*(0)}$. Then if all $\rho_i^{*(0)}$ in $\rho_i^{*(0)}$ are binary, the root problem is terminated and the optimal to the original problem (3) is found. If not, the root problem on the first non-integer ρ_i, which is named as the branching variable, will be split into two more subproblems $S(\mathcal{P}_1^{(0)})$ and $S(\mathcal{P}_2^{(0)})$ by adding two upper bound and lower bound constraints. The new formed sub-problems can be generally expressed as

---

Algorithm 1. PBBA

Set L_{max} = (available TBS - RN Un overhead) and $L = 0$;
Initialize T_p and T_{max}^p for each queue p;
while packet arrival $== TRUE$ **do**

    The incoming packet i is put into one of virtual queue p according to it's priority;

    Starts the waiting timer t_i for the incoming packet i and update L and T_p;

    if $L \geq L_{max}$ && $T_p \geq T_{max}^p$ **then**

        Update the value v for all the incoming packets;

        Get ρ via algorithm 2;

        Aggregate all the packets that satisfy $\rho_i = 1$;

        Send large aggregated packet to RN PHY via RN Un protocols;

        Add RN Un protocols overhead;

        Route multiplexed packet to DeNB in next TTI;

        Update L_{max} from the DeNB;

        Break;

    end if

end while

$$\max_{\rho} \quad \mathcal{P}(\boldsymbol{\rho}),$$

$$s.t. \quad \sum_{i=1}^{n} l_i \rho_i \leq L_{max}, \forall i, (A)$$

$$\rho_i \geq 0, \forall i \backslash (i'), \forall i \in I, (B')$$

$$\rho_{i'} = 0$$

(4)

and

$$\max_{\rho} \quad \mathcal{P}(\boldsymbol{\rho}),$$

$$s.t. \quad \sum_{i=1}^{n} l_i \rho_i \leq L_{max}, \forall i, (A)$$

$$\rho_i \geq 0, \forall i \backslash (i'), \forall i \in I, (B')$$

$$\rho_{i'} = 1$$

(5)

where i' is the index of the branching variable. The depth first strategy [14] is adopted, where the search goes down the tree until it reaches the first binary solution or reaches infeasibility, and then it backtracks the non-visited nodes recorded by a last-in-first-out stack. Therefore, we first go down to sub-problem (4). The optimal variables and optimal objective function is solved as $\boldsymbol{\rho}^{*(1)}$ and $\mathcal{P}^{*(1)}$ respectively. Again if any value of $\boldsymbol{\rho}^{*(1)}$ is not binary, problem (4) is split into two more sub-problems. This branch and bound process will be repeated until the optimal solution to the relaxed sub-problem satisfies all constraints with maximum objective function.

Algorithm 2. BBA

Set the best lower bound $\mathcal{P}^{(low)} = 0$ and $\rho = \emptyset$;
Initialize the problem stack with the root problem as $S = \{\widehat{S}(\mathcal{P}^{(0)})\}$;
while $S \neq \emptyset$ **do**
    Pop a node problem $\widehat{S}(\mathcal{P}^{(j)})$ from stack S;
    Solve $\widehat{S}(\mathcal{P}^{(j)})$ to obtain the optimal variables; $\rho^{*(j)}$ and the optimal objective value $\mathcal{P}^{*(j)}$;
    if $\mathcal{P}^{*(j)} \geq \mathcal{P}^{(low)}$ **then**
        if $\rho^{*(j)}$ are all integers **then**
            Set $\mathcal{P}^{(low)} = \mathcal{P}^{*(j)}$ and $\rho^* = \rho^{*(j)}$;
            Delete $\widehat{S}(\mathcal{P}^{(j)})$ from stack S, i.e., $S := S\backslash\widehat{S}(\mathcal{P}^{(j)})$;
            Continue;
        else
            Branch $\widehat{S}(\mathcal{P}^{(j)})$ into two sub-problems $\widehat{S}(\mathcal{P}_1^{(j)})$ and $\widehat{S}(\mathcal{P}_2^{(j)})$ as (4) and (5);
            Push $\widehat{S}(\mathcal{P}_1^{(j)})$ and $\widehat{S}(\mathcal{P}_2^{(j)})$ to S;
        end if
    end if
    Delete $\widehat{S}(\mathcal{P}^{(j)})$ from stack S, i.e., $S := S\backslash\widehat{S}(\mathcal{P}^{(j)})$;
end while

3.3 Priority Aggregating Heuristic

The OAS improves performance by maximizing the utilization efficiency of PRB, while the potential loss in performance comes from increase of the waiting time, especially in high arrival rate, a sharp increase of the waiting time. Therefore, we design a Priority Aggregating Heuristic (PAH) that can be implemented in real system. The PAH is identical to adopting the greedy algorithm (GA) instead of BBA in PBBA. The GA has given in Algorithm 3. It work as follows. First, define six pointers, which respectively point to the HOL packet of the six virtual queues. Then get the packet which is the largest weight value among six packets that the six pointers point to. If the size of the aggregating buffer is smaller than L_{max} when the packet is put into the aggregating buffer, the packet is marked as $\rho = 1$ and put into the aggregating buffer. If not, marked as $\rho = 0$ and the pointer of the corresponding packet is moved to the next packet, until all the packets of the virtual queues have been marked. This is a low-complexity implementation of OAS that does not consider complex BBA. The PAH is an online algorithm that generates one aggregated packet at a time. If there are n packets in the virtual queues, the algorithm is O(n).

4 Performance Evaluation

4.1 Simulation Setups

The network model Setup: The $1000 \times 1000 \, \text{m}^2$ square simulation scenario is set up, where RN is placed near the centre, UEs are uniformly and independently

Algorithm 3. GA

Set six pointers which point to the head-of-line (HOL) packet in virtual queues;
The current size $S == 0$;
for all the packets in virtual queues **do**
    $CP ==$ the packet of the maximum weight value v among six pointers;
    if $S +$ the size of packet $CP > L_{max}$ **then**
        Set $\rho_{CP} = 1$;
        $S = S +$ the size of packet CP;
    else
        Set $\rho_{CP} = 0$;
    end if
    The corresponding pointer of CP point to the next packet;
end for

---

distributed in RN's coverage, and DeNB is randomly dropped beyond RN's coverage but can smoothly communicate with RN to perform packets aggregation. RN's coverage radius is approximately 350 m. Each UE send packet to RN randomly with the access link (Uu). We assume that the number of packets arrived in RN is satisfied with poisson distribution. The small-sized M2M data packets are considered in the simulation, and have the randomly size between 21 and 120 bytes and the randomly priority between 1 and 6. The DeNB allocates only five PRBs to the RN, and the position of RN corresponds to MCS 20 with a TBS 2344 bits per TTI of 1 ms duration.

Comparison Scenarios: (a) In the first group, M2M data packets are forwarded in PDCP of RN without aggregating. (b) In the second group, the data packets are aggregated at the Uu PDCP layer, in which the aggregated packet are served when their size is equal to the maximum total sizes L_{max} for all the packets or the waiting time reach the maximum waiting time T_{max}. (c) In the third group, the data packets are aggregated at the Uu PDCP layer by PBBA, but set different T_{max} for each queue. (d) In the fourth group, we the data packets are aggregated by PBBA but use the GA to replace BBA. The four groups respectively are No Aggregating Scheme (NAS), Simple Aggregating Scheme (SAS), the proposed Optimal Aggregating Scheme (OAS) and the proposed Priority Aggregating Heuristic (PAH). The maximum waiting time of the second group are set as 10 ms. However, the maximum waiting time T_{max}^p are set as {0, 0.01, 0.1, 1, 10, 100} seconds for the virtual queues p={1, 2, 3, 4, 5, 6}.

4.2 Performance Analysis

The simulation results in Fig. 4 clearly show the efficient utilization of PRBs in all four aforementioned schemes. In the NAS scenario with 200 data packet, the average number of PRBs usage is almost utilize 1 PRB, and in the case of SAS, only half of the PRBs are used with 200 data packets. However, in the case of OAS, the average number of PRBs usage is the lowest in comparison of NAS, SAS and OAS. The average number of PRBs usage is slightly higher than the

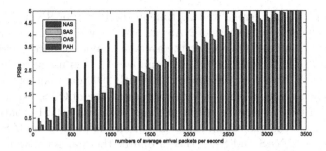

Fig. 4. Average number of PRBs usage for the four groups.

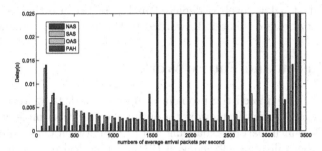

Fig. 5. Average waiting delay of all the packets for the four groups.

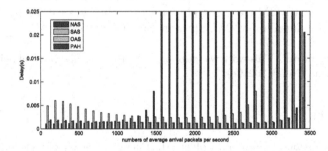

Fig. 6. Average waiting delay of the highest priority for the four groups.

case of SAS between 400 and 1000 data packets. Because the high priority data packets are sent quickly when reach the RN, and the size of all the packets aren't fill with the its maximum capacity. In particular, in low loaded scenarios, the average number of PRBs usage in the case of OAS is lower than the case of SAS, because the packets of lower priority are aggregated that the waiting time T_{max} of the lower priority is set more longer than the second group. Compared with the case of OAS, the average number of PRBs usage is slightly of lower in the PAH scenario, but the total delay is slightly higher. Because the purpose of OAS is to use the least amount of time, while PAH is to get to send more packets.

Figure 5 plots the average waiting time in the PDCP of RN in all four aforementioned schemes. In the case of NAS, its average waiting time more than the waiting time of SAS and OAS when the average number of packet arrival exceed 1400 data packets, because its average number of PRBs usage reach the maximum capacity. However, in the case of SAS with 2900 data packets, the average number of packet arrival is much larger than the case of OAS, because its average number of PRBs usage also reach the maximum capacity. In contrast, in low loaded scenarios, the average waiting time of all the packets of OAS are higher than the cases of NAS and SAS, this is due to the maximum waiting time of lower priority queue is higher than the high priority queue and thus the whole waiting time increase. However, the average waiting time of the highest priority is maintained at a low level as depicted in Fig. 6, because the packets of the highest priority are immediately forwarded to DeNB when arriving at the RN.

5   Conclusion and Future Work

In this paper, we explored the problem of optimal packets aggregation among M2M applications. A new framework for optimal aggregation implemented in the PDCP of RN, which features balancing a tradeoff between QoS requirements of packets and the utilization efficiency of PRBs. Numerical results illustrate that OAS achieves a tradeoff of QoS and PRB utilization efficiency in comparison with four existing schemes. Last but not least, OAS provides an optimal scheduling scheme for uplink M2M traffics, and more key techniques will be systematically studied for the downlink M2M traffics in our future work.

Acknowledgments. This work was supported by the National Natural Science Foundation of China (No. 61302108).

References

1. Wang, K., Alonso-Zarate, J., Dohler, M.: Energy-efficiency of LTE for small data machine-to-machine communications. In: Proceedings of the IEEE ICC, pp. 4120–4124 (2013)
2. Wu, G., Talwar, S., Johnsson, K., Himayat, N., Johnson, K.D.: M2M: From mobile to embedded internet. IEEE Commun. Mag. **49**(4), 36–43 (2011)
3. Mehmood, Y., Khan Marwat, S.N., Görg, C., et al.: Evaluation of M2M data traffic aggregation in LTE-A uplink. In: Proceedings of the ITG-Fachbericht-Mobilkommunikation, pp. 24–29, August 2015
4. Marwat, S.N.K., Mehmood, Y., Görg, C., Timm-Giel, A.: Data aggregation of mobile M2M traffic in relay enhanced LTE-A networks. EURASIP J. Wirel. Commun. Networking **2016**(1), 1–14 (2016)
5. Devi, U.M., Goyal, M., Madhavan, M., et al.: SERA: A hybrid scheduling framework for M2M transmission in cellular networks. In: Proceedings of the IEEE COMSNETS, pp. 1–8 (2015)
6. Majeed, A., Abu-Ghazaleh, N.B.: Packet aggregation in multi-rate wireless LANs. In: Proceedings of the IEEE SECON, pp. 452–460 (2012)

7. Sawabe, A., Tsukamoto, K., Oie, Y.: QoS-aware packet chunking schemes for M2M cloud services. In: Proceedings of the IEEE WAINA, pp. 166–173 (2014)
8. http://www.3gpp.org/technologies/keywords-acronyms/97-lte-advanced. Accessed 12 Sep 2016
9. 3GPP TS 23.107, 3rd Generation Partnership Project. Technical Specification Group Services and System Aspects. Quality of Service (QoS) concept and architecture (Release 13), V13.0.0, December 2015
10. Liu, R., Wu, W., Zhu, H., et al.: M2M-oriented QoS categorization in cellular network. In: Proceedings of the IEEE WiCOM, pp. 1–5 (2011)
11. 3GPP TS 36.300, 3rd Generation Partnership Project. Technical Specification Group Radio Access Network. Evolved Universal Terrestrial Radio Access (E-UTRA) and Evolved Universal Terrestrial Radio Access Network (E-UTRAN) (Release 12), V13.4.0, June 2016
12. 3GPP TS 36.213, 3rd Generation Partnership Project; Technical Specification Group Radio Access Network; Evolved Universal Terrestrial Radio Access (E-UTRA); Physical layer procedures (Release 13), V13.2.0, June 2016
13. Sahni, S., Gonzalez, T.: P-complete approximation problems. J. Assoc. Comput. Mach. **23**(3), 555–565 (1976)
14. Lawler, E.L., Wood, D.E.: Branch-and-bound methods: A survey. J. Oper. Res. **14**(4), 699–719 (1966)

Millimeter Wave Mobile Network
with Full-Duplex Mode

Baiqing Zong[✉], Xiaohong Zhang, Jianli Wang, Xiaotong Li,
and Zhiyong Zhao

R&D Center (Shanghai), ZTE Corporation, Zhangjiang High-Tech Park,
Shanghai 201203, China
Zong.baiqing@zte.com.cn

Abstract. To converge full-duplex and mm-wave is attractive to high spectral efficiency and huge capacity in 5G mobile networks. However, this conjunction will bring more difficulties to design mobile networks. Except for the previous problems of inter-site interference and UE-UE interference, new challenge of ultra-broadband self-interference cancellation about wider bandwidth of mm-wave band occurs. In this paper, we propose a hierarchical mobile network of FDD/TDD massive MIMO and full-duplex mm-wave communications, which has the features of beam division multiple access and filtered sub-band reuse against inter-site interference and UE-UE interference. In addition, we also give a feasible analysis and system consideration of ultra-broadband self-interference cancellation based on microwave photonics and integrated polarization based antenna.

Keywords: Full-duplex · 5G · mm-wave mobile communication
Beam division multiple access · Self-interference cancellation
CU split · Microwave photonics

1 Introduction

In communication research, 5G is now one of the most popular events. There are several initiatives proposed for 5G, in which spectral efficiency is one of the most important ones. To improve the spectral efficiency by full-duplex (FD), in which transmission and reception can occur simultaneously in the same frequency band, is one of the most promising techniques. In our previous presentation, we investigated the challenges and potential application scenarios of FD in future 5G network [1]. For macrocell (with 47 dBm of average output power), 147 dB self-interference cancellation (SIC), and about 87 dB dynamic range of receiver are needed, which are great challenges for algorithm and receiver frontend. For smallcell (with 27 dBm of average output power), 127 dB self-interference cancellation, and about 67 dB dynamic range of receiver are needed, which are somewhat less than macrocell. Furthermore, for FD cellular network, inter-site interference and UE-UE interference are big issues. Simulations show 36 dB and 23 dB UL SINR degradation for macro and small cell respectively due to inter-site and UE-UE interferences. As for massive MIMO, large scale analog and digital cancellation matrix will bring much complexity. So our

K. Long et al. (Eds.): 5GWN 2017, LNICST 211, pp. 622–629, 2018.
https://doi.org/10.1007/978-3-319-72823-0_57

previous studies conclude that FD could be applied in the scenarios of single TX output power <27 dBm, the numbers of antenna less than 8, new spectrum and new air interface. This implies that possible application scenarios of FD would be smallcell, new introduced mm-wave band, and wireless fronthaul and backhaul.

The mm-wave frequency bands (defined as frequency band in 6–100 GHz) have much more available bandwidth than the legacy bands in the sub-6 GHz used today. They can therefore support the much higher data rates that are required in future mobile broadband access and backhaul networks. Although the conjunction of FD and mm-wave is more attractive to improving spectral efficiency and data capacity of 5G mobile networks, FD mm-wave communications would bring new challenges. The feature of wider bandwidth of mm-wave band results in more difficulties in designing FD SIC transceivers, especially analog front end (AFE).

In this paper, to deal with the problems of inter-site interference and UE-UE interference, we propose a hierarchical mobile network of FDD/TDD massive MIMO and FD mm-wave communication, which has the features of beam division multiple access (BDMA) and filtered sub-band reuse (FSR). In addition, we also introduce and discuss microwave photonics based SIC and integrated polarization based SIC antenna suitable to ultra-broadband FD mm-wave AFE.

2 Architecture of FD mm-wave Mobile Network

2.1 CU Split and Hierarchical FD mm-wave Mobile Network

As mentioned above, FD is suitable for using in new frequency band and new air interface. Therefore, new introduced mm-wave band can be considered as a FD frequency band in the future 5G because backward compatibility is not required. In order to ensure the robustness of control signaling, we consider the split of control plane and user plane of hierarchical FD mm-wave mobile network. Macro coverage by FDD/TDD massive MIMO below 6 GHz band mainly carries signaling, some data services such as broadcasting services (mobile CDN), as well as data services in the areas of coverage hole of mm-wave. 28 GHz or 38 GHz mm-wave band builds mm-wave smallcell. Figure 1 shows the hierarchical network of FDD/TDD massive MIMO and FD mm-wave networks, in which the C-plane and the U-plane are decoupled from each other by ensuring that the C-plane signaling seamlessly covers the whole networks. The high data rate is served by the mm-wave base stations. In the macro-coverage cells, radio resource control (RRC) manages signaling, traffic control and low data rate services.

At the same time, for a UE within a coverage area of the mm-wave base station, it keeps dual connections with mm-wave base stations and macro stations. The mm-wave base station is only responsible for the dynamic resource allocation of U-plane while the RRC connection and mobility control remain in the C-plane based on FDD/TDD macro station. In addition, macrocells and mm-wave cells are coordinated with each other through CloudRAN. The information such as the user's preferred content, moving speed and direction of the user beam is stored and held in the mobile edge computing (MEC) node, which front hauls all related services and information to the base station.

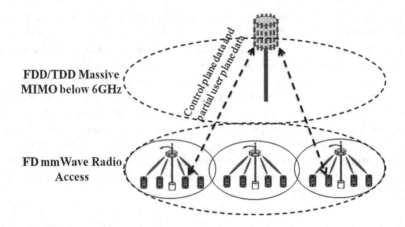

FDD/TDD Massive
MIMO below 6GHz

FD mmWave Radio
Access

Fig. 1. Architecture of FD mm-wave mobile network.

2.2 Filtered Sub-band Reuse Between FD mm-wave Smallcell

For FD mobile networks, inter-cell interference is the biggest challenge. Although the narrow-beam characteristics of mm-wave reduces the interference of line of sight (LOS), interference of none line of sight (NLOS) caused by reflection becomes the main problem. Related research shows that in the worst case, due to the reflection caused by environments the background noise floors up about 46 dB. In order to solve the challenge of inter-cell interference of FD mm-wave networks, the mm-wave frequency band can be divided into several sub-bands of 300 MHz–500 MHz. Fortunately, there is about 1–3 GHz bandwidth of the candidate spectra of mm-wave bands in several main areas around the world [2]. Filtered sub-band reuse (FSR) is used throughout the FD mm-wave mobile network. Figure 2 is a typical 1 × 3 FSR or multiplexing. For example, the available mm-wave band of 28 GHz or 38 GHz is divided into three filtered sub-bands FS1, FS2 and FS3. Each cell is in a single sub-band FD, meanwhile, the self-interference cancellation of single sub-band full-duplex can be achieved through various cancellation technologies in Sect. 3.

For FSR, sub-band filter is added on top of OFDM, UFMC of FBMC, without any change on existing OFDM. Independent subcarrier spacing, CP length and TTI configuration could be for each sub-band. Rather low guard tone overhead between neighboring sub-band can be designed. FSR also supports asynchronous inter-band transmission due to perfect OOB performance.

Furthermore, dynamic FSR can be employed, i.e., different bandwidths are dynamically allocated to different cells according to traffic conditions.

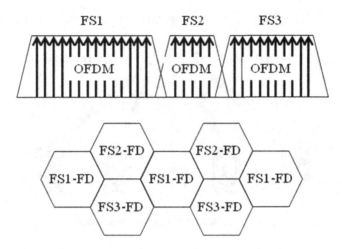

Fig. 2. Filtered sub-band reuse of FD mm-wave mobile network.

2.3   FD mm-wave Smallcell and BDMA

UE-UE interference is also a major challenge for FD mobile networks. To the interference of UE-UEs, beam division multiple access (BDMA) is introduced, as shown in Fig. 3, which can compress the interference of UE-UE in mm-wave FD scenario, on the other hand, achieve the virtual personal cell.

BDMA is the latest resource allocation technique in which orthogonal beams are allocated to each UE. Several beams of base station will be formed and point to different UEs to provide multiple accesses. If the UE and the base station are in LOS, they can transmit beams pointing to each other for proper communication without causing any interference to the other UE. The base station, after evaluating the position and the moving speed of the UE, assigns a separate beam to each UE. Based on the position and the moving speed, the base station also calculates the widths and the directions of the beams of all the UEs. Usually, all beams are different for each UE, so that different UEs can simultaneously transmit data at the same frequency with different angles.

Narrow and strong directional beam is the inherent property of mm-wave transmission. If coupled with beamforming, the mm-wave beam can be much narrower, which is more benefit to BDMA and FD transmission. Depending on various propagation environments, the base station can also more flexibly change the directions, numbers and beam-width of the beams.

For CU-separated and hierarchical FD mm-wave mobile networks, the UE will be a dual-connected terminal. The UE is assigned a signaling beam from FDD/TDD massive MIMO macro-cell as well as being assigned a mm-wave beam from FD smallcell.

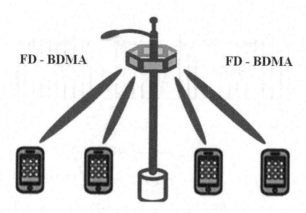

Fig. 3. BDMA of FD mm-wave smallcell.

3 Key Enabling Technologies: FD Ultra-Broadband Analog Frontend

3.1 Integrated Polarization-Based Antenna

Although, to a certain extent, the FD mm-wave mobile network architecture solves the interference of BS-BS and UE-UE, the ultra-broadband SIC, especially ultra-broadband analog SIC, is still the most critical technology, because to achieve ultra-broadband analog SIC is more difficult. At first, analog SIC can be performed at the antenna. Fortunately, an ultra-broadband polarization-based SIC antenna has been proposed and designed, as shown in Fig. 4 [3]. An auxiliary port AUX is introduced on the RX antenna that is co-polarized with TX and terminated with a reflective termination to achieve ultra broadband SIC.

The cross-polarized TX and RX antennas are used to improve the initial isolation between the TX output and the RX input. This increases the TX-to-RX isolation from 12–22 dB to 32–36 dB at 54–66 GHz. To improve TX-to-RX isolation and further suppression from ambient scattering, the SIC is aided by introducing a sub-antenna co-polarized with TX antenna. The sub-antenna is set on the AUX port on the RX antenna. The AUX port creates an indirect path from the TX output to the RX input. The indirect path indicates that the first cancellation signal is coupled to the AUX port and then reflects the reconfigurable terminal from the reflector chip and eventually couples to the RX input to cancel the self-interference from the direct path. The SIC bandwidth depends on how well the amplitude and phase match across the frequency band. A detailed algorithmic design technique for the SIC antenna is described in reference [3], in which 50 dB isolation over 300 MHz at 4.6 GHz is achieved. Reflective termination can be reconfigured to combat the variable self-interference scattering from the environment. Total self-interference suppression >70 dB over 1 GHz bandwidth at 59 GHz is demonstrated even in the presence of an environmental reflector [3]. RF canceller does not have any effect on RX noise floor due to antenna cancellation.

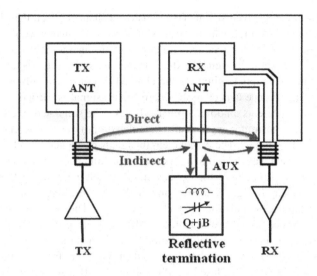

Fig. 4. FD integrated polarization based mm-wave antenna.

3.2 Ultra-Broadband RF Self-interference Cancellation Based on Microwave Photonics

For ultra-broadband analog SICs, the need for accurate amplitude and phase matching of large bandwidths places a heavy burden on the RF circuits, which are limited by the poor frequency flatness. In particular, RF delay lines and phase shifters are inherently narrowband and lack of the precision to achieve high performances of SIC. In the microwave photonics based SIC, simulated interference signals and received signals are all modulated onto the optical carriers and processed in the optical domain. In spite of exploiting the small portion of the bandwidth of the RF modulated optical signal, the microwave photonics based SIC can show an ultra-broadband cancellation.

In microwave photonics based ultra-broadband SIC system, each RF signal passes through an orthogonal bias M-Z modulator that modulates the RF signal onto an optical carrier. By high-precision channel matching, the amplitude and phase of the interference signals should be nearly the same in both receiver and cancellation paths, if subtracted by a balanced photodetector.

However, in the application scenario of mm-wave mobile network, the multipath and reflection of the beam must be considered in the ultra-broadband SIC. This is also the most critical factor to realize ultra-broadband SIC. Due to the antenna beamforming in the mm-wave system, the LOS interference is suppressed and the NLOS interference is amplified. In some environments, NLOS interference may be the primary interference. Because of the delay associated with the NLOS reflection, the interference canceller will need to adapt to larger dynamic delays. Therefore, multi-tap microwave photon FIR filter is a viable option. Considering the compactness and applicability, the photonic integrated circuits (PIC) is promising for the ultra-broadband SIC. Figure 5 is the ultra-broadband SIC system architecture based on PIC [4]. The PIC-based SIC replicates the transmitter interference as really as possible before subtracting the real interference from the received signal. To estimate the channel effect, the PIC based SIC uses a channel matched filter, which consists of N pairs of tunable weights and delays. Each pair may be used, for example, to represent different multipath effect in the transmitter-receiver path. In general, the channel matched filter is an optical FIR matched filter that attempts to simulate the channel response as really as possible and maximize self-interference cancellation. The received signal is carried by the top path in the Fig. 5 and represents a normal optical RF link. The simulated interference signal is tapped from the transmitter antenna and modulated onto the N different wavelengths in the bottom path of Fig. 5. The N wavelength signals propagate to a channel matched filter that assigns each wavelength to a separated tap. After each component is weighted and delayed by the semiconductor optical amplifier (SOA) and the true time delay (TTD), the wavelength signals are recombined. The resulting sum represents the estimated interference signal after the channel effect. The received signal and the estimated interference signal are then fed to the opposite port of the balanced pho- todetector to perform the subtraction. It should be noted that the balanced photodetector subtraction is suitable for both in-band and out-of-band interference, making it more efficient than simple filtering. Based on PIC, about 40 dB SIC over 1 GHz RF band- width has been demonstrated [4].

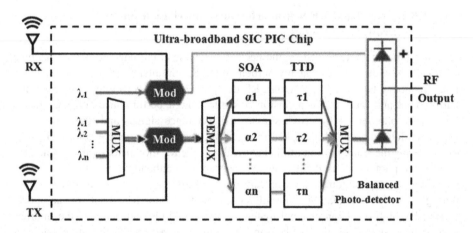

Fig. 5. FD mm-wave ultra-broadband SIC based on integrated microwave photonics.

4 Conclusion

In summary, to combine FD and mm-wave can boost the spectral efficiency and data capacity. A hierarchical network of FDD/TDD massive MIMO and FD mm-wave communications has the potential to realize FD mm-wave mobile networks, in which the features of CU split, BDMA and FSR make a true FD mobile network more feasible. On the other hand, PIC based ultra-broadband SIC and integrated polarization based antenna have respectively achieved self-interference suppression about 40 dB and 70 dB over 1 GHz bandwidth, opening a promising future of FD mm-wave mobile network of 5G.

References

1. Baiqing, Z., Shenlin, Z.: Challenges and potential application scenario of full duplex in future 5G network. In: VTC2015-Spring Workshop on Full Duplex, 11–14 May 2015, Glasgow, Scotland, UK (2015)
2. Shimodaira, H., Tran, G.K., Sakaguchi, K., Araki, K.: Investigation on millimeter-wave spectrum. In: 2015 IEEE Conference on Standards for Communications and Networking (CSCN) (2015)
3. Dinc, T., Chakrabarti, A., Krishnaswamy, H.: A 60 GHz CMOS full-duplex transceiver and link with polarization-based antenna and RF cancelation. IEEE J. Solid-State Circ. **51**(5), 1125–1140 (2016)
4. Chang, M.P., Tait, A., Chang, J., Prucnal, P.R.: An integrated optical interference cancellation system. In: WOCC (2014)

Modeling and Simulation on Cooperative Movement of Vehicle Group Based on the Behavior of Fish

Daxin Tian[1,4,5,6(✉)], Lu Kang[1,4], Kunxian Zheng[1,4], Xuting Duan[1,4], Hui Rong[2], Peng Guo[2], Wenyang Wang[2], and Haijun Zhang[3]

[1] Beijing Advanced Innovation Center for Big Data and Brain Computing, Beihang University, XueYuan Road No.37, Beijing 100191, China
dtian@buaa.edu.cn
[2] China Automotive Technology and Research Center, Automotive Engineering Research Institute, East Xianfeng Road No.68, Tianjin 300300, China
[3] School of Computer and Communication Engineering, University of Science and Technology Beijing, XueYuan Road No.30, Beijing 100083, China
[4] Beijing Key Laboratory for Cooperative Vehicle Infrastructure Systems and Safety Control, School of Transportation Science and Engineering, Beihang University, XueYuan Road No.37, Beijing 100191, China
[5] Jiangsu Province Collaborative Innovation Center of Modern Urban Traffic Technologies, Si Pai Lou. 2, Nanjing 210096, China
[6] Key Lab of Urban ITS Technology Optimization and Integration, The Ministry of Public Security of China, Hefei 230088, China

Abstract. Fatigue driving might affect the traffic safety when the vehicles are on the cruising state in highway. Trying to solve this problem, this paper uses the movement pattern of the fish to the vehicles fleet, and develops a model of vehicle group with realistic restrictions based on the existed fish algorithms, the mobile behavioral model and cluster behavior model, and then demonstrates the feasibility of applying the fish behavior to the cooperative movement of vehicle groups through analyzing the trajectory, velocity and spacing of vehicles.

Keywords: Fish behavior · Internet of vehicle · Groups move · Vehicle cruise

1 Introduction

Vehicles stay a long-term cruise state on highway or urban expressway. Relative to the general road, the vehicles are in a simple status where there are no traffic lights and reverse traffic interferences. But in this situation, it is easy for driver to feel fatigue, which will affect the safety and comfort of driving. And fatigue is the major reason resulting traffic accidents. In this case, we urgently need an auxiliary driving system or automatic driving system which can replace the driver to operate in a relatively simple closed environment.

© ICST Institute for Computer Sciences, Social Informatics and Telecommunications Engineering 2018
K. Long et al. (Eds.): 5GWN 2017, LNICST 211, pp. 630–639, 2018.
https://doi.org/10.1007/978-3-319-72823-0_58

Internet of Vehicles is a simply self-organizing network which is different from the ordinary. Because it uses the radio frequency to identify different Vehicles which equipped with electronic labels in the road, so that to achieve the extraction, supervisory and efficient use of state information from all vehicles in the net [1]. It implements the network interconnection between vehicles and travel environment by gathering a lot of basic information, such as the states of vehicles, road congestion and so on, and then communicates with other vehicles, thus make the travel of vehicles more secure, more convenient and more intelligent.

On the other hand, however, there is a certain defect in the existing communication technology, in spite of AODV showing better performance in average End-to-End delay and throughput under DSDD and SSDD techniques [2]. Moreover, the simulation results in [3] show that building and vehicle obstructions significantly attenuate the signal thus resulting in lower received signal strength, lower packet delivery ratio, and shorter effective transmission range, and the growth in the number of heterogeneous interconnected systems, as well as the emergence of new requirements in applications and services are progressively changing the original simplicity and transparency of the Internet architecture [4].

And the 5G network, which is proposed in recent years, can be a good solution to these problems [5]. And there are lots of works have studied in 5G network and vehicular network. For instance, in [6], Haijun Zhang present an overview of the challenges and requirements of the fronthaul technology in 5G LTE-U UDCSNets. In [7, 8], Shanzhi Chen present a potential step change for the evolution toward 5G, and propose long-term evolution (LTE)-V as a systematic and integrated V2X solution based on time-division LTE(TD-LTE). In [9], a delay-optimal virtualized radio resource scheduling scheme is proposed via stochastic learning. In [10–12], Chunxiao Jiang propose a credible information-sharing mechanism capable of ensuring that the vehicles do share genuine road traffic information (RTI), and study the outage probability of road traffic information sharing in underlay cognitive vehicular networks under both a general scenario and a specific highway scenario. In [13], a unified networking architecture is presented, starting from the inside of the vehicle and the interconnection of various control units and ultimately targeting Car-to-Car communications which enable smarter, safer and more efficient transportation.

In addition, the scientists get inspirations from some specific behavior of the biological community, such as Ant Colony Optimization (the ACO) and particle swarm Optimization (PSO), which are the most widely applied. And we will apply fish behavior into this paper.

So far, the Fish Principle has been widely used in Combinatorial optimization, grid planning, wireless coverage and other various fields [14, 15], and in the transportation field: Wang Jian and Ren Zihui proposed the application of artificial fish algorithm in vehicle behavior under serious traffic incident [16]; Scientists in Ministry of Transport Highway Science Research Institute, Jiang Shan put forward artificial fish school algorithm in the field of traffic distribution applications [17]; Lai Lei carried out the idea of applying the fish group model to the direction of multi-vehicle coordination driving control [18]; The core idea of Fish Principle is that the fish's behavior at the next time depends on the state and the environment mostly. At the same time, it will also affect the activities of the fish around it. We can easily think of the vehicle group from the fish group. The driving condition of every vehicle at next time depends on the condition of surrounding vehicles at this time and the road conditions, and its conditions at this time will also affect the activities chosen by the surrounding vehicles at next time [19]. Vehicles which cooperate with others just like the fish swimming in the highway.

Aim at the problems like long-time driving, low efficiency, and traffic accident, this paper put forward an improved model which based on the swarm intelligence, fish behavior and vehicle cruise state. We use the simulation software to analysis the trajectory, speed changes and separation distance between vehicles, then achieve the formation of team driving within the limits of road and avoid collisions. So as to improve the traffic efficiency, enhance driving comfort and make unmanned driving become true. Simultaneously, it is also benefit to driving safety and energy conservation.

2 Cooperative Model of Vehicle Group

There is a finite observable vehicle in the agreed two-dimensional road space, and each vehicle moves at its own speed. At the same time, each vehicle can exchange information, such as position, speed and acceleration, with other vehicles within a certain range in the surrounding area, we call this range R_0, and these vehicles neighborhood. Based on the current vehicle communication distance, the communication range of each vehicle is set to 300 m [20].

The target vehicle, which is randomly defined, is denoted as vehicle i. The position of vehicle i at time t is denoted as $P_i(t) = [x_i(t), y_i(t)]$. The neighbor of i is defined as

$$N_i(t) = \left\{ j : [x_i(t) - x_j(t)]^2 + [y_i(t) - y_j(t)]^2 \leq R_0^2 \right\}$$ (1)

And the number of neighbor is donated as $n_i(t)$.

At the same time, the speed of i and j at time t is denoted as $v_i(t)$ and $v_j(t)$, the acceleration of i and j is $a_i(t)$ and $a_j(t)$.

According to the analysis, the forces which are acting on vehicle i at time t can be described as

$$F = F_1 + F_2 + F_3 + F_4$$ (2)

In which, F_1 is mobile behavioral model, F_2 is the cluster behavior model, F_3 is the force from lane line. And they can be described as follow:

(1) Similar to the alignment principle of fish group mentioned in [21], each vehicle also tends to maintain a consistent orientation with its neighbor vehicle, that is, the moving direction of i at time t is the average acceleration of its neighborhood at time t − 1.

The moving direction of i is expressed as

$$a_i(t) = \frac{1}{n_i(t-1)} \sum_{j \in N_i(t-1)} a_j(t-1) \tag{3}$$

And F_1 is

$$F_1 = m_i a_i(t) \tag{4}$$

In which, m_i is the mass of vehicle i, and the value of m_i is 1 in simulation.

(2) Suppose that $j \in N_i(t)$ and j is front of i, the position of j is $P_j(t) = [x_j(t), y_j(t)]$. The distance between i and j is

$$d_{ij}(t) = \|P_i(t) - P_j(t)\| = \sqrt{\left(x_i(t) - x_j(t)\right)^2 + \left(y_i(t) - y_j(t)\right)^2} \tag{5}$$

If the vehicle j brakes, j will slide forward for a while. The distance traveled by vehicle j during this time is denoted as $s_j(t)$, and $s_j(t)$ can be described as

$$s_j(t) = \frac{\left(v_j(t)\right)^2}{2\mu g} \tag{6}$$

In which, g is the gravitational acceleration, and μ is the friction coefficient between tire and road. In general, the friction coefficient of asphalt pavement is 0.4–0.8 [22]. In order to facilitate the calculation, and considering that the road may be put into use for many years, the friction coefficient is set as 0.5.

As we mentioned previously, the information of target vehicle i is known to its neighbor vehicles in the environment of IOV. If i receives the information that j is broken, i will also brake immediately.

Likewise, if i brakes

$$s_i(t) = v_i(t)(t_r + t_d) + \frac{\left(v_i(t)\right)^2}{2\mu g} \tag{7}$$

In which, t_r is the reaction time of machine, t_d is the delay time for information exchange of vehicles, $(t_r + t_d)$ is set to be (0.75 s + 0.054 s) [23, 24]. And during the time $(t_r + t_d)$, i is still running in the speed $v_i(t)$.

The distance difference of sliding forward between the two cars is donated as $s_{ij}(t)$, and

$$s_{ij}(t) = s_i(t) - s_j(t) = \frac{\left(v_i(t)\right)^2 - \left(v_j(t)\right)^2}{2\mu g} + v_i(t)(t_r + t_d) \tag{8}$$

According to the works in [25], we can know that the force between the vehicles is divided into repulsion force and attraction force. When the distance $d_{ij}(t)$ between i and j is further than $s_{ij}(t)$, F_2 is attraction force, recorded as $F_{attract}$. And the larger $d_{ij}(t)$ is, the greater $F_{attract}$ is. If vehicle i accelerate toward vehicle j, the distance between i and j becomes smaller, and thereby the transportation efficiency can be improved; when the distance $d_{ij}(t)$ between i and j is shorter than $s_{ij}(t)$, F_2 is repulsive force, recorded as $F_{exclude}$. In order to avoid collision, vehicle i slows down to maintain the distance with the vehicle j; when $d_{ij}(t)$ is equal to $s_{ij}(t)$, $F_2 = 0$ As shown in Fig. 1, the force between i and j exerted on vehicle i is expressed as an attractive force.

In order to ensure traffic efficiency, we compress the distance between the front and rear vehicles to a safe distance $s_{ij}(t)$. The traffic accidents generally occur between the front and rear vehicles on the highway, So in this paper, we give priority to the front and rear vehicles. That is, the range of the force of i applied to the surrounding vehicle is all set to be $s_{ij}(t)$

Here we introduce a negative exponential function to characterize the forces acting on the vehicle which is changing with the distance. So, the attraction force and repulsive force can be expressed as:

$$F_{attract} = m_i A_0 exp\left(-d_{ij}/s_{ij}(t)\right) \times \frac{p_j(t) - p_i(t)}{\left\|p_j(t) - p_i(t)\right\|} \tag{9}$$

$$F_{exclude} = m_i A_1 exp\left(-d_{ij}/s_{ij}(t)\right) \times \frac{p_i(t) - p_j(t)}{\left\|p_i(t) - p_j(t)\right\|} \tag{10}$$

Finally, F_2 can be expressed as

$$F_2 = \sum_{j \in N_i(t)} F_{attract} + F_{exclude} \tag{11}$$

Where, A_0, A_1 are parameters of system. And after a number of tests, A_0, A_1 are set as 5,25 finally, and $\frac{p_j(t)-p_i(t)}{\left\|p_j(t)-p_i(t)\right\|}$, $\frac{p_i(t)-p_j(t)}{\left\|p_i(t)-p_j(t)\right\|}$ are the direction of force.

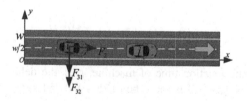

Fig. 1. The diagram of forces acting on the vehicle i

(3) In order to ensure that the vehicles are running within the limits of the lane, i will be subjected to the forces from both road sides. When i is in the position shown in Fig. 1, the vehicle will be repelled by the upper boundary, and attracted by the lower boundary at the same time. Similarly, the closer (farther) vehicle i approaches (gets away from) to upper (lower) boundary,, the greater the repulsive (attraction) force is. When the vehicle is in the middle of the road, the total force

from both sides of the road is 0. Suppose the upper bound is b_1, lower bound is b_2, the force between b_1 and vehicle i is F_{31}, the other is F_{32}, just as shown in Fig. 1.

Therefore, we can get the expression of F_3.

$$F_3 = F_{31} + F_{32} \tag{12}$$

Where,

$$F_{31} = \begin{cases} m_i A_2 exp\left(-\frac{w-y_i(t)}{w/2}\right), & w/2 < y_i(t) < w \\ -m_i A_3 exp\left(-\frac{y_i(t)}{w/2}\right), & 0 < y_i(t) < w/2 \end{cases} \tag{13}$$

And

$$F_{32} = \begin{cases} m_i A_4 exp\left(-\frac{w-y_i(t)}{w/2}\right), & \frac{w}{2} < (w - y_i(t)) < w \\ -m_i A_5 exp\left(-\frac{w-y_i(t)}{w/2}\right), & 0 < (w - y_i(t)) < \frac{w}{2} \end{cases} \tag{14}$$

Finally,

$$F_3 = \begin{cases} m_i A_2 exp\left(-\frac{y_i(t)}{w/2}\right) - m_i A_5 exp\left(-\frac{w-y_i(t)}{w/2}\right), & \frac{w}{2} < y_i(t) < w \\ 0, & y_i(t) = \frac{w}{2} \\ -m_i A_3 exp\left(-\frac{y_i(t)}{w/2}\right) + m_i A_4 exp\left(-\frac{w-y_i(t)}{w/2}\right), & 0 < y_i(t) < \frac{w}{2} \end{cases} \tag{15}$$

Where, A_2, A_3, A_4, A_5 are parameters of the system, and $A_2 = 1, A_3 = 20, A_4 = 2,$ $A_5 = 15$. And w is the width of road, w is equal to 3.75 in general.

(4) In addition to controlling the initial vehicle speed, we also need to keep the vehicles in the model running within the range of speed limit like the actual situation of highway.

For the above reasons, we introduce the vehicle speed control model [26].

$$F_4 = \begin{cases} A_6 v_i(t - 1), & when \quad v_i(t - 1) < 15 \\ -A_7 v_i(t - 1), & when \quad v_i(t - 1) > 30 \end{cases} \tag{16}$$

Where, A_6, A_7 are positive constants, $A_6 = 2, A_7 = 4$, and the unit of $v_i(t - 1)$ is m/s.

When the speed is too fast, for example, it exceed the maximum speed of highway, i will be subject to a force whose direction is opposite to that of the speed in order to ensure traffic safety.

When the speed is lower than a certain value, i will be subject to a force whose direction is the same as that of the speed, which is set to ensure high driving efficiency and avoid congestion.

3 Simulation and Analysis

The simulation experiments and analysis are all accomplished by MATLAB in this paper. At the beginning of the simulation, 10 cars are randomly generated in the initial simulation area of 20 × 200 m, the initial speed of all vehicles is set to be 15–30 m/s, and the simulation time is set to be one hour. In addition, the information of all vehicles is updated every 0.01 s.

3.1 Analysis of Vehicle Trajectory in Simulation

First of all, we establish a Cartesian coordinate system in the plane of road, and the x coordinate is lateral distance of road, y coordinate is longitudinal distance of road. The schematic view of vehicle locus is shown in Fig. 2(a) and (b) is an image obtained by enlarging the initial trajectory of the vehicle in Fig. 2(a), different curves represent the travel trajectories of different vehicles, we can see from the picture that the trajectories overlap together after the initial small amplitude swing. It indicates that vehicles are running in a row at this time. And it's consistent with the expected objectives of the paper. In addition, the total driving distance of vehicles is 110 km during the simulation time, and it is basically consistent with the actual situation of highway.

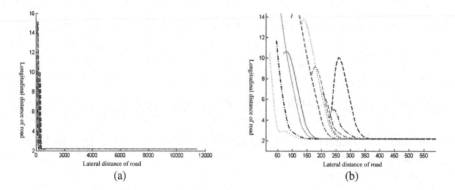

Fig. 2. (a). The schematic view of vehicle locus, (b). The initial trajectory of the vehicle in simulation

3.2 Analysis of Vehicle Speed in Simulation

Figure 3 shows the relationship between speed of vehicles and time, the horizontal axis represents time and the vertical axis represents vehicle speed. We can see that the speed remaining at 30 m/s finally. It is also consistent with the initial goals set by the simulation.

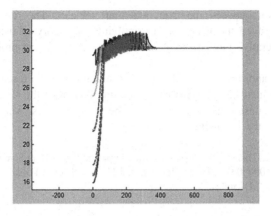

Fig. 3. The relationship between speed of vehicles and time

3.3 Analysis of Relative Distance of Vehicles in Simulation

Figure 4(a) is a graph showing the change in the distance between any two vehicles with time, there are $C_{10}^2 = 45$ lines for ten vehicles. And the horizontal axis represents time and the vertical axis represents distances. We can see the distances between any two cars maintain stability finally. Likely, Fig. 4(b) is an image obtained by enlarging the initial distance between the vehicles in Fig. 4(a). And due to the instability of vehicle speed and location in the early simulation, the range of changes of vehicle spacing is large. The spaces of vehicles also maintain steady after the speeds become stable.

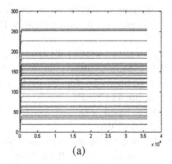
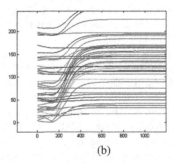

(a)   (b)

Fig. 4. (a). The change in the distance between any two vehicles, (b). The initial distance between the vehicle in simulation

4 Conclusion

In this paper, the group moving model is established based on the fish behavior model and the actual situation of vehicle cruising, we not only ensure the speed, acceleration and trajectory of vehicles are all within the reasonable range during the simulation, but also make all vehicles driven in a line and ensure the stability of the vehicle, so that to avoid the collision between the front and rear vehicles. The results of simulation experiment are proved the feasibility of applying the theory of fish behavior to the research of cooperative movement of multi-vehicle in the environment of Internet of Vehicle.

In the other hand, there are still many shortcomings in the research of this paper. For example, we treat all the vehicles as an individual with the same motion characteristics, without considering the differences between vehicles. And further improvement is needed in the following studies.

Acknowledgments. This research was supported in part by no. Beijing Science and Technology Program no. D171100000317003 and the National Natural Science Foundation of China under Grant nos. 61672082, U1564212.

References

1. Chen, G., Guo, D.: Research and development on internet of vehicle. J. Mob. Commun. **17**, 23–26 (2011)
2. Gaamel, A.M., Maratha, B.P., Sheltami, T.R., Shakshuki, E.M.: Fault-tolerance evaluation of VANET under different data dissemination models. Int. J. Veh. Telemat. Infotain. Syst. (IJVTIS) **1**(1), 54–68 (2017)
3. Mir, Z.H., Filali, F.: A simulation-based study on the environment-specific propagation model for vehicular communications. Int. J. Veh. Telemat. Infotain. Syst. (IJVTIS) **1**(1), 1–18 (2017)
4. Cortéspolo, D., Callecancho, J., Carmonamurillo, J., Gonzálezsánchez, J.: Future trends in mobile-fixed integration for next generation networks: classification and analysis. Int. J. Veh. Telemat. Infotain. Syst. (IJVTIS) **1**(1), 33–53 (2017)
5. Zhang, H., Liu, N., Chu, X., Long, K., Aghvami, A.H., Leung, V.C.M.: Network slicing based 5G and future mobile networks: mobility, resource management, and challenges. IEEE Commun. Mag.
6. Zhang, H., Dong, Y., Cheng, J., Leung, V.C.M.: Fronthauling for 5G LTE-U ultra dense cloud small cell networks. IEEE Wirel. Commun. **23**(6), 48–53 (2016)
7. Chen, S., Zhao, J.: The requirements, challenges and technologies for 5G of terrestrial mobile telecommunication. IEEE Commun. Mag. **52**(5), 36–43 (2014)
8. Chen, S., Hu, J., Shi, Y., Zhao, L.: LTE-V: a TD-LTE based V2X solution for future vehicular network. IEEE Internet Things J. **3**(6), 997–1005 (2016)
9. Zheng, Q., Zheng, K., Zhang, H., Leung, V.C.M.: Delay-optimal virtualized radio resource scheduling in software-defined vehicular networks via stochastic learning. IEEE Trans. Veh. Technol. **65**(12), 9479–9492 (2016)
10. Jiang, C., Zhang, H., Han, Z., Cheng, J., Ren, Y., Leung, V.C.M., Hanzo, L.: Information-sharing outage-probability analysis of vehicular networks. IEEE Trans. Veh. Technol. **65**(12), 9479–9492 (2016)
11. Jiang, C., Zhang, H., Han, Z., Cheng, J., Ren, Y., Hanzo, L.: On the outage probability of information sharing in cognitive vehicular networks. In: Proceedings of IEEE International Conference on Communications (ICC), Kuala Lampur, Malaysia, 23–27 May 2016
12. Huang, Y., Wang, J., Jiang, C., Zhang, H., Leung, V.C.M.: Vehicular network based reliable traffic density estimation. In: Proceedings of the IEEE Vehicular Technology Conference (VTC), Nanjing, 15–18 May 2016

13. Pressas, A., Özpolat, M., Sheng, Z., Ali, F.: Performance evaluation of networking protocols for connected vehicles. Int. J. Veh. Telemat. Infotain. Syst. (IJVTIS) **1**(1), 1–14 (2017)
14. Zhu, Y., Chen, H., Shen, H.: Bio-inspired Computing Individual, Swarm and Community Evolution Models and Methods, pp. 35–38. Tsinghua University Press, Beijing (2013)
15. Huth, A., Wissel, C.: The simulation of the movement in fish schools. J. Theor. Biol. **156**, 365–385 (1992)
16. Wang, J., Ren, Z.: Application if artificial fish algorithm in vehicle behavior under serious traffic incident. J. Syst. Simul. **23** (2011)
17. Jiang, S., Ji, Y.: Artificial fish swarm algorithm for solving road network equilibrium traffic assignment problem. Comput. Simul. **28**(6), 326–329 (2011). ISSN 1006-9348
18. Lei, L., Shiru, Q.: An effective swarm vehicle coordinative traffic control design based on fish swarm grouping behavior. J. Northwestern Polytechn. Univ. **30** (2012)
19. Ban, X., Ning, S.: Research on advanced self-organization behavior for artificial fish school. Acta Automatica Sin. **34**(10), 1328–1331 (2008)
20. Tang, A., Yip, A.: Collision avoidance timing analysis of DSRC-based vehicles. Accid. Anal. Prev. **42**(1), 182–195 (2010)
21. Chu, T.G., Wang, L., Mu, S.M.: Collective behavior analysis of an anisotropic swarm model. In: Proceedings of the 16th International Symposium on Mathematical Theory of Network and Systems. Mathematical Theory of Network and Systems (2004)
22. He, S., Xia, L.: Friction coefficient mesurement and evaluation for lane surface of expressway. J. Highway Transp. Res. Devel. **19** (2002)
23. Johansson, G., Rumar, K.: 'Driver's brake reaction times', human factors. J. Hum. Factors Ergon. Soc. **13**, 23–27 (1971)
24. Taoka, G.: Break reaction times of unalerted drivers. ITE J. **59**, 19–21 (1989)
25. Tian, D., Zhu, K.: Swarm model for cooperative multi-vehicle mobility with inter-vehicle communications. IET Intell. Transp. Syst. **9**, 887–896 (2015)
26. Yang, D., Pu, Y., Yang, F.: Car-following model based on optimal distance and its characteristics analysis. J. Northwest Transp. Univ. **47** (2012)

Propagation Characteristics in Indoor Scenario with Different Transmitter Locations at 3.5 and 6 GHz

Xinzhuang Zhang[1(✉)], Yawei Yu[1], Lei Tian[1], Yu Han[1], Yu Zhang[3], and Jianhua Zhang[1,2]

[1] Key Lab of Universal Wireless Communications, Ministry of Education, Beijing University of Posts and Telecommunications, Mailbox NO. 92, Beijing 100876, China
{zxzhuang,tianlbupt,jhzhang}@bupt.edu.cn
[2] State Key Laboratory of Networking and Switching Technology, Beijing University of Posts and Telecommunications, Mailbox NO. 92, Beijing 100876, China
[3] Qualcomm Inc., 6/F, Tower C, Beijing Global Trade Center, 36 North 3rd Ring East Road, Beijing 100013, China
zhangyu@qti.qualcomm.com

Abstract. This paper presents results from the measurement in indoor conference scenario at 3.5 GHz and 6 GHz. The measurement was performed by using multiple-input multiple-output (MIMO) antennas including uniform planar array (UPA) at transmitter end (Tx) and omni-directional array (ODA) at receiver end (Rx). Two cases including UPA on the wall and the ceiling, have been measured and comprehensive propagation characteristics have been investigated in detail. Based on the measurement, delay and spatial parameters are analyzed and then compared with the standard model. The delay spread measured shows smaller value than standard model due to the small size of the scenario and the elevation angle spread is presented for establishing three-dimensional (3D) channel model. Further, the capacity performances of the channel in different cases are evaluated, and the results indicate that the system with transmitter antenna mounted on the wall performs better.

Keywords: MIMO channel · Elevation angle spread
Channel capacity

1 Introduction

With the continuous development of mobile internet, as well as the emergence of new technology such as Virtual Reality (VR) and Augmented Reality (AR), the demand for data rate has increased greatly. The fifth generation (5G) communication has been widely researched to provide higher data rate and frequency efficiency to satisfy this requirement in the near future. MIMO technology has

© ICST Institute for Computer Sciences, Social Informatics and Telecommunications Engineering 2018
K. Long et al. (Eds.): 5GWN 2017, LNICST 211, pp. 640–649, 2018.
https://doi.org/10.1007/978-3-319-72823-0_59

been verified as a key technology for 5G system. In order to achieve better performance of the technology, understanding the MIMO channel characteristics deeply is necessary. The field measurement is an essential way to obtain the channel properties. Meanwhile it can also provide guideline for system designing and network planning.

As an important deployment scenario for 5G, indoor scenario has been depicted in 3GPP TR 36.900 [1]. So the study of channel characteristics and modeling in indoor scenarios arises researchers' great interests. There are plenty of measurements conducted by different researchers for various channel environments. In [2], the comparison of channel parameters at 3.5 GHz in room-room, room-corridor and corridor-corridor cases was made, the result indicates that the root mean square delay spread (rms DS) in corridor-corridor case has the maximum value for existing obvious reflection paths. And in [3], Central Hall as indoor scenario was measured at three frequency band including 2 GHz, 4 GHz and 6 GHz, and the analysis results demonstrate that the delay spread has no clear dependency on carrier frequency.

In [1], indoor scenarios include office environments and shopping malls, with transmitter antennas mounted on the ceilings or walls. However, there is little literature on investigating the channel characteristics difference between dissimilar Tx location in indoor environment. The attention should be paid more on that.

In this paper, propagation characteristics in indoor conference scenario at 3.5 GHz and 6 GHz were investigated. Two cases including Tx antenna array on the wall and on the ceiling have been measured in detail. We present and compare the key channel parameters such as delay spread and angle spread in two cases. Further, the performances of antenna system in two cases are discussed. The results can provide guideline for 5G communication system design, especially for small cell system.

The rest of this paper is organized as follows. Section 2 gives a detailed description of the measurement campaign. Data post process methods are introduced in Sect. 3. Then analysis results follow in Sect. 4 and Sect. 5 draws the conclusions.

2   Measurement Description

2.1   Measurement System

In field measurement, the channel sounder described in [4] was utilized to conduct the measurement campaign. It consists of three units: transmitter sounder, receiver sounder, and receiver baseband processing unit (RBPU). The RBPU is used to store the raw data received by the receiver sounder. With different radio frequency converter placed in the sounders, measurement at different frequency band such as 3.5 GHz and 6 GHz can be achieved. To capture propagation rays in 3D environment efficiently, full dimensional arrays are equipped at both sides of a measurement link. During our field measurements, dual-polarized ($\pm45°$) ODA consisting of 56 antenna elements is used at the Rx, while UPA with 32 antenna elements at the Tx, as described in Fig. 1. The array elements are microstrip patches and their 6 dB beamwidths are approximately 110° in both vertical and horizontal planes. The gain of each antenna element is 6 dBi, and angle resolution is 2°. In Table 1, measurement parameters including antenna height are listed.

(a) UPA (Tx)

(b) ODA (Rx)

Fig. 1. Layout of antenna arrays

Table 1. The specifications of measurement

Items	Tx-W	Tx-C
CF (GHz)	3.5/6	3.5/6
Bandwidth (MHz)	100	100
Length of PN code (Chips)	127	127
Transmitter antenna/Number	UPA/32	UPA/32
Receiver antenna/Number	ODA/56	ODA/56
Polarized	±45°	±45°
Height of Tx antenna (m)	1.8	2.4
Height of Rx antenna (m)	1.2	1.2

2.2 Measurement Scenario

We carried out the field measurement for 3D channel impulse response (CIR) in a conference room for indoor scenarios. The room is 5.85 m long, 5.10 m wide and 2.40 m high with gypsum ceiling and concrete block wall. And there are no windows in the room. In the middle, there is a long wooden table. The UPA is fixed on different locations-the wall and the ceiling, namely Tx-W and Tx-C case, respectively. The UPA location for Tx-C case is showed in Fig. 2(a).

And the ODA is positioned at the marked spots from number 1 to 20 for static measurement in each case, as depicted in Fig. 2(b). There is no obstruction between transmitter and receiver, so all the measurements are line of sight (LoS) condition. For each case and each central frequency, approximately 20 different spots are measured with 500 snapshots collected for each spot.

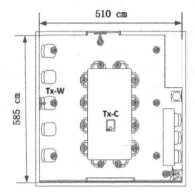

510 cm

585 cm

Tx-W

Tx-C

(a) The Propagation Environment in Tx-C case for UPA

(b) The location of the measured spots for two cases

Fig. 2. The overview of the measurement scenario

3   Data Post-processing

After measurement, post processing is implemented with two steps: firstly, obtaining CIR from the measured raw data; then extracting channel parameters such as delay, power and angle from CIR. The CIR is converted from the raw data through eliminating the system impulse response by correlating the received signals with calibration signal. When extracting channel parameters, channel model needs to be introduced. The 3D channel model for LTE has been introduced in 3GPP TR 36.873 [5] and for any given delay τ, it is given by

$$h_{u,s}(\tau_l;t) = \sum_{l=1}^{L} \begin{bmatrix} F_{rx,u,\theta}(\mathbf{\Omega}_l) \\ F_{rx,u,\phi}(\mathbf{\Omega}_l) \end{bmatrix}^T \begin{bmatrix} \alpha_{l,\theta,\theta} & \alpha_{l,\theta,\phi} \\ \alpha_{l,\phi,\theta} & \alpha_{l,\phi,\phi} \end{bmatrix} \begin{bmatrix} F_{tx,s,\theta}(\mathbf{\Phi}_l) \\ F_{tx,s,\phi}(\mathbf{\Phi}_l) \end{bmatrix}$$
$$\times \exp(j2\pi\lambda_0^{-1}(\mathbf{\Omega}_l \cdot \bar{r}_{rx,u})) \exp(j2\pi\lambda_0^{-1}(\mathbf{\Phi}_l \cdot \bar{r}_{tx,s})) \times \exp(j2\pi f_{d,l}t) \tag{1}$$

Where, L is the total number of multiple components (MPC), λ is the wavelength of the carrier frequency. The SAGE algorithm [6] is applied in order to estimate channel parameters from CIRs. As an extension of the maximal likelihood estimation (MLE) algorithm, taking the antenna pattern into account, the SAGE algorithm provides a joint estimation of the parameter set, $\theta_l = \{\tau_l, \mathbf{\Phi}_l, \mathbf{\Omega}_l, f_{d,l}, \mathbf{A}_l\}, l = 1, 2, ..., L$, where $\tau_l, f_{d,l}, \mathbf{\Phi}_l, \mathbf{\Omega}_l$ and $\mathbf{A}_l$ denote the propagation delay, the Doppler shift, the direction of departure, the direction of arrival, and the complex polarization matrix of the lth path, respectively. Specially, $\mathbf{\Phi}_l = (\theta_{T,l}, \phi_{T,l})$, $\mathbf{\Omega}_l = (\theta_{R,l}, \phi_{R,l})$, where $\theta_{T,l}$, $\phi_{T,l}$, $\theta_{R,l}$ and $\phi_{R,l}$ denote the elevation of departure (EoD), azimuth of departure (AoD), elevation of arrival (EoA), and azimuth of departure (AoA) of the lth path, respectively. For each measurement snapshot, $L = 200$ paths are estimated by the SAGE algorithm.

3.1   Delay Parameters

The main parameters of time domain dispersion include mean excess delay τ_{mean} and rms DS τ_{rms}. They can be determined from a power delay profile (PDP). The rms DS is defined as the root mean square of second central moment of the power delay profile. So rms DS can be calculated as below [7]

$$\tau_{rms} = \sqrt{\frac{\sum\limits_{l}(\tau_l - \tau_{mean})^2 P_l}{\sum\limits_{l} P_l}} \tag{2}$$

where

$$\tau_{mean} = \frac{\sum\limits_{l} \tau_l P_l}{\sum\limits_{l} P_l} \tag{3}$$

These delays τ_l are measured relative to the first detective arriving path at the receiver.

3.2   Spatial Parameters

Root mean square angle spread σ_{AS} is a key factor to characterize the dispersion in spatial domain. As mentioned in the former part of Sect. 3, the azimuth and elevation angles of the MPC can be extracted from CIRs. The mean angle spread $\mu(\Delta)$ and the circular angle spread (CAS) [8] σ_{AS} can be calculated by [7]

$$\sigma_{AS} = \min_{\Delta} \sigma_{AS}(\Delta) = \sqrt{\frac{\sum\limits_{l=1}^{L}(\phi_l(\Delta) - \mu(\Delta))^2 P_l}{\sum\limits_{l=1}^{L} P_l}} \tag{4}$$

$$\mu(\Delta) = \frac{\sum\limits_{l=1}^{L} \phi_l(\Delta) P_l}{\sum\limits_{l=1}^{L} P_l} \tag{5}$$

$$\phi_l(\Delta) = \phi_l + \Delta \tag{6}$$

$$\phi_l = \begin{cases} 2\pi + \phi_l & \phi < -\pi \\ \phi_l & |\phi| \leq \pi \\ 2\pi - \phi_l & \phi > \pi \end{cases} \tag{7}$$

where L, P_l, and $\phi_l(\Delta)$ denote the number of paths, the power of the lth path and the angle of the lth path adding a shifted angle which denotes a certain angular shift.

3.3   Channel Capacity

The channel capacity is an important metric of the MIMO channel. For the CIR of each measurement location, the Discrete Fourier Transform is applied to obtain the channel response matrix $\boldsymbol{H}_{U,S}(f;t)$, where f denotes the subcarrier indice. The mean capacity of frequency selective fading channel over all subcarriers at all fixed spots of different ones is given [9] by

$$C = \frac{1}{Q} \sum_{q=1}^{Q} \log_2 \det(I_N + \frac{\rho}{\beta M} H_{u,s,q} H_{u,s,q}^H) \tag{8}$$

Where Q is the number of channel realizations, ρ is the signal to noise ratio (SNR) and β is a common normalization factor for all channel realizations within one snapshot which satisfies

$$E[\frac{1}{\beta} \|H_{u,s,q}\|_F^2] = US \tag{9}$$

where $\|\bullet\|_F^2$ denotes the Frobenius norm.

4   Results of Measurements

4.1   Delay Characteristics

Delay spread expresses the delay dispersion of the channel and is probably the most important metric describing a radio channel characteristics. When considering delay spread from PDP, the noise cut threshold has to be mentioned. A 20 dB noise threshold criterion [10] has been utilized meaning that incoming paths with higher than 20 dB power difference compared to the most powerful path have been removed. According to the former part, the rms DS is obtained for two cases, and then summarized in Table 2. CF denotes central frequency. The mean excess delay and rms DS obey the lognormal distribution. For example, the fitted cumulative probability density curve of the rms DS obtained in Tx-C case at 6 GHz is depicted in Fig. 3.

From the Table 2, we can observe that the mean excess delay's variation range is from 20 ns to 28 ns in all cases. And in Tx-C case at 3.5 GHz it is smaller than that in Tx-W case, while at 6 GHz, it shows opposite tendency in

Tx-W case. So there is no obvious changing rules for excess delay when Tx location vares. In terms of rms DS, the values in two cases are almost the same, for the tiny difference in a few nanoseconds can be ignored. So there are no obvious dependency between rms DS and frequency. Compared to the InH scenario in [10], the value is smaller as a result of the small size of the room.

Table 2. Delay parameters for two cases

CF (GHz)	3.5		6		3.4
Case	Tx-C	Tx-W	Tx-C	Tx-W	InH
τ_{mean} (ns)	20.08	24.00	28.37	22.68	N/A
τ_{rms} (ns)	10.41	13.38	14.23	13.50	19.95

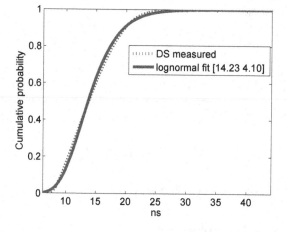

Fig. 3. Fitting results of DS in Tx-C case at 6 GHz

4.2 Spacial Characteristics

The rms AS including EoD, EoA, AoD and AoA can be calculated according to Eqs. 4, 5, 6 and 7 in Sect. 3.2 and the mean values of rms angle spread for Tx-C and Tx-W cases are listed in Table 3.

It is easily observed that arrival angle spread is larger than departure angle. For example, ASA is greater than ASD in Tx-C case as well as Tx-W case. This is due to that Tx antenna is mounted at one place while Rx antenna is set along the measured route so receiver enjoys more scatters than transmitter. As we predict, AS decreases when the frequency increases in a given case, for arrival azimuth angle spread shows greater value at 3.5 GHz than that at 6 GHz in identical case. It is due to the fact that the smaller the wavelength of carrier is, the less scattering paths arrive at the receiver. It is worth noting that ESA

Table 3. The statistical spatial parameters in two cases

CF (GHz)	3.5		6		3.4
Case	Tx-C	Tx-W	Tx-C	Tx-W	InH
ASD (°)	30.2	33.8	28.8	25.7	39.8
ESD (°)	24.0	30.2	26.9	26.9	N/A
ASA (°)	53.7	58.8	50.1	51.3	41.7
ESA (°)	27.5	42.6	26.9	38.9	N/A

in Tx-C case is much smaller than that in Tx-W case at 3.5 GHz and 6 GHz. It is resulted from the fact that there are more reflection and scattering paths from the walls and table arriving receiver when the UPA is equipped on the wall. As for ASA, the variation is not obvious. Above all, in conference room, the Tx antenna location has an obvious influence on angle spread, especially for elevation angle. The deep understanding of spacial parameter can be utilized for beamforming.

4.3 Capacity Analysis

Using the channel matrix H from the CIR, channel capacity can be obtained by Eq. 8. The capacities were calculated in two cases to predict the capacity in conference scenario. For the inter element spacing impacts the capacity, here half wavelength spacing is adopted for 3.5 GHz and 6 GHz, respectively.

From Fig. 4, the antenna-on-wall system performs better compared to the antenna-on-ceiling system no matter at 3.5 GHz or 6 GHz. At an SNR of 30 dB, the antenna-on-wall system at 3.5 GHz provides an ergodic capacity of

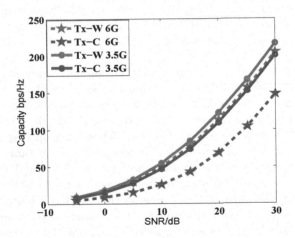

Fig. 4. The capacity of 56 receiving antenna and 32 transmitting antenna

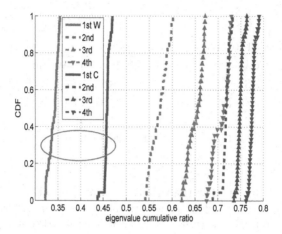

Fig. 5. The cumulative ratio of eigenvalues of channel for two cases at 3.5 GHz

216.5 bits/s/Hz. It is known that channel correlation between subchannels impacts the channel capacity. So the eigenvalues of the MIMO channel were analyzed to find the reason. We chose spot 7 described in Fig. 2(b) for example. The CDF curves for cumulative ratio of the first four eigenvalues in Tx-C case and Tx-W case are depicted in Fig. 5. As emphasized by the rad ellipse, We can find that the main eigenvalue in Tx-C case is larger than that in Tx-W case, indicating antenna system in Tx-W case has lower correlation between subchannels, so it obtains better capacity performance.

5   Conclusion

In this paper, we have reported the results from the measurement in indoor conference scenario. The 3.5 GHz and 6 GHz frequency bands are candidate bands for 5G system, and the measurement scenario is of importance to indoor scenarios.

In LoS condition, two cases including Tx antenna array on the wall and the ceiling at 3.5 GHz and 6 GHz have been measured with UPA and ODA to obtain delay and spacial domain parameters, as well as capacity performance. We compared channel characteristics in two cases in detail. For delay domain dispersion parameters, rms DS has no clear dependency on frequency, and the values are around 14 ns in two cases. For spacial domain parameters, elevation arrival angle spread shows a large difference between Tx-W and Tx-C case, and in Tx-C case it is about ten degrees larger than that in Tx-W case. And the MIMO system with transmitter antenna on the wall has a better performance at 3.5 GHz, obtaining up to 216.5 bits/s/Hz. So transmitter antenna mounted on the wall may be a good choice for indoor small cell system deployment.

Acknowledgments. This research is supported in part by National Science and Technology Major Project of the Ministry of Science and Technology (2015ZX03002008), and by National Natural Science Foundation of China (61322110, 6141101115), and by Doctoral Fund of Ministry of Education (20130005110001), and by Qualcomm Incorporated.

References

1. 3GPP TR 36.900: Study on Channel Model for Frequency Spectrum above 6 GHz (Release 14) (2016)
2. Zeng, J., Zhang, J.: Propagation characteristics in indoor office scenario at 3.5 GHz. In: 8th International ICST Conference on Communications and Networking in China (CHINACOM), Guilin, pp. 332–336. IEEE Press (2013)
3. Li, J., et al.: Measurement-based characterizations of indoor massive MIMO channels at 2 GHz, 4 GHz, and 6 GHz frequency bands. In: 83rd Vehicular Technology Conference (VTC Spring), Nanjing, pp. 1–5. IEEE Press (2016)
4. Zhang, J.: Review of wideband MIMO channel measurement and modeling for IMT-advanced systems. Chin. Sci. Bull. **57**(19), 2387–2400 (2012)
5. 3GPP TR 36.873: Study on 3D Channel Model for LTE (Release 12) (2014)
6. Fleury, B.H., Jourdan, P., Stucki, A.: High-resolution channel parameter estimation for MIMO applications using the SAGE algorithm. In: International Zurich Seminar on Broadband Communications Access - Transmission - Networking, Zurich, p. 30-1 (2002)
7. Rappaport, T.S.: Wireless Communications: Principles and Practice. Prentice Hall, New Jersey (2001)
8. 3GPP TR 25.966: Spatial Channel Model for Multiple Input Multiple Output (MIMO) Simulations (2003)
9. Yu, K., Bengtsson, M., Ottersten, M., McNamara, D., Karlsson, P., Beach, M.: Modeling of wide-band MIMO radio channels based on NLoS indoor measurements. IEEE Trans. Veh. Technol. **53**(3), 655–665 (2004)
10. ITU-R M.2135: Guidelines for Evaluation of Radio Interface Technologies for IMT-Advanced (2009)

Social-Aware Data Caching Mechanism in D2D-Enabled Cellular Networks

Miao Liu[1], Jun Li[1(✉)], Tingting Liu[1], and Youjia Chen[2]

[1] School of Electronic and Optical Engineering,
Nanjing University of Science and Technology, Nanjing, China
{miao.liu,jun.li}@njust.edu.cn, liutingting1026@hotmail.com
[2] College of Photonic and Electronic Engineering,
Fujian Normal University, Fuzhou, China
chenyoujia@fjnu.edu.cn

Abstract. In this paper, we investigate the problem of content caching in wireless cellular networks (CN) using device-to-device (D2D) transmission method to reduce subscriber's download delay. We focus on how to efficiently allocate files to the selected important nodes (INs), and propose a novel approach for minimizing the downloading latency. In particular, we first model the problem of minimizing delay as a matching game. Then we tackle this game by exploiting the popularity of contents as well as users' social properties to generate the utility functions of two-side players: INs and files. Based on the utility function, the preference lists of cache entities is developed. For solving this game, we design a user-file caching (UFC) algorithm to achieve a stable matching between INs and files. Simulation and analytical results show that the proposed mechanism is capable of offering a better delay performance than benchmarks, e.g., random caching and recent-used-file caching scheme.

Keywords: Cellular network · Content caching · D2D
Social property

1 Introduction

With the proliferation of smartphones and other derivative intelligent equipments, the network traffic has witnessed a trend of explosive growth. It is expected to increase by 40 fold over the next five years [1], due to mobile video stream and social network traffic. This increasing need for high rate transmission and low-cost power has impelled mobile operators to redesign and find more efficient techniques to meet the increase. In this respect, device-to-device (D2D) communication [2,3] has emerged as a promising technique to achieve high efficiency. User equipments can obtain data from other mobile devices or small base station rather than the cellular base station (BS) by employing D2D communications [4]. Although it is a promising technology for the next generation communication to meet unprecedented traffic demands, D2D has to overcome

© ICST Institute for Computer Sciences, Social Informatics and Telecommunications Engineering 2018
K. Long et al. (Eds.): 5GWN 2017, LNICST 211, pp. 650–662, 2018.
https://doi.org/10.1007/978-3-319-72823-0_60

some challenges such as mutual interference and transmission distance limitation. However, most researches on D2D communications have focused on the physical layer. In fact, the social-aware networks among the D2D participators can be investigated to further increase the transmission rate.

Social network provides various platforms to users for the purpose of online content sharing with their friends, or searching someone who has common interests in the virtual network. Interestingly, the connection established in the virtual network actually is tightly associated with our offline life. For example, on campus our connected friends in Facebook, Twitter, Youtube, or Sina Blog, usually have a very close physical distance. The authors in [5] make a detailed summary and analysis to the features of social network and propose a social-aware D2D communication architecture. As shown in [5], the social network characteristics consist of ties, community, centrality and bridge. Moreover, eigenvector centrality, closeness centrality and betweenness centrality are commonly used in the identification of social importance. In [6], the authors present a novel approach utilizing eigenvector centrality to judge the relationship in social network. Recently, social network has been proposed to combine with the caching mechanism [7,8]. In [9], the placement of popular content is proposed considering the importance of nodes in social layer. However, how to efficiently match the contents with users remains a challenge.

Matching theory is an effective method for solving the combinatorial problem of matching players in two distinct sets. In [10], the classic classification of matching problem includes one to one matching, many to one matching and many to many matching. Specially, the many to one matching game is utilized in resources allocation, where two players have different preferences towards network resources [11]. Additionally, many to many has been widely applied to the resource and spectrum allocation in wireless network [12].

In this paper, we are inspired to research on the social-aware content allocation in wireless cellular networks (CN) using matching algorithm. Popular contents and important nodes (INs) are modeled as two sides of the matching game. To this end, we model the content allocation problem as a matching game. Our main contributions can be summarized as follows:

1. We present an framework of INs selecting where three social characteristics are considered.
2. We propose a many to one matching game to solve the content allocation problem. In this game, the two sides of players establish their preferences towards each other considering content popularity, social connection features, and the wireless physical layer metrics.
3. The stability of the proposed matching algorithm is proved. Simulation is carried out to evaluate the performance of the proposed algorithm.

The rest of this paper is organized as follows. In Sect. 2, we describe the system model in detail and present the content allocation problem. In Sect. 3, we propose the many to one matching framework. In addition, we design a novel matching algorithm and prove that the algorithm is stable. Simulation results are shown in Sect. 4, the performance of the proposed method is analysed. Finally, we draw the conclusions in Sect. 5.

2   System Model and Problem Formulation

We focus our attention on a cellular network consisting of one BS and an amount of mobile users randomly located in the cellular area. Mobile users would like to acquire some interested files that belong to content providers, such as YouTube and Youku. A sample model of combination of social network and D2D communication is shown in Fig. 1. Such a system can be divided into two layers: the physical layer and social layer and each node in social layer can be projected onto a real user equipment in physical layer. In the social layer, the virtual connections between social users can reflect their offline activities [13]. Thus, we can infer the close degree of user's relationship by observing their behaviors in social network platform. Besides, in the physical layer, users can access to the cellular network or establish D2D connection to obtain required files. Taking the social characteristics of D2D communication pairs into account, we can select INs for caching popular files. For example, in physical layer of Fig. 1, if V_6 and V_9 are active in social layer, the popular files can be downloaded within their storage capacity for disseminating to their linked users. The problem of how to select INs will be introduced in the following. However, there exists some difference between social layer and physical layer. For example, node V_6 has social link with node V_8, but in physical layer the D2D link does not exist between them due to the faraway distance. Also, In physical layer, V_1 and V_3 have close distance, but they don't have a social link.

In this paper, we construct the network model considering both the social layer and physical layer [14]. If the D2D link and social link exist simultaneously between two users, we say that the two users are connected, which means that if the connection exists, the connecting users are not only within the transmission range but also have certain social relationship. We denote the set of M user equipments by $\mathcal{V} = \{V_1, \cdots, V_m, \cdots, V_M\}$, where V_m, $m \in \{1, 2, 3, \cdots, M\}$ represents the mth user equipment. Moreover, the set of INs is $\mathcal{M}_c = \{1, 2, \cdots, m_c\}$, which is chosen by BS for sake of proactive caching within their storage. The set of $\mathcal{M}_d = \{1, 2, \cdots, m_d\}$ represents the general users. In addition, $\mathcal{F} = \{f_1, f_2, \cdots, f_L\}$ denotes requesting file set controlled by content provider.

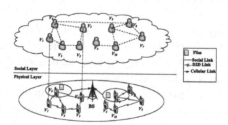

Fig. 1. A detailed description of combination of social network and D2D communication.

2.1   System Description

We suppose that the probability of content requests p_q obeys the Zipf distribution

$$p_q = \frac{1/q^\alpha}{\sum_{i=1}^{L} 1/i^\alpha}, \quad \text{for} \quad q = 1, \cdots, L \tag{1}$$

where α characterizes the skewness of the distribution, reflecting different content popularity. However, generally speaking, people usually have different preference towards files. Thus, The content popularity matrix for all users is given by $\mathbf{P} \in R^{M \times L}$ where each entry P_{m,f_i} represents the probability that the mth user requests the ith file f_i. The relation between $P_{m,i}$ and p_q is illustrated in [15] in detail.

Here, we use $\mathcal{G} = (\mathcal{V}, \mathcal{E})$ to denote a social relationship graph, in which $\mathcal{V} = \mathcal{M}_c \cup \mathcal{M}_d$ represents the set of all nodes and $\mathcal{E}$ is the set of edges connecting $\mathcal{M}_c$ and $\mathcal{M}_d$. Adjacent nodes (m_c, m_d) are connected by a bidirectional edge $e(m_c, m_d) \in \mathcal{E}$, where $m_c \in \mathcal{M}_c$ and $m_d \in \mathcal{M}_d$. For simplicity, $e(m_c, m_d) = 1$ represents the connection between m_c and m_d, while $e(m_c, m_d) = 0$ represents the disconnection.

We suppose that a dedicated frequency band of bandwidth W is allocated to the downlink channels. The wireless channels with path-loss is considered here. For the purpose of offloading data from BS, we assume that each user will firstly try to download data from its connected INs. If a user cannot find its requested files from INs, it will then turn to BS for help. The cellular BS contains the whole content library and can serve all user terminals in the system. Moreover, the channels of D2D connection and cellular connection is assumed to be orthogonal in the frequency domain.

In general, BS is far away from the mobile users. Therefore, the download rate supported by the base station is generally lower than that supported by the D2D link. It will not only encourage the users to download from the D2D transmission first, but also effectively reduce the data traffic of BS imposed by files downloading. In addition, general users can only communication with INs that the connection exists between them.

According to the CN model, the transmission rates of directly cellular network and D2D connections can be expressed as

$$R_{b,V_m} = W \log_2 \left(1 + \frac{P_{b,V_m} G_{b,V_m}^2}{\sigma^2} \right), \tag{2}$$

and

$$R_{m_c,m_d} = W \log_2 \left(1 + \frac{P_{m_c,m_d} G_{m_c,m_d}^2}{\sum_{m_d' \in \mathcal{M}_d} P_{m_c,m_d'} G_{m_c,m_d'}^2 + \sigma^2} \right), \tag{3}$$

respectively [9], where P_{m_c,m_d}, and P_{b,V_m} denote the transmission powers by the m_cth IN and BS, respectively. G_{m_c,m_d} is the D2D channel gain and G_{b,V_m} is BS's the channel gain, and σ^2 is the noise variance.

2.2   Social Importance Analysis

Taking social importance and battery capacity into account, to choose the INs, we define the following importance measurement matrix $\mathbf{X}$

$$\mathbf{X} = \mu \mathbf{B} + \nu \mathbf{S} + \upsilon \mathbf{C}, \tag{4}$$

where $\mathbf{B} = \{b_{j,k}\}$, $\mathbf{S} = \{s_{j,k}\}$, and $\mathbf{C}$ denote the matrices of betweenness centrality, similarity, and battery capacity, respectively, and μ, ν and υ are adjustable parameters with constraint $\mu + \nu + \upsilon = 1$. $b_{j,k}$ is the edge betweenness of the link between nodes j and k, and $s_{j,k}$ is the degree of similarity between j and k. Betweenness centrality is one commonly used way to measure the nodes centrality property. The betweenness centrality of node i can be calculated as

$$b_{j,k} = \sum_{j,k \in \mathcal{V}} \frac{d_{jk}(i)}{d_{jk}}, \tag{5}$$

according to [16]. In this equation above, d_{jk} is the number of shortest distance paths of connecting from node j to node k, and $d_{jk}(i)$ is the number of geodesic paths including node i. In order to facilitate the calculation, a normalized element (j, k) of matrix $\mathbf{B}$ is as follows

$$B(j, k) = \frac{b_{j,k}}{(M - 1)^2}. \tag{6}$$

Similarity Matrix: in [9], for a pair of nodes, (j, k), their similarity matrix is defined as

$$s_{j,k} = \begin{cases} \sum_{z \in M(j) \cap M(k)} \frac{1}{k(z)} & \text{if } j \text{ is connected with } k, \\ 0 & \text{otherwise}, \end{cases} \tag{7}$$

where $M(j)$ is the set of neighbors of j, $z \in M(j) \cap M(k)$ denotes the set of the common neighbors between node j and k. $k(z)$ is the number of nodes connected with z. Similarly, in order to facilitate the calculation, the simple additive weighting (SAW) method is considered. Also, the normalized entries of $\mathbf{S}$ are

$$S(j, k) = \frac{s_{j,k}}{\max s_j}, \tag{8}$$

where s_j denotes the jth row of $\mathbf{S}$. In the Eq. (4), because of the adjustability of parameters, we formulate a constraint on the value as shown below

$$\sum_{n=1}^{h} R_{m,n} \geq \gamma, \tag{9}$$

where $n \in \Theta \triangleq \{1, 2, \cdots, h\}$ denotes the nodes connected with node m, and γ represents the predefined minimum sum-rate threshold according to network performance. In this case, if the node m is selected as IN, it transmission should meet the limitation.

Through analysis and calculation of the centrality of all nodes, we sort the element of $\mathbf{X}$ in a descending order and then choose top $|\mathcal{M}_c|$ as INs. A number of vital users in our cellular network are selected. Thus, these nodes can be exploited for proactive caching. We will elaborate on the problem of content allocation to the INs and will focus on this issue in the next subsection.

2.3 Problem Formulation

To formulate the allocation problem between files and INs, we set up a file distribution matrix $\mathbf{A}^{|\mathcal{M}_c| \times L}$, where L is the total number of files cached. The entry $\lambda_{m_c, f_i} \in \{0, 1\}$ in $\mathbf{A}^{|\mathcal{M}_c| \times L}$ indicates whether f_i is cached by the m_cth IN or not as follows

$$\lambda_{m_c, f_i} = \begin{cases} 1, & \text{if } f_i \text{ is cached by } m_c\text{th IN,} \\ 0, & \text{otherwise.} \end{cases} \tag{10}$$

In the CN, the strategy of D2D users is selecting caching files for sake of minimizing the transmission delay by optimizing the matrix $\mathbf{A}^{|\mathcal{M}_c| \times L}$. According to the consideration, the delay of downloading the file f_i by user n can be calculated as

$$T_{n, f_i} = \begin{cases} \dfrac{Y}{\max\{R_{m_c, n}\}}, & \exists \lambda_{m_c, f_i} \neq 0, \, e(m_c, n) = 1, \\ \infty, & \exists \lambda_{m_c, f_i} \neq 0, \, e(m_c, n) = 0, \\ \dfrac{Y}{R_{b, n}}, & \text{otherwise,} \end{cases} \tag{11}$$

where Y denotes the size of the requested file f_i. In this case, If general users request the INs that have no connection between them, we suggest that the delay is infinite. Based on the request probability of each file, the delay for user n to download a file from $\mathcal{F}$ can be written as

$$T_n = P_{n, f_i} \cdot T_{n, f_i} \quad \text{for } f_i \in \mathcal{F}, \tag{12}$$

where $f_i \in \mathcal{F}$ and $P_{n, f_i} \in \mathbf{P}$. Thus, the content allocation strategy can be solved by the following optimization problem

$$\min_A \sum_{n \in \mathcal{M}_d} \sum_{m_c \in \mathcal{M}_c} \sum_{i=1}^{L} \lambda_{m_c, f_i} T_n,$$

$$\text{s.t.} \quad \textcircled{1} \sum_{i=1}^{L} \lambda_{m_c, f_i} \leq 1, \quad m_c \in \mathcal{M}_c,$$

$$\textcircled{2} \, \lambda_{m_c, f_i} \in \{0, 1\}, \tag{13}$$

$$\textcircled{3} \sum_{m_c=1}^{|\mathcal{M}_c|} \lambda_{m_c, f_i} \leq Q, \quad f_i \in \mathcal{F}.$$

In the above optimization, constraint ① states that a maximum number 1 of files can be matched for an IN, and condition ② guarantees that λ_{m_c, f_i} is a binary variable. Also, condition ③ denotes a maximum number Q of nodes that can be selected for caching by file f_i. The optimization problem (13) is a NP-hard combinatorial binary optimization problem [17]. However, since (13) contains only one binary variable, it can be modeled as a matching problem. Thus, in the next section, we propose a matching algorithm to solve the optimization problem.

3   Matching Algorithm

Caching files in INs can make other users to require files directly from the caching nodes rather than from the cellular network. In this section, we propose a novel content allocation method of utilizing matching game in allocating files.

3.1   Matching Related Definitions

We first introduce some notations to facilitate the solving process. There are two non-intersect sets of participants: $\mathcal{M} = \{\mathcal{M}_i\}_{i=1}^{I}$ and $F = \{F_j\}_{j=1}^{J}$. Here $\succ_{\mathcal{M}} = \{\succ_{\mathcal{M}_i}\}$ and $\succ_F = \{\succ_{F_j}\}$ denote, respectively, the set of preference relations of two players.

Definition 1. *A matching relationship Φ is defined as a function from the set $\mathcal{M} \cup \mathcal{F}$ based on the preference list.*

Let $V_m(\cdot)$ and $U_f(\cdot)$ denote the utility function of user m and pre-cached file f, respectively. Given these utilities, we can get the following instructions

$$V_m(f_i) > V_m(f_j) \Leftrightarrow f_i \succ_m f_j, \tag{14}$$

Above shows that a user m prefers file f_i to f_j. Similarly, a pre-cached file f prefers user m_i to m_j can be expressed as

$$U_f(m_i) > U_f(m_j) \Leftrightarrow m_i \succ_f m_j. \tag{15}$$

Consequently, we denote this matching function $\Phi:(\mathcal{M}_c, \mathcal{F}, Q)$, where $(\mathcal{M}_c, \mathcal{F})$ is the set of matching pairs and Q denotes the maximum number of INs that per file can be cached in.

3.2   Proposed Matching Algorithms

User-file caching (UFC) problem is further comprised of two types of game players including D2D users and files regulated by BS. The matching problem that we elaborate on is a many-to-one game. Based on the above definition, in the system model, limited by the storage capacity of mobile users, an IN can save only one file set but one file can be stored many times at INs of D2D links.

The strategy of both D2D users and BS is to maximize their respective profits in matching algorithm based on the preference over opposite sets. On the other hand, BS makes its content allocation decision based on its local information without relying on a central coordination. So the UFC matching algorithm attend to solve the optimization problem in (13). To design the algorithm, we first design an algorithm for allocating files for one BS. Denote by $\mathcal{H}_{m_c} = \{H_{m1}, H_{m2}, \cdots, H_{mh}\}$ the index set of nodes connected with IN m_c.

Based on this consideration, D2D utility function over the file f_i is defined as

$$V_{m_c}(f_i) = \frac{1}{|\mathcal{H}_{m_c}|} \sum_{n \in \mathcal{H}_{m_c}} P_{n,f_i}, \qquad (16)$$

where P_{n,f_i} represents the connected node n's preference degree to the file f_i and the above equation illustrates that the INs' preference over files is ranked based on the degree of content popularity. Furthermore, the favourite file can be obtained by sorting the utility function in a descending order. Similarly, the utility for file $f_i \in \mathcal{F}$ to be matched with the m_cth IN can be written as

$$U_{f_i}(m_c) = \frac{1}{|\mathcal{H}_{m_c}|} \sum_{n \in \mathcal{H}_{m_c}} P_{n,f_i} T_{n,f_i}. \qquad (17)$$

The utility function over D2D users is affected by the average transmission delay and social network structure. Besides, by sorting the utility function in a ascending order, we can obtain the preference list.

The matching problem proposed in this paper is not a traditional matching game, since the preference lists of files and INs depend not solely on the information available locally but on the character of social-layer architecture. Our proposed matching problem exhibits externality such as peer effects, which means that the users and files may change their preferences during the game, due to the constantly updated social relationship among users. Nevertheless, traditional matching game algorithm may not be able to converge to a stable matching, especially when the game has peer effects [3]. Therefore, we need to develop a new algorithm to find a stable solution of this problem in this paper.

Let $\mathbb{A}(\mathcal{M}_c, \mathcal{F})$ denotes the set of ultimate matching pairs, and $\eta(m, f)$ denotes the subset of $\mathbb{A}(\mathcal{M}_c, \mathcal{F})$, where (m, f) are matched. Thus, the concept of blocking pair and stability is introduced as follows.

Definition 2. *A matching $\eta^*(m, f') \nsubseteq \mathbb{A}(\mathcal{M}_c, \mathcal{F})$, but comparing with the matching pair $\eta(m, f)$, there exists relation that $\eta^* \succ_m \eta$, that it to say, the current matching does not maximize the utility. We define this matching pair $\eta^*(m, f')$ as the blocking pair. If and only if there is no blocking pair, the proposed matching algorithm is stable.*

The UFC matching algorithm considers one BS, and is the solution to the problem in (13). The algorithm is displayed in Table 1. In the following, we describe the process of the algorithm briefly. The preferences are calculated by INs and files, respectively. Then, INs make proposals to the most prefer files, and in turn, the content provider's files decide to accept or reject these proposals based on their preference lists. For a particular user, if it requests for the top of file f_i within the set $\mathcal{F}$, the file f_i updates its utility and accepts the request if the action do not yield a degradation of its utility.

Table 1. Proposed UFC matching algorithm

Algorithm 1 :

Input: B, S, C, X, Q;
Output: $\mathbb{A}(\mathcal{M}_c, \mathcal{F})$;
Steps:
1: **for** $q = 1$ to L **do**
2:    $p_q = \frac{1/q^\alpha}{\sum_{i=1}^{L} 1/i^\alpha}$;
3:    P_{m,f_i};
4: **end for**
5: Calculate the $V_{m_c}(\cdot)$ based on the equation (16);
6: $V_{m_c}(\cdot)$ are sorted in descending way;
7: Set all INs request the most preference file and create request matrix R;
8: Then, the requested file make decision to choose the optimal $U_{f_i}(\cdot)$ based on the equation (17);
9: **while** quota<Q **do**
10: The most popular file is cached by the optimal IN, and quota=quota+1. In addition, $U_{f_i}(m_c)$ of remove the selected IN is set 0;
11: Return step 7;
12: **end while**
13: **if** quota==Q **do**
14:    Select the second most popular and repeat the step 8;
15: **end if**
16: Then according to the next popular ranking, the files are allocated to their prefer INs;
17: Obtain the optimal matching pairs;

We prove the stability of the algorithm proposed in Table 1. Here, we merely discuss the situation in a stable community, which means all the nodes may not readily add or remove any connections established between them. This condition guarantees that the peer effects cannot make any change in community. Observing from our algorithm, the preference is strictly monotone and subjects to (13). In this case, the blocking pairs can not exist because all the players select their matching pairs based on the preference. Moreover, the number of storage is finite and our matching pair selecting method always adheres to the utility maximum principle. Accordingly, under the situation of a stable community, our proposed algorithm is stable.

4   Simulation Results

In this section, we study a wireless network consisting of one BS. This BS is designed as a regulator with 300 meters coverage. And in this range, $M = 20$

and user equipments are randomly distributed in the community. The relationship among them considers both the social online connections and their off-line physical locations.

In this simulation, we set the path-loss exponent $\beta = 4$, noise power $\sigma^2 = 10^{-10}$ and transmission power of BS $P_{b,V_m} = 20W$ and D2D transmission power $P_{m_c,m_d} = 2W$. In addition, we assume that there are $L = 10$ files and the distance between equipments and BS is randomly generated within a certain range, besides, $Q = 2$, the tunable variables μ, v and ν are set to 1/3.

In this simulation, we compare the proposed UFC matching algorithm with random file allocation (randomly choosing files), RUC (caching most recent used files) [18], and no caching algorithms. In the random allocation algorithm, we assign the files randomly to the INs. In the RUC algorithm, the recently used files are allocated to the INs. Figure 2 shows the average download delay for different caching strategies varying with the number of INs. It can be seen that as the INs number increases, all the three algorithms employing caching mechanism show a declining trend. While the download delay of no caching algorithm is fixed at 15 units, due to the reason that no caching method acquires files only through the BS. However, it is clear that the proposed UFC algorithm yields significant performance improvements compared with other methods.

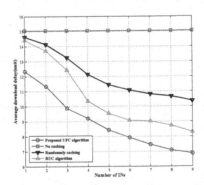

Fig. 2. Average download delay vs. the number of INs

In the file allocation stage, it is critical to choose the INs. Figure 3 depicts the differences between the proposed algorithm and the random file allocation algorithm. As we expected, the proposed algorithm taking the social importance into consideration can bring prominent improvement than the random file allocation algorithm. It can be seen from Fig. 3, when the number of INs is 6, the proposed algorithm's average transmission delay is 8.47 units, while the random file allocation algorithm is 9.24 units.

Figure 4 illustrates that the quota value has a great impact on the transmission delay. We set the quotas to be 1 and 2, respectively. It inspires us that we need to make full use of the storage space of user equipments for the purpose of gaining low transmission delay.

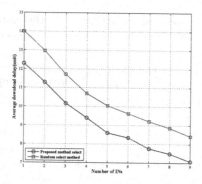

Fig. 3. Average download delay vs. different selecting method of INs

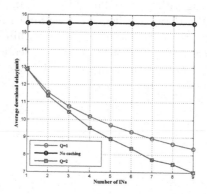

Fig. 4. Average download delay vs. different matching games

5   Conclusion

In this paper, we design a novel distributed caching optimization algorithm to solve the cache allocation problem in D2D underlaid cellular networks. We formulate a many to one matching game combining the social relationship with physical locations in order to minimize the average transmission delay. To solve the D2D transmission problem, we propose a UFC matching algorithm. Also, we prove the stability of the proposed algorithm. At last, the simulation results are provided to demonstrate the validity of this algorithm that considering the social importance can greatly reduce the transmission delay. Furthermore, increasing the quota of files can also reduce the transmission delay.

Acknowledgement. This work is supported in part by the National Natural Science Foundation of China under Grant (Nos. 6150123861602245 and 61472190), in part by the Jiangsu Provincial Science Foundation under Project BK20150786 and BK20150791, in part by the Specially Appointed Professor Program in Jiangsu Province, 2015, in part by the Fundamental Research Funds for the Central Universities under Grant 30916011205, in part by the Open Research Fund of National Mobile Communications Research Laboratory, Southeast University, under grant No. 2017D04, in part by he China Postdoctoral Science Foundation (2016M591852), and in part by Postdoctoral research funding program of Jiangsu Province (1601257C).

References

1. Cisco: Cisco visual networking index: global mobile data traffic forecast update, 2013–2018. http://www.cisco.com/c/en/us/solutions/collateral/service-provider/visual-networking-index-vni/white_paper_c11-520862.pdf
2. Doppler, K., Rinne, M., Wijting, C., Ribeiro, C.B., Hugl, K.: Device-to-device communication as an underlay to lte-advanced networks. IEEE Commun. Mag. **47**, 42–49 (2009)
3. Hakola, S., Chen, T., Lehtomaki, J., Koskela, T.: Device-to-device communication in cellular network - performance analysis of optimum and practical communication mode selection. In: 2010 IEEE Wireless Communication and Networking Conference, pp. 1–6 (2010)
4. Zhang, H., Liu, H., Jiang, C., Chu, X., Nallanathan, A., Wen, X.: A practical semidynamic clustering scheme using affinity propagation in cooperative picocells. IEEE Trans. Veh. Technol. **64**(9), 4372–4377 (2015)
5. Li, Y., Wu, T., Hui, P., Jin, D., Chen, S.: Social-aware D2D communications: qualitative insights and quantitative analysis. IEEE Commun. Mag. **52**(6), 150–158 (2014)
6. Hu, J., Yang, L.L., Poor, H.V., Hanzo, L.: Bridging the social and wireless networking divide: Information dissemination in integrated cellular and opportunistic networks. IEEE Access **3**, 1809–1848 (2015)
7. Shanmugam, K., Golrezaei, N., Dimakis, A.G., Molisch, A.F., Caire, G.: Femtocaching: wireless content delivery through distributed caching helpers. IEEE Trans. Inf. Theory **59**(12), 8402–8413 (2013)
8. Li, J., Chen, Y., Lin, Z., Chen, W., Vucetic, B., Hanzo, L.: Distributed caching for data dissemination in the downlink of heterogeneous networks. IEEE Trans. Commun. **63**(10), 3553–3568 (2015)
9. Ma, C., Lin, Z., Marini, L., Li, J., Vucetic, B.: Learning automaton based distributed caching for mobile social networks. In: 2016 IEEE Wireless Communications and Networking Conference, pp. 1–6 (2016)
10. Gu, Y., Saad, W., Bennis, M., Debbah, M., Han, Z.: Matching theory for future wireless networks: fundamentals and applications. IEEE Commun. Mag. **53**(5), 52–59 (2015)
11. Semiari, O., Saad, W., Valentin, S., Bennis, M., Poor, H.V.: Context-aware small cell networks: how social metrics improve wireless resource allocation. IEEE Trans. Wireless Commun. **14**(11), 5927–5940 (2015)
12. Jiang, L., Cai, H., Chen, Y., Zhang, J., Li, B.: Many-to-many matching for combinatorial spectrum trading. In: 2016 IEEE International Conference on Communications (ICC), pp. 1–6 (2016)
13. Boyd, D.M., Ellison, N.B.: Social network sites: definition, history, and scholarship. IEEE Eng. Manage. Rev. **38**, 16–31 (2010). Third
14. Wang, L., Wu, H., Wang, W., Chen, K.C.: Socially enabled wireless networks: resource allocation via bipartite graph matching. IEEE Commun. Mag. **53**, 128–135 (2015)

15. Chang, Z., Gu, Y., Han, Z., Chen, X., Ristaniemi, T.: Context-aware data caching for 5G heterogeneous small cells networks. In: 2016 IEEE International Conference on Communications (ICC), pp. 1–6 (2016)
16. Ashraf, M.I., Bennis, M., Saad, W., Katz, M.: Exploring social networks for optimized user association in wireless small cell networks with device-to-device communications. In: 2014 IEEE Wireless Communications and Networking Conference Workshops (WCNCW), pp. 224–229 (2014)
17. Gale, D.: College admissions and the stability of marriage. Am. Math. Mon. **69**(1), 9–15 (1962)
18. Gu, J., Wang, W., Huang, A., Shan, H., Zhang, Z.: Distributed cache replacement for caching-enable base stations in cellular networks. In: 2014 IEEE International Conference on Communications (ICC), pp. 2648–2653, June 2014

Two-Tier Matching Game Design for Wireless Caching in Pico-Cell Networks

Guowei Shi[1], Jun Li[1(✉)], Haijun Zhang[2], Feng Shu[1], and Tingting Liu[1]

[1] School of Electronic and Optical Engineering,
Nanjing University of Science and Technology, Nanjing, China
{guowei.shi,jun.li,shufeng}@njust.edu.cn, liutingting1026@hotmail.com
[2] School of Computer and Communication Engineering,
University of Science and Technology Beijing, Beijing, China
zhanghaijun@ustb.edu.cn

Abstract. Wireless caching brings network content close to mobile users (MU), and has been identified as an effective solution for reducing MUs' transmission delay. In this paper, we concentrate on how to efficiently allocate network files to the storage of pico-cells and associate MUs with the pico-cells. To deal with the series of resource allocation problems, we first separate these problems as two distinct many-to-one matching games. Then, we tackle these problems by proposing different concepts to generate the preference lists respectively. The deferred-acceptance algorithm is designed in this paper to achieve stable matchings in these two separated games. It is shown in numerical results that our proposed design demonstrates a better performance compared to state-of-the-art benchmarks.

Keywords: Matching game · Wireless caching
Content-oriented communications · Pico-cell networks

1 Introduction

Along with the developments of mobile communication technologies, mobile users (MUs) show growing interests in using various multimedia services [1]. To deal with the explosive growth of demands in high speed data transmissions by MUs, an low-cost and low-power pico-cell access architecture is proposed which can coexist with any wireless technology and can be deployed in any area underlaid on Macro-cell network [2]. But when pico-cell network density increases, backhaul capacity limitations would be a big problem [3].

Content caching is one of the efficient solutions to effectively handling this problem. With observations that a large amount of data traffic is caused by a small portion of popular network contents, i.e., movies, as well as the price of storage medium is relatively cheaper compared to the price of backhaul,

© ICST Institute for Computer Sciences, Social Informatics and Telecommunications Engineering 2018
K. Long et al. (Eds.): 5GWN 2017, LNICST 211, pp. 663–674, 2018.
https://doi.org/10.1007/978-3-319-72823-0_61

caching in network facilities, such as small-cell, femto-cell, pico-cell and D2D nodes, to release backhaul pressure becomes a potential solution in these years [4–6].

Specially in [4], a fetmo-cell caching system is proposed for assigning files to the femto-cells, in order to minimize the downloading time. Moreover, the authors of [5] proposed a caching system for D2D based cellular network relaying on the MUs' caching of popular files, in order to increase the throughput of networks. In addition, the authors of [6] have proposed a distributed caching scheme using Stackelberg game, in order to deal with resource allocation problems in a small cell network. Although many problems have been solved as above, how to effectively allocate resource in pico-cell networks still remains a great challenge to face.

In this paper, we leverage matching game theory to handle resource allocation problems in cache enabled system. As in [7], authors introduce fundamentals and conventional classification of matching theory for future wireless networks, where matching games are split into three kinds, i.e., one-to-one matching games, many-to-one matching games and many-to-many matching games. In [8], authors utilize many-to-one matching games in wireless small cell networks with a combination of context-aware of information about trajectory profile and quality of service requirements of users, in order to maximum satisfaction ratio and reduce downloading delay. Many-to-many matching games has been used in [9] to reduce backhaul loads and the experienced delay in small cell networks. From discussion above, we are motivated to use matching game theory in pico-cell networks to explore the optimal allocation with caching.

In this paper, we concentrate on proposing a two-tier matching game in wireless caching systems to handle the resource allocation problem. We firstly match network contents with pico-cells and then match the pico-cells with mobile users. The key contributions can be summarized as follows.

1. We model a pico-cell based caching system with the objective to minimize the system transmission delay.
2. We decouple the resource allocation problems into two many-to-one matching games, and address them by using the deferred-acceptance algorithm. We then generate preference lists in the two matching games to obtain a stable matching.
3. We demonstrate that the proposed algorithm has near-optimal outcomes with numerical results.

The rest of this paper is organized as follows. We describe the system model and formulate system objective in Sect. 2. We then decouple the optimization problems and propose matching games to solve the optimization problems in Sect. 3. Our numerical results are illustrated in Sect. 4, while our conclusions are draw in Sect. 5.

2   System Model and Problem Formulation

Let us consider a pico-cell based caching network composed of M MUs which have priorities to connect to pico-cells. As shown in Fig. 1, there exists a Macro-cell serving MUs in its coverage assisted by N pico-cells. Also, we define the set of M MUs by $\mathcal{M} = \{\mathcal{M}_1, \mathcal{M}_2, \cdots, \mathcal{M}_M\}$ and the set of pico-cell by $\mathcal{N} = \{\mathcal{N}_1, \mathcal{N}_2, \cdots, \mathcal{N}_N\}$ which are both randomly located in system. We assume that each pico-cell has the same storage size that could cache only one file.

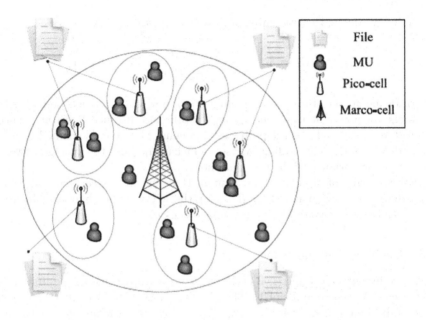

Fig. 1. Pico-cells based caching system model

There are two resource allocation problems in this network. In the first stage, files are allocated to pico-cells and then MUs are associated to pico-cells in second stage. In what follows, we will introduce some key concepts to facilitate the problem formulation.

2.1   File Popularity

Firstly, we model the popularity of files. Let us denote the file set by $\mathcal{V} = \{\mathcal{V}_1, \mathcal{V}_2, \cdots, \mathcal{V}_V\}$ consisting of V popular files which belong to content providers (CP). Intuitively, the majority of MUs request popular files more frequently than the others. Thus, we assume that the popularity profile of files characterized by the Zipf-like distribution as the requests of any files are inversely proportional to file's rank in the request table [6]. Then, the popularity distribution q_v of $\mathcal{V}_v$ is characterized as

$$q_v = \frac{1/v^\beta}{\sum_{j=1}^V 1/j^\beta}, \quad \forall v, \tag{1}$$

where the exponent β is a positive skewness parameter and v means v-th file. Also, the file with a small index v corresponds to a high popularity.

2.2   Transmission Rate of MUs

Secondly, we define the transmission rate of each pico-cells to MUs as

$$R_{mn} = W \log_2 \left(1 + \frac{P_n d_{mn}^{-\alpha} h_{mn}^2}{\sum_{n' \in \mathcal{N} \backslash n} P_{n'} d_{mn'}^{-\alpha} h_{mn'}^2 + \sigma^2} \right), \tag{2}$$

where W means the transmission bandwidth of downlink channels and P_n is the transmission power at pico-cell $\mathcal{N}_n$. d_{mn} represents distance between pico-cell $\mathcal{N}_n$ and MU $\mathcal{M}_m$ and α is the path-loss exponent. The random channel between $\mathcal{N}_n$ and $\mathcal{M}_m$ is Rayleigh fading, whose coefficient h_{mn} has the average power of one. σ^2 is the variance of the Gaussian noise.

For the sake of simplicity, we assume that the Macro-cell will support a fixed download rate, denoted by R_{ma}, for the MUs in the channels which are orthogonal to those spanning from the pico-cells to MUs.

2.3   Caching Related Issue

Next, we introduce the pico-cell caching system with details. In the first stage, each pico-cell cache one file of $\mathcal{V}$. The file placement commence during off-peak time on backhaul links. It is clear that MUs show different preferences towards different files. Thus, we could define the preference from MU $\mathcal{M}_m$ to file $\mathcal{V}_v$ as

$$p_{mv} = \alpha_{mv} q_v, \tag{3}$$

where α_{mv} is a factor that influence MUs' preferences to file $\mathcal{V}_v$ and q_v is the popularity of the file $\mathcal{V}_v$. Then, the pico-cells will download a file relying on collecting the serving MUs' preferences. We define the preference p_{nv} of pico-cell $\mathcal{N}_n$ to file $\mathcal{V}_v$ as

$$p_{nv} = \frac{1}{\mathcal{C}_n} \sum_{k \in \mathcal{C}_n} p_{kv}, \tag{4}$$

where k means the k-th serving MU of the pico-cell and $\mathcal{C}_n$ is the serving MUs set of $\mathcal{N}_n$. Pico-cells will cache the most preference file of its serving MUs according to (4) during off-peak time.

In the second stage, MUs start to request files. In general, an MU can be covered by multiple pico-cells. When an MU $\mathcal{M}_m$ request file $\mathcal{V}_v$, it tries to connect to the nearest pico-cell which cached file $\mathcal{V}_v$. Otherwise, the MU $\mathcal{M}_m$

will download the requesting file from Macro-cell directly. Thus, the transmission delay τ_{ml}^v of MUs can be represented as follows.

$$\tau_{ml}^v = \begin{cases} \tau_{ma}^v = \frac{S}{R_{ma}} \text{ if MU connects to Macro-cell,} \\ \\ \tau_{mn}^v = \frac{S}{R_{mn}} \text{ if MU connects to pico-cell,} \end{cases} \tag{5}$$

where S is the file size.

2.4   Problem Formulation

In this subsection, we formulate the file allocation problem to minimize the transmission delay of MUs. The problem can be formulated as

$$\min_{X,Y} \sum_{n \in \mathcal{N}} \sum_{m \in \mathcal{M}} \sum_{v \in \mathcal{V}} x_{nv} y_{nm} \tau_{ml}^v,$$

$$\text{s.t. } (a) \sum_{v \in \mathcal{V}} x_{nv} \le 1,$$

$$(b) \sum_{n \in \mathcal{N}} y_{nm} \le 1,$$

$$(c) \sum_{n \in \mathcal{N}} x_{nv} \le Q_1,$$

$$(d) \sum_{m \in \mathcal{M}} y_{nm} \le Q_2,$$

$$(e) x_{nv}, y_{nm} \in \{0,1\}, \tag{6}$$

where x_{nv} is the element of matrix X and $x_{nv} = 1$ represents the pico-cell $\mathcal{N}_n$ caches the file $\mathcal{V}_v$, otherwise $x_{nv} = 0$. y_{nm} is the element of matrix Y, and $y_{nm} = 1$ denotes that the pico-cell $\mathcal{N}_n$ is serving MU $\mathcal{M}_m$, if not $y_{nm} = 0$. Condition (a) guarantees that each pico-cell could only cache one file, condition (b) states a user will be served by one pico-cell, condition (c) concerning file variety is to make sure that file $\mathcal{V}_v$ could only be cached Q_1 duplication in this network, condition (d) assures that each pico-cell can serve Q_2 MUs at most, and condition (e) states that the values of x_{nv} and y_{nm} can be neither 0 or 1.

3   Proposed Matching Algorithm

3.1   Decoupling the Optimization Problem

The optimization in (6) is a generalized knapsack problem which is proved to be an NP-hard combinatorial problem [10]. It is hard to find a global optimal solution for these association problems. Hence, to solve the optimization problem in (6), we resort to a suboptimal approach and split the optimization problem into two independent sub-problems: (i) optimal file selection problem, (ii) optimal pico-cell selection problem.

Optimal File Selection Problem

$$\min_{X} \sum_{n \in \mathcal{N}} \sum_{v \in \mathcal{V}} x_{nv} \tau_{ml}^{v},$$

$$\text{s.t. } (a) \sum_{v \in \mathcal{V}} x_{nv} \leq 1,$$

$$(b) \sum_{n \in \mathcal{N}} x_{nv} \leq Q_1,$$

$$(c) x_{nv} \in \{0, 1\}. \tag{7}$$

Optimal Pico-Cell Selection Problem

$$\min_{Y} \sum_{n \in \mathcal{N}} \sum_{m \in \mathcal{M}} y_{nm} \tau_{ml}^{v},$$

$$\text{s.t. } (a) \sum_{n \in \mathcal{N}} y_{nm} \leq 1,$$

$$(b) \sum_{m \in \mathcal{M}} y_{nm} \leq Q_2,$$

$$(c) y_{nm} \in \{0, 1\}, \tag{8}$$

These two suboptimal problems are still NP-hard combinatorial problems [10]. Since they both contain one binary variable, they can be modeled as two distinct many-to-one matching problems respectively [11].

3.2   Matching Related Definition

Matching has been introduced in [12] as a effective way to solve the allocate resource problem. These resources will be divided into two finite and disjoint sets of players. Different sets of players have different preferences over the opposite sets. To construct the preference lists in our model, we use the symbol $\succ$ to represent that the players prefer one player to another player in the opposite set. For example, when a pico-cell $\mathcal{N}_n$ shows $\mathcal{V}_1 \succ \mathcal{V}_2$ in its preference lists, it means that $\mathcal{N}_n$ prefers file $\mathcal{V}_1$ than file $\mathcal{V}_2$. In this paper, we use μ_1 to represent the first many-to-one matching of sub-problem 1.

For $\mathcal{V}_v \in \mathcal{V}$ and $\mathcal{N}_n \in \mathcal{N}$, a matching μ_1 is $\mathcal{V} \bigcup \mathcal{N} \to 2^{\mathcal{V} \cup \mathcal{N}}$, which satisfies

1. $\mu_1(\mathcal{N}_n) \in \mathcal{V}$ and $|\mu_1(\mathcal{N}_n)| \leq 1$,
2. $\mu_1(\mathcal{V}_v) \in \mathcal{N}$ and $|\mu_1(\mathcal{V}_v)| \leq Q_1$,
3. $\mu_1(\mathcal{V}_v) = \mathcal{N}_n \Longleftrightarrow \mu_1(\mathcal{N}_n) = \mathcal{V}_v$.

The second many-to-one matching μ_2 of sub-problem 2 has the following properties.

For $\mathcal{M}_m \in \mathcal{M}$ and $\mathcal{N}_n \in \mathcal{N}$, a matching μ_2 is $\mathcal{M} \bigcup \mathcal{N} \to 2^{\mathcal{M} \cup \mathcal{N}}$, which satisfies

1. $\mu_2(\mathcal{M}_m) \in \mathcal{N}$ and $|\mu_2(\mathcal{M}_m)| \leq 1$,
2. $\mu_2(\mathcal{N}_n) \in \mathcal{M}$ and $|\mu_2(\mathcal{N}_n)| \leq Q_2$,
3. $\mu_2(\mathcal{M}_m) = \mathcal{N}_n \Longleftrightarrow \mu_2(\mathcal{N}_n) = \mathcal{M}_m$.

3.3   File Selection Algorithm

Next, Deferred Acceptance (DA) algorithm [11] is proposed to solve these two many-to-one matching games. We first focus on modeling the preference lists in the first matching.

Definition 1. *For MUs* $C \subseteq \mathcal{M}$, *the corresponding pico-cell's preference over file* $\mathcal{V}_v \in \mathcal{V}$ *is*

$$\mathbf{\Gamma}^v = p_{nv}, \tag{9}$$

where $\mathbf{\Gamma}^v \in \mathbb{C}^{N*V}$ *is pico-cells' preference matrix over files.*

Also, the files of CPs have certain preference towards different pico-cells considering their transmission delay. A pico-cell can serve C MUs so that we take the average transmission delay of C_n serving MUs as CP's preference over this pico-cell. We define it as follows.

Definition 2. *For* $\mathcal{V}_v \in \mathcal{V}$, *its preference over pico-cell* $\mathcal{N}_n \in \mathcal{N}$ *can be given as*

$$\mathbf{\Gamma}^n = \frac{1}{C_n} \sum_{k \in C_n} \tau_{kn}, \tag{10}$$

where $\mathbf{\Gamma}^n \in \mathbb{C}^{V*N}$ *is the files' preference matrix over pico-cells.*

The detailed algorithm of sub-problem 1 is shown in Algorithm 1. We propose a distributed algorithm where both files and pico-cells selfishly and rationally interact in a way that the MUs sum-transmission delay is minimized. As shown in Algorithm 1, we use $\mathbf{\Gamma}^v$ and $\mathbf{\Gamma}^n$ as preference lists. We assume that the number of files is far more larger than the number of pico-cells. At first, the pico-cells send their first choices according to their preference lists. Since a file can be

---

Algorithm 1. File Selection Matching Algorithm

Require: $\mathbf{\Gamma}^v$ $\mathbf{\Gamma}^n$

   Initialize:
   Set Q_1 and construct lists of Unmatched pico-cells to files as sets of $Unmatch_1 = \{\mathcal{N}_1, \mathcal{N}_2, \cdots, \mathcal{N}_n\}$
   Main Process:
   (1)Each pico-cell sends offer to first file in its preference list.
      (**a**)If the number of offers is more than Q_1, then the CP choose most preferred pico-cells and remove these Q_1 pico-cells from $Unmatch_1$ and the others will be rejected.
      (**b**)Else the offers will all be accepted.
   (2)The rejected pico-cells will remove the most preferred files from its preference lists and go on to take part in $Unmatch_1$.
   (3)The algorithm continues until $Unmatch_1$ is empty.
Ensure: stable matching μ_1.

---

cached in Q_1 pico-cells, we need judge whether the requests from pico-cells for a file are more than the quota Q_1. If there are more than Q_1 pico-cells requesting the same file, CP will select its most preferred Q_1 pico-cells. If the requests for a file are less than or equal to the quota Q_1, files accept these requests all. Then, the remaining pico-cells will be rejected and continue to take part in next round of offers until each pico-cell gets a file to cache.

3.4   Pico-Cell Selection Algorithm

After the file allocation problem solved by Algorithm 1, we turn- to handle the pico-cell selection problem. The transmission delay from the pico-cell to each MU is employed to construct the preference of this pico-cell. Thus, the preference of pico-cell over MU is written as follows.

Definition 3. *For a pico-cell $\mathcal{N}_n \in \mathcal{N}$, its preference over MU $\mathcal{M}_m \in \mathcal{M}$ can be given as*

$$\Gamma^m = \tau_{mn}^v, \tag{11}$$

where $\Gamma^m \in \mathbb{C}^{N*M}$ is the pico-cells' preference matrix over MUs.

Moreover, the preference over pico-cells by MUs will be effected by sub-problem 1. When the pico-cells cached files, they broadcasts information about the cached files to all serving MUs. Accordingly, the MUs' preference over pico-cell is also based on p_{mv}, since different files have different attraction for MUs. Then, the MU's preference over pico-cells is written as follows.

Definition 4. *For $\mathcal{M}_m \in \mathcal{M}$, its preference over pico-cell $\mathcal{N}_n \in \mathcal{N}$ can be given as*

$$\Gamma^{n'} = \tau_{mn}^v p_{mv}, \tag{12}$$

where $\Gamma^{n'} \in \mathbb{C}^{M*N}$ is the MUs' matrix preference over pico-cells.

The specific algorithm of sub-problem 2 is shown in Algorithm 2. The distributed Algorithm 2 has been proposed to minimize sum-transmission delay by allocate the MUs to pico-cells effectively. The distributed Algorithm 2 progresses as MUs send their offers to most select pico-cells. Then, if the requests for a pico-cell are more than the quota Q_2, the pico-cell will decide to accept the more preferred MUs according to preference lists, and reject the others. Else, pico-cells will accept all requests. The rejected MUs remove the most select pico-cells and continue to take part in progress till all pico-cells could not construct more links to MUs. At the last, if there still exists a MU without links, it will connect to Macro-cell.

Algorithm 2. Pico-cell Selection Matching Algorithm

Require: Γ^m $\Gamma^{n'}$

   Initialize:

   Set Q_2 and construct lists of Unmatched MUs to pico-cells as sets of $Unmatch_2 =$ $\{\mathcal{M}_1, \mathcal{M}_2, \cdots, \mathcal{M}_m\}$

   Main Process:

   (1)Each MU makes an offer to pico-cell which is in first place in MUs' preference list.

      (a)If the number of offers is more than Q_2, then the pico-cell choose most preferred MUs and remove these MUs from $Unmatch_2$. The others are rejected and still be active in $Unmatch_2$.

      (b)Else, the all offers will be accepted by pico-cells.

   (2)The rejected ones delete the most preferred pico-cell from its preference lists.

   (3)The process repeats (1) and (2) until $Unmatch_2$ is empty or all pico-cells can not accept any other MUs.

   (4)The unmatched MUs will have a connection with Macro-cell.

Ensure: stable matching μ_2.

3.5   Stability of Matching

At last, it is critical to find a stable matching between two opposite sides, because it guarantees that none of players have motivations to change their matched players. Since the matching μ_1 obeys the similar matching rules with μ_2, we will analysis the stability of the second matching μ_2 for brevity.

    We prove it by contradiction. Given a blocking pair $(\mathcal{M}_1, \mathcal{N}_1)$ for μ_2. In this case, $\mathcal{N}_1$ prefers $\mathcal{M}_1$ to $\mu_2(\mathcal{N}_1)$ and $\mathcal{M}_1$ prefers $\mathcal{N}_1$ to at least one element in $\mu_2(\mathcal{M}_1)$, i.e., the MU matches with another pico-cell which is in a higher order in preference list than its previous matched player, and hence both opposite sides will improve their outcomes. But it is contrary to the original definition of matching, i.e., the opposite two sides will change its order in preference list firstly in order to get a better outcome. Thus, there exists no blocking pair in matching games and μ_2 is proved to be a stable matching.

4   Numerical Results

In this section, we evaluate the performance of the proposed two algorithms by some numerical results. We assume the quota of $\mathcal{V}$ is 20 and $Q_1 = 2$. Moreover, the quota of $\mathcal{M}$ is $\in [16, 34]$ and the quota of $\mathcal{N}$ is $\in [8, 20]$. In this simulations, we assume all MUs and pico-cells are randomly located and the physical layer parameters are set to be practical. The transmit power of a pico-cell is typically 2W, the pass loss α is 4 and the noise power is set to 10^{-10}.

    In the following figures, we compare our proposed algorithms with no caching, random allocation and exhaustive searching algorithms. In the no caching algorithm, the pico-cell caches no file. If MUs connect to the pico-cells, the pico-cells would download the requesting files via backhaul channels firstly and then transmit the files to MUs. Thus, no caching algorithm will lead to high latency. In the random allocation algorithm, we assign that files are randomly cached. In the exhaustive searching algorithm, the problems are addressed by centralized solution with high complexity.

In Fig. 2, the number of MUs is 60 and the pico-cell number varies from 8 to 20 with each pico-cell serving at most 2 MUs. As observed from Fig. 2, with the increasing of pico-cell number, the average delay of both the exhaustive searching algorithm curve and proposed algorithm curve have a decreasing trend. Though the exhaustive searching algorithm shows better performance to the proposed one, the proposed algorithm has less computation complexity $\mathcal{O}(\mathcal{M} \times \mathcal{N})$ while the exhaustive searching algorithm complexity increases exponentially over network size. It is easy to verify that with low complexity, the proposed algorithm will reduce a big cost of server processing power. Also, it can be observed that no caching algorithm's average downloading delay is fixed with the 0.5 s delay. And we find that random allocation algorithm exhibits a inferior performance compared with proposed algorithm.

In Fig. 3, we fix the pico-cell number to be 10 and vary the MUs' number from 16 to 34. Figure 3 displays that the proposed one has similar delay performance with the exhaustive searching algorithm, and they both descend as the increase of MUs' numbers. In random allocation algorithm, it shows inferior performance compared with proposed algorithm.

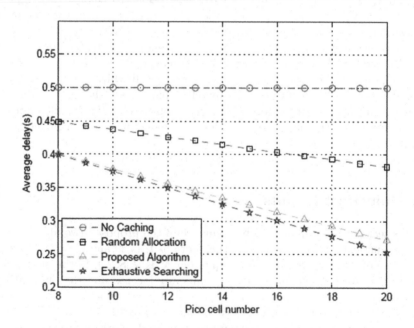

Fig. 2. Average delay vs Number of pico-cells

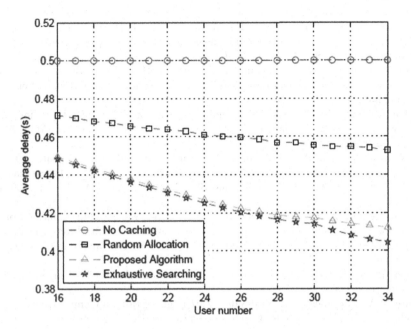

Fig. 3. Average delay vs Number of MUs

5   Conclusion

In this paper, we solve the resource allocation problems in a pico-cell based caching network. The problems are firstly decoupled into two sub-problems. Then, we construct the preference lists of pico-cells, MUs and CPs, respectively. Then, two algorithms is proposed to find stable matchings in these two matching games. At last, simulation results are shown to demonstrate that the proposed algorithm has similar performance with the exhaustive searching algorithm in reducing average transmission delay and shows better performance than the random allocation and no caching algorithms.

References

1. Golrezaei, N., Molisch, A.F., Dimakis, A.G., Caire, G.: Femtocaching and device-to-device collaboration: a new architecture for wireless video distribution. IEEE Commun. Mag. **51**(4), 142–149 (2013)
2. Zhang, H., Liu, H., Jiang, C., Chu, X.: A practical semidynamic clustering scheme using affinity propagation in cooperative picocells. IEEE Trans. Veh. Technol. **64**(9), 4372–4377 (2015)
3. Quek, T., De, G., Guvenc, I., Kountouris, M.: Small Cell Networks - Deployment, PHY Techniques, and Resource Management. Cambridge University Press, New York (2013)
4. Shanmugam, K., Golrezaei, N., Dimakis, A.G., Molisch, A.F., Caire, G.: Femtocaching: wireless content delivery through distributed caching helpers. IEEE Trans. Inf. Theor. **59**(12), 8402–8413 (2013)

5. Golrezaei, N., Mansourifard, P., Molisch, A.F., Dimakis, A.G.: Base-station assisted device-to-device communications for high-throughput wireless video networks. Comput. Sci. **13**(7), 7077–7081 (2012)
6. Li, J., Chen, H., Chen, Y., Lin, Z., Vucetic, B., Hanzo, L.: Pricing and resource allocation via game theory for a small-cell video caching system. IEEE J. Sel. Areas Commun. **34**(8), 2115–2129 (2016)
7. Gu, Y., Saad, W., Bennis, M., Debbah, M., Han, Z.: Matching theory for future wireless networks: fundamentals and applications. IEEE Commun. Mag. **53**(5), 52–59 (2015)
8. Namvar, N., Saad, W., Maham, B., Valentin, S.: A context-aware matching game for user association in wireless small cell networks. In: 2014 IEEE International Conference on Acoustics, Speech and Signal Processing (ICASSP), pp. 439–443, May 2014
9. Hamidouche, K., Saad, W., Debbah, M.: Many-to-many matching games for proactive social-caching in wireless small cell networks. In: 2014 12th International Symposium on Modeling and Optimization in Mobile, Ad Hoc, and Wireless Networks (WiOpt), pp. 569–574, May 2014
10. Boyd, S., Vandenberghe, L.: Convex Optimization. Cambridge University Press, New York (2004)
11. Roth, A., Sotomayor, M.: Two Sided Matching: A Study in Game-Theoretic Modeling and Analysis, 1st edn. Cambridge University Press, Cambridge (1989). Ideas Help Page
12. Gale, D., Shapley, L.S.: College admissions and the stability of marrige. Am. Math. Mon. **69**(1), 9–15 (1962)

A Resource Allocation Scheme Based on Genetic Algorithm for D2D Communications Underlaying Multi-channel Cellular Networks

Ying Sun[1], Xijun Yan[1], Xujie Li[1,2(✉)], Yan Gu[1], and Chenming Li[1]

[1] College of Computer and Information, Hohai University,
Nanjing 210098, China
lixujie@hhu.edu.cn
[2] School of Engineering, University of Warwick, Coventry CV4 7AL, UK

Abstract. In this paper, a resource allocation scheme based on genetic algorithm for device-to-device (D2D) communication underlaying Muti-channel cellular networks is proposed. In our scenarios, N cellular user equipments (CUEs) and M D2D user equipments (DUEs) coexist and share total channel resources. One DUE pair includes a D2D transmitting user equipment (DTUE) and a D2D receiving user equipment (DRUE). The introduction of additional between CUEs and DUEs leads to increases in complexity of resource allocation. First of all, the system model of D2D communications is presented. Then the resource allocation problem based on genetic algorithm is formulated. Next a resource allocation scheme based on genetic algorithm is proposed. Finally, the analysis and simulation results show the performance of proposed scheme outperform that of random algorithm and is very close to that of exhaustive algorithm. This result can provide an effective solution for resource allocation and optimization of D2D communications.

Keywords: D2D communications · Resource allocation · Genetic algorithm

1 Introduction

With the development of society, demands of users for data service increase rapidly. The rare of frequency resource makes the problem more troublesome. Device-to-device (D2D) communications is proposed as an efficient method to resolve this problem [1–3]. As the key technology of 5G, D2D communications can effectively improve resource utilization for cellular networks [4–6].

Resource allocation is a crucial issue in D2D communications [7–12]. In recent years, many researchers adopt various traditional optimization methods to solve resource allocation problem in various application scenarios [13–20]. Meanwhile, there are some papers about the resource allocation based on genetic algorithm. In [21], a genetic algorithm based joint resource allocation and user matching scheme is proposed to minimize the intra-cell interference. This algorithm is used to globally search optimal user matching solution to maximize system throughput. In [22], a genetic algorithm

© ICST Institute for Computer Sciences, Social Informatics and Telecommunications Engineering 2018
K. Long et al. (Eds.): 5GWN 2017, LNICST 211, pp. 675–684, 2018.
https://doi.org/10.1007/978-3-319-72823-0_62

based user machine scheme with optimal power allocation to achieve the multi-dimension optimization is proposed and discussed. The genetic algorithm is applied to obtain the near-optimal user matching in the whole network. In [23], based on the optimization target focusing on device energy efficiency under certain system throughput insurance rather than the traditional system throughput, a modified genetic algorithm-based scheme is applied to address the facing non-deterministic polynomial-time hard problem with higher convergence and lower complexity. In [24], the authors consider the design of link assignment, channel allocation and power control in D2D-aided content delivery scenario for both user fairness and system throughput under QoS requirement. The genetic algorithm is adopted optimize link assignment. And when deriving the fitness of each chromosome, power control optimization will be involved. In [25], a heuristic genetic algorithm to evaluate the secrecy rate is represented. In addition, the authors also propose approximated optimization solutions by considering power allocation of upper and lower bounds to simplify the problem, by leveraging the fractional programming oriented Dinkelbach-type algorithm. In [26], the authors investigate the optimization of the connectivity of different UEs with the target to minimize the total transmission power. An optimization framework and a distributed strategy based on Q-learning and softmax decision making is presented.

However, these papers mainly focus the situation that one CUE and one DUE pairs share the channel resource. To full use of the superiority introduced by D2D technology, we analyse the resource allocation problem under the condition that the number of DUE pairs is far than that of CUEs. In this paper, a resource allocation scheme based genetic algorithm for D2D communications underlaying Muti-channel cellular networks is proposed. In our scenarios, the number of DUE pairs is far more than that of CUEs. The main contributions of our work are as follows:

(1) We propose a resource allocation scheme based genetic algorithm for D2D communications underlaying Muti-channel cellular networks.
(2) We evaluate the capacity of D2D communications and the average transmission power of CUEs.

The rest of this paper is organized as follows. In Sect. 2, we elaborate our system model. We then propose a resource allocation scheme based genetic algorithm for D2D communications and evaluate the capacity of D2D communications and the average transmission power of CUEs in Sect. 3. Simulation results are presented in Sect. 4, and the conclusion is drawn out in Sect. 5.

2   System Model

2.1   Network Model

In cellular networks such as frequency division duplex long term evolution (FDD-LTE), at most one CUE can be allocated to a single sub-channel generally. We assume that the communication system only provides N sub-channels. The means that the communication system can accommodate up to N CUEs. Let us consider a single cellular network, where N CUEs and M DUE pairs coexist, as illustrated in Fig. 1. Every DUE pair consists of a D2D transmitting user equipment (DTUE) and a D2D receiving user equipment (DRUE). Meanwhile, we consider that the CUE and the DTUE follow a uniform distribution in the cell with the radius of R and the DRUE uniformly locates in the circle with center at the DTUE and radius equal to L (the allowed maximum communication distance for D2D communications). Every CUE occupies one sub-channel, and M DUE pairs share the total sub-channel resources. To full use of the superiority introduced by D2D technology, we analyze the resource allocation problem under the condition that the number of DUE pairs is far than that of CUEs. Because it is advantageous to use uplink resources for the D2D link, we only focus the case that the D2D links use uplink cellular resources in this paper.

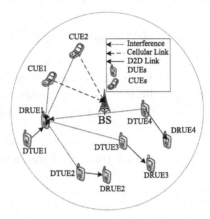

Fig. 1. System model of D2D communications

2.2   Channel Model

In conventional cellular network, power-control scheme is applied into CUEs. Given the complexity of implementation for D2D communication, power-control scheme is not applied into DUE pairs. Here we assume that the transmitting powers for all DTUEs are the same and denoted as P_T. Meanwhile, we assume that the UE links follow a median path loss model having the form $P_r/P_t = 1/r^\alpha$ [27]. Here P_r is the received power at the UE or BS, P_t is transmitting power of the UE, r is the distance between the transmitter and receiver of a pair of DUEs, α is path loss exponent.

3   Problem Formulation and Solution

As mentioned above, N CUEs and M DUE pairs share total sub-channel resources. Let $S = (N, M)$. In cellular networks such as frequency division duplex long term evolution (FDD-LTE), at most one CUE can be allocated to a single sub-channel in general. We assume that there are N sub-channels. Then each CUE is allocated one sub-channel, and all DUE pairs share total sub-channels. For the convenience, we assume that CUE

i use ith sub-channel. Now, we can consider one sub-channel as one package. Then there are N packages. What we need to do is to allocate all DUE pairs to N packages. The goal we pursue is the maximum capacity. The ith package is denoted as $\Re_i$, $i = (1, 2, \cdots, N)$. The diagram below shows an example of $S = (3, 8)$ (Fig. 2).

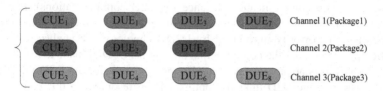

Fig. 2. An example of channel resource allocation

The genetic algorithm can be divided into five main steps:

1. *Coding*

   For CUEs, CUE i is allocated to ith sub-channel (package i) by default. For DUE pair j, the corresponding gene-bit is the sequence number of the assigned package for DUE pair j. Then every chromosome is coded as a M dimensional row vector like $G = (g_1, \cdots, g_j, \cdots, g_M)\, g_j \in (1, 2, \cdots, N)$.

   For example of $S = (3, 8)$ as shown above, the corresponding chromosome is $(1, 2, 1, 3, 2, 3, 1, 3)$. That means DUE pair 1, 3, 7 are allocated to package1, DUE pair 2, 5 are allocated to package2 and DUE pair 4, 6, 8 are allocated to package3.

2. *Population Initialization*

   We initiate the population number as $10 * N$. For every chromosome, the element g_j in G is a discrete random variable between 1 and N. We define the probability mass function $p(a)$ of X by $p(a) = P\{X = a\}$. We assume that the every DUE pairs is equivalent. For g_j, we have

   $$p(1) = p(2) = \cdots = p(M) = 1/M \tag{1}$$

3. *Set Fitness Function*

   In D2D communications, we need to get the maximum capacity. To guaranty the QoS of UEs, the signal to interference plus noise ratio (SINR) value should greater than SINR threshold. Therefore, for the CUE i, the SINR can be written as

   $$\beta_i = \frac{P_i/r_i^\alpha}{\sum\limits_{k \in \Re_i} P_T/d_k^\alpha + N_0} \tag{2}$$

   Here, P_i is the transmitting power of CUE i, r_i is the distance between CUE i and the BS, P_T is the transmitting power of the DTUE k, d_k is the distance between DTUE k and the BS, α is the path loss exponent, N_0 is noise power.

   At the same time, for the DRUE j, the SINR can written as

$$\gamma_j = \frac{P_T/l_j^\alpha}{P_m/d_{m,j} + \sum\limits_{\substack{k \in \Re_m \\ k \notin m}} P_T/d_{k,j}^\alpha + N_0} \tag{3}$$

Here, l_j is the distance between DTUE j and DRUE j, $d_{m,j}$ is the distance between CUE m and DRUE j, $d_{k,j}$ is the distance between DTUE k and DRUE j.

Obviously, the total capacity consists of two parts: CUEs and DUE pairs. For CUE i, the capacity is written as

$$Cc_i = B \log_2(1 + \beta_i) \tag{4}$$

Here, B is the bandwidth of one sub-channel.

Similarly, for DUE pairs, we consider that DUE pairs j is belong to package m, i.e. $j \in \Re_m$. Then, we have

$$Cd_j = B \log_2(1 + \gamma_j) \tag{5}$$

Therefore, the fitness function is denoted as

$$C(U_x) = \sum_{i=1}^{N} Cc_i + \sum_{j=1}^{M} Cd_j = B \sum_{i=1}^{N} \log_2(1 + \beta_i) + B \sum_{j=1}^{M} \log_2(1 + \gamma_j) \tag{6}$$

Here, U_x represent some chromosome.

4. *Breeding Process*

The population of genetic algorithm evolves toward the optimal solution by breeding process, which consists of 4 steps: selection, crossover, mutation, amendment.

(1) Selection

Based on classical roulette wheel selection scheme, individual U_k is selected with probability $p(U_k)$ which is denoted as

$$p(U_k) = \frac{C(U_k)}{\sum\limits_{x=1}^{10*N} C(U_x)} \tag{7}$$

(2) Crossover

The function of crossover is to get the better next-generation. A single point crossover operator is adopted in our algorithm. The crossover point of the chromosome is selected randomly, and the right parts of points of two parent chromosomes are exchanged to generate next-generation. We denote the crossover probability as P_0. The algorithm of crossover is as follows:

```
Begin
    k=0;
    While k < 10*N
            if random number < P₀  then
                    Uₖ is selected as the parents for crossover.
            End
            k = k + 1

            End
    End
```

The crossover point is randomly selected between 1 and M.

(3) Mutation

We denote the probability of mutation as P_1. If the value of the gene bit is x, then the mutated value is randomly selected from the set $\bar{x}$ (The universal set is $S = 1 \cdots N$).

(4) Amendment

To guaranty the QoS of UEs, the SINR value must be greater than SINR threshold ($\beta_i \geq \Gamma$ for $i = 1...N$, $\gamma_j \geq \Gamma$ for $j = 1...M$, here Γ is the SINR threshold). Sometimes, for one chromosome, the corresponding channel allocation result maybe violates the QoS conditions. This can happen during three statuses: population initialization, mutation, amendment. Therefore, we need repeat the relative process to amend the chromosome.

(5) Stopping criteria

Usually, by iterating for *Num* generations, the population will eventually evolve to a convergence. Finally, we get the best chromosome and calculate the optimal result.

4   Simulations and Discussions

In this section, we discuss some important observations obtained from the simulation results. In our simulations, we assume that CUEs and DTUEs follow a uniform distribution in the cell with the radius of R and the DRUEs uniformly locates in the circle with center at the corresponding DTUE and radius equal to L. Simulation parameters are summarized in Table 1.

Table 1. Simulation parameters

Parameter	Value	Parameter	Value
Cell radius (R)	600 m	Crossover probability P_0	0.2
L	20 m	The number of DUE pairs	10
Path loss factor (α)	4	The maximum transmission power of CUE	2 W
SINR threshold (β)	6 dB	The transmission power of DTUE	0.001 W
N_0	−105 dBm	The number of CUEs	3
Iteration number	50	Probability of mutation as P_1	0.2

Figure 3 shows the capacity comparisons of D2D communications among these three algorithms. Obviously, exhaustive algorithm can get the maximum capacity because every feasible solution is calculated. The capacity performance based on genetic algorithm is very close to the optimal value based on the exhaustive algorithm, and far greater than that based on random algorithm. Meanwhile, it can be seen that the proposed genetic algorithm has fast convergence speed. We can get the objective function's optimal value only go through about 11 iterations.

Similarly, Fig. 4 demonstrates the average transmission power of CUEs based on the three algorithms. The genetic algorithm proposed in this paper can get the minimal average transmission power of CUEs compared with exhaustive algorithm and random

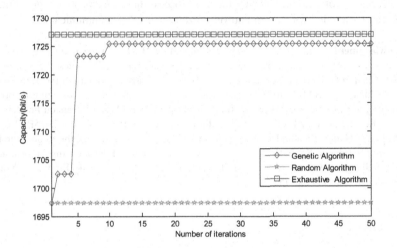

Fig. 3. The capacity of D2D communications

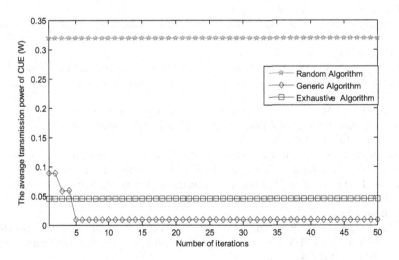

Fig. 4. The average transmission power of CUEs

algorithm. This is because the power control scheme for CUEs is applied into our algorithm. Likewise, the proposed genetic algorithm can obtain very fast convergence speed.

5 Conclusions

In this paper, D2D system model where M DUE pairs and N CUEs coexist is described. Then the resource allocation problem based on genetic algorithm is formulated and analyzed. Next, a resource allocation scheme based on genetic algorithm is proposed. Finally, the analysis and simulation results show the performance of proposed scheme outperform that of random algorithm and is close to that of exhaustive algorithm. This result can be applied for design and optimization of D2D communications.

Acknowledgments. This work was supported in part by "Technical research and demonstration of emergency operation and distributed control of the main and middle routes of South-to-North Water Diversion Project" of the National Key Technology R&D Program in the 12th Five-year Plan of China (2015BAB07B03), "Key technology integration and demonstration of optimum dispatching of pumping stations of east route of South-to-North Water Diversion Project" of the National Key Technology R&D Program in the 12th Five-year Plan of China (2015BAB07B01), the Project of National Natural Science Foundation of China (61301110), the Project funded by the Priority Academic Program Development of Jiangsu Higher Education Institutions, and the Project of Jiangsu Overseas Research & Training Program for University Prominent Young & Middle-Aged Teachers and Presidents.

References

1. Li, X., Wang, Z., Sun, Y., Gu, Y., Hu, J.: Mathematical characteristics of uplink and downlink interference regions in D2D communications underlaying cellular networks. Wirel. Pers. Commun. **93**, 917–932 (2017)
2. Li, X., Zhang, W., Zhang, H., Li, W.: A combining call admission control and power control scheme for D2D communications underlaying cellular networks. China Commun. **13**, 137–145 (2016)
3. Li, X., Zhang, H., Zhang, W., Yan, F.: A call admission control scheme on the uplink of D2D communications underlaying cellular networks. Intell. Autom. Soft Comput. **22**, 605–612 (2016)
4. Khoshkholgh, M., Zhang, Y., Chen, K., Shin, K., Gjessing, S.: Connectivity of cognitive device-to-device communications underlying cellular networks. IEEE J. Sel. Areas Commun. **33**, 81–99 (2015)
5. Zhang, H., Dong, Y., Cheng, J., Hossain, M.J., Leung, V.C.: Fronthauling for 5G LTE-U ultra dense cloud small cell networks. IEEE Wirel. Commun. **23**, 48–53 (2016)
6. Zhang, H., Liu, N., Chu, X., Long, K., Aghvami, A., Leung, V.: Network slicing based 5G and future mobile networks: mobility, resource management, and challenges. IEEE Commun. Mag. (2017)
7. Zhang, H., Jiang, C., Beaulieu, N.C., Chu, X., Wen, X., Tao, M.: Resource allocation in spectrum-sharing OFDMA femtocells with heterogeneous services. IEEE Trans. Commun. **62**, 2366–2377 (2014)

8. Zhang, H., Jiang, C., Beaulieu, N.C., Chu, X., Wang, X., Quek, T.Q.: Resource allocation for cognitive small cell networks: a cooperative bargaining game theoretic approach. IEEE Trans. Wirel. Commun. **14**, 3481–3493 (2015)
9. Zhang, H., Jiang, C., Mao, X., Chen, H.-H.: Interference-limited resource optimization in cognitive femtocells with fairness and imperfect spectrum sensing. IEEE Trans. Veh. Technol. **65**, 1761–1771 (2016)
10. Liu, D., Zhang, H., Zheng, W., Wen, X.: The sub-channel allocation algorithm in femtocell networks based on ant colony optimization. In: 2012-MILCOM, pp. 1–6 (2012)
11. Zhang, Z., Zhang, H., Liu, H., Jing, W., Wen, X.: Energy-efficient resource optimization in spectrum sharing two-tier femtocell networks. In: 2013 IEEE International Conference on Communications Workshops (ICC), pp. 571–575 (2013)
12. Zhang, Z., Zhang, H., Lu, Z., Zhao, Z., Wen, X.: Energy-efficient resource optimization in OFDMA-based dense femtocell networks. In: Energy-Efficient Resource Optimization in OFDMA-Based Dense Femtocell Networks Telecommunications (ICT), pp. 1–5 (2013)
13. Han, J., Cui, Q., Yang, C., Tao, X.: Bipartite matching approach to optimal resource allocation in device to device underlaying cellular network. Electron. Lett. **50**, 212–214 (2014)
14. Li, Y., Jin, D., Yuan, J., Han, Z.: Coalitional games for resource allocation in the device-to-device uplink underlaying cellular networks. IEEE Trans. Wirel. Commun. **13**, 3965–3977 (2014)
15. Song, L., Niyato, D., Han, Z., Hossain, E.: Game-theoretic resource allocation methods for device-to-device communication. IEEE Wirel. Commun. **21**, 136–144 (2014)
16. Xu, C., Song, L., Han, Z., Zhao, Q., Wang, X., Cheng, X., Jiao, B.: Efficiency resource allocation for device-to-device underlay communication systems: a reverse iterative combinatorial auction based approach. IEEE J. Sel. Areas Commun. **31**, 348–358 (2013)
17. Wang, F., Li, Y., Wang, Z., Yang, Z.: Social-community-aware resource allocation for D2D communications underlaying cellular networks. IEEE Trans. Veh. Technol. **65**, 3628–3640 (2016)
18. Zhang, R., Cheng, X., Yang, L., Jiao, B.: Interference graph-based resource allocation (InGRA) for D2D communications underlaying cellular networks. IEEE Trans. Veh. Technol. **64**, 3844–3850 (2015)
19. Ye, Q., Al-Shalash, M., Caramanis, C., Andrews, J.G.: Distributed resource allocation in device-to-device enhanced cellular networks. IEEE Trans. Commun. **63**, 441–454 (2015)
20. Hoang, T.D., Le, L.B., Le-Ngoc, T.: Resource allocation for D2D communication underlaid cellular networks using graph-based approach. IEEE Trans. Wirel. Commun. **15**, 7099–7113 (2016)
21. Yang, C., Xu, X., Han, J., Rehman, W.U., Tao, X.: GA based optimal resource allocation and user matching in device to device underlaying network. In: 2014 IEEE Wireless Communications and Networking Conference Workshops (WCNCW), pp. 242–247. IEEE (2014)
22. Yang, C., Xu, X., Han, J., Tao, X.: GA based user matching with optimal power allocation in D2D underlaying network. In: 2014 IEEE 79th Vehicular Technology Conference (VTC Spring), pp. 1–5. IEEE (2014)
23. Yang, C., Xu, X., Han, J., Tao, X.: Energy efficiency-based device-to-device uplink resource allocation with multiple resource reusing. Electron. Lett. **51**, 293–294 (2015)
24. Tang, R., Zhao, J., Qu, H.: Joint optimization of channel allocation, link assignment and power control for device-to-device communication underlaying cellular network. China Commun. **12**, 92–100 (2015)

25. Wang, L., Wu, H., Liu, L., Song, M., Cheng, Y.: Secrecy-oriented partner selection based on social trust in device-to-device communications. In: 2015 IEEE International Conference on Communications (ICC), pp. 7275–7279 (2015)
26. Pérez-Romero, J., Sánchez-González, J., Agustí, R., Lorenzo, B., Glisic, S.: Power-efficient resource allocation in a heterogeneous network with cellular and D2D capabilities. IEEE Trans. Veh. Technol. **65**, 9272–9286 (2016)
27. Gupta, P., Kumar, P.R.: The capacity of wireless networks. IEEE Trans. Inf. Theor. **46**, 388–404 (2000)

Comparison of Isotropic and 3D Beamforming LTE Systems Using Simulation

Cheng Xu$^{(\boxtimes)}$ and John Cosmas

Department of Electronic and Computer Engineering, Brunel University,
Uxbridge, Middlesex, UK
{Cheng.xu,John.cosmas}@brunel.ac.uk

Abstract. 4G LTE system uses an isotropic antenna to transmit radio wave power uniformly in all directions. In contrast, 3D beamforming is a 5G technology that directs the radio wave beam power towards those user equipment intended for communication thereby increasing SINR and decreasing the BER experienced at the User Equipment (UE). This paper compares the performance of an isotropic LTE system with a 3D beamforming system by quantifying the average Signal Noise Ratio (SNR) and Bit Error Rate (BER) received by all UEs in its coverage area.

Keywords: 3D beamforming · 5G · LTE · Simulation · BER

1 Introduction

There are several technologies for 5G designers that promise improved system performance and the 3D MIMO beamforming is one of the key technologies for 5G system [1]. This paper develops a methodology for estimating the parameters of the beamforming weighting function of a 3D antenna array and shows how the 3D MIMO beamforming is applied in the LTE system. This idea is based on "Study on 3D channel model for LTE, 3GPP TR 36.873" [2]. The advantage of directing a 3D beamforming to a group of users is that the very high bandwidth channel can be shared between a large number of users using time and frequency division multiplexing in Orthogonal Frequency Division Multiplexing (OFDM) without significantly changing the beamforming direction thereby simplifying the control at the BS and simplifying the synchronization of the user terminals with the transmitted channel. The cost is that the user terminals experience a range of BER qualities.

This paper simulates a 3D beamforming system to quantify the range of BER qualities that are obtained when directing a beamforming towards a group of user terminals. The simulation results show better performance than the original LTE system. The energy from each antenna is focused so the received signal strength at the user terminal is strong, which influence the signal quality. For example, if mobile phone may not receive a signal when the user is in the building or is far from the base station then a weighting function is necessary, which can focus the total energy from antenna array so that the signal can be sent further and the signal quality is enhanced at the user equipment. The simulations show that mean BER for the population of user terminals is improved compared to an isotropic LTE system.

© ICST Institute for Computer Sciences, Social Informatics and Telecommunications Engineering 2018
K. Long et al. (Eds.): 5GWN 2017, LNICST 211, pp. 685–694, 2018.
https://doi.org/10.1007/978-3-319-72823-0_63

Section 2 establishes the channel model and the weight matrix for directing the 3D beamforming towards the UEs. Section 3 explains how the 3D beamforming technology is applied to LTE system. Section 4 explains the parameters in the simulation. Section 5 presents and analyses the results from the simulation. Section 6 provides a conclusion for the whole paper.

2   3D Beamforming Channel Model

2.1   Calculating Channel Coefficients

The channel coefficients have been obtained from "3GPP TR 36.873" [2]. In next paragraphs, the H is the channel coefficient. Figure 1 shows the two kinds of path in the channel model. One of them is Non-line of sight (NLOS) and other is Line-of-sight (LOS).

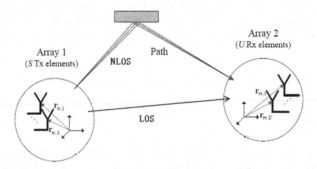

Fig. 1. The single channel model. In figure, the NLOS is Non-line of sight and the LOS is line of sight. The lines are the path.

There are two kinds of channel coefficients. The channel coefficient for the NLOS is [2]:

$$
\begin{aligned}
H_{u,s,n}(t) = \sqrt{P_n/M} \sum_{m=1}^{M} & \begin{bmatrix} F_{rx,u,\theta}\left(\theta_{n,m,ZOA}, \varphi_{n,m,AOA}\right) \\ F_{rx,u,\varphi}\left(\theta_{n,m,ZOA}, \varphi_{n,m,AOA}\right) \end{bmatrix}^T \\
& \begin{bmatrix} exp\left(j\Phi_{n,m}^{\theta\theta}\right) & \sqrt{\kappa_{n,m}^{-1}}exp\left(j\Phi_{n,m}^{\theta\varphi}\right) \\ \sqrt{\kappa_{n,m}^{-1}}exp\left(j\Phi_{n,m}^{\varphi\theta}\right) & exp\left(j\Phi_{n,m}^{\varphi\varphi}\right) \end{bmatrix} \\
& \begin{bmatrix} F_{tx,s,\theta}\left(\theta_{n,m,ZOD}, \varphi_{n,m,AOD}\right) \\ F_{tx,s,\varphi}\left(\theta_{n,m,ZOD}, \varphi_{n,m,AOD}\right) \end{bmatrix} \\
& \cdot exp\left(j2\pi2_0^{-1}\left(\hat{r}_{rx,n,m}^T.\bar{d}_{rx,u}\right)\right) \\
& \cdot exp\left(j2\pi2_0^{-1}\left(\hat{r}_{tx,n,m}^T.\bar{d}_{tx,s}\right)\right) \cdot exp\left(j2\pi2_{n,m}t\right)
\end{aligned}
\tag{1}
$$

The channel coefficient for the LOS is [2]:

$$H_{u,s,n}(t) = \sqrt{\frac{1}{K_R+1}} H'_{u,s,n}(t) + \delta(n-1) \sqrt{\frac{K_R}{K_R+1}}$$

$$\begin{bmatrix} F_{rx,u,\theta}(\theta_{LOS,ZOA}, \varphi_{LOS,AOA}) \\ F_{rx,u,\varphi}(\theta_{LOS,ZOA}, \varphi_{LOS,AOA}) \end{bmatrix}^T$$

$$\begin{bmatrix} exp(j\Phi_{LOS}) & 0 \\ 0 & -exp(j\Phi_{LOS}) \end{bmatrix} \qquad (2)$$

$$\begin{bmatrix} F_{tx,s,\theta}(\theta_{LOS,ZOD}, \varphi_{LOS,AOD}) \\ F_{tx,s,\varphi}(\theta_{LOS,ZOD}, \varphi_{LOS,AOD}) \end{bmatrix}$$

$$\cdot exp\left(j2\pi2_0^{-1}\left(\hat{r}_{rx,LOS}^T \cdot \bar{d}_{rx,u}\right)\right)$$

$$\cdot exp\left(j2\pi2_0^{-1}\left(\hat{r}_{tx,LOS}^T \cdot \bar{d}_{tx,s}\right)\right)$$

Since the propagation paths over which the signal is transmitted is not deterministic, the probability of existence for each path must be set. The calculation for probability of the LOS is defined in Ref. [2]. This probability defines how the power is distributed for different paths. If the power is less than −25 dB, then this path is ignored.

2.2   Calculating the Weight Matrix

A BS (base station) is equipped with antenna array that consists of MN antenna elements which is shown in Fig. 2.

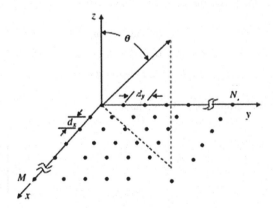

Fig. 2. There are N elements in the y-direction and M elements in the x-direction.

In order to represent the different location of antenna elements, the direction matrix D is introduced.

$$D = \begin{bmatrix} d_{11} & d_{12} & \cdots & d_{1M} \\ d_{21} & d_{22} & \cdots & d_{2M} \\ \vdots & \vdots & \cdots & \vdots \\ d_{N1} & d_{N2} & \cdots & d_{NM} \end{bmatrix} \qquad d_{ik} = e^{j[(i-1)\beta_x + (k-1)\beta_y]}$$

where $\beta_x = -\frac{2\pi}{\lambda} d_x \sin \theta_0 \cos \phi_0 = -\pi \sin \theta_0 \cos \phi_0$, $\beta_y = -\frac{2\pi}{\lambda} d_V \sin \theta_0 \sin \phi_0 = -\pi \sin \theta_0 \sin \phi_0$.

2.3   Calculating the Weight Vector

In order to allow the desired signal to be received without modification and reject the undesired interfering signals, we let AF = 1 in the desired direction and AF = 0 in the undesired interfering direction. That is in the desired direction, we hope $AF_x = 1$ is for a_m and $AF_y = 1$ is for bn. in the undesired direction, we hope $AF_x = 0$ and $AF_y = 0$.

(1) Calculating the weight vector in x-direction $\begin{bmatrix} a_1 & a_2 & \cdots & a_M \end{bmatrix}^T$

$$AF_x = \sum_{m=1}^{M} a_m e^{j(m-1)(kd_x \sin\theta in\theta\varphi + \beta_x)}$$

$$= \begin{bmatrix} 1 & e^{j(kd_x \sin\theta in\theta\varphi + \beta_x)} & \cdots & e^{j(m-1)(kd_x \sin\theta in\theta\varphi + \beta_x)} \end{bmatrix} \begin{bmatrix} a_1 \\ a_2 \\ \cdots \\ a_M \end{bmatrix} \qquad (3)$$

In our paper, there are four beams, so we can let the one desired direction is $\theta = \theta_0$ and $\varphi = \varphi_0$; three undesired direction are respectively:

$$\theta = \theta_1 \text{ and } \varphi = \varphi_1$$
$$\theta = \theta_2 \text{ and } \varphi = \varphi_2$$
$$\theta = \theta_3 \text{ and } \varphi = \varphi_3$$

In the desired direction, from (3), we have:

$$AF_x = \begin{bmatrix} 1 & e^{j(kd_x \sin\theta_0 \cos\varphi_0 + \beta_x)} & \cdots & e^{j(m-1)(kd_x \sin\theta_0 \cos\varphi_0 + \beta_x)} \end{bmatrix} \begin{bmatrix} a_1 \\ a_2 \\ \cdots \\ a_M \end{bmatrix} = 1 \qquad (4)$$

In undesired direction, from (3), we have

$$AF_x = \begin{bmatrix} 1 & e^{j(kd_x \sin\theta_0 \cos\varphi_0 + \beta_x)} & \cdots & e^{j(m-1)(kd_x \sin\theta_0 \cos\varphi_0 + \beta_x)} \end{bmatrix} \begin{bmatrix} a_1 \\ a_2 \\ \cdots \\ a_M \end{bmatrix} = 0 \qquad (5)$$

$$AF_x = \begin{bmatrix} 1 & e^{j(kd_x \sin\theta_0 \cos\varphi_0 + \beta_x)} & \cdots & e^{j(m-1)(kd_x \sin\theta_0 \cos\varphi_0 + \beta_x)} \end{bmatrix} \begin{bmatrix} a_1 \\ a_2 \\ \cdots \\ a_M \end{bmatrix} = 0 \qquad (6)$$

$$AF_x = \begin{bmatrix} 1 & e^{j(kd_x \sin\theta_0 \cos\varphi_0 + \beta_x)} & \cdots & e^{j(m-1)(kd_x \sin\theta_0 \cos\varphi_0 + \beta_x)} \end{bmatrix} \begin{bmatrix} a_1 \\ a_2 \\ \cdots \\ a_M \end{bmatrix} = 0 \qquad (7)$$

According to (4)–(7), we obtain

$$\begin{bmatrix} 1 & e^{j(kd_x \sin\theta_0 \cos\varphi_0 + \beta_x)} & \cdots & e^{j(m-1)(kd_x \sin\theta_0 \cos\varphi_0 + \beta_x)} \\ 1 & e^{j(kd_x \sin\theta_1 \cos\varphi_1 + \beta_x)} & \cdots & e^{j(m-1)(kd_x \sin\theta_1 \cos\varphi_1 + \beta_x)} \\ 1 & e^{j(kd_x \sin\theta_2 \cos\varphi_2 + \beta_x)} & \cdots & e^{j(m-1)(kd_x \sin\theta_2 \cos\varphi_2 + \beta_x)} \\ 1 & e^{j(kd_x \sin\theta_3 \cos\varphi_3 + \beta_x)} & \cdots & e^{j(m-1)(kd_x \sin\theta_3 \cos\varphi_3 + \beta_x)} \end{bmatrix} \begin{bmatrix} a_1 \\ a_2 \\ \cdots \\ a_M \end{bmatrix} = \begin{bmatrix} 1 \\ 0 \\ 0 \\ 0 \end{bmatrix} \qquad (8)$$

To obtain the weight vector $\begin{bmatrix} a_1 & a_2 & \cdots & a_M \end{bmatrix}^T$, we solve the equation

$$AX = b \qquad (9)$$

where

$$A = \begin{bmatrix} 1 & e^{j(kd_x \sin\theta_0 \cos\varphi_0 + \beta_x)} & \cdots & e^{j(m-1)(kd_x \sin\theta_0 \cos\varphi_0 + \beta_x)} \\ 1 & e^{j(kd_x \sin\theta_1 \cos\varphi_1 + \beta_x)} & \cdots & e^{j(m-1)(kd_x \sin\theta_1 \cos\varphi_1 + \beta_x)} \\ 1 & e^{j(kd_x \sin\theta_2 \cos\varphi_2 + \beta_x)} & \cdots & e^{j(m-1)(kd_x \sin\theta_2 \cos\varphi_2 + \beta_x)} \\ 1 & e^{j(kd_x \sin\theta_3 \cos\varphi_3 + \beta_x)} & \cdots & e^{j(m-1)(kd_x \sin\theta_3 \cos\varphi_3 + \beta_x)} \end{bmatrix} \qquad b^T = \begin{bmatrix} 1 & 0 & \cdots & 0 \end{bmatrix}$$

Since $X = pinv(A) * b$ is the solution of (9), we obtain

$$\begin{bmatrix} a_1 & a_2 & \cdots & a_M \end{bmatrix}^T = pinv(A) * b$$

Repeat these steps to calculate the weight vector in Y-direction; and then combining those two weight vectors and direction matrix D obtained in Sect. 2.2 to determine the weight for transmitted signal.

3   Applying the 3D Beamforming in LTE System

The simulation of LTE system is according to "PDSCH Throughput Conformance Test for Single Antenna (TM1), Transmit Diversity (TM2), Open Loop (TM3) and Closed Loop (TM4/6) Spatial Multiplexing" from the LTE System Toolbox in Matlab 2016a. The downlink reference measurement channel configuration is from "3GPPTS 36.101, Table A.3.1.1-1" [3] as Table 1 shown.

Table 1. Overview of DL reference measurement channels.

Reference channels	Reference channels
R.0 (Port0, 1 RB, 16QAM, CellRefP = 1, R = 1/2)	R.26 (Port5, 50 RB, 16QAM, CellRefP = 1, R = 1/2)
R.1 (Port0, 1 RB, 16QAM, CellRefP = 1, R = 1/2)	R.27 (Port5, 50 RB, 64QAM, CellRefP = 1, R = 3/4)
R.2 (Port0, 50 RB, QPSK, CellRefP = 1, R = 1/3)	R.28 (Port5, 1 RB, 16QAM, CellRefP = 1, R = 1/2)
R.3 (Port0, 50 RB, 16QAM, CellRefP = 1, R = 1/2)	R.10 (TxDiversity|SpatialMux, 50 RB, QPSK, CellRefP = 2, R = 1/3)
R.4 (Port0, 6 RB, QPSK, CellRefP = 1, R = 1/3)	R.11 (TxDiversity|SpatialMux|CDD, 50 RB, 16QAM, CellRefP = 2, R = 1/2)
R.5 (Port0, 15 RB, 64QAM, CellRefP = 1, R = 3/4)	R.12 (TxDiversity, 6 RB, QPSK, CellRefP = 4, R = 1/3)
R.6 (Port0, 25 RB, 64QAM, CellRefP = 1, R = 3/4)	R.13 (SpatialMux, 50 RB, QPSK, CellRefP = 4, R = 1/3)
R.7 (Port0, 50 RB, 64QAM, CellRefP = 1, R = 3/4)	R.14 (SpatialMux|CDD, 50 RB, 16QAM, CellRefP = 4, R = 1/2)
R.8 (Port0, 75 RB, 64QAM, CellRefP = 1, R = 3/4)	R.25 (Port5, 50 RB, QPSK, CellRefP = 1, R = 1/3)
R.9 (Port0, 100 RB, 64QAM, CellRefP = 1, R = 3/4)	R.11-45RB (CDD, 45 RB, 16QAM, CellRefP = 2, R = 1/2)

The simulation program chooses the R.0 and R.5 to simulate because the LTE system is a SISO system and the environment channel is Rayleigh fading channel model. The modulation method is 16-QAM, which is R.0 and it is 64-QAM, which is R.5.

4   The Simulation of Program

The simulation program is about the LTE system using the 3D beamforming technology. The simulation results compare with the LTE system. The GUI Fig. 3 is:

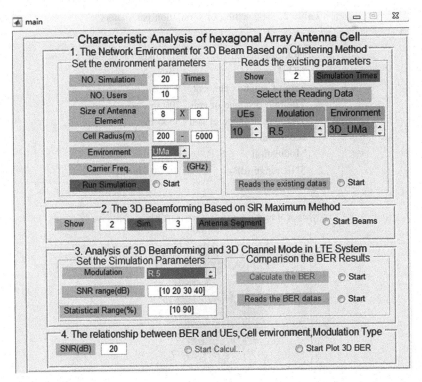

Fig. 3. The first box is the options of parameters for the simulation. The second box is the options for showing which beam. The third box is the options for calculating the BER. The last box is choice of the SNR for BER in 3D LTE system.

The operating time takes more than 8 h so there is the option about reading the data from operated in before.

5   Analysis Results

Choose a 10 users random distribution in one cell. The each beam is sent from 8×8 antenna array. The environment is UMa and the modulation is 64-QAM (R.5). More parameters for simulation are shown in Table 2. Figures 4 and 5 show the constellation diagram of received symbols for one user when the modulation methods are 64-QAM in LTE system and 3D LTE system respectively.

Table 2. The setting of simulation parameters.

Options	Parameters
NO. Simulation	20 times
NO. Users	10
Size of antenna element	8×8
The min distance of cell	200 m
The max distance of cell	5000 m
Environment	UMa
Modulation	R.5
SNR range (dB)	[10 20 30 40]

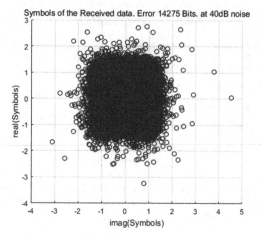

Fig. 4. The constellation diagram of received symbols in 64-QAM LTE system

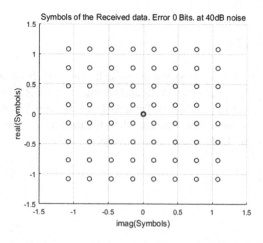

Fig. 5. The constellation diagram of received symbols in 64-QAM 3D beam LTE system

Comparing Figs. 4 and 5, the received symbols in 64-QAM 3D beam LTE are better than the 64-QAM LTE system.

The Fig. 6 shows the comparison with BER between LTE system and 3D beam LTE system in 64-QAM.

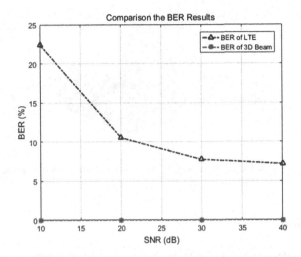

Fig. 6. The red line is the BER of 3D beam LTE system and the blue is the BER of LTE system. (Color figure online)

In Fig. 6, if the modulation method is 64-QAM, the BER of 3D LTE system is closed zero, but the BER of SISO LTE system is more than 7%, which is larger than the BER of 3D LTE system too much.

Therefore, the 3D LTE system has a better BER than the SISO LTE system when the modulation method is 64-QAM. Then we test the effect from the number of users and different environments on the BER in 3D LTE system when the SNR is 20 dB. The results are shown in Fig. 7 and the Table 3 explains the significance of all parameters in Fig. 7.

Table 3. The setting of simulation parameters.

Name	Explain
BER (%)	The median values of all BER
UEs	The number of users
UMiR.5	The modulation methods is 64-QAM in UMi
UMiR.0	The modulation methods is 16-QAM in UMi
UMaR.5	The modulation methods is 64-QAM in UMa
UMaR.0	The modulation methods is 16-QAM in UMa

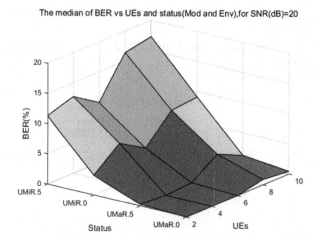

The median of BER vs UEs and status(Mod and Env),for SNR(dB)=20

Fig. 7. The BER for different environments in 20 dB when the number of users are 2, 4, 6, 8 or 10.

6 Conclusion

This paper first develops a methodology for estimating the parameters of the beam-forming weighting function of a 3D antenna array for directing the beam towards one user terminal. The weighting makes the direction of energy from each antenna to be focused on one direction. Moreover, the weighting makes the SINR between every two beams to be smaller. The simulation of 3D beamforming applied to the LTE system show that mean BER for the population of user terminals is improved compared to an isotropic LTE system transmission but this is at the cost of the variability of the BERs experienced by a small number of user terminals.

References

1. Agiwal, M., Roy, A., Saxena, N.: Next generation 5G wireless networks: comprehensive survey. IEEE Commun. Surv. Tutor. **18**(3), 1617–1655 (2016)
2. Study on 3D channel model for LTE (2012). http://www.3gpp.org
3. User Equipment (UE) radio transmission and reception (2016). http://www.3gpp.org

Author Index

Printed in the United States
By Bookmasters